Add

AREA HANDBOOK
for
BOLIVIA

Coauthors

Thomas E. Weil

Jan Knippers Black
Howard I. Blutstein
Hans J. Hoyer
Kathryn T. Johnston
David S. McMorris

Research completed July 1973

Second Edition

Published 1974

(This handbook supersedes DA Pam 550–66, August 1963)

DA Pam 550–66

Library of Congress Cataloging in Publication Data

Weil, Thomas E.
  Area handbook for Bolivia.

  "DA Pam 550-66."
  "One of a series of handbooks prepared by Foreign Area
Studies (FAS) of the American University."
  "Supersedes DA Pam 550-66, August 1963."
  Revision of 1963 ed. issued by the American University
Foreign Area Studies Division.
  Bibliography: p. 359-
  1. Bolivia. I. American University, Washington, D.C. Foreign Area Studies.
II. American University, Washington, D.C. Foreign Area Studies Division. Area
handbook for Bolivia. III. Title.

F3308.W44   1974   918.4'03'5   73-600327

For sale by the Superintendent of Documents, U.S. Government Printing Office
Washington, D.C. 20402—Price $6.15

FOREWORD

This volume is one of a series of handbooks prepared by Foreign Area Studies (FAS) of The American University, designed to be useful to military and other personnel who need a convenient compilation of basic facts about the social, economic, political, and military institutions and practices of various countries. The emphasis is on objective description of the nation's present society and the kinds of possible or probable changes that might be expected in the future. The handbook seeks to present as full and as balanced an integrated exposition as limitations on space and research time permit. It was compiled from information available in openly published material. An extensive bibliography is provided to permit recourse to other published sources for more detailed information. There has been no attempt to express any specific point of view or to make policy recommendations. The contents of the handbook represent the work of the authors and FAS and do not represent the official view of the United States government.

An effort has been made to make the handbook as comprehensive as possible. It can be expected, however, that the material, interpretations and conclusions are subject to modification in the light of new information and developments. Such corrections, additions, and suggestions for factual, interpretive, or other change as readers may have will be welcomed for use in future revisions. Comments may be addressed to:

The Director
Foreign Area Studies
The American University
5010 Wisconsin Avenue, N.W.
Washington, D.C. 20016

PREFACE

Significant developments in political and economic conditions underline the desirability of revising the *Area Handbook for Bolivia* published in 1963. Of particular importance are the changes in government that took place between 1964 and 1971; the growing importance of petroleum and natural gas production; the continuing efforts of the government to bring Indian elements into the mainstream of national life; and the programs designed to improve the lot of the masses.

This book supersedes the area handbook researched and written by Edwin E. Erickson, Susan G. Fortenbaugh, Bela C. Maday, Nathan S. Popkin, Suzanne Teleki, and John O. Weaver under the cochairmanship of Lyman H. Legters and Wendell Blanchard. It represents an effort to provide a compact and objective exposition and analysis of the dominant social, political, and economic characteristics of Bolivian society. It is designed to give readers both within and outside the government an understanding of the dynamics of the elements of the society and an insight into the needs, goals, and achievements of the people. Consultants with firsthand knowledge of the country have provided data not available in printed sources. The authors alone are responsible for the final draft.

Spanish words and phrases, used only when adequate English equivalents are lacking, are defined at first appearance. If employed frequently, they are listed in the glossary. Spanish is based on *Appleton's New Cuyas Dictionary* (Fifth Edition). The spellings of place names used are those established by the United States Board on Geographic Names. Unless otherwise stated, tons used in production and commodity figures are metric tons.

COUNTRY SUMMARY

1. COUNTRY: Republic of Bolivia—República de Bolivia.

2. SIZE, TOPOGRAPHY, AND CLIMATE: Area of about 424,000 miles makes country fifth in size in South America. Dominant features of landform are separate chains of Andes Mountains that flank heartland plateau with elevations of 13,000 feet and more; on east, tropical lowlands make up two-thirds or more of national territory; between high plateau and lowlands, Andean valleys and basins constitute intermediate regions. Climate varies from humid-tropical in lowlands to cold and semiarid on plateau. Rainfall increases from west to east and from south to north, with considerable seasonal and year-to-year variations; floods and droughts are both common.

3. POPULATION: Estimated at slightly over 5 million in early 1970s, but no complete census results since 1950. Limited information available indicates rates of population growth and of urbanization increased during 1950s and 1960s but remained below average for Latin American countries. With 70 percent of population still living in countryside during early 1970s the country remained among the most rural and least densely populated in Latin America.

4. ETHNIC GROUPS AND LANGUAGES: Indians form largest single ethnic grouping, constituting an estimated 50 to 60 percent of the population in the early 1970s. Of these, the Quechua and Aymara, both of the highlands, constitute an overwhelming proportion and have retained their cultural and linguistic heritages. As much as one-third of the population are mestizos—those of mixed European and Indian ancestry. There is also a small percentage of whites of European descent. Both mestizos and whites speak Spanish, the official language of the country. Mestizos are usually bilingual in Spanish and one Indian language; a large percentage of the Indian population is monolingual in Quechua or Aymara, neither speaking nor understanding Spanish.

5. RELIGION: Ninety percent of the Bolivians profess Roman Catholicism, although the church itself holds little economic, social, or political power as a national institution. Many nationalities and outlooks are represented in its clergy. A historic scarcity of priests in the rural areas has encouraged the development of a folk Catholicism among the Indians—a synthesis of Christian and pre-Hispanic religious practices. Constitution guarantees freedom of religion.

6. EDUCATION: During 1960s number of students in primary schools

increased from 50 percent to 70 percent of children of primary-school age. Although population primarily rural, over half of primary and nearly all of secondary and higher school enrollments are urban. Fundamental changes in school system in late 1960s and early 1970s included unification of previously separate urban and rural primary-school programs and increasing number of years in primary school.

7. HEALTH: Medical personnel and facilities concentrated in major cities; nearly half of population without ready access to medical care other than that provided by generally effective preventive programs against endemic diseases such as malaria and yellow fever. Continued reliance on traditional medical practices limits demand for modern care, and supply of physicians exceeds demand for them. High infant mortality rate and incidence of respiratory ailments; diseases attributed in large measure to poor nutrition and sanitation.

8. GOVERNMENT AND POLITICS: Centralized republic in which nine political subdivisions (departments) have limited autonomy. Departmental officials appointed by central government. Constitution of 1967 provides for traditional executive, legislative, and judicial branches, but national congress was dissolved in 1969, and in 1973 government continued to rule by decree. Government of General Hugo Banzer Suárez, who seized power in August 1971, composed of coalition of two leading political parties and armed forces.

9. INTERNATIONAL MEMBERSHIPS: The country is a member of the Organization of American States, the Inter-American Development Bank, the Latin American Free Trade Association, the Andean Common Market, and the United Nations and many of its specialized agencies. Also a party to the Inter-American Treaty of Reciprocal Assistance and the Latin American Nuclear Free Zone Treaty.

10. COMMUNICATIONS: The National Enterprise for Telecommunications, a state-owned company, was installing a national microwave system in 1973. Many local telephone systems in operation. Government provides domestic telegraph service; three private companies offer international telegraph service.

11. RAILROADS: Two major systems totaling over 2,100 miles, owned by the National Railways Company. One short line operated by the Mining Corporation of Bolivia. Another short line is an extension into Bolivia of the Southern Railroads of Peru.

12. ROADS: From 12,000 to 17,500 miles of roads and highways, depending upon criteria used in defining a road. Less than 700 miles paved as of 1973; 2,400 miles of all-weather improved roads; balance passable only in dry weather.

13. CIVIL AVIATION: Bolivian Air Lloyd is major domestic airline and also provides international service. Seven unscheduled airlines, thirty-one air taxi companies, and a commercial branch of the armed forces also provide domestic air service.

14. PORTS: Bolivia has use of ports in Argentina, Chile, Peru, and Brazil under terms of various treaties and agreements.

15. INLAND WATERWAYS: More than thirty large rivers of the Amazon drainage system are navigable for an estimated 12,000 miles in small vessels. Lake Titicaca used as means of communication with Peru.

16. AGRICULTURE: Techniques mainly traditional and production of many crops has not kept pace with growth of population. An agrarian reform program has drastically altered the land tenure system. Major crops are potatoes, corn, sugarcane, cassava, barley, rice, and wheat.

17. INDUSTRY: Manufacturing is in early stages of development, and all plants are small. More persons work in craft shops than in factories.

18. LABOR: In late 1960s some two-thirds of labor force engaged in agriculture; over half of remainder in commercial and personal service activities; in small manufacturing sector, a large majority engaged in artisan work. Most of population over age of fifteen was economically active; when unpaid family workers on farms included, proportion of population as a whole in labor force was among highest in Latin America. Excess of labor supply over effective demand for it results in massive underemployment.

19. CURRENCY: The Bolivian peso is the unit of currency. Its symbol is $b; the official exchange rate was $b20 to US$1 as of mid-1973.

20. IMPORTS AND EXPORTS: Exports are mainly minerals, with tin composing about half of total annual exports. Other major exports are tungsten, antimony, zinc, copper, silver, lead, cotton, and coffee. Imports consist mainly of mechanical equipment, vehicles, iron and steel, wheat and flour, electrical equipment, and fats and oils.

21. ECONOMIC AGREEMENTS AND AID: Bolivia is recipient of aid from many sources—international lending organizations, foreign governments, foreign banks, and private foreign suppliers. Total aid received from end of World War II through mid-1973 totaled the equivalent of over $US1.1 billion.

22. ARMED FORCES: Armed forces number about 17,000—army 14,000; air force 2,000; navy 1,000. Navy operates a small flotilla on Lake Titicaca on the border with Peru and maintains a small river force. The army includes twelve infantry regiments, one motorized regiment, three ranger battalions, one paratroop regiment, and three artillery regiments. Air force includes about twenty-five combat aircraft, twenty transports, a number of communication aircraft, and fifteen helicopters. The armed forces are engaged in civic action programs. Bolivia has about 5,000 armed police and frontier guards.

23. PEOPLE'S MILITIA: The People's Militia, a paramilitary organization designed to serve as a reserve for internal security, numbers about 16,000.

BOLIVIA

TABLE OF CONTENTS

Page

FOREWORD iii

PREFACE v

COUNTRY SUMMARY vii

SECTION I. SOCIAL

Chapter 1. General Character of the Society 1

2. Historical Setting.. 7
Before the Conquest—The Spanish Conquest and Colonial
Rule—Independent Bolivia—Developments, 1952-64

3. Geography and Population 45
Boundaries and Political Subdivisions—Natural Features—
Settlement Patterns—Population Structure and Dynamics—
Population Problems—Labor Force

4. Ethnic Groups and Languages 77
Highland Indian Ethnic Groups—Mestizos and Cholos—
Lowland Groups—Blancos

5. Social System 99
Social Stratification and Organization—Family—Religion

6. Education 137
Historical Development—Administration and Finance—The
School System—Literacy and Adult Education—The Teaching
Profession

7. Living Conditions 165
Diet and Nutrition—Dress—Housing—Health—Welfare—
Pattern of Living and Leisure

8. Cultural Life and Mass Communication 191
Artistic and Intellectual Expressions—Mass Communication

SECTION II. POLITICAL

Chapter 9. The Governmental System 215
The Constitutional Structure—Structure and Functioning of
Government at Subnational Levels—The Electoral System—
The Civil Service

10. Political Dynamics 229
The Development of Political Attitudes—The MNR and Its
Opponents, 1952-64—The Demise of the MNR Government—
Military Rule—Political Forces and Interest Groups

			Page
	11.	Foreign Relations	257

11. Foreign Relations 257
   Historical Background—Relations with Neighboring Coun-
   tries—Relations with the United States—Extrahemispheric
   Relations—International Organizations and Commitments

SECTION III. ECONOMIC

Chapter 12. Character and Structure of the Economy 275
   National Accounts—Role of Government—Public Finance—
   The Balance of Payments and Foreign Aid—Currency, Bank-
   ing, and Credit

13. Agriculture and Industry 291
   Land Use, Resources, and Practices—Land Tenure and
   Agrarian Reform—Crops—Livestock, Fishing, and Forestry—
   Mining and Metallurgy—Petroleum and Natural Gas—Elec-
   trical Energy—Manufacturing

14. Trade and Transportation 317
   Domestic Trade—Tourism—Transportation and Communi-
   cation—Foreign Trade—Regional Economic Integration

SECTION IV. NATIONAL SECURITY

Chapter 15. National Defense and Public Order 337
   Police—Laws and the Penal Code—Court and Criminal
   Procedures—Incidence of Crime—Internal Security—The
   Armed Forces

BIBLIOGRAPHY 359

GLOSSARY 405

INDEX 407

LIST OF ILLUSTRATIONS

Figure   Page

1 Political Divisions of Bolivia xiv
2 Structural Features of Bolivia 49
3 Mineral Resources of Bolivia, 1973 59
4 Ethnolinguistic Divisions of Bolivia 82
5 Transportation Systems of Bolivia, 1973 322

LIST OF TABLES

Table   Page

1 Bolivia, Estimated Size of Labor Force by Sector of Economic Activity, 1967   71
2 Household Expenditure of a Bolivian Peasant Family, 1966 186
3 Structure of Bolivian Gross Domestic Product, Selected Years, 1965-71 277
4 Estimated Agricultural Production of Bolivia Listed by Crop Year, 1967-72   300
5 Minerals Production of Bolivia, Selected Years, 1961-72 306
6 Bolivian Exports by Value, 1967-72 329
7 Structure of Bolivian Exports, 1967-72 330
8 Structure and Value of Bolivian Imports, 1967-71 331
9 Structure of Bolivian Foreign Trade by Trading Partners, 1968-71 332

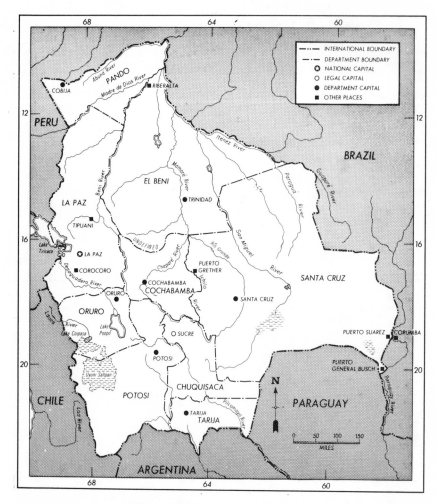

Figure 1. Political Divisions of Bolivia

SECTION I. SOCIAL

CHAPTER 1

GENERAL CHARACTER OF THE SOCIETY

The people of the Republic of Bolivia live in a land noted for striking contrasts in terrain and climate. The majority inhabit a chilly plateau from which peaks of the Andes Mountains rise to heights of more than 21,000 feet, whereas others live in the tropical lowlands of the eastern part of the country. Ever since the Spanish conquest in the second quarter of the sixteenth century a major element in the country's economy has been income from the mining of metals in the highlands, but in 1973 profits from natural gas and oil production in the eastern lowlands promised to strengthen the country's economic position.

Bounded on the west by Peru and Chile, on the north and east by Brazil, and on the south by Paraguay and Argentina, Bolivia is landlocked but carries on its foreign trade through seaports on the Pacific and Atlantic coasts and through river ports in the Amazon valley and in the La Plata Basin.

In 1973 Indians constituted at least half of the country's population. The majority of the Indians were Aymara and Quechua who resided in the high plateau of the north and intermontane valleys of the Andes. The balance of the population was composed of mestizos—descendants of Indians and the Spanish conquerors—and a small proportion of whites, principally of Spanish descent. The people were divided by ethnic and linguistic differences as well as by regional barriers. Beginning in 1952, however, successive governments undertook to improve the status of the Indians, to increase their political consciousness, and to integrate them more effectively into the national society.

In 1973 the population was largely rural, but urbanization was increasing—notably in and around the capitals of the country's principal political subdivisions. In the face of an extremely uneven distribution of population the government was endeavoring to colonize valleys in the north and parts of the eastern lowlands. Likewise, more and more people were being attracted to plantations and to natural gas and oil-producing centers in the eastern part of the country. Population pressures, however, were apparent in the highlands, where a large proportion of the population continued to live.

In many respects the lives of the people are a direct reflection of the

1

history of the country. Large numbers of people speak the Indian languages of their ancestors—notably Quechua and Aymara—despite the fact that Spanish, introduced by the conquistadores in the sixteenth century, has been the official language of the country for five centuries. A large portion of the Indian population tills the land, as was the case when the Spaniards arrived, and Indian cultures and life-styles survive. At the same time the Spanish heritage is preserved among whites and mestizos and is important in religious life, in literature, and in social relationships.

When Francisco Pizarro, the Spanish conquistador, invaded and conquered the Inca Empire in 1532 the Indians lived under an authoritarian government that required them to work for the state to keep the government granaries filled. When the Spaniards took over the Inca administrative machinery the Indians continued their position as virtual serfs—cultivating the land and working in the mines—and after the establishment of the republic in 1825 their position remained much the same until the twentieth century. In the 1930s resentment against the ruling class, composed mainly of members of the white elite, surged to a new high when tens of thousands of Bolivian Indians died in the Chaco War (1932-35)—a war fought over tropical lands claimed by Bolivia and Paraguay. During the 1940s Indians became increasingly conscious of their place in the nation and, in the Revolution of 1952, led by the Nationalist Revolutionary Movement (Movimento Nacionalista Revolucionario—MNR), they won an important position in the political life of the country.

Throughout much of the history of the republic, rivalry among political leaders has generated civil wars, rebellions, and dictatorships. Historians record as many as sixty major uprisings, scores of lesser uprisings, and more than fifty presidents, a number of whom were assassinated. Constitutions promulgated at various times during more than a century after the founding of the republic provided for elected governments, but during this period only a small percentage of the people went to the polls. Laws affecting working conditions and land tenure were usually designed to favor the interests of the elite; and governments often depended on the armed forces for survival. Although constitutions provided for executive, legislative, and judicial branches, the power of the president was seldom checked by the legislature or the judiciary, and presidents frequently ruled by decree and by military force. New constitutions were often drafted with a view to giving an appearance of legitimacy to a president's exercise of power.

The Revolution of 1952, supported by miners, students, and other civilian groups, including members of the middle class, had far-reaching effects on the lives of the people. The MNR government sponsored extensive agrarian reform and universal suffrage, nationalized the largest of the privately owned mining corporations, and undertook to expand the educational system. The power of the established armed forces was greatly reduced and was counterbalanced by militias recruited primarily among Indian miners and peasants. As a result of infighting within the MNR and growing opposition, the MNR regime was overthrown by a military junta in 1964. Most of the basic reforms introduced by the MNR were retained, and a constitutional election was held in 1966, but in 1969 power was again seized by the armed forces, and an army general was entrusted with the formation of a revolutionary civilian-military government. In 1970 guerrilla activity and student and other civil disturbances led to the resignation of this government under pressure from the armed forces high command, but an army officer who did not enjoy the support of the high command, General Juan José Torres Gonzáles, seized power in October 1970 and was installed as president of a leftist nationalist government.

Although the Torres government purportedly represented an alliance of workers, students, peasants, and the armed forces, political instability increased. The government nationalized or expropriated a number of foreign-owned enterprises and terminated the United States Peace Corps program. Peasants seized land, and in 1971 the government tolerated the formation of an assembly of labor unions organized along the lines of a workers' soviet, which leftist sponsors hoped would become an effective legislative branch of the government.

In the face of this turbulence and the accompanying extremist tendencies, two of the country's most important political parties, the MNR and the Bolivian Socialist Falange (Falange Socialist Boliviana—FSB), and other middle-class groups formed an alliance with the armed forces that, in the course of a four-day revolt, overthrew the Torres government in August 1971 and installed army Colonel Hugo Banzer Suárez as president.

Political instability has been matched by economic problems affecting the great majority of the people. The Spanish conquerors fixed their attention on the highland regions because of the discovery of deposits of high-grade silver ore, and during the nineteenth century and the first half of the twentieth the national economy depended almost entirely on the mining of industrial minerals—notably tin. Although there were large agricultural holdings, especially in the fertile parts of the valleys on the eastern Andean slopes, their importance was distinctly secondary, and it became necessary to import foodstuffs. Until the middle of the twentieth century the wealth derived from the mines covered the cost of imports needed by the small white population, but most of the people continued to subsist on the yields of traditional low-productivity agriculture.

The Revolution of 1952 brought about changes that resulted in some redistribution of wealth, but in 1973 more than 50 percent of the active population, including unpaid family workers on the land, were still engaged in agricultural pursuits. Owing to the inability of the industrial sector to create new jobs, the bulk of the remainder was engaged in service activities, and only a small percentage was employed in mineral production—still the country's most important industry. Although unemployment in urban centers was increasing, a more serious problem was widespread underutilization of manpower. Thus, problems of poverty persisted, and the living standards of the majority of the people continued at a low level.

Physical conditions under which Bolivians live vary from those in the highest mining camps in the world to those prevailing in the steaming jungles of the Amazon Basin. Kinds of housing range from the mud huts in the highlands to the handsome colonial homes of old Spanish families. In the 1950s and 1960s, after the nationalization of the largest mining enterprises and the departure of their extremely wealthy owners, the gap between income levels of well-to-do Bolivians and those of the majority of the people began to narrow, and food and housing of both rural and urban dwellers showed some improvement. In 1973, however, most Bolivians found it necessary to spend much of their limited income on foodstuffs. Although some endemic diseases had been brought under control, the government's efforts to improve the health of the people were hampered by poor environmental sanitation, by inadequate nutrition, and by a widespread lack of understanding of the practice of modern medicine. Most of the hospitals and other medical facilities were located in urban centers.

In the early 1970s the government was endeavoring to expand the educational system. Before the Revolution of 1952 attendance at the predominantly urban secondary schools and universities had been largely confined to whites, whereas mestizos and a few Indians attended primary schools for a few years, and most of the Indians received no formal education at all. School enrollments increased rapidly in the late 1950s and during the 1960s—especially in the rural primary schools—but in the early 1970s illiteracy among rural dwellers continued at a high level. Progress in education was affected by student unrest and by differing ideas regarding ways and means of increasing the effectiveness of the educational system. Its overall usefulness to the nation was questioned because of the disproportionate number of students in liberal arts and theoretical-oriented studies as compared with those taking courses to develop technical skills needed for development of the national economy. Most rural dwellers remained illiterate, and many university graduates with degrees in law, medicine, or academic subjects were leaving the country to find employment.

Limited educational opportunities were reflected by the fact that in a country of more than 5 million people only a small percentage read newspapers or books. Until the beginning of the twentieth century literary and artistic activity had been meager. The Spanish elite, however, preserved their cultural heritage, and the Indians passed on their legends from generation to generation. During the colonial period most

4

of the writing dealt with religious speculation or history; and in the nineteenth century some important historical works were published. In the first half of the twentieth century, however, Bolivians began to write critically of their society. Reacting to the disastrous Chaco War, writers praised the Indians, who had been oppressed through the centuries, and called for revolutionary changes. These writings contributed to the growth of a national literary tradition, but in mid-1973 there was still a wide gulf between the intelligentsia and the people they glorified and hoped to influence.

In mid-1973 the most effective channel of communication in the country was radio—a medium that reached virtually all the people and contributed to their awareness of the mainstream of national life. Radio broadcasting played a major role in the government's efforts to incorporate the isolated Indian population into the national society and to increase literacy in Spanish.

Since the establishment of the republic in 1825, Bolivia's foreign relations have been significantly affected by the country's geographic position—surrounded as it is by nations that are stronger militarily and economically, by its dependence on mineral exports that are subject to fluctuations of world prices, and by its dependence on foreign nations for investment and technical skills. Although relations with Paraguay, which gained territory from Bolivia in the Chaco War, were friendly in mid-1973, irredentist sentiment generated by the War of the Pacific (1879-83), in which Bolivia lost its coastal lands to Chile, persisted. Bolivia maintained normal relations with its other neighbors and with the United States and was strengthening its relations with the Republic of China (Nationalist China), the Republic of Korea (South Korea), Israel, Spain, Japan and the Philippines. Economic ties with other Andean nations, and with Argentina and Brazil, were gaining in importance.

In 1973 the government was looking to other governments and to international lending agencies to provide financial assistance for programs designed to stabilize the country's economy and to improve social conditions. Likewise, the government was encouraging private investment, both foreign and Bolivian. With the support of the armed forces, the government was engaged in efforts to increase exploitation of the country's natural resources and to expand educational facilities and health services.

CHAPTER 2

HISTORICAL SETTING

In 1973 Bolivian society clearly reflected the country's history—the role of the indigenous population; the effect on the people of physical factors in the environment; the consequences of traditional dependence on mineral resources; and the impact of authoritarian rule by the Incas, by the Spaniards, and by most of the presidents of the republic.

Over a period of at least five centuries the Indians, constituting the great bulk of the population, occupied virtually the same position in the relationship between the rulers and the ruled. Their services were exploited by the Incas to fill the state granaries and by the Spanish colonists and their successors in the republic to cultivate the land and work the mineral deposits. Until the middle of the twentieth century the perspective of most Indians was confined to their own traditional communities and their struggle for survival.

Not until the middle of the twentieth century did the Indians begin to develop a consciousness of nationalism and an urge for social revolution. Conscripted during the early 1930s to fight in the Chaco War (1932-35), in which an estimated 50,000 Bolivians died, tens of thousands of Indians came to resent more than ever the power of the ruling class, composed principally of members of the white elite. The ruling class lost most of its control and influence, and power-seeking politicians began to court Indian support.

The Revolution of 1952—often compared with the Mexican Revolution (1911-40) for its far-reaching effect—established elements of the Indian population as a major factor in Bolivian politics. The Nationalist Revolutionary Movement (Movimiento Nacionalista Revolucionario—MNR), a broad-based party whose supporters included miners, civilian groups, and students, assumed power in April 1952.

During its twelve years in office the MNR introduced important measures of revolutionary significance, among which were agrarian reform, expansion of the educational system, universal suffrage, and nationalization of the largest privately owned mining enterprises. The strength of the regular armed forces was radically curtailed, and the army's power was offset by militias, composed principally of Indian miners and peasants, which had played an important role in the revolution. Factionalism within the MNR and increasing opposition to its rule led to its overthrow by a military junta in 1964, but the junta retained the basic reforms introduced by the MNR.

7

The lives of the people have been profoundly affected by the physical environment and by the character of the natural resources. The country's topographic and climatic extremes; its natural barriers to communications and transportation; its patterns of vegetation; and its mineral deposits—all have made their mark on political and social conditions. Bolivia's physical inheritance has constituted a challenge to leaders interested in nation-building—in social and political integration and the infusion of modern technology into economic processes.

Between the seventh and tenth centuries A.D. it was in the relatively comfortable climate of the Altiplano that the Indians of Aymara origin developed a highly advanced culture. In the steaming jungles of the eastern lowlands the Indians still live under primitive conditions in the twentieth century. It was in the highlands that the Incas, invading around 1200, and the Spaniards, settling during the second quarter of the sixteenth century, established their power centers. Neither the Inca nor the Spaniards gained full control over the lowlands, and in the twentieth century this region is still sparsely settled.

Silver and tin have played major roles in the economic and political life of the country. The Spaniards' discovery of rich silver deposits at Potosí, south of La Paz, made the colony of vast importance to the Spanish crown; and Potosí became the most populous city in South America in the sixteenth century. The great wealth and prestige of the colonists in the Altiplano probably contributed to a spirit of independence that in turn facilitated the termination of Spanish rule early in the nineteenth century.

Tin production began in the 1870s, and after 1900 tin surpassed silver as the principal export commodity. It became the cornerstone of the Bolivian economy, the main source of government revenue, and the major source of national wealth. In the second quarter of the twentieth century powerful tin-mine owners, who virtually controlled governments, were the targets of revolutionary movements. The success of the MNR in 1952 was attributable in large measure to the support of armed tin miners.

Two disastrous wars were fought over territories containing mineral deposits. The War of the Pacific (1879–83) was waged for control of rich nitrate deposits in the Atacama Desert on the Pacific coast. Chile defeated Bolivia and its ally, Peru, and Bolivia lost all of its coastal territory. The Chaco War (1932–35) with Paraguay was fought over unexploited petroleum resources in the eastern lowlands. Again Bolivia was defeated and lost most of the disputed territory. The resulting exasperation of the people may well have constituted a turning point in the social and political life of the country that led to the Revolution of 1952.

BEFORE THE CONQUEST

In the period ending with Francisco Pizarro's invasion and conquest of the Inca Empire in 1532, the highland territory now within the boundaries of Bolivia was part of the greater cultural and political complex of Andean South America. Most of this territory fell, late in the period, under Inca sway; but, as in much of the rest of the region, the influences of a series of pre-Inca cultures were only partially obliterated by Inca rule.

The most impressive single evidence of pre-Inca development in Bolivia consists of the remains of Tiahuanaco culture. The ruined site just south of Lake Titicaca from which the culture takes its name is one probable center of this cultural flowering and is associated by some observers with the forebears of the Aymara-speaking Indians (see ch. 4). Its principal remnants in stonework and pottery have been compared in architectural achievement and technological skill to Etruscan art.

Although the advent of Inca domination over the whole region marked a break with the past, it is all prehistoric in the sense that there were no written records before the arrival of the Spanish. Much light has been shed on the prehistoric epoch by chronicles of the Spanish invaders, but they were written from the particular standpoint of the alien invader. Hence, their validity is questionable, especially as they project their conjectures into the past, and most of the little we know of Inca and pre-Inca culture emanates from archaeological findings.

Archaeological evidence combines with the oral tradition of conquered Indians to date the Inca period as one of relatively short duration. In and around Cuzco in present-day Peru, where the Inca system arose, it goes back at least as far as A.D. 1300, although radiocarbon dates suggest something nearer A.D. 1000. Most authorities agree in placing the expansion of Inca rule in the century after about 1440. The process of conquest was gradual, but some time before Pizarro arrived, Inca rule had been extended to take in most of Andean and coastal Ecuador, Peru, Bolivia, northern Chile, and parts of adjecent regions.

This century or so of domination by the Quechua-speaking Incas created a cultural, political, and economic overlay resting on the varying local substrata. Little is known of the precise nature of the local societies brought under Inca sway, and perhaps least of all of the local groups within present-day Bolivian boundaries. In general, in all the territory of lowland Bolivia, the societies encountered by the Spanish during the colonial period revealed a traditional character without Inca features. Linguistically and politically diverse, the Indian groups of the eastern two-thirds of Bolivia preserved their ways of life well into modern times in relatively unchanging social patterns. The highland areas, on the other hand, constituted a most important segment of the Inca domain, and the native ways of the pre-Inca groups had been partially obliterated by the time the Europeans arrived.

The establishment of Inca hegemony had far-reaching consequences on the Altiplano. The Inca system exercised absolute autocracy through a highly effective decentralization that took into account and even fostered local customs of social and political behavior. Local chiefs usually retained a great measure of their former powers and, in general, were reinforced by the imperial authority. Inca rule thus combined absolute authority in matters fundamental to its own preservation and to the well-being of the ruling group with a significant measure of local autonomy and impartial adaptation to local practices where nothing vital was at stake. Nearly a hundred years of such relatively benevolent subjection, however, did little to prepare the peoples of highland Bolivia to resist what turned out to be a harsher alien domination.

The local social and economic patterns of the Inca as well as the pre-Inca period are obscure; the most that can be said with certainty is that a communal tradition of landholding and agrarian production runs through all of Andean prehistory. The communal structure, the *ayllu* (see Glossary), predated Inca rule and remained a fixture in the centrally administered Inca system of production. Communal ownership and economic operation survived the Spanish colonial period.

The attributes of the central Inca administration remain important in the light of developments that followed the empire's fall. When the Inca invaders moved into a new territory, as they did in the Bolivian Altiplano around 1450, they crushed local resistance and then proceeded to enlist the local leaders as allies and imperial representatives. The goal was always pacification, and the means employed were usually geared to the minimum force required to establish imperial dominance.

The state that followed pacification was a skillful venture in public administration. In the Altiplano this occurred during the latter half of the fifteenth century. By 1493 the empire extended into Chile, the Maule River marking its southern boundary; and Huayna Capac, last ruler of an undivided domain, was able to devote himself largely to administrative consolidation. This meant the introduction of the division of cultivation and production whereby the central authority extracted the tribute needed both for its own support and for an elaborate scheme of centrally administered social welfare, part of the quid pro quo for accepting Inca hegemony, which ensured Inca subjects against crop failures and other natural calamities. Inca exactions were not only confined to produce but also included military service and a kind of labor draft.

Central regulation also entailed efforts to introduce the Quechua language as lingua franca, as well as the ritual and tributary features of the official religion. When imperial needs so dictated, large population movements might be ordered either as a means of removing dissident groups or as a colonization device. This practice is often invoked to account for the pockets of Quechua speakers on the Bolivian Altiplano (see ch. 4).

The efficiency and extent of the Inca administration were remarkable by any standards of the time and made a deep impression on the Spanish invaders. Yet the elements of prehistory most relevant to the unfolding of recorded Bolivian history are the less striking continuities that emerged before the Inca expansion and survived Spanish rule. The communal social and economic patterns and the localized structure of political power have persisted and continue to resist the centralizing efforts of the modern regimes.

THE SPANISH CONQUEST AND COLONIAL RULE

Discovery and Settlement

Enormous efforts were required to place Spain's conquered territories in the New World under a manageable administration and to begin the process of settlement. Spain was enriched by the mineral wealth of its colonies and by the profits of its trade monopoly; but the mother country was partly depopulated by the effort, and the state bore a heavy burden as underwriter of expensive expeditions and a far-flung colonial government.

By the time what is now Bolivia entered history, Spain was well along in the process of devising a political and economic framework for the control and management of the great areas that discovery and conquest were bringing to the crown. Notwithstanding the numerous local differences from one Spanish colony to another, Spain attempted to weave a single imperial fabric for its entire New World dominion. The Council of the Indies (Consejo de las Indias), formally established in Spain in 1524, oversaw the whole enterprise on behalf of the crown; laws were devised for the entire territory; and policies were adopted for universal colonial application.

Spanish America was a possession of the crown of Castile, deriving from the legacy of Queen Isabella. The Spanish monarch made its laws, acting through the Council of the Indies. That body had supreme legislative, judicial, and administrative authority in the Indies while serving also as an advisory body in connection with all civil and ecclesiastical appointments. The council also supervised the Bureau of Trade (Casa de Contratación) that had been established at Seville in 1503 to control commerce with the New World. The legislative output of the council forms the basis of the monumental codification of 1680, the Compilation of Laws (Recopilación de Leyes), which contains most of the story of official policy for the period. Only during the eighteenth century did the council begin to lose its authority to other institutions.

The king's personal representative in Spanish America was the viceroy. When the Viceroyalty of Peru was established in 1542, its jurisdiction began with the Isthmus of Panama and included all of Spanish

South America except Venezuela, which belonged to the Viceroyalty of New Spain and had its seat in Mexico City. Such a vast territory inevitably invited division, but Alto Perú, or Charcas, as present-day Bolivia was variously known, remained a part of Peru until it was allotted to the new Viceroyalty of La Plata (Buenos Aires), created in 1776. The viceroy of Peru was the highest ranking personage in Spanish America.

The viceroy's duties were numerous and his authority great. He was aided by his *audiencia* (council), which was simultaneously the highest court of appeal in the jurisdiction and, in the absence of a viceroy, also a governing body. The territory of an *audiencia* did not necessarily coincide with that of a viceroy, for lesser *audiencias* were attached to executives of lower rank—presidents and captains general. In some cases these officials became almost independent of the viceroyalty to which they belonged. Apart from the restraining influence of the *audiencia*, the actions of a viceroy—and those of lesser officials too—were checked mainly by the institution of *residencia*, an inquiry of variable duration into the official's conduct in office.

Smaller administrative units were superseded late in the eighteenth century by the intendancy system, the officials of which were vested with far-reaching powers and directly responsible to the crown. Municipalities also enjoyed a distinctive governmental institution, imported like the others from Spain; but the town council (*cabildo*) seldom exercised the independent self-governing function for which it was designed and, except for such important towns as Potosí, the municipalities were frequently dominated by royal officials.

Although the colonial enterprise is remembered more for the strenuous feats of the conquistadores and for the impressive material consequences than for moral content, the intellectual problems posed for Spain by its commitment to justice are crucial to any understanding of Spanish American history in its fuller dimensions. The association of temporal and ecclesiastical authority was exceptionally close in the Spanish empire. Several papal bulls had, by the time the conquest was well begun, conferred on the crown an exclusive jurisdiction over the Indies in the religious sphere. The missionaries who accompanied the expeditions of the conquistadores were agents of the crown as well as of the church. The responsibilities of the crown for bringing Christianity to the Indians were clear and acknowledged. The spreading of the faith was an unmistakable motive in the establishment of the empire in Spanish America.

Both civic and ecclesiastical representatives were serving the crown, but they were moved by varying considerations in deciding what the monarch's policy should be in his new domains. The moral issue turned on the conquerors' treatment of the Indians and expressed itself in questions about the right of Spain to rule, the possibility of peaceful colonization and transmission of the faith, the nature of the Indian, and the circumstances under which a just war might be waged against

Indians. A major question was the validity of the *encomienda* system, whereby rights over Indian labor and tribute were granted to individual colonists, and the *mita*, a compulsory labor system used in working the mines. In general, the conquerors themselves took a harder line than did the crown or church in all these matters, for the ease with which they could extract the material gain for which they had risked their lives depended largely on the continued exploitation of Indian labor and possessions.

On the other hand, the theory in favor of the more compassionate alternative was vigorously argued by such men as the Dominican father Bartolomé de las Casas. In the learned disputations waged for the purpose of guiding the king, the humane theory tended to prevail, a fact reflected in the laws and official policy directives. The remarkable feature, which has been obscured by histories of unrelieved Spanish brutality and exploitation, is the serious intent with which the debate was pursued and the genuine moral concern animating the crown's policies.

The more humane New Laws of 1542, largely the result of las Casas' protestations, provoked the debate of the century over colonial policy. The colonists contended that the empire depended on the preservation of the *encomienda* and exactions of tribute and labor from the Indians, whereas las Casas and his allies argued vehemently that peaceable settlement and conversion of the Indians were required by the dictates of justice. The problem was never fully solved during Spanish rule. For the most part exploitation prevailed, notably in the mines of Alto Perú. But on occasion, as in the Jesuit missions of the eastern lowlands, Indians were protected from exploitation by the settlers.

Years of Turbulence

Francisco Pizarro and Diego de Almagro, partners in the discovery and conquest of the Inca Empire and eventually enemies in the management of their victory, were both long-time residents of Panama when they sailed south in 1524. The isthmus had long been aware of stories of untold riches in South America, and some unsuccessful efforts had already been made to uncover them. In the course of eight years the two adventurers made three voyages following the coastline southward in quest of the reputedly wealthy empire and finally gained a foothold in northern Peru in 1532.

The Inca domain fell with extraordinary ease, owing in part to a civil war preceding Pizarro's arrival and in part to the overly hierarchical organization of central authority, which made the capture of the person of the Inca, or emperor, tantamount to total victory. There was, then, little need for expeditions to the far ends of the Inca Empire, and none of the events of the conquest took place in the northern Altiplano region.

Bitterness had already developed between Pizarro and Almagro when the latter concluded that his associate had dealt unfairly with him on a trip to Spain to secure royal backing for the Peruvian conquest. After the victory Pizarro built his capital at Lima (Peru) and was granted authority over a territory called New Castile; Almagro received a similar award under the name of New Toledo that was to extend southward from the vaguely defined southern limit of Pizarro's domain.

In 1535, before the boundary between these territorial grants was established, Almagro left on an expedition to Chile, following the Inca military road past the silver-laden mountains that were to become so important in a few years. A member of this party established the first colonial settlement—near the present-day city of Oruro. Unsuccessful in Chile, Almagro returned (in 1537) in time to put down a revolt led by Manco Capac, whom Pizarro had designated as puppet Inca, and seized Cuzco (in present-day Peru), which he regarded as being within his grant. This act led to armed conflict with Pizarro, who defeated and executed Almagro early in 1538.

In 1541 Francisco Pizarro was assassinated by Almagristas, and civil war broke out again. Charcas, the *audiencia* in the territory that later became Bolivia, declared for the king and the king's representative. A military contingent dispatched to Cuzco was instrumental in defeating Almagro's son, Diego, and Gonzalo Pizarro, who had proclaimed the right to succeed his brother Francisco as governor in Lima, was sent off to his *encomienda* in Charcas to enjoy his princely revenues.

After the New Laws were promulgated in 1542 with the intent of abolishing the *mita* and at least limiting the *encomienda*, Blasco Nuñez de Vela was sent out from Spain with express orders to apply the New Laws in Peru. No mission could have been less welcome, and the opposition gathered around Gonzalo Pizarro, who left Charcas for Lima. Under some intimidation, the *audiencia* there invited Gonzalo to head the government and to lead the resistance against Nuñez and the crown.

Fighting spread the length of the viceroyalty. La Plata (later known as Chuquisaca and, after independence, Sucre) was loyal to the king; it was taken and retaken several times. Only in 1548 did the crown succeed in reasserting its power through the skillful efforts of its new representative, Pedro de la Gasca. Gonzalo Pizarro was beheaded after his army had melted away in the face of Gasca's advance at the head of the greatest military force yet assembled in Peru.

Gasca's administration of the viceroyalty concluded the stormy era of conquest. He reformed the government and moderated the burdens of taxation and forced labor in behalf of the Indians (without imposing the New Laws strictly). He celebrated the inauguration of peace and stability by dispatching Captain Alonso de Mendoza on an expedition in the course of which Mendoza founded the city of La Paz southeast of Lake Titicaca.

Colonial Administration

With the advent of relatively stable colonial government in Lima (capital of the viceroyalty), developments in Charcas began to follow a distinctive course. Apart from an unsuccessful but bloody revolt led by Francisco Hernández Girón in 1553 and the severe consequences for the Indians of Spanish eagerness for quick profit, activity in Charcas tended to be mainly constructive. Within slightly more than half a century, all the major urban centers of modern Bolivia had been founded. By 1575, in addition to La Plata, La Paz, and Potosí—which arose at the foot of the mountain of silver—the towns of Cochabamba, Tarija, and Santa Cruz had been founded (under different names, and Santa Cruz on a different site from the one it occupies in the present day). Oruro dates from 1601.

The Audiencia of Charcas, necessitated by remoteness from Lima and by the wealth and the lawlessness of the mining communities, was decreed in 1559 and began to function in La Plata two years later. Its jurisdiction was first defined as covering a radius of 100 leagues around La Plata, but this was soon extended to Santa Cruz and to Tucumán (Paraguay) and Río de la Plata—the latter two in territory outside modern Bolivia. Cuzco and its environs in southern Peru also belonged to Charcas until 1568, when the royal Audiencia of Lima absorbed it.

Officially, the executive functions of the *audiencia* were divided; the one at Charcas had a president of its own, but the functions of governor and captain general were vested in the viceroy at Lima, leaving the *audiencia* empowered to deal only with routine matters. This situation led to a competitive attitude and, therewith, to Charcas' reputation for assertiveness, a condition reinforced by the economic importance of the province.

Location accorded Alto Perú a distinctive function in the second half of the sixteenth century. The Spanish, at home and on both sides of the South American continent, were concerned about Portuguese rivalry and the danger that Portugal might extend its territory in the New World. This, along with an unassuaged appetite for new sources of wealth, prompted concerted efforts to penetrate and explore the lowland to the east of the Altiplano. Both Buenos Aires and Alto Perú participated in such ventures. Although success of any kind was limited, the two sides of the continent were linked by expeditions setting out from both the east coast and Alto Perú. It was one such expedition, proceeding from the south under Ñuflo de Chávez, that founded Santa Cruz about 1560 at a site 180 miles east of the present-day location, to which it was moved in 1595. The Portuguese were forestalled, but the rivalry arising between the two groups of Spaniards prefigured subsequent hostilities between Paraguay and Bolivia over this lowland territory.

The great distinction of Alto Perú remained, however, the seemingly inexhaustible mineral wealth pouring from its mountains. The glitter of silver frustrated efforts to better the conditions of the Indians and diverted most of the attention that the Spaniards might otherwise have devoted to agriculture. The embodiment of the social and economic order based on silver was Potosí.

Potosí

The event of greatest import for the future of Alto Perú occurred early in the period of Spanish rule. Scarcely more than a decade after Francisco Pizarro's initial victory over the Inca, the richest silver deposits ever known were discovered in the place that was rapidly to become famous throughout the world as Potosí. This city of silver had overwhelming importance as a determinant of the country's future development.

Potosí in the period after the silver discovery has been described as a boomtown, and indeed the available evidence suggests something very like the temporarily prosperous, often rough and brawling atmosphere of mining towns in the North American West of the nineteenth century. The principal difference lay in the relatively prolonged productivity of the Potosí mines, attributable in part to the richness of the veins and in part to the primitive extractive technology that served to delay exhaustion of the mines.

Moreover, Potosí held a unique position by reason of its immense riches and the demand for its wealth; it was not merely one of several silver-producing towns. The mine operators therefore enjoyed a strong bargaining position in relations with the crown and its local agents and were able to secure special consideration corresponding to the city's official designation as the Imperial City of Potosí (Villa Imperial de Potosí). A petition of the times reveals the miners' desire to reduce the royal share from a fifth of the silver output to a tenth, to be exempted from a sales tax, to be assured of ample supplies of merchandise for the vigorous municipal market and of the mercury from Peru so necessary to silver extraction, and to protect their labor force against conscription and other diversions of manpower. Here as elsewhere, the crown was skillful in substituting fine words for costly performance, but it did accede to some of the demands, thereby demonstrating its recognition of Potosí's importance.

Population statistics afforded another measure of the city's importance. Some twenty-five years after the mountain of silver (the Cerro Rico) began to be worked, Viceroy Francisco de Toledo ordered a census that registered 120,000 inhabitants in Potosí. A century after the silver boom began the population was reported to total 160,000, much the largest urban concentration on the continent. Such figures are perhaps no more reliable than the widely varying estimates of silver production—one treasurer of Potosí calculated that between 1556 and 1783 miners had derived 820,513,893 pesos and the crown, 151,722,647 pesos worth of silver from the Potosí mines—but all available figures can be discounted heavily and still effectively demonstrate the city's importance.

The fame of Potosí spread far and rapidly. The name was placed by Cervantes in the mouth of Don Quixote and became current in English as a symbol of riches. The city was located on the Jesuit Father Lorenzo Ricci's Chinese map of the world toward the end of the sixteenth century and appeared on European maps as Spain's enemies learned of this important source of revenue.

The internal life of Potosí during the approximately two centuries of mining prosperity was in keeping with the boomtown image. Continued prosperity supported handsome dwellings and palatial official buildings as well as public works, which survived the city's fall from prominence; but it never contributed to the establishment of a permanent economic foundation capable of sustaining a populous urban concentration after the demise of the silver economy. The recklessness that typifies even a prolonged mining boom doubtless contributed to the record of almost uninterrupted intrigue and revolt. With so much at stake, the more or less permanent tension between Spanish-born and American-born residents and between entrepreneurs and agents of the crown were here exacerbated, and occasions for conflict and conspiracy were never lacking.

Spaniards flocked to the mines, and Indians either found their way there in the hope of enrichment or were driven there as labor. Negroes were imported for work in the mines, and foreigners abounded—to the discomfiture of both officialdom and the Inquisition—wary respectively of unrest and of heresy. Ethnic mixing was prevalent, and many an Indian laid claim to mestizo status as a means of avoiding compulsory mine labor.

The impersonal requirements of silver production overrode all considerations of human welfare and community development. The toll in Indian lives was overwhelming and brought Potosí squarely into the controversy over the nature of the Indian. A disciple of las Casas, defender of the Indian and foe of both *encomienda* and *mita*, gave the Council of the Indies a report vehemently denouncing Potosí's exploitation of the Indians, but the mines still needed workers and Peru, as well as Spain, needed silver. Official enforcement of the *mita* system of forced labor prevailed except for brief interludes, and no amount of smuggling by the laborers, of which there was an incalculable amount, could make Potosí attractive to the Indians.

Silver production, described as the "jugular vein" of the Viceroyalty of Peru, became a technological problem of major import as soon as the first high-content ores had been exhausted. Hydraulic power then took on increased importance in the process of refinement, and by 1621 several wealthy mine operators had accomplished what a modern engineer has called "a remarkable feat of engineering." A system of artificial lakes was created with a storage capacity of several million tons of water, thus regularizing the supply for the refineries.

Nearly as much attention was given to the development of improved refining techniques as to the discovery of new veins. Before the end of the eighteenth century an academy of metallurgy had been founded in Potosí. Nevertheless, foreign technicians of the same period remarked upon the absence of technical facilities and sophistication, which, had they been available, might have combated the inordinate waste that hastened the city's economic collapse. The retarded state of mining technology prefigured the conditions prevailing much later in a national economy built not on silver but on tin.

Alto Perú and the Road to Independence

By the end of the sixteenth century the pattern was established for Alto Perú that was to prevail with only moderate change through the remaining two centuries of the Spanish American empire. The economy was built on the extraction of silver. The population was divided into strata that permitted only slight mobility; the *peninsulares* (Spanish born) reserved for themselves the most attractive positions, and the bulk of the population were consigned to permanent exploitation in the mines. The Audiencia of Charcas had by that time made its relative autonomy a tradition within the Viceroyalty of Peru, and the Roman Catholic Church was firmly ensconced as sole spiritual guardian of Spaniard and Indian alike. The two centuries were not, however, rich in events. Only the end of the period began to manifest significant new tendencies.

During the seventeenth century the mining boom was still strong, and a stable mode of life crystallized slowly. Gradually the Audiencia of Charcas evolved a majestic disregard of both external authority and external affairs that brought it into conflict with the viceroyalty and finally produced a state of parochialism at once self-isolating and self-defeating. The arrogance of this final stage, when members refused even to kneel during religious observances, coincided with the greatest power that the body ever held.

It was near the end of the eighteenth century, from 1780 to 1783, when the revolt of Tupac Amaru mobilized practically all the Indians of the Peruvian and Bolivian Andes in an effort to expel the Spanish and restore the Inca Empire. The Audiencia of Charcas, by rallying the Spanish inhabitants, was instrumental in putting down the revolt, during which La Paz was besieged for more than a hundred days by some 40,000 Indians. The insurgents were not easily overcome and, even after Tupac Amaru was captured through treachery among his own followers and executed, the revolt continued for two years. Its final suppression was accompanied by terrible reprisals. Among its effects, it kept alive the sense of Indian identity in the face of continued subjugation. Likewise its occurrence so late in the colonial period and the effort it cost the Spanish to quell it undoubtedly strongly reinforced their conviction that rigid suppression of the Indians and their exclusion from society was a continued necessity.

The zenith of majesty and power of the Charcas *audiencia* was very quickly overtaken by other events. In 1778 Charcas was transferred to the jurisdiction of the new Viceroyalty of La Plata, administered from Buenos Aires, and new *audiencias* were set up that cut into the sphere of influence of Charcas. Still more important, in 1782 the intendancy system was instituted as a step in the process of executive centralization in the colonies, which was designed to improve the control mechanism of the mother country. Eight intendancies were established in the Charcas jurisdiction, each intendant being directly responsible to the viceroy. This bypassed the *audiencia*, making it more of a court of appeal than a governing body, and at the same time reinforced the judges' concern with details of ceremony. By concentrating on the fine points of their status, the members of the *audiencia* lost sight of important issues and became unconscious tools of the minority of radicals desirous of separation from Spain.

Equally important in its way was the decline in prosperity that accompanied the falling off of mineral wealth. Technology had not kept up with the exhaustion of high-grade ores and was unequal to the task of refining the ores of lower silver content that had once been disdainfully cast aside. And, since no other economic base had arisen to take up the slack, the Indians continued to be driven to extract mineral wealth despite the many attempts to lighten their burden—a circumstance closely related to the ferocity that characterized the Tupac Amaru revolt.

A final trend that characterized the last period of colonial rule manifested itself in the intellectual realm. Chuquisaca (as La Plata was by this time called) was not only the seat of the *audiencia* but also a university town. The Royal and Pontifical Higher University of San Francisco Xavier of Chuquisaca had been founded there by the Jesuits early in the seventeenth century. After that order was expelled in 1767, the university became subject to the conflicting influences of the archbishop (who was also chancellor of the institution), the president of the *audiencia*, and the internal university organization. One result was to shift emphasis from theology to law. In this connection a royal academy was founded in 1776 to serve as a final internship for advanced law students.

Partly because of its university life, which drew students from outside Alto Perú, Chuquisaca contested Bogotá's claim to the title, "the Athens of America." Its intellectual life, and especially the student discussions current by this time, reflected the impact of the Enlightenment on Spanish America. The Inquisition had not kept the writings of Machiavelli, Benjamin Franklin, Thomas Paine, and Jean-Jacques Rousseau out of Spanish America, and the ideas of these men were often discussed. Such ideas, especially pronounced among the so-called generation of 1809, the fomenters of the initial break with royal authority, had a profound impact when the Napoleonic invasion of Spain complicated the hitherto simple question of legitimacy.

Despite its frequently independent course, Charcas was fundamentally loyal to the crown (see ch. 8). Yet, when it became difficult to determine just where the crown resided or just who was wearing it, the radical lawyers understood how to exploit the confusion to turn Alto Perú in the direction of independence.

INDEPENDENT BOLIVIA

Liberation

A critical event leading to the independence struggle was the invasion of the Iberian Peninsula in 1807 and 1808 by Napoleonic forces. The overthrow of the Bourbon dynasty divided local sentiment in Charcas into three main camps: those loyal to the deposed dynasty, those loyal to Spain irrespective of royal incumbency, and those desirous of pursuing an independent course in the Spanish American territories. Charcas had already made significant contributions to the third camp through the intellectual ferment of its academies and through its relatively iconoclastic behavior in the face of royal authority over a period of three centuries.

Like all Spanish America, Charcas was rent by the standing quarrel between *peninsulares* and criollos, the latter resentful of the privileges reserved to the former and consequently open to radical ideas that promised them an improved position. At the same time, among those loyal to Spanish rule were conservatives, most of them prepared to wait for the question of legitimacy to resolve itself in Spain, and liberals, eager to welcome the reforms of colonial rule and practice that the Bonapartist victory seemed to promise.

In 1808 José Manuel de Goyeneche, a Peruvian general representing the junta of Seville—an organ of popular Spanish support for the Bourbon Ferdinand VII against the Napoleonic forces—arrived in Chuquisaca. He came to press simultaneously the claims of Ferdinand and his sister Carlota, then governing Brazil with her husband, the Prince Regent John of Portugal, and anxious to extend her position into Spanish America. Goyeneche sowed confusion in the Audiencia of Charcas and gained the support of the president, Ramón García León de Pizarro. When Pizarro attempted to arrest the judges of the *audiencia* for their resistance to Goyeneche and their general intransigence, the people of Chuquisaca rose against the president, arrested him, forced the archbishop to flee for safety, and established their own government under the recalcitrant *audiencia*. This move in the direction of indepedence (although based on proclaimed loyalty to the deposed Ferdinand) made May 25, 1809, an important date in Bolivian history.

La Paz was the next city to fall to the forces of independence and, indeed, went further than had Chuquisaca in demanding independence from Spain. By November Cochabamba, Oruro, and Potosí had followed suit. Although the movement received sharp setbacks at the hands of royalist forces sent to La Paz under Goyeneche by the viceroy of Peru and to Chuquisaca by Viceroy Liniers of La Plata, Alto Perú was never again wholly subdued.

In Spain the defeat of Napoleon Bonaparte brought Ferdinand back to his throne in 1814. The Spanish Cortes (legislature) was favorably disposed toward the interests of the overseas Spaniards and, during a constitutional interlude in 1821, passed measures designed to conciliate them. But Ferdinand set aside the liberal Constitution of 1812 and, in 1823, reestablished his absolutist regime. In Alto Perú he enjoyed the unquestioning loyalty of General Pedro de Olañeta, an unswerving monarchist who resisted appeals by independence forces and Spaniards with equal vehemence. As commander of the absolutist forces, Olañeta was the paramount force in Alto Perú for the last years of the Fifteen Years' War. He finally found himself in the curious position of trying to found an independent kingdom in that territory for the sake of preserving it intact for Ferdinand. It was Olañeta's pocket of royalist resistance that confronted Simón Bolívar in 1825 after the rest of Spanish America had been liberated.

Apart from the hardship inflicted on the countryside by marauding troops and on the cities as they changed hands repeatedly, economic life and social organization were disrupted; the population probably numbered fewer than 1 million by this time. Although Marshal Antonio José de Sucre, Bolívar's Venezuelan-born lieutenant, was impressed by the patriotism of the partisans of independence in Alto Perú, he had a premonition of what awaited him when Bolívar appointed him to lead an army in pursuit of Olañeta. Not wishing to assume the task, he expressed the fear that he and his forces would get themselves "into a maze of trickery."

After a bloodless campaign in which the remaining Spanish forces gradually melted away and, after Olañeta had been killed, Sucre witnessed the convocation of the General Assembly of Alto Perú in Chuquisaca on July 10, 1825. In accordance with the marshal's decree of the preceding February, the delegates to the assembly were chosen by the five provinces—La Paz, Cochabamba, Chuquisaca, Potosí, and Santa Cruz—to decide on the future political status of the country. Although Bolívar was cool to Sucre's initiative in this matter, the latter did his best to ensure honest elections so that the voters could choose freely among the alternatives. He even withdrew the army of liberation to avoid any hint of pressure on the delegates.

Despite Sucre's good intentions, the assembly was less interested in faithful representation of the country's interests than in furthering the ambitions of the delegates. Almost all of them, however, desired sovereign status for Alto Perú and, after much rhetoric, rejected two alternatives—attachment to the Viceroyalty of La Plata and reunion with Peru. Not altogether absent from their consideration was the factor of balance among the nations of the southern part of the continent. By choosing independence the assembly hoped to prevent Argentina from assuming undue weight in the regional configuration. Before the assembly completed its work, it adopted the Declaration of Independence, proclaimed on August 6, 1825; and five days later the assembly resolved to name the new nation after Bolívar, not without the hope that this act would placate Bolivar's reservations about independence for Alto Perú.

On August 18, 1825, Bolívar entered La Paz and was greeted by elaborate ceremonies to honor him as Liberator—recognition that he never failed to share with Sucre. But Bolivar was outspoken about his doubts as to the ability of Bolivians to govern themselves. In all official acts from that time until his departure at the end of the year, he was careful to avoid recognition of Bolivia's independence, always referring to it as Alto Perú and signing his many decrees as dictator of Peru. Only in January 1826, when he turned the country over to Sucre, did he promise approval by the Peruvian congress of Bolivia's independent status.

Bolívar's tenure as dictator of Bolivia was marked by energetic attempts to impose his ideas as a blueprint for the country. His decrees covered matters of landholding, education, public works, and the ordinary affairs of government, and he showed his awareness of the Indian problem by seeking to inculcate respect for manual labor in the rest of the population, hoping thereby to overcome the liability of continued exploitation of the indigenous population. Even after he had left Bolivia late in 1825, Bolívar, on request, supplied the General Constituent Assembly with the draft of the country's first constitution (see ch. 9).

Marshal Sucre inherited Bolívar's mantle of authority in January 1826 and continued to govern by decree. He was an able administrator and farsighted in such matters as encouraging immigration. Formally installed as president after the General Constituent Assembly convened in May, he carried on the Bolivarian policies already elaborated. At the end of the year he was confirmed in office under the new constitution. The country seemed at this point to have been placed on a firm footing, enabling it to look forward to a national development that would restore some of its former prosperity.

Foreign and domestic machinations led to Sucre's downfall in 1828, by which time fears had arisen that Bolivia might continue indefinitely as an appendage of Gran Colombia, the new republic composed of Venezuela, Colombia, and Ecuador, to which both Sucre and Bolívar properly belonged. The foreign author of Sucre's downfall was Agustín Gamarra, dictator of Peru, who engineered the Bolivian revolt against Colombian influence. Gamarra invaded and, with the connivance of certain Bolivians, forced Bolivia to expel Sucre in August 1828.

Assessments of the Bolívar-Sucre regime vary considerably. Their detractors emphasize the non-Bolivian character of their rule, the naïveté of their attempts to alleviate conditions for the Indian, and the baneful military influence they established as the basis of their positions. Their defenders can point, with at least equal justice, to the enlightened nature of their administrations as compared with much of what followed.

Problems of Independence

The president put into office by Gamarra ruled five days and was assassinated. Bolivians then elected their first native-born president, Andrés Santa Cruz, marshal in the armies of Bolívar, whose previous military and political experience had been mainly in the service of Peru. The son of a Spanish official and María Calahumana, direct descendant of the last Inca, he had joined the Spanish army as a youth. After capture by the forces of José de San Martín in Peru in 1820, he changed sides and thereafter had a brilliant career in the patriot cause. There was reason to believe that his mother had thoroughly imbued him with a consciousness of his Inca heritage, which may explain his later ambitions.

Santa Cruz assumed office in 1829 and, while watchful of events in Peru, devoted the first few years of his administration to highly constructive work in Bolivia. He ruled without a legislature for two years but called one in 1831 that united extremely capable men. They produced a constitution that year to supersede the Bolivarian one and approved a legal code drawn up at the direction of Santa Cruz, the first law code to be enacted in the new Spanish American republics. The Higher University of San Andrés in La Paz also dates from this period. Making full use of his wide powers, Santa Cruz did much in his first four years of rule to order the affairs of the country, encouraging trade and industry and making advances in education, public works, and pacification.

In 1835 Santa Cruz signed a treaty with President Luis José de Orbegoso of Peru that permitted Bolivian intervention in Peru for the purpose of pacification. Acting in support of the agreement, Santa Cruz led forces to Peru and defeated in turn two competing would-be dictators, Gamarra and Felipe Santiago Salaverry. He then proclaimed the Peru-Bolivian Confederation with himself as "Protector." The potential power of this combination aroused the opposition of neighboring countries. Brazil and Argentina both protested, and the latter unsuccessfully invaded Bolivia, but it was Chile that proved the decisive opponent. Its invasion of Peru, culminating in the battle of Yungay, brought the confederation to an end in 1839 and with it the career of Bolivia's ablest nineteenth-century president.

Santa Cruz was succeeded in June 1839 by José Miguel de Velasco.

The new Peruvian president, Gamarra, believing it safe to absorb a Bolivia now lacking a Santa Cruz, invaded. General José Ballivián, distinguished revolutionary soldier and erstwhile Santa Cruz lieutenant who had been exiled from Bolivia, was recalled and became a national hero by repelling the invader at Ingavi, southwest of La Paz, in 1841, a battle celebrated in the country's annals as placing the final seal on Bolivia's independence.

Ballivián then succeeded in overthrowing Velasco and making himself provisional president in 1842. With his position later secured by electoral mandate, he drew up a new constitution notable for its concentration of power in presidential hands. In some five years of autocratic rule, Ballivián aroused forces of opposition but maintained at least essential order in the country, in contrast to his equally dictatorial successors in office.

Velasco enjoyed a brief return to the presidency after Manuel Isidoro Belzu had, in 1847, instigated a revolt that brought about Ballivián's fall. A year later Belzu repeated the performance with Velasco as victim and succeeded to the presidency.

Himself a La Paz *cholo* (an accultured Indian—see Glossary) of little education, Belzu injected a temporary innovation into the country's political life during his tenure in the presidency from 1848 to 1855. Whereas his forerunners, all of aristocratic origin, had never seriously contemplated the participation of the lower classes in the affairs of government and national life, Belzu encouraged the *cholos* to rise against the ruling class and preached vengeance for the years of exploitation to which they had been subjected. The result was a succession of atrocities and reprisals producing a state of anarchy. The regime of Belzu consisted of a series of repressions of revolts rather than any program of reform that might have seemed implicit in his espousal of the *cholo* cause. Belzu resigned in 1855 after securing the accession of his relative Jorge Cordova as his successor. Ten years later he returned to public life in characteristic fashion, leading a revolt against President Mariano Melgarejo, who held office between 1864 and 1871. This time Belzu lost his life in the attempt.

The country's first civilian president, José María Linares, who engineered the overthrow of Cordova in 1857, was no less dictatorial than Belzu but otherwise of completely different stripe. A member of the elite and supporter of Ballivián, he had served the latter as minister to Spain and secured official Spanish recognition of Bolivian independence in 1846. His rule, from 1857 to his overthrow in 1860, reestablished the educated class in the seats of government but was so harsh that it paved the way for the Reform Constitution of 1861. The junta that succeeded Linares ordered elections to choose deputies for the national legislature—an exceptionally able group as it turned out—which then drew up the new basic law. The ensuing year was one of struggle between the elected president, General José María de Achá, a foe of the liberal constitution, and Colonel Adolfo Ballivián, son of the ex-president and advocate of the 1861 charter. The revolution that resulted in 1864 brought into office the most flamboyant of Bolivia's military dictators, Mariano Melgarejo.

Melgarego, whose origin was similar to that of Belzu, was a man of impressive native ability and military valor, but he was also without restraint in the use of power, and his tenure has been recorded as "the acme of dictatorship" in Bolivia. His natural shrewdness, however, kept him in power through six years of intrigue and revolt. It was during his dictatorship, in 1867, that the first large loss of Bolivian-claimed territory occurred—not through military defeat, but through negotiation.

In return for navigation rights on Brazilian rivers, including the Amazon, of which Bolivia was in no way prepared to take practical advantage, Melgarejo ceded approximately 100,000 square miles of territory. In this way Bolivia lost claim to its access to the Paraguay River in its northern reaches and about half its claims to lands in the Amazon basin (see ch. 3). In keeping with Bolivian tradition a revolt unseated Melgarejo in 1871. According to a contemporary diplomatic dispatch, his assassination while living in Lima as an exile "caused a profound sensation throughout the country but excited little sympathy."

Agustín Morales, in spite of his avowed preference for "more liberty and less government," represented little improvement as president. Only with the accession of Tomás Frías, a man of education and cultural attainment, did Bolivia enjoy a respite from the military style of dictatorship. The relief was of short duration, however, for only two years later, in 1876, Frías' war minister, Hilarión Daza, overthrew him. Daza restored the military tradition in the presidency and, partly to strengthen his internal position, recklessly involved his country in the disastrous War of the Pacific.

Bolivia's Atacama Desert and Pacific coast territories had become a coveted region because of their fertilizer resources—guano and nitrates—for which there was a ready market. Chilean companies had obtained concessions for exploitation of these resources earlier, but Daza saw an opportunity for increasing Bolivia's revenue by imposing higher charges. Chile seized the Bolivian ports, and in 1879 a war for which Bolivia was unprepared resulted. Bolivia's troops in its coastal province were easily defeated, and Chilean forces moved by sea to attack Bolivia's ally, Peru. Daza led a force to the coast to take part in the defense but soon deserted his troops and was exiled in ignominy. His successor, General Narciso Campero, led another force to help Peru; but the combined armies were defeated in 1880, and Bolivia withdrew, leaving Peru to fight alone for two years. It was not until 1904 that a treaty of peace was agreed upon by Bolivia and Chile, but the diminishing verbal disputes of the intervening years only underscored the futility of the Bolivian position. Its landlocked condition was as much the result of inept leadership as of foreign depredation (see ch. 3; ch. 15).

The alternatives of continuing the war or accepting defeat and a landlocked status became the basis for the formation of the country's first political parties that were to be other than mere factions associated with ambitious men. The Liberal Party was originally formed by those who would not accept defeat and consequently drew the support of army leaders like General Campero and his wartime chief of staff, General Eliodoro Camacho. The Conservatives, the peace party, nevertheless won the election of 1884 and succeeded in remaining in power for fifteen years.

During this period a degree of relative prosperity returned, owing to a resurgence of mining. Not only did the world price of silver increase for a time, but also the industrial ores, hitherto almost disregarded, appreciated in value. Copper, lead, zinc, and, most of all, tin began to be valuable as exports. The construction of the railroad from Oruro to Antofagasta, on the coast, in the 1890s facilitated the transport of ore. On the cultural side, there was a modest increase in the availability of schooling, but its benefits were reserved for the prosperous. The lot of the Indian remained unenviable, for increased economic benefits still depended on cheap Indian labor in the mines and in agriculture.

Writing about the period around the turn of the century, a Bolivian author, Alcides Arguedas, applied the term "a sick people" (*pueblo enfermo*) to his countrymen, in recognition of the persistence of national problems. Mining remained the principal earner of the costs of the government and the chief means of employment for wages; but the general diminution of returns from the exploitation of mineral resources had long since foreclosed any possibility of national prosperity under existing conditions. Only in the first two decades of the twentieth century did tin emerge as a large-scale mining enterprise capable of substantial earnings on the international market.

Although the business of tin extraction contributed notably to improvements in the country's rail network, its domination by a few large firms, controlled in substantial measure from outside Bolivia, prevented the kind of prosperity that silver had earlier provided for the country. Enrichment did not spread far outside the small group of owners and operators, and minimal wages and unsafe working conditions continued to bear heavily upon the workers. At the same time, agricultural production remained primitive, settlement thin and spotty, illiteracy high, and public life the province of only the well-to-do upper stratum.

Revolution and violent change of government came again in 1898 and 1899. The Liberal Party, by now the party of the newly emergent and prosperous tin-mine owners and other entrepreneurs, ousted the Conservatives and, after interim rule by a junta, General José Manuel Pando became president in 1900. Besides dissatisfaction with the long-continued rule of the Conservatives, regionalism and federalism were also at the root of dissension. The Liberals were strong in the mining area to the north and west, and the Conservatives, led mainly by the great landowners, controlled the south. The immediate cause of conflict was the Liberal demand to move the capital from Sucre to the larger, more vigorous and accessible La Paz, which thereafter became the de facto capital.

The so-called Federal Revolution failed to achieve its announced goals, principally the substitution of federalism for the unitary system of government and the separation of church and state, but there became evident a new inclination to approach soberly, and to act with deliberation toward, the nation's problems. The reasoning of the Liberal movement was that the unitary arrangement had failed to produce national unity or political democracy and that federalism would be more in keeping with the nation's physical and mental regionalism. A national convention debated the alternatives for months in 1899 and found itself so evenly divided that no decision could be reached. Notably, its decision to adjourn was reached without undue rancor and was not followed by violence.

On the religious question, the Liberals opposed the official status of the Roman Catholic Church and the privileges that such status afforded. The church-state question remained alive longer than the issue of federalism and actually brought about some changes. The right of public worship in faiths other than Roman Catholic became law for the first time in 1905. Later certain special privileges of the church were denied, and civil marriage was made a requirement in 1911.

Highland Bolivia's remoteness from its eastern borders again contributed to its dismemberment. When the increased demand occasioned by the tire industry made Amazonian rubber highly profitable, Brazilian rubber gatherers and other adventurers working up the tributaries encroached on Bolivia's Acre territory. As early as 1899 one of these armed his men and proclaimed an independent republic, which was suppressed by a Bolivian expedition. Thereafter there was commercial competition and diplomatic negotiation with Brazil that finally resulted in a convention by which Bolivia relinquished its claims in return for two small areas on the Madeira and Paraguay rivers, the equivalent of US $10 million, and the use of a railroad to be constructed around the rapids of the Madeira in Brazilian territory (see ch. 3; ch. 11).

The Liberal Party retained power for twenty years without any outbreak of internal violence. This unprecedented situation in the country's history is attributable in part to the party's successful identification with the sources of real power and also to its shrewd and often wise use of the position it gained thereby.

Most significant was the rise of the three great mining interests: Patiño, Aramayo, and Hochschild. Their growth was favored by the Liberal group, which was committed to a laissez-faire policy toward private enterprise. The tin magnates provided the government's principal tax source and soon came to carry so much weight in the Bolivian economy that they became a potent political force. In effect the nation was run for over forty years with a sharp eye on the interests of the tin-mining group, for the national welfare was almost as dependent on its support as upon the world price of tin.

The Liberal Party, having come to power through military support, was most favorable to projects leading to the development of a strong, well-trained army and, by reason of funds derived from the mining interests, able to contribute to them. Conversely, its purchases of military equipment, its approval of improvements in organization and training, and its employment of a German military mission all helped to ensure the support of the army's senior officers.

In addition to taxes and fees from the mining industry, the government received substantial sums through its treaty settlements. In addition to the equivalent of US $10 million received from Brazil, the country in 1904 finally concluded a treaty with Chile under which it received US $8.5 million, less the value of the Bolivian section of a new railroad Chile would construct from La Paz to the sea at Arica. With these funds in hand other railroads were constructed, and by 1917 Sucre, Potosí, Cochabamba, and the lake port of Guaqui were all connected in one system.

The long rule of the Liberal Party came to an end in 1920, not from any resurgence of Conservative strength, but because of an internal split. A faction calling itself Republican was defeated at the polls in 1917 but seized the government by a bloodless coup in 1920. The Republican period lasted through the 1920s and was marked by hectic financial operations backed by loans contracted abroad, mainly in the United States. Some of the money was put to good use—for example, a rail link connecting the Bolivian system with that of Argentina was built—but in general the national economy benefited little, and graft was rampant. The loans were supposedly secured by pledges against national revenue, and finally the foreign creditors insisted on the appointment of a resident commission to oversee collection. With the arrival of the world depression in 1929 the whole system collapsed, and with it the administration of Hernando Siles, the last Republican president.

The immediate cause of Siles' downfall was his attempt to bypass the constitutional provision forbidding reelection by resigning in order to run again. The revolt that unseated him brought about rule by a military junta until 1931, when Daniel Salamanca was elected as a coalition candidate. Supposed by many to have been backed by Patiño money, he was nevertheless highly respected for his competence and personal honesty. In turn, however, he fell victim to the frustrations stemming from Bolivia's series of defeats in the Chaco War.

The dispute with Paraguay over a region in the Gran Chaco, to which neither country had clear title, and its development into the greatest conflict to take place in the Western Hemisphere since the American Civil War constituted an ironical tragedy. Whereas the War of the Pacific had concerned a territory of great importance, both as to economic potential and the obvious Bolivian desire to retain its outlet to the sea, the Chaco dispute concerned terrain that was largely undeveloped. There may have been hope of oil discoveries in the area, but evidence indicates this to have been a rationalization of postwar origin. By the 1920s, although Bolivians still professed to yearn for access to the sea, they showed little if any bitterness toward Chile and had apparently come to terms with the arrangements agreed upon for Bolivian use of Pacific ports in Chile. Hostile feelings toward Paraguay, on the other hand, rose to a significant level.

From the late 1920s, despite conciliation attempts by other countries, border incidents multiplied. Bolivia's determination to see the dispute through to victory was traceable to an overweening confidence in its resources and population, significantly greater than those of its neighbor, and its armed forces which, German trained for a decade past, appeared to outclass those of Paraguay. Moreover, and here is the principal irony in the contrast between the War of the Pacific and the Chaco War, the loss of its important Pacific territory had aroused a desire to open up avenues of transport and communication with the Atlantic to the east, in seeming disregard of great impracticalities. Even complete victory would confront Bolivia with the problem of providing means of land transport across 400 miles of roadless semidesert and swamp to river ports still nearly 1,000 miles from salt water.

The war raged openly from 1932 to 1935, while continuous efforts by several groups of conciliators, including the League of Nations, failed to mediate the controversy. From the first the Bolivians were tactically outclassed and, although at times able to win small local successes, were consistently defeated in the more important engagements. By the end of 1934 they had been driven back 300 miles from their original positions deep in the Chaco to the foothills of the Andes, where a final stalemate was reached. Their German training and their superior numbers were canceled by inadequate logistical arrangements, poor intelligence, inept leadership, and dissension between military and civil officials. Not the least of the army's handicaps was the excessive rate of nonbattle casualties stemming from the inability of the highland Bolivian to become acclimated to the heat and the alternating drought and excessive rains in the low-lying Chaco (see ch. 15).

Frustrated by their own lack of success, a group of senior officers in the field—including the commander, General Enrique Peñaranda, Colonel David Toro, and (then) Major Germán Busch—took the opportunity afforded by a visit of President Salamanca to seize him and force his resignation. In his stead, his vice president, José Luis Tejada Sorzano, known to favor a cessation of hostilities, was accepted as president.

An armistice, arranged in 1935 by a commission of neutral nations (Argentina, Brazil, Chile, Colombia, Peru, and the United States), was followed by a prolonged effort to reach a final settlement and a new boundary line (finally established in 1938). As loser in the war, Bolivia could not hope for satisfaction in the postarmistice deliberations; nevertheless, there ensued a wave of bitterness against the neutral nations involved, especially the United States. The bitterness was partially responsible for the seizure of Standard Oil properties in 1937.

Seedbed of Revolution

The period immediately following the Chaco War bears many similarities to the era of military dictatorships in the nineteenth century. From 1936 to 1946 most transfers of power occurred by means of revolt, and the heads of government were all military men, most of whom resorted to dictatorship in the face of economic and social disruption. There was the same absence of political participation by the vast majority of the population. The traditional dissension among leaders continued. The social fabric was still strained by regional sentiment, reinforced by physical separation and a continued disregard of the lower classes on the part of those in positions of power.

There was, however, a difference of signal importance. In the midst of chronic floundering in matters of policy, there was a growing awareness that, after all, corrective steps could be taken to deal with the basic national problem other than the acceptance of one version of dictatorship after another. This awareness, and a willingness to act accordingly, represented a developing revolutionary situation based on ideological rather than purely personalist grounds. Even the postwar military *caudillos* (political strong men) were moved to make some accommodation to mounting tension, although they failed to develop promising programs that would have forestalled more radical attempts at finding solutions.

The Chaco War was an important factor in the awakening. It not only revealed the inadequacies of the traditional system but also afforded opportunities for many Bolivians to catch their first glimpse of the world around them. Many Indians of the Altiplano obtained their first perception of the meaning of the term Bolivia, and groups of the population established their first contacts with each other. Furthermore, the war left large elements of the population with a sense of injustice and the conviction that they had been used and misused by the national leaders. This feeling was especially apparent among veterans of the war, many of whom joined together in associations aiming at redress of their specific grievances.

The initial manifestation of active unrest took the form of a general strike fomented by unemployed Chaco veterans in May 1936. This brought about a coup d'etat, organized by some of the officers who had deposed Salamanca and who were backed by students. Calling itself the National Socialist Party, this movement upset the government and established Lieutenant Colonel Germán Busch at the head of a military junta in which socialist leanings were well represented. Colonel David Toro, who was responsible for many of the blunders of the war, was invited by the junta to assume the presidency. In July 1936 Toro suspended the constitution and decreed the conscription of workers to counter the labor shortage afflicting the country. Ironically, the veterans opposed the move, since their pensions were worth more than current wages. To carry out his announced purpose of creating "gradual socialism," Toro then inaugurated a quasi-syndicalist program that was designed to do away with political parties in favor of the organization of all employers and employees into two compulsory associations. His policies aroused such dissatisfaction, especially among veterans, that another coup in July 1937 easily displaced him in favor of Busch.

The Busch government abandoned state socialism, restored political parties and, in 1938, promulgated a new constitution. By 1939 economic conditions had again deteriorated to such an extent that Busch was moved to adopt police state methods to maintain order. At the same time the government undertook a barter agreement with Germany to exchange minerals, oil, and hides for manufactured goods. Busch announced his intention of establishing a planned economy with wide controls for the purpose of raising living standards. His death, reportedly a suicide but called murder by his supporters, prevented him from revealing details of his program.

After a few months' interregnum under the provisional presidency of General Carlos Quintanilla, an election was held that placed another Chaco veteran, General Peñaranda, in the presidency in the spring of 1940. The new executive oriented his policies to secure North American support, particularly with regard to tin purchases. The Japanese capture of Thailand, Malaya, and the Netherlands East Indies in the early years of World War II made Bolivia the principal source of tin for the United States and its allies, and arrangements of mutual benefit were made. A remunerative agreement to produce tungsten was also negotiated.

Despite the attainment by the country of a degree of relative economic prosperity, the Peñaranda administration found itself subject to growing hostility. During the late 1930s agents of the Rome-Berlin axis had been active in the country, working through the German Legation, cultural groups, and the then German-managed Bolivian Air Lloyd (Lloyd Aereo Boliviano). Long-established Nazi elements in Argentina had made many converts who were active in Bolivia, and the Italian Fascists—members of an air force mission—also preached the virtues of totalitarianism. Converts to Marxist thought, which had gained a foothold during the 1920s among intellectuals and had had some impact within the labor movement since the Chaco War, also began to manifest opposition to the Conservative regime. Still another group was influenced by the example of Franco's Spanish Falangists.

Out of the ideological ferment developed first factions, and then parties. The oldest of these was the Bolivian Socialist Falange (Falange Socialista Boliviana—FSB), patterned on the Spanish model, which in its early days attracted little strength. The extreme Left produced two parties: the Revolutionary Workers Party (Partido Obrero Revolucionario—POR), adhering to Trotskyite principles, which also was of little force and effect at the time; and the Party of the Revolutionary Left (Partido de la Izquierda Revolucionario—PIR), representing itself as an independent Marxist group but consistently following the Stalinist line of international communism. The PIR gained considerable strength in the labor unions, notably that of the railroad workers, and was the only party to nominate a candidate to oppose Peñaranda in the election of 1940.

The party, also emerging in 1940, that was in the end to demonstrate the greatest potential was the Nationalist Revolutionary Movement (Movimiento Nacionalista Revolucionario—MNR). It had originated somewhat earlier as a small group of middle and upper class intellectual dissidents representing a wide range of political persuasions from Right to Left and united by their discontent with the whole trend of events, which seemed to be reverting to type. Among its earliest leaders were Víctor Paz Estenssoro, a brilliant lawyer; Hernán Siles Suazo, son of the former president; and several prominent and influential writers. Intensely nationalistic in purpose, it aimed to unite the dissatisfied of whatever origin and to create from mass support a broadly based national party. Its early pronouncements were highly chauvinistic and contained ideas borrowed freely from socialism, Nazism, and the new Peronism of Argentina. To achieve its ends, it was willing to use all means that came to hand.

The MNR found its ally, strangely enough, in the army. There was already in existence a secret military society named Reason for the Fatherland (Razón de Patria—RADEPA). It had cells in most military units and key institutions, such as the high command and the military schools, and exercised control to a far greater degree than its numerical strength would indicate. As nationalistic in character as the MNR, it was also totalitarian in principle, and its influence within the army was capable of supplementing the MNR's political astuteness (see ch. 15).

Opposition to the Peñaranda government was not limited to that arising from ideological difference. The outwardly moderate tone of the regime did not extend to advocacy of any measures to improve the lot of the Indians, especially the miners, who continued to work under appalling conditions. The miners' growing resentment, given new force by unionization, led them to strike in December 1942. The government backed the management in its efforts to break the strike and sent troops to Catavi, one of the Patiño mines. The severity used in subduing the strikers, involving the machinegunning of men, women, and children, occasioned wide revulsion. The indignant interrogation of government ministers in the congress was led by Paz and resulted in the rise of MNR influence with the miners.

A year later the RADEPA-MNR alliance came to fruition in a coup unseating President Peñaranda. The affair was a typical palace revolution carried out by the officers in the secret society, and the influence of their cells in high military circles was such that army interference with the execution of the plot was forestalled. A junta was set up with Major Gualberto Villarroel as president. In his cabinet were three MNR members, of whom one, Paz, was finance minister. The United States and all Latin American nations except Argentina denied recognition to the new regime on the grounds that its revolt had been supported and financed by Nazi Germany and Argentina. Six months later recognition was granted after Villarroel had gone through the motions of dismissing the MNR members of his cabinet.

The MNR won a majority by questionable means in the July election, and its cabinet members returned to their posts. Villarroel then took measures to convert his police into an arm of repression and set about eliminating all opposition to the regime. Several prominent citizens, opposition leaders, and former officeholders were assassinated or kidnapped, properties were confiscated, and, in general, all potential opposition was repressed by terroristic methods. The effect was the opposite of what was intended, and people and groups found themselves united against the regime.

The reaction finally came in July 1946 when mobs in La Paz, largely unorganized and composed of students, teachers, and workers, took to the streets. The army remained aloof in its barracks, and only the police supported the regime. Villarroel dismissed his MNR officials but refused demands that he resign. The mob seized arms from the arsenal and moved on the palace, where Villarroel was captured and shot and his body suspended from a lamppost in the main plaza.

That rare manifestation in Bolivian politics, a civilian junta, governed until a constitutionally elected government supported by all moderate centrist parties took over early in 1947. The new president, Enrique Hertzog, formed a coalition cabinet that included members of most opposition parties, including the PIR. Neither the MNR nor their allies, the Trotskyite POR, were represented, although both were able to elect senators and deputies. Aside from ousting many leaders and members of the MNR (several thousand, including Paz, fled to Argentina), the new government was moderate in its conduct of affairs. It was, however, a regime devoted to the status quo and, although it did propose some liberalizing reforms, it showed enough political ineptness to render it vulnerable to constant MNR propaganda and agitation, vigorously led from outside the country. One result was the increase of MNR representation in congress after the elections of 1949. The government's evident hope that the lid might be held down by a program of mild and gradual reform, combined with a policy of enforcing peace and quiet by repressing the threats it considered most serious, in the end offered no satisfactory alternative to the radical revolutionary solution toward which the country had been drifting since the Chaco War.

The government's arrest and exile of Juan Lechín Oquendo after his election as senator in 1949 initiated a chain of events that in the end proved fatal to it. Lechín, long the popular leftist leader of the miners' union, was a firm MNR supporter and, as the agitator responsible for many strikes, was anathema to both the government and the mine owners.

The arrest brought on a violent strike, again at Catavi, in the course of which two United States mining engineers were murdered and others hurt. Troops again put down the strike with severity, killing many. This brought on sympathy strikes and finally a widespread civil war in which MNR-POR forces succeeded in gaining temporary control of Oruro, Potosí, Cochabamba, Sucre, and Santa Cruz. A revolt in La Paz was narrowly averted, and exile forces from Argentina invaded. The army remained loyal, however, and suppressed the revolt in a matter of weeks, thus earning the lasting hatred of the MNR. After the uprising the ailing President Hertzog, who had already turned his administration over to Vice President Mamerto Urriolagoitia, resigned.

The year 1950 was marked by a general strike, suppressed without difficulty, and by preliminary preparations for the presidential elections of May 1951. Overconfident by reason of recent successes, the group of centrist parties that had supported the government failed to unite behind a single candidate—an action that might have ensured a clear mandate from the little over 200,000 enfranchised citizens. Instead, each party put up its own man. The MNR, on the other hand, already supported by the POR, established a firm and formal alliance with the newly formed Bolivian Communist Party (Partido Communisto Boliviana—PCB), and with Lechín's Mine Workers Federation of Bolivia (Federación Sindical de Trabajadores Mineros de Bolivia—FSTMB). The FSB, on the Right, and the PIR, on the Left, also nominated candidates.

When the votes were in, the MNR candidate, Paz, was found to have won a substantial plurality, 43 percent of the 126,000 votes cast (only 49 percent of the registered electorate). In the congressional elections the trend was reversed, with the centrists gaining twice as many seats as the MNR. The constitutionally provided method of resolving the situation where no presidential candidate had a majority would have been to throw the election into the congress. Instead the president— fearful of the show of unexpected strength by the MNR, of the results of its announced policies of nationalization and land reform, and of

34

its known alliance with the extreme Left—persuaded the army, against its initial reluctance, to take over the government and resigned. Thus again the country was denied a peaceful alternative to violent revolution, and the inevitability of the latter was brought closer.

The military junta, under General Hugo Ballivián, negotiated favorable international contracts and granted amnesty to all political exiles, but it alienated labor by prohibiting strikes and demonstrations and antagonized all by press censorship. Further, it disregarded its promise to hold new elections and, perhaps most serious of all, it lost much of the otherwise sympathetic support of moderates by the illegality of its very existence.

It took less than a year for the MNR to complete its plans for seizing control. Mass support, toward which the party had for years been working, was strongest among the organized miners and other labor unions but also present to a limited extent in some agricultural areas. Many of the weapons taken by the mobs of 1946 were in the hands of men now supporters of the party, and the MNR had supplemented these with other acquisitions over the years. A final accession of strength to the revolution was the defection to its cause of the ambitious minister of government, General Antonio Seleme, the junta member in control of internal administration, and the National Police. The insurgents rose in La Paz on April 9, 1952, but within a day the army seemed to be getting the upper hand and agreed to a truce urged by the papal nuncio and foreign ambassadors. Armed miners from outside La Paz, however, occupied the heights of El Alto above the city, blocking all hope of reinforcement. The army surrendered on April 11. Paz assumed the presidency four days later.

DEVELOPMENTS, 1952–64

Although political stability, compared with conditions in the nineteenth century, had improved to some extent during the first decades of the twentieth century, the war with Paraguay had discredited the traditional ruling classes and exhausted the economy of the country. By 1951 the people had tired of political turbulence. The tin producers were troubled by demands for higher wages; and peasants wanted to own land.

The revolt of April 1952, inspired by the MNR and led by Lechín and Siles Suazo, was supported by the tin miners, by the national military police, and by civilian and student groups. During a period of three days of fighting, between 2,000 and 3,000 people were killed. As a result of their major role in defeating the regular army, the tin miners became the most powerful single group in the country.

On April 15 the MNR leaders moved into the presidential palace, and Siles Suazo announced the victory from the balcony. Paz, who was in Buenos Aires, promised to return to assume the presidency. A week later he told thousands of citizens who welcomed him at the airport that the government would use the wealth of the mines for the benefit of the people.

After the inauguration of Paz in April the MNR put into effect a number of plans and programs that the party had developed during the preceding twelve years. Never published in detail, their trend had been forecast in party pronouncements and commitments made at various times. In July 1952 universal adult suffrage, without literacy or property requirements, was decreed for the first time in Bolivia's history. Its implementation, however, was delayed four years, as the MNR continued to rule by decree during that period. The next important step, in October, was the nationalization of all the mines of the three great companies, Patiño, Aramayo, and Hochschild. In 1952 the Indian *campesinos* (peasants) on their own initiative began to seize the land. In 1953 the government issued a decree establishing a program of expropriation and distribution of large underexploited agricultural properties (see ch. 9; ch. 13).

In addition to these dramatic reforms, the government issued a decree in 1955 to provide rudimentary educational opportunities for the whole population and, despite great difficulty, tried to make it more effective than earlier laws with the same objective. After an unsuccessful attempt at fiscal reform in 1953, the government undertook a more thorough and effective program in this area in 1957 (see ch. 6; ch. 12).

Although accomplished without bloodshed, these sweeping changes in social and political organization brought in their wake dislocation and disorder. Large numbers of the educated class occupying executive and managerial positions left the country in fear of the new regime and in the face of considerable persecution. Stricken by the rapid loss of foreign technicians employed in industry—particularly in the mines and the railroads—urban life was thrown into near paralysis.

Another feature of the early revolutionary period was the serious constriction of personal liberties that took place under the first Paz administration. Extremely sensitive to the danger of overthrow, the MNR government moved against those forces that, in the light of their previous history, were likely to pose threats. Political opponents, many of them holders of high office in former governments, were sent to detention centers in outlying parts of the country, where they led an uncomfortable existence under the surly supervision of the miners and their armed militias. Some accusations of political assassination were leveled at the MNR but, apparently mindful of the mistakes of the Villarroel government, the party was not openly associated with the murder of any prominent opposition politician during this period. Violence directed against less important persons, however, was reportedly common (see ch. 15).

Nationalization of the mines had for so long been an announced

36

principle of the MNR that, regardless of predictable effects on the economy, it became a prime political necessity once the party had seized the government. Far from swelling the treasury, nationalization proved a substantial burden of the republic's finances. The three great mining companies had for years been operating as internationally owned concerns and maintained their headquarters and all but the minimum operating capital abroad. With the advent of the MNR all readily convertible funds were sent out of the country in expectation of the takeover. For some years little capital had been expended in modernizing or even in repairing the mining plants. When the government moved against the mining companies, it inherited run-down equipment and—after more than half a century of intensive exploitation—nearly depleted deposits of low-grade, complex ore. There was, in addition, the problem of meeting the payroll for a large labor force in the mines which, because of its great power and influence in the new government, could not be reduced and was even increased by nearly 50 percent. Skyrocketing internal inflation and dropping tin prices on the world market combined to make the mines a net burden.

In agriculture, too, land reform, admirable as social justice, brought initially diminished production. The *campesino*, unused and formerly unable to produce for a market economy, failed to plant for a marketable surplus. Consequently the food supply for the urban population was significantly smaller than it had been before the land reform. Declining revenues from the sale of tin meant that there was less foreign exchange to underwrite the import of food; thus the continuance of shortages was reinforced.

The revolutionary step of admitting the Indian majority to citizenship and accompanying electoral privileges brought a salutary change in the attitude of this group toward the country and their place in it; however, the newly broadened electorate had elections in which to make its voice heard for four years. Along with the increased self-respect that the revolution brought to the lower class—both in the cities and the countryside—came a general loss of social discipline. In the rural areas the Indians celebrated their newly won independence by terrorizing, at least in some localities, the non-Indian population, thus contributing to a general decline of law and order. In the cities the new power of the trade unions was used to enforce demands—sometimes excessive—on the MNR and, ironically, often produced a strained state of labor relations with a government that was basically prolabor and seemingly more concerned with the general welfare than any of its predecessors.

A leading representative of the government characterized the change wrought by the revolution in the economics of the republic as a "socialization of poverty." But in spite of this, the effects of the changes earned the MNR, and Paz in particular, the loyalty of much of the population. By 1956 the revolutionary party felt secure enough to permit elections for both congress and the presidency.

The MNR nominated the president's more conservative associate Siles Suazo, who was generally respected for his integrity and selfless interest in the goals of the revolution. Most opposition strength coalesced in the FSB, which nominated Oscar Unzaga de la Vega, a figure of considerable personal appeal, as Siles Suazo's chief opponent. In an election marred by extensive manipulation and coercion by the MNR and threatened abstention by the FSB, nearly 1 million Bolivians voted—most of them for the first time. The MNR received 786,792 votes—84 percent of all votes cast. The FSB received 130,494, and the Trotskyite POR and the PCB received a total of 14,602. Legislative cooperation with the MNR executive was assured when the party won all eighteen Senate seats and all but five seats (which went to the FSB) in the Chamber of Deputies.

The Siles Suazo regime was marked by a slight turn toward the Right as the government attempted to cope with the problems created by the great changes of the preceding four years. The first task of the government was to deal with the inflation, which had reached great proportions. Since 1952 the official import rate of exchange of the boliviano (later called the Bolivian peso) had dropped from BS60 to US$1 to nearly BS7,800 to US$1, the free-market rate approaching 13,000. Supported by advice from the United States government and the International Monetary Fund (IMF) implying clearly that subsidies essential to the maintenance of the economy could not reasonably continue if stabilization through reform were not achieved, Siles Suazo and his advisers decided to act. A program of politically dangerous measures was drafted, including the abandonment of the government-subsidized miners' commissaries, the freezing of wages and salaries, and other measures extremely distasteful to many of the government's strongest supporters (see ch. 12).

In late 1956 and early 1957, when Siles Suazo pressed the stabilization program, Bolivians witnessed the first serious rupture of the MNR coalition. Radical elements in the Bolivian Labor Central (Central Obrera Boliviana—COB) called for a general strike, which threatened chaos in the already disrupted economy. The threat was avoided only by a personal tour of the mining camps by the president and by the unwillingness of the more moderate unions to carry through the strike. This internecine dispute brought the resignation of Vice President Nuflo Chávez Oritz and continuing bitterness on the part of Lechín, Chávez, and other party members who had opposed Siles Suazo's action as a betrayal of the revolution.

Meanwhile, under Siles Suazo the complex machinery set up to administer the agrarian reform program continued with the time-consuming process of examining legal appeals, settling the inevitable disputes, and forwarding tentative titles to the president for his signature. Siles Suazo was criticized for the slowness with which the

38

new owners received title to their lands during his term. Though there was no doubt that the more conservative-minded Siles Suazo favored a deliberate approach in distributing land titles, it was also true that by June 1956 even the Paz government had succeeded in expediting the legal expropriation of only 109 large estates. Because of the numerous opportunities for appeal, thought to provide safeguards for smaller landowners, the title-granting process was of necessity a time-consuming one. The complexity of the reform law itself—which exempted medium-sized estates and larger properties that had been rationally utilized and in which significant capital had been invested—prevented its immediate implementation. Though dissatisfaction continued over the expense *campesinos* were subjected to in having their titles searched and the government's failure to provide technical assistance to new owners, the *campesinos*, with relatively few exceptions, continued to support the MNR.

In the latter part of Siles Suazo's term, disaffection began to grow on the right of the MNR spectrum. Wálter Guevara Arze, foreign minister and then minister of government in the first Paz government and perhaps the most fervent orator of the revolutionary movement, had aspired to accept the mantle from President Siles Suazo in 1960. Just as the left wing of the MNR under Lechín and Chávez had been frustrated during Siles Suazo's term, so too was the right wing under Guevara. When Paz returned to Bolivia from his post as ambassador in London and indicated that he was available for nomination in 1960, Guevara pulled away from the MNR to become the first formal dissenter and, with a large personal following, formed the Authentic Nationalist Revolutionary Movement (Movimiento Nacionalista Revolucionario Auténtico—MNRA). Charging betrayal of the revolution by the MNR, Guevara posed formidable opposition in the presidential elections of 1960. With the nomination of Paz by the MNR, a political understanding awarded the vice-presidency to Lechín, in the hope that strong support for the ticket would thus be generated from the left wing to offset the anticipated defections from the right wing.

Although the MNR had successfully avoided major embarrassment at the polls, disillusionment was clearly evident in the results. The cities, afflicted by food shortages and high prices, had given heavy support to the rightist opposition. The FSB nearly matched the government's vote in La Paz. The opposition increased its representation in the Chamber of Deputies from the five seats the FSB had held since 1956 to a total of seventeen seats, the FSB's representation dropping to three seats and the MNRA gaining fourteen seats, under the proportional representation system. The official party, however, retained control with fifty-one seats. The eighteen-member Senate remained solidly MNR, as it had been since 1956.

During the second Paz administration the government's position became more tenuous. The interest groups to which it had looked for support became increasingly divided. The heavy involvement of Lechín, leader of the FSTMB, in national politics weakened the bonds of communication and identification that he had enjoyed with the miners. The COB itself never fully recovered from the divisions engendered in the bitter general strike dispute of 1957.

The *campesinos*, too, organized in their *sindicatos* (syndicates), found their previous unity of purpose—in many ways more nominal than real—diminishing. After achieving their goal of landownership, the most critical purpose of the *sindicatos* had been accomplished, and tendency to focus on local issues and needs hampered their effectiveness as a national interest group. This disunity within the major pro-MNR interest groups was matched by conflict within the ranks of the party itself. After 1959 the leftists within the movement coalesced into the left sector, under the general leadership of Lechín, and cells and an embryo organizational structure were formed by the sector, particularly around La Paz. A similar group, the socialist sector, grew up on the Right. The central leadership of the party, under Paz, had good reason to be disturbed by this polarization of what had always been an extremely loose coalition of disparate groups drawn together for their own pragmatic reasons.

The June 1962 congressional elections were held against this background of internal disunity. Outside the revolutionary movement, however, the opposition was also afflicted with increasing problems. Guevara had become convinced that the MNRA must establish its own identity separate from that of the MNR. Rechristened the Authentic Revolutionary Party (Partido Revolucionario Auténtico—PRA)—except for a small band of dissidents, who deserted Guevara's leadership and retained the old name—it was prepared for an even more serious challenge to the MNR's leadership.

The natural affinity of the two largest rightist parties brought some talk of a united front against the MNR. This idea, however, soon foundered on the refusal of either Guevara or the FSB's leader, Mario Guitérrez Gutiérrez to relinquish primacy to the other. These two parties, considered by the MNR to be by far its most serious opposition, centered most of their fire on each other, and their campaigns deteriorated into personal attacks on one another's leaders rather than on the MNR.

Nonetheless, with the degree of widespread dissatisfaction that existed, particularly in the cities and certain specific areas such as Oruro, the MNR campaign was a bitter one. Deeply disturbed at the possibility that the election might indicate a shift of the popular consensus away from the revolution, the party, by report of both foreign observers and the La Paz press, engaged in massive coercion and fraud, directed from the top level of the party and the government. Affronted by the heretical nature of the PRA and seriously concerned by its strength, the MNR strategy was to reduce that party's vote by all available means. Deals were made with other parties, and the votes of the Social Christian Party (Partido Social Cristiano—PSC) and PCB were artificially inflated as a means of frustrating the election of PRA candidates to the legislature.

Another party active in the early campaign was the rump of the MNRA. On the formation of the PRA it fell under the control of loyal members of the MNR. The MNR kept the name in reserve during the spring in order to provide the official party with a front for formal opposition in the event the other opposition parties abstained. When this did not occur and it became clear the election would be bitterly contested, the MNRA was withdrawn.

With a reduced number of the electorate voting in the off-year elections, the MNR received a vote of approximately 347,000; the FSB, 51,000; the PRA, 26,000; the PSC, 13,000; and the PCB, 11,000. The government party won all senatorial seats being contested; of the thirty-eight seats in the Chamber of Deputies up for election, the MNR won twenty-seven; the FSB, six; the PRA, four; and the PSC, one. The PRA suffered the most from MNR manipulation. In La Paz Department the PSC's electoral strength was inflated in such a way that Guevara lost his seat there under the system of proportional representation. In the city of Oruro the FSB vote exceeded that of even the MNR, though a desire to see the PRA lose its position as the most important opposition party may have played some part in the manipulation of returns there.

Regardless of appearances, the election represented a significant setback for the government. With abstention running to nearly half the electorate and the fraudulent nature of the elections widely reported both inside and outside Bolivia, the government lost considerable prestige at a time when it could poorly afford it. The postelectoral period produced the usual round of charges and countercharges. The PRA leader, Guevara, left for self-exile in Chile, charging the government with the theft of his seat in congress. In August an event of some significance occurred when Gutiérrez of the FSB signed a pact of unity with Guevara's associates on behalf of the PRA.

The government's problems in early 1963 were, if anything, more serious than before the congressional elections. An immediate concern was the question of the presidential ambitions of Lechín, regarded by many as potentially the most powerful man in the country.

In spite of these preoccupations the Paz government continued, with external assistance, particularly from the United States, to develop and expand the programs with which it hoped eventually to pull the republic out of economic chaos and political disorder. An attempt to put national planning on a long-range basis, abjuring previous practices of ad hoc programming, had been made with the announcement in July 1961 of an ambitious and comprehensive ten-year plan for economic and social development; in early 1963 it was under revision after review by Alliance for Progress agencies. In addition, further

41

economic programs involving international aid were planned.

As the government attempted, often ineffectively and wastefully, to move toward these goals, it was hampered by the very improvements that had occurred in the country. By raising questions never before faced by Bolivians, the revolution had brought about a marked increase in the level of expectations of the population. By endowing previously deprived groups—miners, workers, and *campesinos*—with a new sense of their own worth and power, the government found itself in the position of having to accede to the exactions of its principal sources of political support, even though the satisfaction of such demands was beyond the capacity of the economy.

At the same time that increased demands were being placed on the government and the MNR, the room for maneuver had been significantly reduced. Sectors of the urban population were impatient for the material rewards of a decade-long revolution, as the 1960 and 1962 election results graphically illustrated. The demands of this group became increasingly difficult to meet, and strikes became endemic.

Confronted with the prospect of the increasing fragmentation of the initial, nearly countrywide, support it received, the MNR—and consequently the government—faced a self-created dilemma. Born of violence, it had continually to pay for its existence by trying to satisfy the turbulent elements that brought it to power, and any effort by government or party to curb excessive demands or opposition only increased the trend toward divisiveness.

By the end of 1963 the disagreement between Paz and Vice President Lechín, boss of the miners, as to how the tin mines should be operated led to an open break. Depending primarily on the army, Paz continued to repress dissent and to exile or imprison uncooperative subordinates. When Paz compelled the congress in 1964 to amend the constitution to permit him to run for the presidency again, he aroused bitter opposition in the universities, in the labor Left, and among politicians in his own party. Paz' opponents refused to participate in the elections, which they charged were rigged. Supported by the army, the police, and the peasants of the Altiplano, Paz was reelected in June 1964.

Paz lost his ablest allies. Guevara had alienated himself when he aspired to the presidency in 1960; and immediately before the 1964 elections Siles Suazo and Lechín staged a hunger strike to protest what they called Paz' "dictatorship." On the eve of Paz' inauguration, Lechín was severely beaten by a street mob said to have included political police; and in September Siles Suazo was exiled.

The country was on the verge of anarchy. Paz' vice president, General René Barrientos Ortuño, attacked Paz openly. Barrientos left La Paz for Cochabamba and, declaring himself a rebel, sided with students who were demonstrating and miners and factory workers who were striking. When workers and students were fired on, all opposition groups urged the army to intervene, and on November 4, 1964, after a

42

two-day insurrection by most units of the army, Paz fled to Lima.

Barrientos was sworn in as president of a military junta early in November 1964, a junta presided over jointly by Barrientos and General Alfredo Ovando Candia, commander in chief of the armed forces. Political prisoners were released. Exiled politicians returned. Confiscated property restored to its owners; and Barrientos and Ovando promised to achieve the goals of the 1952 revolution—agrarian reform, nationalization of the mines, industrialization, and social advancement (see ch. 10).

CHAPTER 3

GEOGRAPHY AND POPULATION

Bolivia has an area usually reported at slightly more than 424,000 square miles, but a complete survey has never been conducted and slightly smaller measurements are sometimes recorded. It is fifth in size among the countries of South America. Ringed by Peru, Brazil, Paraguay, Argentina, and Chile, it is entirely landlocked in the heart of the continent.

Structurally the country consists of a high plateau flanked on west and east by separate cordilleras of the Andes Mountains and by an extensive tropical lowland farther to the east. The ridges and valleys of the mineral-rich mountain systems separating the plateau from the lowlands form portions of the national territory so extensive that they constitute intermediate geographical regions.

Bolivia lies entirely within the tropics, but the extreme differences in elevation—as low as 300 feet along the Brazilian border and more than 21,000 feet on the highest mountain peaks—produce a great variety of climatic conditions. These, coupled with a wide diversity in soils, result in kinds of vegetation ranging from the sparse cover of scrub in the semiarid highlands to lush rain forest in the abundantly watered plains of the east.

The demographic data available are few and of limited reliability, but in the early 1970s the population was believed to number a little more than 5 million. Its rate of growth was somewhat slower than that of Latin America as a whole, but it was increasing as a consequence of a sustained high rate of birth coupled with a high, but declining, death rate. Life expectancy was low but on the rise.

Bolivia as a whole remained underpopulated, but the distribution was extremely uneven. Population pressures had developed on the barren plateau and in the valleys and basins of the southern cordillera region. At the same time, efforts were being made to colonize fertile but empty lands in the cordillera valleys farther to the north and in the broad eastern plains. The population was predominantly rural, and urbanization was proceeding at a moderate pace. Most of the urban population sector resided in the capitals of departments, the country's principal political subdivisions.

The proportion of the total population belonging to the labor force was the highest in South America, the consequence of a high rate of participation by women. Most of these, however, were unpaid family agricultural workers. Well over half of the active population was engaged in agriculture, and most of the remainder was occupied in service activities as a consequence of the industrial sector's inability to generate new jobs (see ch. 13).

In general, the largely unskilled labor force was increasing at a rate considerably faster than that of the number of jobs being created, and unemployment in the cities was high and increasing. It was, however, less serious a problem than that of underemployment. As a whole, the economy was characterized by underutilization of manpower.

BOUNDARIES AND POLITICAL SUBDIVISIONS

The borders between Bolivia and its five neighboring states have been fully delineated and demarcated, although minor questions remain concerning the border with Brazil (see fig. 1). For the most part, boundary lines follow such natural features as mountain ridges and streams, but surveyed straight lines predominate in the lowland frontiers of the southeast.

The boundary with Paraguay, delineated in a 1938 treaty signed following the conclusion of the Chaco War, was demarcated by 1941. It consists almost entirely of surveyed straight lines drawn across the featureless plain of the Chaco. The Argentine border consists of similar lines, the courses of rivers, and mountain features. The Chilean boundary, generally delineated by a treaty signed following the War of the Pacific, was entirely demarcated by 1906. Throughout its length, it follows ridges and peaks of the Andes.

The Peru border also follows mountain features in its southern sector. Farther to the north, it follows colonial-era hacienda property lines and cuts across Lake Titicaca. It is so drawn that the Bolivian portion of the Copacabana Peninsula in the lake is isolated from the remainder of the country; overland, it can be reached only by travel through Peru. In the extreme north, a virtually straight line of about 125 miles in length extends to the Brazilian tripoint.

In the north and northeast, the frontier with Brazil is formed primarily by large rivers, such as the Abuná, Madeira, Mamoré, Iténez, and Guaporé. In the southeast, it consists principally of straight lines. Sovereignty over the Isla de Suárez, a large island in the Mamoré River, remained in question in the early 1970s because of a disagreement with respect to where in the river the boundary line should be drawn.

A straight-line segment in the extreme southeast is interrupted by an eastward bulge at the frontier town of Puerto Suárez, a station on the line of a railroad connecting the city of Santa Cruz with the town of Corumbá, across the Brazilian frontier at the head of navigation of the Paraguay River. In addition, at the tripoint with Paraguay, a small wedge-shaped protrusion of Bolivian territory that includes the settlement of Puerto General Busch extends southward. Both of these extensions into what would ordinarily have been Brazilian territory were designed to give Bolivia access to the Atlantic through the navigable Paraguay River. In 1972 Puerto Suárez had yet to be opened to navigation, but docks were under construction at Puerto General Busch to make possible movement of the first hematite shipments from Mutún iron mines (see Natural Features, this ch.).

There is considerable free movement of people across the borders. A large number of subsistence farmers move seasonally into Argentina to participate in the sugarcane harvest, and the distinctive costumes and llamas of Bolivian peasants are familiar sights in the port cities of northern Chile. People on both sides of the border with Peru in the vicinity of Lake Titicaca are ethnically identical. The semiannual fairs in the lakeside town of Copacabana draw Peruvian visitors from considerable distances.

The movement of people in both directions across the border with Brazil was a matter of some concern to the Bolivian government during the early 1970s. Bolivians crossing into Brazil often remained and became Brazilians, but Brazilians entering Bolivia tended to impair the national identity of the territory entered by making Portuguese the principal language used and Brazilian currency the principal medium of exchange.

At the root of the problem was the fairly extensive colonization that had taken place on the Brazilian side of the border as compared with the relative emptiness of the corresponding zone in Bolivia. Bolivian children, lacking schools of their own, attended classes across the border, and Bolivian frontier dwellers, unable to find work in their own territory, could sometimes find it in Brazil. It was estimated that the Brazilian border town of Corumbá, alone, had more Bolivian residents than most of the border settlements on the Bolivian side combined.

Concern over the Brazilian penetration of the frontier increased at the beginning of 1973 when a Brazilian newspaper published reports of a movement into the valley of the Abuná River in remote Pando Department. The newspaper reported that this movement, by rubber gatherers and hunters, had commenced some sixty years earlier and that some 30,000 Brazilians were currently in the area—more than the total Bolivian population of the department. The movement had been peaceful, but a mild flurry in the daily press in La Paz echoed the Brazilian report, the government of Pando Department called for an alien census in the northeast, and the government in La Paz issued several statements of reassurance. The evident need for placing settlers in the frontier zone where Bolivia had never established effective sovereignty added a new dimension to the country's program for colonization in the sparsely populated eastern plains (see Settlement Patterns, this ch.).

Bolivia was created—at least in part—as a buffer state amid five neighbors. Its presence in the middle of the South American continent has probably served to ease tensions among the neighbors, but during the course of its history it has lost territory to all of them in a process that has meant the trimming off of more than half of the territory originally claimed (see ch. 11). Given this historical background, it is inevitable that irredentism to some extent colors political thought. It has not exercised a seriously adverse effect on the generally amicable relations that the country has enjoyed with its immediate neighbors during the years since World War II, but the loss in the War of the Pacific of what is now the Chilean province of Arica had not been forgotten in the early 1970s (see ch. 11).

The principal political subdivisions of the country are its nine departments. These are divided in turn into provinces (ninety-nine as reported in 1972) and sections. Each provincial capital, together with an immediate hinterland, makes up the first provincial section. Other towns are the centers of the second, third, and other sections. Rural areas of sections are called cantons, each with a village as its administrative center. In addition, the departments of Cochabamba, Tarija, and Santa Cruz contain delegations (*delegaciones*) that lie outside the jurisdiction of the departments. The administrative officer in charge of each of the three delegations is responsible for encouragement of colonization and for the welfare of Indian tribes in his area.

Only to a limited extent do the departments correspond to geographic regions. For example, although La Paz is thought of as an Altiplano (high plateau) department, most of its territory lies in other regions. Among the nine departments, only Oruro in the Altiplano and Pando in the eastern lowlands are clearly located entirely in a single region. Nor is there much uniformity in territorial extent or in size of population. Santa Cruz Department alone contains more than one-third of the national territory. Tarija Department, the smallest, contains a little more than one-thirtieth. Tarija, on the Argentine frontier, and Pando, in the northeast—populated largely by tribal Indians—were established as separate departments primarily because of their remote locations and poor communication with the rest of the country. The origins of the departments are historical. Six came into being with the establishment of independence in 1826, and Tarija and El Beni (the Beni) were added in 1831 and 1842, respectively. Finally, Pando was detached from El Beni in 1938. Despite the early establishment of the departments, however, in the early 1970s most of the border between Cochabamba and El Beni had yet to be defined.

NATURAL FEATURES

Landform and Drainage

Rising to their greatest average elevations in Bolivia, the Andes Mountains consist of two chains separated by the lofty intermontane plateau that is the country's heartland (see fig. 2).

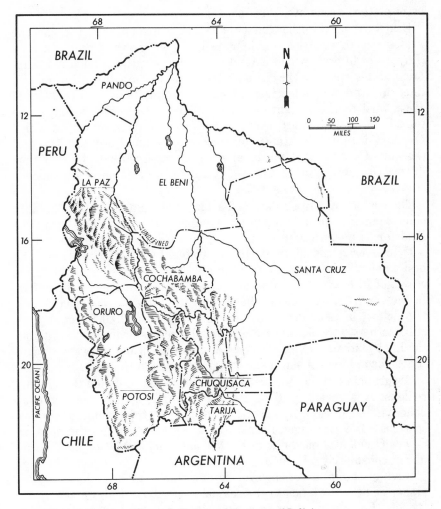

Figure 2. Structural Features of Bolivia

On the west, the Cordillera Occidental (Western Cordillera) forms the border with Chile and has crests in excess of 13,000 feet above sea level. Various perpetually snowcapped peaks rise to more than 16,000 feet, and the loftiest in the chain—Sajama—has a 21,391-foot elevation. For the most part, they are either quiescent volcanoes or solfataras—volcanic vents producing sulfurous gases. The scanty number of streams originating in the chain drain both eastward to the interior plateau and westward to the Pacific Ocean, although the Loa River is the only watercourse to the Pacific that maintains a year-round flow. The Lauca River, which rises in the Chilean Andes, drains eastward to Lake Coipasa, the remnants of a much larger lake that once existed at the foot of the Cordillera Occidental. Chilean diversion of the waters of this river in the early 1960s has been the subject of a lively controversy

49

between the two countries (see ch. 11).

Eastward, on the other flank of the high plateau of the Altiplano, the Andes rise to even greater heights in the narrower Cordillera Real (Royal Cordillera), which extends southeastward to a line drawn approximately between the cities of Oruro and Cochabamba. Beyond this line, the Andes broaden into a complex mountain system that bends southward to the Argentine border. This southern extension of the Cordillera Real includes several ranges, the most prominent of which are the Cordillera Central (Central Cordillera) and Cordillera Oriental (Eastern Cordillera). Occasionally, the name Cordillera Real or Cordillera Oriental is given to identify the entire system of the eastern Andes.

The eastern mountains are of Paleozoic origin and are considerably older than the volcanic mountain system to the west. The Cordillera Real forms an impressive array of peaks rising above the snow line, with an average elevation of over 18,000 feet for most of its extent. The best known of the crests are Illampu, at 21,500 feet, and the triple crown of Illimani, which rises to 21,300 feet behind the city of La Paz. In the southern extensions, the crests rarely rise above 16,000 feet in the vicinity of Lake Poopó, but peaks again rise to 19,000 feet or more still farther to the south. Various small streams drain westward onto the high plateau, but the larger watercourses drain eastward toward the Amazon Basin or southward toward the La Plata Basin.

Geographers are at odds concerning how best to divide Bolivia into regions. It is variously divided into two, three, or four regional components, and lines of demarcation vary. With the exception of a few scattered and tiny agricultural communities in the north, the Cordillera Occidental on the west has virtually no population and is ordinarily considered a boundary rather than part of a region. The high plateau of the interior, however, is universally identified as the Altiplano, and the lowlands to the east of the eastern Andes make up the Oriente (East). This great area is also known as the *llanos* (plains), and its extensive open areas are sometimes known as pampas. English-language writers occasionally refer to the region as a whole as the Eastern Plains.

There is nothing resembling a consensus with respect to the proper means of identifying the eastern Andes that separate the Altiplano from the Oriente. Often, this transitional territory is referred to generally as the intermediate region or zone. The eastern flank of the Cordillera Real, however, is specifically identifiable as a series of steep semitropical valleys called the Yungas, a word of Aymara origin roughly definable as "warm lands." South of Cochabamba, the physical characteristics of the intermediate region have characteristics very different from those of the Yungas, and it is often known as the region of the Valles (valleys). Although a majority of writers choose to treat the Yungas and the Valles as a single region, the topographical, cli-

50

matic, and demographic characteristics are so different that the two may be considered as separate regional entities.

There is no consensus with respect to the size of the several regions. Most writers consider the Altiplano to constitute 14 to 16 percent of the national territory, but some choose to count the Yungas as part of the Altiplano. A majority regards the Yungas and the Valles as constituting about 15 percent of the territory, with about two-thirds of the total belonging to Valles. At the foot of the eastern Andes, however, lies a belt of sub-Andean terrain that makes up about 8 percent of the national territory. It is considered part of the Oriente but is sometimes assigned to the Yungas and Valles. Accordingly, the great eastern lowlands of the Oriente can be considered to constitute as much as 70 percent or as little as 62 percent of the total area of Bolivia.

Altiplano

The forbidding lunar landscape of the Altiplano extends southward from Peru to the Argentine frontier for a distance of 500 miles and an average eighty-mile width at altitudes varying between 12,000 and 14,000 feet. It tilts upward from the center toward both eastern and western cordillera systems and descends gradually from north to south. The plateau floor is made up of sedimentary debris washed down from the adjacent mountains and reaches enormous depths that are probably greater in the north where rainfall is heavier and the more numerous mountain streams have created larger alluvial fans.

The material frequently appears to consist of rock, but it is in fact made up of compressed sandy materials, clays, and gravels. It powders readily, is highly susceptible to erosion, and has so great a capacity to absorb moisture that the scanty rainfall drains away promptly to leave the topsoil permanently parched. There is so little organic material in the soil's content that fields are left fallow for periods of up to eight years.

The Altiplano is the largest basin of inland drainage in South America. Lake Titicaca, straddling the Peruvian border in the north, is at once South America's largest lake and the world's highest body of navigable water. The remainder of a much larger ancient body of water, Titicaca has an extent of 3,500 square miles and contains twenty-five islands, which played an important role in Inca mythology.

Its volume of contained water is sufficient to exercise influence on the climate in its vicinity, and the mediterranean conditions prevailing in the surrounding territory have made it the most heavily populated and the most agriculturally productive section of the Altiplano.

Lake Titicaca is drained to the south by the Desaguadero River. Flowing southward for 200 miles to Lake Poopó, the river is the only major stream on the surface of the Altiplano. Titicaca has depths of up to 700 feet, and its icy waters are only slightly saline. In contrast, Poopó is a shallow body of very brackish water with depths of ten feet or less. After heavy rains it occasionally overflows toward the Coipaso

51

saltpan, immediately to the southwest, but it more customarily loses its water through evaporation and, as a consequence, is saline. Some geologists believe the Altiplano lakes and saltpans are remnants of a single ancient inland sea. Underground water of good quality but unknown extent is reported still to exist in the vicinity of the town of Patacamaya, about halfway between the cities of La Paz and Oruro.

In the southern part of the Altiplano the land becomes progressively more barren and the rainfall and vegetation scantier. The landscape is somber, and it is possible to travel for hours without seeing man or habitation. Much of the land is occupied by the great saltpans of Coipasa, Uyuni, and Chiguana. Elsewhere, stones adorn the surface in such profusion that, although many have been moved and formed into cairns and fences, the fields have the look of dried-up riverbeds. At the southern extremity of the plateau near the Argentine border, transverse hill systems span the gap between the eastern and western cordilleras of the Andes.

Yungas

The Yungas is a region made up of the sharply tilted mountain valleys that descend eastward from the crests of the Cordillera Real. The region is sometimes referred to by English-language writers as the *montaña* (mountain), the customary name of the corresponding eastern Andean slopes in Peru. The Yungas consists of three zones. The highest, sometimes called the *ceja* (eyebrow), has characteristics similar to those of the Altiplano; the lowest, or tropical zone, is related to the Oriente. Between, at levels of from 3,000 to 9,000 feet lies the true semitropical Yungas—a series of narrow river valleys with rich soils, heavy rains, and lush vegetation.

All three elevation zones, including the heavily forested ridges that separate the valleys, are generally thought of as part of the Yungas region. It lies almost entirely in La Paz Department, but a transitional area in the south lies in Cochabamba Department. The Yungas lands are the most fertile in Bolivia, and their location is relatively close to the city of La Paz, but the region's steep slopes and deep and eroded gorges have challenged highway and railroad builders. In the early 1970s it remained a thinly populated region in an early stage of development.

Valles

South of the Yungas, the descent from the Andean heights to the lowlands is more gradual and occurs in a series of steps. This is the Valles region, in which the valleys and basins are broader and more extensive than in the Yungas. Their alluvial soils—notably those of Cochabamba, Sucre, and Tarija—support the country's most intensive agriculture. The high ridges and plateaus of the region, known as the *puna*, are unproductive and sparsely peopled. The removal of much of the vegetation has resulted in poor water retention leading to alternating droughts and floods, which have ruined many terraces and fields.

Although broader than the valleys of the Yungas, those of the Valles region are also deeply entrenched. The drainage pattern is divided between the system of the Pilcomayo River, which rises in the heart of the region and flows southward to join the Paraguay River near Asunción in Paraguay, and the system of the Chaparé, Ichilo, and Río Grande rivers, which join in the Oriente to form the Mamoré, whose waters eventually reach the Amazon.

Oriente

The Oriente includes all of the country located to the east of the Andes. The region slopes gradually from south to north, and from elevations of 2,000 to 2,500 feet at the foot of the Andean piedmont in the west to as little as 300 feet along parts of the Brazilian border in the east. Politically, it includes all of Pando Department, nearly all of the departments of El Beni and Santa Cruz, and parts of the departments of La Paz, Cochabamba, Tarija, and Chuquisaca. Containing about two-thirds of the national territory and less than one-sixth of the population, the Oriente is frontier Bolivia.

The flat northern part of the region—made up of the departments of Pando and El Beni—consists of tropical rain forest and the Plains of Moxos (Llanos de Moxos), which cover most of the basin of the Mamoré River. Because the topsoil is underlaid by a clay hardpan, drainage is poor, and much of the area is converted seasonally to swamp. In the plains that make up the northern part of Santa Cruz Department, the terrain becomes gently rolling and better drained. Savannas alternate with forests, and cultivated areas are more numerous. In general, however, it is estimated that no more than one-tenth of 1 percent of the Oriente is under cultivation. In the southern part of Santa Cruz, a low line of hills marks the beginning of the Bolivian part of the Chaco that continues southward into Paraguay.

The luxuriant tropical growth that covers much of the Oriente has given rise to a belief that the region is extraordinarily fertile. Alluvial soils of good quality exist along the courses of rivers and support high forest growth. Even these soils, however, are generally less fertile than those of the Yungas, and between the watercourses much of the land consists of pampa negra (black plain) that supports only sparse natural vegetation. About half of vast Santa Cruz Department consists of poor quality sandy soil known as pampa blanca (white plain).

The few streams of the Chaco drain southward into Paraguay. Elsewhere, the drainage of the entire region is part of the system of the Madeira River, one of the major tributaries of the Amazon. It is formed by the junction of the Beni and Mamoré rivers near the extreme northeast corner of the country. The rivers of the plains are wide and sluggish but of sufficient depth to permit navigation in certain sections by shallow-draft paddle wheel steamers or launch-towed barges. Interconnection between the greater watercourses of the Mamoré-Madeira system is prevented, however, by a series of granite outcrops that

53

produce rapids and cascades, which effectively block them to navigation. The upper limits of power-driven navigation of any sort are reached at considerable distances short of the Andean foothills; as a consequence, water transport is of local importance to the river settlements but contributes little to the national distribution system (see ch. 14).

Climate

Climatic conditions vary sharply, both interregionally and within the regions. From west to east, mean annual temperatures increase progressively from the chill of the Altiplano to the tropical warmth of the Oriente. Precipitation is lightest in the Altiplano and heaviest in parts of the Oriente; in all regions of the country, it tends to decrease from north to south. Most of the rainfall occurs between October and April, during the southern hemisphere summer, but it varies considerably from year to year as well as seasonally, and both floods and droughts are common. In 1956 and 1957 a sustained drought virtually destroyed the Altiplano crops; in 1968 a state of emergency was declared in five of the country's nine departments as a consequence of heavy flooding.

The mean annual Altiplano temperature is between 45°F and 50°F, but on hot days in summer the thermometer may reach above 80°F. Nights are cold, even in summer, however, and during winter nights 0°F is sometimes recorded. Because it lies in a deep canyon, the city of La Paz is spared the extremes of the plateau climate. Although Lake Titicaca is of sufficient size to exert a moderating influence on the temperature of the surrounding countryside, a weather station near the lake recorded only ten months without freezing temperatures during one forty-month period.

The rain-bearing winds of the Altiplano are easterlies from the Amazon Basin that reach the high plateau only after having dropped most of their moisture on the Oriente and the eastern slopes of the cordilleras. The amounts vary from about forty inches annually around Lake Titicaca to as little as two inches in the semideserts and saltpans of the south, where potable water can be found only in a few scattered localities. Around the city of Oruro, large stretches of land are usually encrusted in salt, but when rain comes at the turn of the year, it falls in torrents, and the city may be inundated for several days. Irregularity of rainfall and freezing temperatures, even around Lake Titicaca, are said to result in the almost total loss of a crop on the average of once every five years and a loss so appreciable during three years that only a single crop during the five-year period is considered a really good one. The snowline on the mountain slopes occurs generally at about 16,000 feet, but most of the Altiplano surface is subjected to hail and frosts.

The thinness of the Altiplano air produces a variety of unusual phenomena. The landscape is seen with intense clarity, color, and a kind of luminosity. Writers frequently call attention to the stimulating quality of this visual effect and the physical response to the strong sunlight and cold, thin air. Some suggest that the indigenous population's ability to survive through centuries of hard labor and malnutrition can be attributed to this natural heliotherapy. The same natural conditions, however, have other, and less desirable, consequences. For example, the thin air can result in altitude sickness, and severe sunburn can result from even a short exposure to sunlight penetrating the thin blanket of air. In addition, as a consequence of the thinness of the atmosphere, water boils at temperatures so low that pressure cookers are in considerable demand in La Paz. Because of the reduced oxygen content, however, fires start with such reluctance that there is little work for the city's fire department.

In the Yungas the climate ranges by altitude from tropical through subtropical to temperate, and humidity is generally high. The upper reaches are draped in a constant pall of cloud during most of the year, and in the lower reaches the atmosphere is heavy with heat and moisture. The region is exposed to the rain-bearing easterly winds, and precipitation ranges up to sixty inches annually.

Southward, in the Valles, temperatures are similar to, but slightly lower than, those of the Yungas. Humidity is considerably lower, and the sheltered and densely populated valleys and basins have precipitations averaging from twenty-five to thirty inches annually. In the relatively dry area surrounding Sucre, however, an extensive system of dikes has been built because streams sometimes rise to flood level in a matter of hours.

In the rain forest and savannas of the northern Oriente, temperatures average up to 80°F annually, and there is little diurnal or seasonal temperature change. It is a land of humid haze and abundant rainfall, which is heaviest in the summer months, causing the sluggish rivers to overflow their banks to form vast, shallow lakes. Summer rainfall in the savannas is as heavy as that in the selva, but winters are relatively dry.

In the Santa Cruz Plains to the south, the heat, humidity, and rainfail decline. Annual precipitation is from forty to sixty inches. Temperatures average 75°F or less, and a sharp drop occurs when dust-laden winds called *surazos* are blowing up from Paraguay. In the far south of the Oriente—the Bolivian Chaco—the climate becomes semitropical and the rainfall is further reduced. The thirty-five to forty inches that are recorded during the year, however, fall during the three-month period from December through February and turn much of the area into seasonal swamps. During the remaining months, the watercourses dry up, and the land becomes parched.

Vegetation

The natural vegetation is sparse throughout the Altiplano. It decreases progressively to the south and virtually disappears south of the saltpans. The most common growth is *ichu*, or *paja brava* (savage grass), a spiky bunchgrass, which serves as food for the llamas and as matting and thatch for houses. Thinly interspersed are such hardy shrubs as the twiggy *tola* and a resinous herb called the *yareta*; both these species are important sources of fuel. Cacti are also found, and the banks around Lake Titicaca are thickly grown with *totora* reeds, which are lashed into tight bundles to make the Indian boats called *balsas*.

There are no native trees, but occasional willows grow in hollows near La Paz, and sheltered valleys and the area around Lake Titicaca are dotted with eucalyptus trees, which were introduced from Australia during the nineteenth century.

All modern kinds of potato are believed to have derived from a primitive tuber first domesticated thousands of years ago in the vicinity of Lake Titicaca. Another indigenous root crop is the *ocu*; indigenous grains include barley and native cereals called *quinoa* and *cañahua*.

The natural vegetation of the Yungas is the montane rain forest (low selva), which differs from the true tropical rain forest or selva (sometimes called high selva) of the Amazon in the smaller size and more open distribution of the trees and the greater density and variety of the undergrowth. The two forest types are also known respectively as the low selva and high selva—not because of their elevations above sea level but because of the difference in height of their largest trees. The descending lateral highlands of the Yungas are relatively barren, but the intervening valleys support plant life of immense vigor and variety. Tree species include mahogany, cedar, walnut, laurel, lignum vitae, ceiba, and dyewoods. In the lower reaches, many kinds of palm appear. The trees are draped in lianas, and creepers, ferns, succulents, lichens, and mosses abound.

Yungas slopes are terraced for the cultivation of coca bushes, the economic mainstay of the region (see ch. 13). A product of past importance to the area was the bark of the cinchona (*quina*) tree, from which antimalarial quinine was produced. Other medicinal and aromatic species include vanilla, sarsaparilla, saffron, and the *vilca*—a shrub that yields tannin. Below 6,000 feet, semitropical and tropical fruits, such as bananas, pineapples, avocados, custard apples (*chirimoyas*), mangoes, and Indian figs are found.

The natural vegetation of the Valles at higher elevations consists mainly of rough mountain grassland and occasional stunted trees, blown asymmetrical by the mountain winds. In valleys and basins, drought-resistant scrub and small trees predominate, and along the eastern rim of the region, a strip of semitropical deciduous forest extends from a point near the city of Santa Cruz to the Argentine border. The most usable of its trees are the walnut and the quebracho, a tree of extremely hard wood that is a source of both timber and tannin.

The entire northern part of the Oriente west of the Beni River and the northern section between the Beni and the Mamoré are occupied by the selva, or tropical rain forest, which is largely evergreen and requires heavy rains. The giant trees reach from eighty to 100 feet, without branches for most of their height. The crowns form dense canopies so impervious to sunlight that there is little underbrush; but lianas, parasitic vines, orchids, and other air plants festoon the trees. Skeletons of dead trees remain erect, supported by the tangled vegetation, and there is a thick ground cover of decaying vegetation. The selva contains many valuable hardwoods, but difficulties of transport have hindered their exploitation. Rubber trees are occasionally tapped, and Brazil nuts are an important export item.

To the southeast, and covering most of western Santa Cruz Department, is a large belt of semideciduous tropical forest with vegetation that is intermediate between the rain forest of the selva and the dry forest of the Chaco. Woodlands alternate with areas of natural grassland and low vegetation. The vegetation in the seasonally flooded Plains of Moxos consists of coarse tropical grasses mixed with scrub, palms, and heavier tropical woodland in the vicinity of rivers.

South of the Santa Cruz Plains and the low range of hills to the east, the Bolivian portion of the Chaco is an area of dry forest with quebracho trees, thin scrub and cacti. There are also stretches covered by coarse savanna grass interspersed with stunted trees, and communities of palms appear in moister places.

Wildlife

The animals most closely identified with Bolivia are the three Western Hemisphere members of the camel family—the llama, the alpaca, and the vicuña. Natives of the Altiplano, they are also common in high Andean plateau regions of Peru. The llamas are the commonest and most useful of the three breeds. The most used beasts of burden, they are also the main source of the wool used for weaving textiles for clothing and blankets. Dried llama dung, called *taquia*, is preserved carefully for fuel in the treeless region. Eventually, the animals provide meat and skins. The alpaca is similarly useful, although its smaller size precludes its use for carrying purposes. The vicuña, rarest of the group, is an endangered species protected by law. Unlike the llama and alpaca, it cannot be tamed, and hunters seek its pelt for the extraordinarily fine wool.

Also indigenous to the Altiplano are the increasingly scarce chinchilla and the still scarcer vixcacha, a long-tailed rodent of the chinchilla family. Other animals include the Patagonian hare and the guinea pig, which has been domesticated as a source of meat.

Species of animals are found in the greatest variety and abundance in the forests of the Oriente and in the lower reaches of the Yungas. Among the most common are the *tigre*, or jaguar, wild pigs, various monkeys, squirrels, badgers, peccaries, anteaters, ocelots, armadillos, opossums, and sloths. The large marsh deer is found in the Bolivian Chaco. River turtles, capybaras, or river hogs, alligators, and otters are found in Oriente rivers.

Best known and most spectacular of the birdlife species in the Altiplano and the surrounding Andes is the condor, known to the Incas as the messenger of the gods. The rhee, or South American ostrich, is found in the southern part of the highlands, and a wide variety of species inhabit the vicinity of Lake Titicaca. Curlews, plovers, snipes, and ibises live in bordering swamps; and lake birds include gulls, grebes, ducks, geese, and curlews. Among the principal birds of the Oriente forests are wild turkeys, parakeets, hornbills, toucans, and herons. Various hummingbirds are common from the tropical lowlands to Andean elevations of 18,000 feet, where flowers cease to grow.

The waters of Lake Titicaca provide several kinds of fish for the tables of La Paz. Among them are a kind of bass called the *boga*, rainbow trout, and enormous salmon-trout. The Pilcomayo River, which flows through the heart of the Valles, provides fish for the cities of that region. They are so numerous that great numbers are stranded and die on banks and sandbars during low water seasons. There is a similar abundance in the streams of the Oriente, where the carnivorous piranha and a kind of stingray as well as edible fish are found.

Minerals

Bolivia has enormous mineral resources, both in terms of size of deposits and variety of ores. Although they represent the lifeblood of the economy, the emphasis on mineral exploitation and marketing has been a mixed blessing to the economy. Until after World War II the few roads and railroads built were installed almost entirely with an eye to providing means of moving the mineral wealth from the Andean mines westward toward the Pacific for shipment abroad. The development of a transportation network linking the Altiplano with the fertile but empty lowlands to the east remained virtually neglected.

Copper and tin, as well as gold and silver, were extracted during the pre-Columbian period, but the early Spaniards had little interest in the base metals. Alluvial gold continued to be exploited, and silver became the principal source of extractive wealth during the colonial period. The great silver mines of Potosí alone are believed to have produced metal worth the equivalent of US$1 billion. By the beginning of the nineteenth century the richest precious metal resources had been exhausted, and during the twentieth century silver has been recovered principally as a byproduct of industrially important base metals. Some production of gold has continued, particularly near Tipuani in the Yungas, where operations have shifted from mining to panning and dredging in the rivers.

Tin deposits are distributed in a belt that follows the Cordillera Real and its southern extensions almost to the Argentine border (see fig. 3). Bolivia has a virtual Western Hemisphere monopoly on reserves of tin, the mainstay of the economy since the late nineteenth century when the growth of the food-canning industry stimulated its production. Production peaked during the 1920s, but a subsequent decline in the quality of ores has caused the closing of many of the mines and a scaling down of operations in others. During the late 1960s the tin reserves were still extensive, but the 1.25 to 2.25 percent metallic tin contained in the ores extracted severely limited profit margins.

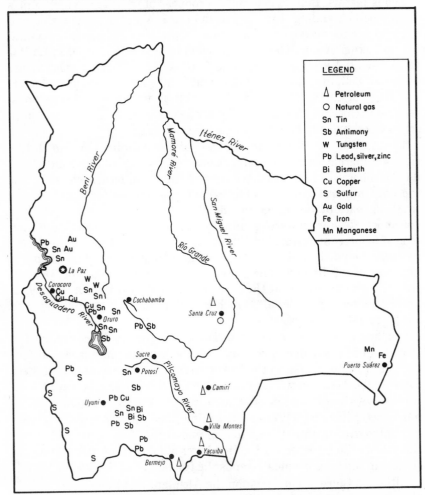

Figure 3. Mineral Resources of Bolivia, 1973

Tin is often found in lodes that also contain other metals, such as zinc, silver, lead, bismuth, antimony, and tungsten. The concentration of these minerals in the vicinity of Oruro makes the city the hub of the mining industry to the same extent that the silver mines of Potosí made it the hub city of the colonial era.

Zinc, occurring most frequently in association with silver and lead, is of high quality, and its proven reserves in tonnages of ore far exceed those of tin. Copper is found in the Altiplano near the town of Corocoro, as well as in the tin belt of the cordilleras. The most important bismuth production centers are in highlands of the Valles region, close to the Argentine border, and in the Yungas. In the late 1960s bismuth reserves were estimated at 500,000 tons of ore with a metallic content of 1.41 percent, much of it associated with copper and limited quantities of precious metals. Bolivia is a major producer of tungsten, which comes from a belt extending from La Paz to Potosí. Asbestos, magnesite, and gypsum are found near Cochabamba. Deposits of 2.2 percent uranium ore and extensive molybdenum deposits have been reported in La Paz Department. Nickel, mercury, and fluorite occur in the northern part of the tin belt, and there are many small antimony mines on the western flank of the Cordillera Real, as well as in the Valles highlands. Wolframite occurs throughout the tin belt, and in 1972 asbestos properties were reported being developed in the Yungas.

The Andean cordilleras to the west of the Altiplano are much less rich in minerals than those on its eastern flank. Small lead-zinc deposits are reported in the northern part of the Cordillera Occidental, but the only mineral resource of importance is the sulfur found in the southern part of the range on the slopes of the Tacora and Ollagüe volcanoes. Resources were estimated during the late 1960s at 22 million tons of 58 percent sulfur, but the enormous heights at which the deposits were found, combined with extreme transport problems and the high cost of refining volcanic material, has limited production. In addition, the great saltpans at the eastern rim of the Cordillera Occidental are the sources of crude salt, which is sold throughout the country, and are potential sources of borax.

Iron and manganese deposits in Tarija Department were reported in 1969, but of far greater importance are the iron and manganese at Mutún near Puerto Suárez on the Brazilian frontier. The existence of these deposits has been known for many years, but poor transportation facilities have discouraged development, and in the early 1970s development was still in an early stage. The mineralized area, however, is huge, estimated to contain 40 billion tons of more than 55 to 60 percent hematite ore, and to be associated with a layer of 50 percent manganese ore six feet in thickness, which extends the full length of the iron deposit.

Although there is some peat on the Altiplano and lignite in the Cochabamba and Tarija basins, there are no known coal deposits and, in much of the country, desert scrub growth and animal dung are the principal sources of fuel. There are, however, substantial petroleum resources that in the early 1970s had not yet been fully explored. The oldest oil fields, some of which also produce natural gas, lie in the Bolivian Chaco. More recent and more productive fields have been developed in the general vicinity of the city of Santa Cruz. Test drilling in the Altiplano aroused interest in 1972 when a gas well was brought in at Vilque, and an early report on the 1973 national budget indicated that the equivalent of US$15 million would be devoted by the national petroleum authority for oil prospecting and exploration, principally on the Altiplano and in Santa Cruz Department.

SETTLEMENT PATTERNS

In the early 1970s Bolivia remained one of the least urbanized countries of Latin America. Urbanization had quickened, however, following the 1952 Revolution and the enactment of agricultural reform legislation the following year. Before the revolution, the peasant had been virtually bound to his parcel of land, and the development of the urban labor market was insufficient to encourage migration of surplus workers from the farms.

The 1950 census classified as urban all administrative centers of departments, provinces, and cantons. On this basis the 1950 census report found 33.7 percent of the population to be urban. Many or most of the smaller administrative centers, however, included in their populations many persons dependent on agriculture for their livelihoods. On a basis that defines urban localities as those with populations of 2,000 or more, the Ministry of Planning and Coordination in 1970 estimated the urban population sector as having increased from 25.4 percent in 1950 to 29.3 percent in 1970 and projected a further growth to 32 percent by 1980. Another series of estimates shows the annual rate of urban growth during the 1950-60 and 1960-70 periods to have increased from 3.1 to 3.5 percent; rural increases during the same periods were 2.2 and 2.3 percent.

In the early 1970s the cities of La Paz, Cochabamba, and Santa Cruz had populations in excess of 100,000. Oruro, Potosí, and Sucre had populations of more than 50,000; Tarija and Trinidad had populations of about 20,000. These eight cities represented eight of the country's nine departmental capitals. Only little Cobija, the village capital of remote and sparsely populated Pando Department, had less than 10,000—and in the early 1970s it appeared unlikely that any other Bolivian urban center had as many as 10,000 residents. On the basis of the definition that urban places are those with populations in excess of 2,000, it appeared that the department capitals represented as much as 80 percent of the urban total.

The national seat of government of La Paz, also capital of the department of that name, is by far the country's largest city. Although Sucre is designated by the constitution as the legal capital, all government departments with the exception of the Supreme Court are located in La Paz (see ch. 9). The 1950 census showed La Paz to have a population of 321,000. Preliminary results of a carefully organized 1970 census of that city showed its population to have increased to about 564,000, but postal workers at once complained that the total should have been at least 800,000. A late 1970 estimate set the population at anywhere from 600,000 to 800,000, and a 1972 estimate fixed it at 700,000, including an increase of 200,000 during the preceding five years. The city, however, was reaching the physical limits of reasonable growth. The rift in which it was located had become fully packed with residences, and the migrants from the countryside had built their homes up the mountainside to the El Alto airport on the Altiplano surface far above the city.

With a population of 158,000 in 1969, the city of Cochabamba had doubled its population since 1950. It owes its growth to urban migration from the surrounding Cochabamba Valley, the most densely populated rural area in the country, and to the growth of a substantial manufacturing industry, which includes such products as footwear, furniture, and processed and canned foods. In addition, with the opening in 1954 of a highway to the city of Santa Cruz, it is important as a gateway to the vast Oriente region.

The third city in size, Santa Cruz, had a population in 1969 of about 109,000—nearly three times the population recorded in 1950. The only city of considerable size in the Oriente, it was the center of an agricultural colonization zone, of a cattle industry, of recently developed oil fields, of cotton produced for export, and of sugarcane and rice production in quantities sufficient to meet domestic demand (see ch. 13).

Oruro, the country's principal mining center, had a population of 93,000 in 1969, and after 1950 grew at a rate somewhat below that of the country as a whole. Potosí had a population in 1969 of about 64,000. At the height of its splendor as center of the silver mining industry in the mid-seventeenth century, 160,000 people had lived there.

Sucre, the legal capital of the country, in 1969 had a population of 48,000; an old colonial city, its pace of life and growth was leisurely during the 1950s and 1960s. The small city of Tarija had some 23,000 inhabitants in 1969; a crowded but relatively infertile hinterland and poor communications with the rest of the country had kept it apart from the mainstream of urbanization. Surplus agricultural workers from the area tended to migrate to other Bolivian urban centers or southward into Argentina, rather than to the local departmental capital.

Trinidad, the capital of the Beni Department, was also isolated; but it was a major cattle center, and the trade in beef, transported by air to the cities of the Valles and Altiplano, made possible a healthy growth rate and a population in 1969 of more than 17,000. Among the departmental capitals, only Cobija—the capital of Pando Province—had a population of less than 3,000 and thus failed to warrant city status.

By geographical region the distribution of settlement is extremely uneven. In the Altiplano and the Valles it is extremely dense in relation to the amount of arable land available. In the Yungas it is moderate, and in the Oriente vast tracts of land still await settlement.

The unevenness of the pattern of settlement is also evident within the regions. In the vicinity of Lake Titicaca, relatively mild climate and good growing conditions have resulted in a population density in excess of 125 per square mile in some localities. Population diminishes progressively to the south, but settlements are numerous the full length of the Desaguadero River, wherever sufficient moisture exists. East of Lake Poopó, settlements are strung along the west-facing foot of the Cordillera Real on alluvial fans that have been built up by streams issuing from the mountains. On the western flank of the Altiplano, occasional small valleys in the northern Cordillera Occidental support scanty populations on narrow sections of bottom land. In the southern part of the cordillera and in the saltpans and semideserts of the plateau surface, the land is almost devoid of people other than occasional seminomadic shepherds.

In the Valles region most of the population is clustered in the crowded valley hinterlands of the major cities of Cochabama, Sucre, and Tarija. The fourth major Valles city, Potosí, has no agricultural hinterland population of significance.

Northward, in the Yungas, soils and climate are beneficient, but the convoluted terrain has caused roadbuilding to proceed slowly and, as a consequence, in the early 1970s most of its population was concentrated in areas relatively close to La Paz. Otherwise, the pattern of settlement has been one in which most of the scanty population is found at middle elevations and adjacent to access roads. After enactment of the 1953 Agrarian Reform Act, some effort was made to preserve intact some of the more efficient of the larger landholdings. In contrast, population pressure in the Valles region resulted in the expropriation and distribution to peasants of many estates entitled to preservation under the legislation.

The population of the Oriente is small and widely scattered, except in the vicinity of the departmental capital of Santa Cruz. There has been considerable progress in agricultural colonization along the highway between Santa Cruz and Cochabamba, but the prevailing pattern of settlement is one of large commercial farms producing cotton, rice, and sugarcane in localities accessible to the transport center of the city of Santa Cruz and of great ranches and small towns and hamlets clustered along riverbanks in the areas where no roads exist. The rain forest of the north is virtually empty, except for tribal Indians, rubber and Brazil nut gatherers, and trading post hamlets on the riverbanks.

Primarily on the Altiplano, but also in the Valles and Yungas, the haciendas, with clustered hamlets located near the manor houses, formerly existed side-by-side with Indian communities consisting of small, dispersed farms. During the second half of the nineteenth century, there was a progressive decrease in the number of communities in all provinces of the Altiplano, and in a majority of those in the Yungas and Valles regions, as the communities were absorbed by haciendas. The Indian population remained in a kind of peonage in which they were permitted to farm small plots of land in return for labor performed on the estate lands. By the time the hacienda system was brought to an end by the Revolution of 1952 and the Agrarian Reform Act of the following year, it was estimated that although there were still well over 3,000 communities in existence (nine-tenths of them in the departments of La Paz, Oruro and Potosí), about two-thirds of the agricultural land was occupied by haciendas, many of enormous size.

By the end of 1959 over 400,000 plots of land had been distributed (but only in a minority of cases had titles been received) under the agricultural reform program to former hacienda Indians who now were officially referred to not as *indios* (Indians) but as *campesinos* (peasants) because of the pejorative connotation that had become attached to the term formerly used. The events of 1952 and 1953 caused a considerable number of mestizos to migrate to La Paz but, as the direct effect of the agrarian reform program was to give land to landless *campesinos* rather than to resettle them on new lands, they did not otherwise immediately alter the pattern of settlement.

The breakup of the haciendas released the *campesinos* from their peonage and made them to some extent participants in the cash economy. New markets were needed and, as a consequence, a series of completely new market towns came into existence around Lake Titicaca, along the road leading to La Paz, and in more accessible parts of the Yungas (see ch. 5). They were usually formed at intersections of former haciendas and at freeholding community boundaries, places usually utilized as loading points for hacienda produce and, accordingly, logical sites for developing market centers.

Beginning as small nucleated settlements, their growth has been in large part spontaneous. They have grown into towns; they include several hundred or more houses, a school offering instruction in the lower primary grades, a municipal building, and a church. Some have become administrative centers. By 1970 at least eight of the new towns had been established in an area of 150 square miles at the southeast corner of Lake Titicaca. The first of several new towns to be developed in the Yungas was Arapata in La Paz Department; it had grown into a town of about 750 full-time and part-time residents by 1964.

At least in the early stages of development, the new towns were remarkable in that during most of the week they were virtually empty. The householders were farmers from the nearby countryside who continued to derive their livelihood from agriculture and who resided during the week on their properties. On market and festival days, they would occupy the second homes that they had constructed in the new towns. As the little population clusters grew in size, however, *campesinos* without agricultural lands gravitated to them to engage in service activities and to reside in them on a permanent basis.

64

Colonization of virgin agricultural lands in the Yungas and Oriente regions is not a new concept, but it was limited in scope until the Agrarian Reform Act of 1953 made it a collateral part of the land distribution program. During the succeeding twenty years, the pace of colonization quickened, but estimates of the number of persons resettled vary from as many as 500,000 to far less than half of that number.

The three principal zones of colonization have been in the Oriente region—in the general vicinity of the city of Santa Cruz—and in the Yungas valleys of Alto Beni and Chaparé. Colonization zones of secondary importance have been located in Chuquisaca Department and along the Bermejo River in Tarija Department.

In Santa Cruz colonization has been heaviest in lands to the north of the city and along the highway leading to Cochabamba. Among the most successful of the colonies established have been those consisting of Japanese, Okinawan, Italian, and Mennonite immigrants. The Alto Beni program, centered in a fertile valley covered by virgin forest and located about 125 miles north of La Paz, has been unique in the sense that it has included the establishment not only of farms but also of agricultural cooperatives and industrial undertakings. The Ministry of Planning and Coordination, however, has noted that too often the transfer of *campesinos* from old to new lands has resulted only in moving them at considerable social cost from subsistence farming in one region to subsistence farming in another.

Colonization has taken place in the form of projects fully planned and directed by the government, in semidirected projects in which limited assistance has been furnished, and in spontaneous colonization by individual families. Semidirected colonization has tended to be the most successful in the sense that spontaneous resettlement has usually resulted only in the creation of more subsistence farms, and colonists in directed programs have tended to be overly dependent on the sponsoring agency. Estimates of the numbers engaged in the three categories vary widely, but most authorities believe the number of spontaneous colonists to be in a considerable majority. Surveys taken in sponsored colonies, however, indicate that many of the colonists have learned of the program through friends and neighbors rather than from an official source and that many of the spontaneous colonists may have been unaware of the government-sponsored alternatives.

In all three categories, substantial proportions of the colonists have abandoned their holdings and returned to their former homes or have migrated to urban centers, and in some cases entire colonies have been terminated. The highest rate of failure is believed to have occurred in the government-sponsored projects, where as many as 40 percent of the colonists have abandoned their new properties. Among the probable reasons for abandonment have been difficulty in adapting to a new social environment, major differences in crop techniques, and the effect of a radical difference in climatic conditions on people conditioned to the thin Altiplano air. In addition, it has been possible to clear the new lands only slowly; middlemen have received the bulk of the scanty profits, and the shortage of technical assistance and credit has often made necessary the limiting of production to a few relatively unprofitable crops.

Campesinos colonizing the Alto Beni zone have come principally from freeholding communities of the northern Altiplano and from more heavily populated parts of the Yungas; most of those migrating to Chaparé and colonies in the Yapacani-Puerto Grether area of Santa Cruz Department have come from the Valles departments of Cochabamba, Chuquisaca, and Potosí. Quechua speakers have predominated.

Although poverty coupled with the hope of economic improvement has played a major part in causing people to participate in the colonization program, successful colonists represent a kind of *campesino* elite that is much better educated and more adventurous and enterprising than the average. A survey of colonies in the Santa Cruz zone found that nearly all of the men and a majority of the women spoke Spanish, and 75 percent of the men and 30 percent of the women were literate. Nearly half of the heads of families had lived in one or more localities other than their places of birth. A large majority found themselves much better off as colonists and achieved economic positions that permitted them to contract for paid labor to help them in the fields.

POPULATION STRUCTURE AND DYNAMICS

The population was officially estimated at about 5,100,000 in 1971, as compared with a total calculated at 3,019,000 for 1950, including an upward adjustment of 8.4 percent to compensate for underenumeration in the census conducted during that year. The annual rate of increase was estimated at 2.3 percent annually during the 1950-55 period, 2.5 percent during the 1955-65 period, and 2.6 percent during the 1965-70 period. The rate in 1965 through 1970 remained somewhat below the 2.8 or 2.9 percent estimated for Latin America as a whole during the 1960s, but it was far above the Bolivian rate of 1.2 percent estimated for the years from 1900 to 1950.

A census originally scheduled for 1972 had not yet taken place in early 1973. The rural population, widely scattered over sometimes impassable terrain, has never been fully counted, and the various partial counts and estimates recorded probably tend to be underestimates. Urban counts tend also to be incomplete; the 1970 census of the city of La Paz resulted in an underenumeration estimated at 10 percent or more. The official 1971 estimate of the total population was considerably higher than estimates for immediately preceding years but, in view of the general tendency toward underenumeration and underestimates, it was probably more nearly accurate.

The crude 1950 census data, without adjustment for underenumeration, showed females to have exceeded males in number by about 50,000. A reported tendency of men to evade enumeration because of fear that it might lead to conscription for military service suggests that the enumerated margin may have been excessive, and an official 1969 estimate listed the margin at less than 15,000.

The 1969 estimate showed males to have been in a small majority at birth and at all ages under thirty. Females were in a majority in all subsequent age groupings. Some 41.8 percent of the population as a whole were under the age of fifteen, and 52.4 percent were under the age of twenty. Some 80.1 percent were under the age of forty, and only 3.5 percent were sixty-five years of age and older. Moreover, the median age of the population was believed to be decreasing. According to estimates from another source, between 1960 and 1970 the dependency ratio (number of children under the age of five years per 1,000 women between the ages of fifteen and forty-nine) rose from 688 to 728.

Population dynamics during the 1960s were characterized by a sustained high crude birth rate, a high but declining crude death rate, and a rising rate in infant mortality. Data available are incomplete, but representative estimates indicate that between 1960 and 1970 the rate of birth remained stable at about forty-four per 1,000, the crude death rate declined from twenty-one to nineteen per 1,000, and the number of infant deaths per 1,000 of the population rose from 103 to 108. For Latin America as a whole in 1970, crude birth and death rates per 1,000 averaged thirty-eight and thirty-nine, respectively, and the 1967 infant mortality rate averaged about eighty-one.

No ready explanation is available for the rise in infant mortality in Bolivia during the 1960s, but the total number of recorded deaths at all ages during the late 1960s was only about one-third of the highest estimates of the actual figure, and the apparent increase in infant deaths may have reflected only an estimate based on an increase in the proportion recorded. About one-fourth of all deaths recorded in 1966 were of infants under the age of one year, however, and a study issued by the Ministry of Planning and Coordination indicates that the actual rate of infant mortality during the 1960s may have been even higher than the estimate reported.

All estimates available show the rate of life expectancy at birth to have increased progressively during recent years, but the estimates vary widely. Ministry of Planning and Coordination figures show expectancy in 1960 and 1970 to have increased from forty-eight to fifty-two years for males and from fifty to fifty-four years for females, but other estimates show it to have averaged forty-seven years or lower for the two sexes in 1970. No comparative vital statistics are available for urban and rural dwellers, for the several ethnic groups, or by occupational status. Fragmentary data do, however, indicate that tuberculosis and silicosis take a heavy toll in the mines and that the life expectancy of miners is far shorter than that of the population as a whole (see ch. 7).

The scattered data available indicate that immigration to Bolivia during the years since World War II has been insufficient in volume to have much effect on population dynamics. The 1950 census counted 4,470 persons whose first language was Portuguese, presumably those persons from Brazil. There were 3,559 speakers of German, some of whom may have been members of a 500-family Mennonite agricultural colony established in Santa Cruz and Jews who fled from Europe during the 1930s. There were also 2,500 speakers of English and small numbers speaking Arabic and other languages. Immigrants who arrived after 1950 include some 1,500 Japanese and 3,000 Okinawan families in agricultural colonies. In addition, a considerable number of Brazilians are reported to have taken up residence in Bolivian territory close to the frontier in the northern part of the Oriente region (see Boundaries and Political Subdivisions, this ch.). Migration from neighboring Spanish-speaking countries, however, appears to have been negligible.

Emigration has far outstripped immigration. Describing the situation as "alarming," an official 1970 study reported that Argentina was the principal destination of emigrants. During the 1952–66 period there had been 279,831 officially recorded departures for Argentina, many of them presumably seasonal farmworkers. There had, however, been only 169,088 returns—an apparent population loss of 110,743 during the fourteen-year period. The same study noted that during 1965 some 26.4 percent of the Bolivian residents leaving the country had departed with visas for Argentina. Visas for travel to Chile had represented 21.5 percent, to Peru 13.9 per cent, to the United States 13.3 percent, and to other countries 11.4 percent.

The official study may have greatly understated the case. A large number of Bolivians without documentation are generally recognized to have left the country permanently or on a long-term basis in response to the promise of better job opportunities and higher standards of living in Brazil, in Chile, and—especially—in Argentina. One writer estimated that in the late 1960s there were as many as 700,000 Bolivians in Argentina alone. Of this number about 200,000 were seasonal farmhands who cross and recross the frontier. About 100,000 were itinerant hands who moved from farm to farm in various parts of Argentina, and half or more of the Bolivian émigré population lived in the shantytown suburbs of Buenos Aires and other Argentine cities. In 1967 the Inter-American Development Bank estimated that Bolivians made up as much as 20 percent of the populations of the northern Argentine provinces of Salta and Jujuy.

The official concern over the flow of emigration, which has also been expressed editorially in La Paz newspapers, relates to the qualitative as well as the quantitative aspects of the outflow. Most of the emigrants have been young adults with some degree of education, persons of maximum value to the society. The number of professionals emigrating seems small, but it has been relatively high in proportion to the limited size of the cadre of professionals. According to data compiled by the Organization of American States, during the 1959–67 period an average of 162 professionals departed Bolivia annually with emigrant documentation. The figure represented 14.1 percent of the number graduating annually from the Bolivian universities, the sixth highest proportion among seventeen Latin American countries studied.

POPULATION PROBLEMS

The Bolivian government regards as its primordial population problem an uneven distribution of people by geographic region, which is such that too many are crowded on relatively poor lands while enormous stretches with fertile soils remain virtually unpopulated. Nearly all of the Oriente and much of the Yungas await development at a time when the population of the Altiplano and the Valles has outstripped its capacity to feed itself (see Settlement Patterns, this ch.).

Overall, Bolivia is among the least densely populated countries of Latin America, and its rate of population growth is somewhat below the average for the region. For these reasons, the attention directed toward population control has been limited. In addition, literacy rates and per capita incomes are among Latin America's lowest, and in almost all countries the degree of consideration given to limiting the sizes of families varies in direct proportion with education and income.

In the Bolivian countryside contraception is virtually unknown, although abortion (prohibited by law, even when medical reasons are involved) is sometimes attempted by drinking infusions of herbs. In urban localities family planning and the use of contraceptives occur with a frequency in almost direct proportion to socioeconomic status. Even at higher levels, however, there is appreciable resistance to the concept of organized planning. In one La Paz radio program a scare announcement was made to the effect that a woman who had taken contraceptive pills had given birth to twenty miniature infants. In 1969 a La Paz newspaper editorialized that the great powers should not attempt to pressure developing countries to sponsor birth control programs as elements of their overall programs for economic and social development. The editorial noted that the domestic film *Yawar Wallku* (Blood of the Condor), playing at the time in La Paz theaters, had a story line repudiating the policy of manipulating people sexually as though they were animals. It added that there had been published reports of foreign assistance workers secretly sterilizing the wives of Bolivian peasants and miners.

A few planning measures have been undertaken. The National Family Center was established in late 1968, with a Governing Council composed of representatives of the government, the medical profession, and private organizations. Its first undertaking was the preparation of a study of the prevalence of induced abortion and the use of contraceptives. In addition, a day care center in La Paz was converted into a maternal and child health unit with the objective of providing integrated, responsible parenthood orientation and related services. In this undertaking, the National Family Center was joined by the National Council for Minors and the Ministry of Health and Social Welfare.

In 1970 the Ministry of Health and Social Welfare's Department of Family Protection included family planning matters among its responsibilities, and training courses related to family planning were offered by the Higher University of San Andrés in La Paz. External assistance in family planning was being made available in varying but generally limited degrees by the United States economic assistance program, by the United States-based Pathfinder Fund, by World Neighbors, by Church World Services, and by Oxfam—a voluntary British relief organization.

LABOR FORCE

Scattered estimates during the early 1970s indicated that well over 2 million people were numbered in the labor force. In 1967 it was officially estimated to consist of 1,910,000 people, including 100,000 unemployed workers actively seeking employment, as compared with 1,361,277, counted in the census of 1950 (see table 1). The figures cited indicated a sharp decline in the participation rate (labor force as a percentage of total population) of from 50.3 percent in 1950 to between 42 and 43 percent in 1967. Evident deficiencies in the 1950 census, however, prevent the data from being fully comparable. The participation rate was calculated on the basis of actual enumeration without the 8.4 percent upward adjustment for underenumeration, and it appears unlikely that underenumeration of the labor force occurred at the same rate as that of the population as a whole. Estimates by the International Labor Organization (ILO) based on different criteria and indicating much lower participation rates show the labor force to have been made up of 1,049,000 workers, or a participation rate of 34.8 percent in 1950; and of 1,560,000 workers, or a participation rate of 33.5 percent in 1970.

The sharp disparity between the official Bolivian data and the ILO estimates is largely explained by the fact that the former included and the latter appeared to have excluded most of the females who were unpaid family agricultural workers. For example, the 1950 census found that there were more than 397,000 female agricultural workers, of whom nearly 374,000 were unpaid. The ILO estimate for 1950 showed that there were 51,000 female members of the agricultural labor force.

70

Table 1. *Bolivia, Estimated Size of Labor Force by Sector of Economic Activity, 1967*

Sector of Activity	Employment (in thousands)	Percent
Agriculture and related activities	1,205	66.6
Industry		
Manufacturing	145	8.0
Mining	49	2.7
Petroleum	6	0.3
Construction	40	2.2
Public utilities	5	0.3
Subtotal	245	13.5
Services		
Commerce and finance	110	6.1
Transport and communications . . . . : . .	50	2.8
Government (direct employment)	48	2.6
Other services	152	8.4
Subtotal	360	19.9
Total*	1,810	100.0

* Does not include estimated 100,000 persons unemployed and actively seeking employment.

Source: Adapted from Bolivia, Ministerio de Planificación y Coordinación, *Estratégia socio-económica del desarrollo nacional, 1971-1991*, La Paz, 1970, p. 507.

Although several reporting entities in addition to the ILO appear to have excluded female family workers, there is good reason for regarding them as valid labor force members. During the period that preceded the 1953 agricultural reform, the heads of households on the haciendas were required to give so much of their time to work in the hacienda fields in return for their small plots of land that the job of working these plots fell largely to their women. It is not reasonable to suppose that the pattern of extensive female participation changed significantly as a consequence of agricultural reform. Moreover, even in the freeholding communities outside the hacienda system, the women's economic importance has traditionally been as great as the men's. In addition to performing her household duties, she has prepared seeds and manure, played the principal role in care of the livestock, and contributed labor to plowing and to the harvest. When unpaid family workers are included in the labor force, the scattered data available indicate that the overall participation rate in Bolivia during the years since World War II may have been the highest in Latin America, after Haiti. Excluding females working without remuneration, the rate is below the Latin American average.

Comparative statistics do not permit an exact judgment on employment trends by sector of employment. General considerations indicate that the proportions of the labor force in the agricultural and manufacturing sectors have declined and that the proportion in services

71

employment has risen. A moderate but increasing country-to-town migration has substantially increased the urban proportion of the population (see Settlement Patterns, this ch.). As a consequence, the already saturated urban labor market was assailed by new job demands, but industrial employment has had relatively little to offer. Employment in the construction sector rose considerably with a gain in housing and highway construction during the late 1950s and the 1960s. In large measure, however, it was seasonal work occupying Altiplano farmers. Demand for manufactured goods rose sharply, but it was mainly for imported durable goods, such as bicycles, sewing machines, and radios. Moreover, as much as five-sixths of the manufacturing employment was in traditional handicraft operations producing items for which the demand increased at a flagging rate.

As a consequence of the limited demand for industrial workers, most of the swollen urban labor force has found work in the services sector. Many urban migrants have gravitated to marginal service activities in such fields as street vending and a peculiarly Bolivian service occupation, that of the *aparapita*. The word *aparapita* is Aymara and means literally "bring it to me." Persons in this category are not regularly employed, but they are constantly available in the streets of La Paz to carry messages or bear any load from a bag of groceries to heavy household furniture. The 1950 census set off against the 1967 labor force estimates indicates an increase in the services sector of the labor force of from 13 to 19.9 percent of the total.

Lines between sectors of employment are poorly defined. For example, a 1969 official study of family income based on the kind of employment from which the income was derived placed amounts earned by families of independent artisans and amounts earned by farm families in the same category. This arrangement made indistinguishable the income of farmers and the income of a large majority of the economically active persons in the manufacturing industry.

The only data available concerning employment by income category are those from the 1950 census. More nearly current data are not available, and the land reform program that commenced in 1953 has eliminated whatever validity the 1950 figures may have had. In general, specialization is so limited that the urban worker may shift between self-employment and wage occupation on the basis of work available, and in the countryside the two are often combined. The farm wife may combine unpaid family labor with self-employment as an artisan. In the Yungas day laborers may be landless local personnel, who receive a regular cash wage, and *utawawas*, usually self-employed operators of a small Altiplano plot of land who, as seasonal migrants, receive bed and board as part of their wages. A similar kind of seasonal movement takes many subsistence farmers from Tarija Department into Argentina for the sugar harvests, and many Altiplano farmers migrate seasonally to La Paz for construction work. In early 1973 it could be generalized that most of the rural and a large part of the urban labor force were self-employed but that a large portion of both were seasonal wage earners.

Labor legislation classifies certain personnel working for wages or salaries either as laborers (*obreros*), who customarily perform work of a manual nature, or employees (*empleados*), who customarily work in offices and perform work of a nonmanual nature. The distinction is important because conditions of employment prescribed by law are somewhat different for the two categories. The distinction is not invariably between blue-collar and white-collar personnel; in some instances, legislation has been enacted to give employee status to manual labor groups as a means of making available to them benefits applicable only to employees.

Not all personnel working for pay are placed in one of the two categories. For example, the Ministry of Planning and Coordination reported that in 1967 of the 145,024 persons employed in the manufacturing industry, the 21,740 engaged in factory production (*produccion fabril*) included 3,666 employees and 18,074 laborers. The 123,284 workers engaged in artisan production were not classified.

By age, in 1970 the estimated participation rate in the labor force for males between the ages of ten and fourteen was estimated at 30 percent of the total in that age category. Between the ages of fifteen and nineteen the rate increased to about 68 percent and reached a maximum of 98 percent between the ages of twenty-five and forty-four. It declined progressively in older age groupings, but remained at nearly 68 percent for those sixty-five years of age and older. The 1970 estimate for female employment by age group, which apparently excluded unpaid family labor, showed participation to have risen from less than 6 percent among those between ten and fourteen to a maximum of about 27 percent between the ages of twenty and twenty-four and to have declined progressively in older age groups to 10 percent for those sixty-five and older. The 1950 census, however, had recorded a maximum female participation rate of nearly 67 percent between the ages of fifteen and nineteen.

The productivity of the labor force is low in all sectors of employment, largely because of an absence of skills. In one study it was estimated that only 5 percent of the labor force could be regarded as skilled. The general level of education is low, and the few who reach the secondary or university levels show little interest in vocational studies (see ch. 6). It is probable that productivity suffers also because of simple lack of energy on the part of many workers; diets average far below minimum standards, and a substantial portion of the population suffers from some degree of malnutrition (see ch. 7). In addition, the proliferation of small business establishments, such as artisan shops and small stores, tends to militate against efficiency. It has been calculated that in the industrial and services sectors in the early 1970s nearly two-thirds of the labor force was self-employed or working in enterprises employing five people or fewer.

Substantial gains in productivity would mean a socially unacceptable increase in overt unemployment. Significantly, during the 1965–70 period about half of the new industrial investment was absorbed by the petroleum and the transport and communications industries, which contributed only about 3 percent of the new employment becoming available. In 1970 it was estimated that the equivalent of US$7,000 would be required to create an additional modern industrial job and that, as a consequence, most of the new members of the nonagricultural labor force gravitated to marginally productive work as artisans or in retail trade and personal services.

According to a report based on surveys in the seven largest cities during the late 1960s, overt unemployment in these cities averaged about 13 percent. It was lowest for young people under the age of fifteen and highest for the elderly over the age of sixty. The highest recorded was about 18 percent in Cochabamba; the lowest was 10.5 percent in La Paz. The trend appeared to be upward; estimates from another source indicated that the rate in the major cities rose from an average of 14 percent in 1965 to 16 percent in 1970, and in early 1973 the La Paz press quoted President Hugo Banzer Suárez as stating that 30 percent of the available manpower was unemployed.

Because persons living on farms can almost always find some work to do, overt unemployment is largely confined to the cities. Half or more of the rural labor force, however, is believed to be underemployed. On the miniature plots of farmland on the Copacabana Peninsula in Lake Titicaca, for example, agricultural work occupies only about one-tenth of the time of one person, frequently the wife. Under these circumstances, husbands and older children look for work elsewhere, and the wife devotes her own surplus time to handicraft and the preserving of foods. In the Cochabamba Valley, more than 6,000 farm families during the late 1960s occupied parcels of land less than one hectare (2.5 acres) in size, which required little more than one-fourth of their available time.

Although there was an estimated 25 percent increase in the number of *campesino* families working in the rural sector between 1953 and 1970, there was no specific evidence of increasing underemployment or the appearance of a landless agricultural labor force. The Agrarian Reform Law of 1953 gave people freedom of movement and an increase in free time to look for seasonal employment. The Yungas in particular had benefited from an increased seasonal flow of workers from the Altiplano. Planned and spontaneous migration to agricultural colonization zones in the Yungas and Oriente has also eased some of the rural population pressure and attendant underemployment in crowded areas of the Altiplano and Valles regions (see Settlement Patterns, this ch.). In addition, the sharply increased opportunity for rural trading resulting from the breakup of the haciendas has given employment to an appreciable part of the rural labor force. There also has been some shifting from traditional staple crops to labor-intensive produce, such as the vegetables grown to meet the demands of the growing urban centers for foodstuffs.

CHAPTER 4

ETHNIC GROUPS AND LANGUAGES

The population of modern Bolivia traces its ethnic origins from two major components: the linguistically and culturally diverse native Indian groups; and the white Spanish speakers who, in the mid-sixteenth century, imposed their rule upon the area and its peoples. In spite of more than four centuries of contact and considerable interbreeding, these disparate ethnic elements have never been welded into a single people; in modern times the descendants of the conquerors and the conquered continue to be sharply divided into socially isolated ethnic groups by language and by differences in life-styles.

Interbreeding between Spaniards and Indians from the earliest days of colonial rule gave rise to a distinct group of mestizos as well as introducing a racial admixture to the ranks of both ethnic groups. As the population of mestizos grew, its members developed an increasingly strong sense of social identity and, by the middle of the seventeenth century, they composed a third recognizable ethnic grouping. In 1973 Indians constituted between one-half and two-thirds of the population. Whites and mestizos made up the remainder, mestizos considerably outnumbering whites.

Regionalism has always been one of the keys to understanding the Bolivian ethnic situation, particularly that of the indigenous population. Geographic barriers have kept groupings more or less isolated, preserving ancient cultural patterns at the expense of an integrated national society. Consequently, many of the indigenous groups have been socially, economically, and politically marginal throughout history, and in the late 1960s and early 1970s there was still an estimated 40 percent of the Indian population who could not communicate in Spanish, the official language of the country. Nevertheless, there has been some cultural drifting over the years, resulting in hazy ethnic boundaries. In areas touched by two or more groups, it is not uncommon to find persons who are bilingual and even trilingual.

The greatest geographic divergence and the greatest ethnic differences are found between the Andean highlands and the eastern lowlands. When the Spaniards arrived in the highlands they encountered a relatively dense population of sedentary agriculturalists, predominantly Quechua or Aymara speakers. These peasant peoples had achieved a high level of technological efficiency and sociopolitical organization and had been united under the rule of the powerful Inca

Empire (see ch. 2). In the lowlands, by contrast, the white invaders found a sparsely settled population of culturally varied and politically autonomous peoples speaking several dozen tongues affiliated with the Arawakan, Guaranian, and other less widespread linguistic families. None of the lowland groups had achieved the high level of technology and organization of the highlanders. These early differences continue to characterize the two regions and have resulted in differing applications of reform measures and differing degrees of subsequent social change.

Over the years, the concept of race has come to have more of a social and cultural connotation than the purely biological one. Thus, members of the white group are often racially mixed, and certain members of the mestizo group are racially Indian but culturally Hispanic. The term *indio* technically means Indian, but it is attached to a myriad of social characteristics to describe someone who lives in an indigenous community, speaks an indigenous language, goes barefoot and wears homespun clothes, and bears an Indian surname. Historically, it has been an epithet used to imply racial inferiority.

The 1952 Revolution touched many aspects of the ethnic situation in Bolivia. The most notable change was the official abandonment of the title *indio* and the substitution of the word *campesino*, or peasant. The terminological change heralded the government's attempt to raise the Indian's status from a powerless tenant farmer to a landholding participant of the national society. The effects of the reform are seen in varying degrees throughout the country but are most obvious in the highlands. Aymara and Quechua groups are more cognizant of the national state and are working through local *sindicatos campesinos* (peasant syndicates) to effect changes in education and public welfare. In many cases the increased dynamism of the Indians and the fluidity of the social structure have caused a worsening of interethnic relations. These relationships now range from mild paternalism to bitterness and animosity.

HIGHLAND INDIAN ETHNIC GROUPS

Successive waves of invading peoples left the Bolivian highlands with a uniquely layered and diverse ethnic configuration. Several ethnolinguistic groups developed before the Spanish conquest, the Aymara and the Quechua being the most advanced. The Spanish imposed another culture and language and effectively came to dominate the national scene. They established a racially stratified and feudalistic socioeconomic system in which the whites and privileged mestizos were the wealthy *patrones* (landowners) and in which the Indians were reduced to virtual peonage.

Throughout the 2,000 years of preconquest history the Indians of highland Bolivia closely resembled those of Peru. Most early groups based subsistence on intensive agriculture and herding of llamas and alpacas, although archaeological evidence indicates the development of advanced technologies and social organization capable of supporting fairly sophisticated cultures. The most important of these early cultures was Tiahuanaco, centered a few miles south of Lake Titicaca. The Tiahuanaco developed an impressive artistic and architectural style around the year A.D. 1000, which spread northward over the highland and coastal sections of what is now Peru. The identity of the builders of Tiahuanaco has never been definitely established, but many archaeologists hold that they were the ancestors of the present-day Aymara.

The periods between the decline of Tiahuanaco and the advent of the Incas are not well known archaeologically, but it is possible to establish a definite link between certain Altiplano cultures and the Aymara. Some non-Aymara groups included the Uru and the Chipaya, who lived around lakes Titicaca and Poopó and who spoke Puquina, a language unrelated to Quechua or Aymara. The Aymara themselves were organized into several small states—each apparently under a hereditary ruler—which were involved in a continuous series of shifting alliances. It was by exploiting these divisions that the Quechua-speaking Inca entered the northern Altiplano around 1450 and later extended their rule over the territory of what is now highland Bolivia.

The scant eighty to 100 years of Inca rule had resulted, by the time of the Spanish conquest, in the imposition of considerable cultural and linguistic uniformity over the entire area. Inca polity was designed primarily to effect the rapid incorporation of alien ethnic groups into the empire and to foster absolute loyalty to its rule. The method used to achieve these aims usually included mandatory instruction in Quechua, the imposition of sun worship, and the forced migration of potentially hostile people to distant parts of the empire and their subsequent replacement by groups of unquestioned loyalty.

These measures were applied with considerable rigor in the Bolivian area. Large groups of Aymara speakers were moved to other sections of the empire where they were settled among peoples known to be loyal to the Inca. In addition, numerous Quechua speakers were brought in to colonize many of the valleys, particularly Cochabamba and Sucre. One exception to usual policy was the dispensation extended to many Aymara speakers that permitted them to retain their native tongue. Other groups did not fare so well in the retention of their linguistic and cultural identity. By the time of the Spanish conquest only the Aymara and Uru languages had not passed into extinction. The deportation of some Aymara speakers and the enforcement of Quechua on others, along with the introduction of settlers from the north, resulted in a radical shift in the ethnic and linguistic balance of the country. By the middle of the sixteenth century Quechua speakers predominated.

The institution of Spanish rule in the former Inca territories had immediate and profound effects upon the Indian population and its way of life. War, famine, and social disorganization caused a drastic decline in population. The destruction of the Inca imperial system and the undermining of traditional authority reduced what had been a complex society to an undifferentiated subordinate caste. New agricultural techniques and products were introduced and caused radical changes in economic and social organization. Old priesthoods and temple cults were suppressed, and Christian forms were substituted in religious life (see ch. 2).

Estimates of the highland Indian population at the time of the conquest, based upon early Spanish censuses of doubtful accuracy, vary widely. A reasonable estimate for the Indian population of what is now highland Bolivia would be about 800,000 in 1532. The early years of colonial rule were marked by a sharp decline in native population, conservatively estimated for the entire viceroyalty of Peru at approximately 50 percent in the first thirty years following the conquest. A major part of this disastrous population loss is accounted for in the civil wars of the period. Not only were large numbers of Indians killed in physical combat but the disruption of food production caused many local famines. Another factor in the drastic decline in numbers was migration to lowland areas not yet affectively penetrated by the conquerors.

The Spanish colonial government's Indian policy was guided essentially by two aims: religious conversion of the native population and exploitation of its labor for the extraction of the mineral and agricultural wealth of the colony. These aims were formally implemented by measures intended to concentrate the population in areas accessible to Spanish control and to distribute colonial authority as widely as possible. One of the most important measures was the forced resettlement of dispersed populations in planned villages close to Spanish towns. To effect the distribution of Spanish authority, colonial law provided for the *encomienda,* a system by which individual colonists were given the right to collect tribute from Indian communities in return for assuming the responsibility of supervision and religious education of the Indians (see ch. 2).

If the institutions of Spanish colonial policy were humane in conception, their application was most often fraught with abuse. Holders of *encomiendas* used their positions of authority to exact excessive tribute and, in some cases, to appropriate Indian lands for their own use. The system of *mita* (labor conscription), which required that all able-bodied Indian men present themselves periodically for short periods of paid work in the mines, was abused by inhumane treatment of the conscripts, by arbitrary extensions of the service period, and by placing such large demands upon individual communities that they were left virtually devoid of adult males.

Many Indians sought refuge from intolerable conditions by becoming *yanaconas* (members of the class of urban servants and artisans), who were free from *mita* and tribute burdens. An individual assuming the status of *yanacona* was in general forced to abandon his native language and way of life for those of the Spaniards he served. Cut off from his communal roots, language, and way of life, the *yanacona* quickly became assimilated to an urban class that was not identifiably Indian in either a cultural or a social sense.

Interbreeding between the Spaniards and Indians, quite common throughout most of the colonial period, rapidly gave rise to a large population of mestizos, whose position in society was often equivocal. Mestizo offspring of legitimate marriages were generally assimilated by the elite group. Illegitimate children of lower status Indian women and Spanish men were either absorbed into their mother's group or, if they had been given a rudimentary education, they entered the urban trades as artisans or petty merchants. The growing ranks of mestizos merged socially with elements of the *yanacona* group to form a burgeoning urban lower class. In general, members of this class were Spanish speaking and culturally much closer to the European elite than to the Indian masses.

By the end of the colonial period, the mining enterprises of Potosí were in nearly total decline, and most Spanish fortune seekers had turned their attention to another area of economic interest—large-scale commercial agriculture on huge landed estates, worked by entailed Indian labor. Through various means, largely illegal, the European elite had acquired control over most of the better farmlands and the Indians resident upon them. Thus, the great majority of highland Indians became tenant laborers, bound for life to their estates, a position that was to be typical of their status until the 1952 Revolution (see ch. 13).

Independence from Spanish rule produced virtually no changes in the social and economic lot of the Indian population. Except for the departure of a few crown officials, the small white elite remained unmodified in power and outlook. Indeed, throughout the nineteenth century, white control over the most productive lands and over Indian labor was further consolidated, and the landed estates with their populations of entailed Indian tenants grew in size and number. The necessity of maintaining close control over the *campesinos* led the whites to oppose any attempts at Indian education or their employment outside of agriculture. The bulk of the Indian population was thus shielded from further culture change, and the way of life laid down in colonial times was perpetuated into the twentieth century.

The Aymara

The Aymara compose the oldest Indian group in Bolivia and are the second largest after the Quechua (see fig. 4). Estimates of their numbers range from 750,000 to nearly 1 million, but lack of an accurate

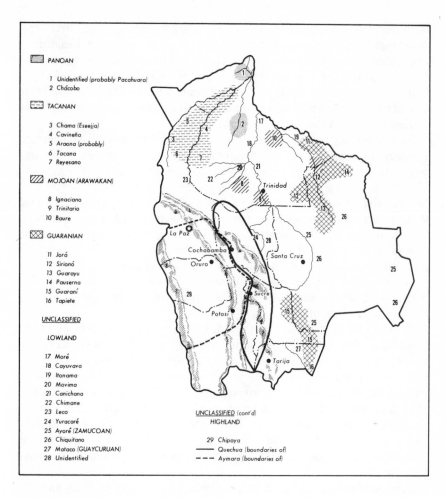

Key:

PANOAN

1 Unidentified (probably Pacahuara)
2 Chácobo

TACANAN

3 Chama (Eseejja)
4 Cavineño
5 Araona (probably)
6 Tacana
7 Reyesano

MOJOAN (ARAWAKAN)

8 Ignaciano
9 Trinitario
10 Baure

GUARANIAN

11 Joró
12 Sirionó
13 Guarayu
14 Pauserna
15 Guaraní
16 Tapiete

UNCLASSIFIED

LOWLAND

17 Moré
18 Cayuvava
19 Itonama
20 Movima
21 Canichana
22 Chimane
23 Leco
24 Yuracaré
25 Ayoré (ZAMUCOAN)
26 Chiquitano
27 Mataco (GUAYCURUAN)
28 Unidentified

UNCLASSIFIED (cont'd)
HIGHLAND

29 Chipaya
——— Quechua (boundaries of)
– – – Aymara (boundaries of)

Source: Adapted from Harold Key and Mary Key, *Bolivian Indian Tribes: Classification Bibliography, and Map of Present Language Distribution*, Norman, Oklahoma, 1967; and William E. Carter, *Bolivia, A Profile*, New York, 1971.

Figure 4. Ethnolinguistic Divisions of Bolivia

census since 1950 leaves the matter open to question. They are scattered in small settlements throughout the Altiplano, but some 90 percent of the entire Aymara population resides in La Paz Department. In 1973 they were still characterized by a distinctive language, religion, social organization, personality, and material culture. The historic isolation of the Aymara helped to preserve their culture, but it was at the expense of national integration. Only since 1952 has this group—which represents one-fifth or one-sixth of Bolivia's population—begun to be integrated into the national life.

Before 1952 the social isolation of the Aymara was extreme. There was little sense of community with neighboring groups or with the

82

nation. Political participation was nil. Aymara communities were self-sufficient, noncash-oriented societies in which the basic social unit was the nuclear family. Strong extended family and ritual kinship ties contributed to the social cohesion, but there was little intracommunity solidarity or mutual aid beyond this. In fact, although each community had a high degree of internal integration, few were truly communal insofar as mutual aid was concerned. Family existence centered on communally farmed land and a complex system of work and fiesta obligations. Aymara religion was a synthesis of Roman Catholic and ancient Indian beliefs, incorporating fiestas celebrating Catholic saints and daily propitiations and prayers to Pachamama, the earth goddess (see ch. 5). Socialization and religious practices were closely tied to land cultivation, as is evidenced by the practice of giving a seven-year-old child full responsiblity for cultivating a small plot of his father's land.

Before the revolution the Aymara communities were divided into two types: the large agricultural estate, or hacienda, and the marginal freeholding community (see ch. 13). In the former the Indians were called *colonos* (tenant farmers), bound for life to the landlord through indebtedness and lack of alternatives. The *colonos* had little contact with the world outside their immediate estate; they were both exploited and insulated from the national life by their landlord. In terms of social isolation the *comunarios*, their counterparts in the freeholding communities, fared worse than did the *colonos*. These free Aymara survived the onslaught of white overlordship, largely because their lands were so poor and inaccessible to markets that they were regarded as undesirable. Reinforced by geographic isolation, the *comunarios* of a freeholding community developed a strong in-group feeling and strenuously resisted all contact with outsiders. Any *comunario* who attempted to sell his land to an outsider was subject to severe sanctions, and young people were exhorted to marry within the community. Local government officials had little success gaining entrance for purposes of taxation or military conscription, and even visiting parish priests were seldom invited to spend the night within the community.

The feudal isolation of the *colono* and the self-imposed isolation of the *comunario* gave rise to numerous denigrating stereotypes concerning the Aymara personality. In the past they have been characterized as "harsh, brutal, cruel, and stupid" by Bolivians and foreign anthropologists alike. Studies of their culture and folktales portrayed them as unhappy, hostile, and unable to communicate with outsiders. Nevertheless, recent studies with a more humanistic approach have put the Aymara personality into a different perspective. His outward character, to the extent that it can be generalized, is seen as the result of five centuries of exploitation by successive waves of Inca, Spanish, and mestizo overlords. The fear of unreasonable taxation, military conscription, and land expropriation made the Aymara understandably reluctant to divulge basic information concerning the location of his fields or the names, ages, and numbers of his children. Furthermore, the closed and hostile attitude maintained toward outsiders has not been found within the communities themselves. Interpreted in this light, these traits appear as a clever, resourceful adaptation to a socially and geographically hostile environment historically threatening to the Aymara, his family, and his property.

When his status was raised from peon to that of a landholding *campesino*, the outlook of the Aymara began to change. This change was reflected both individually and communally through interpersonal relations and political activities. Openness, self-esteem, and status mobility are now replacing the mistrust and xenophobia that long characterized Aymara contact with the outside world. Where once Indians would greet white Europeans with meek genuflections and hand kissing, they now shake hands or give each other a firm *abrazo*, the bearlike embracing gesture popular between social equals throughout the continent. The disequilibrium of the social scene has also produced its share of animosity, and traditional, daily interethnic patterns have been disrupted and remain unstable. Anthropological studies have demonstrated the disruption of such common practices as interethnic social drinking. As the old etiquette breaks down between *campesino* and former landlord, it may be supplanted by a new etiquette based on the ambitiousness of the former and the resentment of the latter.

As their collective consciousness is being awakened to the world outside the immediate locality, the Aymara are expressing an increasing desire for schools and teachers. The exposure to formal education and outside contacts has meant a rise in the number of Spanish speakers. The Aymara language is still widely spoken in the home and marketplace, especially by the women, but the number of monolingual Aymara speakers is declining. Another consequence of the 1952 Revolution was the organization and proliferation of the *syndicatos campesinos*. Through these unions the *campesinos* have been able to increase their bargaining power with reform agencies and the government (see ch. 5).

Changes in the Aymara community have been paralleled by changes in personal appearance and in costume. Traditional male costume, consisting of tight homespun trousers and jacket, has gradually given way to industrially produced clothes. Nevertheless, the poncho remains universally popular among both Aymara and Quechua men. This garment is the remnant of pre-Columbian times and one that has been popularized throughout the Andean region and the Western world because of its warmth and practicality. Although the art of spinning and weaving homespun cloth is also on the decline, the Indians continue to make their ponchos from alpaca or llama wool, using styles, patterns, and weaving techniques dating back hundreds of years.

The change affecting women's dress has been slow. Nevertheless, studies indicate that Aymara women not only perceive the difference

84

in styles but also attach higher status to Western dress. The traditional costume consists of a number of varicolored and superimposed skirts, or *polleras*, an embroidered blouse, a homespun shawl, and a felt hat of ancient Spanish design. The archaic headgear has been gradually and almost universally replaced by the felt derby, the style worn by the more urbanized *campesinas*. (The incongruence of encountering British derbies in the Bolivian Altiplano is often noted by tourists. Supposedly the custom came into vogue when a British merchant discovered a surplus of these hats and unloaded them to the *campesinas* for a low price). Women who are dressed in the traditional fashion, which is called *de pollera*, are automatically categorized as country people. An increasing awareness of Western fashion has caused some socially ambitious women to adopt modern dress, which is termed *de vestido* (lit., of dress). Although changing patterns of dress are only a minor point of social change as a whole, they reflect the depth and pervasiveness of the Bolivian metamorphosis (see ch. 5).

Opinions vary concerning the character and depth of the social reform that followed the Revolution of 1952. Some indicators point to the greater integration of the native population through their accelerating politization, participation in the *syndicatos campesinos*, and awareness of such national values as education and the Spanish language. On the other hand, some scholars feel that the actual integration has not been so great. These observers stress that, although the agrarian reform changed *patrón-peon* (landowner-peon) relationships, it did little to break the traditional land tenure patterns among the Indians themselves. The sluggishness of the integration process was caused by the failure of agrarian reform to modify the stratification system within the ex-hacienda communities.

Indigenous communities have become even more stable and self-sufficient because of *campesino* landownership, and the social order has remained reinforced through internal cohesiveness and social criticism of innovation and deviance. Traditional practices have endured, and daily life is still centered on conventional concepts concerning land and the family. Furthermore, many *patrones* adapted to their new landless status by becoming local merchants and acting as economic middlemen between the Indians and trading centers such as La Paz. In this manner they also retain their positions as cultural brokers for the nonintegrated Aymara communities, continuing to serve as a filtering mechanism for the social and economic, if not political, institutions and values on the national level.

The Quechua

It has been difficult to calculate the total number of Quechua speakers and to generalize about their culture because of tremendous geographic and cultural differences. They are part of the largest language group in

South America and follow the Aymara in populating the Bolivian highlands. There are nearly 1 million Quechua speakers in Bolivia alone; fewer than half of these speak Spanish. They are found throughout the Altiplano and intermontane valleys of central and southern Bolivia, particularly in the departments of Cochabamba, Oruro, Potosí, Chuquisaca, and Tarija. They occupy areas extremely varied in altitude, climate, and proximity to urban centers and markets. In the face of such divergence it is not surprising that the only thing many Bolivian Quechua have in common is their language, and even that may be tempered by distinctive regional dialects.

A few limited generalizations concerning the Quechua can be made, however. All communities are overwhelmingly rural; land is the most vital commodity. As in the prereform Altiplano, Quechua communities were dominated by the hacienda, although a few indigenous freeholding communities were formed around Cochabamba. The basic social unit in all groups has been the nuclear family, which has been reinforced through extended and ritual kinship ties. Despite differing degrees of cultural change and bilingualism, outsiders have tended to consider all Quechua as members of the same social class, basing their judgment on traditional dress patterns and other social—rather than physical—indicators. Among Quechua themselves, however, variations in dress are duly noted as are levels of education and knowledge of Spanish. Industriousness is highly prized, as evidenced by the popular commandments dating from Incaic times: "Ama qella, Ama llulla, Ama sua" (don't be lazy, don't lie, don't steal). Community fiestas and the organizational structure surrounding them have also played an important role in most Quechua communities, as has individual status with regard to landownership.

Before the 1960s most research and contact with Quechua-speaking peoples dealt with the Indians living in the Cochabamba Valley. Broad generalizations were made concerning the urbanity and adaptability of the Quechua personality on the basis of these limited observations. Moreover, hopeful predictions were made surrounding the increased assimilation of Quechua. In the light of more recent research among the more isolated groups in Chuquisaca and Tarija, stereotypes and forecasts have been pushed aside for a more complete picture.

Quechua speakers can be differentiated on a number of levels affecting their status and participation in Bolivian national life. Community location is of primary importance. For example, gross mistreatment and exploitation of the Indian population by whites and mestizos never reached the Cochabamba Valley to the same degree it did in the other highland areas. Feeling less threatened by their non-Indian neighbors, the Cochabamba Quechua never developed the extreme xenophobia that characterized other Indian groups. Friendly contact between groups was facilitated by the fact that many mestizos were not large landholders but small farmers who lived interspersed among the Quechua at roughly the same level of subsistence. Finally, Cochabamba's strategic location between cities of the Altiplano and the lowlands made its inhabitants an important part of the integrated heart of the country. The unique ethnic situation of the Cochabamba area has made it significant in the social history and political development of the entire country.

This advantageous location is contrasted with the isolation of the valleys of southern Bolivia. Topography, lack of transportation and communication, the nature of the economy, and settlement patterns— all worked to the detriment of highland Chuquisaca. Haciendas in this department were often owned by white landlords who lived in Sucre and had little direct contact with their lands or the Indians who worked them. Not only was the region fragmented on a spatial scale but on a social plane as well, between city and town and between urban and rural.

The effect of the agrarian reform and *syndicatos campesinos* among the Quechua is directly related to the type and nature of the prereform community. For the most part, the southern regions, unlike Cochabamba, had agrarian reform experience based on the intact transfer of lands following hacienda land tenure patterns. The effect was similar to that among Aymara, namely, to abolish the hacienda by removing the landlords without actually changing the land base of the indigenous community. In most cases, Indians did not receive title to land other than the plot they were already working. Preexisting inequalities of plot size and soil quality continued to differentiate individual holdings. Rather than promoting rapid social change and assimilation of the Indian, the agrarian reform may have underscored local introversion and self-reliance.

There has been little change in traditional dress or consumption patterns. The fiestas tend to be centered on personal ceremonies such as weddings and baptisms, rather than on patriotic or patron saint observances. In general, life-style and values have remained more stable in this area than elsewhere in the highlands. Data also seem to indicate that the Chuquisaca and Tarija *syndicatos campesinos* are the weakest in the country and have exerted little of their potential power. The economic power of the *patrón* is still strong, and there has been little corrosion of traditional authority patterns. Corruption at police and government levels has encouraged the *campesinos* to seek solutions to their legal problems through traditional means rather than through the *syndicatos*.

In the total context of highland agrarian reform, the Cochabamba Quechua stand out as somewhat of an anomaly. Because of a relatively fluid social structure, a weak hacienda system, and the formation of prereform *syndicatos campesinos*, Cochabamba precipitated the actual agrarian reform. It is now in a state of internal flux and social change that has not been paralleled anywhere else in the nation. Cochabamba has been the only area in which the hacienda tradition has not been dominant in the maintenance of social patterns.

The former landowners have been irrevocably separated from their properties and have fled the area, probably to a greater degree than anywhere else in Bolivia. The *syndicatos campesinos* have been strong and viable, in some cases functioning as armed militia. The agrarian reform movement has accelerated an already existing process of social homogenization between Quechua and mestizo elements in the area. Although they habitually speak Quechua the Indians of Cochabamba have had higher percentages of bilinguals than any other native groups. Literacy also seems to be more widespread. Their dress and mannerisms have been similar to those of the mestizo population, the men wearing industrially produced work clothes and the women opting for factory-made shawls and the high-crowned white enameled hats of the mestizas. There is growing participation in the market economy, both as consumers and as producers.

Other Highland Ethnic Groups

The Uru and Chipaya

Of the two groups of Puquina speakers that survived both Incaic and Spanish invasions, apparently only one remained in 1973. The ethnic story of the Uru is one of gradual deterioration and eventual extinction. They were a very numerous pre-Columbian tribe living near Lake Poopó and giving the region its current appellation—Oruro—which is a corruption of Uru-Uru, meaning much Uru. They were always despised by the numerically superior Aymara who, throughout known history, have encroached increasingly on their lands. Significantly, the only oral tradition of any antiquity to survive among the Uru recounted that the pre-Inca Aymara made a regular practice of hunting the Uru for use in human sacrifice.

Thus, the Uru were already an oppressed and backward people at the time of the Spanish conquest. They eked out a meager existence on floating rafts on Lake Titicaca, their staple food being raw fish and roots. The Uru population continued to dwindle throughout this century, many being assimilated into urban settings or through intermarriage with the Aymara. By 1931 it was estimated that there were no more than 100 Uru in the entire Desaguadero region and, according to one anthropologist, the last Uru died in 1960.

The Chipaya of the Charangas area are apparently still in existence. They make their living largely from trading llamas, sheep milk, and cheese to neighboring Aymara farmers for quinoa and potatoes. They practice some agriculture, but the terrain in which they live is the driest and least hospitable portion of the Altiplano, and their crop production consequently satisifies only a small part of their need. This group still uses a mode of dress imposed on them by the Spaniards four centuries ago.

Although they have not suffered as intensely at the hands of the Aymara as have the Uru, the Chipaya are also a dwindling population. Various estimates would suggest that there are no more than 300 of them. Surrounded by a large and probably growing population of Aymara, the Chipaya have increasingly intermarried with their neighbors. Aymara influence has been so strong that members of the group have been adopting that language for everyday use. Most Chipaya are bilingual in Puquina and Aymara, and recent reports indicate that many of the younger members of the group have never learned their ancestral tongue. Between the acculturation of the Chipaya and the drastic disappearance of the Uru, their common language, Puquina, will probably be extinct within a very few years.

The Callahuaya

The Callahuaya, who live in the provinces of Muñecas and Caupolicán, La Paz Department, are historically a subtribe of the Aymara, but for centuries they have considered themselves to be ethnically distinct. They are supposed to have been court physicians to the Incas, and there is some conjecture that Callahuaya became the secret language of the royal Inca family. The Callahuaya were little affected by the conquest. If anything, they seemed to profit by it, especially by the introduction of horses. Their survival rests on their position as famous traveling curers and charm sellers throughout the entire Andean region.

The Callahuaya continue to practice their aboriginal folk medicine and retain their customs, language, and prestigious position despite the advent of modern medicine. The continuance of pre-Incaic indigenous beliefs has helped to perpetuate their respected status and useful position within the Andean society. Their status and wealth are reflected in their expensive indigenous costume and the silver-worked saddles and stirrups of the Callahuaya horsemen. Members of this ethnic group may speak as many as four languages—Callahuaya, Quechua, Aymara, and Spanish. Except among themselves, they ordinarily speak one of the predominant Indian languages.

The herbal remedies known to the Callahuaya number in the thousands and are prepared from plants of both the highlands and the Oriente. Several historians credit the Callahuaya with having introduced quinine and ipecac to the Spaniards. In addition to their empirical remedies, they manufacture and dispense a large number of charms and amulets, designed not only as protectors against illness but also as bearers of good luck.

At some time in his life almost every man of the group leaves his home village, carrying a sack of herbal remedies and amulets, and travels the length of the Andes, visiting the weekly fairs held in virtually all market centers. The wandering Callahuayas have supposedly traveled as far north as the United States and as far south as Buenos Aires. A small band lives in La Paz and may "visit" in Peru for as long as thirty years, only to return to their native village. The Callahuayas have effected cures and divined fortunes for every class of people. They are proud of the fact that a Callahuaya was called to cure the daughter of the Peruvian president—Augusto Leguía (1908-12 and 1919-30)—and succeeded.

MESTIZOS AND CHOLOS

Mestizos, technically those people of Spanish and Indian descent, constitute as much as one-third of the population. Geographically, this is the most widely distributed and pervasive of all ethnic groups; economically and socially their position in the Bolivian society is equivocal. The ambiguity surrounding their status also surrounds their nomenclature, and mestizo and *cholo* are applied indiscriminantly and often interchangeably, depending upon the cultural criterion or the situation. A wealthy, upper class mestizo may be regarded as *blanco*, or white, whereas a poorer mestizo truckdriver might be called *cholo*. An urbanized Indian might be called *campesino* in one village and *cholo* in another. There would be little apparent physical difference between the three, and the terms chosen would refer to social status rather than biological race.

During the colonial period *cholo* was apparently a general synonym for mestizo, meaning someone of mixed blood. Over the years, however, a more specific and value-charged definition was developed for *cholo*. Although it still carries a purely racial connotation, it may also describe an upwardly mobile Indian—often one who is considered an aggressive social climber. Some writers have grappled with this semantic problem by classifying the *cholo* as a transitional group between the Indians and mestizos. In this context the term *cholo* denotes low status town *campesinos*, whom other mestizo town dwellers regard as "refined" Indians.

Part of the reason for the social ambiguity and lack of solidarity within this group stems from the rigid two-class system of prereform days that discouraged the advent of cohesive intermediate groups. In many cases the mestizo was the hacienda manager, and he identified with the ruling class, although he was not considered a social equal by them. Under him were the Indian peons, who had little chance for upward mobility. The Revolution of 1952 broke down these class barriers, often reducing the *patrón* and his staff to genteel poverty, while appreciably raising the status of his *campesinos*. Since 1950 some *campesinos* have become more urbanized and "choloized." Their goals have become education and a higher standard of living. Not only did the reform awaken the *campesinos* to possibilities outside their traditional life-styles but it increased both the confusion and animosity between various intermediate elements.

Regardless of status differences between mestizo and *cholo*, both are defined by the cultural criteria of language, urban orientation, occupation, manners, and dress. The hallmark of this complex group is its ability to speak Spanish along with one or more of the Indian languages. The degree of bilingualism varies greatly from the *cholo* who resides in the urban periphery and understands Spanish but speaks it haltingly, to the mestizo merchant who has a fluent command of Spanish and two Indian languages. The prestige attached to Spanish is particularly enhanced among members of this group, and especially among incipient speakers, because the degree of fluency reflects personal status. Spanish is always used in more formal situations, even if one speaker is barely intelligible and both are fluent in an Indian tongue. Among certain mestizo segments Spanish may also be the language spoken at home, although the Indian language is the mother tongue and is more commonly employed in informal conversations.

A close correlate of the ability to speak Spanish is literacy. Most mestizos are at least marginally literate. Here again there is a great disparity between the *cholo* who had had two years of primary education and the fully literate mestizo. Education, like speaking Spanish, is seen as a key to upward mobility and is avidly encouraged. Such is often the case among impoverished former landlords who may send a son to the provincial university despite financial hardship incurred by the family.

Language is not the only criterion for distinguishing mestizo status, for some Indians may be fluent in several languages, including Spanish, without having made the transition to *cholo* status. Another important distinction concerns occupation and orientation. Mestizos and *cholos* are overwhelmingly urban oriented; for the most part they are not *campesinos*. Those who do own land usually derive only part of their income from this source. Only in the Cochabamba, and, to some extent, the Chuquisaca valleys have they engaged in subsistence farming and taken on the rural orientation of their *campesino* neighbors.

Traditionally, mestizos have filled the middlemen positions and occupations, such as clerk, merchant, hacienda overseer, and government official. Those who have only recently made the transition to *cholo* status are usually occupied as unskilled laborers or craftsmen. A prestigious occupation in highland Bolivia often filled by *cholos* is that of the truckdriver. He serves as the vital link between the produce of the *campesino* and the regional market and is regarded as the pinnacle of highland bravery, owing to his courageous navigation of the less-than-perfect Bolivian highway system. He is not referred to as *el chofer* (the chauffeur) as are urban taxi and bus drivers, but as *el piloto*, or the pilot. Upwardly mobile *campesinos* and returning military conscripts often perceive this occupation as a mode of elevating their own status.

Mestizos (including *cholos*) are highly adaptable, entering the more complex world of La Paz from their Altiplano villages with minimum culture shock. They have already adapted to industrially produced clothes, if not to Western-style dress, and soon adapt to other facets of urban living. Nevertheless, they rarely completely abandon local folk

91

culture and Indian heritage. Indian folk religion, magic, and curing techniques are an accepted part of the *cholo* way of life in most areas of the country. Even in the more cosmopolitan areas such as La Paz, there is an entire marketplace devoted to the sale of amulets, magical remedies, and llama fetuses (used for burial sacrifices in the dedication of new houses). The Indian folk belief and practice have an entirely different social significance for the *cholos* than for the Indians, however. For the latter they are community rituals; for the *cholos* they represent merely a set of traditions retained largely as a matter of individual choice.

In their position as cultural go-between, mestizos and *cholos* have managed to introduce and incorporate many features of local folk culture into the national life. An outstanding example of the way in which *cholos* have served to introduce local Indian custom into the wider popular culture is the nationwide celebration of Alacitas, the January festival in honor of Ek'eko, the Aymara god of fertility and good luck. Small statues of an Ek'eko laden with material goods are sold to all who wish to augment their wealth in the coming year. Originally an Indian custom, the observance of Alacitas (which means "buy me" in Aymara) was introduced to La Paz by the *cholos* during colonial times and became a popular practice among all classes. From La Paz, the Ek'eko celebration spread to the *cholo* population of virtually the entire highland area and has more recently come to be celebrated even by the Quechua speakers of the Cochabamba area.

LOWLAND GROUPS

The eastern two-thirds of present-day Bolivia was, in preconquest times, an area of extreme linguistic and cultural diversity. The peoples who occupied the area extending from the dry grasslands of the Gran Chaco on the south to the hot, rainy jungles of Pando on the north spoke several dozen languages affiliated with probably more than a dozen linguistic families. The area was apparently the terminus of numerous migrations because many Indian groups there speak languages of the Guaranian and Mojoan (Arawakan) families, whose centers of distribution are far from the Bolivian lowlands.

The preconquest peoples of eastern Bolivia varied widely in subsistence technology, population, and level of sociopolitical organization. At one extreme were the numerous, small, kinship-organized bands of hunting and gathering nomads of the Gran Chaco or the wandering Sirionó farmers and hunters of the forests of Santa Cruz and Beni departments, whose only form of political organization was the informally appointed headmen, who had little power. At the other extreme were the sedentary agricultural chieftainships, such as those of the Arawakan-speaking Moxos (Mojos), whose larger villages often had populations of some 1,500 people and were connected by causeways built above the level of the seasonal floodwaters.

Although the Inca sent several expeditionary forces into the eastern lowlands, they were never successful in subduing any of the numerous Indian groups of the area. There was, however, considerable trade between Indians of the Inca-dominated highland areas and those of the lowland chieftainships.

One of the largest and best organized of the preconquest groups in the east was the Chiriguano, sedentary farmers whose formidable military forces made occasional forays against Inca outposts. The Chiriguano were a Guaranian subtribe that, by a rapid series of migrations during the fifteenth and sixteenth centuries, spread out from a center of origin probably to the south of the lower Amazon in Brazil to reach northeastern Peru and present-day eastern Bolivia, covering a significant part of tropical South America. Their dispersal was apparently motivated by a burst of religious fervor, which sent whole communities on pilgrimages in search of the mythical Land of the Grandfather, a sort of earthly paradise. A part of the group, which penetrated and settled in Paraguay in the fifteenth century and came to be known as the Guaraní, later returned northward (across the Chaco) to the area of Santa Cruz, where they formed the powerful Chiriguano chiefdoms.

Spanish control over the Oriente and the Indian populations was established largely by two means. On the one hand, religious orders, particularly the Jesuits, set up a widespread system of mission settlements in which many Indian groups were induced to settle by peaceful persuasion or by force. Numerous expeditions of Spaniards set out, both from the Inca highlands and from Paraguay, in search of the fabled land of the Great Tiger Lord (El Gran Paititi), whose wealth was said to rival that of the Inca Empire. Certain of these expeditions resulted in permanent settlements of Spaniards. From such population centers military forces were sent out periodically against the surrounding Indian groups. The paucity of European women in the early days of colonization in the Oriente encouraged mass miscegenation between settlers and lowland Indians. Consequently, an ethnically and culturally distinct mestizo class developed in many of the settled areas.

Jesuit missions were established among both the sedentary and populous chieftainships and the smaller nomadic groups. From their earliest establishment until 1767, when the Jesuits were expelled from the South American colonies, the missions maintained a very tight control over the Indians in their charge. The process of conversion to Christianity was completed quite early, and the Indians became subjects of what amounted to theocracies, the priests occupying all positions of supreme authority. By royal decree mission territories were forbidden areas to the encroaching Spanish civil and military settlers. Hence, their populations were free of the gross exploitation (and often downright slavery) imposed upon other groups. The missionaries spoke to the Indians in the Indians' native languages, and those aspects of native culture not in conflict with Christian morality and belief were not suppressed.

In 1767, with the expulsion of Jesuits, many of the formerly subject Indian groups fled to the forests and resumed a totally independent existence. Both they and the groups that remained settled on the old mission grounds soon came to suffer intensely from the mistreatment and exploitation that followed the influx of new settlers. For example, the Moxos, who had thrived under mission rule, were hunted and sold as slaves. Many were compelled to work under inhuman conditions, practicing the high level of weaving skill taught them by the Jesuits. Others were forced to work as boatmen and carriers along Spanish trade routes. The influx of white settlers also brought new diseases— particularly smallpox and influenza—which made terrible inroads on the population. The major blow to the once numerous Indians of the missions came with the rubber boom of the late nineteenth century, when forced labor and slave trading reached all-time highs.

Many Indians successfully evaded the slave traders by retreating within the forests, where they attached themselves to groups that had migrated earlier. Others escaped by assuming the way of life characteristic of lower class townsmen, becoming general hangers-on in white population centers. Such large-scale abandonment of the traditional way of life, along with the extremely high mortality rates, has led to an almost total extinction of Indian cultures in the most accessible parts of the Oriente.

The remnants of lowland Indian groups that were extant in 1973 are probably not so well known as were their ancestors of the mid-seventeenth century, when missionary activity was at its height. In fact, knowledge has been so scanty that members of the Summer Institute of Linguistics who studied the region in the late 1960s discovered several tribes that were not known previously. The Oriente, especially the northeastern part, remains one of the few areas in the world where there is unknown land in ethnographic terms. Population figures are scant and sketchy; the last official estimate of 87,000 forest Indians was made twenty years ago. In view of the work done by the Summer Institute of Linguistics the number would seem much lower than that, probably closer to 60,000. In any event, it is evident that the population of the lowlands Indians and their traditional ways of life continue to decline.

The remaining Indians are classified into four identifiable linguistic groups—Panoan, Tacanan, Mojoan (or Arawakan), and Guaranian— and one unrelated linguistic group. These, in turn, are divided into over thirty extant tribes whose estimated speakers range from ten people to 20,000. The largest of these linguistic groups is the Guaraní, whose members live in southeastern portions of Tarija and Chuquisaca, close to the Paraguayan border, and in the northeastern frontier zone of El Beni. Still residing in the Tarija portion are the Chiriguano, linguistically related to the Guaraní, and estimated at 15,000 speakers. They settle in small autonomous bands throughout the region, apparently wherever they feel inclined. The *patrones* do not depose them and, in fact, seem glad of the potential labor force during peaks of the agricultural season. The largest single tribe unrelated to the Guaraní peoples is the Chiquitano, who are sandwiched between the various Guaraní tribes in Santa Cruz Department. This group, of the Amazon cultural type and unclassified linguistically, comprises about 20,000 speakers.

In general, attempts made by the national government to protect the dwindling population of forest Indians have been no more than desultory. The white settlers have continued to commit abuses against them, and diseases brought in by outsiders continue to decimate them. A few small groups of lowland Indians live under the protection of missionaries, and such groups are well insulated from contact with outsiders.

The marginality of many of these tribes is extreme, especially around the Santa Cruz area. They subsist at a very low cultural level and have little notion of modern techniques or their national government— unlike their contemporaries in the highlands. They are shunned by the other ethnic groups living in the Oriente and invariably are called savages or barbarians by their more "civilized" neighbors. They emerge from the jungle only occasionally, as often as not to attack their unsuspecting white neighbors. As recently as the early 1960s there were reportedly unseen Indians with bows and arrows attacking an oil prospecting truck around the Santa Cruz area. As yet no group serves as a truly effective liaison between these forest Indians and the twentieth century.

Although the lowland Indian tribes—generally isolated and dwindling in numbers—are of little importance to the national society, their detribalized and urbanized members form part of a growing population with at least incipient political and economic significance. They have merged socially and racially with the lower class of service workers, agricultural tenant laborers, and subsistence farmers. They are usually regarded as *campesinos* and consider themselves an ethnic mixture of various tribes and non-Indian elements. In the relatively populous region surrounding the city of Santa Cruz the lower class mestizos form a distinct and self-conscious group popularly called Cambas.

No more than isolated vestiges of their various Indian traditions remain in the life-styles of the Cambas of Santa Cruz. Their costume consists entirely of Western-style garments, and their only language is Spanish. Nothing of aboriginal belief and practice remains in their religious life. Although they are not fervent Catholics, they obey sacramental requirements of the church. The scattered nature of Camba settlement patterns, along with a general lack of specialization in agricultural work, has led to a very loose social structure. There is nothing resembling the highly integrated community organization typical of

Altiplano settlements. Family organization is quite casual, marriages often being the common-law type and easily dissolvable.

The term *camba* is used in several other closely related senses. In the Oriente outside the Santa Cruz area it is often used to refer to an upwardly mobile *campesino*, often in a derogatory context. It can also be used as a noun or an adjective pertaining to the Oriente or a native from that region. It is contrasted with the term *kolla*, meaning highlands or highlander. The difference reflects a fundamental and pervasive duality in popular Bolivian thinking that is far more than topographic. Both terms carry pejorative connotations of social and geographic stereotypes, especially when used in reference to a person from another region. Many times Cambas are portrayed by highlanders as lazy and immoral and their environment depicted as a "green hell" filled with frightening beasts, whereas Kollas are scorned by their neighbors in the lower altitudes as dirty, ignorant, lazy, and superstitious people living in a barren and inhospitable land.

The ethnic resentment follows the traditional polarity of the two regions. Both the lands and the people inhabiting them are physically different from each other. Kolla *campesinos* often come down to the Oriente to work as migrant farm laborers. They often fill the more technical and specialized occupations and are subsequently resented by lowland *campesinos* for their higher salaries and greater buying power. Upper and middle class lowlanders recognize the fact that the majority of politicians and public works have been centered in the highlands. A secessionist movement based in Santa Cruz and led by dissatisfied members of the upper class gained momentum until it was finally crushed by armed Kolla militiamen in 1959. Anti-Kolla slogans remained painted on walls in Santa Cruz as late as the mid-1960s, adding fuel to the continuing interregional animosity (see ch. 10).

BLANCOS

At the top of the ethnic pyramid are the *blancos*, who are also referred to as *gente decente* or *gente buena* (decent or good people). Studies indicate that they represent 15 percent of the population, although this may be an exaggerated estimate. *Blanco* status is defined by socioeconomic and cultural boundaries rather than by strictly racial criteria and closely corresponds to the traditional upper class (see ch. 5). Furthermore, it is generally dependent upon ascribed characteristics— those assigned at birth—rather than attributes acquired during one's lifetime. Standards for membership in the *gente decente* vary with the locality, as does the degree of traditionalism and adherence to the Spanish heritage. Although *blancos* claim descendancy from the original Spanish settlers or later European immigrants, there are very few who have no Indian ancestry.

Blancos do not occupy as broad a geographic spectrum as do mestizos and *cholos*, but they are found in both large cities and small towns and are traditionally employed in high status positions as professionals, wealthy merchants, or high government officials. In the rural areas the historical epitome of the *blanco* was the wealthy *patrón*. *Patrón* status implied not only wealth, but a European life-style, level of culture and education, and Spanish as their mother tongue. It also implied adherence to a particular code of moral behavior, a lineage traceable to colonial roots, local origin, and the cultivation of a leisurely attitude toward work. Loss of wealth and land could not by themselves lower a *blanco* to mestizo status; conversely, a wealthy mestizo might be denied *blanco* status because of his origin and life-style.

Although whites are well aware of the admixture of Indian blood in their ranks, their highly exclusive group consciousness and sense of superiority rest largely upon the notion of *limpieza de sangre*, or "purity of the blood." This concept of purity is not strictly racial but arises in part from a strong sense of aristocracy and good lineage. A person of good lineage can trace legitimate descent from one of the traditional upper class families. Legitimate marriages between Spaniards and Indians were fairly common in early colonial times before the arrival of large numbers of European women and the formation of a rigid society.

The notion of *limpieza de sangre* has always been strong among *blancos* in the Oriente and particularly in Santa Cruz. Founded in the mid-sixteenth century, it was a small isolated settlement surrounded by primitive Indians who had retreated into the jungle with the arrival of the first settlers. Unlike the highland areas of Bolivia, there was little intermarriage in Santa Cruz. The original Spanish stock remained unmixed into the twentieth century, explaining the famed Andalusian beauty of the women of Santa Cruz. The settled population of the Oriente in general is largely of European extraction, often white colonists from Paraguay and Argentina. These people have not only remained aloof from the surrounding tribes but have also developed certain denigrating racial attitudes regarding the Indian population.

The *blanco* elite have remained culturally homogeneous and true to their Spanish heritage despite the influx of other European groups— English, German, and Italian—and the social Revolution of 1952. Members of this group are bearers of the Hispanic traditions, which have always dominated the national society, even though they are not shared in great degree by the Indian and mestizo majority. The Spanish quality that still pervades many aspects of urban life is particularly strong in the larger valley towns except for Cochabamba. Conservatism and regionalism characterize the *blancos* in places such as Sucre and Tarija. Their values rest on a sense of aristocracy and innate privilege and are strongly entwined with a cultural cosmopolitanism based on European rather than indigenous models.

The social attitudes that underlie *blanco* ethnic consciousness are extremely ambiguous and stem from a confusion of racial and cultural stereotypes. Relations between *gente decente* and their social under-lings range from warmly paternalistic to blatantly exploitative and from cordial to scornful. Since many *blancos* possess an obvious degree of Indian ancestry themselves, their prestigious position cannot rely on physical features alone. But the general trend in traditional thought on the subject of race has been a profound conviction that the Indians and *campesinos* are innately inferior and that *cholos* and mestizos have in-herited the worst characteristics of both races.

Blancos believe themselves to have a stronger sense of honor and morality than the other ethnic groups. Such behavior as theft, drunk-enness, premarital pregnancies, and physical violence are strongly censured among *decentes* but are expected behavior patterns among the *campesinos*. *Cholos* have been viewed as incurable social climbers by their *blanco* neighbors. Even men who have risen to positions of national prominence and have amassed great fortunes have been con-sidered pretentious *cholos* in the eyes of the *gente decente*. Neverthe-less, mestizos and even *cholos* have gained marginal acceptance of *blanco* groups through marriage to the daughter of an impoverished *decente*. The children of these matches, depending upon the good for-tune of their parents and their education, are usually considered *blancos*.

Since 1952 the society has been in a state of flux, which has shaken the traditional basis of *blanco* supremacy. Although some regions have remained relatively isolated and traditional, other areas have wit-nessed increasing fragmentation and obfuscation of racial stereotypes. *Blanco* characteristics are still prestigious, but upper class occupation, wealth, life-style, and education are no longer monopolized by the *gente decente*. Increasing racial tension in certain areas has often been the result of the accelerating fluctuation of racial boundaries. The bit-terness of former *patrones* is well documented by researchers in the area.

CHAPTER 5

SOCIAL SYSTEM

The structure of Bolivian national society has been undergoing fundamental and far-reaching changes over the past four decades in basic institutions, in socioeconomic and ethnic groupings, and even in underlying attitudes. Although these changes were most dramatic and visible in the years following the 1952 Revolution, their roots lie in economic and social changes that followed in the wake of the mining boom of the late nineteenth and early twentieth centuries and in the political pressures that became apparent in the aftermath of the Chaco War (1932–35). In a sense, the formal institutional changes wrought by the revolution were merely the culmination of social movements that had existed for at least half a century.

The major outlines of the traditional social structure, as it existed well into the twentieth century, were derived by a process of orderly and gradual evolution from patterns laid down in colonial days. Institutions that had grown up in the sixteenth century continued to exist—in name and function—down to the eve of the Revolution of 1952.

Perhaps the outstanding characteristic of the traditional society was its extreme regionalism, which was partly the result of geographic barriers and underdeveloped communication facilities but was also rooted in a long history of political jealousies and conflicts of economic interest often underscored by great differences in language, culture, and race (see ch. 4). In the highland areas—most particularly in the Altiplano—social isolation was pronounced even between neighboring and ethnically similar Indian community groupings. Mobility had traditionally been minimal, because of a lack of transportation facilities and active restrictions on travel, which were imposed upon Indian peasants by prerevolutionary governments.

For virtually all of the 63 percent of the population estimated (in 1950) to be linguistically and culturally Indian, the significant social reality was not Bolivian nationality or even membership in a nationwide ethnic grouping but simply residence in a small, largely self-contained community. National life signified occasional contact with regional markets, infrequent (and preferably avoided) dealings with local government officials, and certain onerous obligations—taxes and conscription.

Capital wealth—particularly land—was overwhelmingly concentrated in the hands of a small, largely closed circle of families that formed a highly self-conscious upper class. This group also enjoyed a virtual total monopoly of national political power. Although wealth was one of the prime attributes of the upper class, commerce and industry were not the major concern of most of its members, who generally sought to live at a high standard from the proceeds of passive investment, mostly in land. The keystone of elite status was a concept of group privilege, seen as a birthright deriving from the distinction of pedigree.

Far below the numerically small elite—in both power and privilege—were the great masses of farmers, laborers, artisans, and petty merchants who formed the group usually called the common people. Not only poor but also disfranchised—for the great majority could meet neither the literacy nor the property requirements for suffrage of pre-revolutionary constitutions—members of the lower groups had little opportunity to improve their positions because educational facilities were sharply limited, as were routes to economic advancement.

Only partly bridging the gap between the elite and the masses was a small and poorly defined middle class of relatively recent origin. This class drew its membership largely from among professionals and successful merchants whose background did not include the distinction of pedigree necessary for acceptance by the elite.

The most important component of traditional ethnic and social stratification was an amalgam of culture and language. Both Quechua- and Aymara-speaking Indians—who have traditionally occupied the lower status position—can be differentiated from other Bolivians by their inability to speak Spanish and by numerous features in their way of life, such as total engagement in subsistence farming, essential lack of national consciousness, and a religious life that shows many holdovers from preconquest days. The rare individual who managed to divest himself of the linguistic and cultural stigmata of the Indian usually found it possible to join the *cholo* group (literally, mestizo group, but also possessing a social connotation of urbanized Indian—see Glossary), provided he moved to an area in which his Indian background was unknown.

The effects of land reform and the institution of universal suffrage have been dramatic. Within a very few years after the 1952 Revolution, the bases of the elite monopoly on economic and political power began to show signs of erosion. The most important social effect of the revolution has been the emergence of a significant national consciousness on the part of the previously isolated Indians. This consciousness has resulted partly from their sudden introduction to national political life by constitutional reforms and partly from an incipient awareness of their membership in a defined socioeconomic bloc.

In early 1973 it was evident that Bolivian society was still in a state of flux traceable to the cataclysmic events of the early 1950s. Both upward mobility of the common people and downward mobility of former elites brought accelerating fluidity to a once rigidly stratified society. Traditional class lines were becoming obscured as the significance of traditional class criteria changed. Upper class members who once had a triangular base of support in wealth, political power, and prestigious pedigree were finding their social position precariously balanced solely on the last criterion. Wealth providing the ability to cultivate and maintain a certain standard of living had taken on increasing importance as a determinant of status.

Old institutions, such as the family and the Roman Catholic Church, have weathered the social storm with a minimum of adjustments. Certain models for individual behavior have also remained stable despite changes in the criteria for the achievement of social status. Thus patronage and the definition of manly behavior are still vital elements in social interaction. Nevertheless, new institutions and forms of social organization—the *sindicatos campesinos* (peasant unions) and the nucleated settlement patterns being two of the most outstanding— have arisen to meet the demands of rapidly assimilating Indian groups. The irreversible and dynamic character of the social revolution has been gradually changing a traditional society and integrating formerly peripheral elements into the national life.

SOCIAL STRATIFICATION AND ORGANIZATION

Historical Background

Evidence points toward the existence of a stratified society among pre-Incaic Aymara tribes of the Altiplano. In any case, with the advent of complete Inca rule of the highlands during the middle of the fifteenth century, a complex and rigidly stratified society clearly emerged. Inca government was rigidly pyramidal. The ruling Inca nobles formed the highest stratum of local society and were followed by regional officials, drawn from local populations, who acted as liaisons between the nobles and the conquered tribes. Community-level government was virtually untouched. The lines of Incaic authority were arranged to form a vertical hierarchy. Communication occurred within the hierarchical framework but rarely between peers of neighboring communities. Consequently, there was little basis for political cooperation among such communities, and a truly regional integration never developed (see ch. 2).

Neither did a system of regional economic units or markets develop under Incaic administration. The Inca encouraged maximum agricultural production to ensure individual community needs, but any surpluses were siphoned off as taxes. Thus, the state became the focus of storage, and little intercommunity marketing occurred. The patterns of economic self-sufficiency and political fragmentation continued to complement and perpetuate each other and left only a small basis for

regional or national integration. This pattern was to continue throughout most of Bolivia's history (see ch. 2).

The ease with which Spanish rule was instituted and consolidated in
the highlands was at least partly a result of the rigidity of the Inca
power structure. Within a very few years of the initial conquest the
Spanish were able to eliminate the powerful Inca nobles from the top
of the social pyramid and establish themselves at the pinnacle of the
society. The colonial social system was then founded on definite ideas
of status stratification and associated privilege, which became inexor-
ably tied to the concepts of race (see ch. 4). Native-born Spaniards held
the highest and most lucrative positions, followed by those whites born
in the colonies. Despite the internal inequality of privilege and rank,
however, both Spanish groups occupied a status immeasurably above
that of the nonwhite groups. Light skin and Hispanic background were
established as positive values, whereas Indian life-style and heritage
were accorded little, if any, prestige.

The Hispanic political and economic systems were designed to maxi-
mize Spain's control over the Indian populations while integrating
them into the colonial economy at chattel status. These objectives became the basis for policymaking and institutions not only in Bolivia
but throughout Latin America. They were carried out through the implementation of three successive institutions: the *reducción*, the *encomienda*, and the *mita* (see ch. 2). The *reducción* was a resettlement
program that involved the relocation of dispersed highland Indians
into compact and planned settlements. The *encomienda* was the basic
institution in the early period. It gave the fiduciary grant of collection
rights over Indian tribute to individual settlers. The *encomienda* was
chronologically followed by the *mita*—a form of forced labor in which
all Indian men were liable to service in labor gangs conscripted to meet
the demands of mining centers.

Instead of replacing each other these institutions were often overlapping and mutually supportive. The *reducción* reorganized Indian
society along Spanish lines, and the *encomienda* was crucial in implanting direct Spanish control at the community level. *Encomenderos*
(those in charge of *encomiendas*) frequently abused this system by
exacting tribute in precious metals and nonlocal produce that could
be obtained only through cash purchases. The *mita* was designed to
correct some of these abuses, but it neither replaced the *encomienda*
nor was more humane in practice. Impossible working conditions and
exploitive administration made the *mita* one of the most hated aspects
of Indian colonial life. The net result of these institutions was a
thorough disruption of traditional patterns of labor organization and
distribution, further hastening the breakdown of older sociopolitical
forms and the reduction of Indian society to capitve status.

Another important development was the social homogenization of
the diverse Indian groups. The once stratified Inca society was uni-

laterally lowered to the status of a subordinate caste with virtually no internal differentiation. The great mass of Indians fell into the tributary class under the *mita*, regardless of their preconquest status. Only a few who had escaped to the urban centers—the *yanaconas*—and a few nobles who had submitted to Spanish rule and were now in positions of local authority—the *curacas*—were able to escape *mita* service and were in separate and distinct classes. Whereas the Spanish colonial rule dismantled the pre-Columbian stratification system, it served to perpetuate the fragmentation of the Indian communities themselves. The colonial structure was no more conducive to social integration on an intercommunity basis than it had been under Inca rule. Although all lives were profoundly affected by the actions and influence of colonial government, those effects were mediated through the community and its white officials. They were not designed to facilitate interaction among local Indian groups through markets, political participation, or exogenous social contact.

Early in the colonial period another social class arose that was racially a cross between the white and the Indian but was culturally ambivalent toward both. These were the mestizos—often the illegitimate children of Spanish fathers and Indian mothers. The child was usually raised by his mother, and felt a certain loyalty to her people, yet was also cognizant of the socially superior status held by his father. Mestizos were accorded special status by virtue of their Spanish antecedents and were often given the opportunity to integrate themselves into the white status group through education and wealth. Because they also possessed Indian background, however, the great majority were never accepted by the white elite, and their frustration at this social rebuff continued to grow throughout the colonial period.

By the end of the eighteenth century mestizos formed a significant and powerful, yet dissatisfied, segment of the population. Mestizo dissatisfaction with the status quo added to the increasing frequency of Indian revolts and led to the gradual weakening of the colonial structure. The indigenous revolts were not attempts to eradicate Spanish influence but were rather sporadic expressions of social unrest. Actual Indian participation in the War of Independence (1825) was, in fact, negligible. Quechua and Aymara fought on both sides. After independence the status of the Indians in the national society remained virtually unchanged. The only major change was a shift in power from an elite of Spanish born to one of light-skinned native born.

The despoliation of Indian lands and the exploitation of the Indians themselves continued unabated into republican times. The governments of the nineteenth century perceived the Indian as a national labor pool to be employed for the benefit of the small national upper class and therefore to be driven off their independent peasant holdings and into economic dependence, first upon the large landowners (*hacendados*) and later upon the mine owners. The great haciendas became an entrenched feature of the social scene and did more to influence the character of class relations than any other element. Because of this system highland Indian communities remained in isolated, serflike groupings, self-sufficient in food production but dependent upon the landowner in every other respect (see ch. 13).

The vast highland population traditionally resided in three types of rural communities characterized by a dispersed pattern of dwellings: the *comunidad*, or freeholding community, the hacienda, and the mixed mestizo and Indian village. The *comunidad* and the hacienda closely resembled each other in organizational details because the hacienda often originated from an expropriated *comunidad*. Cohesiveness within these communities was strongly reinforced through dislike for outsiders, marriage within the group, and a comprehensive fiesta system. Social organization within them was based on land cultivation and on a local hierarchy closely linked to a system of fiesta sponsorship.

The development of mining as Bolivia's economic mainstay in the earlier part of the twentieth century, along with the initiation of a national communication system, produced a trend toward urbanization, shown by the accelerated growth of city populations. Its social effects were most apparent in the establishment of a proletarian group—the mineworkers—and in the growth of the number of acculturated Indians, often referred to as *cholos* (see ch. 4). For the Indians collectively, industrialization and accelerated urbanization meant little, except for the addition of a few more opportunities for acculturation into the national milieu. For the great mass the basic institutions of the hacienda and the socially isolated community continued to be the significant realities of life.

The stratification system and basic community organization patterns remained stable until the middle of the twentieth century, although the groundwork for change had been laid earlier during and after the Chaco War. For the first time large numbers of Indians participated in a united and national effort, and it broadened cultural perspectives considerably. Veterans of the war, especially those in the Cochabamba region, joined in loosely organized associations that were later welded into a prototype of the *sindicatos campesinos*. These groups were far more politically aware than their ancestors had ever been, and along with an increasingly self-conscious labor bloc they formed the backbone of the recent transformation of the national social structure.

Changes in the Social Structure Since 1952

Since 1952 Bolivian national society has reflected a continuing and irreversible process of social change. This metamorphosis appears in all levels of relationships, from interpersonal to intercommunity and from interethnic to intergenerational, and in all levels of organization, be they social, political, or economic. Although the social system still has a distinctly two-sided character—that of the European-based urban versus that of the indigenous rural—the gap between the two is narrowing because of the growing awareness on the part of rural people. Here again is division between the highland and the lowland rural areas, indigenous populations in the former being far more advanced and dynamic than in the latter.

Bolivian society is divided not only within the classes but also regionally and within the rural-urban continuum. City life and the Hispanic traditions concentrated there have always carried high prestige. The wealthy elite rarely lived on their highland haciendas, considering the life there backward and unpleasant. They preferred the cities, especially Sucre and La Paz, because of the westernized cultural atmosphere and greater social contact. Historically, the great majority of the Indians were isolated from the magnet of urban life or were immune to it altogether.

The agrarian reform left a vacuum within many *campesino* (peasant) communities. For the first time there were no haciendas to command the use of agricultural surpluses, and a need for regional market mechanisms developed. For the first time isolated Indian groups had a voice in the national government, thus creating a need for the organizational and educational *sindicatos campesinos.* For the first time the Indian was given a sense of pride and self-worth. In an attempt to upgrade his social position the government began to refer to him as *campesino* rather than as *indio* (Indian), hoping to imply his new landholding status in the process. The departure from the hacienda system brought the *campesinos* a growing awareness of the world outside their traditional localities and resulted in a dynamic and changing rural sector.

One of the changes is reflected in the rural settlement patterns of the northern Altiplano and subtropical valleys of the Yungas. In these areas nucleated settlements, called new towns, have sprung up spontaneously, often on the land of an expropriated hacienda. They are clearly distinguishable from the widely scattered residential patterns that characterized the area before 1952 (see ch. 3). New towns have been created as a response to governmental or economic stimuli and correspond to the increased aspirations of the *campesinos* for a better life through urban living. The larger of these settlements may have administrative functions, serving as the bases for *sindicato* activities or as the local canton centers (county seats), or they may serve as regional centers for weekly markets. Residents whose adjacent farm plots are too small to support their economic needs may generate extra income by engaging in petty commerce or service activites.

Migrants prefer new towns to such large urban centers as La Paz. Even householders who are not full-time residents consider themselves urban. They are also permitted continuing contact with their land and familiar rural patterns and thus inherit the best of both worlds. Furthermore, *campesinos* often reject the already-established market centers in favor of establishing a new center inhabited entirely by people of rural origin. A historic animosity exists between the Indians and nearby mestizo towns whose inhabitants have tried to exploit the surrounding indigenous populations whenever possible. New town dwellers do not form a class distinct from the rural community around them. Nevertheless, they are viewed with envy and respect by those not participating and consider themselves superior to workers who continue to live exclusively in the countryside. The term *vecino*, meaning neighbor, has been adopted to distinguish new-town householders from the *campesinos* of the surrounding area.

Most importantly, new towns represent the growing desire of *campesinos* for life in an urban environment. Their perceptions of an urban situation revolve around a nucleated settlement pattern, regardless of size. Consequently, an area containing only five to ten houses that stand empty most of the week while *vecinos* are farming subsistence plots is still regarded as an urban nucleus. The image of the urban way of life is also associated with social advance—in particular, an improved physical environment, increased opportunities for social mobility, better housing, availability of electricity, drinkable water, and a better school. These advantages are not usually seen in terms of concrete and measurable improvements but are more intangible and involve life-style. *Vecinos* hope their children will learn Spanish, be literate, and wear nonpeasant clothes so that they may better adapt to a changing world.

With the demise of the hacienda system and the emigration of mestizo officials, certain cantons and their capitals faced reorganization. The mantle of power passed to peasant-organized localities, and some new towns have become canton capitals. If a new town comes to act as nodal point for two or more systems—educational, marketing, or syndicatal—it may gain enough power to become a canton capital. People living there often have strong links with La Paz. For example, local store owners may be migrants returning from the capital who turn their familiarity with the products of both areas into a commercial venture. Thriving new-town cantons may attract doctors, teachers, and other professionals educated in La Paz. The progressive atmosphere in such settlements often encourages the children of prosperous *vecinos* to continue their studies in the capital (see ch. 3).

Change since 1952 has not only been reflected in a shift in geographic settlement patterns among rural residents but has also been noticed within the economic and political structures of entire rural populations. Even though the *campesinos* ultimately depend on a centralized government and centralized economy, a growing political acumen and a developing market system have given them greater power over their destinies than ever before.

Since market mechanisms have been one of the most important educational structures within the community, their role cannot be undervalued in the process of rural social change. Although some authors feel that *campesinos* still fail to perceive the relationship between what they produce and the national welfare and believe the majority of their produce is for household consumption, a study of market processes indicates the contrary. Interviews with Bolivian farmers show that the hacienda-based production system has changed substantially in the last twenty years. The *campesino* has not remained a mere subsistence farmer but has also come to play a large role in the marketing of his produce. Estimates indicate that only one-eighth of the produce is sold at the farm level; the rest is sold through weekly agricultural fairs. Growth of these fairs has mushroomed since 1952; there are fifty to seventy-five each week in the Altiplano alone. They serve as both market points for produce and supply points for manufactured goods. No real effort, however, has been made by La Paz merchants to capture the consumer potential generated by increased *campesino* income, despite the increased demand for such consumer goods as transistor radios, sewing machines, and bicycles (see ch. 14).

Unlike the inhabitants of many rural areas in Latin America, the Bolivian *campesino* seems to function in a strictly commercial environment, free of blood or ritual kinship ties. Only a very few *campesinos* interviewed reported a family or *compadre* (godparent) relationship existing between himself and his buyer. The producer himself is braving the risks of the open market, thus making the marketplace more competitive and providing a more progressive kind of selling activity. This situation has facilitated both geographic and social mobility among rural dwellers and especially among aspiring *cholos*. There is evidence in the more dynamic areas that once a nuclear family has reached a certain economic level the next step is to disown all poor relatives. Although this is not the prevalent pattern throughout rural Bolivia, it does indicate a certain break with economically oriented extended family relationships.

Before the reform, Indians had little opportunity for political leadership or participation on a national scale. Prestige and leadership within the communities rested on a system of fiesta sponsorship and the rotating positions meted out by the landowners. The power vacuum left by vacating landowners and their staff was gradually filled by Indian-run *sindicatos campesinos* and their leaders, the secretaries general. This was a new kind of formal social organization and the only one to exist in most communities. It was not modeled on the preexisting hacienda structures but on industrial labor unions. Nevertheless, in a great percentage of communities the prestige and leadership patterns of the *sindicatos* have been greatly influenced by such traditional Indian structures as fiesta sponsorship.

The functions, strength, and effectiveness of the *sindicatos campesinos* vary from region to region. They have been especially influential in the Cochabamba Valley, the Altiplano, and the Yungas, where they brought about significant changes in local attitudes. Their activities have included political demonstrations, arbitrating land claims, resolving disputes between *campesinos*, and organizing support for public works projects. Although motivation toward a communal effort is not a common characteristic among highland Indians, there is evidence to indicate an increasing ability to coalesce around a common cause. In fact, certain *campesino* groups have kidnapped mining and industrial officials, hoping to force government action on promised improvements in schools, roads, and soccer fields. Gradually these people are becoming aware of industrial progress, but their frustration is outstripping the benefits they have reaped.

The secretary general within each *sindicato* holds a powerful role in the development and change of his community. A man need not have been a board member, nor must he ascend through hierarchy, in order to fill the office. Nevertheless, it is a highly prestigious position, usually requiring a person of responsibility who has some knowledge of Spanish. Any outsider who wishes the cooperation of the community must first make contact with the secretary general, otherwise the outsider is regarded with suspicion. In the early days of the agrarian reform some ambitious *campesinos* took advantage of the post to further their own aims, but in the early 1970s this was far more the exception than the rule.

In many highland communities the position of secretary general has become a primary focus for the patterns of prestige surrounding community service that were once exclusively channeled through fiesta sponsorship. In prereform days fiestas served to maintain community cohesion better than any other factor. The language of social relations was expressed through fiestas and punctuated by alcoholic consumption. Traditional consumer goals were based on accruing enough wealth to sponsor a first-class party.

Recent studies indicate a shifting of attitudes and a gradual erosion of the fiesta system since the advent of the *sindicatos campesinos*. An increasing number of younger individuals are indifferent or antagonistic toward sponsoring fiestas because of the cost, thus implying that this is no longer the unqualified vehicle for gaining status. These persons are often socially ostracized and called *evangelistas* (evangelists) by the rest of the community, particularly in the Quechua-speaking zones and more isolated areas where traditional sponsorship patterns are most persistent. It appears that consumer goals of those still participating are geared largely toward fiesta giving; spending has not notably shifted toward consumer goods to the detriment of fiesta expense. Nevertheless, the prestige of sponsorship must compete with the prestige of *sindicato* officeholding, and it has been noted that the former does not necessarily lead to a position within the *sindicato* because of the distinct requirements of the latter office. Despite the shifting of prestige patterns within the communities themselves, the value of selfless community service remains intact.

Although little evidence points to family breakdown in Bolivia, there are some indications of change in family structure and in attitudes surrounding extended and ritual kinship since the 1952 Revolution. Upward mobility has caused some *campesino* families to preserve their nuclear character but to avoid contact with extended or ritual kin. On the other hand, downward mobility among elites and the generally precarious position of the upper class in rural areas have caused resentment of lower classes and increasing refusal to participate in *compadrazgo* (coparenthood) rites. Although there is consensus that family roles have not changed appreciably, one observer noted a decrease in family cooperation and solidarity. This is underscored by the opinion expressed by some *campesinos* that business is easier when one does not feel an obligation to deal through his ritual kin. Shifting interests and alliances have also been noted among the younger *campesino* families, whose attitudes contrast with those of older family members. Young rural Bolivians who have grown up and married since the revolution have difficulty understanding the fear, respect, and loyalty evinced by older persons for former *patrones* (landowners). Because this young segment has greater freedom and opportunity, it is likely that they will rely less and less on the protection provided by traditional family patterns.

The Upper Class

Members of the traditional upper class in Bolivia built their status on the triangular foundation of wealth, political power, and Spanish heritage. Their wealth was based on a virtual monopoly of agricultural production, mineral resources, and control over commerce. For most of Bolivian history they were the only educated members of society and the only ones who had contact with, and understanding of, the world outside the national borders. Although generally of mestizo origin, they considered themselves white and identified solely with the European culture. They formed a self-conscious and cohesive enclave whose members kept their status intact through intermarriage and looked upon their privileged position as a birthright. As with the rest of the society, however, the upper class has suffered the disruptive effects of historic regionalism and the 1952 Revolution, and in 1973 only one of the three original bases of power—social prestige—remained unchallenged.

Upper class notions of racial superiority and purity of the blood have always been and continue to be at the heart of their tenacious class consciousness (see ch. 4). Despite the loss of wealth and power, impoverished members of the upper class strenuously resist redefinition of their status. Outsiders, except for European Christians, have always found acceptance by this group difficult. An aspirant to upper class status faces a critical appraisal of his physical features, his name (for possible Indian derivation), and his province of origin. There is blatant dislike for social climbers, and often this is expressed as an ethnic prejudice toward those of obvious *cholo* or Indian origin.

Upper class ideology has been shaped by notions regarding the relative worth of work and leisure. The ethic of work as an innate good has never been a prevalent idea among the upper echelons of the society and, in fact, most remunerative activity has been regarded as degrading. Conversely, a generous amount of leisure time has been the mark of upper class status and considered necessary for the cultivation of a gracious and gentlemanly life.

Thus wealth, along with racial and cultural background, evolved into a prerequisite that could only be inherited rather than acquired. Certain occupations came to be more or less desirable according to the degree of remunerative effort and manual labor involved. A distinguished professional practice has never been enough to admit someone to the ranks of the privileged, yet *patrón* (landholding) status—which involved very little labor on the part of the landowner—has always been a sine qua non for membership in the upper class. Education and academic activity were viewed in similar perspective. Although the great majority of upper class men received a university education, it was not perceived as a stepping-stone to a professional career but rather as the finishing touches to a polished and cultured individual.

The Bolivian upper class patterned its values on those brought from Spain. This orientation toward life diverged markedly from that of the Indian and brought about a dual system of norms that has never been successfully synthesized. At the heart of personal action and social interaction among the upper class is the ethic of *personalismo*. This is a complex of precepts and behavioral norms exalting self-expression and the inner dignity and uniqueness of the individual. *Personalismo* accords each individual a personal status separate from his social status. In consequence, a strong respect for individuality is in no way contradictory to equally strong social patterns of stratification and inequality of opportunity. An upper class Bolivian is not constrained to imply equality in his behavior toward one of lower rank, but he is expected to treat the other with a courteous respect and deference that acknowledges the personal level of their interaction.

Although the notions defining individuality dominate behavior patterns, they are circumscribed by a fairly rigid Hispanic sexual differentiation concerning both ideal personality and social role. A man is expected to be aggressive, competitive, and strongly self-expressive, whereas the woman is his gentle and ornamental antithesis. Traditionally governing male behavior have been the twin concepts of the *macho* (male) and the *caballero* (gentleman). *Machismo* is the barometer of a man's maleness and is measured in terms of heroism, personal force, a zest for action, and constantly demonstrated sexual prowess. Within this context the man judges himself and is judged by his coparticipants in the activities of love, politics, intellectual life, and business. In all fields of male endeavor greater prestige is accorded to those who demonstrate their *machismo* than to those who make contributions by simple but unobtrusive and pedestrian competence.

The achievement of personal status as measured by *machismo* is open to all men regardless of class. Within his own sphere a man can exert himself and be accorded much prestige as a *macho*. Not so with the ideal of the *caballero*, which is generally used to prescribe the behavior of high-status men only. The *caballero* is the gentleman whose behavior and attitudes emphasize qualities of noblesse oblige, chivalry, generosity, and paternalistic leadership. Wealth is a prerequisite for the *caballero*, who ideally devotes his life to dabbling in politics and the arts, manifesting a total lack of interest in purely materialistic aims and activities. He must command sufficient resources to enable him and his family to live in a genteel style while cultivating a benevolent and generous paternalism toward those less fortunate than he. The prestige accrued to the successful *caballero* indicates why so many upper class Bolivians have chosen to become wealthy *patrones*. The stereotyped behavior of both these behavior patterns dovetailed into one another and are practically inseparable.

The traditional concept of ideal womanhood is antithetical to *machismo*, emphasizing the qualities of passivity, modesty, sacrifice, and maternal nature. A woman's realm ideally centers on the home, relatives, and the Roman Catholic Church. Upper class women are expected to be ornamental, cultivating a lady-of-leisure attitude and limiting their activities to charity and good works. This enhances the feminine, genteel, maternal image these women would like to create about themselves. Social realities since the revolution have added a new dimension to the woman's character. High-status women are becoming educated professionals and participating in the national life to an ever greater extent. They are sponsoring seminars attended by all classes of women and are consequently awakening to the national problems. Traditionally isolated and protected from the harsh life of the Bolivian poor, upper class women have begun to demonstrate a genuine concern and dynamic vitality for innovative social action.

Bolivian men have also felt the heavy hand of the social revolution as many of their traditional privileges were curtailed by loss of wealth and political power. Increased fluidity in the social structure of both the downwardly and upwardly mobile has made it possible for a broader spectrum of Bolivians to adopt behavior patterns of the elite. Some wealthy middle-class men have been able to assume the aspect of *caballeros* and *patrones*, whereas the loss of wealth and land has relegated some of the upper class to regular jobs in the city or even to indigence and dependence upon relatives. Despite the change in actors, it appears that the roles of *macho, patrón*, and *caballero* have remained fairly stable. One study of *campesinos* in the Yungas indicates that they often retain their peon-like demeanor and dependency despite a considerable change in status. They continue to rely upon *patrón-peon* (landowner-peon) kinds of relationships in both personal and business interactions. In other areas where traditional patterns have been little changed by the agrarian reform—such as the valleys of Chuquisaca and Tarija—the upper class has easily retained its position as fatherly mediator of lower class interests.

Since the upper class families owned most of Bolivia's productive capacity, passing family wealth from one generation to another was no problem until 1952. With the cataclysmic loss of their economic base of power, however, many members of the upper class have had to resort to their professional training in order to remain economically solvent. In towns where agrarian reform was particularly successful, the flight of hacienda families left few upper class families in the area. In many cases the children of local landowners were being educated in La Paz at the time of the reform and chose to remain in the larger cities engaged in a professional capacity rather than to return to their provincial homes and fragmented land. In these areas the only upper class people remaining are the elderly people who live on the last vestiges of their pre-1952 wealth.

Despite a common heritage and value system, the Bolivian upper class has been divided along regional lines that helped to build independent and isolated social groupings with unique lineages and traditions. At the pinnacle of Bolivian society and occupying a supraelite status are the *rosca* (literally, the screw). Membership in this subclass has declined drastically since the revolution, largely because of emigration, and only a few hundred families remain. This elite segment has retained its essentially urban character, living in either Sucre or La Paz. Paradoxically, although Sucre sparked off the rebellion against Spanish rule, it is the most intrinsically Hispanic city in Bolivia. It is the traditional seat of the Bolivian aristocracy (some of whom purchased titles to their nobility), and throughout the republican period it has supplied numerous names to the roster of Bolivian presidents. The *rosca* of Sucre have jealously guarded their heritage, reinforcing it by sending their children to study in Europe and making frequent shopping trips for porcelain and French furniture. The popular stereotype of the gentleman of Sucre is of a conservative intellectual dressed in the stiff high collar of the nineteenth century.

The *rosca* of La Paz placed less emphasis on lineage and more on land and cash wealth. Theirs has always been a more modern and commercial city where government bureaucracy plays an important part. Consequently, during the Nationalist Revolutionary Movement (Movimiento Nacionalista Revolucionairo—MNR) years (1925-64) it was easier for the La Paz *rosca* to integrate themselves into the revolutionary government and to retain some of their pre-1952 influence and wealth. Their social clubs are still exclusive, as are their residential patterns, yet there is evidence that wealthy persons of nonelite origin are gaining entrance to even such closed circles as these.

Although regional upper strata exist throughout the rural areas and medium-sized towns of highland Bolivia, they are not generally referred to as the *rosca* but as *gente buena* (good people) or *gente decente* (decent people) and are a step below the *rosca* in wealth and prestige (see ch. 4). Their status has been defined in terms of local landownership and is generally not transferable to another locality. This has kept them a fairly immobile segment within the upper class. Lacking a broad base of economic support, many members of this group were left destitute and bitter after the agrarian reform. Some, especially those in the valley towns of the south, managed to keep their lands and prestige intact; but the less fortunate left the country or moved to urban regions in Bolivia where they had to accept a decline in status. Others remained in their original communities, bereft of power and wealth. This latter group assiduously avoided contact with other townspeople, rarely attending social functions or serving willingly as *compadres* to *campesino* children as once was demanded by popular custom. Their voluntary seclusion was sometimes carried to extremes, as in the case of the *decente* woman who refused to send her child even to the local parochial school because it admitted *campesinos*, although she could no longer afford to send the child to school in another town.

The case of the Oriente is a special one within the Bolivian stratification system because it did not develop from a classical colonial pattern. The scarcity of Indian labor and the general intractability of these populations made labor, not land, the more valuable commodity. Consequently, lowland estate owners have traditionally lived on or near their land in close contact with their workers. Unlike the highland tradition, urban residence is not an important factor in determining upper class status. Moreover, the series of erratic economic booms that characterized the area allowed fortunes to be made and lost with remarkable rapidity. This instability caused greater emphasis to be placed on maintenance of wealth in lowland than in highland areas, where a stable economic situation was taken for granted until the middle of the twentieth century. Thus, those occupying the *gente buena* or *gente decente* stratum in the highlands are often called *los ricos* (the rich) in the lowlands.

On the other hand, because the racial balance between whites and Indians was much more equal and upwardly mobile, Indian groups presented less of a social threat; and because intermarriage was early and extensive, a racial basis of social stratification never assumed the monumental significance it did in highland areas. The bulk of the Oriente upper class is clearly mestizo, yet they consider themselves white and in fact propagate the notion that they are of purer Spanish descent than their counterparts in the highlands.

Over the years closed social circles developed around Santa Cruz and, to a lesser extent, Trinidad, where upper class elements retained a refined European culture and followed intellectual pursuits. Fiesta giving among the upper class has been a useful mechanism for defining and stabilizing class lines because the invitation to an upper class party assumes the guest to be a status equal. The more spectacular social functions of *los ricos* take on a showcase effect, for it is not uncommon for crowds of common people to gather at the doors and windows of a wealthy home to watch the guests at their leisure.

Throughout much of the region, status lines have hardened around wealth and the positions of cattlemen, landholders, merchants, and professionals. These people form an upper class enclave whose elite position has been affected by the hacienda reform. They have kept a great deal of their local power and wealth intact. Relations between social strata in the Oriente have remained similar to those of *patrón-peón* in the highlands and are still those of deference on one side and privilege on the other.

The Middle Class

The middle class in Bolivia is at least as regionally fragmented as the upper class and is far less ideologically cohesive. This class occupies an equivocal position in both urban and rural sectors and runs the gamut of prestige and position from rural truckdriver to urban professional. In fact, there is almost as much range within this stratum as between two adjoining classes. Lack of commonality and class consciousness makes the middle sector an incipient class at best and one that is extremely difficult to conceptualize through all-inclusive generalizations. For the most part, the middle class consists of bilingual individuals who can be identified as neither upper class—generally for lack of a proper pedigree—nor as lower class—for their significant ideological and economic differences.

To a large extent the middle class is a joint product of social mobility and elite exclusiveness. It was initiated with colonial mestization, but dates effectively from the explosive boom in the mining industry. This boom created demands for educated, skilled administrators, thus greatly expanding the occupational opportunities for a middle sector traditionally tied to commercial endeavor. Both upward mobility of *campesinos* and downward mobility of elites brought individuals into an intermediate status position.

For lack of common criteria, the middle class is largely defined in terms of occupational specialization and economic status within each community. In the urban sector its members tend to be successful merchants, white-collar workers in commerce or government service, and less wealthy professionals lacking an upper class pedigree. For the most part, members of the rural middle class are considered *cholos* and are employed in similar positions. This group has come to form the backbone of the rural middle class, their interests traditionally bound up in commercial activity, such as marketing, transporting local agricultural produce, and petty retail trade.

Although, like the upper class, they may be employed in high prestige positions, the middle class traditionally depends upon salaries, fees, or commercial profit for sustenance rather than upon passive investment. Even the gentle forms of work performed by the upper middle class in rural areas is still a kind of remunerative activity and distinguishes them from the *gente decente*. The range of income in the middle class, and hence the range of life-style, is very broad and falls between the monthly wage of a primary-school teacher (the equivalent of US$70) and the comfortable income of a successful physician.

Regardless of their economic level, however, members of the middle class aspire to upper class status and perform incredible financial gymnastics in trying to achieve it. They tend to live far beyond their economic means, often placing a severe strain on their personal resources. Wealth takes on a particular importance for this element because it is the delimiting factor between them and the lower classes. Although impoverished members of the elite can often survive on the prestige of their heritage, the status of the middle class is directly tied to wealth and fluctuates with their financial fortunes.

Although wealth is enough to lift them out of the lower classes, it is insufficient to elevate them to upper class status. A high degree of social integration must also take place and must be accompanied by education and good breeding in a bid for upward mobility. Education is considered a vital goal throughout the stratum and is one of the few universally held values. Educational and ideological orientations have paralleled those of the upper class, especially in the urban areas where the Hispanic heritage and elite influence are strongest. In contrast to the upper class image of education, however, schooling is perceived as a true stepping-stone to a prestigious and professional career. In fact, earlier in the twentieth century, professional training had been sought as a path to socioeconomic advancement by so many urban *cholos* that the practice of law had lost prestige among many members of the elite and had come to be regarded as the mark of a social climber.

Racially speaking, the middle class is fairly homogeneous. Most middle-class members are Indian or of Indian extraction, although some urban middle class are clearly mestizo. Few are eager to claim their Indian origins, for it is still a sign of backwardness (see ch. 4). Because they cannot properly identify with the upper class either, they live in a culturally ambivalent atmosphere that does not lend itself to a strong sense of group identification. Aside from universal deprecation of their Indian heritage, middle class self-perceptions and the perceptions held by others around them vary with the local situation. In a large sense, then, status is a nontransferable regional phenomenon. In many cases this means that an individual and his family will be excluded from local society should they decide to move. Even though they may become wealthy middlemen and prosper materially, they are still considered outsiders by long-standing members of the local middle class.

Generally speaking, the wealthier, more urban, and westernized the individual is, the greater is his tendency to perceive himself as mestizo, comply with Hispanic norms, and follow the lead of the upper class. Moreover, the closer he comes to imitating the upper class, the greater is his desire to be assimilated, and the greater is his frustration at rejection. Bitter relations have often resulted between upwardly mobile middle-class members and those members of the elite who consider them ostentatious social climbers.

The middle class of the rural areas are usually *cholos* who occupy merchant positions within the community. These people are at least bilingual in Spanish and one or more Indian languages and usually are at least marginally literate. They do not follow Spanish norms as closely as their urban counterparts, actually deriving some behavior patterns from their Indian backgrounds. Of all the peoples of Bolivia, the *cholos* come the closest to being a synthesis of the Indian and Hispanic strains. They value education and material comforts yet, unlike the upper class and urban middle class, they do not resent working for them. In fact, they often criticize the *gente decente* for laziness. There seems to be some dichotomy between the sexes concerning their roles, however; *cholo* men seem much more dissatisfied with their position than the women. They have a greater orientation toward Hispanic values than the *cholas*, wearing European styles and attempting to adopt Hispanic norms concerning sexual adventure and love of leisure.

These desires are sharply constrained by economic reality and by the fact that the *chola* women often control the purse strings of the family. In contrast to their men, *cholas* have adopted a self-identity that is far from Hispanic in origin and have come to constitute a unique and unified enclave within the Bolivian middle class. These are aggressive and self-assured businesswomen who possess formidable business acumen. In a society where few realistically assess their status, *cholas* provide the exception to the rule. They have few delusions concerning their relationship to upper classes and tend to ridicule those among themselves who put on airs or Western clothes in hopes of changing their status. They often form unions to protect their interests and have taken part in the national process to an ever-increasing degree. They are fiercely energetic in the pursuit of education for their children, exhorting them to use Spanish and become literate.

The Urban Working Class

As in the case of the middle class, the advent of a recognizable urban working class as a self-conscious socioeconomic bloc is a phenomenon dating from the beginning of the modern mining boom. The core of this group is the labor force employed in the mines, but workers in several other branches of industrial activity, notably transportation and textile manufacturing, constitute important segments of this class. Also assimilated into the group are most of the domestic servants, petty merchants, and small artisans of the cities, by virtue of being quite similar to the industrial workers in economic status and ethnic and educational background.

The lower class industrial workers, artisans, and petty merchants are recruited from among both urban *cholos* and translocated *campesinos*. Except for the miners' group, such personnel stem overwhelmingly from town and city *cholos* who sought each new economic opportunity as it opened up. The miners and, to a great extent, the railroad workers are of predominantly Indian origin. Culturally and linguistically all components of the working class have come to be quite similar. Typically, a member of this group speaks fluent Spanish (which, however, often bears a heavy Quechua or Aymara accent) and considers himself a Bolivian national. Although literacy is by no means generalized, urban school attendance has long been relatively high in comparison to the rural situation.

Members of the core groups, particularly miners and factory workers, show a class consciousness and awareness of common interest almost as strong as that of the elite. These groups are united not only by strong ties of labor organization but also by a sort of group ideology arising out of a long history of social strife. Thus, it is easy to mobilize political opinion and action through the use of propaganda that appeals to the memory of such incidents as the massacres of Uncía (1924), Catavi (1942), and Villa Victoria (1949).

Although the ideology of working-class consciousness exists at the national level, the social life of the typical member of that group is usually quite circumscribed. All labor unions are affiliated with national and departmental organizations, but the interests and activities of the average worker do not take him far beyond the boundaries of his own local group. Thus, even though mass political action can be mobilized on a national scale, such mobilization must always take place through leadership at the most local level.

Particularly in the larger cities, lower class neighborhood social life is organized around a wide variety of associations. In addition to the labor union locals, such districts in La Paz often have women's associations, soccer teams, and neighborhood councils that serve to mobilize civic action. In several typical lower class neighborhoods of La Paz, such associations draw their members from the majority of families resident in the area. Overlapping membership in neighborhood-based associations provides a tie that crosscuts occupational speciality. Thus, factory workers, petty merchants, artisans, and railroad workers are often drawn into an active social life that reinforces the group consciousness of the urban lower class. In purely local matters this pattern of overlapping association usually overcomes differences in economic interest and political orientation.

Class consciousness among the urban proletariat and its associated groups extends to the definition of fairly sharp boundaries with respect to other social groupings. The typical member of the lower class, if pressed to identify his position in urban society, will most frequently place himself among the working people. On the other hand, the working people see themselves as quite distinct from rural *cholos* and *campesinos*. The social rift between the proletarian groups and the *campesinos* has long been underscored by divisions of economic interest and political jealousy. Although both groups have consistently supported the MNR and revolutionary reforms, they always stood as opposing units within the party. This long-standing rift has been exploited frequently by party leadership and the government, as in the use of *campesinos* to break a miners' strike in 1959.

The Campesinos

Campesino is a blanket term that legally superseded *indio* in the Bolivian vocabulary after 1952 (see ch. 4). The application of this term to the ethnically diverse and socially isolated masses of peasant farmers who constitute the bulk of Bolivia's population implies an identity that is only incipient. Insurmountable barriers to integration, traditionally reinforced by an exploitive and prejudiced upper class, have begun to disappear only recently and only in certain areas. Internal differences in language and culture, mistrust of outsiders, and profound regionalism prevent the *campesinos* from carrying the collective weight within the society that their sheer numbers would suggest. Despite profound internal divisions, however, the *campesinos* are gradually acquiring a national class consciousness as they assimilate into the political, economic, and even social mainstream of the society.

This rural lower class is composed principally of Indians from three major groupings: Quechua of the valley zones, Aymara of the Altiplano, and Spanish-speaking mestizos of the Oriente. They may be referred to by different names—such as *mozo* in Chuquisaca or Camba in Santa Cruz—and many follow distinctive land tenure patterns, yet they are all considered within the general category of *campesino*. Their commonality lies in their non-Spanish heritage, traditional ties to a purely agricultural existence, and disadvantaged position within the stratification system.

Unique land tenure patterns developed to shape the character of the lower class within each geographic region. The agrarian reform has been only partially effective in changing these traditional patterns and giving *campesinos* the economic means to acquire the physical trappings of mestizo status. In areas where the changes have been successful, such as Cochabamba, the Altiplano, and the Yungas, the social order has become much more fluid, and *campesinos* have come to form a dynamic element within the local community. In certain isolated areas of the south and the Oriente, however, traditional patterns have persisted, and *campesinos* remain relegated to a powerless position.

The Cochabamba valleys have always been the most progressive of the rural areas in Bolivia. Instead of being characterized by large, isolated haciendas like those of the Altiplano, the thickly settled Quechua areas of Cochabamba were divided into numerous small farms centered in a well traveled area. These were frequently leased out by their owners (often church bodies) and had a fairly high turnover in landlords. Moreover, the rural settlement pattern was one containing a mixture of *comunarios* (freeholding farmers) and *colonos* (tenant farmers) in an open structure that minimized the isolation of the individual social units. The *colonos* enjoyed a freer access to markets than those in the Altiplano and were correspondingly less dependent upon their landlords. Finally, Indian farmers were interspersed with *cholos* who operated with a technology and market behavior identical to their Indian neighbors. Cochabamba is the only area where significant numbers of *cholos* also kept their *campesino* status. *Campesinos* were also exposed to urban mestizos and were familiar with the norms of that culture.

Consequently, the integrated nature and fluid atmosphere of the Cochabamba valleys facilitated and in part precipitated the national agrarian reform. As early as 1936 one group of *campesinos* in the province of Cliza formed a union to further their interests, thus predating the *sindicatos campesinos* by nearly two decades. Since 1952 a strong *sindicato* movement has encompassed the entire area, and former *patrones* have been separated from their holdings—perhaps to a greater degree than in any other region in Bolivia. Most important, observers have noticed a growing mobility and fluidity of the social structure of the region, an increasing homogenization of diverse classes, and the broad-spectrum acculturation of *campesinos* into the national society.

Criteria of race and cultural background do not play a very important part in the social stratification of the Cochabamba valleys. *Cholos* and *campesinos* dominate the area and possess nearly identical life-styles and patterns. Rather, social stratification is determined by language, dress, occupational activity, and the wealth and productivity of one's lands. In contrast with the Hispanic tradition, Cochabamba *campesinos* exalt hard work and place no particular value on leisure. In fact, being poor is equated with being lazy. Cooperation is encouraged over personalistic displays of individualism, and to be a good community member one must participate in community activities as well as face other villages with a friendly and hospitable air.

Isolated and self-sufficient kinship units have never developed as they have among the Aymara, although marriage within their community is the rule for both. Despite crowding, land is commonly available for cash purchase in Cochabamba. It is customary for young

Cochabambinos to leave their native communities to work in the mines or cities, then return with sufficient funds to buy land and start a family. They seem to make the transition from rural to urban worker and back again with a minimum of hardships. Although rural workers continue to be called *campesinos*, their wives may be called *cholas*. These women wear the many-skirted *chola* costume and participate directly in the local economy by selling vegetables at the market or train station.

The Aymara Indians of the Altiplano are another *campesino* group that has undergone considerable change. Unlike the Cochabambinos, whose *campesinos* have always been more or less integrated into the national society and whose status actually antedated agrarian change, numerous isolated, xenophobic groupings in the vast Altiplano remained well outside the national life until 1952. The landholding system in the Altiplano also differed from that of Cochabamba by being dominated by the hacienda instead of the mixed mestizo town. Estimates show that two-thirds of the land was incorporated by haciendas or estates that were still undergoing expansion well into the twentieth century. The progress achieved by Altiplano *campesinos* since 1952 in eradication of the hacienda, in integration, and in political and market organization has been phenomenal, making the Altiplano the true showcase for the agrarian reform program.

Before the reform the *colonos* depended entirely upon their landlord and the small plots of land granted them. Cash wages were nonexistent or nominal, for landlords were loath to permit their *colonos* the economic independence implied in wage labor. Aside from very limited opportunities afforded by regional markets, *colonos* were forced to rely upon the landlord for any commercially manufactured goods or nonlocal produce that they might want. Landlords often abused this monopoly, charging outrageous prices and bringing about a system of debt peonage that helped bind the Indians to their haciendas. Estate owners also enjoyed the right to exact free labor and household service from their *colonos*. Severe abuse and hopeless debt often caused peons to flee the hacienda, although it meant giving up all claim to what little land they possessed. Since these minuscule land plots were the center of their existence and the only means of remaining in the community, most Aymara thought twice before abandoning them. On the other hand, so important were *colonos* as a servant caste that estates put up for sale were advertised on the basis of their *colono* population (see ch. 13).

Isolation and suspicion were two important patterns that characterized the interaction of the Altiplano Aymara before 1952 (see ch. 4). Indians from the estates were generally denied even minimal intercommunication with *comunarios* or other *colonos*. *Comunarios*, in turn, lived in constant fear of expropriation or absorption by a neighboring hacienda and developed xenophobic attitudes toward all outsiders. The immobility, localism, and hostile environment that surrounded both communities encouraged the development of parallel stratification systems. The organization of haciendas followed that of the *comunidad*, probably because of their close continuity in historical process and the general adaptability of the *comunidad* hierarchy to the hacienda system.

The typical prereform community consisted of perhaps 250 to 500 nuclear families living in scattered adobe dwellings, each bounded by a piece of land varying in size from one-half to several acres. Clusters of these dwellings constituted a zone, which was then bounded by extensive lands for cultivation. Clusters of zones constituted a community, which was the hacienda or *comunidad*. The hierarchy within these communities was rigid and complex, based on a socioreligious system of fiesta giving.

Ideally, each adult male could move upward by giving a series of fiestas. Because of the prohibitive cost, however, only a few could realistically compete for the ultimate honor of being *jilakata*, or headman. So great was the honor of the position and so great the personal sacrifices incurred that aspirants would spend as many as seven years in planning the coup de grace that would elevate them to this office. The prestige of this position was undermined in hacienda communities, where the *jilakata* was chosen to please the *patrón* or where he was an ineffectual buffer against the abuses of the overseer. Nevertheless, certain structural and organizational features and the orientation toward community service remained intact and helped form a base for the *sindicatos campesinos* that followed the revolution.

Aymara values have traditionally centered on hard work and service to one's fellow man and therefore closely resemble those of their Quechua neighbors. Among the Aymara this service is seen strictly in terms of one's immediate community, however, and does not extend to surrounding settlements. Unlike the Hispanic ideal of *personalismo*, where prestige accrues to those who demonstrate force of character and an aggressive competitive nature, the Altiplano *campesinos* disparage self-expression and self-preoccupation. Children are taught stoic self-control, responsibility, and conformity from very early childhood and that social ties demand self-sacrifice. A common reprimand for an obstreperous child is "people are watching you." Whereas such an observation would elicit no end of attention-getting antics from the Hispanic child, it carries the opposite effect with Aymara *campesino* children. These children grow up to be circumspect and fairly conformist, likely to subjugate personal feelings to group cooperation.

Many observers have stated that this quality produces a more democratic atmosphere than that in communities dominated by the Hispanic traditions of authoritarian and personalistic leadership. The phrase "first among equals" has often been used to describe both the *jilakata* position within the fiesta system and the office of secretary general among the *sindicatos campesinos*. This egalitarian atmosphere is heralded as the cause of the success enjoyed by the *sindicatos* in the Altiplano. On the other hand, other observers attribute the effectiveness of *sindicatos* to the dynamic and autocratic role played by the leaders of the more apathetic *campesino* groups. Whichever is the cause, the effect has been the same: increasing integration of once-isolated Aymara communities.

Another factor helping to integrate Altiplano *campesinos* is the accelerated mobility and interaction with urban market centers, especially La Paz. Many *campesinos* no longer feel tied to their traditional communities. They have moved into towns or set up new settlements, sharing economic and political responsibility and entering jobs once held exclusively by *cholos*. Their children are attending schools, where they are available, and gaining a knowledge of Spanish, the vital tool in understanding the concept of Bolivian nationhood. *Campesinos* are actively interested in educating their children and energetically campaign for schools and teachers, often erecting the buildings themselves from their own limited resources.

Although there have been profound changes at the macrocosmic level, there is little evidence of alteration within or between Aymara communities in an individual's status or role. Former landlords were effectively separated from their traditional holdings and eliminated from the scene, but the distribution of the land followed preexisting tenure divisions. Consequently, the status differences based on land tenure have continued among the *campesinos*. The only avenue open to those with poor or insufficient holdings is moving into town, employment in a new town, or sharecropping. At least these options are viable means of increasing personal fortune, which did not exist prior to 1952. Moreover, even though communities continue to be integrated into the national system, it is through a one-to-one vertical relationship. Horizontal cohesion and cooperation between communities is still rare, as old feuds and suspicions tend to preclude interaction. *Campesinos* maintain their strongly local orientations, and some observers feel that the reform has actually reinforced a concentration on local subsistence.

The nuclear family is still the foundation of *campesino* society. Little evidence suggests a changing of roles within this traditional unit, in which women occupy a paradoxical position. They are given a voice rarely found in Hispanic groups, and within the household the female opinion predominates. Incidents of wives beating their husbands support the popular notion that physically women are nearly as strong as men. Women share in the heaviest farm labor and often manage the family finances, as is the case among the *cholos*. (Actually, the reported aggressiveness and forthright character of the *cholas* is probably largely an inheritance from their Indian ancestors.) Nevertheless, women realize that their role is clearly subordinate to that of men.

The educational goals that *campesinos* hold for their sons do not extend to their daughters. This attitude is frequently noted, and an air of general dissatisfaction has caused the formation of numerous women's clubs throughout rural areas and even resulted in the First National Seminar on the Problems of Peasant Women in April of 1973. *Campesinas* and *cholas* representing the departments of El Beni, Cochabamba, La Paz, Pando, Potosí, Santa Cruz, and Tarija came to the capital to air their views and exchange ideas. These *campesina* leaders expressed a need for better health and educational facilities—for their daughters as well as their sons—and the need for a more receptive government attitude toward *campesino* problems in general. The women present represented an astute and growing number of dynamic *campesinas* anxious for equal participation alongside their men.

The *campesinos* of the Yungas, like those of Cochabamba and the Altiplano, are enjoying postreform changes. The Yungas, a fertile eastern area settled fairly late by Altiplano landowners and freedmen of Aymara descent, developed patterns that were somewhat similar to both the Altiplano and the Oriente. A hacienda system developed as it did on the plateau, but it was quite different and bore a resemblance to the patterns in eastern lowlands. Many Yungas landowners were not absentee but lived on their properties as they did in the Oriente. There was a great deal of available land and a relative scarcity of labor, which gave tenants greater freedom from their *patrones*. Rural workers found it quite easy to obtain and cultivate new land, and they devoted a good portion of their resources to the production of cash crops to be sold at local markets.

Although no studies were made of social patterns among *campesinos* in the prereform Yungas, it is assumed that the Aymara of this region bore a close resemblance to their predecessors on the Altiplano. The actual organization of hacienda workers followed traditional highland models. Officers were selected from the community to supervise the fulfillment of rent obligations, but neither offices nor obligations were as prolific as on haciendas in the Altiplano. A fiesta system flourished but was not connected to a socioreligious hierarchy as it was among Aymara of the plateau. Even though isolation and dependency were not as debilitating among *campesinos* in the Yungas, the existing sociocultural system did not provide direct access to regional or national institutions. Consequently, most contacts were made within the community or with the *patrón* acting as mediator, as was the case in the Altiplano.

Since the agrarian reform, numerous changes have made the *campesinos* of the Yungas a more dynamic element in the national society. The most outstanding change has occurred in traditional local attitudes and patterns. Some observers feel that there has been greater change here than among Aymara in the Altiplano. Yungas *campesinos* have become increasingly mobile both geographically and socially. They have moved to mestizo towns or established a dual residence to gratify the desire for urban residence. Hacienda owners who actively discouraged merchants from setting up market centers near their traditional sphere of influence have found their positions as distributors and brokers usurped by new town merchants.

There is a growing emphasis on conspicuous consumption of prestige manufactured items as more *campesinos* adapt to a "choloized" existence through changing their language and dress patterns. As a result of the pressure of upwardly mobile *campesinos, cholos* are beginning to use the *decente* tactic of reliance on refined manners and traditional family names to distinguish old *cholo* families from newer ones. Fiestas have remained popular, but the shift has been from an individually sponsored event to one involving communal preparations.

Sindicatos campesinos have played an extremely important part among peasants in the Yungas. The organizations have been well led, have received strong support, and have been highly effective. They strengthen the work ethic among the *campesinos* and help to structure the internal prestige system of the community. If a *campesino* fails to work his land, his claim is weakened in the eyes of the community, and he suffers loss of prestige. *Sindicatos* have performed such diverse duties as setting up a local system of weights and measures and drawing up plans for armed defense. The power of the *sindicatos* is so great in some areas that *campesinos* feel their *sindicato* actually controls the land. Likewise, the secretary general has been an important leader in *campesino* communities. His judicial duties have corresponded to those of the traditional hacienda overseer, but the method of selection has followed fiesta patterns. In fact, *sindicato* officials are often the sons of former fiesta sponsors.

In sharp contrast to other rural areas, the southern valleys of Chuquisaca and Tarija have not experienced much change and remain among the most static and isolated areas of highland Bolivia. The historical background and unique development of the hacienda system in this Quechua-speaking area had helped to determine the traditionalism of the *campesinos* throughout the region. The southern valleys were not in the mainstream of east-west traffic as was Cochabamba and never developed anything but the most primitive transportation facilities. This, plus the striking agricultural self-sufficiency of each locality, enhanced isolation and impaired hopes of integration with the national system.

The hacienda complex evolved earlier and came to dominate the area to a greater degree in the south than in the Altiplano. There were far fewer *comunidads* in the south, and the organizational system that developed was not founded on the norms or patterns of this Indian-based agrarian structure. In addition, a scarcity of land and a concomitant crowding produced a pattern of subletting and a rigid stratification system among the *campesinos* themselves, which never arose on the Altiplano.

124

The *colonos* of the southern valleys, often called *arrenderos*, obtained their grants of land directly from the owner. They were divided into several categories, according to size of plot and obligations, and actually controlled the bulk of the land. Very little land was set aside by the landlord as unrented property. Beneath the *arrenderos* in status were the *arrimantes* and the *vivientes*. *Arrimantes* were subtenants who rented from the *arrenderos*, and *vivientes* were peripheral hangers-on who entered the household of the *arrendero* through marriage or adoption and had few rights or privileges. Although *vivientes* were an additional burden, they also added prestige, for they were proof that the *arrendero* could support more than just his immediate family. Under this system many *arrenderos* became petty *patrones* in their own right, exacting labor and taxes from those below them.

Furthermore, the hierarchical system of fiesta sponsorship so characteristic of Altiplano communities did not develop to the same degree throughout the south. In areas where it did not develop at all, there was no organizational structure for the presentation of either secular or religious fiestas. Fiesta giving did not take on the symbolic import it did in the Altiplano or even in Cochabamba, and community members greeted ceremonies with a casual attitude. This lack of an overriding socioreligious pattern to structure community interaction has been noticed by several observers. Moreover, the status hierarchy that did exist was based directly upon land and wealth, not upon service to others in the community.

The effect of agrarian reform and *sindicatos campesinos* in the southern valleys has been the least impressive in highland Bolivia. Very little land actually changed hands after the agrarian reform for, although the *patrones* were removed, true redistribution never took place. *Arrenderos* gained titles to the plots they had farmed for generations, whereas *arrimantes* and *vivientes* remained landless. Overcrowding remained a salient characteristic of land tenure patterns. Thus, the land-based stratification system among *campesinos* was reinforced. The failure of the reform to modify the relational base of ex-hacienda communities has been cited as the most important single factor in the continuing lack of integration with the outside world.

Sindicatos campesinos have never gained the foothold they did in the other rural areas and consequently have done little to propel the southern *campesino* out of isolation and into the twentieth century. Internal fragmentation has made unification of various *campesino* elements difficult. Because there was no hierarchical system that lent itself to adaptation to *sindicato* structure (as did the fiesta system in the Yungas), many communities did not develop *sindicatos*. There were a few groups in the south, such as the Camba migrants, who expressed genuine antagonism toward the *sindicatos*. For the most part, however, *campesinos* greeted the *sindicatos* with the same passivity and apathy they did the agrarian reform. In this region, unlike other highland areas, there seems to be little connection between fiesta sponsorship and *sindicato* offices, thus underscoring the weakness of authority patterns among southern *campesinos*. Where *sindicatos* have existed in this area, they have often been characterized by a lack of strong and effective administrators who have understood and appreciated community problems.

Campesinos of the Oriente, often called Cambas, bear little resemblance to any parallel groups in the highlands. Development of the eastern area was very late. (Not until the rubber boom of 1880 was there interest in the northeast, for example.) Ecological conditions of plentiful land and scarce labor contrasted sharply with the Altiplano and the southern valleys and caused the growth of nontraditional hacienda patterns. The near absence of indigenous peoples and the results of an early and extensive mestization process brought about a rural lower class of mixed ancestry and heterogenous cultural background. This element eventually abandoned most of the vestiges of its diverse Indian background, adopting the Spanish norm and language at an ever-increasing rate.

In social stratification and organization, the Oriente diverged sharply from the rest of the country. The connotations of "*campesino*" and "*indio*" were not equated here as elsewhere. Being a *campesino* held few racial implications because both landlords and tenants considered themselves *blancos*. On the other hand, the word *indio* was reserved for the primitive tribes inhabiting the jungle. Status among Cambas was therefore based on wealth and not race. Upward mobility was less restricted because of the linguistic and cultural similarities between *campesinos* and the *patrones*.

There was little solidarity between *campesinos* working for the same *patrón*, mainly because strongly cohesive and traditional patterns like fiesta sponsorship never developed. Intracommunity relations were cordial but not warm. Locality never became an important element in group identity as it did in the highlands. The only feelings of commonality were held about the lowlands region as a whole. Cambas contrasted themselves with the highlanders, reinforcing mutually chauvinistic attitudes.

Camba communities developed as the need for tenant farmers grew. They usually consisted of between twenty and 200 families loosely grouped around the hacienda manor house. In addition to being self-sustaining units they were also more independent of their *patrones* than most of the highland groups. Some Camba families lived in isolated household units. Frequent isolation of individual families and a high degree of geographic mobility were not conducive to extensive family ties and added to the solitary character of Camba existence. Neither locality groups nor voluntary or kin associations fostered local social solidarity, and there was little hierarchy around which *sindicatos* could coalesce.

Although the impact of the 1952 Revolution was negligible in some areas of the Oriente, it was pronounced in others. Most *campesinos* were not as ruthlessly eager to overthrow their landlords as were their compatriots to the west, and the friendly relations that had existed between *patrón* and tenant before the revolution were a factor in the generally peaceful situation that existed after the land reform. Gradually more landlords have been separated from their holdings until in 1973 only a few Cambas remained as tenants, whereas the great majority had succeeded in becoming small landholders.

Little information is available concerning the overall effect of *sindicatos campesinos* in the Oriente. In some areas wooed by the MNR, *sindicatos* took on a great deal of significance. One very important effect was the building of a sense of identity among the members, who came to call each other *compañero*, or comrade. The shared sense of community lay virtually dormant until awakened by the reform process.

FAMILY

For the majority of Bolivians a stable family life and widely extended bonds of kinship loyalty provide the most effective source of personal security. Although there are wide variations in family and kinship patterns among the disparate Bolivian ethnic groups, the prevailing value traditions, Hispanic and Indian, place great stress upon bonds of responsibility and affection among kinsmen and upon the faithful fulfillment of marital duties. No other institution—social, economic, or political—has evinced the degree of stability and endurance characteristic of the family, and none has commanded the degree of loyalty accorded the latter by most Bolivians.

The basic unit of family organization among the upper and urban middle classes is the nuclear household—a father and mother with their unmarried and dependent children. It is within this household that children are reared, women play their major social roles, and men owe their primary obligations of economic support. Almost invariably based upon formal matrimony—both religious and civil—the nuclear family is extremely stable.

Despite its functional importance and stability, the basic family seldom exists as a totally independent unit. As a result of both the strong traditional familism and the social and economic conditions of Bolivian life, bonds of loyalty, affection, and mutual responsibility with the more distant kinsmen of both spouses are strong and abiding. There are few activities or decisions of an individual and his immediate family that do not, in the Hispanic view, affect the wider circle of kin.

The ties of solidarity among kinsmen are expressed in an active and highly ceremonial pattern of social life. The nuclear family spends much of its time making formal calls upon relatives and receiving such calls. Weddings, baptisms, and funeral masses are virtually command appearances, even when those involved are distant cousins. Indeed, such ritualized visiting and compulsory attendance at weddings, funerals, and the like form almost the entire social life of many women. Kinship solidarity is also expressed most graphically by the assumption of mourning garb—particularly by women—on the death of relatives, whether close or distant.

For the Quechua- and Aymara-speaking Indians, who constitute the majority of Bolivians, family and kinship loyalties have always provided a first line of defense against their precarious economic and social position. In many communities cooperative sharing of goods and labor among the members of closely knit kin groups has served to maintain their almost total independence in relation to the markets dominated by whites and *cholos* and hence to reinforce the shell of self-isolation assumed by the Indians as a matter of protection. In many areas, also, the cohesive kin groups exercise a control over inheritance and sale of lands held both collectively and individually by their members, and thus they effectively protect themselves from encroachments by outsiders. Strong bonds of kinship unity, along with networks of intermarriage among kin groups, reinforce cohesion and esprit de corps within the local communities.

Among all highland Indian groups the basic family is highly stable. On the one hand, prevailing social values lay great emphasis upon the endurance of marriage and the fulfillment of marital duties by both husband and wife. A man's neglect of duty or purposeful injury to his spouse calls forth strong reactions from his neighbors and kinsmen. On the other hand, a marriage usually not only entails relationships between the spouses but also involves ties of trust and cooperation between their respective circles or kin. In consequence, many people feel that their interests are bound up with the success of the marriage.

The bonds uniting the parents of a nuclear family are ideally, but not necessarily, both civil and religious marriage. The church wedding and the fiesta that inevitably accompanies it are generally seen as highly important acts solemnizing the relationships established between individuals and their kinsmen. In many communities isolation and poverty combine to make church marriage somewhat rare, although in general the Indians desire it. In such cases the expressed intention of a man and woman to live together, along with the act of establishing a household, is sufficient, in the local view, to make a valid marriage. Such couples often seek religious solemnization of their union after years of cohabitation, when they have accumulated the necessary amount of money to pay for the ceremoney.

The strength of familism at all levels of Bolivian society is such that those who are unrelated to persons of wealth and power very often seek to establish bonds of fictional kinship with them through the institution of *compadrazgo* (the set of relationships that exists between a child's parents and his godparents). In the Hispanic tradition persons related through *compadrazgo* are seen as ideally sustaining the highest regard and loyalty toward one another. For many of the traditionally dominant whites, *compadrazgo* represents, on the one hand, the extension of kinship bonds to a wider circle and, on the other, a means of formalizing and ritualizing pre-existing ties of friendship. For the great mass of lower status Indians and *cholos*, *compadrazgo* has been one of the few relations in which trust could be established outside the bounds of the local community.

Cholo merchants and local officials still seek to establish bonds of *compadrazgo* with wealthy citizens and prominent political officials. In many areas Indians attempt to obtain *padrinos* (godfathers) for their children from among the local gentry of *cholo* merchants and petty officials. Camba *campesinos* of the Oriente frequently ask upper class planters or cattlemen to stand as *compadres* (godparents) to their children. In every case the man who asks another of greater power and wealth to serve as *padrino* to his child expects thereby to enhance his own status. Not only does his stature increase in reflection of the importance of his *compadre*, but he most often enjoys at least a minimal claim upon the latter's aid and protection as well. Although in the case of great social distance between the parents and *padrinos* the relationship can never develop any degree of intimacy, the *padrinos* seldom fail to maintain at least a mild interest and to render economic or political assistance when needed. Powerful and affluent Bolivians are not usually averse to accepting invitations of ritual kinship with the more humble, for personal loyalties thus generated can bear significant psychological, economic, and political benefits.

RELIGION

The Roman Catholic Church

The Roman Catholic Church has not been a particularly dominant or dynamic institution in Bolivian national life, although Catholicism is still at the heart of many traditional values and roles, particularly with reference to women. It is faced with the problems of regionalism and duality of culture that encourage fractionalism within the social system as a whole. Diverse political and national elements characterize the Bolivian clergy, making it difficult for the conservative elements in Santa Cruz to reconcile the actions of more liberal clergy in La Paz and Cochabamba. Although over 90 percent of the Bolivians profess Catholicism, a much smaller portion participate actively. The burden of religious activity falls on the women. Bolivian men feel no negative sanctions by other members of the society if they refrain from church attendance and Catholic practices. Moreover, the lack of an empathetic clergy, and sometimes the lack of any clergy, has caused a unique brand of Catholicism to evolve among the Indians in rural areas. There was some evidence that the church was beginning to realize and deal with its weaknesses in 1973, but the obstacles precluded much rapid or effective change on the institutional level.

The Catholic church became an initially powerful and influential force in Latin America soon after the conquest. The conquerors of Bolivia were accompanied by six priests, who established the first Christian community in 1535 near the present city of Oruro. With the founding of the city of Charcas (later to become Sucre) as the seat of authority for Upper Peru, missionary work had a center in the area. As early as 1540 four religious houses had been established there. The extensive missionary effort, carried out through the instruments of the *encomienda* in the highlands and the rural settlements established by priests throughout the country, eventually brought the majority of the Indians under the influence of the church and served as the fundamental colonizing force in the eastern lowlands.

In addition, the church and its representatives performed the valuable service of organizing and administering educational and charitable institutions. In the social sphere the church acted as chief promoter of arts and letters and maintained its traditional role of protector of the poor, sick, orphaned, and aged. It also preserved and disseminated traditional Catholic values regarding morality and interpersonal relations. In a broader sense the church closely touched the lives of all society because that society was the child of a culture more medieval than modern, which had not yet been strongly affected by the liberal influences that were reshaping northern Europe.

During the colonial period Spain had great power over ecclesiastical affairs and united church and state in the colonies more completely than it had been able to in Europe. By the end of the sixteenth century civil control and administration of patronage were consolidated, and no major changes occurred during the rest of the colonial period. Although it is true that civil authority over the church and its dignitaries was great, the latter exerted considerable influence in its spiritual function and its economic power. Its wealth was increased as a result of its role as colonial banker. By extending loans or mortgages to the landed aristocracy (also holders of high political positions) and by investing church funds in real estate, it eventually had complete or partial ownership of most of the large estates of the colony. The Inquisition and the religious services performed by the church, instruments through which great moral pressure could be applied, provided another means of influence. Thus church and state, while closely aligned, possessed considerable power and influence over each other. Conflicts seldom arose; the general attitude was one of mutual appreciation and support.

The first hundred years of independence brought little change in official church-state relations. The new national government inherited control over church affairs from their Spanish antecedents—despite the opposition of clergy and church supporters who wanted more freedom from state interference. On the other hand, the church retained its favored position in the eyes of the government—despite advice to the contrary by such notables as Simón Bolívar. Catholicism became the official religion of the state, to be protected by the state and to be the professed religion of the head of state. During the beginning of the twentieth century the Liberal Party tried to separate church and state, favoring freedom of worship, lay education, and civil marriage. Although they did not succeed completely, they did loosen church control over education, civil and penal matters, and marriage. Freedom of worship was also instituted.

In 1961 the government relinquished the right to mediate in church affairs. No longer could it hold sway over the approval of conciliar decrees, briefs, bulls, or rescripts emanating from the pope or have a voice in the selection and appointment of major church officials. Thus, although once closely interwoven, the actions of church and state in Bolivia have been gradually separated. The church continues to receive financial support through the budget but, aside from this, each structure is supposed to operate exclusively in its own sphere of influence.

Actual relations between church and state have been ambiguous ever since the 1952 social revolution and subsequent reinstatement of a status quo military regime. Relations between the Catholic church in Bolivia and the MNR were officially cordial. Unlike many successful revolutionary parties in Latin America, the MNR never adopted a strongly anticlerical position. For its part, the church expresses a position of noninterference in politics, largely because of division within its own ranks. The strong anticommunist sentiment of some clergy caused this element to be wary of certain aims of the MNR government. These conservatives incurred the irritation of other lay and clerical people who felt that the church's policy of noninvolvement was a cover for its refusal to cooperate with social reforms.

A partial explanation for the division within the church and its weakness as a national institution arises from the heterogeneity in age and nationality of the clergy. An overwhelming number of priests are foreign. A study in the late 1960s indicated that nearly 80 percent of the clergy were not Bolivian nationals. Another study showed that between 1950 and 1960 the number of native diocesan priests dropped from 204 to 172 despite a population increase from 3 million to 4.5 million. The priesthood has never been a popular vocation for Bolivian men, who prefer positions that will allow them to be dominant, competitive, and have an active social life to a career demanding humility and abnegation. Moreover, the priesthood was often used by poor families as a means of educating their children and came to be regarded as an avenue for potential social climbers. The dropout rates in Bolivian seminaries are impressive—at the lower levels they vary between 40 and 50 percent. These percentages help to explain why only thirty-eight new clergy were ordained in the thirty-year span between 1935 and 1965. The number of inhabitants per priest—5,419 to one—is about average for Latin America.

The high number and strong influence of foreign priests have been resented by Bolivian nationals. Foreign priests have been elevated to commanding positions within the church hierarchy and have generally made their presence known in the political circles of the country. Sometimes the limited knowledge of well-intentioned foreigners brought about disastrous consequences, as in the case of the Sirionó tribe in the Oriente. Missionaries converted this jungle tribe and removed them from their traditional environment. By 1967 about 90 percent of the Indians had contracted tuberculosis, and their numbers had decreased from 1,000 to 600 in a very few years.

In the late 1960s and early 1970s Catholic clergy became increasingly concerned with defining their religious, social, and political role in Bolivia. One manifestation of their concern was a statement signed by 12 percent of the priests in the country that discussed their feelings of ineffectiveness. Although the Catholic church has traditionally maintained numerous charitable activities, the consensus was that this had been insufficient. At a congregation of clergy and laity in 1968 a concerned group stated that the church must serve the people and not vice versa. Those in attendance criticized the clergy for lack of sensitivity, saying that, to be effective, clergy would have to adopt a life-style similar to those with whom they worked.

Despite their concern, the Bolivian Catholic clergy continued to vacillate politically in the early 1970s. Their ambivalence was demonstrated in simultaneous backing and denunciation of rightist status quo groups and the government of Hugo Banzer Suárez. Even so, church property became subject to periodic raids by police in search of subversive materials, and a few clergy were imprisoned on suspicion of involvement with leftist groups.

In the early months of 1973 there appeared to be a break in the stalemate of church-state relations when the statement "Gospel and Violence" appeared. This document was subsequently endorsed by the Episcopal Conference of Bolivia (comprising all the country's bishops) and gave the first unified support to sentiment of this nature. The tenor of this statement was antiviolent, criticizing government practices, past and present, and citing acts of violence committed by both Left and Right. It concluded by saying that the only way to eliminate violence in Bolivia is to eliminate injustice, hunger, and repression.

In addition, the clergy demanded more freedom to preach and to do social work among the disadvantaged. They recognized the need to make profound changes in the existing social and economic structure and pleaded that their efforts in this vein not be construed as subversive or extremist. They also asked for a more expeditious mediation of justice for both political prisoners and common criminals, respect for human dignity through the elimination of alleged torture techniques, recognition of the right of asylum, and the right of workers to bargain for a just wage.

Foreign clergy who have become involved in politics have received sharp reprimands from the government, especially if the two have been at odds. The antigovernment document "Gospel and Violence" was signed by nearly 100 priests, the great majority of whom were foreign. In an angered reply to this statement, one government official expressed surprise at the number of foreigners and criticized the signers for meddling in Bolivian politics, when they had never done so in their home countries. He advised that foreign priests who signed the document take a special collection at Sunday masses for return fare to their countries. The initial outburst was later mitigated by a statement issued by the cabinet and supported by President Banzer himself that stated that "Gospel and Violence" was an "intelligent assessment of national political life."

Indian Practices

Indian beliefs today are an intricate blend of Roman Catholicism and pre-Hispanic religion. Necessary adaptations were made with ease by the Indian. The Inca had introduced new gods that were incorporated into the local pantheon so that, when the Spaniards came, the Indians were easily able to graft foreign beliefs and practices onto the existing religious culture. The Indian, however, does not divide his religious beliefs into Spanish and indigenous elements, nor does he concede greater or lesser power to the supernaturals on the basis of origin. The basic lack of system in the synthesis is partly a result of the absence of a priestly cult dedicated to the study and formulation of a theology. Although this lack leads to confusions and incongruities, it is not a source of concern for the Indian.

The older religious beliefs have tended to persist more strongly among the Aymara than among the Quechua, but the two groups are generally characterized more by their similarities than by their differences. The Aymara world is densely populated with spirits that are constantly influencing everyday events. They are related to and explain his economic state (in agriculture), his health, his personal relations with other members of his community, and the fearful unknown. Most commonly, spirits are place spirits, living in the air, in or around a natural phenomenon, or wandering with no fixed dwelling. The association of the spirits with place reveals the Aymara's preoccupation with his natural environment, which plays such an important role in his life, and also explains the variations in objects of veneration from town to town or area to area.

Other supernaturals include ghosts, demons, the souls of the dead, and Roman Catholic saints. These spirits are considered ambivalent, if not malevolent, in their attitude toward the Indian, concerned with his

133

affairs but not necessarily with his welfare. For this reason the individual must attempt to remain on good terms with them through propitiation and the use of magicians and diviners who can speak with or interpret the actions of the supernaturals for him. The rank accorded the spirits is based on their intelligence and power. Their positions progress from those most intimately associated with everyday life, who are relatively weak and unintelligent, to those who are supreme but very remote. At the bottom of the scale are the individual house guardians, the only spirits who are consistently kindly disposed toward the Indian; next, the place spirits, ghosts, souls, demons, and devils; then, the spirits that inhabit important physical phenomena like large rivers and mountain peaks; and finally, the saints.

The Virgin Mary and God, the latter often confused with Christ and at times with the sun, occupy the position of supremacy but are also so remote that they do not figure significantly in the Indian's life. God and Christ, as the Indian envisions them, are white men who are not interested in his affairs and who are potentially threatening. God is not seen in relation to a final judgment because the Indian is not essentially concerned with the hereafter; nonetheless, it is considered a good idea to remain in his good graces.

The Virgin Mary, referred to even less than God or Christ, is seen as a white woman, a wealthy señora whose attitude is one of casual and patronizing benevolence. At the same time she is strongly identified with the earth mother, Pachamama. To the Indian there are as many Virgins as there are representations of her, and each is a different being. There is no comprehension of the Holy Spirit. Of all the supernaturals in the Roman Catholic religion, the saints have been incorporated most effectively, usually to the degree to which they can be associated with indigenous deities. Often they are confused with the more important place spirits, mountains, rivers, and lakes, which now bear the names of the saints as well as their own.

The view of the soul is at great variance with the Christian concept. First, the Indian has not one but several souls, which leave the body not only at death but during life—in a dream or through the machinations of a practitioner of black magic. Because children's souls are thought to be less securely attached to the body than those of adults, they are particularly subject to loss. Wandering souls are a source of fear, and exposure to a corpse can cause sickness. For this reason death and the dead are greatly feared, and elaborate precautions are taken to remove all traces of the dead. Because the souls wander at night, the Indian is highly reluctant to go out after dark. Propitiation of souls is also common for the purpose of discouraging their suspected malevolent intentions toward the living.

Generally, Roman Catholic rites and celebrations are seen primarily as an outlet for social activity, whereas indigenous practices are the means by which spiritual and material difficulties are resolved. Of all the Catholic observances, the most notable among the Indians are the fiestas, held on the numerous saints' days, which are celebrated with extended festivities that include drinking, music, and feasting. Except on fiesta days, more solemn functions such as mass are not popular and are attended, if at all, out of fear. According to some observers, the Catholic practice of confession is seen by the Indian as a form of punishment, and he therefore rarely goes on his own initiative. Catholic morality has not been adopted by the Aymara, whose ethical behavior is based on indigenous cultural tradition.

Rural Bolivia has never possessed an abundance of clergy. Some villages would see a priest every two years, and some villages never. What priests there were found themselves frustrated in their efforts to impose Roman Catholic morality. They often used the concern of the *campesino* for his crops as a leverage in instituting Catholic practice, warning farmers that failure to comply with Catholic obligations would mean crop failure. Consequently, for those Indians—largely Aymara—religion became another form of oppression, which included duties and expenses, such as candle lighting, providing dancers for religious fiestas, taking part in processions, and contributing flowers to decorate the church. Over the years the mixture of Catholic and Indian beliefs has resulted in a rigid and somewhat confusing complex of beliefs, appropriately suited to the Indian concept of a threatening world.

Protestantism

After more than sixty years of missionary work in Bolivia, the Protestants still command only a fraction of believers. Although the number of actual converts is not impressive, the number is growing. Significant inroads have been made in the fields of education and social work, which have gained Protestant missionaries the respect of the people.

In the 1880s the American Bible Society succeeded in getting three of its agents into the country, but it was not until the arrival of the Canadian Baptists in 1898 that a real missionary program was established. Within a few years the Methodist Episcopal Church, the interdenominational Indian Mission, and other groups began work there also. Initial activity was concentrated in education because the practice of faiths other than the Roman Catholic was forbidden by law. Even with the enactment of legislation introducing religious freedom, Protestants still had their greatest success in the areas of education and medical assistance.

The numerous fundamentalist groups that followed the pioneering denominations have located primarily in the rural sectors. In fact, the largest Protestant denomination in Bolivia is the Seventh Day Adventist, whose work has been concentrated among the Indians of the Lake Titicaca area. Although the Indians are conservative and often strongly attached to the Roman Catholic Church through custom, the appeal of its ceremony, and fear of the local priest, the evangelistic approach employed by the fundamentalist groups has created an atmosphere of social acceptance and comradeship that the Indian finds attractive. Other appealing factors include the few economic demands the Protestant missionary makes on the Indian in contrast to his Catholic counterpart, a greater concern for the individual's temporal state, the strong emphasis on the virtue of physical labor, and the conviction that all fellow believers share equal status in the community.

In most rural areas Protestants represent a small but respected enclave within the local society. Interaction between Roman Catholics and Protestants is high, expressing itself in friendship, *compadrazgo*, and even intermarriage. Both Seventh Day Adventists and Baptists have done considerable work in the Titicaca region, forming cohesive groups within their communities. In La Paz Baptists and Methodists have maintained a nursery school, a primary-secondary school, a hospital, and a radio station. In Santa Cruz the Church of the Brethren has organized livestock clubs, and the Methodists have promoted 4-S clubs for children, which are similar to the 4-H clubs that flourish in the rural United States. The four S's stand for Saber (to know), Sentir (to feel), Servir (to serve), and Ser (to be) and, in this sense, to express oneself.

CHAPTER 6

EDUCATION

The Bolivian educational program during the late 1960s and early 1970s was in a state of almost incessant change. During preceding years it had evolved slowly, with little that was innovative and without adequate planning to define objectives and priorities. Beginning in the late 1960s, however, a variety of measures for reforming the administration, structure, and curricula of all kinds of schools at all levels of the system were introduced in a politically chaotic atmosphere marked by frequent student strikes and school closings.

Up to the time of the Revolution of 1952 the educational system had been one in which whites attended secondary schools and universities, mestizos and a scattering of acculturated Indians attended a few years of primary school, and nearly all of the Indians, who made up half or more of the population, remained illiterate. During the late 1950s and most of the 1960s school enrollments at all levels gained rapidly at accelerating rates, particularly in the rural primary school, which continued to offer the only education of any kind available to Indian people, few of whom resided in urban localities. Qualitative reforms of any significance, however, died aborning.

Three basic themes made up the litany of the educational reformers. First was the demand that the separately administered rural system be improved and coordinated or unified with the urban program. Second was the demand that the theoretical and liberal-arts-oriented curricula be restructured to place much greater emphasis on practical studies at the secondary and higher levels in order to provide technical skills needed by the economy. Third was the demand that steps be taken to reduce a student attrition rate that was critically high throughout the system. Collateral to all of these demands was the plea for an accelerated school construction program to alleviate a situation in which it was often necessary to hold classes in multiple shifts and to remedy an acute shortage of books and teaching aids of all kinds.

The reforms that commenced in the late 1960s were addressed directly to these basic problems and, in particular, progress was made in the building of schools and the provision of teaching materials. Most of the rural population in the early 1970s remained illiterate, however, and an inability to find suitable professional-level jobs was causing an alarming number of university graduates to emigrate at a time when secondary students were engaged in preuniversity courses of study to the virtual neglect of studies providing training in practical skills.

HISTORICAL DEVELOPMENT

Education during the colonial era was administered almost exclusively by the Roman Catholic Church. The Jesuit order provided most of the teachers until its expulsion from Spain in 1767. Theology and moral teachings were the mainstays of a curriculum that included some instruction in philosophy, the arts, and languages. Priests and lay tutors for the most part confined their teachings to the male children of elite families; education for women was frowned upon as tending to distract them from their more important religious and domestic duties.

Little education was made available to the indigenous population. Male children of tribal leaders were given some formal instruction, but most of the teaching was aimed at conversion to the Christian faith, implanting attitudes of acceptance toward the new masters, and the learning of useful crafts. Because few of the teachers were fluent in the Quechua or Aymara languages, however, many of the students acquired a rudimentary command of Spanish by accident rather than by intent.

With the coming of independence in 1825 education passed into the hands of the government, and at the beginning a spate of decrees was issued calling for the formation of public primary, secondary, and vocational schools in all capitals of departments. No vocational schools were established at the time, however, and attempts to introduce vocational and agricultural schooling were sporadic and generally unsuccessful until well into the twentieth century.

During the remainder of the nineteenth century, chronic political unrest, punctuated frequently by military coups, confined educational growth to the opening of a few urban schools for children of the upper class. Most of the country's universities were established during this period, and legislation enacted in 1895 set forth some of the foundations of university autonomy. An 1872 law making primary education free and compulsory had little discernible effect. The spirit of liberalism was growing, particularly among university students, but the indigenous people were generally regarded as constituting a race apart, and dominant political factions saw as dangerous to their own interests all schemes for the schooling of the Indian population.

Soon after the beginning of the twentieth century, a Belgian teaching mission was invited to Bolivia by the incumbent administration to establish teacher training schools. It was to remain in the country for nearly thirty years and to exercise a strong influence on the development of rural education. It brought about the creation of the first lasting and successful normal school and the introduction of vocational and agricultural subjects into the public school curriculum and conducted the first systematic studies of the problems of Indian education.

Several abortive efforts to establish schools for the training of Indian teachers were made during the early years of the century, and 1929 legislation called for the establishment of schools for the children of workers on the larger haciendas. The law was largely ineffective, however, and a majority of the few rural schools in existence were concentrated in those indigenous farming communities that had not been absorbed by the hacienda system of land tenure.

The year 1931 was enshrined as a landmark date in the history of educational development as a consequence of the establishment in that year of a school center for Indians at Huarisata, near Lake Titicaca. The school, which was to serve as a prototype for indigenous educational institutions, included a large nuclear school (*núcleo escolar*) surrounded by smaller satellite school units. This pattern was to become the characteristic one in the organization of rural education in Bolivia and to be adopted in Peru and Ecuador (see The School System, this ch.). The creation of the Huarisata school was regarded as of such importance that August 2—the official date of its inauguration—was selected as the date for promulgation of the Agrarian Reform Act of 1953 and officially set aside as the Day of the Indian (El Día del Indio).

At about the same time, an overall reform of the administrative apparatus was undertaken to permit greater local school autonomy and to reduce the influence of political appointees. The quasi-autonomous National Council of Education, created to direct the administration of all primary and secondary schools, was given authority to manage funds and to draft annual budget proposals. The allocation of moneys remained in the hands of the central government, however, and the council proved ineffective as a means of reducing partisan political influence.

The disastrous Chaco War (1932–35) brought the educational program to a virtual halt, and for the first time Indians in considerable numbers left the Altiplano and the high valleys to join in the fighting. The socially broadening influence of this movement may have been overemphasized, but the conflict did prompt socially conscious members of the elite to accelerate their demands for education of the rural masses.

Soon after World War II an effort was made to restructure the rural curriculum by introducing practical studies to replace or supplement the existing urban-oriented course selections that bore little relevance to the needs of farm children. The project had the assistance of the newly established Inter-American Cooperative Education Service (Servicio Cooperativo Inter-Americano de Educación—SCIDE), a joint venture of the Bolivian and United States governments that, during the succeeding twenty years, was to play an important part in the development of rural and vocational schooling.

Growth of rural enrollments during the remainder of the 1940s remained negligible, and the outbreak of the Revolution of 1952 found all but a scattering of the primary students enrolled in urban schools. Between 1952 and 1954 alone, however, rolls in rural primary establishments rose sharply, and the 1955 Code of Education provided— inter alia—the first real charter for rural education. The dominant political party at that time was the Nationalist Revolutionary Movement (Movimiento Nacionalista Revolucionario—MNR) which, coming into power with the 1952 Revolution and destined to remain in power until 1964, had linked its prestige with the goal of educational progress (see ch. 10).

During the 1960s and early 1970s the pace of enrollment growth accelerated at all school levels, and educational reform became a matter of increasing concern to everyone. The variety of reform plans that were introduced involved sweeping administrative, organizational, and substantive changes. In particular, the need for greater emphasis on practical studies at all educational levels and on the upgrading of rural education was stressed.

Beginning in 1969 a series of reforms was enacted, but in early 1973 these appeared likely to be superseded by a new blueprint for educational change that was reported under preparation by the government.

ADMINISTRATION AND FINANCE

Under the 1955 Code of Education, responsibility for the school system was divided between the Ministry of Education and Fine Arts and other public entities, particularly the then Ministry of Rural Affairs, which was assigned responsibility for what was specifically defined as fundamental peasant education (*educación fundamental campesina*). As the system developed, the Ministry of Education and Fine Arts administered most of the urban schools at the primary and secondary levels. The Ministry of Rural Affairs administered the rural primary units and the secondary-level normal schools for the training of rural teachers, which together constituted virtually the only rural educational institutions of any kind. Various other public ministries and agencies maintained separate school systems, however, and by the late 1960s a total of seventeen public entities participated in the public educational program.

Increasing demand for a simplification of this cumbersome assignment of responsibilities led to issuance in early 1970 of a decree giving the Ministry of Education and Culture (formerly, the Ministry of Education and Fine Arts) direct responsibility for rural as well as for urban schooling. Most of the other public entities maintaining educational programs were stripped of their direct responsibilities, and in the early 1970s only the government-owned mining corporation and the state petroleum enterprise continued to operate separate systems.

Directors of the country's school districts are responsible for the inspection and supervision of all public and private primary and secondary units; they also appoint teaching staffs and prepare budget estimates at the district level. School inspectors, acting as intermediaries between the districts and the individual schools, issue directives, interpret curricula and instructions, supervise work programs, and evaluate teacher competence.

Local administration of rural schools falls within the province of an administrative council, or school assistance board. This civic group is made up of leading members of the community and includes a school mayor (*alcalde escolar*), who monitors the attendance of students and the performance of teachers. The position of school mayor is a traditional one that predates the Revolution of 1952 in the freeholding communities. During more recent years the responsibility of the position has sometimes been shared with a secretary of education named by the local peasant syndicate.

Private education plays a substantial part in the national program; in 1971 some 17 percent of the primary school and 25 percent of the secondary school students were in private institutions. Since 1960 the private primary enrollment growth had been somewhat slower, and the private secondary enrollment growth had been somewhat faster than the rates in schools of the public sector. Tuition-charging private units are administered by religious congregations, lay organizations, and foreign communities and entities. Also counted in the private sector are schools administered by business enterprises whose workers and employees have twenty-five or more children of primary-school age—which, as a consequence, are required by law to maintain primary school facilities—and the schools maintained by the government mining and petroleum programs.

The country's eight public universities have traditionally enjoyed autonomous administration. Legislation enacted in 1972, however, had the effect of limiting this autonomy (see The School System, this ch.). The eight public institutions and the country's one private university are administered by the National Council on Higher Education, established under the 1972 legislation.

Virtually all of the costs of public education at the primary and secondary levels, as well as of public literacy and adult education programs, are borne by the central government. Its budget expenditures for education increased irregularly from less than 19 percent of the total outlay in fiscal 1961 to about 30 percent in 1971.

A proportion of 24.4 percent budgeted for education during 1973 suggests a relative decline since 1971, but expenditures on education have consistently exceeded budget estimates by substantial margins, and the proportion spent on education has consistently been among the highest in Latin America. In only seven of the countries in the region were the budgets in excess of 20 percent.

Private schools derive their incomes from tuition fees, donations, boarding charges and, occasionally, central or local government subsidies or subsidies of foreign or international public or private organizations. In order to qualify for tax exemption, private schools must provide scholarships covering tuition and costs of textbooks to at least 10 percent of their enrollments, the scholarship students to be named from lists prepared by the government. Certain business enterprises required by law to maintain schools for children of workers and employees bear the costs of these institutions, and schools maintained by the public mining and petroleum programs receive their own budget allocations.

Central government budget expenditures for education have consistently been devoted almost entirely to current expenses; during the 1960s and early 1970s the proportion allocated to salaries of teachers and the large corps of administrative personnel exceeded 90 percent of the total. Little remained for the construction, maintenance, and equipping of the schools. A substantial portion of the limited amounts spent on construction and maintenance (about one-third of the total in 1972) consisted of foreign credits and school construction funds derived from a 2 percent tax on payrolls.

Departmental and municipal governments are required to contribute 10 percent of their revenues to school construction, and organizations of parents and teachers and other civic groups at the community level are theoretically required to contribute labor and materials to the construction of school buildings. Enforcement of these statutes is uneven, but peasants (*campesinos*) often assist in construction and maintenance work, either directly or through local peasant syndicates.

The amount of new construction completed during the 1960s fell far short of minimum needs, however, and in 1970 the Ministry of Planning and Coordination estimated that the amount of classroom floorspace available to public school students in the primary and secondary systems amounted to little more than one-third and one-half, respectively, of the minimum square footage recommended by the United Nations Educational, Scientific and Cultural Organization (UNESCO). According to a government survey, less than 1 percent of the schools were considered to be in good condition, and nearly 70 percent either were in need of major repair work or should be abandoned.

Teaching aids and equipment have been in similar short supply. Libraries and laboratories have been almost nonexistent, and the shortage of demonstration equipment for scientific and technical courses has limited teachers to the teaching of theory. Rural schools, in particular, have lacked public utility services, and blocks of adobe have served as desks for students seated on the earthen floor.

Textbooks of any kind have been few, and virtually none have been produced domestically. A beginning in domestic compilation and production of school texts was made in the late 1960s, however, and in early 1973 it was reported that the newly established National Service of Technical School Assistance had placed in circulation basic texts in such fields as mathematics, chemistry, technical and vocational studies, literature, and language.

There appeared also to be a quickening of activity in school construction. In mid-1972, through another recently established public entity, the National Council for School Construction (Consejo Nacional de Edificaciones Escolares—CONES), some forty-three schools consisting of 647 classrooms for an anticipated 25,800 students were reported under construction. An unreported number of existing facilities were under repair, and work on an additional thirty-four new schools for 26,640 students was to commence before the end of the school semester.

The public universities are located in the departmental capitals, and much of their financial support is derived from departmental governments. In addition, the universities accept donations and during recent years have benefited from international loans. Between 1964 and 1970 the Inter-American Development Bank extended credits totaling US $2.4 million to Bolivian universities. Some also benefit from specific taxes (the Higher University of San Andrés received an earmarked portion of the levy on beer sales) and, in some instances, from the proceeds of university-owned enterprises.

THE SCHOOL SYSTEM

During the politically turbulent late 1960s and early 1970s changes and proposed changes in the organizational structure of the school system came too rapidly for a clearly discernible pattern to emerge. The 1955 Code of Education had prescribed a structure consisting of two optional years of kindergarten followed by six primary and six secondary years. In 1962 President Víctor Paz Estenssoro, whose MNR government had sponsored the 1955 legislation, proposed a new pattern giving much greater emphasis to practical or vocational schooling. Under it the number of preprimary years would be increased to five by adding three prekindergarten years of nursery school. The regular primary cycle would be reduced to four years, and schooling at the secondary level would consist of four years of vocational schooling followed by four years of specialized studies.

The proposal was opposed by teachers and by the international organizations that had been counted on to provide support for its implementation, and the preexisting structure remained in effect until 1968. At that time the then-existing Supreme Council of Education announced a schedule including the two years of kindergarten but extending the primary school to eight years and reducing the secondary cycle to four years. Concurrently, new course schedules were to come into force to replace curricula that dated from 1948 in the primary and 1956 in the secondary cycle and 1966 in the normal school for training rural primary teachers. At the same time the previously separately

143

administered rural and urban school systems were gradually to be unified.

The reform plan became operative in 1969, but its initial effect was more apparent than real. School enrollment figures reported by grade reflected a shift from the six-year primary and six-year secondary division of classes to the new eight- and four-year division, but in the early 1970s at least some of the schools continued to operate on the six-and-six basis. The proposed curriculum changes were to have emphasized courses designed to provide needed additional practical schooling. With respect to the announced substantive changes, however, the National Conference of the Chiefs of School Districts that convened in 1969 reported that the so-called reforms accomplished during the 1969 school year had consisted of no more than superimposition on the existing educational structure of confusing plans and programs that bore no relationship to reality. A newspaper editorial stated that the curricula were still excessively theoretical and encyclopedic in content and that—particularly at higher levels—dictation, rote memorization, and subjection of students to long and difficult examinations continued to be regular practices.

In August 1971 President Hugo Banzer Suárez took control of the government. The country's eight universities were closed immediately and were to remain closed for more than a year while a new basic statute for these institutions was prepared and implemented. A short time later primary and secondary classes were suspended, and the Ministry of Education and Culture announced that the entire educational program was archaic and must be restructured.

At the end of the year the National Commission for Integral Education was appointed to prepare the draft of a new reform of the primary and secondary systems. According to scattered reports appearing during 1972, the new program, which had yet to be placed in effect at the beginning of 1973, would—like preceding reforms—eliminate the differences between urban and rural schools and place increased emphasis on practical studies. Early in 1973 President Banzer announced that in the future the student graduating from general secondary school with the baccalaureate (*bachillerato*) certificate would have technical training enabling him to engage at once in productive activity as well as academic training qualifying him for university matriculation.

According to basic rules, presumably unchanged by pending reforms, students in both the primary and the secondary cycles are evaluated on both classroom performance and twice-yearly examinations. Work is marked on a uniform scale consisting of five levels of grading for proficiency. The regular school year is divided into two terms and covers a minimum of 200 days, which extend from January to June and from July to October. A winter holiday occurs during June, and a summer holiday during November and December marks the end of the school year.

The university year is organized into three periods of four months each, which are called *cuadrimestres*. During the late 1960s and early 1970s student and teacher strikes and shortages of classroom space severely restricted the number of hours in which classes were held in the primary and secondary systems. The universities were closed altogether during late 1971 and most of 1972.

According to a 1970 press report, during a period of unspecified duration the urban primary schools had been able to cover no more than 65 percent of the program material in classes held during little more than half of the number of hours required under the 1955 Code of Education. In the somewhat less turbulent and crowded rural schools, 85 percent of the program material had been covered in 75 percent of the required number of hours.

Preprimary and Primary Education

Preschool classes, tuition free in the public sector, are optional parts of the educational system. For children under the age of three years, the Ministry of Labor and Trade Union Affairs maintains a few urban nurseries. Two years of kindergarten are available as part of the regular urban school program under teachers prepared in the National Teacher Training Institute in La Paz.

In the countryside preprimary Spanish instruction for Quechua and Aymara speakers is occasionally provided by primary-school teachers. In 1969 some 24,000 children were enrolled in kindergarten classes, more than one-third of them in private units, and girls about equaled boys in number. A majority were five years of age, and most of the remainder were aged four and six, but a few were eight years of age or older.

In 1971 the enrollment was about 746,500 in the new eight-year primary cycle. In 1968 it had been 612,000 under the previous six-year program. About 22 percent had been in private schools, and girls had made up about 40 percent of the total. Between 1960 and 1968 the number of children between the ages of six and fourteen enrolled in primary classes increased from less than 50 percent to nearly 70 percent of the total. According to a widely publicized statement made in 1970 by an official of the Ministry of Education and Culture, some 460,000 children in that age bracket (about half of the total) were not in school; but the statement appeared not to have made allowance for the considerable number over the age of six years who had not yet entered school and the number over the age of fifteen who were still attending primary classes. In addition, a great many young people still in the six- to fourteen-year age bracket and not currently in school had already terminated a complete or partial primary education.

In 1968 about 90 percent of the primary school enrollment was between the ages of seven and fourteen years, the age bracket at which school attendance was mandatory under legislation that could not be enforced because schools were not always available. During the 1960s the median age for commencing primary studies in urban localities, however, was only slightly less than nine years, and in the countryside it tended to be even older. By North American standards school began at an advanced age.

Although about 70 percent of the country's population in 1968 was rural, more than half of the primary enrollment was in urban schools. Girls made up nearly half of the urban student body, but in the countryside—where schooling was traditionally considered unnecessary for females—girls made up not much more than one-third of the total. The urban and rural distribution by sex had not changed significantly since the mid-1950s.

The 375 nuclear schools in existence in 1968 made up the core of the rural primary system and included most of its enrollment. They consisted of complete six-year central schools surrounded by fifteen to thirty outlying sectional units (seccionales), in each of which a single teacher taught all of the classes—usually three or fewer—offered. In addition to offering a complete six-year curriculum, the central schools in theory had teachers specially trained in agriculture and animal husbandry, hygiene and sanitation, and domestic science. Only about half of the units had staffs that included such specialists, however; and, although in theory the students finishing the incomplete sectional programs could continue their primary education in the central schools, lack of boarding facilities coupled with the long distances involved between central and sectional units usually precluded this transfer.

Outside the nuclear school program, there were fewer than 100 complete and numerous incomplete independent primary units scattered about the countryside in localities where the rural population was too widely dispersed for application of the nuclear system. Most of the more than 1,500 rural private schools were small, incomplete units maintained by Roman Catholic and Protestant missions, a large proportion of the latter located in frontier areas.

Efforts to generalize with respect to the availability and utilization of rural school facilities tend to be frustrated by regional and local variations. Schools of some kind are available to most of the school-age population in the densely populated countryside near Lake Titicaca, in the rural hinterlands of the cities in the Valles, and in the colonization zones of the Yungas and the Oriente. Moreover, in these areas both children and parents tend to be more receptive to the idea of formal schooling than those in more isolated localities. Similarly, schools were much more numerous and attendance in them higher in the freeholding farm communities that were never absorbed by haciendas than in the former hacienda zones. Hacienda proprietors had rarely maintained schools, and in the 1960s and early 1970s the former colonos (hacienda farmworkers) lagged behind their freeholder compatriots in understanding and accepting the value of schooling. Although families of former *colonos* far outnumbered those of freeholders, the 1965 student body at the Tarija school for training rural primary-school teachers included thirty-five students from freeholding community families and only three from families of *colono* origin. The Tarija student body was a select unit that may not have been fully representative of the rural population, but the school was a boarding institution drawing students from all parts of the country.

In both urban and rural schools the teaching methods are didactic and stereotyped; students learn to copy from blackboards, take dictation, and recite lessons by rote. The extensive urban curriculum provides, essentially, an introduction to liberal arts schooling, to which manual training for boys and home economics courses for girls are added in the upper class years. The much simpler rural curriculum, at least before the beginnings of change in the late 1960s, has reflected a basically different objective, which was stated in the 1955 Code of Education. Emphasis has been on literacy training and a few basic studies that may contribute to making the student a more useful member of the rural community and a more successful farmer. It has not prepared him for further studies at the secondary level and has not contributed materially to upward social mobility.

Attrition rates in urban as well as in rural schools are high, but the proportion of students who successfully complete the primary cycle of studies is higher in the urban schools, where in 1969 the number graduating represented 40 percent of the number that had commenced studies six years earlier. In rural institutions the proportion was less than 3 percent. Between urban and rural sectors the incidence of dropouts and grade repeaters differs sharply. During the six-year primary cycle ending in 1969, grade repetitions in urban classrooms were so numerous that in some grades the number actually exceeded the number promoted from the lower grade. In the rural sector repeaters were relatively few, and all except a few dropped out of school before graduating.

The reasons for the far higher rural attrition rate are understandable. For most of the country children there are either no schools available that offer the higher primary grades or the schools are available but discouragingly distant. Classes are conducted in a language unfamiliar to a majority of the entering students. Urban parents are less likely than parents of rural children to require their full-time labor after a few years of schooling.

Schools are great sources of pride to members of peasant communities, and parents willingly contribute labor—and sometimes funds— to their construction. Many, however, believe that one or two years is sufficient to acquire literacy and that further education is superfluous once literacy is acquired. In urban families attainment of literacy is seldom regarded as the ultimate educational goal.

A 1970 evaluation of the Bolivian school system cited an earlier study of 2,000 urban and rural children as providing a likely explanation for the relatively greater reluctance of peasant young people to repeat grades of school. In tests assigned, rural children had demonstrated great initial enthusiasm when undertaking an unfamiliar task but to abandon it much more readily than their urban counterparts upon encountering the first obstacle.

Secondary Education

Education at the secondary level is offered in general or academic schools designed to prepare students for university entrance, in vocational schools, and in normal schools for training teachers for schools in the rural primary system. On the basis of the shortened four-year course of study, the 1971 enrollment in secondary schools of all kinds was about 102,000. Between 1960 and 1968 (before the course was reduced from six to four years) enrollments almost doubled, and the four-year program registered an enrollment increase of about one-third between 1969 and 1971.

In 1968 virtually all of the school units, with the exception of the rural normal schools, were located in cities and towns. Girls made up about two-fifths of the total enrollment, and about one-third of the students were in privately operated institutions. About one young person in five of secondary-school age was enrolled in the system. As in the primary school program, students were primarily occupied in note taking and memorizing predominantly theoretical course material. Laboratories, shops, and libraries were few.

Academic Schools

In 1971 nearly 86,400 students, or 86 percent of the secondary level enrollment, were engaged in academic or general studies, a proportion slightly higher than the 83 percent recorded in 1960. Boys' schools were called *colegios* and the schools for girls, who constituted about one-third of the enrollment, were called *liceos*. Most of the students at the secondary level come from urban families with, or aspiring to, middle class or higher status.

Coupled with the social and intellectual prestige associated with the academic courses of study, this circumstance does much to explain the continued strong show of preference for the preuniversity academic curriculum—to the frustration of the efforts of administrators who sought to put greater emphasis on practical career studies in the vocational classrooms. The academic school curriculum was aimed essentially at university matriculation and the primary school facilities available to most rural children offered nothing above the third grade. From the fourth grade onward, the educational system was geared largely to the objective of placing young people in universities, which were already producing graduates at rates beyond the economy's absorptive capacity.

Private academic schools, with about one-third of the total enrollment during the 1960s, are of particular importance because of the quality of education that they offer as well as because of the number of students that they attract. Their retention rate and their record of securing university admissions for their graduates are substantially higher than those of the public sector. Most of the institutions are located in La Paz and in the larger provincial capitals.

A provision of the 1955 Code of Education requires that private schools give scholarships to poor children in proportion to their enrollments, and additional scholarships are sometimes offered by schools operated by Roman Catholic orders. For families of limited income, however, the cost of supporting children in their late teens even in the tuition-free public academic institutions is a severe one. At this age most Bolivian children are already working to help contribute to the family support, and parents of children in academic schools must look forward to the possibility of years of university attendance.

In 1968 the students graduating from academic schools represented 26.8 percent of those who had matriculated six years earlier; the proportion was moderately higher than the 24.2 percent registered in 1965. Attrition was most serious—one-third of the total—at the end of the first year.

Vocational Schools

In 1971 a little less than 11,000 students, or about 10 percent of the secondary-level student body, were enrolled in vocational school classes. The rate of enrollment increase since 1960 had been a high one but not quite as high as that registered in the academic schools. About two-fifths of the students were in privately operated institutions. So large a proportion were in the commercial schools devoted largely to teaching office skills to girls and in home economics schools for girls that the vocational school system was predominantly a female one; girls and young women made up nearly 80 percent of the 1968 enrollment.

The retention rate, varying considerably in the various kinds of study courses, had a collective average about the same as that for academic schools but was not readily comparable because of durations varying from two to six years. Most courses required a completed primary education, but some admitted students after completion of four primary years.

The home economics schools for girls, with over 3,200 students in 1971, and the commercial schools, with over 3,800 students, represented about two-thirds of the total vocational enrollment. The four-year home economics program consists of some academic courses plus training in such fields as dressmaking, cooking, and nutrition. Commercial courses vary in length and offer studies ranging from instruction in dictation and operation of office machines to bookkeeping and accounting. Secretarial schools operate in all of the major cities and towns—even the remote Oriente town of Riberalta has its school for

149

secretaries—and the Institute of Higher Commercial Studies in La Paz has sections in commerce, accounting, customs procedures, and business administration. The commercial secondary schools are the only ones in the school system in which the enrollment in private units predominates.

Industrial schooling for boys is offered in a four-year course at the Pedro Domingo Murillo National Industrial School and in a six-year course at the Don Bosco school operated by the Roman Catholic Church. The 1971 industrial enrollment was a little more than 600. The limited popularity of industrial courses is in part explained by the inability of graduates to find suitable jobs. According to one study, in 1968 only a minuscule percentage of the graduates receiving the technician (*técnico*) diploma had been able to find employment in their fields of specialization; employers had almost invariably preferred to give on-the-job training to unskilled personnel.

In 1971 over 1,000 students were enrolled in secondary schools of arts and music, which offered courses of up to six years. In addition, more than 2,000 students were trained in a variety of vocational courses conducted under the independent school program maintained by the national mining corporation.

A public agricultural vocational school, the first in the country, was established with United States assistance in 1958 at Muyurina, near the city of Santa Cruz. In 1960 its administration was assigned to the Roman Catholic order of the Salesian fathers. Statistical tables appearing during the late 1960s and early 1970s, however, included no figures for agricultural enrollment in secondary level schools.

During the early 1960s a system of labor secondary schools (*colegios laborales*) was established outside the regular school system to give instruction to young people in agrarian and artisan techniques and at the same time to give them some grounding in academic studies. By 1967 about thirty of these entities had been established, and more than 1,600 students were receiving instruction in a nine-month course of study. A majority were public institutions, but the fact that many of the number had been established through the initiative of parents in rural communities indicated the degree of popular interest that the program had aroused.

The schools had been started primarily to offer prevocational training to rural children who had completed all of the primary schooling available to them and who had no secondary schools to attend. By the late 1960s, however, the schools were coming more and more to resemble regular secondary institutions, apparently as a consequence of peasant demand for formal education rather than practical training. In addition, their number was growing precipitously despite a precarious lack of funds, facilities, and adequately trained teachers. UNESCO, which had provided guidance in initiating the program, had envisioned limiting the number of units to one in each of the country's ten rural school districts, the curricula to be tailored to the needs of the district. Popular demand coupled with political pressure brought to bear by the peasant syndicates, however, had brought the number of units to fifty-six before the end of 1968, and rural leaders were beginning to talk about the possible creation of peasant universities (*universidades campesinos*).

Rural Normal Schools

More than 4,700 students were engaged in studies in rural normal schools in 1971 as compared with 3,465 in 1967. The first school for preparing rural primary teachers had been established in 1915, but at the time of the 1952 Revolution a scant 360 students were enrolled in the system. During the late 1960s male students somewhat outnumbered females. The minimum age for enrollment was fifteen years, and the student body included a few adults.

The fourteen public and four church-operated normal schools were widely but unsystematically distributed about the countryside; they ranged in number from four in La Paz Department to a single school for the entire Oriente region. The most prestigious was Rural Normal School Number One, located at Huarisata in La Paz Department, the site of the prototype nuclear primary school (see Historical Development, this ch.). The Huarisata institution has played a prominent role in the training of student teachers in practical subjects designed to raise community living standards and to encourage personal habits of sanitation and good nutrition.

The rural normal school teaching staff is more fully prepared than that of the secondary system as a whole. In the late 1960s all normal school personnel were listed as qualified (*titulado*) either through graduation from the Higher Institute of Rural Education in Tarija or by other means of qualification, which in some instances included schooling abroad. In a 1969 seminar, however, the National Directorate of Rural Normal Schools noted that the instruction furnished was excessively informational and did little to encourage students to think deductively and develop values. In addition, the assignment of personnel has not always been to positions best suited to their qualifications, and classroom presentations have as a consequence often been improvised. Instruction in technical subjects has been particularly deficient.

Students come from varied cultural backgrounds and from various parts of the country, including a large minority from urban localities. Boarding facilities are frequently provided, however, and a considerable number of government scholarships are available. The four-year course of study includes practical teaching during the last year. Until 1968 only completion of the primary school cycle was required for admission, but in that year the requirement was raised to include the first two years of secondary school (eight years of primary school), and completion of the secondary cycle was to be required as of 1972.

Institutions of Higher Education

In 1971 a reported 32,550 students were enrolled in the country's institutions of higher education, as compared with fewer than 13,000 in 1961. A little more than one-fourth were girls, and almost all of the students were in public schools. Three-fourths of the total were in eight public universities. The remainder were in a single private university, in a higher technical institute, and in postsecondary teacher training schools.

The universities, which represent the heart of the higher education system, are defined collectively under the law as the Bolivian University. All are located in the capital cities of departments (only Cobija, the village capital of Pando Department, is without one). All are frequently referred to by the name of the cities in which they are located, but most have other official names, in most instances prefixed by the term "higher university" (*universidad mayor*).

The largest of the eight is the Higher University of San Andrés, located in La Paz. During the early 1970s it offered the widest range of studies. In addition to several attached institutes and schools, it was composed of nine faculties (*facultades*)—quasi-independent academic units offering complete courses of study in an academic discipline or in several related disciplines. The faculties were those of law, economics, philosophy and letters (including pedagogy), medicine and surgery, dentistry, pharmacy and biochemistry, architecture, civil engineering, and industrial engineering.

Second in size is the Higher University of San Simón of Cochabamba. Like the Higher University of San Andrés, it was founded soon after independence in the early nineteenth century. Smaller schools have complained that these two institutions received disproportionately large proportions of the public funds available to the university system.

The oldest Bolivian university—and one of the oldest in the Americas—is the Royal and Pontifical Higher University of San Francisco Xavier of Chuquisaca, located in Sucre. Despite the ecclesiastical flavor of the elegant name that reflects its Jesuit origin, it is a state-operated institution. The Higher and Autonomous Tomás Frías University, located in Potosí, and the Gabriel René Morona Higher University in Santa Cruz were founded in the late nineteenth century, and the Higher and Autonomous Juan Misael Saracho University was established in Tarija in 1946. The Technical University of Oruro was founded in 1892, and the José Ballivián University in El Beni opened its doors until 1967 as a school of exact and natural sciences.

The country's only private institution of higher education—the Bolivian Catholic University—was established in 1966 by the Roman Catholic Church as a school of business administration. In 1973 it maintained departments of administration, humanities and education, economics, psychology, and sciences of communication in facilities located in La Paz and Cochabamba.

The bulk of the postsecondary enrollment outside the university system is gathered in two institutions for the training of urban primary and secondary level teachers supervised by the Ministry of Education and Culture. The older of these, the National Higher Institute, was founded in 1909 in Sucre by the Belgian educational mission that was active in Bolivia in the early twentieth century. The second, the National Teacher Training Institute, was founded in 1917 in La Paz for the training of secondary teachers but later added primary school and kindergarten divisions.

In addition, rural primary teachers are trained at a higher normal school founded in 1963 in Tarija, and there is a small institute for training teachers of physical education. Collectively, the postsecondary teacher training units had a 1971 enrollment of about 7,600.

In 1971 about 300 postsecondary students were enrolled in the Higher Technical Institute. Founded in La Paz in 1961, this entity provides training in mining, metallurgy, petroleum technology, and related technological fields of study. Also offering postsecondary studies, but not ordinarily included in postsecondary enrollment statistics, is the Higher School of Fine Arts in La Paz.

During the 1973 school year the institutions making up the Bolivian University offered studies in fifty-eight fields of study (*carreras*) leading to undergraduate or graduate degrees. These fifty-eight fields ranged from highly specialized ones such as Altiplano agronomy to broad ones such as architecture. Specific enrollment data available for 1968 showed that economics, medicine and surgery, law, and engineering attracted more than half of the total. Agronomy and veterinary surgery together attracted a little more than 3 percent. It should be noted, however, that a considerable number of students were enrolled in university-sponsored technical schools that offered subprofessional courses to students who had completed part of the secondary cycle. In addition, in 1968 about 7 percent of the university enrollment was in popular universities (*universidades populares*) (see Literacy and Adult Education, this ch.).

In 1968 about 60 percent of the university degrees granted were in the prestigious disciplines of law, economics, and medicine. The problem of providing a larger cadre of university graduates with a variety of professional skills better adapted to the needs of the society, however, is second to the larger problem of providing employment for graduates in all disciplines that at once makes use of their skills and provides conditions of employment sufficiently attractive to stop their emigration (see ch. 3).

Data on the Bolivian "brain drain" are frequently conflicting but, according to one unofficial series of estimates, professionals of all kinds have emigrated in very substantial numbers. Among the proportions of professional groups living abroad, for example, were more than

50 percent of all agricultural engineers. The estimate is so high as to seem fanciful, but in the early 1970s it was clear that the universities were producing graduates at a rate far beyond the effective absorptive capacity of the economy.

Successful completion of secondary studies and an entrance examination are customarily required for matriculation in regular university courses of study. Most courses are from four to seven years in duration, and in some of the faculties doctoral (*doctorado*) degrees are offered after additional study and presentation of a thesis. Among the four-year courses are agronomy, veterinary surgery, and nursing; architecture, law, economics, pharmacy and chemistry, philosophy and letters, dentistry, and geology require five years. Engineering and medical degrees require six and seven years of study, respectively. Because a large proportion of the university enrollment is also employed full or part time, however, the average graduating student has spent more than the indicated number of years in completing his course of study.

The physical plant in most of the universities is much more nearly adequate than in the schools of the primary and secondary systems. The buildings are scattered irregularly about the cities in which they are located, however, and demonstration equipment and teaching aids of all kinds tend to be inadequate. In particular, libraries leave much to be desired. The number of volumes is limited (with fewer than 100,000 volumes, the library of the Higher University of San Andrés is the largest), and the selection tends to be dated. A North American visiting professor at one of the universities found that the economic section of its library consisted largely of standard texts by such nineteenth century authorities as Adam Smith and John Stuart Mill—and a shelf of works by Karl Marx.

In the late 1960s less than half of the first-year students were promoted, although promotion rates improved progressively thereafter to more than 70 percent in the fourth year and still higher in the fifth, sixth, and seventh years.

An excessive rate of failure in the first year is attributed in large measure to preparation at the secondary level so often inadequate that several of the universities maintain schools for preuniversity studies. In addition, the academic structure of the universities is such that students matriculate directly into a faculty or school without benefit of orientation programs in general studies, such as those offered in the lower undergraduate classes at North American universities. As a consequence, the entering student often finds himself locked into an unsuitable course of study.

Academic failure or dropping out as a consequence of discouragement is often prompted by poor study conditions. The consequences of inadequate laboratories and libraries are compounded by a system in which most of the teaching staff is made up of persons practicing the various professions who teach only on a part-time basis and to whom students as a consequence have limited access (see The Teaching Profession, this ch.).

The consuming interest evinced by university student groups in partisan political activity has been an important factor in academic failure, in expulsion or jailing of students, and in intermittent closing of the universities. In addition, the necessity of simultaneously studying and holding a job imposes a sometimes impossible burden on serious students. The burden becomes so severe when the student comes from another part of the country, and must usually provide himself with food and lodging, that some educational authorities have urged the establishment of dormitories and additional dining facilities as important means of raising the student retention rate.

Students and University Reform

The autonomy of universities and the academic freedom of action enjoyed by these institutions are sources of national pride. The safeguarding of these prerogatives against government interference has been considered by students and faculty alike to be a personal obligation of the highest importance. During the politically turbulent late 1960s, however, expression of the prerogatives of autonomy increasingly took the form of political demonstration.

In the last days of June and the first days of July in 1971, university delegates played active roles in the first plenary session of the Popular Assembly (Asemblea Popular). This remarkable paralegislative body was convoked by the then-dominant central labor organization and was likened to the Paris Commune of 1871 and the first Soviet meetings of 1905 and 1917. Delegates elected to its presidium gave clenched-fist salutes at their swearing-in ceremony.

Among the important acts of the nonelective Popular Assembly was the determination taken to transform the universities into a streamlined structure consisting of a single technological or labor university for the entire country with its center at the Catavi-Siglo XX mining complex at Oruro. It was to be based on replacement of the traditional liberal arts program with technological training and would bring about a gradual closing of the gap between manual and intellectual labor. Although the proposal meant abandonment of the concept of university autonomy, the student delegates voiced no strong objection to it.

In August 1971 a revolt against the government of President Juan José Torres González erupted in Santa Cruz and spread quickly to La Paz (see ch. 10). Students, supporting the government, seized the main building of the Higher University of San Andrés, but aircraft of the insurgent forces strafed the building in an attack during which ten students died and twenty-five or more were wounded.

The revolt toppled the incumbent government, but students in San Andrés were among the last to surrender. Under the new administration of President Banzer, some 300 students were promptly arrested, and a substantial number of students and professors went into exile. Banzer closed all eight of the country's universities, announced that henceforth students would not be permitted to engage in national or international politics, and appointed the National Commission on University Reform to prepare a new basic set of rules governing the university system.

The universities were still closed in June of 1972, when the new Fundamental Law of the Bolivian University was promulgated by decree as the legal instrument governing the structure and operations of the universities. The 239-article document was greeted with expressions of disapproval by spokesmen of students and professors, but it incorporated several important reforms that had previously been recommended by educational authorities.

Article 9 of the new law specifically reaffirmed the principle of university autonomy with respect to purely administrative and academic matters but limited it to these areas of concern. It specified, inter alia, that autonomy was not to be interpreted to include immunity for university properties or the license to violate public order; this point was later repeated by President Banzer in a 1972 Independence Day address in which he also stated that he regarded the new law as essentially preserving the principle of autonomy.

The right of students to organize was confirmed, but the activities in which student groups could engage were specifically limited to those directly concerned with university matters. Students and professors were to share responsibility for governing the internal functioning of the universities, the students playing a minority role. Previously, the equal cogovernment by students and professors had been incorporated in the legal statutes of the several institutions.

The new supreme directive body for the Bolivian University, the National Council on Higher Education, was made directly responsible to the executive power and assigned broader authority over the universities than that assigned to its predecessor body, the National University Council.

The new law called for restructuring the preexisting system of faculties by the creation of departments responsible for the individual academic disciplines taught, which were to be grouped in six schools — architecture and arts, health sciences, social sciences, pure and natural sciences, humanities, and education and technology. Not all universities would be permitted to offer the disciplines taught in all departments; in order to reduce costly duplication of effort, the National Council on Higher Education was to assign teaching responsibilities to the universities on a regional basis, with three universities in a northern, three in a central, and three in a southern zone. In commenting on this innovation, one educational authority pointed out that seven of the universities were currently offering programs in law and in economics and that implementation of the new system would make possible a reduction of this number by three or more.

University teaching and administrative staffs were to be named by the governing bodies of the universities themselves. A transitory article of the new law, however, assigned to the National Council on Higher Education a one-time responsibility for making these appointments.

Under the new program, the universities commenced to reopen late in the year. The catalog of the Bolivian University for the 1973 academic year reported that uniform academic programs, school calendars, teaching methods, and performance evaluation had been designed to facilitate transfer of teachers and students between institutions. This, in turn, would facilitate the structuring of departments within the faculties and the reduction of duplication in teaching programs.

LITERACY AND ADULT EDUCATION

In the late 1960s and early 1970s widely varying estimates concerning the rate of literacy for the population aged fifteen years and over averaged about 40 percent of the total, as compared with an estimated 37 percent reported by the Organization of American States (OAS) for 1960. Data from the 1950 census, as adapted by the OAS, showed the rate to have been about 32 percent. The adapted census figures were based on a definition of literacy as the ability to read and write a simple paragraph in any language; persons whose hard-earned ability had been eroded by lack of use or lack of relevance of the skill to their daily needs were ranked among the illiterate.

Illiteracy is seldom absolute. A series of late 1960s surveys concerning reading ability alone conducted in all four of the geographical regions of the country found that there were pronounced regional differences but that, overall, the proportion "partly able" to read exceeded both those "unable" and those "fully able" to understand written material.

At the root of the literacy problem is the language barrier in a country where half or more of the population consists of Aymara- and Quechua-speaking Indians whose knowledge of Spanish—the language of instruction in the regular school system—is for the most part limited or nonexistent. The 1955 Code of Education prescribes that Aymara and Quechua are to be used as a means of teaching reading and writing in Spanish in those localities where they are predominantly spoken. Quechua- and Aymara-speaking teachers are not always available, however, and in practice the adults who acquire literacy are those who already have some command of Spanish.

The barrier represented by the Spanish language is the factor that contributes most heavily to illiteracy among Quechua- and Aymara-speaking women. The traditional indigenous prejudice against female education extends also to the learning of another language. No overall data are available on the degree of rural literacy by sex, but the limited information available indicates that the rate for men is as much as twice that for women. Conversely, the ability of most urban people to speak Spanish probably contributes as much to the higher urban literacy rate as does the greater availability of schools in urban localities, where the rate of literacy among females is probably not significantly lower than that among males.

According to one late 1960s estimate, the literate 40 percent of the adult population included 85 percent in the cities and towns and 14 percent in the countryside. In rural localities literacy tends to be highest in those areas relatively close to urban centers, where schools are more numerous and where there is more practical need for the acquisition of reading and writing skills.

The origins of recent literacy programs can be traced to the establishment in 1956 of the National Office for Literacy and Adult Education. Since that date numerous plans and campaigns have been inaugurated, but accomplishments have fallen far short of the overly ambitious announced goals. According to an estimate reported by the Inter-American Development Bank, an average of some 12,000 adults became literate annually during the 1960s, less than 1 percent per year of the illiterate population. During the decade there was no clear evidence that the annual rate had increased.

During the late 1960s and early 1970s the public program for adult literacy training was provided in small centers scattered about the countryside, which were presided over by regularly assigned teachers. The announced focus of the program was on a few key economic development areas and on young adults who were already employed in jobs contributing to development of the economic process.

The work of the regular literacy teachers was supplemented by that of specially trained military conscripts as part of the military civic action program, by teachers in classes sponsored by a few peasant syndicates, and occasionally by volunteers from the universities. In at least one instance, however, a group of universitarians was found to have volunteered in order to distribute Marxist propaganda rather than the literacy-training materials that had been furnished them by the Ministry of Education and Culture.

The 1955 Code of Education prescribed that, in addition to reading and writing, the national adult literacy program was to include instruction in fundamental education and in practical skills. During the late 1960s and early 1970s, a substantial proportion of the adults receiving scholastic training was enrolled in the regular primary and secondary institutions and in subuniversity practical courses offered in several of the universities.

In addition, several universities maintained units called popular universities. The functions of these entities had little to do with the higher education program; in the 1955 Code of Education they were assigned the role of providing for workers "cultural, politico-social and labor-union training." An innovation of the MNR political party, the popular university was devised as a symbol of the revolutionary concern for mass education.

Outside the regular school system, the Center for Technical and Craft Training was established in La Paz in 1966 under the auspices of various entities including the Ministry of Labor and Trade Union Affairs, the National Chamber of Commerce, and the United States assistance program. Also outside the regular school system, beginning in the early 1960s a number of schools were established in the country-side to teach scholastic and practical courses at the secondary level to young peasant adults in localities where no regular schools were available (see The School System, this ch.).

In the early 1970s an accelerated adult program was reported available for the completion in three years of the equivalent of the regular six-year course of study. At the secondary level, centers for intermediate adult education (*centros de educación media de adultos*) were reported in operation in early 1973 in La Paz, Cochabamba, Santa Cruz, and Sucre for persons twenty-one years of age and older.

Not all of these centers had yet established complete courses of study, which were to cover the equivalent of six regular years (seventh through twelfth grades) in a three-year period. The program led to a certificate of *bachiller por madurez* (literally, bachelor by maturity), qualifying the holder for university matriculation.

The increasing use of inexpensive transistor radios has brought about a corresponding increase in the use of radio broadcasts for educational purposes. Some of the sets, as well as educational materials for use in connection with educational radio programs, have been contributed by public and private welfare-oriented organizations. In the early 1970s educational broadcasts were being transmitted from La Paz, Cochabamba, Sucre, Oruro, and Potosí.

A program conducted by the Maryknoll order of the Roman Catholic Church outside La Paz covers a range of sixty miles from the transmitter and thus can theoretically be received by half of the country's Aymara population. No information is available concerning the number of regular listeners, but during the late 1960s a reported average of between 2,500 and 3,000 people participated in study groups formally organized to hear the broadcasts, and about one-fourth of these received certificates of satisfactory course completion.

The study groups, organized in communities, were led by unpaid volunteers who had received a short course of training conducted by the Maryknoll fathers in La Paz, and students paid a small amount per month in order to participate. The core element in the curriculum was the use of Aymara as a means of teaching literacy in Spanish, but the inclusion of basic instruction in arithmetic, geography, hygiene, farming, and religion made it possible, in theory, for the persevering student in eight months of study to achieve the equivalent of three years of regular primary education. A similar Maryknoll program, using the

Quechua language, was broadcast from Cochabamba.

THE TEACHING PROFESSION

There is no quantitative teacher shortage at any level of instruction. Statistics on numbers of teachers are sometimes conflicting—in part, perhaps, because urban personnel frequently occupy two or more teaching positions—but the student-teacher ratios of about twenty-seven to one and eighteen to one at the primary and secondary levels, respectively, in 1971 compared favorably with those in other Latin American countries.

The necessity of holding multiple sessions in urban institutions resulted from a shortage not of teachers but of classroom space and, as a consequence of this shortage, many teach only a few hours daily. It has frequently been suggested that an accelerated building program would make it possible to use staff services more fully, thereby leaving funds available for other badly needed educational purposes.

Qualitatively, a serious shortage does exist. According to undated material published by the Ministry of Planning and Coordination in 1970, only 36.5 percent (30.8 percent rural and 41.6 percent urban) of the primary and 44.5 percent of the secondary personnel were qualified. Data from other sources show both higher and lower proportions, but all figures indicate a moderately rising proportion of qualified personnel during the 1960s and early 1970s.

Most of the qualified teachers are graduates of urban or rural normal schools. Other teachers hold temporary, or interim (*interino*), appointments. After ten years of service, interim personnel may become assimilated (*asimilado*) by successfully passing a special examination and thus attain the rank of qualified teacher.

There are relatively few assimilated teachers—in 1967 fewer than 500 of the nearly 8,000 rural primary teaching staff were assimilated, and the proportion in urban schools was probably much lower. In theory, entering teachers who are not qualified by virtue of graduation from a normal school must at least have completed the general secondary school cycle. In practice, however, many of the teachers in rural localities have completed only a few primary school years, and in the few schools scattered along the frontiers the instructional personnel are themselves often little more than literate.

Teachers in the public system must by law be between the ages of eighteen and sixty years, although the requirement of retirement at sixty is not regularly enforced. Despite the fact that many normal school graduates leave the teaching profession after a few years, the average teacher is a mature person. During 1965 more than 40 percent of the personnel in urban primary and secondary schools were between the ages of thirty and thirty-nine, as compared with 6 percent under the age of twenty-five. Complete data are not available concerning the proportion of teachers by sex, although in 1967 some 43 percent of the rural personnel were reported to be women. The proportion of women is believed to be far higher in urban primary and secondary schools.

Before the Revolution of 1952 teacher employment, dismissal, and promotion often depended on political affiliation. An unprecedented number of teachers were appointed and promoted during the years immediately after the war, and legislation enacted in 1957 on seniority limited dismissal and demotion to instances of gross incompetence or immorality and established rules governing employment, promotion, transfer, and retirement. The resulting degree of job security has been such that it has caused some critics to complain that teachers have been encouraged to neglect self-improvement through the several available inservice training courses. There are no programs in the private school system for upgrading qualifications, for social benefits, or for employment security. Salaries tend to be higher than in the public system, however, and private teaching appointments are in relatively high demand.

The normal schools have little trouble in filling enrollment quotas. A variety of room-and-board scholarships are available, and—in addition to the good social standing and the job security offered by the professions—the generally low demand for labor in Bolivia encourages many young people to enroll. Cochabamba, chronically the department with the highest rate of unemployment, is the highest in the rate of normal school matriculation. Moreover, the continued hiring during the 1960s of teachers who were not graduates of normal schools is believed to have resulted from a compelling desire to create jobs rather than from a need for the services.

The several attractions of the teaching profession do not include good pay. During the late 1960s the average amount received in all parts of the country came to less than the equivalent of US$70 per month; the rural average was closer to US$40—well below the average of miners and factory workers. Fringe benefits include such features as long vacations and short working hours, and some rural personnel receive housing and the right to farm small plots of land attached to the school. Many of the teachers, however, hold outside jobs and are sometimes absent from their classes.

The attitude of members of the teaching corps toward their profession differs less between teachers in urban and in rural schools than between teachers who come from urban and from rural backgrounds. There are several reasons for this pattern of differentiation. Although all or almost all of the personnel in the urban system are urban bred, a large proportion of the rural personnel also come from urban homes. Teachers in urban schools are better educated and, for the most part, are drawn from a higher socioeconomic class than their rural school counterparts, but their relative status in the local community is lower.

The rural teacher—whether of rural or urban origin—enjoys a high social status in the community to which he is assigned and lives as well as, or better than, other members of the community. The urban-bred teachers who make up the entire urban teaching corps, on the other hand, frequently find it necessary to live in poor housing in undesirable localities and to mix with social classes lower than those to which they have been accustomed.

Within the rural teaching corps, the country bred are likely to see teaching both as a lifetime career and as a means of upward social movement. The city bred are more likely to regard teaching as a transitional occupation. They often foresee a lack of opportunity in the urban labor market and secure scholarships in rural normal schools in the hope of ultimately securing a supervisory assignment in the rural system, an appointment to a normal school staff, a position with one of the peasant syndicates, or entry into the political arena. Others expect to remain in the countryside a few years and then to return to the city and establish themselves in other urban occupations.

The Aymara and Quechua young people who enter normal school directly from the farm are considerably changed by their years at normal school. Spanish has been spoken, the curriculum has been urban inspired, and the values of urban schoolmates have been at least partially assimilated.

As a consequence of this process of change, the peasant normal school graduate accepting his first teaching assignment is no longer regarded as fully a part of the rural community. His social status is superior to that of the temporary or assimilated teacher, but this status has been achieved at the cost of becoming to some extent an outsider who is neither of the country nor of the town. It is significant, however, that these teachers think of themselves as normal school graduates (*normalistas*) rather than as qualified teachers.

Although they make up a minority of the rural teaching corps, the normal school graduates are the leaders. They represent an elite of the only permanent representatives of the central government in the countryside and, as such, play a significant role in the integration of the countryside into the national life. Their collateral work in community development activities is often opposed by local peasant syndicates, which tend to regard them as competitors.

University professors are appointed by the rectors. In 1968 fewer than 100 of the nearly 2,000 people engaged in university teaching were women. The teaching staff consists for the most part of professional men who devote a few hours daily or weekly to teaching. Inadequate salaries and chronic irregularities in the academic schedule have contributed to the prevalence of part-time university teaching, which is customary in most of the Latin American institutions of higher learning. The administration of President Banzer announced its intention of establishing a program that would encourage more university teachers and researchers to work on a full-time basis and its belief that the provision of the 1972 university reform legislation for concentrating particular fields of study in particular universities would increase the opportunities for full-time employment.

CHAPTER 7

LIVING CONDITIONS

Bolivians live under physical conditions that range from those experienced in the world's highest mining camps to those in the jungles of the Amazon Basin. Culturally, their life-styles are reflected both by the patios of the aristocratic old city of Sucre and by the mud hutments of the Altiplano. By income, the population formerly included both the tin barons, who enjoyed the most conspicuous wealth in South America, and a rural majority that had the continent's lowest per capita income.

The social and economic change precipitated by the Revolution of 1952 has been uneven in its impact, but it has tended to alter living conditions in the countryside and to accelerate migration to the cities, where the transplanted countrypeople live under profoundly different conditions.

In the early 1970s the food and housing of the majority, urban as well as rural, had improved somewhat since 1952 but remained well below the average for Latin America. The *campesinos* (peasants) were beginning to adopt modern dress but continued to show a fondness for colorful traditional costumes.

Where available, motion pictures were the most popular of the relatively few recreational outlets. In the countryside, however, the dullness of everyday life was still relieved principally by the feasting and dancing that accompanied the traditional village fiesta. In both country and town, most of the limited income was spent on food. Incomes were somewhat higher than before 1952, however, and the variety of things purchased has been increasing.

Some of the country's worst endemic diseases had been brought under control, but poor nutrition and environmental sanitation as well as a lack of awareness of modern medical practices militated against further improvement in health conditions. A social security program provided extensive coverage, but the level of benefits paid was low, and the rural people had yet to be included in its benefits. Public social programs, such as those concerned with health, welfare, and housing, were carried on by a proliferation of small agencies serving such occupational groups of clients as miners, factory workers, and teachers. Similar services were brought to rural areas by the National Community Development Program.

DIET AND NUTRITION

Estimates of caloric intake per capita during the 1960s varied from less than 1,800 to slightly over 2,000 calories daily. According to one 1968 survey conducted by a government agency, the average was 1,890 calories for the country as a whole and showed slight regional variation. The national average included forty-nine grams of protein per day, of which only fifteen—less than an ounce—were of animal origin. Animal protein consumption in the Altiplano was slightly less than that in the other regions.

The average diet appears to have improved somewhat in recent years. According to one source, between 1958 and 1964 caloric and protein consumption were each up by more than 10 percent. The average caloric intake during the late 1960s, however, appears to have been only about 80 percent of that recommended by the United Nations Food and Agriculture Organization (FAO), and the protein intake was deficient by a narrower margin.

In some of the communities in the Antiplano over half the intake by weight is in the form of potatoes, and most of the remainder is in the form of grains, such as barley and quinoa. Green vegetable consumption is minimal, and the scanty meat consumption consists largely of the flesh of superannuated llamas, domesticated guinea pigs, and fish from Lake Titicaca. In the Yungas and the Valles corn, wheat, and potatoes are the principal staples; and green vegetable, fruit, and meat consumption is somewhat heavier and more varied than in the highlands. In both the Altiplano and the intermediate regions a large proportion of the protein is derived from beans. In the Oriente, however, beef, pork, and some chicken make up an important part of the diet. Meat not infrequently appears at all of the day's meals. Lowland staples consist principally of cassava, rice, plantains, and bananas.

Because of a lack of storage and shipment facilities, only small amounts of fresh fruits, dairy products, and meat reach small town markets. More variety is available in the cities where, in addition, fish from Lake Titicaca or the Pilcomayo River are available as important protein supplements. The average working-class family in La Paz, however, must devote half or more of its expendable income to food purchases (see Patterns of Living and Leisure, this ch.).

In urging the public health authorities to expand their studies in nutrition, a La Paz newspaper in 1971 attributed many of the country's social and economic problems to quantitative and qualitative food deficiency and estimated that two-thirds of the population suffered from some degree of malnutrition. The proportion seems excessive, but malnutrition is known to be widespread, particularly among children. A 1965–68 government survey found that 38 percent of the rural children under the age of fifteen suffered malnutrition of the first grade (10 to 25 percent under normal weight), 17 percent suffered second grade malnutrition (25 to 40 percent underweight), and 4 percent suffered malnutrition of the third grade (40 percent or more under normal weight).

In many parts of the country the foods are badly lacking in some nutrients. Iron, thiamine, and ascorbic acid are present in adequate proportions, but a 1964 study showed the quantity of vitamin A to be about 40 percent under FAO standards, riboflavin to be less than half, and calcium to be not much more than one-fourth of the standards recommended by the FAO. In addition a 1962 survey by the Interdepartmental Nutrition Committee for National Development found that endemic goiter resulting from iodine deficiency was widespread, particularly in the Oriente. Countrywide, it was reported to affect 15.4 percent of the population under the age of fifteen and 10.5 percent in older age brackets. The scattered information available, however, indicated a gradual improvement in the diet during the 1950s and 1960s. The land reform program had given farmers the opportunity to produce more food both for their own consumption and for sales that made possible the purchase of previously unavailable diet supplements. The improvement was limited, but an increase in the height and weight of army conscripts since the early 1950s indicated either higher levels of caloric consumption, a general improvement in the quality of the diet, or both.

The potatoes that make up most of the Altiplano diet are frequently preserved by conversion into *chuño*, a processed form of the vegetable that has been popular since Inca times and has acquired an almost religious significance. Produced by dehydration and a primitive kind of freeze-drying, *chuño* emerges as a hard lump about the size of a walnut. It keeps indefinitely, and some eaters find its distinctive flavor attractive. A similar product, *tunta*, is more costly because it requires a month of careful preparation. Both are popular in cities as well as in the countryside, but by 1970 the price of *chuño* in La Paz had risen to the equivalent of US$0.30 a pound; and the price of a pound of *tunta*, the equivalent of US$1.20, had removed it from the tables of most consumers.

In the cattle country of the lowlands, beef is the major element in the diet to almost the same extent that potatoes are staples in the rural highlands. With the exception of a few regional variations such as these, the menu of rural people and of the lower income urban population is standard in composition.

Breakfast consists of a lightly sweetened cup of strong black coffee or a cup of tea or a herb infusion. The midday meal is made up of a thick soup of tubers, greens, and an occasional piece of meat. There may also be a second dish based on beans, cereal, or potatoes. The evening meal may be leftovers from lunch or may be limited to coffee and bread. Cheese is a frequent diet supplement, but milk and eggs are seldom used.

Traditional Bolivian dishes are relatively few in number. *Ocapa* is made from dried shrimp that has been soaked overnight and mixed with nuts, tomatoes, garlic, and yellow peppers. Oil is added to the mixture, which is served over potatoes and lettuce leaves. Ceviche, common everywhere in South America, is made of pieces of fish that are marinated in lemon or lime juice. The generally tasteless diet of the rural Altiplano is often enlivened with a fiery sauce of peppers, tomato, and the herb *quilquiña*.

Picana, a traditional Christmas Eve dish, is made from beef, turnips, carrots, and onions boiled in watered red wine and served with potatoes. *Salsa jallpahuiaca*—a specialty of the Oriente—is made from tomatoes, red or yellow peppers, onions, and herbs and salted to taste.

The mild narcosis produced by chewing leaves of the coca plant is so much a part of the tradition of the Altiplano that Inca death masks frequently show a swelling in the cheek, representing the wad of coca being chewed. The tea-like plant that produces the leaves was once the economic mainstay of the Yungas and remains a major cash crop in that region. Chewing of the leaves—together with lime ash, which helps to release the active ingredient in the leaf—tends to reduce both sensitivity to cold and hunger pangs for brief periods and to increase ability to perform hard manual labor.

The longtime effect of the chewing of coca—the raw material for the production of cocaine—may be habit forming and has an adverse effect on productivity. The government has discouraged its use, the Yungas terraces where it grows best have increasingly been put to tea and coffee plantings, and the scattered data available suggest that the traditional chewing of coca leaves may be on the decline (see Patterns of Living and Leisure, this ch.).

DRESS

There are many differences in customs of dress characteristic of the Bolivian population. Cutting across these multiple differentiations, however, is a universal fondness for possession of some good raiment. This fondness can be seen in the startlingly colorful costumes that *campesinos* wear for important occasions. Increasingly, conventional Western garments are used for everyday wear, but vividly colored ponchos and many-colored petticoats are still to be seen. In the cities all but the very poor will take pains to dress well when they go out into the streets, where much of the social life takes place, and a late 1960s survey of consumption patterns in La Paz found that the families of the poorest wage earners devoted the same proportion of their limited income to clothing as did other families with five times as much money to spend.

Concern over raiment reaches a peak in the countryside in the number and kinds of hats worn by women. Sometimes they are shapeless and greasy, but the number of hats in a wife's wardrobe has important bearing on her husband's status. Region and ethnic origin are factors in the determination of headgear. Around La Paz, the women wear bowlers; southeastward into Quechua country white tophats are encountered, their elegant contours made more distinctive by distinguishing loops of ribbon that show not only the community of origin but also the matrimonial status of the wearer.

The traditional Indian costumes of both Quechua- and Aymara-speaking areas consist of a few basic garments (knee- or ankle-length trousers, long-sleeved shirts and, very often, ponchos for men and skirts, blouses, and shawls for women) made of homespun wool. Regional variations in color and cut of the native costumes are so rich and detailed that they often serve to identify the home village of the wearer. Topping the basic costume is the hat with its distinctive style.

Cholo (acculturated Indian or lower class mestizo) people who live in the provincial towns have taken on the language and some of the cultural characteristics of the urban whites and of the mixed-blood mestizos (see ch. 4). In this ethnic in-between land, difference in dress patterns between males and females is most evident. The *cholo* men tend to adopt the Western patterns of dress of the urban whites, but women exercise more choice in finding for themselves a hybrid kind of dress.

Traditional patterns of dress that to some extent continue to prevail in the Altiplano and the Valles tend to be forgotten in the lower Yungas and in the Oriente. The heavy wool uniforms of every day are discarded in favor of factory-made cottons that blur cultural distinctions in the lowland areas. For men, in particular, the transition in dress is conspicuous. In contrast to the Altiplano, where the somber everyday attire of men seems designed to hide them against the adobe-colored terrain, in the lowlands ponchos and scarves are frequently flamboyant in color. For transplanted urban people, boots and khaki garments are the rule. Among some tribal Indians, the conventional garb is a kind of T-shirt worn by both sexes.

HOUSING

In the late 1960s and early 1970s it was generally agreed that three-fourths or more of the population lacked adequate housing. In particular, a 1970 newspaper article attributed to a Bolivian public housing agency the statement that there was a housing deficit of more than 700,000 units, including substandard housing that should be replaced. Altogether, there were fewer than 1 million units in the country.

According to a 1964 series of estimates, less than 12 percent of the country's houses were in good condition. Another 22 percent were in need of repair, and the remaining 66 percent should be replaced. A distinction was drawn between rural and urban areas. In the former, 80 percent were in need of replacement; in cities and towns, 60 percent of the housing was in poor condition but could be repaired. According to another series of estimates, in the late 1960s there was no absolute shortage of housing in the countryside, but 60,000 or more additional urban housing units were needed.

The design of the traditional *campesino* house has remained essentially unmodified since colonial days. Typically, it is a rectangular adobe box no more than about ten by twelve feet in dimensions, with walls five to six feet high and a steeply gabled roof of thatch. Simple to an extreme, it is usually well constructed and makes effective use of the limited variety of raw materials available.

There are some regional variations in layout and construction materials, but the pattern is a generally consistent one in which the dwelling is designed not only as a shelter for its occupants but also as a workshop and storage facility. The house—or group of houses—is constructed in a compound that may or may not be fenced or walled, depending on local custom and resources. In the compound are smaller service structures, such as storehouses and kitchens, although cooking is more frequently done inside the house. Dried manure for fuel is stacked in corners, and animals often use the area as a nighttime corral.

Traditional housing in the tropical lowlands is different in detail from that of the highlands because of the variations in raw material available and because the owners are often seminomadic people who practice the slash-and-burn system of agriculture, in which the families move to other lands after the soils under exploitation have become exhausted. The mobility of the lowland farmers is often reflected in the relatively impermanent look of their dwellings.

No statistics are available with regard to construction materials put to use, but by a wide margin common earth is the most usual building material. On the Altiplano, in particular, the brown mud adobe houses appear to the viewer to be in imminent danger of subsiding into the brown earth that produced them.

Floors are of unprocessed or pounded earth. Walls are customarily of adobe brick made with straw temper. In some of the newer dwellings the bricks have given way to forty-pound adobe blocks with mud used as mortar. Sometimes, in highland dwellings, mud for the walls is poured into temporary wood frames and pounded into place with heavy wood mallets. In the lowlands a common form of construction that involves the use of earth is called *bahareque*, a kind of wattle and daub in which sticks, tied laterally to upright poles, are smeared thickly with straw-tempered mud. In the lower part of the Yungas and in the Oriente, walls are frequently constructed of open bamboo or bamboo framework.

In all rural areas thatch of some kind predominates as roofing material. The roofs are steeply gabled because, even in the drier parts of the country, rain comes in deluges. Materials used for thatch include reeds from Lake Titicaca, scrub from the Altiplano, and palm fronds from the lowlands.

Rural housing during the period that ended with the 1952 Revolution was substandard by any measure, particularly on the haciendas. Since 1952 so many of the manor houses have fallen into disrepair that they tend to give the countryside a dilapidated look, but the housing of *campesinos* has improved somewhat as labor and materials that once went to the hacienda have been diverted to *campesino* homes. Particularly in areas near cities, tile or metal sheets have sometimes replaced the thatch for roofing, and a few concrete floors have been installed. Exteriors of walls are sometimes plastered with mud and whitewashed or painted in pastel colors, and in villages a few two-story houses have appeared. Of particular significance is the fact that increasing numbers of dwellings have windows, some with panes. In the traditional home the only aperture was the door, kept low in order to conserve heat in the interior; in newer homes windows serve as a kind of badge of improved status.

Traditionally, the kitchen was a small clay stove that burned llama dung or scrub. Cooking and eating utensils were of wood or clay. The bed was a raised area made of adobe upon which sheep and llama hides and excess clothing were placed. In the lowlands, hammocks slung from corner poles were common. Furniture of any kind was virtually nonexistent.

The years since 1953 have seen little improvement in the furnishings of homes in remote localities, but in more accessible rural places the progress has been considerable. In a late 1960s survey of several rural communities near Lake Titicaca, it was found that half the families interviewed slept on metal or wooden beds. Although in the early 1970s not more than 5 percent of the rural population had access to electricity, the traditional *mecheros* (lamps made by inserting a wick into a can or bowl of kerosine) were beginning to give way to proper kerosine lamps. Increasing numbers of households had some purchased tableware and kitchen equipment. One 1967 survey found that only 7 percent of the families interviewed owned tumblers, but 83 percent had empty tin cans, which served the same purpose very adequately.

Urban housing ranges from the adobe huts of recent migrants from the countryside to the elegant houses of the wealthy. Migrants have flocked principally to La Paz, where in the early 1970s they made up as much as half of the population. They lived for the most part in crowded neighborhoods, perched on cliffs that descend steeply from the El Alto airport to the canyon occupied by the city. Known locally as *barrios altos* (high neighborhoods) or *barrios marginales* (marginal neighborhoods), the houses are closely packed on terrain so steep that they are sometimes washed from their foundations by heavy rains. They differ from the adobe houses of the countryside principally in the frequency with which corrugated roofing is used.

Farther down the canyon more prosperous residences are clustered in the Obrajes district, where older homes are found, and in the Calacoto district, where most of the foreign colony lives in California-style stucco homes with tiled roofs. With the precipitous growth of the city since the 1950s numerous modern apartment buildings have appeared.

The capital cities of the departments house most of the remainder of the urban population (see ch. 3). Sucre, in particular, is a city virtually without growth. A place of the traditional past, its white-walled street exterior is pierced only by grilled doorways that give onto galleries and flagstoned patios. Potosí is a traditional city with up-and-down streets and old plaster and stone construction. In contrast, Cochabamba is a fast-growing urban center of middle-class prosperity, in which concrete houses of one or two stories are geometrically arranged and neat front gardens replace the traditional interior patios.

The country's principal public housing entity is the National Housing Council (Consejo Nacional de Viviendo—CONAVI), founded in 1964 to meet the serious and increasing housing deficit. An autonomous agency under the general supervision of the Ministry of Urban Affairs and Housing, it has delegated a large part of its actual building responsibilities to committees formed for the benefit of families of workers in particular sectors of employment. Initially the bulk of the work was performed by committees representing workers in the mining and petroleum industries; they were established soon after the creation of CONAVI. In addition, early in 1973 the government announced formation of units for the teaching profession and for workers in the factory, construction, and printing-industry sectors. There is also a program for construction of housing for families of armed forces personnel.

The CONAVI and delegated projects are operative principally in the large urban centers where the greatest actual shortage occurs, although in 1969 the government established the legal basis for creation of a commission to study the problems of rural housing. Plans under study at the time involved encouraging development of voluntary brigades of *campesinos* to participate on a part-time basis in housing and sanitation projects. In 1973 the establishment of *campesino* housing cooperatives remained under consideration, but the greater urgency of the urban housing shortage relegated rural plans to a lower priority.

CONAVI is supported financially by the National Housing Fund, an entity created to finance low-income housing, defined legally as being of *interés social* (social interest). The fund is supported by employer contributions based on the wage bill of workers covered in the social security program and by a sales tax on the revenue derived from factory manufacture, construction, and the printing industry. During the 1960s it also benefited from US$9.5 million in two credits extended by the Inter-American Development Bank (IDB). The funds were used largely in government-sponsored self-help programs in which most of the work was provided by the beneficiaries. In late 1972 a third IDB credit was reported under negotiation.

The National Savings and Loan Housing Fund is a public institution founded in 1963 to encourage development of savings and loan institutions. By 1971 some eight of these units with 8,000 members had come into being. Most of the building in this sector was designed for middle and higher income groups.

During the early 1970s there was a mounting volume of criticism over both the lack of coordination between the public and private building sectors and the lack of a comprehensive, central funding organization. In this connection, early in 1973 the government announced plans for a national housing bank that would be financed through measures such as savings withheld from worker wages and that would serve as a central point for the procurement of credits from abroad.

Overall data on housing construction during recent years on the basis of figures such as the number of housing starts are not available. Scattered data, however, indicate that the accomplishments of the public and private sectors have been moderate. Between 1962 and 1969 it was reported that 9,500 housing units had been constructed — including 6,400 in the public sector—or an average of 1,350 per year. The total included urban construction only and was confined to commercially constructed units. In his Independence Day speech in 1972 President Hugo Banzer Suárez reported that, before the end of the year, 1,562 homes with *interés social* would be constructed by the public sector, the highest yearly amount ever accomplished. He added that with the expected third IDB loan some 7,000 homes would be constructed between 1973 and 1975 and that the government was lending assistance to a private savings and loan project involving construction of 3,700 homes for middle-class families. The rate of construction did appear to be somewhat on the increase, but in 1970 the Ministry of Planning and Coordination had speculated that, with a continuation of the then-current rate of public and private home building, the urban housing shortage would increase by almost 60 percent by 1980.

HEALTH

Administration of Health Programs

According to a manual prepared in the late 1960s for the training of public health doctors, the coparticipation of various social security funds (*cajas*—see Glossary) offering medical care for their individual participants has made the public program of medical care one of competition and duplication rather than one of unity and cooperation (see Welfare, this ch.). Generally confirming this judgment, a Ministry of Planning and Coordination publication reported that in 1969 some six of the then-existing thirteen cabinet ministries and fourteen other public institutions had a hand in public health administration. In addition, a small urban elite that probably numbered under 100,000 chose to pay for the good service available in a few private clinics and offered by a few carriage-trade doctors in private practice.

The public health training manual noted that, with responsibility for the care of 78 percent of the country's population, the public health

173

ministry had 1966 appropriations sufficient for a per capita expenditure of $b0.59 (for value of the Bolivian peso—see Glossary) monthly (equivalent to US$0.04) as compared with $b18.3 (equivalent to US $1.50) per capita available for persons covered under the individual social security programs.

In general, in the early 1970s the medical care program was an urban one. Most of the rural care available was confined to immunization programs and the occasional first-aid and sanitation practices instruction available from mobile health teams. The public health training manual reported that, by political department, availability of service ranged downward from 86.6 percent of the population in Chuquisaca to 19.5 percent in Pando.

Health Hazards and Preventive Medicine

Only a fraction of the country's deaths are reported, and a substantial portion of those reported are not defined by cause. Acute diseases of the respiratory tract are, however, recognized as the principal causes of death. According to one official report, in 1967 respiratory ailments were followed in order of incidence as causes of mortality by diseases of early infancy; senility and poorly defined causes; diseases of the digestive and intestinal tract; tuberculosis in all forms; rheumatic fever; accidents and violence; arteriosclerosis; and cancer.

There was some regional variation in the causes of death. In all of the country's nine departments acute respiratory ailments ranked either first or second in incidence. In La Paz, Chuquisaca, and Oruro accidents and violence constituted the other principal cause. Digestive and intestinal tract ailments were most important in Sucre, Tarija, Cochabamba, and Pando. Intestinal parasites were listed in El Beni and bacterial infections in Santa Cruz.

It has been officially estimated that diseases causing 10 percent of mortality (such as yellow fever, smallpox, rabies, and typhus) can be completely eradicated and that those causing 80 percent (such as tuberculosis, diphtheria, tetanus, and polio) can be substantially reduced in incidence. The campaign against these ailments would involve combating traditional health attitudes, improving nutritional and sanitation levels, and better utilizing the already available resources for health improvement. In particular, unsanitary and crowded housing combine with poor ventilation to result in a dangerously ready interchange of communicable diseases, particularly during sleeping hours.

Mortality is by a wide margin highest among the very young. One-fourth or more of all infants die during the first year of life, and almost half of all deaths reported in 1968 involved children under the age of five years. The number of deaths under the age of five was almost ten times that between the ages of five and fourteen.

In the more remote parts of the countryside, delivery is presided over by an unschooled midwife or family member who severs the umbilical

174

cord with a broken piece of pottery—in the belief that use of a metallic instrument may cause the child to develop a belligerent character. No attempt is made at sterilization, and the baby is made particularly susceptible to respiratory ailments by the frequent practice of wrapping it in swaddling clothes in the belief that the child will thus be endowed with a strong, straight body. Parts of the anatomy are released from the swaddling for increasing lengths of time, but the child may be two years of age or older before swaddling is altogether discontinued. Because breast feeding is believed to be conducive to strong muscles and virility, boys are frequently not weaned until they are old enough to attend school.

An immediate goal proposed by public health authorities during the late 1960s involved medical or paramedical care for at least half of the rural deliveries. It would include three or four consultations during pregnancy, and most deliveries would be handled at a health post by a trained midwife or a nursing auxiliary; difficult deliveries would be handled by a doctor at the nearest rural hospital. These modest objectives appeared still far from attainment. A 1968 survey of eighteen rural communities in Cochabamba (a department with better than average availability of medical care) found that 8 percent of all births were attended by doctors and 21 percent by midwives who probably had little if any training. Some 15 percent were attended by traditional practitioners (*curanderos*), and the remaining 56 percent were attended by family members or neighbors. Some 92 percent of the deliveries were in the home.

Mining is the employment sector with the most serious health hazards. Estimates of the proportion of miners afflicted with silicosis range as high as 40 percent. A smaller proportion contract silicotuberculosis, and the average age for retirement with disability pension was reported to be forty-one years during the late 1960s. In addition, intense heat in the mine shafts followed by exposure to the outside chill of the high altitudes made mineworkers particularly susceptible to respiratory diseases.

There has been an increase in the reported countrywide incidence of tuberculosis since the end of the Chaco War (1932–35), a trend which may at least in part be the result of a greater frequency of migration of *campesinos* to the tropical lowlands, where they are believed to be more susceptible to the disease. The apparently greater incidence may, however, be a reflection only of improved medical reporting. In any case, the combination of crowded and unsanitary housing and low nutrition levels makes much of the population highly susceptible to the several forms of tuberculosis that the World Health Organization in its 1962 annual report declared to be Bolivia's principal health problem. The government estimated that there were 55,000 active cases in the country in 1961, and new cases reported rose from 1,471 in 1964 to 2,947 in 1969.

175

The two mosquito-borne scourges of the lowlands, malaria and jungle yellow fever, seem to have been brought under a degree of control by recent eradication campaigns. In 1970 the examination of 167,265 slides resulted in detection of only 6,862 positive malaria cases. The number of reported cases of yellow fever declined from thirty in 1960 to two in 1970, and eradication of the aëdes egypti mosquito, which acts as the vector, had been declared complete in all areas of the country believed initially to have been infested.

Until recent years Bolivia had the highest reported incidence of smallpox in the hemisphere. A mass vaccination campaign, begun in 1958, continued intermittently, and no cases were reported during the years 1966 through 1970. As a precautionary measure, however, more than 300,000 vaccinations were administered during 1970.

Leprosy is increasing in reported incidence, particularly in the Oriente. In mid-1969 there were 1,560 active cases, all under surveillance, in the recovery center at Los Negros in Santa Cruz Department and in the Monteagudo program in Chuquisaca Department. The Monteagudo program has received assistance from the German Mission for Aid to Leprosy Patients.

Plague has been a constant concern of health authorities. Between 1960 and 1970 there were 460 cases reported, the fourth largest number in the Americas, and some were reported every year except 1962. All forty-one cases in 1970 occurred in La Paz Department, where there had been a violent outbreak in 1969.

In 1956 yaws was discovered in the provinces of Nor Yungas and Sur Yungas in La Paz Department, and studies revealed that 5,000 persons in a population of approximately 50,000 had contracted the disease. An eradication campaign reduced the incidence by 50 percent in a little more than a year, however, and no new cases were reported in the late 1960s and 1970.

Medical Personnel

The 1,702 physicians reported in practice in 1968 by the Pan American Health Organization represented 3.6 per 10,000 of the population. Although the proportion was little more than half the average reported for South America, the number reported in practice may have been too high. At about the same time, an Organization of American States (OAS) publication estimated that there were probably not more than 1,200.

Physicians and surgeons are trained in seven-year courses at the universities in La Paz, Cochabamba, and Sucre (see ch. 6). Medicine is a profession commanding the highest order of prestige, and the medical schools never suffer from a shortage of applicants. The average of 140 graduated annually during the late 1960s, however, exceeded the country's effective demand for doctors.

The problems of the Bolivian doctor are legion. As an intern he may be required by law to serve for two years in a rural hospital. If called into rural service he finds himself in a kind of halfway state between modern and traditional medical practitioner; sometimes his appointments with patients are made by peasant syndicate secretaries who make the determination as to whether the illness involved can best be served by a twentieth-century doctor or by a witch doctor. The story is told of one physician in rural practice who was unable to attract patients until he gained the trust of the community by ministering effectively to a sick donkey.

Returned to the city, the doctor is unable to find work. Bolivia has so chronic an oversupply in relation to the effective demand that the training manual for public health physicians described young doctors as "the army of the professional unemployed." In the late 1960s the number of unemployed registered physicians was estimated at 18 percent of the total, and there was a heavy flow of emigration in the medical profession (see ch. 6). According to one report, there were some fifty Bolivian doctors in the city of Chicago alone.

In 1969 the number of dentists in practice was listed at 627, or about 1.3 per 100,000 of the population. The limited data available indicate that a majority of the dentists, unlike the physicians, engaged in private practice. Dental work consists primarily of extractions, and in rural localities visiting doctors and paramedical personnel are frequently pressed into service for tooth pulling.

In 1969 there were reported to be 612 graduate nurses and 1,549 nursing auxiliaries in the country. These numbers represented 1.3 and 3.2 respectively per 100,000 of the population. Graduate, but not auxiliary, personnel tend to be clustered in private practice.

Graduate nurses receive a thorough professional education. Until 1962 some three years of university level training was required; during that year the course was extended to four years, and various fields of specialization were added. Recognition of the nurse as a trained professional has yet to be fully accepted in Bolivia, however. Even trained medical personnel tend to think of anyone capable of administering first aid or an injection as being a nurse. Salaries are low, and during the late 1960s it was estimated by the public health ministry that 50 percent of the country's graduate nurses had gone abroad.

Medical Facilities

In 1968 the country's 318 hospitals maintained a total of 10,734 beds. Hospitals with fewer than fifty beds constituted 38.7 percent of the total, those with fifty to ninety-nine constituted 15.3 percent, and those with 100 to 499 constituted 40.6 percent. The 532-bed Miraflores General Hospital in La Paz was the only unit with more than 500 beds. Nearly 90 percent were general hospitals; most of the remainder were equally divided between hospitals for mental illnesses and tuberculosis sanitariums.

177

Hospital units were about equally divided between those supported by the public health program and those supported by the several social security entities. Among the few privately operated institutions was the Clinica Americana operated in La Paz by the Methodist church. Early in 1973 the government announced that it had begun negotiations with the Inter-American Development Bank (IDB) for a credit with which to finance the new 500-bed public health Hospital de Clinicas in La Paz, construction to begin in 1974.

The number of beds in relation to the size of the population as a whole, reported at one per 522 of the population in 1968, was among the lowest in Latin America. The occupancy rate of less than 60 percent of the beds, however, was also among the lowest. Nearly all the units were located in urban places, but the incomplete data available indicate that the bed occupancy rate was higher in the big urban institutions than in the small rural hospitals. In the relatively few places where rural hospitals were available, in the early 1970s people had not yet become fully aware of their utility: the cornerstone of the first rural unit had not been laid until 1960.

In the mid-1960s the military hospital in Riberalta was the largest in El Beni Department, and the ten-bed military unit in Cobija provided the only service in Pando Department. For some of the more remote places where no regular hospitalization facilities exist, the government maintains a small flotilla of hospital vessels. In early 1972 it was announced that two additional vessels would be added to those already in operation in the Oriente region on the Beni and Madre de Díos rivers. In addition, a naval hospital craft was reported to be following a regularly scheduled itinerary of sixteen ports on Lake Titicaca.

Traditional Medical Practices

Minor respiratory ailments, headaches, and toothaches are believed to result from minor causes and are treated largely by herbal remedies. Coca leaves are commonly used as poultices for the relief of pain, and a variety of herbal teas are used in cases of digestive upset. An infusion concocted from specified quantities of four different herbs serves to regulate menstruation. Together with the herbal remedies, many of which have considerable pharmacological value, incantations and magic charms are used in treatment of real and fancied ailments. In the treatment of goiter and lymphatic swellings, for example, a mouse is sometimes applied as a poultice, and llama fetuses are sold as protection against witchcraft.

Severe diseases are seen as the direct result of supernatural causes. Both Quechua and Aymara speakers believe in the possible detachment or disappearance of the soul, a condition that can cause death if the condition is not treated promptly. In particular, the loss of the soul can occur as a consequence of sudden fright (*susto*), a cause to which many infant deaths are attributed.

The treatment of supernaturally caused ills almost invariably involves divination in an attempt to discover the human agent, if there is one. Where there is evidence that a malevolent person has worked black magic on the victim, a common practice is to bathe the victim and to splash the bathwater over the doorstep of the malefactor. Another common practice, used whenever the curer believes the disease to have been supernaturally caused, is to place objects of the patient's clothing in a conspicuous spot on the road in the hope than an unsuspecting stranger will pick them up and thereby contract the disease, freeing the ill person of the curse. In times of epidemic a similar practice is sometimes followed: a black llama is loaded with personal effects of the diseased victims and driven from the village.

There are various kinds of specialists in the traditional diagnosis and treatment of disease. A majority make use of both practical and magical treatment. In most communities there are practicing midwives, and in most there are men who specialize in the setting of bones. The best known of the folk practitioners are the Callahuayas of Muñecas Province in La Paz Department, who travel the length of the country selling herbal remedies, charms, and amulets. The arrival of one of these itinerants is a village event of great importance.

Traditional medical practices are not entirely confined to the countryside. A substantial section of the street market in central La Paz is occupied by vendors of folk remedies and charms. Attitudes of the rural people toward modern medicine reflect a considerable eclecticism. Those for whom medical facilities are readily available will often use modern and traditional cures—and curers—on an alternative basis. In some areas there has been resistance to practices such as vaccination, but the opposition mounted has seldom been strong.

In the Altiplano towns, and occasionally in the cities as well, the pharmacy may represent a hazard as well as a cure. Most drugs are available without prescription, and the druggist may also be a traditional practitioner. In the La Paz press a regularly carried advertisement concerns a product guaranteed to restore male virility. In the towns, sophisticated but little-tested European drugs are available, and the prescribed doses are given in languages certainly meaningless to the druggist as well as to the purchaser who, as often as not, is illiterate. The druggist has often received some training, however, and the products sold are frequently of value. Hazardous as they sometimes are, the village-store products probably save many more lives than they destroy.

Sanitation

In the early 1970s the water and sewerage systems were seriously deficient. Virtually all of the rural and most of the urban populations had direct access to neither, and the OAS had estimated that 15 percent of the country's disease could be attributed to unsafe water. According to official data, in 1969 about 34 percent of the urban population was served by water systems, and about 21 percent had sewerage outlets. In rural areas, service in both was virtually nil.

In Bolivia, as in most Latin American countries, water service is customarily described as service with *agua potable* (potable, or drinkable, water). It is often something quite different; it can better be defined as water of any quality delivered through a system of conduits. Of those households served with *agua potable* it is probable that in the early 1970s about half had interior connections and the remainder were within a short walking distance ("easy access") of a public fountain or tap.

Water, sewerage, and refuse collection are conveniences available only in the larger urban communities. Only a small proportion of the farm population has provided itself with latrines, and few public facilities are available in cities and towns.

The public environmental sanitation program is under the general direction of the National Potable Water and Sewerage Corporation (Corporación Nacional de Agua Potable y Alcantrillado—CORPAGUAS), created in 1967 to determine the general policy of water and sewerage supply on a national scale and to provide systems in localities unable to provide them. The general public policy—reaffirmed by President Banzer early in 1973—is for local governments, where possible, to install these services. A summary of expenditures on water and sewerage during the late 1960s showed that about half the funds came from domestic sources and about half from foreign credits. Details showed that participating agencies had included the CORPAGUAS (water supply for thirty-five small towns), Ministry of Defense (rural water supply), Ministry of Social Service and Health (water for rural schools), and several municipal and departmental water and sewerage entities.

The urban water supply problem is at its most acute in La Paz, a direct consequence of the city's rapid growth. The piping was installed in 1923, and by the early 1970s it had been mended and extended many times. Mains had eroded, cracked, and rusted—and sewer lines laid in the same trenches sometimes resulted in contamination of the water supply.

The best sewerage is provided in Santa Cruz, where a model system was installed in 1970 with IDB assistance. There are no sewerage mains other than those in La Paz and the departmental capitals, and the manual for public health doctors noted that in the late 1960s no more than 4 percent of the rural population had any installations for the disposal of human wastes.

Refuse collection in the larger urban localities is generally satisfactory, although it is in some part accomplished by private contractors. In towns and villages much of the refuse is simply thrown into the street, where it is devoured by dogs and pigs. In general, economic imperatives are such that very little trash and garbage are generated. Empty tins, bottles, and cartons find ready use, and animal excrement is used for fuel or fertilizer.

WELFARE

The Social Security Code of 1956 unifies and expands a voluminous body of law enacted since 1924 in the fields of social insurance and workmen's compensation. It entrusts administration of most funds and programs to an autonomous public agency, the National Social Security Fund (Caja Nacional de Seguridad Social—CNSS). Specifically exempted from the supervision of the national agency are the funds (cajas) administered on behalf of the railroad workers, bank workers, military personnel, and petroleum workers, each of which is administered autonomously. Both the national fund and those of the occupational groups are, however, subject to regulation and audit by the Ministry of Labor and Social Security. Financing of all social security funds is by contributions of the employer, the covered employee, and the government.

As set forth in the 1956 code the social security system operates through two broad undertakings—social insurance and family subsidies. Participants in the various funds are insured against the risks of illness, maternity, occupational disease and injury, old age, and death through the provision of free medical care and through the payments of pensions and indemnities. Family subsidies, intended to aid all covered families to achieve a minimum standard of living, are paid partly by the fund and partly by the employer. They include monthly allotments (in addition to basic wages) to legally married participants, lump-sum payments and gifts of infant clothing to new parents, free distribution of milk to children under one year of age, monthly child support payments, and burial benefits.

The difficulties plaguing the program have been attributed to its extraordinary intricacy. In a 1970 study the Ministry of Planning and Coordination counted eighteen agencies that were in varying degrees concerned with social benefits. It has tried to do many things. The basic code concerns itself not only with social security per se but also with labor and health matters. The document regulates salaries and spells out the rights of organized labor. The CNSS and the several other funds also maintain complete medical programs.

Coverage varies for various categories. In 1970 the CNSS and the fund for petroleum workers covered sickness, maternity, occupational injury, old age, death, and family allowances. The fund for railroad workers covered old age and death and medical care for pensioners. Active workers were covered directly by employers. The fund for chauffeurs covered old age pensions and certain other benefits. Sickness and maternity cases were covered under separate legislation. Career military personnel were covered under a retirement fund; health services were covered by the regular military health program. The Complementary Fund for Public School Teachers (Caja Complementaria del Magisterio Fiscal) provided a supplementary old age pension for teachers in the public school system. Different degrees of protection were applicable in a few other participating entities.

Campesinos, artisans, and domestic servants were in effect excluded from social security coverage under the 1965 code by a provision stating that "independent workers are to be incorporated in the system when the socioeconomic conditions for such an inclusion are appropriate." In 1971 a decree law extended medical provisions to all agricultural workers. At approximately that time, however, the daily press was commenting that the CNSS was bankrupt and, in any event, that the CNSS medical facilities were virtually confined to the larger cities.

A new element was added to the welfare hierarchy in early 1972 by the creation of the autonomous Bolivian Institute for Social Security (Instituto Boliviano para la Seguridad Social) to coordinate and supervise technical aspects of the operations of the existing funds and similar organizations. President Banzer, in announcing the establishment of this new entity directly responsible to the office of the president, stated that it would not replace any of the already existing entities and that no discharge of personnel was contemplated.

According to the OAS, in 1970 about 137,000 workers and 360,000 dependents were under the umbrella of social security coverage. According to a 1973 report by the CNSS, that organization covered more than 500,000 workers and employees. Benefits, however, were small. A 1971 press report stated that monthly retirement pensions averaged only between $b100 and $b150, a figure that made it necessary for people to continue working into old age.

Informal mutual aid and cooperation among kinsmen and neighbors provide an important measure of defense against hardship and adversity, supplementing and, in many cases, replacing formal welfare institutions. The value traditions of both the Spanish-speaking whites and the major Indian groups place great moral stress upon kinship loyalty, and most Bolivians look, as a matter of course, to relatives in time of need. Under conditions of extreme poverty and social stress in the larger cities, many individuals violate the traditional precepts of family duty, but in stable communities orphans, the very old, and the infirm normally find shelter in the households of their relatives. Women who migrate from rural areas to the cities and there give birth to illegitimate children frequently entrust such offspring to the care of kinsmen in their home villages. The wives and children of *campesinos* who migrate to urban work centers or to the mines, often for periods of years, commonly seek shelter in the houses of relatives and in-laws.

Indian communities, both Quechua- and Aymara-speaking, are organized around extensive patterns of mutual aid and cooperation. *Aini*, the traditional practice of agricultural labor sharing, makes assistance available to those whose fields overtax the work abilities of their own households. The erection of a house for a newly married *campesino* couple almost always calls forth dozens of willing neighbors and kinsmen whose cooperation is rewarded with a fiesta.

The peasant syndicates that came into being after the breakup of the hacienda system have represented a bridge between the old and the new and, to some degree, have preserved traditional community attitudes. In addition, the syndicates have provided some socially important services, such as school construction.

Traditionally, most Indian communities have expected of their members a certain number of days of unpaid labor in public works projects. Throughout both the Quechua and the Aymara areas, village schools, roads, and communal irrigation systems have been built and maintained by the spontaneous enterprise and cooperation of *campesinos*. Technical aid personnel and social workers have encountered some success in mobilizing this spirit of common effort in the organization of producers' and marketing cooperatives.

A similar spontaneous cooperation is sometimes encountered in urban lower class neighborhoods. Poor districts of La Paz, for example, have neighborhood associations whose volunteer members organize locally recruited work gangs for the construction of streets and school buildings and petition municipal authorities for assistance in efforts in behalf of the common welfare. Direct interpersonal charity is also common. With the quickening of the pace of country-to-town migration and the rise of urban crowding, however, the incidence of child abandonment and of street begging during the early 1970s had increased to an extent that gave rise to editorial comment in the La Paz press.

The rise in the employment rolls that followed nationalization of the major mining industries—and a concurrent drop in production—has been described as a kind of "low order welfare effort." The description is not necessarily a frivolous one. Various reasons can be advanced for the increase in mining employment, but the economy's inability to generate enough jobs to keep the labor force employed represents a socioeconomic problem of the first importance. In this sense the government's willingness to employ more people than it needs is, consciously or unconsciously, identifiable as a welfare undertaking comparable to that of the Works Progress Administration (WPA) that played an identical part in the United States during the depression-ridden 1930s.

PATTERNS OF LIVING AND LEISURE

Holidays and Business Hours

A 1936 decree listed sixteen holidays, not including Sundays and local holidays, which the departments may declare. The sixteen holidays are: New Year's (January 1); carnival (Monday, Tuesday, and Wednesday at the outset of Lent); Holy Thursday, Good Friday, and Holy Saturday; Labor Day (May 1); Corpus Christi (May 28); Bolivian Independence Days (August 5, 6, and 7); Family Day (October 12); All Saints' and All Souls' days (November 1 and 2, respectively); and Christmas (December 25). Additional days have been declared as legal days of rest for certain workers, such as the miners who are honored on December 21. Ceremonial days involving some suspension or curtailment of work include the Day of the Martyrs of the National Revolution on July 21, the Day of the Indian on August 2, and the Day of the Student on September 21. Abaroa Day on March 23 commemorates the name of a civilian hero in the War of the Pacific. July 16 is the La Paz Municipal Holiday, and there are several departmental holidays.

There are also various local holidays—patron saints' days for the most part—but there are also many annual fairs and other days of local significance. The catalog of national and local holidays and other days of a festive or ceremonial nature is so extensive that no general total can be given. After the devaluation of the currency in late 1972, however, and the issuance of various announcements that people must work harder during an austerity period, the La Paz press blossomed with a series of statements to the effect that the number of holidays had got out of hand and was in need of drastic surgery.

Business hours in La Paz are customarily from 9:00 A.M. to 12:00 noon and from 2:00 P.M. to 6:00 P.M. Saturday is a half day. Government offices are closed on Saturdays. In La Paz there are several twenty-four-hour pharmacies, and others are open around the clock on a rotating schedule.

Financial and commercial establishments are closed from 1:00 P.M. Saturday to Monday morning, although restaurants and stores selling necessities, such as food, fuel, and medicines, remain open. The general suspension of business activity from Saturday afternoon to Monday morning is traditionally a comprehensive one, at least until recently: from noon on Saturday to the opening of business on Monday La Paz was isolated from the outside world by the closing down of international telephone and telegraph connections.

In early 1973 it appeared likely that the customary noontime siesta break in the working day might be curtailed. It was announced that three public agencies were being placed on an experimental schedule of continuous worktime (*horario continuo*), interrupted only for thirty minutes at noon. Initial reactions were mixed, but on balance they appear to have been favorable. In La Paz, at least, many people seemed to find an early end to the working day a welcome alternative to spending most of a two-hour siesta going to and from home on a crowded bus or lunching in a correspondingly crowded, and too expensive, restaurant.

Consumption Patterns

In 1966 a survey was conducted with regard to the spending patterns of *campesino* families living in the northern part of the Altiplano in areas formerly occupied by fifty-one haciendas. Calculated in terms of 1966 prices, it compared their patterns of expenditure with their recollections of those for the period immediately preceding the 1952 Revolution. According to this reconstruction, a pre-1952 annual market-basket expenditure of the equivalent of US$30.65, including US$7.85 in barter, had given way in 1966 to a much more extensive equivalent of US$100.95, including a smaller US$5.05 in barter (see table 2).

A comparison between the pre-1952 and the 1966 expenditure patterns shows an increase in sophistication, as well as an increase in volume of cash acquisitions. For example, the old pattern included substantial barter transactions for hides and wool; the new pattern replaced these items with cash-purchased cloth and clothing. In 1966 soap purchases made an appearance; there had been none previously.

Comparison of the pre-1952 and the 1966 figures shows a decline of 50 percent in the quantity of coca leaves acquired. The decline, however, was offset by an increase of two-thirds in the purchased amount of alcohol and a fourfold increase in the number of cigarettes.

In quantity, sugar and bread purchases doubled, and noodles made an appearance as a purchase item. In 1966—as well as before 1952— meat was absent from the list of purchased items; presumably home-raised llama and guinea pig meat plus some fish provided the animal protein. Far from being meat purchasers, the families involved in the survey tended to sell meat and dairy products in local markets in order to derive a large portion of their cash income.

The consumer goods listed were bartered and purchased in local markets. More costly items were usually bought during the course of infrequent visits to La Paz, where they could be acquired more cheaply. Increasingly, however, during the 1960s the newly established village fairs of this region marketed such goods as kerosine stoves, new and used bicycles and parts, and sewing machines. Readymade clothing, radio batteries, nails, hammers, tools of all kinds, yard goods, and school supplies were also becoming familiar stock items. On the lands of one 200-family hacienda in 1952 there was a single house with a metal roof and one bicycle. By 1966 there were forty metal roofs and eighty bicycles on the former hacienda. The number of sewing machines had increased from seven to 120, and the number of radios from one to 100.

More information is available concerning consumption patterns in the northern Altiplano—probably because of its greater accessibility to La Paz—than in other parts of the country. It seems clear, however, that in many other localities the local markets have not developed to a corresponding degree, and as a consequence people still have little cash income. In a series of surveys conducted during the mid-1960s in parts

Table 2. Household Expenditure of a Bolivian Peasant Family, 1966[1]

Article	Quantity	Value[2]
Bartered		
Condiments	. . . .	0.65
Pots for cooking	5	1.65
Salt	3 panes	0.75
Food items in small quantities	. . . .	2.00
Subtotal		5.05
Purchased		
Alcohol	5 quarts	3.50
Soft drinks	20 bottles	1.75
Beer	10 . . . do .	2.50
Cooking grease	3 pounds	0.60
Cooking oil	3 bottles	1.25
Fruit and vegetables	. . . .	2.50
Noodles	15 pounds	1.50
Bread	75 pieces	3.15
Flour (wheat and corn)	50 pounds	3.40
Rice	35 . . . do .	3.00
Sugar	25 . . . do .	2.10
Coca	5 . . . do .	2.10
Cigarettes	20 packages	2.00
Matches	60 boxes (small)	0.95
Kerosine	26 bottles	1.10
Cloth of all kinds	15 yards	7.00
Dyes	. . . .	0.50
Shoes	2 pairs	12.50
Suits	1	12.50
Skirts	1	5.00
Sweaters	1	5.50
Trousers	1	5.00
Shirts	2	2.00
Hats	2	8.00
Shawls	1	5.00
Soap	10 pieces	1.50
Subtotal		95.90
Total		100.95

[1]Most commonly acquired goods by family of five people in Northern Altiplano.
[2]In U.S. dollar equivalents.

Source: Adapted from U.S. Agency for International Development, in *Land Reform in Bolivia, Ecuador, Peru; A.I.D. Spring Review of Land Reform*, VI (2d ed.), Washington, 1970, 70.

of rural Tarija and Chuquisaca, for example, the volume and variety of commodities purchased varied considerably from place to place, but it did not appear that the fifteen years since the Revolution of 1952 had brought with them significant changes in the pattern of consumption.

In the country as a whole during the five-year period ending in 1970 private consumption expenditures increased by about 40 percent, one of the highest rates in Latin America, but the per capita average remained one of the lowest. The higher bracket incomes were those of urban families, but income levels differed substantially by urban locality. For example, a series of 1966 estimates concerning incomes in four major cities found that both the lowest and the highest wages were paid in La Paz but that the highest and the lowest averages were paid in Cochabamba and Sucre, respectively.

A 1966–67 survey of consumption patterns of wage-earning families in La Paz divided these families by income into the lower third, the middle third, and the higher third. Average incomes were cited as the annual equivalents of US$560, US$1,096, and US$2,194, respectively. Food costs ranged downward from nearly 80 percent of income in the lowest third to 43 percent in the highest. In addition, savings patterns were strikingly different. Both the lower and the middle category spent substantially in excess of income; only the higher wage-earning bracket was able to put aside modest savings.

Recreation

The isolation of the country, combined with the wide dispersal of its predominant rural population and the low level of average income, limits the variety of recreational outlets available. Commenting that athletic contests were few and that the legitimate stage was almost nonexistent, a La Paz newspaper observed that motion pictures were the only important form of organized recreation. The relative poverty of organized entertainment, however, is matched by a wealth of informal interpersonal relationships. From birth to death, Bolivians of all classes are intimately involved with other people. The mechanics of relationship vary by socioeconomic class and ethnic group, but among the upper classes in La Paz as well as among the *campesinos* in the countryside, the Bolivian hierarchy of values ranks friendly contact far above competitive aggressiveness.

Soccer is the national sport. Bolivia supports two professional leagues denominated First A and First B that play regularly in La Paz and, occasionally, in other cities. Former Vice President Juan Lechín Oquendo first came into the public eye as a soccer star. The Agrarian Reform Act of 1953 set aside plots of former hacienda lands as playing fields, and postreform peasant syndicates have organized soccer teams supported by quotas paid by members.

Basketball and volleyball are of sufficient importance to support national federations, and cockfighting is popular in the countryside. Bullfights are held occasionally in La Paz, but the effect of the thin atmosphere on both matador and bull limits the quality of the performances and makes performers of international status reluctant to visit the high-altitude city.

The elevation adds a sense of novelty to participation in elite sports, such as skiing, golf, and tennis. The Chacaltaya ski run, an hour from La Paz, is the world's highest; and 300-yard drives on the two golf courses of La Paz are not beyond the range of the average player.

The most popular of the traditional social games is a uniquely Bolivian form of contest called *sapo* (frog). Played both in town and in countryside, it involves tossing disks or coins at a target surmounted by the image of an open-mouthed frog. The maximum score comes from hitting the mouth, but points are also made by hitting other holes in the target. Various dice games are played, and card games range from bridge, poker, and canasta in La Paz to a game called *rocambór* in the countryside. A predecessor of whist, *rocambór* is played with an ancient Spanish deck of forty-eight cards. Considerable prestige among rural people attaches to skill in card playing.

The harsh life of the Bolivian mining camps is reflected in a terrible kind of game involving competition as to who can be last to release a stick of dynamite with a lighted fuse. Missing limbs or parts of limbs serve to identify winning competitors.

Official paid-attendance statistics for motion picture theaters showed the per person average to have been about ten a year during the mid-1960s in La Paz, somewhat higher in Cochabamba, and not much lower in Oruro and Tarija. Low income and absence of electric current in much of the countryside limits rural motion picture attendance but, in places where theaters are available, they are patronized at rates far above the average for Latin America.

As in other Latin American countries, fiestas play a highly important part in the recreational life of the people. The fiesta may be religious, civic, or commercial in character, and patterns of observance differ regionally. For the most part, however, the observances are traditional ones in which the entire community participates but in which the cost is borne by a leading member of the community.

In some communities near Lake Titicaca, ascent up the ladder of official responsibility is marked traditionally by fiesta sponsorship. All males are eligible for participation, but the cost involved restricts the number of participants. The first step may involve sponsorship of a group of dancers taking part in a major fiesta. Later may come individual sponsorship of one or more small fiestas. The climactic event, the staging of the entertainment for a major fiesta commemorating the day of the local patron saint, can lead to candidacy for the position of local headman. Once selected, the headman is expected many times to bear the cost of food, drink, and music at subsequent fiestas and to provide lodging for visitors who come to stay overnight.

A generally similar pattern is followed in the Valles communities, although fiesta sponsorship is less closely linked with attainment of public office. The popularity of the traditional fiesta varies from locality to locality, and in some instances the cost entailed has aroused direct opposition to it. In general, support is strongest in the more remote and conservative communities where traditional values remain the strongest and alternative forms of recreation are the fewest.

Traditionally, the patron saint occasions are the most important,

188

but the local chapel frequently contains images of other saints for whom there are annual observations calling for their own sponsors and expenditures. Fiestas are also held for weddings, wakes, and memorial services. In some instances the entire community shares in the work and expenditure involved. In others the fiesta may be conducted on a commercial basis and the costs covered by selling liquor to the revelers. Such occasions as carnival, national independence, and Holy Week, however, are celebrated on a nationwide basis by private parties for the well-to-do, street dancing for those of more modest incomes in the major cities, and simpler observations in towns and hamlets. Altogether, there are at least fifty local or widespread fiesta occasions. Some last as long as a week, and often the fiesta scheduled for a single day may spread out over a considerably longer period of time.

Although the significance of Lent is either unknown or unobserved in the countryside, both the pre-Lenten carnival and Holy Week are fiesta occasions of the first order of importance in town as well as in country. In parts of Cochabamba and in Santa Cruz carnival activity continues on into Lent, and in every Altiplano hamlet serpentine lines of carnival dancers follow the local band around the village plaza. The most colorful of the carnival features are the devil dancers of Oruro. The ornate costumes of these performers attract swarms of tourists to the city, and the highly organized performances are the result of preparations that have lasted most of the year. Masked dancers in general are carnival features so popular that the making of masks for carnival has been described as a form of expression second only to politics in importance.

Fiestas have individual characteristics. The Alacitas Festival held in La Paz involves the purchase of good luck symbols; the Feast of the Virgin of Copacabana features fireworks displays; and the Feast of San Juan, celebrated in various places, is an occasion for bonfires and water games.

In general, fiestas are times for magnificent and often costly costumes, dances, and parades and much feasting and drinking of *chicha* (a fermented beverage). Countrypeople derive great satisfaction from these brilliant occasions, which contrast sharply with the drabness of their everyday life. Even the *velario* (funeral vigil) is of recreational importance. Eating and drinking to excess during the *velario* are considered proper and worthy acts of remembrance; the guests are doing what the deceased enjoyed during his lifetime.

The fiesta occasions represent an interesting mixture of the religious, the profane, and the cycle of agricultural events. Tuesday of the carnival is associated with an Inca day of observation, and potato planting in December is associated with a being who manages at once to be an Inca god of thunder and the Apostle Saint John.

In its simplest form, recreation in the countryside takes the form of visiting neighbors, made relatively easy by the small size of most farms and the informality of life in the villages. Despite the general poverty, convention and courtesy demand that visitors be greeted with food and drink. In cities and towns the traditional custom of the promenade survives as an important mechanism in social life. After mass on Sundays, young men and women parade in opposite directions along the Prado—a major La Paz thoroughfare—in a custom centuries old. Band concerts in the plaza provide the setting for similar performances in the provincial towns.

CHAPTER 8

CULTURAL LIFE AND MASS COMMUNICATION

Bolivia's physical isolation from the trading posts of culture is reflected in its artistic and intellectual traditions. Most of the important international currents have eventually made their way to La Paz, but only those that have been adaptable to the expression of the Bolivian historical experience or social conditions have been embraced and assimilated.

Although the Hispanic cultural elites now take great pride in the archaeological remains of pre-Columbian cultures and manifest a sense of urgency about recording the legends and the music of the Indians that have been passed down orally from generation to generation, the original Spanish colonizers disrupted and repressed indigenous creative efforts and implanted an alien culture. Development in literature and the arts, however, was scanty and halting until the beginning of the twentieth century. Most of the literature of the colonial period consisted of either religious speculation or historical chronicling, and there was no printing press in the whole of Upper Peru (encompassing part of present-day Peru and Bolivia) until the eve of independence in 1825. The graphic arts and music of the period were generally imitative in both style and subject matter.

The nineteenth century produced some outstanding historical works, but it was not until the early twentieth century that writers began to take a critical look at the society of which they were a part. What began as a literary revulsion against the status quo developed, after the Chaco War (1932–35), into a glorification of the downtrodden Indian and an impetus for revolutionary change. The Indian, conscripted to fight and die in a war he did not understand in order to preserve the prerogatives of an alien exploitative elite, became the protagonist of innumerable novels and interpretive historical treatises. Whether these writers were highly influential as precursors of the revolution or were merely reflective of a national mood is still being debated by historians, but their importance in the development of a national literary tradition is well established.

The focus on the Indian in his natural and societal environment spread in the 1930s and 1940s from literature into painting and sculpture with the assistance of stylistic borrowings from the Mexican

191

muralist school. The figurative approach that prevailed in the earlier nativist or indigenist works had lost ground by the 1960s to abstract expressionism, but the themes remained the same.

The country has never developed a strong tradition in classical music, although the incorporation of native music into some compositions has broadened its appeal. Folk expression in music and dance, on the other hand, has flourished; its vitality is particularly manifest in festivals, often unique to a city or region, involving elaborate costumes and imaginative choreography.

Postrevolutionary governments, especially in the 1950s and early 1960s, have made some attempts to underwrite the efforts of artists and scholars, to disseminate their works to a broader audience, and to expose the educated classes to the country's rich folkloric tradition. Nevertheless, the cultural gap between the intelligentsia and the masses they choose to depict and seek to influence remains immense.

In the early 1970s some observers maintained that creative efforts had been stymied both by lack of interest and by selective limitations on freedom of expression. Seasoned writers and critics have lamented that today's educated young people are more prone to express their passion for social justice and national identity through direct political action than through literature and the arts. Furthermore, since the advent of the government of President Hugo Banzer Suárez, many members of the intelligentsia—who had generally been critical of that government—were imprisoned or went into exile or hiding.

Development of mass communication has long been inhibited by geographic, linguistic, and social barriers. Such progress as was made after 1952 in reducing social and linguistic barriers was largely attributable to the government's efforts to integrate the isolated Indian population into the national society and to promote literacy in Spanish. In 1973, however, the proportion of total illiteracy remained high, and many people who were marginally literate were insufficiently educated to read a newspaper (see ch. 6). The limitations on dissemination of information by the written word were illustrated by the fact that in La Paz, a city with a population of more than 500,000, the total circulation of the five daily newspapers was estimated at 90,000.

In 1973 radio, which reached the majority of the country's population, was by far the most important mass medium. Nevertheless, in many areas word-of-mouth communication continued to serve as a significant channel for the dissemination of information and the exchange of ideas.

In 1973 there was no formal censorship of the press, and some criticism of the government appeared in newspapers. Actions had been taken against selected journalists and periodicals, however, and a number of leftist periodicals that had been circulated during the 1950s and 1960s were no longer published.

ARTISTIC AND INTELLECTUAL EXPRESSION

The Colonial Heritage

The mineral wealth of the colony gave it an economic and political importance that contributed greatly to its artistic and intellectual development. A large colonial administration, the prospect of financial gain, the opportunity for political advancement, and the influx of Spanish priests, to meet the spiritual needs of white and indigenous elements, converted the colony into a thriving population center. With this growth in size came the need for the construction of municipal, domestic, and religious buildings. In turn, the monumental development of colonial cities stimulated the production of the decorative arts—painting and sculpture.

The church and its representatives did not limit themselves to educational activities but served alongside the elite as promoters of the arts by supplying commissions for artists and architects. In literary and intellectual activity the church was the important single factor; early musical development also depended upon its efforts.

During the conquest, Gregorian chants were introduced by the priests. Musical instruments, initially imported from Spain, were soon produced in the colony. In many cases the missionary program of the Spanish priests resulted in the development of Indian choruses that reached a relatively high degree of technical ability and also incorporated something of their own music into Western modes. In higher social circles musical preference was for pure Spanish styles. Young ladies from the upper classes learned to play the harp, lyre, and guitar in the convent schools. For the general public musical experience was limited to the religious procession, popular street music, and military marches.

In contrast to the limited musical activity, the cultivation of the plastic arts was very great. Architecture, foremost of the plastic arts, reached its peak in the eighteenth century. Whereas both Potosí and Cochabamba were important colonial centers, Potosí, the heart of mineral wealth, was the site of the grandest architectural achievements. The early Renaissance plateresque style, with its light, intricate, superficial decoration, was adopted first, but in the seventeenth century—the period of Potosí's greatest economic power—the more impressive baroque flourished. Superimposed on the baroque and plateresque structures, the decorative details clearly show the hand of the Indian and mestizo workmen who realized the plans of Spanish and criollo architects.

The sculptural work of the period was limited to religious artifacts, architectural decoration, and furniture carving. The artisans, mostly Indians and mestizos, were organized into guilds, following the medieval Spanish example. Silver, wood, and stone were the most commonly used materials. The practice of carving life-sized wooden statues, popular in Spain during the seventeenth century, was also cultivated in the colony. Native ceramics were encouraged by the Spaniards and reached a high degree of quality.

A great deal less is known about painting in colonial Bolivia, but significant schools apparently did exist, particularly in Chuquisaca (Sucre); Jusepe Pastorelo, a painter and sculptor who worked on the retable of the Cathedral of Chuquisaca, is one of the few known artists from the first half of the seventeenth century.

The blossoming of a truly brilliant school took place in Chuquisaca during the second half of the century, inspired largely by the arrival of Spanish paintings from Seville. The subject matter is predominantly religious, but historical paintings also exist. The outstanding figure in colonial painting, Melchor Pérez de Holguín, unknown until recently, comes from this period. In his work there is a definite influence of the Spaniards Bartolomé Esteban Murillo, famous for his gentle, luminous virgins and children, and Francisco Zurbarán, painter of mystics and monks.

Although Spanish colonial policy always favored the subordination of culture to political needs, the development of the fine arts was unaffected since there was no conflict. Such was not the case with literary and intellectual activity. Initially Protestant ideology was the threat, and the Inquisition, established in Spain to combat it, was instituted in the colony as well. Although the colonial Inquisition tended to be less rigorous, it too restricted the sale and production of books on political and religious matters. The suppression of dangerous political ideas became particularly significant in the late eighteenth century with the rise of the Encyclopedists and the American and French revolutions. Colonial intellectuals and writers labored under the handicap of enforced isolation from contemporary European currents of thought and the lack of printing facilities, but they did have extensive classical libraries, and locally written manuscripts did circulate. Some manuscripts were also published in Spain.

The main literary effort of colonial writers, the majority of whom were monks and priests, was directed toward the production of chronicles and histories. In addition to accounts of postconquest life and events, much of what was written concerned Inca legend and history. From their contact with the Indian, missionary writers developed a great deal of sympathy for him and often defended his way of life.

Padre José de Acosta, considered by Bolivians the first colonial writer, reveals such an attitude in his *Historia Natural y Moral de Las Indias* (Natural and Moral History of the Indies). Knowledge of the Indian languages led some Spanish priests to write valuable grammars and dictionaries of Aymara and Quechua. After the revolutionary period interest and concern for the Indian was not revived until the twentieth century (see ch. 4).

The important city of Potosí had its chronicler in Nicolás Martínez

Arsanz y Vela, who offers a picture of colonial life in *Historia de la Villa Imperial de Potosí* (History of the Imperial City of Potosí). The first self-taught Upper Peruvian and also the most outstanding writer of the colonial period, Fray Antonio de la Calancha wrote about the work of his own order, the Augustines, in *Crónica Moralizada* (Moralized Chronicle). A humanist, Calancha, like the other writers of the period, reflects the influence of neoclassicism and scholasticism in colonial letters.

In addition to producing the most outstanding writers of the period, the church and its representatives were also responsible for colonial education. The Jesuits, well known for their independence, were the most active in this area and crowned their activities with the establishment of the university in Chuquisaca in 1624. Intellectual life revolved around this university, and its influence extended beyond the confines of the colony. Located in the same city as the powerful Audiencia de Charcas, which held dominion over the area comprehending all Spanish territory south of Lake Titicaca, it became the most important intellectual center in lower South America, attracting students with both political and scholastic ambitions from all over the region. Its studies in philosophy centered on the Aristotelian doctrines of Saint Thomas Aquinas, modified by the interpretation of Francisco Suárez. Suarist contributions included such ideas as royal subordination to law and the justice of regicide in cases where the king transgressed against popular rights. This thinking became useful to revolutionaries at the turn of the nineteenth century as an ideological basis for the justification of their actions (see ch. 2).

By the second half of the eighteenth century, the ferment of ideas had reached its peak. During the reign of Charles III a greater freedom was allowed, permitting some of the works of the Encyclopedists to enter the colony. Their ideas, the ideas of empiricists and naturalists against tradition and authority, were quickly associated with and absorbed into earlier doctrines of Suaristic Thomism. Especially popular was Jean-Jacques Rousseau's *Social Contract*, the most influential work in Bolivia. Although Bolivia was the last South American country to achieve independence, intellectually—through the groups centered in the University of Chuquisaca—it had been a forerunner.

The Evolution of a National Culture

From the activity of the colonial period, Bolivian artistic and intellectual life lapsed into a period of inertia that lasted until the latter part of the nineteenth century. With the departure of the Spaniards, the country became preoccupied with national consolidation and was more isolated than ever before (see ch. 2). Literary activity was limited in general to the production of pamphlets and small publications concerned with the issues of the day.

A few of the early governments tried to stimulate national culture.

By official decree Antonio José de Sucre had made Destutt de Tracy's *Ideology*, based on the principles of the French *Encyclopedia*, required reading in the secondary schools, and Simón Rodríguez, who had spent a considerable length of time in Paris, set up a model school that was to inaugurate the transformation of society by education. Both efforts were of short duration.

José Ballivián's administration also attempted to give impetus to cultural affairs. At that time the national theater appeared, and performances were well received. In 1833 Andrés Santa Cruz had offered large bonuses to any foreign musicians who would come to the country and take on at least two disciples, but it was not until 1845, under Ballavián, that one did arrive, the Italian Benedetto Vincenti. In the same year he wrote the Bolivian national anthem. After these official endeavors came nearly thirty years of rule by the so-called *caudillos bárbaros* (barbarous strong men), who were no more than military adventurers and warlords and showed no concern for cultural affairs.

Around midcentury the ideological climate in Bolivia changed greatly. Eclecticism, more a method for the selection of ideas from a wide variety of sources than a philosophy in itself, enjoyed great acceptance and diffusion in Bolivia. This period marks the appearance of the first artistic and literary movement in the country, romanticism. The Spanish influence was not lost, but the French was by far the stronger. Largely imitative, the work produced in this style is significant, with few exceptions, from a historical point of view alone.

The movement's first manifestations were in political oratory and poetry. Political oratory in Bolivia, as in other Latin American countries, was a popular and frequently practiced art; Santiago Vaca Guzmán's literary history—published in the 1880s—devotes a whole chapter to it. Poetry became the most widely cultivated literary form with the advent of romanticism. Quantity did not mean quality, however, and of the many poets produced during the period, only Ricardo José Bustamante is notable.

Of far greater significance was the novel, which made its first appearance in national letters with the romantics. In the indigenous literature there had been no form similar to the novel; during the colonial epoch Spanish works were read but not imitated by the criollos. The first novel written by a Bolivian, Sebastián Delanze, did not appear until 1861. Delanze's novel, a superficial copy of the French style, was followed by a number of equally imitative and undistinguished works whose authors, in accordance with the romantic tradition, preferred exotic, faraway settings to the national scene. It is noteworthy that during the long period of romanticism, which encompassed the terms of fifteen presidents, a shift from Conservative to Liberal rule, and two wars, nothing of Bolivian reality was reflected in the fictional literature.

The romantic spirit, with its interest in evoking the past, gave rise to the historical novel. Nataniel Aguirre's *Juan de la Rosa*, set in the independence era, is regarded by many as the first Bolivian novel in the sense that its subject matter was specifically Bolivian. In addition to being a novelist, Aguirre was one of the country's few noteworthy playwrights.

During the colonial period dramatic representations had been almost exclusively religious in theme and very simple technically. Although there was some original work, in general, what little was performed had been imported from Spain. There is some confusion as to which was the first play written in Bolivia, but many cite *Odio y Amor* (Hate and Love) by the sentimental poet, Serapio Reyes Ortiz, which was staged in 1859. Early theatrical development faced many obstacles, and politics—the constant antagonist of intellectual activity—often worked to its detriment. There was also a lack of performers and of an interested public large enough to give support sufficient to maintain those involved.

The static conditions of the early republican period were even more obvious in the plastic arts. Painting, the first to emerge after independence, was the most widely cultivated, although it never approached the dimensions that it enjoyed during the colonial era. Early republican works still showed a preference for the old religious themes. Gradually historic scenes and portraits, particularly of national heroes, began to appear. As in most young countries, there was a desire to set down the national past and its protagonists on canvas; these paintings imitated the stiff, sterile styles of European so-called official art. During the second half of the century a kind of romanticism, which differed from the European mode in its patriotic fervor, arose to displace classicism. Although religious themes were still in evidence, portraits were now predominant.

Architecture, the crowning achievement of colonial plastic art, fell into a decline from which it has still not recovered. The few major buildings that were completed in the early years of independence had been begun a number of years before and continued the colonial styles. Throughout the century architecture was imitative; it followed the European periods of classicism and French romanticism and showed Italian influence in religious structures and academic effect in civil works. Without the extensive monumental activity that had characterized the colonial era, sculpture deteriorated greatly.

Romanticism, which continued well into the twentieth century, lasted longer in Bolivia than in most other Latin American countries. After the country's defeat in the War of the Pacific in 1883, however, new attitudes developed and with them a generation that found romanticism unrelated to its interests. Bolivians were made conscious of their nationality and wanted to explore realistically and systematically the various aspects of their own country. The old traditionalist, eclectic, and spiritualist philosophies, which had so adequately complemented the romantic literary and artistic trend, could not provide a suitable ideological context for these new goals and attitudes. Consequently, they took up the more practical, humanistic positivism, which had already spread to the rest of South America. With its predilection for science and belief in the power of man to shape his future through the application of the scientific method, the philosophy generated a spirit of optimism and practicality that was quickly adapted to politics by the more progressive elements.

Politically, the triumph of positivism came after the Liberal revolution of 1899. The ensuing twenty-year period of Liberal government was characterized by mild social reforms (which did not profoundly change national life) and increased commercial activity (which complemented the materialism and practicality of positivism). Positivism remained largely an intellectual concern, however, and it never directly involved the main body of the population (see ch. 2).

The inclination of the postwar generation toward national themes marked the real beginning of Bolivian arts and letters. The shift in orientation and consistently increasing activity did not, however, constitute a complete or immediate transformation. The new interests were held only by the same small group that had always controlled the economy and politics.

The most notable literary product of the period between the War of the Pacific and the War of Acre in 1899 was the didactic prose of a group of writers who worked in the spheres of journalism, science, and the humanities and whose common goal was to explore Bolivia—past and present. They were loosely united in a school that Fernando Díez de Medina has called the Indagadores, or Searchers. Some chose to deal with the traditions, customs, and way of life of the country in reaction against the romantic poetry and novels that still constituted the great body of fiction; others dealt with national history and jurisprudence, the natural sciences, geography, geology, and archaeology.

The first literary history, which was written by Vaca Guzmán, appeared in the 1880s. Scientific activity was stimulated by the efforts of Augustín Aspiazu, who wrote on the natural sciences, medicine, jurisprudence, and economics. Aspiazu was also prominent in some of the numerous cultural and scientific societies that began to appear in the last two decades of the century.

A few of the societies put out publications, and there were also unaffiliated literary and cultural magazines like Daniel Sánchez Bustamante's *La Revista de Bolivia* in Sucre. This period also saw the rise of musical organizations like the Haydn Society of La Paz—the first group devoted to the cultivation of classical music—the Philharmonic Society of Sucre, and the Academy of Military Music in La Paz.

The historian Gabriel René-Moreno is regarded by many Bolivians as the greatest writer of the period. Before the War of the Pacific, René-Moreno had attempted negotiation with Chile on behalf of his country and, for failing to settle the differences that ultimately led to the war, he was accused of being a traitor. The bitter, strongly critical attitude that pervades his work had its origin in his unfortunate political involvement. René-Moreno dealt with sociological analysis, political criticism, and biographical study, but his most significant contribution was in the field of history. His *Los últimos días coloniales en el Alto Perú* (The Last Days of the Colony in Upper Peru) is the best work done on that period.

In addition to a generally critical attitude toward Bolivia, one of the most notable characteristics of René-Moreno's work is the strong prejudice against the Indian. He was a native of Santa Cruz, whose homogeneous population was extremely proud of its reputedly pure Spanish heritage. For him the indigenous inhabitants of the country were of no value, and the pre-Hispanic past was completely negligible. Although Bolivians reject René-Moreno's negative attitude toward the Indian and his colonial mentality, they respect his great contribution to national letters and have honored him by giving his name to the university in Santa Cruz.

The investigative inclination that began with the Indagadores continued in the first decades of the twentieth century, but prose fiction and poetry also reappeared as important literary elements. Two parallel currents tended to work simultaneously during the period. In the novel social realism was dominant, and in poetry the most outstanding work was done by the modernists. Receptive to the realist school of Europe, novelists began to describe city and country life from a social point of view. In 1911 the problem of the miners was first introduced in Jaime Mendoza's *En las Tierras de Potosí* (In the Lands of Potosí). A later work, *Páginas Bárbaras* (Savage Pages), dealt with the rubber collectors and life in the northeastern part of the country. One of the best novels to come out of Latin America in the early twentieth century was Armando Chirveche's *La Candidatura de Rojas* (The Candidacy of Rojas), which concerns rural political life.

A theme that was to become paramount in subsequent years, indigenism, was initiated in 1919 in the Bolivian novel with *Raza de bronce* (Bronze Race) by Alcides Arguedas. One of the few writers known outside the country, Arguedas later turned to historical and sociological themes, as in *Vida Criolla* (Criollo Life) and *Pueblo Enfermo* (A Sick People), which were critical studies of city life at the turn of the century. In his own time, Arguedas' novels were well received, but today his criticism is considered too harsh.

The continuing Indagador school was also susceptible to sociological and indigenist material. Prehistoric culture was described in Belisario Díaz Romero's *Tiahuanaco*, and Bautista Saavedra wrote on Indian sociology in *El Ayllu*. Rigoberto Paredes also took up the question from the cultural viewpoint in *Mitos, Supersticiones y Supervivencias Populares de Bolivia* (Popular Myths, Superstitions, and Survivals [from ancient customs] of Bolivia).

Although inspired by French symbolism, modernism was Latin America's first original contribution to international literature. With its emphasis on physical beauty, exotic settings, sensuous vocabulary, and universalism, modernism represented the antithesis of realism. In Bolivia its outstanding cultivators were Ricardo Jaimes Freyre and Franz Tamayo.

Freyre, well known throughout the continent, was one of the earliest modernist poets. He and the Nicaraguan poet Rubén Darío founded the *Revista de América* in 1894. Three years after Darío published his *Prosas Profanas* (Profane Prose), considered the first manifestation of the movement, Freyre's *Castalia Bárbara* (Bold Castalia) appeared.

Tamayo, although less well known outside the country, holds a more exalted position at present, probably because of his admiration for the Indians. Whereas Arguedas had emphasized their misery, he emphasized their nobility. Like Freyre, who had held diplomatic posts, Tamayo was involved in politics and fulfilled the duties of minister of state, parliamentarian, and diplomat. In addition to poetry, Tamayo occasionally wrote prose works. One of his best known and most important contributions was *Creación de la Pedagogía Nacional* (Creation of the National Pedagogy), an analysis of the Indian and mestizo. Although realism never became a popular literature, it stimulated a more widespread interest, whereas modernism remained the possession of a very small cultured minority.

After World War I, attention was not so heavily concentrated on social themes and national interests. In Europe and North America the postwar period produced radical new movements in art, literature, and philosophy. This was the period of "isms" with wide divergence in artistic tendencies and ideological orientation. In Bolivia there was something of this spirit, although the intensity and scope were, quite naturally, not nearly so great as in areas where the war had had a direct effect.

In the late 1920s and early 1930s, before the Chaco War, Marxism won adherents in intellectual circles, where a logical explanation of Bolivian history was sought in dialectical materialism. Marxism's social concerns also struck an appealing note for those who were interested in the problems that had inspired the realists. The Aprista Party in Peru was another influence; in 1927 one of its writers, Manuel A. Seoane, published a book dealing with the problems of the Indians and the privileged position of the mining oligarchy in Bolivia.

Evidence of intense nationalism in literary circles increased in the late 1920s and finally exploded after the Chaco War. Most of the members of literary groups, such as Potosí's Gesta Bárbara, soon became absorbed in public affairs; but Carlos Medinacelli, initiator of modern criticism in the country, was the exception. Medinacelli's novel *La*

Chaskanahui (Starry Eyes) and Antonio Díaz Villamil's *La Niña de sus Ojos* (The Apple of His Eye) were the best *cholo* (see Glossary) narrations written in Bolivia. Díaz Villamil was the most productive talent of the generation; in addition to novels, he also wrote didactic prose, history, short stories, criticism, and plays.

The stimulus for increased theatrical activity came from Youth Athenaeum (Ateneo de la Juventud), a group that appeared in 1922. Organized primarily to protest the lack of organization and effective contribution of the country's intellectuals, the Youth Athenaeum felt that the state of so-called collective culture might be improved by bringing intellectuals together. Its manifesto was followed by the penetration of members into diverse cultural centers of the country. Under the influence of the Youth Athenaeum, groups with more specific interests were formed. One was the Women's Athenaeum (Ateneo Femenino), the first women's organization with intellectual goals. Its activities were politicocultural in nature and concentrated on raising the cultural level of the Bolivian woman and on campaigning for women's suffrage. These groups continued to flourish, and by the 1960s there were approximately forty of them throughout the country.

The stimulation that the Youth Athenaeum had given to the theater resulted in the formation of the Bolivian Society of Playwrights (Sociedad Boliviana de Autores Teatrales). It was their wish to promote drama, to improve the economic status of artists, and to create a real national stage art. Many of the numerous productions reached the stage, but few were ever published. In theme they generally tended toward national or local subjects with a popular flavor, but there was still some interest in social problems and in moralizing.

Information on developments in music is scant, but it is known that two dance academies were founded in the period. Events in the plastic arts were of much greater significance. There had been a few small private academies that were started in the first decade of the century by artists like Avelino Nogales and Elisa Roche de Ballivián—advocates of the realist school that had succeeded romanticism in painting as well as in literature.

In 1926 the National Academy of Fine Arts was founded. Its first professors were Alejandro Guardio, Humberto Beltrán de Oliveira, both sculptors trained in the European classical tradition, and the French painter Henri Sène. Although the two sculptors had studied abroad, they were not influenced by the new trends that were revolutionizing the form. By bringing together a group of young people who were eager to revitalize the plastic arts, the national academy laid the foundation for a new Bolivian school. Under the tutelage of the painter Cecilio Guzmán de Rojas, who acted as its director in 1930, the students found a leader who established the direction the arts would take in subsequent years.

Contemporary Trends

The young generation of artists was moved by the same spirit that was shaping writers, intellectuals, and musicians—artistic nationalism. Their desire was not just to deal with Bolivian subjects as literature as the Indagadores had done but also to create something distinctly Bolivian in form. Although the scholarly approach was continued, there was an increasing tendency to exploit national themes for their own sake, particularly in the fine arts. Social themes, introduced by the realists of the first twenty years of the century, came into great prominence. They were inspired by the revolutions in Mexico and Russia, the intellectual Marxism of the twenties, and the internal economic state of the period. The Chaco War brought together many elements of the population and contributed to a better defined sense of national identity. The Bolivian defeat was seen as the culmination of the shortcomings of the old order. In an atmosphere of frustration, discontent, and political instability, the postwar generation envisioned a new Bolivia, wrought by social reform, whose particular character would emerge with the spiritual and artistic return to the indigenous. Foreign trends were simply of no consequence, except when related to national interests.

In the discovery and exaltation of indigenous folklore and folk art, the appearance of regionalism and indigenism, and the cultivation of social themes in literature and painting, Bolivia has closely paralleled developments in twentieth-century Mexico. The intensity and wide acceptance on all social levels of these movements in Mexico, however, has not been characteristic of Bolivia. Although sentiment was strong, it was still limited generally to the younger generation of the same small group that had always produced the country's artists, intellectuals, and writers.

Literature

In literature the post-Chaco generation can be said to form a school only in its common preoccupation with the indigenous. The variety and diffusion typical of the eclectics persisted in the subsequent movement. Introspective and critical, the young writers tended toward a realism expressed in rugged and brutal language, somewhat reminiscent of French naturalism. In form they preferred the short story, novel, and essay, although poetry was not completely abandoned. After publishing one or two books, many either turned to newspapers or periodicals or stopped writing altogether, for a great deal of literature that emerged from the Chaco experience was the product of young ex-combatants who, without the necessary technical skills or real literary motivation, were moved to set down what they had seen and felt.

Although Bolivian critics feel that a definitive work on the war is still to be written, several notable novels and collections of short stories appeared in the late 1930s and early 1940s. Inspired directly by the war, they nevertheless indicated the thematic direction literature would take after the conflict itself ceased to be a source of creative production. Surprisingly, these novels and short stories expressed no animosity toward the recent enemy but instead preached a general hatred of war. A strong autobiographical current, as seen in Augusto Guzmán's *Prisionero de la Guerra* (Prisoner of War) and Jesús Lara's *Repete* (a term used to identify Indian combatants), was also typical of the majority. A suggestion of the indigenism that was to become an important aspect of artistic nationalism is reflected in *Sangre de Mestizos* (Mestizo Blood), by Augusto Céspedes. In addition to expressing the common pacifist tendency and criticizing the government in power during the war, Céspedes gives the mestizo ethnic factor an important role in his work.

The poet Oscar Cerruto emphasized the social drama and contemplated the rise of the Indian to his full power. With the use of the geography of the sierra for political and philosophical projections, Cerruto, among others, indicated another trend for postwar literature. The physical nature of the Chaco apparently impressed the Bolivians considerably, for it figures prominently in many war novels and stories. A great interest in national geography developed in the period after the war, which gave rise to regionalism and, consequently, *costumbrismo* (the portrayal of customs and daily life in a given city, town, or region).

Geography, important in its own right, was also linked to man. The *mística de la tierra* (mysticism of the land) philosophy, which developed in the period, was based on the principle that man's natural surroundings produce a fundamental effect on him and make him different from those having another physical environment. For those who held the belief, the great Andes were capable of inspiring Bolivians to new initiatives as they had in the pre-Hispanic past. They claimed that all Bolivians felt the power of the national landscape and that their disassociation from it was a prime cause for the spiritual ills of the nation. The land was to be the new basis for the Bolivian spirit.

One of the foremost adherents of *mística de la tierra* was Roberto Prudencio, an art history professor at the Higher University of San Andrés in La Paz. His most significant accomplishment was the creation in 1939 of the literary magazine *Kollasuyo*, which he intended to be the spiritual expression of the country in which essayists, critics, and authors would have a forum for cultural nationalism and indigenism. Prudencio's most characteristic concept was the "feeling of the land" manifested in individuals and collectivities.

Another proponent of *mística de la tierra* was Fernando Díez de Medina—author, critic, and politician. In 1948 he founded the Pachakutismo Party, moderately nationalistic in ideology, whose initial campaign was against the tin magnates. Under the Nationalist Revolutionary Movement (Movimiento Nacionalista Revolucionario—MNR) government he became minister of education, with ample reflection of his views in an official cultural magazine, *Cordillera*. Díez de Medina, one of the most prolific contemporary Bolivian writers, achieved his greatest success in literary criticism. Although he has never formulated a systematic philosophy, he attributes a spiritual function to the land, considering it a source of aesthetic, ethical, and religious profundity. Indianism often becomes an adjunct of *mística de la tierra* since the indigenous inhabitants have always lived close to the land. Díez de Medina's *Nayjana*, which won the National Grand Prize in 1951, is permeated with this sympathy and concern for the Indian. In a collection of essays on national concerns, entitled *Bolivia y su Destino* (Bolivia and Her Destiny), that came out in June 1962, he continued to display interest in the Indian. In addition, he offered an evaluation of the MNR government after ten years and a discussion of his departure from the party.

Politically, intellectual nationalism also had its effect. Because Bolivian writers rarely limit themselves to their literary activities and invariably have some contact with public affairs, their ideas have often helped to form or modify the political ideology of their particular parties. The postwar atmosphere encouraged the growth of less traditional groups and parties. Most counted intellectual elements of the new generation among their founders or members. Botelho Gosálvez, one of the leading writers, was a socialist. Céspedes and the critic Carlos Montenegro were members of the MNR, and José Antonio Arze, Ricardo Anaya, and Arturo Urquidi belonged to the Party of the Revolutionary Left (Partido de la Izquierda Revolucionario—PIR), a Marxist group.

Arze translated several books dealing with the putatively communist society of the Inca and also wrote original works on sociology. Anaya's political thinking is best delineated in *Nacionalización de las Minas en Bolivia* (Nationalization of the Mines in Bolivia), written in 1952. Rector of the Higher University of San Simón of Cochabamba for more than a decade, Urquidi contributed to the Marxist ideological orientation of that institution. The works of Céspedes and Montenegro are saturated with political doctrine and purpose and are written in language suitable for mass consumption. Céspedes' 1946 novel *Metal del Diablo* (The Devil's Metal), based on the life of the tin magnate Simón Patiño, promoted the cause of nationalization of the mines. His *El Dictador Suicida* (The Dictator Self-Destroyed), published in 1956, is a nationalistic, revolutionary interpretation of Bolivian history. The nationalism and socialism expounded by these groups merges in the Bolivian context with indigenism.

Philosophically and aesthetically, indigenism represented a reaction against modernism, which sought inspiration in remote and exotic sources. Some aspired to the rebirth of indigenous culture and a rediscovery of ancient wisdom, whereas others adjusted the indigenist cult to the contemporary scene by studying the ways of the Indian and copying his art. Lara took up the indigenist theme in *Surumi*, which describes the social problem of the desolation and misery of the Indians, and in *La Poesía Quechua* (Quechua Poetry) the first systematic study of indigenous literature. Few Bolivian writers have been able to escape some aspect of indigenism.

Social themes, revolving principally around the problems of the Indians, miners, and other lower class or rural elements, were vigorously cultivated in the 1940s and, with indigenism and politics, form the major emphasis of contemporary literature. Authors rarely take a purely sociological or an expository position; instead, they combine protest and political orientation with fact and creative fancy. Sympathies usually lie with the economically downtrodden, and the blame is placed on traditional institutions or custom. People and landscape, within the social context, are the focal point. For example, Fernando Ramírez Velarde's *Socavones de Angustia* (Caverns of Anguish) deals with the *campesinos* (peasants) and miners in the Cochabamba Valley, while José Fellman Velarde takes up the exploitation of the Aymara before agrarian reform in *La Montaña de los Angeles* (Mountain of the Angels). When the social problem is general in locale, there is usually a politically propagandist tone. In cases concerned with specific areas, the inclination is toward regionalism.

Two basic trends may be distinguished in the novel of social protest since the 1952 Revolution. One is essentially self-congratulatory, taking the form of nostalgia over the dark days of the struggle itself or glorification of the victory that was won. The other is critical of the revolution and the government it brought to power, either because it went too far in the upheaval of the social structure or because it did not go far enough. Criticism ranges from the moderate admonitions against extremism in the works of Mariano Morales D'Avila to Lara's scathing charges of a sellout.

The persistent themes of indigenism, regionalism, nationalism, and socialism are not without their critics. There have been those who feel that the concentration on national problems and aspects has created too limited a viewpoint. Although they do not advocate the abandonment of Bolivian themes for foreign literary trends, they do suggest the need for a more universal approach. It has also been noted that most contemporary novelists are townspeople and that a strain of artificiality is not uncommon in their indigenist works. And it has been charged that the persistence of themes addressed by the revolution represents an exhaustion of social imagination.

Scholarship

Criticism itself has received greater attention in the postrevolutionary period. Until the publication of Díez de Medina's *Literatura Boliviana* (Bolivian Literature) in 1952 and Guzmán's *La Novela en Bolivia* (The Novel in Bolivia) in 1955, the only major treatment of literary criticism and history was that done by Enrique Finot in 1943. A few essays and scattered references in more general works existed, but interest was apparently slight. In 1953 the first Bolivian history of modern plastic arts was published, Villarroel Claure's *Arte Contemporáneo* (Contemporary Art). Guillermo Francovich's *El Pensamiento Boliviano del Siglo XX* (Twentieth-Century Bolivian Thought) was published in 1956. Francovich, the first in the country to approach the history of ideas systematically, also reflects the more universalist tendency. Expanding on several of his earlier works, in 1960 Lara published *La Literatura de Las Quechuas* (Quechua Literature).

Aside from the interpretive histories inspired by nationalism or social consciousness, most of the country's historical works have been biographies of controversial political figures, in which Bolivian history is not lacking. A biography of Mariano Melgarejo by Paredes, published in 1963, has been judged by critics as superior to earlier portrayals of that colorful nineteenth-century dictator.

Recent works by the country's few professionally trained historians have treated the indigenism theme less dramatically, downplaying extreme interpretations of the noble savage and black legend varieties. The pervasiveness of racial antagonism, however, continues to be stressed, as seen in Gonzalo Romero's well-received *Reflexiones para una interpretación de la historia de Bolivia* (Reflections for an Interpretation of the History of Bolivia) published in 1960.

A fascination with folklore, which has swept the hemisphere since the early 1960s, has provided a stimulus to the social sciences. In musicology Angel Olmos Algreda's *Cancionero Popular en Cochabamba* (The Popular Songbook in Cochabamba) and the more general study *La danza folklórica en Bolivia* (Folkloric Dance in Bolivia) by Antonio Paredes Candia explore the origins and functions of a large number of songs, dances, and musical instruments. Both works were published in 1966.

In linguistics Joaquín Herrera has analyzed a selection of Bolivian idioms and phrases in Spanish that he feels reflect the structures of the Quechua language, and Yolanda Lastra de Suárez has posited a genetic relationship between Quechua and Aymara. Archaeologist Carlos Ponce Sanginés, who has devoted many years to excavation of Tiahuanaco, presents this site as a major urban center of pre-Columbian America in a study published in 1969.

Research in the natural sciences has been limited, but the Higher University of San Andrés supports the Institute of Cosmic Physics of Chacaltaya as well as a center for the study of geology.

The Plastic Arts

The plastic arts have followed much the same course taken by literature. With Guzmán de Rojas and his students, artistic life was regenerated. Following his lead in the development of works inspired by indigenous elements, the new school sought to create a national art. After initial study at the National Academy of Fine Arts, the majority perfected their techniques abroad, principally in the United States and

Europe. Until this time painting had been limited almost exclusively to oils, but with foreign experience many artists began to do water-colors, woodcuts, etchings, and prints. Sculptors learned new techniques and were influenced by more modern trends. In subject matter, however, artists consistently used native themes, such as the Indian, the Bolivian landscape, and local customs. Their work began to appear in foreign exhibitions, winning various forms of recognition.

Of all those dedicated to the exploration and exaltation of native themes, Bolivian critics hold the initiator, Guzmán de Rojas, in the highest esteem. After studying at the San Fernando Fine Arts Academy (Academia de Bellas Artes San Fernando) in Madrid, the artist returned to Bolivia to exhibit for the first time in 1929. In 1930 he became the director of the National Academy of Fine Arts. It was he who introduced the increasingly popular decorative art of muralism to the Bolivian scene. Guzmán de Rojas' contributions are not limited to the works he produced or to the leadership he exercised; he also developed a process for restoring colonial painting and discovered the country's greatest colonial painter, Melchor Pérez de Holguín.

The works of María Luisa Pacheco and Jorge Carrasco Núñez del Prado represent a transition between the figurative nativism of Guzmán de Rojas and the semiabstract and abstract nativism in vogue in the early 1970s. Pacheco's work was strongly influenced by cubism in the 1950s. The approach, however, in one of her most powerful canvases, *Palliri* (1958), is expressionistic. Symbolic of despair, it depicts a woman miner kneeling in a distorted attitude of suffering. Pacheco's paintings in the 1960s have moved toward complete abstraction, although inspired still by native themes. The expressionistic work of Núñez del Prado, who had thirty one-man shows between 1943 and 1963 in Europe and in the Western Hemisphere, has been characterized by freely symbolic associations.

The style of the younger painter Luis Zilveti Calderón has been described as neofigurative. His subject matter does not differ much from that of the earlier nativists, but his rendering has added new technical dimensions. His contemporary Alfredo da Silva became known internationally when he won the highest award for a foreign artist at a competition in Buenos Aires in 1959. Transparency of coloring gives an aura of mystery to his nonobjective works.

Two followers of Guzmán de Rojas, Marina Núñez del Prado and Hugo Almaraz, were responsible for reviving interest in sculpture. None of the plastic arts had suffered more because of the lack of technical training and public interest. Although sculpture has not achieved the prominence of painting, it has made great advances. Never since the colonial era has it received so much attention. Like the painters, sculptors have felt the need to study abroad; both Marina Núñez del Prado and Almaraz have studied in the United States. Indigenous themes were the initial inspiration for both, but Almaraz has since concentrated on funereal pieces.

Marina Núñez del Prado is one of the most widely acclaimed sculptors of Latin America. Her work is characterized by rolling curves and bulk and by the use of such spectacular materials as black granite and white onyx. *White Venus* (1960), a stylized female body in white onyx, is among her most admired works.

Emiliano Lujan Sandoval is the country's only contemporary monumental sculptor. His bronze *Sacred Heart of Jesus*, done for Santa Cruz in 1961, is more than sixty feet tall.

Artists who deal with social themes generally find more opportunities to sell their work than those who produce art for its own sake. Social themes are concentrated in mural art that, although not exclusively a product of the present generation, has come into prominence with it. The Athenaeum (Ateneo) group, organized by Wálter Solón Romero in Sucre, is noteworthy. Strongly influenced by the Mexican school, the work of its members is largely imitative. A number of public and private buildings in Sucre and La Paz, including the government and legislature palaces, were decorated by members of this group.

The other arts have not received the same stimuli felt in painting and sculpture. Architecture, of such great importance in the colonial period, continues to receive little attention. Students interested in architecture can find only inadequate training in the country. Buildings constructed in recent years reveal some awareness of twentieth-century developments, but the modern touches are imitative and superficial. Economics is fundamental in the lack of significant monumental activity in architecture.

Music

Bolivia's formal musical tradition has never been strong. The indigenous movements, however, did promote innovation. Interest was aroused in Indian music, and popular criollo songs were the source of inspiration for many compositions. Attempts were made to set down existing musical folklore in written form or on records. Eduardo Caba (1890-1953) was one of the few Bolivians whose musical efforts were of a serious nature. At the age of thirty-two he began technical studies in Buenos Aires. At first Caba was a folklorist but, finding this approach unsatisfactory, he adapted elements of the indigenous musical tradition to Western techniques. Although Caba was a prolific composer, only fourteen of his compositions were ever published. Jaime Mendoza Nava, one of the most significant contemporary composers in the country, spent long periods in both Europe and the United States and has used the same general approach as Caba.

Indigenous and nationalistic themes have also been prominent in the compositions of a number of others, and José María Velasco Maidana's folkloric ballet *Amerindia* has been widely acclaimed. Among the few who have gained recognition for modern compositions utilizing universal as opposed to nationalistic themes is Alberto Villalpando.

The country has had a symphony orchestra, under the auspices of the Ministry of Education and Culture since 1940, although it has often been dependent upon foreign talent for its direction. A United States Peace Corps volunteer served as its director for the two years before the expulsion of the corps in early 1971. A Soviet conductor was then offered the position and was still serving in that capacity in 1973.

In the performing arts Bolivia's best known figure has been the violinist Jaime Laredo. After the discovery of his unusual gift at the age of eight, Laredo came to the United States to study and in mid-1973 still resided there. The violinist, in 1959 at the age of nineteen, won first prize in an international competition held in Brussels. Bolivian pianist Walter Ponce received rave reviews for his debut recital in New York in early 1973. He had performed previously in other parts of the United States and in several Latin American countries. Although less well known abroad, Raúl Barrigan is noted in Bolivia as an outstanding concert pianist.

Folk Music and Dance

Bolivia's folk music, dances, and the festivals in which they are performed have been described as a living portrayal of the country's historical development. The most important festivals, such as those of Copacabana, Tiahuanaco, and Oruro, are characterized by ornate costumes, careful choreography, and exotic pageantry.

Several dances of the pre-Columbian era are still performed, by men alone, in the fiestas. Some are group dances that represent herders or harvesters. Others, such as the Sun Feast, are identified with Inca religious practices. These native dances vary greatly from one region to another.

Musical forms, instruments, and rites introduced by the Spaniards and modified and adapted by the Indians constitute another category of folklore. In this category is the famous Devil Dance of Oruro, in which an elaborately costumed Satan emerges from a mine shaft to confront the archangel Michael. There are also a number of Indian dances that mimic or satirize Hispanic customs, such as the bullfight, and ridicule Hispanic figures of authority.

The most popular of the criollo dances throughout the Andean countries is the *cueca*; handclapping and the use of the handkerchief are among the Latin American embellishments of the original Spanish *jota*. African influence is apparent in such dances as the *carnavalito* and the *taquiari*, performed in the eastern lowlands. The soft and lilting romantic music popular in Santa Cruz Department is similar to the Guaraní music of neighboring Paraguay. In addition to such native instruments as panpipes, flutes, and drums, modified versions of the Spanish guitar, including the *charango* made of the armadillo's shell, and harp have been incorporated into the folkloric tradition.

Government Activity in Cultural Affairs

After the 1952 Revolution there seems to have been a greater attempt to diffuse the nation's folk traditions and to stimulate cultural activity, but great obstacles still exist. One of the principal problems is the low educational level of the majority of the population. Another is the lack of funds and resources to implement programs of a cultural nature in view of the great needs in other more immediate areas of national development. The upper class has never shown any real sense of responsibility in cultural and artistic philanthropy, although individuals within the class have made minor efforts. The result is that, if cultural activities are to be made available to the general public, their source must be official. In fact, what has been accomplished has come principally from the Ministry of Education and Culture, the municipal cultural councils in La Paz, Cochabamba, and Oruro, and the universities. The ministry has been most active. It has established a number of institutions to study and promote the arts, national folklore, archaeology, and science. The old Tiahuanaco Museum, famed for its excellent collection of pre-Columbian pieces, has been taken over by the ministry, and the National Museum of Art has also been created. On the local level, the municipal cultural councils maintain museums, sponsor music and dance festivals, and hold annual art salons with the ministry. Of the institutions of higher learning, the Higher University of San Andrés has been the most active. The Institute of Historical Research of the Higher and Autonomous Tomás Frías University in Potosí, founded in 1956, has also contributed greatly to the country's output of scholarly works.

The universities have also been working with experimental theater but, as in most of their other efforts, success has been undermined by political involvement, which in some cases (notably in Cochabamba) has been fundamental in limiting official funds. By ministerial resolution, the MNR government also created the Center of Archaeology, which conducts excavations and then exhibits and publishes information on the findings. Publishing facilities, long inadequate in Bolivia, have been increased by the government. The Ministry of Education and Culture and the National Office of Information have sponsored cultural magazines and have published collections of modern works and national classics. Smaller publishing activities have been maintained by the municipal councils and universities. The government-sponsored National Council of Art, created in 1960, has been particularly active in promoting the study and performance of folk dance.

MASS COMMUNICATION

Freedom of Expression

Although guaranteed in most of the country's constitutions, the right of freedom of expression has not been consistently upheld. On a number of occasions during the 1950s the MNR government interfered with press freedom by confiscating individual issues of newspapers, by temporarily suspending publication of newspapers supported by the MNR's political foes, and by imposing censorship when publications tended to exploit situations that in its view jeopardized the public order.

During the early 1960s opposition newspapers freely criticized the MNR government and President Víctor Paz Estenssoro. Articles on alleged corruption and political blundering in the government appealed principally to members of the disaffected middle class. Letters-to-the-editor columns in the opposition press reflected a variety of antigovernment opinions, though these were not necessarily in agreement with the political philosophies that these newspapers represented (see ch. 10).

Toward the end of the MNR regime in 1964, however, criticism of Paz brought on press censorship that provoked strikes by factory workers and miners and sparked student demonstrations. When the army decided to support the strikers and Paz ordered the armed *campesinos* to join the struggle, the resulting turbulence led to the overthrow of Paz in November 1964 (see ch. 2; ch. 4).

The precarious position of the press was demonstrated during the first six months of 1971, during the presidency of General Juan José Torres González, when a number of newspapers and radio stations were taken over by journalist employees and used to advance the process of radicalization. Then, after the fall of the Torres government, President Banzer's government secured the dismissal of scores of Bolivian journalists and created difficulties for foreign journalists; and the communications media quickly switched to an uncritical stance. In 1973 the government did not exercise formal censorship, but most editors and commentators refrained from severe criticism of the government.

Newspapers and Books

The forerunners of today's newspapers appeared shortly after printing presses were brought to La Paz and Chuquisaca (Sucre) in 1825, and freedom of expression was granted in the Constitution of 1826. Newssheets and bulletins containing government proclamations, official notices, and religious items were published at irregular intervals. In addition, handbills and pamphlets were circulated containing excerpts of university debates dealing with ideas and theories of the French and American revolutions (see Artistic and Intellectual Expression, this ch.) (see ch. 6). Excerpts of learned debates and theoretical articles on politics, law, and economics later became the principal items in the more regularly published newspapers and bulletins and helped to determine the eminently political and opinionative character of the press.

The internal disturbances of the 1830s and 1840s curbed the free flow of ideas and sent many authors of political articles into exile. Only one major newspaper, *El Comercio*, published in La Paz, served the entire north. *El Cruzado* of Sucre featured mainly religious items. The ensuing thirty years of disorder were even less favorable to the growth of a healthy press. Journalism and pamphleteering were revived during the 1870s. The press, however, continued to serve a small, educated elite whose interests were theoretical and who had little contact with the practical aspects of national issues. Newspapers featured mainly political articles and platforms with only sporadic and irregular news coverage.

Although the readership of the country increased in numbers in the late nineteenth and early twentieth centuries, its proportion of the population remained about the same. No newspapers of more than local distribution arose until the mid-twentieth century and, although there was some increase in news coverage as national and worldwide communications improved, the press remained for the most part devoted to the political interests of its owners.

In 1973 five daily newspapers were published in La Paz, five in Santa Cruz, two in Cochabamba, and one in Oruro. The most widely read daily was *Presencia* (circulation about 40,000). The leading newspaper in the interior was *Los Tiempos* of Cochabamba (circulation about 15,000).

Presencia, a morning newspaper established in 1962 and published under Roman Catholic auspices, urged its readers to become involved in social problems and consistently opposed communism. It was known for its coverage of international news and had a reputation for objectivity. *El Diario*, another morning newspaper published in La Paz and founded in 1904, had an estimated circulation of 25,000. Like *Presencia*, it had general interest appeal. The other La Paz dailies were *Hoy* (estimated circulation 15,000) and two afternoon newspapers—*Ultima Hora* (about 7,000) and *Nueva Jornada*, which reflected government policies.

Because of the shortage of qualified reporters and lack of funds to dispatch them to foreign capitals or even to the major cities within the country, local news predominates in most newspapers. The same factors are responsible for the relatively widespread practice among the small newspapers of copying items from the metropolitan press without attribution.

The format of newspapers varies between the standard twenty-two- by fifteen-inch and the fifteen- by eleven-inch tabloid size. Some of them, however, do not follow either standard size. Typical weekday editions of the more prominent newspapers have about ten pages; the tabloid size, only eight pages. Only the major La Paz and Cochabamba newspapers use pictures regularly. Those of international events or persons are usually on the front page; local or sports pictures are on the last pages or the back cover. Cartoons usually appear on the editorial page. Advertisements, a principal source of revenue, are featured throughout the newspapers, as are personal notices of births, deaths, and engagements. Professional services of physicians, dentists, and lawyers are also advertised. Foreign, including United States, clients advertise mainly in *El Diario* and *Presencia.* Motion picture programs, social and obituary columns, and horoscopes are featured regularly only in the major newspapers. Nearly all of them carry gossip columns dealing with domestic politics and personalities.

Training in journalism is offered at the Bolivian Catholic University with campuses in La Paz and Cochabamba and at the Royal and Pontifical Higher University of San Francisco Xavier of Chuquisaca in Sucre. Because of low salaries and the lack of job security, however, there are only a few professional journalists. Most of them pursue the profession only part time, supplementing their incomes with another job. In some cases, publishers have had training and experience in journalism and continue to write features and editorials for their newspapers.

In the absence of foreign correspondents, newspapers rely heavily on wire services. Most of the major Western news services, notably Associated Press (AP), EFE—the Spanish news service—United Press International (UPI), the Agence France Presse (AFP), and the Deutsche Press Agentur (DPA) of the Federal Republic of Germany (West Germany), have regularly or intermittently served the major newspapers. Because of the frequent lack of funds, most newspapers are unable to pay the wire services regularly and, therefore, remain without foreign service coverage from time to time.

Because of the limited purchasing power of the small, literate middle class and the poorly organized distribution of books, the country has one of the least active book markets in Latin America. The annual output, including privately published volumes and government publications, has been estimated at 100 titles. Most publications are printed in La Paz, but the universities at Sucre and Cochabamba also produce books. The country's largest suppliers of imported books have been Argentina, Spain, and the United States.

Radio, Television, and Motion Pictures

In 1973 there were eighty-eight radio stations and an estimated 2 million receivers in the country. Broadcasts reached an average weekly audience estimated at 3 million. Eighteen amplitude modulation (AM) and ten frequency modulation (FM) stations were located in La Paz. The industry was regulated by the Directorate General of Radio Communications (Dirección General de Radiocommunicaciones).

The most powerful AM station (20,000 watts), Radio Illimani—the Voice of Bolivia (La Voz de Bolivia)—located in La Paz, was owned and operated by the government. A number of stations were operated by the Maryknoll fathers, by Spanish Jesuits, and by Canadian Oblate fathers. Privately owned stations depended primarily on advertising revenues. A large portion of the broadcasting time of most stations was used for musical programs and related entertainment; educational, informational, and religious programs were transmitted in Spanish, Aymara, and Quechua. Some stations specialized in broadcasts of sports events, and others featured news programs.

During the 1960s the importation of transistor receiving sets made it possible for virtually everyone in Bolivia to listen to broadcasts. Radio has thus become the most significant channel of mass communication in the country.

In 1973 Bolivia had one television station—government-owned Channel 7 in La Paz—which initiated regular telecasts in 1969. It transmitted an average of 7½ hours daily and was received by an estimated 20,000 television sets in La Paz.

Motion pictures are a popular form of entertainment in the cities and in mining centers. In 1973 there were approximately eighty-eight theaters in the country—thirty of these in La Paz. Total seating capacity was in excess of 50,000. Films shown were from the United States, Mexico, and Argentina and from Italy and other European countries. The only Bolivian film producer—Proinca—had made several full-length commercial films—one of these in color.

Foreign Government Activities

A number of foreign countries operated cultural and informational programs in Bolivia in 1973. France maintained Alliance Française organizations offering French courses and conducting cultural activities in seven cities. West Germany sponsored the Goethe Institute in La Paz, which taught German and carried out an extensive cultural program that included the presentation of many performing artists from Germany. Brazil maintained the Bolivian-Brazilian Cultural Institute in La Paz. Argentina sponsored the Bolivian-Argentine Institute (Instituto Boliviano-Argentino) in La Paz. Israel was offering seminars and exhibits in La Paz, Cochabamba, and Sucre; and Italy conducted Italian-language classes at its embassy in La Paz. The Yugoslavian and Czechoslovakian embassies both publish and distribute periodicals dealing with cultural subjects.

The United States Information Service (USIS) maintained a post in La Paz and binational centers in La Paz, Cochabamba, and Santa Cruz. USIS sponsored cultural presentations and an educational exchange program and distributed books to libraries and student and labor groups. It also furnished material to the press and to radio and television stations and distributed sixteen-millimeter films.

SECTION II. POLITICAL

CHAPTER 9

THE GOVERNMENTAL SYSTEM

In 1973 Bolivia was governed under the Constitution of 1967, which is structurally similar to most of the fifteen preceding constitutions. Bolivia's constitutions have been adopted through a variety of methods, including legislative amendment, executive decree, and action by constituent assemblies. Few constitutional changes, except for those made in 1961 and 1967, have reflected any significant change in basic political philosophy or in wording. Each fundamental law has provided for a democratic republic as well as for basic civil rights, an independent judiciary, a representative legislature, and a limited executive.

As in many other Latin American nations, however, the democratic tenets of the constitution have been largely ignored, and the power of the executive branch has grown disproportionately at the expense of other branches of government. Furthermore, until Bolivia's Revolution of 1952 all of its constitutions were written exclusively from the point of view of a small, educated, and propertied upper class that saw itself as uniquely capable of directing the affairs of the nation. Consistent with such a viewpoint, this group established literacy and property-holding qualifications for the exercise of citizenship rights, effectively disenfranchising the great majority of the population.

In the Bolivian presidential elections before 1952, only about 100,000 people out of a population of almost 3 million went to the polls. The Indians and *cholos* (see Glossary) were politically and economically defenseless against the power of the elite. Laws regarding wages, working conditions, and land tenure were generally written in the exclusive interest of upper class citizens, and the few provisions that existed to protect the interests of the poor and powerless were left unenforced. The constitutions of 1961 and 1967 reflected a basic change in political philosophy as compared with the earlier constitutions, which at best paid lip service to the political rights of a very large segment of the population.

Provisions written into all of the constitutions called for an orderly succession of governments through elections; governments, however, rose and fell through the mechanism of revolt and maintained their authority through the fiat of the armed forces. In theory, a separation of governmental powers existed in the form of executive, legislative, and judicial function; but in practice provisions designed to delimit the powers of the president were seldom honored, and the president tended to control all branches and levels of the government. The president and the congress were supposed to be equal partners, but in practice the chief executive dominated the scene through the use of his authority to issue decrees and through military force. Even duly elected presidents often resorted to government by decree. The frequent writing of constitutions reflected little more than attempts by governments to legitimize their rule.

In part, the price of minority rule and disregard of constitutional reform was an extremely unstable government. During the nineteenth century Bolivian history was marked by more than sixty coups d'etat. Between 1925 and 1952 no president completed his term of office. On the one hand, the disenfranchisement of a large segment of the population left all governments with a scant basis of popular support, and most pretenders to power found it easy to recruit armed support for the overthrow of the incumbent government. On the other hand, the tradition of strong personal leadership and disrespect for institutional order encouraged the ambitions of such pretenders.

Political instability before the Revolution of 1952, however, cloaked an unchanging and rigid social stability. If governments rose and fell and presidents exiled their opponents or themselves went into exile, the participants in such affairs were usually drawn from the same social groups. The upper class consistently retained all decisionmaking power. Although many of the presidents who established themselves through force of arms were members of the lower class by birth, they were, in some cases, assimilated into the elite, and their rule faithfully reflected the interests of that group. The overwhelming majority of the Bolivian people did not participate in politics; the social structure effectively removed at least 90 percent of all Bolivians from any contact with the decisionmaking process, and legal provisions for voting disenfranchised many more.

THE CONSTITUTIONAL STRUCTURE

Constitutional Development, 1826–1961

Bolivia's first constitution was adopted by the Constituent Assembly on November 6, 1826. It was written by the Liberator, Simón Bolívar, regarded as the "father and protector" of the new nation. Upon assuming dictatorial powers, Bolívar openly expressed his doubts as to the ability of the Bolivians to govern themselves. Before actually writing the Constitution of 1826, Bolívar issued a number of decrees, resolutions, and orders that clearly reflected his thinking on social, political, and economic matters. For example, he issued a number of decrees abolishing the conditions under which the Indians had lived for several centuries as virtual serfs. In addition to giving much attention to issues of educational reform and road construction, Bolívar also attempted, though with little success, to reduce the influence of the Roman Catholic Church in public matters.

Bolivia's first constitution provided for a unitary republic with sovereignty formally vested in the Bolivian people and a fourfold separation of the powers of government. The government was headed by a lifetime president, responsible to no other branch of government, and supported by a vice president, also serving for life, who was charged with the routine administration of government and was responsible to the legislature. In the tricameral congress, two houses—the Chamber of Tribunes and the Senate—had fixed terms, and members of the Chamber of Censors served for life. The Chamber of Tribunes possessed general legislative power. The Senate was charged with the codification of laws and the reorientation of court and church officials. The Chamber of Censors had general supervisory powers, including the power of impeachment of the members of the executive branch, in respect to the proper observance of constitutional and legal provisions. The judicial branch of government was completely independent.

The fourth branch of government, the electoral body, was selected on the basis of one elector per 100 voters. Not only did the system rest upon a base of indirect referendum, but the indirectness was compounded: the electoral body nominated slates of three people to fill each legislative vacancy, and each chamber made its own selections.

The first constitution (soon decried as a foreign imposition), with its complex and sometimes cumbersome provisions, remained in force for only a short time and was disregarded after the departure of Marshal Antonio José de Sucre in 1828. In both principle and practice, however, it did set certain precedents that proved pervasive in Bolivian political life from that time on.

One effect, still in force in 1973, was the establishment of a system in which a preponderance of power was placed in the hands of the executive, and little effective curb was imposed upon this power. Not only did Bolívar express his lack of confidence in the ability of even the educated minority of the country to govern collectively but, from his observation of the common people in all the northern half of Spanish South America, he had come to believe that a democratic constitution could only bring chaos. Hence, Bolívar thought that a lifetime presidency with great and irrevocable powers offered the best chance for stability.

Distrust of a government founded on a broad electorate was reflected not only in the highly selective manner of establishing the electoral branch of government but also in the restriction of voting rights. The franchise was granted only to those literate in Spanish who either possessed property worth 400 bolivianos (for value of the boliviano—see Glossary) or engaged in an art, in a science, or in some other remunerative position. All personal or domestic servants were excluded from the franchise. Such restrictions, which initially limited the vote to about 10 percent of the population, prevailed in successive constitutions, which differed only in degree until the mid-twentieth century.

Bolivia's second constitution was adopted on August 31, 1831, during the regime of General Andrés Santa Cruz. The new constitution abolished most of the innovative features of its predecessor—the tricameral legislature and the lifetime president, for example—and substituted an organization more in line with other Latin American models. A bicameral legislature and a four-year presidential term, renewable indefinitely through successive reelections, were established.

In 1834 another constitution was promulgated by Santa Cruz. It was basically a rewriting of the Constitution of 1831, and the few changes were of a formal nature. Its historic importance lies in the fact that it was the governing structure for the short-lived Peru-Bolivian Confederation (see ch. 2).

Between 1839, when Santa Cruz and his confederation were overthrown, and 1880, when the nation's first durable charter was adopted, Bolivia was ruled under five constitutions. A sixth was drafted but never adopted. Except for the length of the presidential term and the powers granted to the president, these charters varied little in either language or substance and, for the most part, represented little more than attempted ex post facto legalizations of strong man regimes imposed by force of arms. The constitution promulgated by José Miguel de Velasco in 1839 went far toward weakening the power of the president, probably in reaction to the headstrong and impulsive rule of Santa Cruz. The constitutions promulgated under the regimes of José Ballivián (1843), Manuel Isidoro Belzu (1851), José Maria de Achá (1861), Mariano Melgarejo (1868), and Agustín Morales (1871), on the other hand, provided for the traditionally strong executive. When Velasco was briefly returned to power (1847-48) by the overthrow of Ballivián, a constitution similar to that of 1839 was drawn up, but its promulgation was prevented by the successful coup d'etat staged by Belzu (see ch. 2).

In 1878 the tenth constitution was adopted. This was a document of extreme importance, for its readaptation as the 1880 charter was the first durable constitution, remaining in effect for an unprecedented fifty-eight years. Indeed, some constitutional authorities, seeing in the subsequent charters little more than a reworking of the 1880 document, believe that the spirit of 1878 persisted until the 1952 Revolution.

During the time it was in effect, the 1880 Constitution was amended several times. Among the most significant of the changes were a series of modifications adopted in 1906 with respect to religious freedom and the special privileges traditionally enjoyed by the clergy and by military personnel. Replacing a provision in the original text that forbade the public exercise of any religion other than Roman Catholicism (except in immigrant colonies), the reform of 1906 decreed absolute religious freedom; the Roman Catholic Church, however, remained officially established and protected. Both the clergy and the military lost their traditional right to trial in special courts and came under the jurisdiction of the common court system. Other important amendments were adopted in 1931. A comptroller general's office was established, the judicial branch was made independent, and habeas corpus (previously absent) was specifically introduced.

The 1880 Constitution was explicitly designed to maintain social, economic, and political relationships according to the status quo of the period. It continued to maintain property and literacy requirements for the electorate, denied religious tolerance, and guaranteed the property and special status of the church. It was under this constitution that the basis for the party system developed as it was to continue until the Revolution of 1952.

As a result of the worldwide depression that struck Bolivia in 1930 and the disastrous defeat in the Chaco War (1932–35) against neighboring Paraguay, significant changes began in Bolivian society, giving rise to a new generation that began to revolt against the old patterns of oligarchical rule. The legacy of this combination of the military, nationalists, intellectuals, and Socialists was the 1938 Constitution, a reflection of the new social ferment. The Constitution of 1938, promulgated during the administration of Colonel Germán Busch (1936–39), was in form a revised version of the 1880 document but substantively embodied revolutionary changes within the context of Bolivian society. Human rights were declared superior to property rights, the national interest in the subsoil and its riches was declared preeminent, and there was a hopeful insistence on educational facilities for all children. These pronouncements were extremely radical in the context of the traditional views of the elite, which had consciously rejected universal education in its determination to retain control of the country. A key provision recognized the right of workers to organize and bargain collectively. This was to have influence on future political development, for it was through the armed strength of the unions of miners and peasants (*campesinos*) that Bolivia experienced revolutionary change in the 1950s.

The Revolution of 1952 and subsequent events brought little alteration in the formal structure of government. Between 1952 and 1956, the period of President Víctor Paz Estenssoro's first term, there was, however, a de facto change of the system established in the constitution, for Paz governed without a congress. After 1965 all three branches of government functioned more or less normally. In 1961 a joint session of the congress revised the constitution, incorporating the fundamental changes that the revolution had brought about during the preceding nine years. Agrarian reform, nationalization of the tin mines, and universal adult suffrage were incorporated in the constitution. The workers' and peasants' militias were declared to be regular parts of the national army. The *patronato* (see Glossary) of the church was abolished. The Constitution of 1961 reflected the history and experiences of the Revolution of 1952 and the government that it supported. In form, however, the government that emerged was not radically different from the one that had existed in Bolivia before the Revolution of 1952.

The extent of the revolution can be appreciated by focusing on the platform of the Nationalist Revolutionary Movement (Movimiento Nacionalista Revolucionario—MNR), the revolutionary party that helped bring about the events of 1952, and on the profound structural changes that have since occurred in Bolivian society (see ch. 10). Promulgated during the initial years of the revolution and incorporated into official governmental decrees, the changes that were to lead to a more equitable distribution of power and economic opportunities included the grant of universal voting privileges, the nationalization of the country's three largest mining companies, the dissolution and reorganization of the army, agrarian reform, and acceptance of the principle of participation of workers in the management of national enterprises (see ch. 13). The real efforts of the MNR government to define and serve the interests of the majority of the population were, in a sense, rewarded by a measure of political stability between 1952 and 1964—stability almost unknown in the country's prior history.

Paz was elected for a second term but, when a new constitution was drawn up in 1961, it was deemed prudent to include a provision for the reelection of an incumbent president. By 1964 the political situation had deteriorated, and Paz considered himself the only man who could hold the revolutionary movement together. After pushing through a change in the constitution to allow for a second consecutive term in the presidency, Paz obtained the nomination of the MNR against the opposition of his vice president, Juan Lechín Oquendo, and of the former president, Hernán Siles Suazo. Paz was reelected, but the election was boycotted by all of the opposition groups, and Paz was the only name on the ballot. Meanwhile, he had been forced to put the head of the air force, General René Barrientos Ortuño, on his ticket as vice-presidential candidate.

Paz's election, however, proved to be a Pyrrhic victory. The traditional pillars of support had faded away. His regime was finally overthrown by General Alfredo Ovando Candia and Barrientos, who declared themselves copresidents in 1964. After the overthrow of Paz, the 1961 Constitution was abrogated, and the new document of 1967 was prepared.

The Constitution of 1967

According to the Constitution of 1967, Bolivia retains the democratic representative form and, according to Article 2, assumes that sovereignty resides in the people, that it is inalienable, and that its exercise is delegated to the legislative, executive, and judicial powers. The functions of the public power—legislative, executive, and judicial—cannot be united in a single organ. Nonetheless, Bolivia has not had a democratic election since 1966, when Barrientos was elected to the presidency. Since the military takeover of the MNR government by Ovando and Barrientos in 1964, Bolivia's presidents have made little effort to enforce the Constitution of 1967 or, since 1966, to provide for free elections. That constitution is hardly distinguishable from the previous constitution except that it attempted to legitimize the Barrientos government, reduce the power of labor, and enhance the opportunities for private and foreign investment.

Under the Constitution of 1967 Bolivia continued to have a presidential form of government. As under virtually all Latin American constitutions, the Bolivian president has the right, under certain conditions and for a limited period of time, to suspend specific civil liberties guaranteed in the constitution. He also has powers of legislation by decree and the power to issue regulations governing the administration of laws passed by the congress, which makes it possible to modify statutory law considerably.

The National Government

The Executive

The Constitution of 1967 provides that the executive is a president elected for a four-year term by direct suffrage and by a simple majority. He is ineligible for reelection until another term has intervened. Many officials of the government are ineligible for the presidency, but they become eligible if they resign their positions at least six months before the election. Blood relatives of the president and vice president, as well as relatives to the second degree by affinity, are also ineligible; so are members of the clergy of any faith. A presidential candidate must be at least thirty-five years old, literate, a registered voter, and the nominee of a political party. A vice president, who must meet the same requirements, is elected with the president on a party ticket. The vice president presides over the Senate and succeeds to the presidency if the incumbent dies or is removed from office. If both the president and vice president are unable to serve, the succession goes to the president pro tem of the Senate, followed by the president of the Chamber of Deputies.

By tradition and constitutional law, the president of Bolivia is a strong executive. In addition to the powers granted to all executives— enforcing the law, negotiating treaties, appointing officials, conducting foreign affairs, and commanding the armed forces—the Bolivian president controls all local government and has the power to declare a state of siege. The ministers of the president's cabinet, who serve as the heads of the various executive departments, are appointed and removed by the president. It has been claimed that Bolivia "blends the presidential and cabinet types" of government, because the constitution gives the legislature the power to vote "a censure of the acts of the Executive addressing it against the Ministers of State" and to command a minister to appear before the congress for questioning. But this does not change the presidential type of government. The president is in charge of the executive, and he and his ministers can be removed from office only by legislative impeachment.

The basic problem all Bolivian presidents face is the lack of an effective administrative apparatus and a swollen army of government employees whose number has been rising gradually (see ch. 12). The largest number of employees is in the administration of educational affairs. The Bolivian Ministry of Education is operated at a tremendous cost and enormous duplication of effort. The second largest ministry is the Ministry of the Interior, which includes local government, and the Ministry of Peasant Affairs and Agriculture is next largest. Practically all employees are appointed on a patronage basis, and only the first steps have been taken to set up a modern civil service system.

The president is assisted by a secretary general with cabinet rank who has fifteen people on his staff to supervise the office of the president. A military officer is in charge of the president's security, handles problems of protocol, and supervises the caretakers of the Palace of Government. The budget is prepared by the Ministry of Finance, drawing submissions from the various ministries.

The president has a large measure of fiscal power. He administers the national taxes and can decree the disbursement of state revenue through the various ministers. This latter power is exercised in conformity with both national and departmental budgets. Oversight of municipal government is also entrusted to him. When congress is in session the president is required to deliver a report on the state of the republic to the congress at its first regular meeting. The president is constitutionally required to enforce the decisions of the judiciary. Additionally, he may decree amnesties for political offenses.

The power of appointment is one of the chief executive's most important sources of strength. It enables him to exercise control over the large number of public servants at all levels of government. The president appoints the ministers, the two attorneys general, the comptroller general, and the national superintendent of banks from lists of three candidates submitted by the Senate, as well as the presidents of important state agencies. In his capacity as captain general of the armed forces the president also designates the commander in chief of the armed forces (an optional position) and the individual commanders of the three services within the armed forces: the army, the air force, and the river and lake forces (which substitute for a navy in landlocked Bolivia).

The president also serves as the highest appellate authority in title disputes under the agrarian reform program. He has ultimate authority over the work of the National Agrarian Reform Service, the agency for implementation of the agrarian reform program.

In 1973 the Council of Ministers included the following ministries: foreign affairs and worship (this title is due to Bolivia's historical ties with the pope, in which the latter legitimized Bolivia's conduct in foreign affairs), the interior (which is in charge of internal security); finance; mining and metallurgy; energy and hydrocarbons; industry and commerce; education and culture; peasant affairs and agriculture; social service and health; information; transportation and communications; labor and trade union affairs; urban affairs and housing; planning and coordination; and national defense. Theoretically, the independence of the executive and legislative branches is emphasized by a provision forbidding the ministers to remain in either of the two legislative chambers when voting is taking place. In order to be valid, however, a presidential decree must be countersigned by the minister charged with the administration of affairs in the area of the particular decree.

In addition to the ministries of the central government, the public sector includes various other institutions. In 1973, for example, there were forty-two decentralized institutions (they had branch offices all over the country), such as the social security administration; thirteen semiautonomous government agencies, such as COMIBOL and the National Electricity Company (Empresa Nacional de Electricidad— ENDE); four banks; and all the prefectures, municipalities, and regional development organizations.

In 1973 the government of General Hugo Banzer Suárez appeared to enjoy continued support by the military, and it ruled in coalition with the Bolivian Socialist Falange (Falange Socialista Boliviana—FSB) and the Paz faction of the MNR. The military retained the leadership of the ministries of industry and commerce, peasant affairs, interior, defense, and agriculture; the MNR and the FSB were allotted five ministries each.

The Legislative Branch

Although in 1973 the Bolivian legislature had not met since 1969, the Constitution of 1967 provides for a bicameral congress consisting of the Senate and the Chamber of Deputies, both elected under rules that guarantee representation for the opposition party. The Senate consists of twenty-seven members, three from each department, who are elected for six-year terms. The party winning the most votes in each department is awarded two Senate seats; the party with the second highest vote is awarded the third seat in the Senate. Ordinarily, the twenty-seven senators are divided into three groups, one-third being elected every two years; but in 1966 the entire Senate was divided into three groups by lot. To become a senator one must be at least thirty-five years old, a Bolivian by birth, and a registered voter and must not be a government employee, clergyman, or contractor for public works.

Each department has five deputies plus one more for each 50,000 inhabitants or fraction thereof over 30,000. Vacancies in the congress are filled by alternates, usually the candidates who have failed to win election. To become a member of the Chamber of Deputies one must be at least twenty-five years old and meet all of the requirements for the post of senator.

Theoretically, the two houses of Bolivia's legislature function both separately and in joint session. The constitution lists the powers and duties of the houses in great detail. The president of the republic has the right to veto bills passed by the congress, but the congress can override the veto by a two-thirds majority of each house. According to the constitution, the congress is a very powerful body, but Bolivia's political situation has rendered the constitutional power meaningless except in periods of constitutionally elected government. After the revolution the various political parties and factions developed the custom of having "watchers," mostly women, in the visitors' gallery when the congress met.

Although the constitution provides that a legislative committee, composed of five senators and nine deputies, take the place of the congress when the congress is not in session, such a committee has not convened since the late 1960s. This legislative committee is "to see that the constitution and the laws are complied with" and, in case of emergency, to authorize the president, by a two-thirds vote, to issue decrees with the force of law. Finally, this committee also has the power provisionally to approve a presidential decree of a state of siege.

The Judicial Branch

The judicial power rests in the Supreme Court of ten justices and in a series of subsidiary tribunals. The members of the Supreme Court are elected for ten-year terms by the Chamber of Deputies from a list proposed by the Senate and cannot be reelected. The Supreme Court nominates the justices of the district courts, who are elected by the Senate for six-year terms. The Supreme Court selects the judges of the lower courts for four-year terms.

The power of the Bolivian judiciary is limited. When in session the Supreme Court meets in the city of Sucre, the legal capital of Bolivia. Thus it is physically separated from La Paz, where the executive and legislative powers are located. Past governments have paid some attention to the judicial process, even in times of major change. The MNR, for example, established special agrarian courts to deal with land redistribution. This whole process, however, took place outside the purview of the regular civil courts.

For the lower level of the judiciary, the constitution provides for district courts whose judges shall be elected by the Senate for four years from panels of candidates prepared by the Supreme Court. The jurisdiction of the nine district courts is chiefly appellate, in both civil and criminal matters, from decisions rendered on the trial level by the courts in each territory. The district courts also hear cases against government officials on the local level. Furthermore, they are given cognizance over mayors, municipal council members, and agrarian and labor court judges for offenses committed while they are holding office. In the event that litigants wish to contest a ruling of a district court, it is necessary to prepare a new case and then appeal to the Supreme

Court for a nullification decision.

Scattered throughout the capital cities of the territorial departments and also in towns and cities in the districts in Bolivia are a number of civil and criminal trial courts—territorial courts (*juzgados de partido*). The criminal sections have judges of instruction (*juezes de instrucción*) who investigate and prepare criminal cases for trial whenever it is appropriate. These cases are tried by territorial judges (*juezes de partido*). The civil sections of the trial courts hear commercial and civil matters on personal and property actions generally. Again, the judges are appointed by the Supreme Court from panels drawn up by the district courts.

Bolivia also has a number of small-claims courts, which are scattered throughout the country and are limited to actions involving personal and real property, or personal actions, evaluated at between $b500 and $b3,000 (for value of the Bolivian peso—see Glossary) in the early 1960s. Larger claims can be submitted to the same court, but the parties have the right of appeal to the territorial judge.

At the bottom of the judicial system are the mayor's courts, which consist of judgeships in every parish. The civil jurisdiction of these courts is limited to hearing claims under $b100 in value and in the criminal field chiefly to police and correctional matters.

STRUCTURE AND FUNCTIONING OF GOVERNMENT AT SUBNATIONAL LEVELS

In 1973 Bolivia was divided for administrative purposes into nine departments, which were divided into ninety-six provinces; these in turn were divided into 940 cantons. The governors of the departments are named by the president, and there are no regional legislatures, although there are both city and town councils. Thus, local government is based on the French system, practically all powers being vested in the president. In each department there is a prefect, appointed by the president for a four-year term. Prefects hold the overall authority in military, fiscal, and administrative matters, working in each substantive area under the supervision of the appropriate minister. Centralized control is further ensured by the president's appointment of the subprefects, officials vested with the administration of the provinces. The cantons are in the charge of *corregidores* (administrative officials), who are appointed by the prefect of their department. Traditionally, many of the *corregidores* have been accustomed to serve without formal stipends and thus have been perhaps the governmental link most susceptible to favoritism and corruption. In some areas another category of officials functions under the supervision of the *corregidores*, the agents (*agentes*), who have quasi-judicial-executive functions.

The municipal governments are autonomous, at least in the formal sense, and function under the direction of municipal councils. They are elected in the capitals of all departments and provinces. Although mayors are elected, according to the constitution, by municipal councils, the president actually chooses a mayor from among the members of the municipal councils. Hierarchical supervision of the work of the municipalities within the structure of local government reinforces this control in Bolivian governmental practices.

In some areas the Indians continue to be organized in their traditional community groups (*ayllus*) (see Glossary). Even during the long period that witnessed the disenfranchisement of the Indian on a national level, he continued to make quasi-political decisions in the selection of his local communal leaders (*jilakatas* or *mallcus*). This long-preserved and deeply embedded tradition of local communal responsibility has been considered by some to explain partially the ability of indigenous Bolivians to reenter the stream of national political life with no greater dislocation than has been the case.

THE ELECTORAL SYSTEM

Before the Revolution of 1952 only a small percentage of the Bolivian population voted in any election. With the rise of Bolivia's first labor unions, peasant organizations, and revolutionary parties after the Chaco War, a larger percentage of the population began to be politically active, but the electorate continued to be small until after the revolution. No more than 1.5 or 2 percent ever voted in a Bolivian election before 1952. As expected, and consistent with the changes that occurred in Bolivian society as a result of the events of 1952, a much larger percentage of Bolivians acquired their constitutional right to vote and exercised it until 1966. Bolivia, however, has not had a presidential election since 1966. Although about 36 percent of the total population voted in the election of 1964, it has been estimated that a few years later approximately 50 percent of Bolivia's eligible population participated in the political system either directly or indirectly.

According to the constitutions of 1961 and 1967, Bolivia recognizes the existence of the National Electoral Court, which is made up of representatives of the congress, the Supreme Court, the president of the republic, and the major political parties of the country. The electoral court is charged with the responsibility of supervising all matters pertaining to elections, including the registration of candidates and political parties. In each of the nine departments a departmental electoral court is set up, consisting of three members—one designated by the president, one by the congress, and one by the Supreme Court. The departmental electoral courts supervise the registration of voters and count the votes cast in their departments. Under the departmental electoral courts, there are electoral judges who supervise and organize the many electoral notaries and juries, and select the polling places. The electoral notaries are the men who register the voters and give them their voting cards (*cédulas electorales*). An electoral jury consists of the five persons who conduct affairs at the polling places. They are chosen by lot from among the literate voters registered in each polling place.

Each party's ballot has a distinctive color and symbol to make voting easier for the illiterate. The voter casts his vote for a party. Nothing appears on the ballot except the party's initials and symbol. Much dispute exists about the fairness of elections under this system. There seems to be agreement that the MNR won a majority in the 1956 election, but there is no agreement about the fairness of subsequent elections.

THE CIVIL SERVICE

The patronage system, which functions under the general direction of the president, has severely interfered with the development of a professional body of public servants. Contributing to the continued strength of the patronage system has been public pressure to expand the ranks of civil servants, pressure in part due to the scarcity of private employment. The National Civil Service Office was established in 1956 as a separate directorate in the Ministry of Finance, with the task of organizing a civil service system. The public service, however, remains rudimentary, partly because of mass illiteracy and the general backwardness of the country. Little incentive exists for capable people to enter public service because remuneration is low. Both Bolivian and foreign observers have long decried the widespread acceptance of bribes on the part of public officials. They have commented further that the MNR government (in power until its overthrow by Barrientos and Ovando in 1964) failed to put a high priority on honesty or on improvement of the human factor in public service. According to both Bolivian and North American sources, salary schedules are primitive, and payrolls are often not met on time; inefficient use of the workday by employees is a general complaint.

In addition to the establishment of the National Civil Service Office, other changes in public administration have occurred since the Revolution of 1952. Mechanization of the government payroll operation has resulted in the elimination of considerable waste and overpayment, and an effort has been made toward the establishment of a system of job classification and job analysis for government employees. Customs enforcement assistance (including the construction of a customs warehouse financed by the United States Agency for International Development), intended to help both administration and collection of revenues, has made a considerable impact on the problem of contraband activities. A reorganization of the postal system also has received a relatively high priority. Perhaps most important, a series of important decrees in the late 1960s has greatly increased the authority of the minister of finance, giving him a much more direct control over the operation of the semiautonomous agencies of the government. In the early 1970s there appeared to have been an improvement in the quality of paperwork and reports turned out by the various ministries.

Despite some of these changes, however, inefficiencies continue to hamper the overall operation of the government. Duplication of responsibilities, lack of control, overstaffing, and lack of adequate expertise in the basic principles of public administration may be due, in part, to the absence or inaccessibility of pertinent technical literature.

CHAPTER 10

POLITICAL DYNAMICS

In 1973 overt political activity was contained within the narrow limits delineated by the military-backed government of General Hugo Banzer Suárez. The core of the Nationalist Revolutionary Movement (Movimiento Nacionalista Revolucionario—MNR), the party that had previously dominated national life for more than a decade, and the party that was the MNR's most bitter rival, the Bolivian Socialist Falange (Falange Socialista Boliviana—FSB), had been drawn into the governing coalition but, although the civilian parties had acquired certain patronage rights and had exerted influence on public policy, the military maintained a veto power over most policy decisions.

The coup d'etat of August 1971 that placed Banzer in power was, by some calculations, the country's 187th major uprising against a seated government in its 148 years of independence. A few months before that coup, then President Juan José Torres González, who had himself attained the office through a coup d'etat, commented that the biggest problem for a Bolivian president was survival. This pattern of "barracks revolt" and "palace coup" politics had been broken for a dozen years (1952–64) through a thorough-going revolution and the establishment of a single party, the MNR, loosely embracing all the sectors—peasant, labor, and middle class—whose coalescence in opposition to the old feudalistic regime had made the revolution possible. Víctor Paz Estenssoro, who has been credited to a large extent with both the creation and the dissolution of the MNR, in retrospect attributed the relative political stability of the years of MNR rule to the "equilibrium existing between the armed forces, the police, and the popular militias."

A number of factors, including rampant inflation, the conditions attached to seemingly crucial foreign assistance, and the personal ambitions of competing faction leaders in the MNR, combined to shatter the middle class-labor alliance. And once the peasants had acquired land and the means of defending it, they ceased to be a revolutionary force; in fact, some of the peasant militias were drawn into the efforts of the middle class party leadership to deprive workers, particularly the miners, of the gains they had achieved through the revolution. The military, virtually eliminated after the revolution but reconstituted and, after 1958, strengthened by increased budgetary allocations for equipment and training, moved in to fill the authority vacuum left by the disintegrating MNR.

By the early 1970s the political system was sharply polarized. Organized labor and some sectors of the middle class, including students and the intelligentsia, were calling for a more equitable distribution of wealth and further nationalization of the economy. At the same time the newly rich class of merchants and industrialists, important sectors of the middle class, and the majority of the military officer corps sought to take advantage of the possibilities of foreign investment and to contain the political power of organized labor.

In this polarized yet organizationally fragmented political arena the remnants of the party system had little relevance. The MNR, the only party that ever succeeded on a large scale in aggregating interests across regional and class lines, although still the strongest party, had been badly splintered and had lost a large share of its main base. Most of the other parties were elite cliques or spokesmen of interest groups. Under the Banzer government some moderate and conservative parties had been allowed to assemble openly and, within limits, to criticize government policies. A number of political organizations (most of them small) to the Left of the governing coalition, however, had been declared subversive.

In response to an appeal for elections from a new coalition of parties of the Center-Right, the minister of foreign affairs and worship and the minister of government asserted in March 1973 that holding elections would be a waste of time because they knew that the results would be favorable to the current government. Two months later, however, a former minister of government, Colonel Andrés Selich, was arrested on charges of conspiring to overthrow the government. His death at the hands of his interrogators, together with continuing economic problems, provoked a crisis of confidence in the government. Under such pressures, President Banzer announced in June that the process of returning the country to constitutional rule would begin in 1974 and that for this purpose "the supreme government will dictate the respective rules during coming months." Meanwhile, changes in the cabinet since April had increased the representation of the military in that body.

THE DEVELOPMENT OF POLITICAL ATTITUDES

Before the national Revolution of 1952 only a small segment of the population took an active part in political life, and only a small proportion was more than dimly aware of being a part of a nation-state. Power, political action, and even citizenship were virtually the exclusive prerogatives of the Spanish-speaking whites. Conscious of their supreme position and jealous of their power, members of this small elite consistently relegated the majority of their countrymen— Quechua- and Aymara-speaking Indians and most mestizos (persons of

230

mixed racial and cultural heritage)—to a position of subordination and political passivity. At the same time they tended to justify their dominance by depreciation of both the racial qualities and the cultural traditions of the Indians. Hence, the prerevolutionary society was not only dominated by white men; but it was also sanctioned exclusively by their attitudes, values, and ideas, drawn largely from Hispanic and Western European sources. Stressing their adherence (in theory) to liberal democratic forms and to Christianity, members of the dominant group saw themselves as the natural rulers of the country and the sole repository of national honor.

The submerged Indian and mestizo groups neither participated in political life, except at local levels, nor felt more than a tenuous bond of conationality with their fellow Bolivians. Denied an arena of political action by custom and by restrictive suffrage laws, they seldom had an occasion for expressing opinions on matters of national concern. The trappings of republican government—elections, candidates, issues, and laws—had very little meaning for them because most communication with compatriots was limited by virtue of language differences, and few ever traveled far from their homes. Also important was a tendency on the part of most Indians to withdraw from all but necessary contact with persons and institutions beyond the bounds of the community, a tendency born of an intense distrust of whites and mestizos.

For almost a century after the War of Independence (1825) few Bolivians questioned the established social order. The Spanish speakers continued almost unanimously to express their conviction of racial and cultural superiority. The Quechua and Aymara speakers, for their part, demonstrated attitudes of resignation and acceptance. Such acquiescence was not untempered by resentment, but discontent never resulted in more than local outbreaks of violence.

In the early years of the twentieth century there developed an increasing conviction in certain sectors of the Spanish-speaking group that some modification of the traditional sociopolitical system was overdue. Some, like Franz Tamayo, argued the indigenist view that the nation was being deprived of both useful citizens and a valuable cultural heritage by the oppression and subordination of the Indians. Others pointed to the country's failure to develop a sense of national unity transcending narrower regional interests and jealousies.

At the same time the hitherto quiescent Indians were subject to increasing influences from the national culture. Contact with Spanish speakers and with the cash economy in the mining centers and along the transportation routes, which were developed earlier in the century, provided many Indians with a new perspective on their position in the national society. Furthermore, the forced introduction of thousands of Quechua and Aymara speakers to the duties (and, to some extent, the rights) of Bolivian nationality through military service in the Chaco

War (1932–35) awakened a degree of political awareness that had never before existed.

The introduction of new social and political ideologies—notably fascism, in its several varieties, and Marxism—crystallized this growing discontent, and numerous parties and movements dedicated to reform grew, including the MNR. The inconsistent but revisionist regimes of David Toro, Germán Busch, and Gualberto Villarroel during the late 1930s and the 1940s were expressions of such organized dissatisfaction with the traditional system (see ch. 2).

The 1952 Revolution and the sociopolitical changes arising from it resulted from an uncoordinated ground swell of discontent felt by both a large number of Spanish speakers in the cities, especially the predominantly *cholo* (acculturated Indian or lower class mestizo) miners, and politically awakened Indians in the countryside. The former, under the banner of the MNR, deposed a conservative caretaker government, and the latter forced the beginning of land reform (see ch. 2).

Early policies and party platforms of the MNR were dedicated to the introduction of change not only in the resented socioeconomic and political order but also in basic attitudes underlying that order. Most official pronouncements and actions of party and government were directed at furthering the social integration of the Quechua- and Aymara-speaking Indians into national life and to upgrading the low esteem in which they have traditionally been held by their literate Spanish-speaking compatriots. Government propaganda consistently stressed the value and beauty of the Indian cultural traditions as an integral part of the national heritage, and official cultural agencies fostered the use of indigenous languages as a medium of literary expression.

There was also a concerted effort to develop a sense of nationalism in the traditionally isolated Indian groups not only by broadening the base of political participation but also through the use of expanded educational facilities. Much of the time and energy of rural schoolteachers, army training personnel, and similar functionaries was devoted to lectures on patriotic subjects and to extolling the hopes and accomplishments of the revolution. The MNR attempted to put forth the image of a mass party representing, as the "party of the workers, peasants and middle class," a coalition of nationwide socioeconomic interests rather than, as traditionally, merely representing the followers of personalistic or regional leaders.

The degree of success achieved in implementing these aims was by no means clear in early 1973. That some change in the attitudes underlying the traditional ethnic caste system had taken place was apparent. The newly found political and armed power of the peasants was immediately translated into a new sense of self-esteem and confidence, replacing their former stance of servility and acquiescence. That same power, wielded through the *sindicatos* (rural unions), has resulted, at least in the areas accessible to urban centers, in a degree of communication between the Indians and national institutions and in the growth of at least a nascent sense of national identity. Nevertheless, much of the old pattern of attitudes remains. Although the quality of the Quechua and Aymara speakers and the value of their cultural traditions have been officially recognized, they have not been accepted wholeheartedly by significant numbers of whites and mestizos, who tend to see the Indians as primitives. At the same time probably a majority of Indian communities continue to be socially isolated from their compatriots by linguistic barriers and age-old suspicions.

The strong persistence of traditional political forms—particularly *personalismo* (the exaggerated importance given to personalities and leader-follower relationships over issues and institutions) and regionalism—have to some extent been responsible for the failure of the MNR to institutionalize itself as a mass nationally based party. Rank-and-file loyalty continued to be focused upon leaders of urban or rural unions or of factions within a party rather than on the party itself.

In the countryside the leader of a *sindicato campesino* (peasant syndicate) or a militia force has to some extent replaced the landlord in the role of *patrón* (boss and [or] benefactor). These new *patrones* are the direct and visible sources of leadership and benefit. They are the providers of arms and the intercessors in welfare cases, and they have often influenced the local distribution of central government funds and aid.

A prime example of the reciprocity that traditionally governs interpersonal relationships is found in the obligations of *compadrazgo* (the ties that exist between the parents and godparents of a child), which finds its application also in politics (see ch. 5). The politician or union official is always eager to serve as *padrino* (godfather) to the children of supporters and thereby establish lifetime ties highly advantageous in political situations. The *padrino* takes these assumed obligations most seriously, and so strong is the tradition that any failure to observe them might well be damaging to his political future. Parents are equally eager to enter into the relationship as it is expected to provide them with a modicum of access to the powers that be.

Another historic force that continues to influence political behavior is regionalism. Some parts of the republic, separated from the capital by distance and by varying historical backgrounds and interests, developed separatist traditions, which laid the foundation for strong and sometimes violent resentment against the national government. Santa Cruz, historically restive under government from La Paz, erupted in May 1958 in a revolt, led by the FSB and backed by a multiparty committee, which was suppressed only after considerable bloodshed. Controlled politically by an affluent class of landowners and merchants whose economic interests, between the late 1950s and the late 1960s, had been increasingly linked to the investments of Bolivian Gulf Oil

Company, Santa Cruz was the center of conspiratorial designs against the nationalistic regimes of Alfredo Ovando Candia and Torres. President Banzer is a *cruceño* (native of Santa Cruz) whose government came to power through just such a conspiracy; nevertheless, rumblings of separatist sentiment continued to emanate from Santa Cruz in 1973.

The resentment of *cruceño* elites has been directed against both the peasants and the wage laborers, who profited from the revolution, but the revolutionary coalition itself has suffered cleavages with regional connotations. Political and economic competition, cultivated by faction leaders, between the strongest of the peasant *sindicatos* in the Cochabamba Valley, and the strongest of the urban labor groups—the miners on the Altiplano—often evoked regionalist sentiment.

THE MNR AND ITS OPPONENTS, 1952-64

By 1952 the leadership of the MNR, which was formed in the late 1930s by a group of intellectuals of diverse political beliefs, had coalesced around Víctor Paz Estenssoro, an economist and former cabinet minister in the Villarroel government (1943-46).

The primary units of the party were the cells, which in turn were organized into *comandos* (committees or commandos) on the departmental, provincial, and lower levels. A process of periodic elections was the formal basis for the selection of *comando* leaders. At the top of the structure was the National Political Committee (Comité Político Nacional—CPN), which directed the overall activity of the party. Although the actual assignment of leadership functions on the intermediate and lower levels was not well documented, there is reason to believe that elections among the rank and file for lesser officials were subject to review by the CPN.

Funds to support the party's apparatus and operations were derived from several sources. Dues from the membership constituted a significant part and were obligatory for government workers. Another source of party revenue was money extracted from the general funds of various ministries, a practice extremely difficult to challenge because all the ministers were Movimientistas (MNR members) and opposition representation in the legislature was small and relatively impotent.

The social and economic reforms of the first several years of MNR government so largely satisfied the demands of the Bolivian Left that the MNR drew off a high proportion of its voting strength. Consequently, formal opposition from the Left was restricted to several small parties, such as the so-called independent Marxist Party of the Revolutionary Left (Partido de la Izquierda Revolucionario—PIR) and the Revolutionary Workers Party (Partido Obrero Revolucionario—POR), a Trotskyite group divided within itself. Such groups polled extremely small returns in the elections and therefore were generally tolerated, though conflict was bitter when their activities directly collided with what the MNR saw as its vital interests.

Absorption into the MNR did not occur in the case of the rightist parties. Their appeal was to groups intensely dissatisfied with the course of the revolution and accustomed to active participation in politics. The revolutionary leadership saw potentially serious threats as originating on the Right and shaped its policies accordingly. The Bolivian Socialist Falange (Falange Socialista Boliviana—FSB) attempted several abortive coups against the MNR government and was occasionally suppressed, although it was allowed to participate in the presidential and congressional elections. The Authentic Revolutionary Party (Partido Revolucionario Auténtico—PRA), a personalistic party established in 1960, suffered the disadvantage of speaking not only for the Right but for a "heretical" Right (having been born of dissension in the MNR ranks) and was the subject of more severe measures. The church-oriented Social Christian Party (Partido Social Cristiano—PSC), more moderate than the other two and less popular, enjoyed greater toleration from the MNR.

The PIR had been active during the 1940s under the leadership of José Antonio Arze, an important figure in Marxist circles. About the same time a group of Trotskyite intellectuals formed the POR which, advocating the direct mass action principles of Trotsky, gained considerable influence among workers in the mining and industrial unions as well as in intellectual circles. Much of the membership of the PIR was absorbed by the Bolivian Communist Party (Partido Comunisto Boliviana—PCB)—the first formal Communist party in Bolivia when it was formed in 1950. During the 1950s significant numbers of individuals, who after the revolution joined the MNR, had been active in one or the other of these parties, and this later influence of the Marxists was greater than was any direct impingement of the Marxist parties on politics during the earlier periods.

In the 1960 presidential election the PCB—alone among the three recognized leftist parties—presented a slate of candidates in formal opposition to the MNR, but the PCB nominee for president was Paz. The party polled almost 11,000 votes, a drop of only 1,300 since the election of 1956, about the same proportional falloff as was experienced by the MNR.

Influenced by the political theory and program of the Spanish Falange, the FSB sought a return to the two great traditions of Bolivian history—Hispanicism and Catholicism. They saw the liberalism and egalitarianism of the French Revolution as weakening the fabric of traditional society and encouraging its disintegration into a secular and amoral modernism. For the achievement of social progress, the party advocated that the intelligent and politically conscious minority, with its superior discipline, impose order on the general community.

Founded in 1936 by Bolivian students in Santiago de Chile and consciously modeled after the Falangist Party of Spain, the FSB was strongly influenced by its leader, Oscar Unzaga de la Vega. Unzaga rejected representative institutions and democracy in general, which he castigated as "an artifice of words for the distraction of the people."

During the early 1940s the FSB collaborated with the MNR in university elections, running joint slates for student offices, and shared a common anti-United States orientation with the MNR. During the postwar period the FSB opposed the unpopular conservative governments of Enrique Hertzog, Mamerto Urriolagoitia, and the military junta that succeeded them. Hence, it was in a position after 1952 to profit from the general discredit that overtook almost all the other rightist and centrist parties that had been associated with those regimes.

After 1952 the FSB came to see the MNR more and more as the instrument of communism in Bolivian life, to be opposed by all means, including violence. In November 1953 it attempted a coup in Cochabamba, which set the pattern for the future. In the 1956 elections, inheriting the supporters of the moribund Republican Socialist Union Party (Partido Unión Republicana Socialista—PURS) and the old Liberal Party (Partido Liberal), the FSB ran Unzaga and Mario Gutiérrez Gutiérrez (foreign minister and party leader in 1973) as the only rightist slate to oppose the MNR.

Defeat and the coercive policies of the government in the election reinforced the FSB tendency to violence. In 1958 two serious coups were attempted and put down by the MNR. In April 1959 the party supported still another abortive revolt in the capital, which left Unzaga dead—murdered according to his supporters and a suicide according to the government.

The campaign of the FSB in the 1962 congressional election was extremely negative in tone and tended to dissipate the strength it had retained over the years. Instead of concentrating its fire on the MNR, the party's speakers spent much of their time assailing Wálter Guevara Arze of the PRA. Nonetheless, the FSB retained enough support to defeat the MNR in the city of Oruro, a longtime Falangist stronghold. In La Paz the vote of the FSB together with those of the PRA and the PSC exceeded the MNR's total vote.

It was inevitable that the political, social, and economic upheavals following the Revolution of 1952 should give rise to the development of deep and abiding animosities and frustrations. Those who suffered a loss of political influence, social eminence, or economic fortune believed that the revolution was leading Bolivia down a road that could end only in complete social and economic chaos. Those of Marxian persuasion who originally supported the revolution grew increasingly disenchanted with the regime because they believed that the scope of reform had been too limited and its pace too pedestrian.

Since the MNR embraced such a broad spectrum of political opinion and interests, much of the real political activity of the country between 1952 and 1964 was internalized within the party. By the early 1960s political differences within the party had been formalized in the development of three factions. The left sector led by Juan Lechín Oquendo, executive secretary since 1944 of the miners union and since 1952 of the central labor confederation, represented the more radical elements within the party and the labor movement. The Socialists, or right sector, under the leadership of Aníbal Aguilar and other prominent Movimientistas, reflected a desire to curb the power of the mining unions and also represented the regionalist sentiment in Santa Cruz. Between these two groups was the centrist faction led by Paz, who had served as president from 1952 to 1956 and from 1960 to 1964.

THE DEMISE OF THE MNR GOVERNMENT

Both the disintegration of the MNR and the resurgence of a politicized military, which together foreshadowed the coup d'etat of 1964, were well under way before the election of Paz to his third term in the presidency. The MNR had suffered internal strains from the beginning of its rule. The most serious of the many cleavages that were to come began to develop shortly after Hernán Siles Suazo was elected to the presidency in 1956. Over the vehement opposition of Lechín, powerful spokesman of organized labor, he accepted a monetary stabilization plan (upon which further aid from the United States and the International Monetary Fund was conditional) that placed the social costs of national economic recovery on labor.

The economy began to grow again after the reelection of Paz in 1960, but the foreign assistance that he considered indispensable continued to be conditioned upon acceptance of economic recovery plans that penalized labor, and Paz was under pressure to accept large-scale assistance for the reconstruction of a professional military. Confronted with a spate of strikes and demonstrations, Paz depended more and more on the use of peasant militias and the military as a counterweight to the militant miners and other sectors of urban labor.

In late 1963, alleging a communist coup plot, Paz arrested several important mine union leaders. The miners responded by taking seventeen hostages, whom they claimed they would free only if their own leaders were freed. Paz surrounded the mining complex with army and peasant militia units, and after a few days the beseiged miners capitulated. The outcome of the incident was a short-term victory for the strategy of using the military and the peasants to contain the labor Left, but it was a Pyrrhic victory in that it contributed further to the disintegration of the ruling party.

The presidential candidacy of Paz in 1960 had been launched at the expense of Wálter Guevara Arze, another of the founders of the MNR. Guevara, expelled from the party by a convention dominated by Paz, established his own center-right opposition party, the PRA. At the beginning of the 1960-64 term Vice President Lechín had been led to

237

believe that he was to be the successor to Paz. But Paz pushed through a change in the constitution allowing for a second consecutive term in the presidency. Furthermore, the prevailing image within the military and among sources of foreign assistance of Lechín as a dangerous leftist led Paz and other middle class MNR regulars to believe that his candidacy would be nonviable. Thus Paz was named the candidate for 1964, and Lechín was expelled from the MNR. Taking the important left-wing of the party with him, he established the National Leftist Revolutionary Party (Partido Revolucionario de la Izquierda Nacional—PRIN). Before the elections former president and deputy head of the party Siles Suazo returned from Spain to plead with Paz to withdraw his candidacy for the sake of party unity. His pleas rejected, Siles Suazo joined Lechín in a hunger strike to protest Paz' candidacy. Predictably, Siles Suazo, too, was expelled from the MNR and ultimately established his own party.

Although Paz' control over the core of the MNR was virtually complete, it soon became apparent that the party no longer had the power to make its nomination stick. The convention nominated for the vice-presidency Paz' choice for a running mate, Federico Fortún Sanjines. Fortún's candidacy was contested, however, by air force General René Barrientos Ortuño. After a period of confusion in which Barrientos was shot, transported to the Panama Canal Zone where he recovered rapidly, and greeted with demonstrations of his popularity in Cochabamba upon his return, Fortún abruptly withdrew his own candidacy and was replaced by Barrientos.

The elections of May 31, 1964, were boycotted by all parties except the MNR and three small captive parties established by the MNR to give the appearance of opposition. Paz was elected to a third term with 1,114,717 of the 1,297,319 votes cast. The victory, however, was not long to be savored.

The breadth and depth of the opposition to Paz—incorporating remnants of the groups dispossessed by the revolution, most of the urban middle class, students and the intelligentsia, alienated MNR factions, and the entire labor Left—was only intensified by his uncontested reelection. In the late summer and early fall of 1964 the miners initiated a series of strikes; they were reinforced by teacher strikes, and students struck in support of both groups. With the streets filled with demonstrating strikers, Paz called on the military and the peasants to restore order, but those groups proved to be unreliable pillars of support. Several of the key peasant leaders had already reached an agreement with Vice President Barrientos not to interfere with his moves when, from his political stronghold, Cochabamba, he declared himself in rebellion. On November 3, 1964, army Chief of Staff General Alfredo Ovando Candia escorted Paz to the airport and put him on a plane bound for Lima.

MILITARY RULE

On November 4, 1964, Ovando and Barrientos occupied the presidential palace and declared themselves copresidents. But as the crowd gathered outside the palace persisted in shouting their preference for Barrientos, Ovando allowed Barrientos to assume the formal title alone, while he occupied the post of commander in chief of the armed forces.

Barrientos insisted that his assumption of power was not to be regarded as a counterrevolutionary move. In fact, he pledged a restoration to "the true path" of the 1952 Revolution, from which he maintained the Paz government had grievously deviated. But he began his rule with the same ephemeral base of support—military and peasants—that had crumbled beneath Paz; furthermore, like Paz, he looked to the United States as his principal source of economic assistance and, in so doing, accepted the logic of the stabilization plan that called for the containment of the labor Left. Although many of the peasants tended to identify with Barrientos because he had an Indian mother and spoke Quechua, he was actually dependent for immediate effective support on alliances with key peasant leaders whose competition among themselves inhibited attempts to mold the peasantry into a power block. The peasants failed to constitute an effective counterweight to miners and other workers, and Barrientos was dependent almost exclusively on his military supporters for the imposition of his economic game plan.

In early 1965 the Mining Corporation of Bolivia (Corporación Minera de Bolivia—COMIBOL) was placed under the control of a military director. "Control Obrero" (workers' control), the provision of the nationalization decree empowering union leadership to veto management decisions, was nullified. Miners' pay was halved to the equivalent of about US$0.80 a day, and the COMIBOL work force was cut by 10 percent. The number of subsidized food items in company stores was also sharply reduced. When the miners responded in May 1965 by striking, the military moved into the mines and, after a violent clash, terminated the strike and disarmed the miners' militias. Leaders of the miners' unions were hustled into exile and were soon joined by leaders of other unions that protested the treatment of the miners. Lechín was among those exiled, and the Bolivian Labor Central (Central Obrera Boliviana—COB) was effectively dismantled. In September 1965 the mines were placed under permanent military occupation, and the remnants of independent labor organization in most sectors were eliminated.

Meanwhile, with an eye to legitimizing his rule through elections in 1966, Barrientos attempted to construct a new civilian political organization. The organizing cadres for the Popular Christian Movement

(Movimiento Popular Cristiano—MPC) were to be drawn from right-wing anti-Paz factions of the MNR, and their target group was to be the peasant masses. The organizing campaign was not successful, however, and the MPC remained a phantom party.

Ultimately Barrientos decided on a broad front tactic. Four small parties with nothing obvious in common—the MPC, PIR, PRA, and the Social Democratic Party—plus what the pro-Barrientos peasant leaders had designated the *bloque campesino* (peasant bloc) composed the heterogeneous Frente Barrientista (Barrientista Front). With the bulk of the peasant vote (but with relatively few city dwellers' votes), Barrientos won handily over five lesser known opponents in the presidential elections of July 3, 1966.

In order not to lose his grip on the power base he had started with, Barrientos frequently increased the salaries and perquisites of the military and continued the process of granting land titles; but most attempts to expand that base beyond its original components proved futile. Cultivation of the urban middle class was difficult as the laissez-faire drift of the Barrientos government, offering greater privileges to foreign investors, ran against the nationalistic grain, which was strong in that sector. Most labor organizations remained implacably opposed to his government, and students and teachers became increasingly alienated.

The killing of Ernesto (Che) Guevara in 1967 and the defeat of the guerrilla movement he had led might have consolidated support for Barrientos within the military, but an incident the following year aroused the ire even of a number of military officers. In August 1968 Antonio Arguedas, former minister of government and a close personal friend of Barrientos, announced that he had been an agent of the United States government and that agents of that government had penetrated all levels of the Bolivian government. The importance of the incident lay not so much in what was said (the rumor mill had been circulating the same information for a long time) as in who had said it because Arguedas had been the man in charge of the government's large-scale crackdown on labor, students, and other leftist groups. Nationalistic indignation was aroused, and a cloud of suspicion enveloped the government.

By 1969 Barrientos had dropped many of the formalities of constitutional government and was relying more and more on coercive measures to contain potential opposition. Moreover, as had not been uncommon in Bolivian political life, he was being publicly criticized by his own vice president, Luis Adolfo Siles Salines. Many Bolivians believed at that time that the tenure of Barrientos depended more on the military than on any other political base.

The tenure issue was eliminated rather than resolved when the president was killed in a helicopter crash on April 27, 1969. Ovando was in Washington at the time of the crash, and the vice president, Siles

Salines, received permission from the army high command to assume his mandate.

Elections had been scheduled for July 1970, and it appeared for a few months that Ovando might wait for an electoral mandate and assume the presidency by constitutional means. The death of Barrientos, however, initiated a great deal of political activity and maneuvering among the various political parties and forces. The fluidity of the situation became particularly apparent in July when the popular mayor of La Paz, General Armando Escobar Uría, announced his candidacy for the presidency. On September 27, 1969, however, calling for national pacification and a true nationalist political program, Ovando dismissed Siles Salines and moved into the presidential palace. He installed a new ideologically eclectic and regionally diverse civil-military cabinet, which he described as representative of the national Left, annulled the elections scheduled for 1970, and dismissed the congress. Attempting to harness the political energy contained in the issue of economic nationalism in general and anti-Americanism in particular for the provision of immediate popular support for his new government, Ovando proceeded to nationalize the Bolivian Gulf Oil Company and to nullify the Petroleum Code. He also imposed restrictions on capital movement, gave the state mining bank a monopoly over mineral exports, withdrew the army from the mining camps, and publicly criticized what he viewed as the emphasis the United States placed on military assistance as opposed to economic assistance.

In adopting this populist-nationalist stance, Ovando had rejected his own past associations and allies, who had advocated the acceptance of international economic and military assistance, gambling that sponsorship of popular measures would provide him with a new and stronger power base. But the popularity of his policies did not translate into widespread political support for his presidency. Thus, lacking organized backing from the populist-leftist-nationalistic sector, he had to turn again to those advocating international cooperation in economic and military affairs. Lechín was again exiled for several months, and a miners' hunger march in December 1969 was denounced as subversive. In February 1970 United States military assistance, which had been temporarily suspended, was reinstated, and in September 1970 an agreement in principle was reached with the Bolivian Gulf Oil Company for financial compensation (see ch. 12).

By mid-1970 failure to convert populist rhetoric into real benefits for the masses and concessions he had made to the Right had chipped away much of the diffuse popular support Ovando had originally enjoyed. Thus, he was left in the untenable position of posing as a leftist whose base of support was the predominantly rightist military. Ambivalence and a power vacuum at the highest levels of government seemed to invite conspiracy from both Right and Left.

In October the situation deteriorated. The first move against the

Ovando government came from the Right. On October 4 General Rogelio Miranda led a revolt of the La Paz garrison, forcing Ovando's resignation and claiming the presidency for himself. He was, in turn, forced by some of the more moderate conservatives among his colleagues to step down in favor of a junta. The junta had hoped to unify the armed forces, but a group of younger, more nationalistic officers under the leadership of General Juan José Torres González had different ideas. This group, with some support from students and the Bolivian Labor Central (Central Obrera Boliviana—COB) plus the armed muscle of the air force were enough to topple the junta and install Torres in power on October 7.

From the start Torres faced many of the same problems that had plagued Ovando but, having been dismissed in July as commander in chief of the armed forces, he was not associated with some of the more damaging compromises of Ovando's last months in office, and he enjoyed more organized support from the nationalistic Left. The Workers' Political Commando (Comando Político de los Trabajadores), for example, organized in October to back Torres, embraced the PRIN, the POR, the Siles Suazo splinter of the MNR, and the Moscow-oriented wing of the PCB.

This support made it possible for Torres to weather the first attempt to unseat him. He had held office only three months when it took place. Participants in the abortive coup, led by Colonel Hugo Banzer Suárez, commander of the elite Colegio Militar in La Paz, were isolated within hours as a mass demonstration by workers and students suggested that Torres' faction of the military had strong popular support. Civilian demonstrators had urged Torres to distribute arms to them as a hedge against future coup attempts by right-wing military elements, but Torres, mindful that he had no control over these groups, refused.

Torres made a serious, but ultimately futile, attempt to win the full confidence of the Left. He tolerated the organization in July 1971 of the People's Assembly. The majority of the delegates to this two-week session represented the trade unions, although peasant organizations and students were also represented and six leftist parties were allowed two delegates each. Neither the MNR, the largest political party, nor the military was represented. The assembly lacked the means to implement its program, and proposals to establish a people's militia and to reinstitute trade union control over COMIBOL, among others, served only to unite in opposition the disparate elements who saw their interests threatened by the assembly.

Even more provocative to opponents of the Torres government in general and to the military hierarchy in particular was the emergence of the Military Vanguard of the People (Vanguardia Militar del Pueblo—VMP). A manifesto published by this group in August 1971 noted that the lower ranks of the army were the proletarians in a class-stratified institution and proposed the replacement of the existing

242

hierarchy with a popular army at the service of the people. The VMP, a secret society of junior officers organized on a cellular basis, was active only in La Paz. By publicizing its intentions while lacking a firm base, the VMP merely gave premature warning to its opponents.

In deference to his civilian supporters, Torres had purged a number of right-wing officers from the military, but he was apparently unwilling or unable to allow the predominance of the military among the country's institutions to be undermined. As he wavered between the irreconcilable pressures of the military and the unions, the minimal control he had exercised over each of these groups was eroded.

Meanwhile, Banzer and his principal collaborators, exiled following the abortive coup in January, had returned surreptitiously and were being harbored by military colleagues in Santa Cruz. By August rumors had spread throughout the country that Banzer, supported by such diverse entities as Bolivian Gulf, the Brazilian government, and the FSB, was plotting a coup. The government apparently placed credence in these rumors because on August 18, 1971, Banzer and a number of his colleagues were arrested by the police in Santa Cruz. The remaining conspirators proceeded to organize a demonstration and to occupy the town square, the major radio stations, the university, and the trade union headquarters. By nightfall effective control of Santa Cruz was in the hands of the insurgents, and military garrisons all over the lowlands were declaring their support for the insurrection.

Within a couple of days the garrisons of the Altiplano were wavering in their support of the central government. Workers and students in La Paz organized a large demonstration in favor of Torres and demanded weapons to defend his government. Those supporting Torres had few weapons to distribute. Nevertheless, the violence and loss of life accompanying this change of government was greater than at any time since the 1952 Revolution. In the final confrontation only one military regiment, the Colorado regiment of La Paz, was willing to fight to preserve the government. Many workers, students, and other civilians, however, some with and some without weapons, attempted in vain to hold out against the insurgents. Street fighting in La Paz reportedly left some 200 dead and 500 to 700 wounded.

On August 21 Torres retreated to the Peruvian embassy, and Banzer emerged from imprisonment to assume the presidency. Before dawn on the morning of the following day tanks rolled through the streets of La Paz, their loudspeakers announcing that Bolivia had been saved from communism. The last of the serious fighting took place on August 23, when armored car units and air force fighter planes attacked students at the Higher University of San Andrés in La Paz. The Banzer government announced that seven students had been killed; other sources maintained that casualties were several times that number. About 300 students were arrested. All of the country's universities were closed thereafter for more than a year while faculties and student bodies were purged of opponents of the government, and a new university reform decree eliminating university autonomy was drawn up (see ch. 6).

The power base of the new government consisted of an alliance of groups drawn together for the most part by their fear of Torres' radicalism and their commitment to order, anticommunism, and private enterprise. In addition to Banzer's military allies, the major components of the Nationalist Popular Front (Frente Popular Nacionalista— FPN), as the new ruling coalition was called, were the FSB and the core of the MNR, under the leadership of Paz. Considering the family background (the landowning class of Santa Cruz) of the new president and his consistently conservative stance, the collaboration of the FSB with his government was not surprising. The involvement of the MNR has been seen in part as a consequence of the nearly total exclusion of that party from the government of Torres, particularly in its later days. Paz was invited to return from exile, but he did not assume a formal position in the government.

The two parties were allocated five ministries each, and at the departmental level one party was to nominate the prefect and the other, the mayor. The military retained the ministries of defense, government, and agriculture, and the ministries of industry and of hydrocarbons were filled with representatives of private enterprise. One of the most notable shifts in the power structure was that of regional base; almost half the cabinet members were natives of Santa Cruz.

The precariousness of the collaboration of such traditional foes as the FSB and the MNR was apparent from the start, as fistfights erupted between members of the two groups at the swearing-in ceremonies for the cabinet. Both parties suffered internal dissension as a consequence of their collaboration with each other and with the military. The MNR leaders were constrained by the military in their efforts to mobilize their traditional popular base, and the FSB had never had a mass base, so both parties were to a degree dependent on the pleasure of the military for their continued participation in government.

The new minister of government, Colonel Andrés Selich, head of the ranger unit that had been specially trained by United States military advisers to deal with guerrilla movements, launched a pacification program in which he enjoyed considerable autonomy of action. Predictably, public employees were among the first groups to be purged, both because they had served a government considered radical and because all available patronage was needed to undergird the new government. Other groups that were targets of the government ministry's campaign were labor and student leaders, worker-priests, and journalists. Within a month of the coup d'etat, for example, more than 100 journalists had vanished from their former posts.

By early 1972 the visibility of the rangers and the zeal and apparent

244

lack of discrimination with which Selich had pursued his campaign against those he considered communist subversives had provoked sharp protests from the church and appeared to have brought the shaky government coalition to the verge of disintegration. The presbyterial council of the diocese of La Paz called on the government ministry to end the repression, and the bishop of Corocoro expressed outrage over the unexplained invasion and search of his house by the police. MNR leaders in the government were antagonized by the arrests of many members of their rank-and-file; and the detention of former Vice President Nuflo Chávez Ortiz and of Paz' son, an international civil servant, aroused extreme indignation.

More importantly, the elite status and virtual autonomy of the rangers were resented by many in the upper echelons of the regular military hierarchy. The rangers were far better paid, fed, and equipped than other military units and wore a distinctive uniform. Moreover, many in the upper echelon of the regular military ranks perceived that close ties existed between Selich and the United States military assistance group. At a birthday celebration in December 1971 for a newly appointed commander in chief of the armed forces, the rangers were openly accused of being mercenaries under foreign control.

Banzer announced the dismissal of Selich that same month. Initially, Selich held out in the ministry and threatened to shoot anyone who tried to remove him. He was finally assigned to diplomatic exile in Paraguay and later was forcibly retired from the army. Nevertheless, rumors that he was plotting a coup persisted. The seriousness of such threats to the government could not be reliably ascertained. The majority of subversive plots that the government reported to have uncovered in the course of 1972, however, were attributed to leftist groups.

The semipublic bickering and dissembling within and between the parties in the governing coalition that continued throughout 1972 appeared to enhance the power of Banzer vis-à-vis the civilian leaders, but in July he acquiesced to MNR pressure and permitted the legalization of labor unions (though not of the major federations). The devaluation of the peso from about 12 to 20 to US$1 in October, however, sparked a new crisis. A general strike shut down business activity in the capital, and demonstrations resulted in clashes between strikers and police and in large-scale arrests of labor leaders. On November 23, Banzer, stating that he had uncovered a leftist plot to overthrow the government, declared a state of siege.

In December Banzer announced that his government had uncovered another massive plot, in this case to assassinate him and "vietnamize" Bolivia. The plotters were said to be components of a front group known as the Anti-Imperialist Revolutionary Front (Frente Revolucionaria Anti-imperialista—FRA). More than twenty Bolivian organizations, including virtually every party to the Left of the MNR, were listed as components. Also listed among the plotters were about a dozen leftist organizations from other parts of the hemisphere, including three composed of Chile's Mapuche Indians. The plot was said to be funded by Cuba and supported by the People's Republic of China (PRC) and the Soviet Union and to include an attack by a 7,000-man guerrilla army that was in training in Chile.

A reinvigorated campaign to round up subversives followed this announcement. By January 1973 the number of political prisoners, many of whom were held in special camps in remote areas, was estimated by some sources at more than 1,500. As had been true in several other Latin American countries, the thoroughness of the antisubversive net was such that even personal libraries of suspects were examined for literature that might be considered subversive.

It was announced in January that the coalition of the Christian Democratic Party (Partido Demócrata Cristiano—PDC), formerly the PSC, and the PRA had entered into an opposition pact with the Siles Suazo faction of the MNR, known as the Nationalist Revolutionary Movement of the Left (Movimiento Nacionalista Revolucionario de la Izquierada—MNRI). In early February the coalition appealed to the armed forces to restore constitutional order and guarantee free elections. The armed forces high command responded that "when the social and economic objectives (of the government) are achieved, the political conditions necessary to enter into an institutionalization process will be studied."

The reappearance in Bolivia of Colonel Selich in May 1973 set off a chain of events that resulted in the most severe crisis that the Banzer government had yet confronted. Suspected once again of masterminding a plot to overthrow the government, Selich was arrested on May 14. It was announced on the following day that Selich had died as a consequence of falling down a flight of stairs while attempting to escape. The original official version of the event met with considerable skepticism, and on May 18 a new official version was released. Government Minister Alfredo Arce Carpio announced at that time he had discovered that Selich had been beaten to death by overly zealous interrogators.

The announcement provoked outrage from both military and civilian sectors, and the FSB threatened to withdraw its support from the government if Arce were not removed from office. President Banzer discouraged precipitous action by his opponents by posting army vehicles and troops around the National Palace, while acquiescing to FSB demands and accepting Arce's resignation. The commander in chief of the armed forces, General Joaquim Zenteno Anaya, also resigned, claiming that Banzer's coalition was inoperative, and the president himself took charge temporarily of that vacated post. Meanwhile, President Banzer was reportedly sharing his power to a greater extent with other military officers.

POLITICAL FORCES AND INTEREST GROUPS

Peasants

The acquisition of arms, the vote, land, and organization in the course of the revolution raised the Indian peasants from a position of serfdom to one of considerable collective political power. For at least a decade their position as an internal base of support for contending political factions was rivaled only by the urban unions, predominantly the miners, and later by the reconstituted military. As a corollary of the upgraded status of this approximately 70 percent of the population, their collective designation was officially changed from the traditionally pejorative racial term *indios* (Indians) to the functional term *campesinos* (peasants or farmers) (see ch. 5).

In 1936 Indian tenant farmers who, as a consequence of the Chaco War had been uprooted and exposed to new ideas, formed the first *sindicato* in the Cliza Valley. Despite opposition from the *latifundistas* (estate owners) and, between 1947 and 1952, persecution by the government, the group survived and gradually, during the late 1940s, extended its influence through the general area of Ucureña in Cochabamba Department.

After the 1952 Revolution the countryside fell into chaos as the old socioeconomic patterns were violently changed by the then-armed and belligerent Indian population. The new MNR government, with the support of José Rojas Guevara, the leader of the Ucureña *sindicato*, set about organizing the rural population into groups similar to that of Ucureña.

The *sindicato* soon became the predominant form of social and political organization in the rural areas. Endowed with corporate personality for purposes of litigation in land transactions, it proved also to be the most effective avenue for the expression of rural initiative in pursuit of other tangible goals, such as schools, roads, and irrigation projects. Furthermore, although the newly acquired collective clout in some cases aggravated rather than mitigated the preexisting interethnic suspicions and hostilities, the *sindicatos* provided the first institutionalized links between the peasants and the mainstream of national life or, stated conversely, between the cultural elite and the vast majority of the population.

The *sindicatos* maintained their own armed militias, and while the MNR was in power there was a complex network of linkages between the *sindicatos* themselves and between the *sindicatos*, the party, and the various levels of government. In many cases *sindicato* leaders controlled local government. Leaders lacking influence at the local or departmental level often bypassed those levels and appealed directly to the central government.

In some cases the overlapping membership and leadership of *sindicato*, *comando*, and local government resulted in the rise of regional warlords whose personal control reached all three organizations but was usually most firmly based on the *sindicato*. Through energetic cultivation of local sources of power, these warlords built positions nearly independent of both the national government and the MNR. When rival *sindicato* leaders have clashed, the conflict has involved hundreds of armed men, often severely testing the power of the national government to maintain control of the situation. Nevertheless, the MNR, for about a decade, enjoyed the support of most of the competing groups and was generally able to reconcile regional differences at the national level.

Use of the *sindicatos* and their militias by MNR leaders to further party or factional policy was extensive. They were used to suppress regional and party uprisings, generally organized in Santa Cruz, as well as to quell labor strikes, particularly in the mines. Heavily armed units of miners and *campesinos* were habitually brought into the cities for demonstrations on such holidays as the April 9 anniversary of the revolution or during election time to impress potentially disloyal elements in urban centers with the power available to the MNR. They were also used more overtly at election time to stifle the appeal of the opposition parties for electoral support.

By the early 1960s the National Confederation of Rural Workers of Bolivia (Confederación Nacional de Trabajadores Campesinos de Bolivia), which linked the *sindicatos* and served as their spokesman at the national level, claimed 2 million members. But the unity and militance of the peasants as well as their dedication to the MNR and to Paz had begun to wane.

Like Paz, Barrientos cultivated the peasants as his only civilian base of support. His speeches stressed his ethnic identity with the Quechua speakers, and he accelerated the distribution of land titles. But, leaving little to chance, he intervened directly in local *sindicato* politics to eliminate those leaders whose loyalty to him was in doubt. This tactic was to some extent counterproductive as it alienated the rank and file from the leaders recognized by the Barrientos government. This was demonstrated in 1968 when the peasant leaders "chosen" to attend the First Economic Conference of the Bolivian Peasantry approved a government-proposed tax on all rural land. The formation of the Independent Peasant Block (Bloque Campesino Independiente) and the continued rumblings of discontent from the rural areas ultimately caused the government to abandon the proposal.

After Barrientos' death there was considerable upheaval in the *sindicatos* as leaders who had been ousted by Barrientos reassumed their positions. Since that time there has been little involvement of the *campesinos* in national political life. They played no notable part in the chaotic power plays in which Ovando was deposed, and Torres eventually assumed the presidency. They participated in the short-lived People's Assembly of the Torres government, but as a minority group.

Most observers believed that the political role of the peasants in the early 1970s was basically localized and defensive; that is, they could be expected to defend their land and their communities. In fact, efforts by former *latifundistas* to regain lost land have met with effective armed resistance in some areas since the Revolution of 1952. It appeared unlikely, however, that they could be easily mobilized for the pursuit of governmental or partisan goals that did not affect them directly.

Miners and Urban Lower Classes

Since 1952 miners and other more urbanized industrial workers have shared, along with the peasants, in the most dramatic growth of status and power of any group in Bolivia. The origins of this development may be traced to the turn of the century when, with the quickening pace of industrial growth in the country, an incipient working class began to emerge. In the 1920s trade unions were founded, and Marxist ideas were introduced into the country, largely through the universities. Class consciousness among workers, especially in the mines, rapidly accelerated after the Chaco War.

By 1951 the labor movement had become a major source of strength to the MNR. In April 1952 trade unions throughout the country became members of the newly created Bolivian Labor Central (Central Obrera Boliviana—COB). MNR leadership even experimented briefly with direct labor participation in the government through the system known as cogovernment (*cogobierno*), in which key positions in the cabinet, the National Assembly, and MNR's Executive Committee were assigned to members of the labor movement. This principle, however, proved unworkable in practice and was soon dropped.

In succeeding years the COB developed into an immensely powerful interest group which, if it did not control the MNR government, often held the power of veto over it. The oldest, most disciplined, and strongest of the unions in the COB was the Mine Workers Federation of Bolivia (Federación Sindical de Trabajadores Mineros de Bolivia—FSTMB), through which Lechín rose to national prominence. It had some 35,000 members in 1971. The COB also included unions representing utility workers, commercial sales personnel, bank workers, petroleum workers, printers, building-trades workers, transport workers, millers, and industrial factory workers. In addition, the *sindicatos campesinos* (peasant syndicates) were incorporated into the formal structure of the COB, although the nature of their interests and general outlook prevented them from becoming thoroughly integrated into the organization.

Very early after the revolution the COB's other constituent unions organized their own armed militias in imitation of the miners' militias. When their interests have been threatened the constituent groups of the COB have not hesitated to use this armed power either singly or in concert.

Despite the fact that it was largely through the street fighting of workers' militias that the MNR seized power, the economic gains that initially accrued to organized labor as a consequence of the revolution began to vanish after only four years of MNR rule. Since that time the use of the most effective weapon at their disposal, the actual or threatened general strike, has generally failed to achieve union goals.

Lechín's attempt to call a general strike in 1957 in opposition to the government's economic stabilization plan was frustrated when most of the unions failed to follow his leadership. When strikes have actually materialized they have often been terminated by force. Scores of miners were killed in clashes with the military while Barrientos was in power, and labor leadership was driven underground or into exile. Organized labor enjoyed a brief respite from repression under the government of Ovando and regained considerable power, approaching that of the cogovernment status it enjoyed in the early years of MNR rule, as the main civilian base of the Torres government. But the assumption of power by Banzer once again reversed this.

Lechín, executive secretary of the miners' union and of the COB, reemerged from exile in 1970 when the previously repressed trade union federations were allowed to operate freely. The movement had become atomized, however, and it was Lechín's leadership skills rather than the organizational strength of the COB that temporarily united the Left in the face of threats of rightist coups d'etat in October 1970 and January 1971. Lechín, unable to repeat that performance in the face of Banzer's second insurgency in August 1971, fled into exile, reportedly escaping from La Paz concealed in a coffin.

Labor union activity was severely restricted by the Banzer government until mid-1972. In conjunction with an apparent attempt to depoliticize the unions, all unions and labor federations—with the crucial exception of the FSTMB—were granted legal status in July. And it was suggested that a new COB might be formed provided that it confine its attention to collective bargaining.

In late November in a futile attempt to forestall a violent clash with labor over the peso devaluation that reduced workers' buying power, the government extended recognition to the FSTMB (see ch. 12). Recognition was refused, however, to the Committee for the Defense of Workers, which represented a concerted effort by twenty-four of the country's most powerful unions to negotiate an increase in wages to offset the devaluation. The impasse between the unions and the government resulted in widespread strikes in La Paz in November, accompanied by violent clashes between strikers and police and in the arrests of some eighty labor leaders.

Some groups in the urban lower classes are not associated with the trade union movement. These individuals fall primarily into one of two classes: persons with marginal socioeconomic positions, such as porters, day laborers, and medicants; and persons who are engaged in trade on a scale too small to justify their inclusion in the middle class.

The former category is found in large numbers in the shantytowns that have sprung up on the peripheries of urban communities, where the concentration of such persons with their peculiar needs has led them in some cases to establish dependency relationships with some powerful political patron and in turn to constitute class-conscious political blocs.

The Upper Class

Except in Santa Cruz Department, the political power of the landed aristocracy was broken by the 1952 Revolution. The well-to-do members of Bolivian society found themselves suddenly shorn by nationalization and land reform of the economic power that had served as the foundation of their political position. In the ensuing years exile and emigration sharply reduced their numbers in the country, and the outpouring of hostility against the old regime made the mere identification of an individual as a former *rosquero* (member of the elite class) a potential political handicap. Many of the leaders of the MNR, however, were themselves products of the upper class, and their relatives and friends were in some cases able to escape the rigors of the revolutionary process.

In spite of the loss of most of its political and economic power, the traditional upper class has managed to retain its social prestige and its identity and consciousness as a social unit. Politically, the class has usually divided its support among the parties to the Right of the MNR; the FSB and the PSC have received the strongest support. Significant numbers of younger members of the upper class, however, particularly those who have received their education since 1952, have tended to recognize the MNR's claim to have provided a more just and equitable arrangment of society. It is not uncommon to find younger members of the elite aware, in a way that was seldom encountered before 1952, of the inequities and cleavages of prerevolutionary society.

Although the political influence of the traditional upper class is negligible, the period since the revolution has seen the expansion of a group of *nuevos ricos* (new rich). This group, although it possesses significant wealth, derived in some cases from political connections or, in the case of *cruceños*, from links with foreign investors, does not enjoy the social prestige associated with the *rosca* (traditional landholding aristocracy) (see ch. 5). Although this class stands to gain from the continued expansion of the internal market, it has generally been resentful of the gains made by the lower classes as a consequence of the revolution and has been particularly unsympathetic with the demands of urban labor.

Though their political power has been most apparent in Santa Cruz, the class has been growing also in La Paz and other cities where industry and commerce have expanded. Whereas the political influence of the *rosca* was exerted almost exclusively through interpersonal channels, the *nuevos ricos* have made greater use of collective pressure.

Chambers of industry and of commerce and organizations representing small private mining firms have been particularly active.

The Middle Class

Although some MNR leaders came from the upper class, and the revolution that placed and kept the MNR in power was carried out largely by the lower classes, the MNR was basically a middle class party, and its long rule greatly expanded the opportunities for that class. The statist aspects of the revolution, which transformed the economy from feudalism to incipient capitalism, called for an expanded bureaucracy; and the patronage possibilities, in turn, strengthened the party. It was, however, a highly dependent and vulnerable class. Both the bureaucratic and the more traditional sectors of the middle class suffered from the severe inflation that afflicted the country between 1952 and 1958.

The middle class has never been cohesive politically. The FSB and the PSC probably received the support of most of the members of this group who did not affiliate themselves with the MNR. The MNR made a determined bid for the support of the middle sectors in the hope of welding as broad a progovernment coalition as possible. Its use of the slogan, "Workers, *Campesinos*, and the Middle Class," and its organization of *comandos* composed of scientists, teachers, students, and other professional elements were evidence of this campaign. Although it is difficult to assess the success of this attempt, the generally accepted estimate of a 50-percent abstention rate in the urban areas in the 1962 congressional elections suggests a significant lack of identification on the part of most middle class voters with the leadership of the MNR at that time. In the presidential election of 1966, however, the urban population generally opposed Barrientos, splitting their votes for the most part between the FSB and two MNR factions.

Students

The most active group politically in the middle class has been the students, who have traditionally shared an intense interest in politics. The major student organizations have been influenced by Marxist and Marxist-derived political thought, though other political viewpoints have been represented as well. There has been a tendency, for example, for Catholic students to support the PSC, and the student contingent of the FSB was strong throughout the country in the 1950s and remained strong in Santa Cruz in the early 1970s.

Student organizations on the university level have published newspapers, issued pronouncements on issues involving both foreign and domestic affairs, and staged demonstrations. Student strikes are serious matters and have often resulted in deaths among those involved and in the closing of universities. The university community was represented in the short-lived People's Assembly during the Torres government by groups, such as the Central Revolutionary Committee (Comité Central Revolucionario), embracing faculty and administrators as well as students.

Generally, the issues most subject to agitation among the students have involved foreign affairs. In the early 1960s students, including those affiliated with the MNR, attacked United States aid programs and the Alliance for Progress as an attempt to dominate Bolivia's internal development. In the early 1970s United States military assistance and private investment have been targets of criticism.

Student groups in the Altiplano have generally taken up the cause of urban labor when the interests of that group have been threatened. The Higher University of San Andrés in La Paz was the last focal point of violent opposition to the successful Banzer insurgency; students, therefore, have been particularly suspect and subject to repression by the Banzer government. All of the country's eight universities, which at the time of the coup d'etat had a population of about 32,500, were closed for more than a year after President Banzer assumed power. Many of the faculty members who had been teaching before the schools were closed had been imprisoned or had gone into exile (see ch. 6).

Official suspicion of students extended into secondary schools as well, which the Banzer government stated had been infiltrated by revolutionary organizations. Following the arrests in early 1973 of thirty-two teenagers on charges of subversion, the minister of government called an urgent meeting of the minister of education, the National Council for Minors, the Federation of Parents, and representatives of various church groups to discuss the country's youth problem.

The Roman Catholic Church

The political influence of the Roman Catholic Church has never been strong in Bolivia. Although the church hierarchy in prerevolutionary Bolivia had been identified with the *rosca*, the MNR did not launch any especially strong campaign against the status or position of the church. Probably the relative isolation of the church from crucial national problems and its lack of great properties had much to do with the absence of bitterness toward it after the 1952 Revolution.

The only major formal alteration in relations between church and state resulting from the revolution was the abolition, in the Constitution of 1961, of the *patronato*, an arrangement whereby the president had nominated all candidates for positions in the hierarchy of the Bolivian church. The Constitution of 1961 was abandoned in 1964, but the *patronato* was not reinstated.

Although the church has not had great influence in the political system, governments have generally sought its sanction; and the church, in turn, has sought certain favors from the government. Thus, the church has been unavoidably affected by the clashes of interests and ideologies that have swept the larger community, and this has been particularly true of the polarization that has been increasing since the mid-1960s. Polarization within the church has to some extent followed generational and regional lines, as the younger clergymen from the Altiplano tend to identify with the politically repressed and economically deprived while a small group of older ones from Santa Cruz tend to identify with the rich and powerful (see ch. 5).

A priest believed to be a supporter of Torres was shot at the time of the 1971 coup d'etat by the victorious insurgents who placed Banzer in power, and since that time the left wing of the church has been among the groups considered subversive by the government. Convents and rectories have been raided, and many priests and nuns have been imprisoned or exiled. (The Bolivian government maintains that ELN documents and weapons have been discovered in these raids.) Representatives of the right wing of the church, on the other hand, have been among the most outspoken supporters of the Banzer government.

The bishop's conference initially attempted to occupy a centrist position and was ambiguous in its statements and actions. A statement issued a month after the coup, for example, lamented the number of people who had been killed, wounded, jailed, or exiled but expressed confidence that the country was headed toward "a period of greater tranquility." In early 1973, however, the conference endorsed a document entitled "Gospel and Violence," which urged the elimination of hunger, injustice, repression, and torture and which called for recognition of the right of asylum and the right of workers to bargain for a just wage.

The Military

Historically, the army had been an institution of the greatest importance in political life, where its role, at least until 1952, had been largely directed toward the maintenance of the status quo and the oligarchy and the expansion of its own position in Bolivian society. In consequence, no other group except the *rosca* underwent such a rapid constriction of power after the 1952 Revolution.

During the twelve years immediately preceding the revolution, three of the republic's six chief executives had been military men, and the other three had had effective army support, especially against the serious rebellion engineered by the MNR in 1949. On coming to power the MNR, associating the army with the traditional order in Bolivia, consciously set out to nullify its power. Even the influence of the military group known as the Reason for the Fatherland (Razón de Patria— RADEPA), with which the MNR was allied in the early 1940s, was negligible by 1952 (see ch. 2). Apprehensive about any potential threat to its own government, the MNR moved rapidly against the army through forced retirement of about 80 percent of its commissioned and noncommissioned officers. With the sudden growth of counterbalancing forces of armed militias among the miners and the *campe-*

sinos, the army was rendered virtually impotent in the first year of the revolution. Military expenditures dropped from 23 percent of the national budget in 1952 to 6.7 percent in 1957.

On July 24, 1953, President Paz issued a decree restoring the army and at the same time launched a program to remold the military in the revolutionary image. The army's military academy was directed to adopt admission policies favoring lower class and middle class candidates, and its faculty and curriculum were changed in an effort to ensure the inculcation of the party's revolutionary principles. At the same time a supporting propaganda campaign was launched in the press. During 1953 and 1954 frequent articles appeared in *La Nación*, the MNR daily newspaper, stressing that the army should reflect the new synthesis of social forces emerging under the revolution.

In 1954 there were other signs of government resuscitation of the military. Some career officers, active in the prerevolutionary army, were reinstalled in their former positions on the basis of thorough background investigation and in consideration of their taking an oath to support the MNR. The army's participation in construction and colonization projects in various parts of the country was favorably publicized.

In general, however, the military remained quiescent until 1958 when its fortune changed rather abruptly. At that time the opposition of organized labor to the government's stabilization plan led the MNR leadership to cultivate the military as a counterpoise to the armed militias. Military expenditures rose steadily after 1958. United States military assistance was also accepted, beginning in 1958.

In the early 1960s Paz greatly increased defense expenditures and accepted a sharply increased amount of military assistance. By 1964 the defense budget had increased twelvefold over its 1956 level, and most of the twenty-three senior officers of the Bolivian army had been trained in the continental United States or at the School of the Americas in the Panama Canal Zone.

A number of officers had also been trained in other Latin American countries. With the assistance of the United States and some Latin American neighbors, the Bolivian military had developed a system of educational institutions of its own far more complex than that of most countries of similar size and level of development. Training stressed various means of maintaining internal security, including counterinsurgency and civic action rather than defense against invading forces or operations against neighboring countries (see ch. 15).

The hopes expressed by Paz and other Movimientistas in the early 1950s that selection of officer candidates from lower class backgrounds, who had been nurtured in the goals and principles of the revolutionary party, would produce an officer corps that would play a less active political role proved to have been misplaced. Both Barrientos and

Ovando, who conspired to overthrow Paz in 1964 had been officers before 1952, but both had risen to their influential positions through the military reconstituted by the MNR. The ideological orientation of Barrientos, a mestizo, was very similar to that of Banzer, a member of the upper class, whereas both Ovando, of the upper class, and Torres, a mestizo, assumed a leftist, anti-United States course in the presidency that would have been anathema to Barrientos and that was reversed by Banzer.

Ideological orientations within the officer corps (as well as calculations of expediency) have tended to correspond, at least since the mid-1960s, to the increasing polarization of the larger political community. The self-designated "leftist-nationalist" school, represented by Ovando and Torres, is the minority position among upper echelon officers but reportedly has some support among the younger lower ranked officers. Adherents of this school define the internal enemy as that sector of the population allied with foreign commerce and the external enemy as economic imperialism. They believe that the United States exaggerates the threat of international communism in order to manipulate and exploit its allies, and they view insurgency as a consequence of underdevelopment.

The ideological orientation of the majority of the commissioned officers involves advocacy of Bolivian economic growth without major structural change, and the acceptance of foreign economic and military assistance and foreign investment under specified conditions to achieve that end. They view the insurgency threat as rising primarily from an international communist conspiracy, and they favor a foreign policy alignment with the United States. Regardless of ideological orientation, historically many officers, as reflected in the number who have assumed political leadership, share the belief that the military has the responsibility and capability of overseeing the governing of the nation. This view has been attributed in part to the many years of formal education that are an integral part of the officers' career patterns and to the reputed strengths of the institution itself, such as discipline and administrative efficiency.

CHAPTER 11

FOREIGN RELATIONS

Bolivia's foreign policy alternatives have been severely limited by its geographic position—that of a landlocked state serving as a pentagonal buffer among states all but one of which are decidedly stronger economically and militarily; by its vulnerability to fluctuations in the international market for its tin; by its dependence upon external sources of capital and technology; and by its lack of internal ideological and regional cohesion.

Since gaining its independence Bolivia has been a loser in two major wars, and by 1938 it had lost territory—more than half of that which it originally claimed—to all of its contiguous neighbors. Relations with Paraguay, to which Bolivia lost a sizable chunk of wasteland in the Chaco War (1932–35), have been relatively cordial since Bolivia's Revolution of 1952, as the war and its consequences have been blamed as much on the Bolivian leaders of that era as on Paraguay. The loss of the country's coastal territory to Chile in the War of the Pacific (1879–83), however, has left strong irredentist sentiment. Relations with Chile were severed in 1962 over a dispute concerning the use of the Lauca River and have not been renewed.

Alliance with Peru in two nineteenth-century wars has not left particularly strong ties, as the two countries have generally had little to offer each other in the twentieth century. Among its neighbors Bolivia, in this century, has been most strongly linked economically to Argentina. Although there have been lingering fears of Brazilian expansionism, ties with Brazil have been increasing.

Since World War II Bolivia's relations with the United States have not been consistently cordial, but they have always been highly influential, both in the formulation of Bolivia's domestic and foreign policies and in the distribution of political power among contending groups in the national arena. United States efforts during World War II to remove from Bolivian political life persons considered to be pro-Nazi or unfriendly toward the United States generated resentment that resurfaced forcefully when one of those persons, Víctor Paz Estenssoro, emerged as head of a revolutionary government in 1952.

Nevertheless, since 1954 Bolivia has received more United States assistance per capita than any other South American country. United States assistance contributed greatly to the battle against inflation and food shortages in the 1950s and to the reconstruction of the military in the early 1960s. But the high visibility of United States officials in decisionmaking positions in Bolivia since that time has grated against nationalistic sensitivities, and the undermining of revolutionary programs and of the revolutionary coalition have been widely attributed to the conditions attached to United States assistance. As a consequence, resentment against the United States government and United States-based corporations has been such that Bolivian political figures, in or out of office, have seemingly felt that they had to choose between appealing for United States support and appealing for popular support.

The frequent changes of government since 1964 have been accompanied by some sharp reversals in foreign policies and international political alignments. The government of General Hugo Banzer Suárez, who overthrew a leftist nationalist military government in August 1971, has cultivated close ties with the United States and strongly encouraged foreign private investments. Among neighboring countries the Banzer government has drawn closer to Brazil and has displayed bellicosity toward Chile. Chile has been accused of harboring and assisting Bolivian and international groups plotting the overthrow of the Banzer government, and the Banzer government has refueled the traditional rhetorical campaign for reconquest of seacoast lost to Chile.

In early 1973 an internal committee of the foreign ministry was in the process of drafting a statute on foreign affairs that was to include a restructuring of the foreign service; the foreign service had not previously been regulated by specific provisions of law. Bolivia maintained diplomatic relations with most of the countries of Europe and the Western Hemisphere and with several nations of Africa and Asia, although it maintained only nine resident embassies outside South America. Commercial ties with the United States, Great Britain, the Federal Republic of Germany (West Germany), and Japan have been particularly important. The country is a member of the United Nations (UN), the Organization of American States (OAS), and various other global and regional organizations. Nevertheless, Bolivia remains relatively isolated from the main currents of global affairs.

HISTORICAL BACKGROUND

Although the attention of most Bolivians has been directed toward the ordering of relationships within the society, external affairs—wars with neighbors, isolation from the South American seacoasts, and the crucial importance of foreign economic relations—have been a significant part of Bolivian history since the independence established in 1825.

The formal part of Bolivian history is, to a great extent, a series of territorial disputes with neighbors. Such disputes were rooted largely in two factors. When the republics of Latin America first emerged, it was generally accepted that boundary lines would correspond to those dividing the various Spanish colonial provinces before independence. This general principle resulted in conflict, however, for the viceregal boundaries themselves had never been clearly defined. The second significant factor in the republic's troubled external relations was the uncertain balance of power that existed in the Andean region. The existence of more powerful neighbors on at least three sides made Bolivian territory a tempting target for expansionist aims.

Bolivia's closest initial relationship was with Peru, understandably enough in view of their common history under Spanish rule. Their early relations were marked by hostilities, brought to a close by a treaty of peace in 1828. Thereafter relations between the two ranged from short-lived confederation (1836-39) to open conflict.

A treaty of demarcation between Peru and Bolivia was concluded and ratified in 1902, the problem having been simplified by the intervening losses of both countries to Chile in the War of the Pacific. Later demarcations by commissions took place, and Argentina served as arbitrator in a complicated case, the resolution of which Bolivia refused to accept. Until the late 1940s the definitive settlement of some sections of the boundary between Bolivia and Peru was still pending, though the question was no longer prominent in relations between the two countries.

Problems on the Argentine frontier were rooted deep in the colonial period, when the Viceroyalty of La Plata (Argentina, Uruguay, and Paraguay) had absorbed the Audiencia of Charcas, which was later to become Bolivia. Active negotiations took place in the 1860s, and a treaty was concluded in 1889. Later clarifications and redefinitions were achieved, largely through a "definitive" treaty concluded in 1925.

The government of President Gualberto Villarroel (1943-46) was considerably influenced by Bolivian admirers of the Peronist regime and its immediate predecessors in Buenos Aires. There also had been a significant association between the early theoreticians of the Nationalist Revolutionary Movement (Movimiento Nacionalista Revolucionario—MNR) and Argentine political ideologists. This identification was probably influenced by an early attraction toward national socialism—later disclaimed—of which Argentina was then the outstanding representative in South America. Argentine hostility toward the United States at that time probably also influenced the Villarroel regime, which was the subject of an unsuccessful "quarantine" attempt on the part of the United States. A more durable factor in relations between Bolivia and its southern neighbor is a rail link constructed by Argentina under the terms of a treaty in 1941. This railroad, completed in 1962, connects Yacuiba with Santa Cruz and serves as a direct link to Buenos Aires, the Argentine terminus of the Yacuiba line (see ch. 14).

Conflict with Brazil also began in the colonial period. An early demarcation agreement between Spain and Portugal foundered on the attraction of the rubber-producing territory of Acre. In 1867 Brazil succeeded in gaining the acceptance of its incorporation of the northern half of Acre and the important outlet to the Río de la Plata (see ch. 3).

259

About 60,000 square miles of potentially valuable territory were exchanged for scarcely comparable commercial concessions on the part of Brazil. Feeling in Bolivia was strong over the cession, and the agreement has been regarded as a contributory factor in the fall of the regime of Mariano Melgarejo (see ch. 2). Both Brazilians and Bolivians sought to exploit the remaining area, and pacification attempts by both nations proved futile.

In 1903 the Bolivians, far less interested in their border territories than the Brazilians, adopted the course of least resistance and agreed to the terms of the Treaty of Petropolis. Bolivia gave up the remaining half of the Acre region—about 73,000 square miles—for an indemnification of 2 million British pounds and Brazil's undertaking to construct the Madeira-Mamoré Railway as a means of reaching the sea by way of the Amazon River. The Bolivian government had been no more able to assert its control over the Acre territory ceded in 1903 than it had been with the earlier portion; local plantation owners carried the defense of the rubber-rich area with little effective support from the government. As in the case of most of Bolivia's boundaries, work on clarifying the Brazilian border was still under way during the middle of the twentieth century.

At independence Bolivia had inherited a considerable stretch of the Pacific coastline; the colonial frontier between Chile and the Audiencia of Charcas was fixed at the Salado River, 26°10'S. The usual treaties of peace and friendship were concluded, and Bolivia's coastal rights went largely unquestioned until Chile's interests were awakened by the development of a rich export industry in nitrate deposits from the Atacama Desert and guano from the coastal islands. From the very first Bolivia was at a disadvantage because of its inability to settle and exploit the area. As a result, contractual arrangements with private companies for the exploitation of nitrates were instituted.

A treaty concluded in 1866 and revised in 1874 provided various territorial and commercial concessions to Chile. This, however, proved insufficient, and in 1879 precipitated the War of the Pacific by occupying the entire area. Bolivia, even with the aid of Peru, was able to carry on only ineffectual defense of its rights and withdrew defeated in May 1880. Peru, with a substantial interest at stake in its own coastal province of Tarapacá, fought on for three years. A truce ended hostilities in 1883 and was followed by a treaty conceding the entire Bolivian coast (as well as part of the Peruvian coast) to Chile. The agreements concluding the war were questioned, however, and it was not until 1904 that a treaty was concluded that established the broad lines of a modus vivendi. Under this arrangement the victor retained territorial possession of the mineral-rich coastal area. In return, Bolivia was offered perpetual free port rights in Antofagasta and Arica, and the Chileans agreed to build a railroad linking Arica with La Paz.

The outcome of the War of the Pacific again demonstrated the republic's inability to defend its territory. It also established the setting for the disastrous Chaco War in the next century, which was the product of Bolivia's determination to regain access to the sea, this time by means of the Paraguay-Paraná-La Plata river system.

Bolivia, defeated by Chile on the field of battle, sought redress after World War I through the League of Nations and pressed a request for renegotiation of the coastal question under the terms of Article 19 of the 1904 treaty. This approach, however, was unsuccessful; the league lacked jurisdiction in the matter.

The long and bitter background of the Chaco region dispute extended from the very beginning of Bolivian-Paraguayan relations. In a dispute stemming, again, from the old claims based on the extent of Charcas, both parties tended to be intransigent, and several treaties concluded by the governments failed subsequent ratification. Various international attempts at arbitration—by the United States and Argentina among others—also failed.

By the late 1920s the two nations were engaged in active, though intermittent, hostilities. The discovery of oil in areas adjacent to the Chaco, allied with the increasing desire of Bolivia for a maritime outlet via the Río de la Plata system, contributed to a gradual loss of restraint by both governments. Despite negotiations, increasing intemperateness on the part of the forces in the field finally led to general hostilities. The Bolivians, confident in the ability of their German-trained army and conscious of their superior resources and population, were falsely optimistic. Bolivian tactical and logistical ineffectiveness led to the advance of Paraguayan forces well into Bolivian territory.

The peace settlement in 1938 extinguished Bolivia's claim to more than 90,000 square miles of territory without any provisions for the long-sought maritime outlet. The impact of the Chaco War on internal developments was profound. The politicians had failed, the army had failed, and each blamed the other in the full view and awakening consciousness of the 200,000 survivors of the war. The resulting ferment set in motion the political and attitudinal changes that were the prelude to the Revolution of 1952 (see ch. 2; ch. 10).

Bolivian relations with the United States had been heavily influenced by the nature of their economic ties and particularly by the Bolivian opinion that these relations were basically exploitative. Nationalists contended, for example, that the Standard Oil Company of New Jersey was frustrating the development of the petroleum industry in the country by holding its Bolivian oil fields as reserves. The construction of railroads by United States and British financial interests in the early twentieth century also provided grist for the mills of nationalistic commentators.

The most direct involvement of United States business interests in the internal economics of the republic occurred in the extractive industries. The Patiño mines were incorporated in Delaware as the

Patiño Mines and Enterprises Consolidated, a United States corporation. Other industries were organized under even more evident United States auspices—for example, the American Smelting and Refining Company.

During the 1920s, when official United States diplomacy in Latin America was devoted mainly to protecting its citizens' business interests, United States banking institutions also came into unusual prominence in Bolivian internal affairs. Loans to the Bolivian government were conditioned on its acceptance of the authority of the Permanent Fiscal Commission, an entity controlled by New York financial interests, to collect Bolivian taxes for a period of twenty-five years. Thus, one representative of United States banking interests functioned during the 1920s as director general of Bolivian customs, and still another functioned as head of the Permanent Fiscal Commission and as a director of the National Bank of Bolivia. A general perception of the United States economic presence in the country as allied with the exploitative internal elite further reinforced negative attitudes toward the larger country.

United States-Bolivian relations were not highly developed on the political level, but contacts were present. United States recognition came early, as it did to all the Latin American republics, but involvement in the nineteenth century and the early part of the twentieth was not great. Bolivia was integrated into the inter-American system under the aegis of the United States, which participated in several attempts at arbitration over Bolivian boundaries.

Insensitivity to Bolivian feelings, exemplified by the publicized remark of a former United States diplomat in Bolivia that "a bluff at the use of force was the only way to deal with these people" created ill will. Stimulated by the cynicism Latin Americans felt toward United States interests in general, Bolivians reacted suspiciously to the proposal of Secretary of State Frank B. Kellogg in 1926 that the Tacna-Arica issue be resolved by the transfer of part of the area to Bolivia. Even the prospect of reacquiring the much-desired marine outlet did not allay nationalist suspicions; the motivation behind this suggestion was alleged to be a desire to remove Bolivia from her isolation and thus expose the country to greater United States influence.

Later United States involvement in attempts to arbitrate the Chaco dispute under neutral inter-American auspices further precipitated Bolivian resentment when the ultimately fixed boundary line seemed disadvantageous to Bolivia's interests. Another important factor in hostility was the seeming association of the United States with elitist governments on important policy questions. Thus, the government of Enrique Peñaranda installed in 1940 and heavily dominated by the conservative mining interests, vigorously supported the United States lead against the Axis, promptly breaking diplomatic relations and becoming one of the first countries in the area to associate itself formally with the UN. Moves were also made during this period to compensate United States oil interests expropriated by the government of David Toro in 1937.

Reciprocal support of the interests of the oligarchy appeared forthcoming in the upward adjustments in prices paid for tin by the United States, in reality a largely fortuitous matter created by the wartime shortages of that period. United States refusal to recognize the heavy-handed but revisionist Villarroel government until June 1944, after it had purged itself of Paz and other MNR figures, tended to confirm United States support of the domestic status quo in the minds of many Bolivians. The advent to power of the MNR in 1952, its expropriation of large mining firms involving United States interests, and the unrelated but important decrease in United States need for tin all posed problems in the 1950s. The mutual interest of the two countries in avoiding chaos in Bolivian national life, however, provided grounds for close economic cooperation and amicable political relations during most of the dozen years of MNR rule.

RELATIONS WITH NEIGHBORING COUNTRIES

Among the main factors influencing Bolivia's relations with its neighbors since the mid-twentieth century have been lingering irredentism and other problems relating to boundaries, ideological alignments on regional or international issues, and economic concerns. Overlapping among these factors has at times exacerbated and at times mitigated preexisting frictions in bilateral relations.

Bolivia's desire for an outlet to the sea remains a significant issue in relations with its immediate neighbors. This goal is expressed in various ways in the pronouncements and policies of the republic, as well as in more or less spontaneous popular demonstrations and regular events, such as the annual March to the Sea (Marcha al Mar), which began in 1961. Observers have noted that Bolivian heads-of-state tend to be particularly effusive in their quest for the recovery of territory lost to Chile when they are facing strong opposition in the domestic political arena.

Apart from, but intensified by, the persistent irredentist claims, the most contentious issue in recent years in Bolivian-Chilean relations has concerned Chile's Lauca River development project. In the face of Bolivia's insistence (since 1939) on the mutual use of the river, which rises in Chile and flows into Bolivia, Chile undertook preparations in the fall of 1961 for a unilaterally developed hydroelectric project involving the Lauca River in its Azapa Valley. Diplomatic exchanges took place in November and December, followed by the unanimous adoption by the Bolivian Chamber of Deputies of a resolution condemning its neighbor for "geographic aggression and territorial usurpation." Against this background of antagonism severe anti-Chilean rioting, led mainly by students, broke out in La Paz early in 1962, and diplomatic relations were severed on April 16. Later, the matter was submitted by Bolivia to the OAS council. Following the OAS passage of a resolution appealing to both governments for peaceful settlement, Bolivia proposed mediation by other Latin American governments. After the rejection of this proposal by Chile, Bolivia appealed once again to the OAS.

Increasingly disturbed by the regional organization's inability to force Chile to suspend its action in the area, Bolivia announced in protest on September 3, 1962, that it was suspending "its participation in the OAS council and all of the organizations of the system." The note declaring the move expressed Bolivia's hope that its empty seat would "remind the nations of the continent that she continues to wait a just solution" of the Lauca River issue. This withdrawal from political and administrative activities of the regional organization was ended in December 1964.

The Lauca River dispute remained unsettled in early 1973, and diplomatic relations had not been renewed. Appeals to international forums in the late 1960s and early 1970s, however, generally focused on the larger issue of the country's landlocked status. President René Barrientos Ortuño boycotted the April 1967 meeting of American chiefs-of-state in Punta del Este, Uruguay, because the issue was not included on the conference agenda, and Bolivian diplomats utilized the March 1973 meeting of the UN Security Council in Panama as a forum for reiterating the country's grievance.

Conditions surrounding the use by Bolivia of free port facilities in Chilean ports were the subject of ongoing negotiations in 1973 through the Chilean-Bolivian commission on railroad and port traffic matters. Bolivia, however, has not been satisfied with the results of these negotiations and has taken steps to shift its cargo and mineral exports to Peruvian ports. Bolivia's foreign minister announced in March that resumption of diplomatic relations with Chile was conditional upon revision of the 1904 treaty that ended the War of the Pacific. There had been a great deal of posturing in official and unofficial circles about recovery of the lost territory by 1979, the centennial of that war. The goal had been expressed in virtually all speeches commemorating national heroes and events. Newspapers carried full-page advertisements about the anticipated expansion to the coast, and there was even a locally produced brand of cigarettes called Pacífico.

An agreement between Bolivia and Brazil in the early 1960s, establishing a Bolivian port on the Paraguay River, gave Bolivia an outlet to the Atlantic and improved relations between the two countries. Mindful of Brazil's early acquisition of the rubber-rich Acre region, however, many Bolivians have been disturbed by indications of Brazil's continuing interest in the oil reserves of eastern Bolivia. More recently, Brazilian newspaper reports of the extensive settlement of Brazilians along the Abuná River valley in the Bolivian department of Pando, including the estimation that in 1973 there were more Brazilians than Bolivians living in Pando, aroused a furor in Bolivia (see ch. 3).

Initially moved by the nineteenth-century dispute with Chile, Bolivia has increasingly turned toward more intimate relations with Argentina than with any of its other neighbors. A growing dependence on Argentine wheat and a general attraction to Argentina's dynamic industrialization reinforce the trend. Several loan and trade agreements between the two countries since the Chaco War have promoted the development of highway, railroad, and pipeline links. In 1963 Argentina offered Bolivia a free shipping zone from Barranqueras on the Paraná River, and in 1969 Argentina guaranteed the financing of a crucial pipeline.

Recognition of the principle of condominium over the waters of Lake Titicaca by the presidents of Bolivia and Peru in 1955 resolved the only significant boundary demarcation issue between those countries. As was true of Bolivia's relations with all contiguous states, contraband trade across the border was a problem. There was a large influx of smuggled manufactured goods, particularly textiles produced cheaply and in large quantities by Peruvian industry, across the northwestern border.

Ideological alignments, reflecting the political bases of incumbent governments, have most consistently found expression in multilateral forums, but they have been consequential in bilateral relations as well. Furthermore, such alignments among opposition groups or between an opposition group in one country and the governing elites in another have helped to shape both domestic and international politics. The protection and support afforded Paz, for example, during his exile in Buenos Aires were indicative of a political configuration that extended back to the original affinity between the military forerunners of the MNR and their colleagues in Argentina; the hospitality Paz enjoyed in Buenos Aires was, in turn, reflected in Bolivian-Argentine relations after the Bolivian revolution when Paz became president.

Alignments in the late 1950s and early 1960s related, to some extent, to the issue of representative versus authoritarian government; but, more important, ideological alignments have increasingly been based upon differing conceptual frameworks for the assessment of national interests. In simplified form one framework consists of a North-South confrontation, in which the interests of the rich nations (North) are seen to be at odds with those of the poor nations (South). The other framework postulates the East-West confrontation, in which the capitalist nations (West) are pitted against the socialist nations (East).

In Bolivia's neighborhood the assumption of an East-West confrontation has found expression in acceptance of the leadership of the United States in the formulation of foreign and, in some cases, domestic policy, whereas assumption of a North-South confrontation has been expressed in attempts to diminish economic dependence on, and political conformity with, the United States and to demonstrate solidarity with other developing countries. In the early 1960s the governments of Paz in Bolivia, Arturo Frondizi in Argentina, and João Goulart in Brazil engaged in consultation on means of evolving foreign policies less consistent with those of the United States. After military coups in Brazil and Bolivia in 1964 and in Argentina in 1962 and again in 1966, the civilian governments in each of these countries had been replaced by military governments that favored, as did the government of Paraguay, intimate relations with the United States. Cooperation was particularly marked in counterinsurgency operations. The Argentine government, for example, provided limited military equipment and other types of assistance to the Barrientos government in 1967 for its campaign against the guerrilla movement led by Ernesto (Che) Guevara, and Paraguay increased its vigilance in the Chaco area in cooperation with Bolivian authorities.

General Alfredo Ovando Candia, who assumed control of the Bolivian government in 1969, revised the country's foreign policy and drew closer to the governments of Peru and Chile, which were attempting to resist United States influence on their domestic and foreign policies. Aware of the popular support the new military government in Peru had acquired in 1968 by nationalizing the International Petroleum Company (an affiliate of Standard Oil of New Jersey), Ovando proceeded to nationalize the Bolivian Gulf Oil Company and to declare: "Our revolution is the same as Peru's." Ovando's government had also been encouraged by the chileanization of the United States-owned copper companies, and Chile responded favorably to the nationalization of Bolivian Gulf.

The alignment with Peru and Chile was continued by the government of General Juan José Torres González, which assumed power in October 1970, and relations with Bolivia's neighbors to the east, particularly Brazil, deteriorated. Many Bolivians have expressed concern that the coalition that toppled Torres and placed Banzer in the presidency in August 1971 has become highly receptive to Brazilian influence. The Brazilian government extended immediate recognition and economic assistance to the new Banzer government and, despite expressions of alarm from both right- and left-wing parties in Bolivia that Brazil was encroaching on Bolivian territory, governmental relations between the two countries remained extremely cordial. In early 1973 the Bolivian foreign ministry published details of a border revision, whereby Bolivia was to lose fifty square miles of Santa Cruz Department to Brazil.

Relations with Paraguay and Argentina were also improved, although the election in March 1973 of a Peronist to take over control of the Argentine government from the military had caused some uneasiness in Bolivian official circles, especially since some Bolivian exiles have taken refuge there. Meanwhile, relations with Chile had seriously deteriorated, as many political exiles from Bolivia had taken refuge there, and the Banzer government had accused Chile of complicity in innumerable plots to overthrow it. There was also an intensification, encouraged by the government, of irredentist sentiment regarding the seacoast lost to Chile.

Ideological shifts, however, have had little influence on Bolivia's role in regional economic cooperation. The country's position vis-à-vis the various regional groupings has been conditioned primarily by the fact that its level of industrialization is considerably lower than that of most of its neighbors. Except for gas and petroleum, Bolivia produces few items of interest to its neighbors, and with its small domestic market it has naturally wanted to protect nascent national industries from competitive imports.

Bolivia finally joined the Latin American Free Trade Association (LAFTA) in 1967, when the ten states that had joined since its founding in 1960 agreed to grant Bolivia special status as a "relatively under-developed" country, a designation that entitled the country to certain tariff concessions. The association did not prove particularly advantageous to Bolivia, however, and Bolivia, Uruguay, and Paraguay formed a bloc within it to oppose the discriminatory practices of the larger nations (see ch. 14).

Still interested in participating in a group in which the country would not be overwhelmed by the relatively highly developed economies of Argentina, Brazil, and Mexico, Bolivia—after some three years of negotiation—joined Chile, Colombia, Ecuador, and Peru in 1969 in signing the Andean Subregional Economic Integration Agreement. Already commonly known as the Andean Common Market, the group aspires to actual common market status by 1980. Venezuela adhered to the agreement in early 1973. President Banzer has strongly criticized some aspects of the pact, especially the conditions it places on foreign investment, but he has not indicated any intention of withdrawing the country from it.

Another regional venture into which the country entered in 1969 was a treaty providing for the joint development of the River Plate Basin. The other parties to the treaty are Brazil, Paraguay, Uruguay, and Argentina.

RELATIONS WITH THE UNITED STATES

The advent of the MNR to power in 1952 enormously complicated United States-Bolivian relations. Associating the United States with the foreign capital at whose hands Bolivia's resources had been exploited and recalling the role allegedly played by the United States in ousting Paz from the earlier Villarroel government, MNR leaders were initially antagonistic to the larger country. A large element of United States opinion, on the other hand, viewed with disfavor the uncompensated expropriation of the large mining companies in which United

States investors had a considerable interest. In the light of this background, the paradox of Bolivian-United States relations is that the United States government came to be the main source of economic assistance to the revolutionary government.

The evolution of a modus vivendi that both governments would find acceptable was not easy. The United States maintained that, with a large emergency stockpile of tin and with its Texas City smelter operating at a loss, it was no longer as intensely interested in Bolivian tin as it had been for reasons unconnected with the revolution. Nonetheless, much of Bolivian opinion—official and nonofficial—interpreted the closing of the Texas facility, the nonrenewal of contracts, and the general reluctance to support what the United States considered an inflated international price level for tin as retaliation for the MNR's seizure of the large mining companies and as indicative of general hostility toward the spirit and objectives of the revolution.

The United States decided that the importance of reestablishing viable relations superseded any ultimate assessment that it might make of the MNR government. Milton Eisenhower, the brother of the United States president, who had visited Bolivia in 1953, prompted the expansion of the small technical assistance program that was begun in 1942 to a massive program in 1954. The initial assistance consisted primarily of budgetary support and surplus agricultural commodities. Police training and military assistance were added in 1957 and 1958. After 1963 budgetary support was reduced, and funds for economic development projects were increased. Total assistance from 1953 through 1964 amounted to about US$387 million.

This arrangement proved beneficial to some elements of both United States and Bolivian society but not, in the long run, to the MNR. Assistance both from the United States and from the international lending agencies was conditioned upon the acceptance of an economic stabilization plan that aroused the wrath of labor; this forced an end to the worker-middle class alliance, driving most of organized labor out of the governing party (see ch. 10). Acceptance of the aid program, with its requirement of a severely orthodox monetary policy, meant a retrenchment on some of the social welfare legislation to which the party had been committed; it also meant the opening up of Bolivia's oil fields to United States companies for the first time since 1938 and the reconstitution of a powerful military establishment, trained and equipped by the United States to guarantee order.

In retrospect Hernán Siles Suazo, president from 1956 to 1960, noted that the aid and stabilization plan that the United States had given him had not been an unmixed blessing. And even though Paz had been led to believe by the United States aid mission that aid would be cut off if he failed to run for a second consecutive term in 1964, allowing the radical wing of the party to succeed him, he later expressed the belief that a United States military attaché had been involved in the conspiracy that deposed him a few months after the election. The United States, however, denied any involvement in the event.

Relations between the United States and Bolivia were very cordial during the government of Barrientos (1964-69), who replaced Paz in the presidency. Both military and economic assistance continued to be substantial, especially in 1967 when the Bolivian government was combating the guerrilla movement led by Che Guevara, and United States private investments increased. Relations began to deteriorate, however, with the advent of the government of Ovando (1969-70), and the United States Department of State viewed the trend under the government of Torres (1970-71) as one of "increasing hostility toward the United States."

Ovando publicly expressed his resentment of what he considered the emphasis in United States policy on military assistance over assistance for economic and social development. (His government continued, nevertheless, to receive military assistance.) His nationalization of Bolivian Gulf was also a source of friction between the two countries.

Under the Torres government Bolivia nationalized a United States-owned secondary tin-processing mill known as the International Metal Processing Corporation and the Matilde Mine, owned by United States Steel Corporation and Engelhard Minerals and Chemicals Corporation. In April 1971 the United States-Bolivian Binational Center in La Paz was seized by students, and in May the Peace Corps program was terminated at the request of the Torres government.

With Banzer's assumption of power, relations between the two countries once again became cordial. The United States agreed to provide US$14 million (US$2 million in grants and a US$12 million loan) to Bolivia in special emergency assistance immediately after the coup in August, and in November an additional loan of US$8 million for agricultural development was extended. By June 1973 US$20 million more had been lent for what was described as the "emergency plan" or the "takeoff toward development program." These loans and grants were in addition to the regular aid programs.

The Banzer government enunciated a new policy to encourage private investment. A special investment code was promulgated as well as a hydrocarbons law designed to attract foreign capital for service contract arrangements in the petroleum industry, and the government moved to settle outstanding claims resulting from the expropriation actions of previous administrations. The government, for example, borrowed sufficient funds to pay the owners of the Matilde Mine the amount of their investment in cash. The United States Department of State noted in December 1972 that the Banzer government had emphasized the friendly ties existing between Bolivia and the United States, had stated that it would not tolerate subversive activities, and had particularly pursued the energetic campaign against the guerrilla movement that grew out of Che Guevara's abortive campaign in 1967.

The United States is Bolivia's major trading partner, accounting for about 35 to 38 percent of both its imports and its exports. From fiscal 1946 through 1971 United States economic aid, encompassing loans, grants, and technical assistance, totaled about US$560 million. Military assistance from fiscal 1958 through 1971 amounted to US$25.3 million.

EXTRAHEMISPHERIC RELATIONS

Relatively isolated throughout the nineteenth century and the first half of the twentieth, Bolivia had few important contacts beyond the Western Hemisphere, and the contacts that did take place were not necessarily fruitful. After a British envoy was subjected to a particularly crude indignity by the government of Melgarejo in the 1860s, Queen Victoria ordered the British navy to shell La Paz. Informed that that was not feasible, she literally crossed Bolivia off her map and officially declared that the country did not exist.

Germany played an important role in the training of the Bolivian military during the 1920s, a factor that contributed to Bolivia's willingness to go to war with Paraguay over territorial disputes in the Chaco. In spite of the defeat of the German-trained army, German influence continued strong in the 1930s.

It was not until after the Revolution of 1952 that Bolivia's leaders embarked upon a determined effort to expand the country's global contacts. By the early 1960s Bolivian attitudes and policies in the world arena were oriented toward achieving a wider measure of independence in foreign policy. Politically, this has been sought through increased contact and the beginning of not wholly clear, but nonetheless real, identification with the neutral powers of Africa and Asia and increased but restrained contact with the Soviet-bloc countries. Economically, the same end has been sought by the development of greater self-sufficiency, particularly in the foodstuffs that Bolivia has long imported, as well as by the diversification of Bolivia's industrial and extractive production to end its once critical dependence on world tin markets (see ch. 14).

In 1961 the Paz government issued invitations to President Tito of Yugoslavia and President Sukarno of Indonesia to visit Bolivia. Its relations with the United Arab Republic (UAR) moved toward greater intimacy with the announcement in January 1962 that technical specialists would assist Bolivia in mining, petroleum, and railroad development as part of a technical aid program. (The program, however, never actually materialized.) Later that year the diplomatic missions of both countries were raised to embassy status.

Even more concrete signs of a trend toward nonalignment appeared in late 1961 and in 1962. Bolivia sent an observer delegation—the only Latin American country other than Brazil to be so represented—to the Belgrade conference of neutral states in the fall of 1961. Bolivia then joined Cuba, Mexico, and Brazil in sending a fully accredited delegation to the Cairo international economic conference of nonaligned nations in July 1962.

There were also new contacts with the Soviet Union and Eastern Europe. At the UN General Assembly session of September 1960, Premier Nikita Khrushchev of the Soviet Union offered a substantial line of credit to assist the mining and oil industries. Shortly thereafter there were reports of an offer by Czechoslovakia to underwrite the construction of a smelter for processing the country's rich and relatively unexploited deposits of antimony: in 1962 a contract between Czechoslovakia and Bolivia was successfully negotiated. (The smelter was still under construction in 1973.) These offers of economic assistance came against a background of exchange visits of parliamentarians, students, and trade union leaders that established unprecedented contacts between Eastern Europe and Bolivia.

There were few Bolivian initiatives in contacts beyond the Western Hemisphere between November 1964 and September 1969. President Ovando, who assumed power in September of 1969, asserted that "we hope to have friendly relations with all countries . . . providing they respect our sovereignty." Although Bolivia had recognized the Soviet government since 1945, the two countries did not agree to exchange ambassadors until September 1969. In mid-1970 technical and scientific agreements were reached, and arrangements were made for the sale of Bolivian tin to the Soviet Union. Also in 1970 Bolivia and Poland reestablished diplomatic relations, severed since 1939, and Bolivia and Hungary agreed to raise the rank of their diplomatic representation to ambassadorial level. The country reasserted its common interests with other developing countries by sending observer delegates to the consultative conference on nonaligned nations in Belgrade in 1969.

Since the advent of the Banzer government, relations have been particularly strengthened with the Republic of China (Nationalist China), the Republic of Korea (South Korea), the Philippines, Spain, Israel, and the Khmer Republic (Cambodia). Relations with the Soviet Union have cooled. Tentative plans for visits by the Bolshoi Ballet and other musical groups were canceled following Banzer's assumption of power, although a limited economic assistance program and a scholarship and educational exchange program remain in effect.

In early 1972 the Bolivian foreign ministry announced that the government was expelling a large number of Soviet diplomats. After several weeks of argument between the ministry and the Soviet embassy as to how many Soviet diplomats were actually in the country, the Bolivian foreign ministry concluded that there were sixty-two and that forty-nine of them were to be repatriated. Approximately forty Soviet citizens had left by the end of April 1972.

Aside from the United States, Bolivia's most important economic relations in recent years have been with Great Britain, West Germany, France, and Japan. Great Britain is the principal purchaser of Bolivian tin. Bolivia imports large quantities of manufactured goods from Western Europe, especially Great Britain and West Germany. The country has also received substantial loans and technical assistance from Great Britain, West Germany, and France. Japan's share of Bolivia's imports, especially in electrical equipment, has been steadily increasing (see ch. 14).

Though still small in proportion to the overall volume of the country's foreign trade, trade with the Eastern European countries was also increasing. By 1973 Bolivia was maintaining diplomatic relations with all of the Eastern European countries except Albania and the German Democratic Republic (East Germany).

INTERNATIONAL ORGANIZATIONS AND COMMITMENTS

Western Hemisphere Affairs

Bolivia is a member of the OAS and of the Inter-American Development Bank (IDB). It is a party to the Inter-American Treaty of Reciprocal Assistance (1947, better known as the Rio Treaty), providing for collective defense against attack from within or beyond the hemisphere, and the Latin American Nuclear Free Zone Treaty (1967).

Most of the variation in Bolivia's votes in the OAS has been in matters relating to security and has been attributable to shifts in the country's domestic power configuration. The MNR government, though highly dependent upon the United States for economic assistance, attempted to resist United States pressures in the formulation of its foreign policies and, representing itself as a revolutionary government, expressed sympathy with revolutionary movements elsewhere. Thus, along with Mexico, Argentina, Brazil, Chile, and Ecuador, Bolivia refused to vote in favor of disassociating the Cuban government from the OAS at the meeting of foreign ministers in Punta del Este in January 1962. The final act adopted by that meeting provided for the establishment of the Special Consultative Committee on Security Against the Subversive Action of International Communism. Only Bolivia, still smarting from its experience with the Emergency Advisory Committee for Political Defense during World War II, abstained from approving its creation.

When the Cuban missile crisis occurred in October 1962, Bolivia joined the other Latin American states in the unanimous adoption of a resolution sanctioning, in effect, the quarantine of shipments to Cuba that had been imposed by the United States. Along with Mexico and Brazil, however, it qualified its adherence to the resolution with the assertion that it would not support armed invasion of Cuba.

By the time of the ninth meeting of foreign ministers in July 1964 the MNR had virtually disintegrated, and President Paz was left highly dependent upon the military for the retention of his office. At that meeting Bolivia refused to join the majority in adopting stringent diplomatic and economic sanctions against Cuba. Paz lost his office a few months later to a strongly pro-United States military government; and after the military intervention of the United States in the Dominican Republic in April 1965, Bolivia voted in the OAS council in favor of the highly controversial resolution creating the Inter-American Peace Force to assist the United States troops there.

Along with most of the other Latin American countries, Bolivia opposed the creation of a permanent inter-American force along the lines of the temporary one. But in 1967 Bolivia's foreign minister, after presenting to the twelfth meeting of foreign ministers evidence of Che Guevara's leadership of a guerrilla movement in Bolivia, called for new regional measures to combat subversion supported by Cuba.

A general revision of security policy and, in particular, a rejection of the hard line against alleged insurgents that characterized the leftist nationalist governments of Ovando and Torres was reflected in the country's position at a special session of the OAS in January and February 1971. A resolution providing that persons accused of kidnapping or otherwise assaulting diplomats must be extradited or brought to trial by the country in which they were apprehended was passed; but, objecting to any such limitation on the right of granting political asylum, Chile opposed, and Peru and Bolivia abstained.

The switch once again, under the Banzer government, to a staunchly pro-United States and anticommunist position was manifest in the country's policy toward Cuba. Although a few Latin American states had proceeded to reestablish diplomatic and (or) commercial relations with Cuba and several others had announced intentions of doing so, President Banzer had declared that Bolivia opposed the lifting of the OAS sanctions. The general agreement with the United States on the security issue, however, did not necessarily extend into economic issues. At a meeting of the General Assembly of the OAS in Washington in April 1973, Bolivia joined Peru in sponsoring a resolution expressing concern over the United States decision to sell part of its stockpiles of strategic minerals. The resolution passed overwhelmingly.

Global Affairs

Bolivia is a charter member of the UN and has been duly represented in the important councils of that body. It was, for example, a member of the UN Trusteeship Council in 1961 and 1962 and of the Security Council in 1964 and 1965. In the various forums of the UN, Bolivia has frequently reiterated its need for an outlet to the sea and has consistently expressed its advocacy of the principles of pacific settlement of disputes, the inviolability of territorial integrity, and the nonrecognition of territorial rights gained through conquest. Its representatives have also spoken out forcefully from time to time in favor of international cooperation toward the economic development of poor countries and against colonialism and racial discrimination.

Bolivia is also a member of many of the UN's affiliated agencies and of the International Monetary Fund (IMF) and the International Bank for Reconstruction and Development (IBRD—commonly known as the World Bank). Between 1946 and 1971 the IDB, the IBRD, the UN, and other international organizations have provided Bolivia loans and grants amounting to about US$150 million. In the process these organizations, and particularly the IMF, have influenced the country's policies in regard to combating inflation. The country was also a member of the so-called Group of 77 (by 1973 the group actually had ninety-five members) developing countries, which met periodically to attempt to reach agreements on strategies for gaining concessions from the developed countries through the United Nations Conference on Trade and Development.

SECTION III. ECONOMIC

CHAPTER 12

CHARACTER AND STRUCTURE OF THE ECONOMY

Few nations of Latin America have been endowed with as much natural wealth as has Bolivia; yet it is one of the least developed countries in South America. Tin, zinc, antimony, tungsten, lead, copper, and a variety of other valuable minerals occur in large quantities in the highlands, although the quality of the tin ore has been declining; and petroleum and natural gas resources are sufficiently plentiful in the lowlands, although petroleum exploration needs to be increased. Fertile valleys and wide lowland plains provide good soil and climate for many crops; and even the highlands produce large quantities of certain foods. Two-fifths of the country is covered with stands of valuable timber; there are extensive pastures for cattle in the lowlands and valleys and for sheep and llamas in the highlands. Rivers and lakes provide ample quantities of fish and offer a vast hydroelectric potential (see ch. 3).

The great majority of the population, however, is engaged in low-productivity traditional agriculture. Manufacturing is in a rudimentary state, and only a small fraction of the labor force is employed in producing commodities for export, such as mine products and petroleum (see ch. 3). Mining, however, is the second largest employment sector. Development had been hindered by geographic isolation, regional disparities, political instability and, until 1952, rigid social stratification. The 1952 Revolution changed the historic sociopolitical order, and succeeding institutional change accomplished some degree of wealth redistribution (see ch. 2). Nevertheless, the problems of poverty and underemployment persisted in 1973, and living standards of the majority of the population were still low (see ch. 7).

In the early 1960s the country appeared to be embarked upon a period of consolidation after nearly a decade of disorderly postrevolutionary economic experiments and inflationary pressures. Economic growth was rapid until the 1969-71 period, when there was a resurgence of political instability, a loss of confidence in the economy by the private sector, and a deterioration in government finances. In late 1972 the government of President Hugo Banzer Suárez was forced to devalue the currency and initiate an austerity stabilization program designed to restore equilibrium in the economy. International lending agencies had confidence in the stabilization program, and a number of loans were under negotiation to help support the program.

NATIONAL ACCOUNTS

Users of Bolivian statistics, including Bolivian economists, are often not aware of the fragility of most of the data used in compiling the national accounts and other statistical series. Production and income data before 1950 are found only in scattered form and are difficult to use for purposes of comparison. Statistics compiled since 1950 are frequently inconsistent and are often presented in different units of measurement. Figures related to agriculture are recognized by some outside economists as being the least dependable. All agricultural data are based upon a partially completed survey carried out in 1958 in half of the provinces in seven of the nine departments. Estimates are made of agricultural production consumed by the producers themselves, and an arbitrary percentage is then used to convert production into value. The formula used has not been altered since 1958, and no one in the Ministry of Agriculture in the early 1970s appeared to know why it was devised. Further, the economists in the Ministry of Planning and Coordination utilize their own set of agricultural statistics.

Manufacturing data also suffer; data for all industry are estimated on the basis of a 1958 survey of small-scale industry. Many industrial firms are known to submit false production data, and some do not submit any data at all. Data on commercial activities are also poor. Most commercial data are estimated because there has never been any regular method of reporting commercial statistics. Urban construction statistics are considered fairly accurate, but little rural construction is ever reflected in the national accounts. Data on mineral and petroleum production are reasonably accurate, and statistics for the other economic sectors are also fairly reliable.

According to one set of statistics, the gross national product (GNP) was the equivalent of US$916 million in 1971, and the per capita GNP in that year was US$203. Another set of statistics for 1971 indicated a GNP of US$1.1 billion and per capita income of US$180. The gross domestic product (GDP) was estimated in 1972 at $b14.2 billion (for value of the Bolivian peso—see Glossary) at current prices but only $b12.2 billion at 1968 constant prices, taking into account an inflationary factor. The per capita GDP was estimated at $b2,352 in 1972. Dollar equivalents are not possible for 1972 because of a devaluation of the peso in that year (see Currency, Banking, and Credit, this ch.).

Estimates of growth rates of GNP and GDP vary. According to one set of statistics, the GNP grew by an average annual rate of only 1.1 percent between 1956 and 1961 but by an average annual rate of 5.7 percent between 1962 and 1968. The United Nations (UN) estimated that the GDP grew by 4.5 percent in 1969, by 5.2 percent in 1970, by 3.8

percent in 1971, and by 5.9 percent in 1972. On the basis of UN estimated growth rates the United Nations Conference on Trade and Development ranked Bolivia forty-fourth of ninety developing nations in 1969.

A 1971 survey by international economists indicated that the top 5 percent of the population received almost 36 percent of the total national income, and the poorest 20 percent of the population received only 4 percent of the total income. The highest levels of income were found in Santa Cruz Department, mainly because of petroleum and natural gas production and larger farms with better soil and climatic conditions. The Ministry of Planning and Coordination estimated per capita income of all rural inhabitants at about the equivalent of US$28.40 in 1969 and per capita income of all urban inhabitants at US$241.10. There were also wide divergencies in urban income. A survey of La Paz incomes in the mid-1960s indicated average per capita income in the city to be the equivalent of US$272, but 2 percent of the urban population received annual incomes over US$10,000.

A slight shift has occurred in the relative contribution to GDP of the various economic sectors since the 1952 Revolution. Since 1965, for example, the shares of agriculture and government have declined, and petroleum and services have increased (see table 3). The contribution of manufacturing has been almost stagnant, but the government hopes this sector's contribution can be doubled by 1990. This would entail heavy investments by both the government and private interests.

Since 1937 the country has experienced inflationary pressures, the

Table 3. *Structure of Bolivian Gross Domestic Product, Selected Years, 1965–71*
(in percent)

Sector	1965	1967	1969	1970	1971
Agriculture	28	24	23	22.9	18.0
Manufacturing	13	12	12	13.2	14.0
Commerce and finance	12	12	12	10.9	14.0
Mining	9	9	9	14.1	10.4
Transportation	8	8	9	8.4	8.0
Government	9	9	9	8.9	7.9
Construction	5	6	7	4.6	4.0
Services	7	7	7	10.0	....[1]
Petroleum:					
Extraction	2	6	5	1.9	3.6
Refining	2	3	3	....[2]	....[2]
Energy	2	1	2	1.7	1.9
Housing	3	3	2	3.4	....[1]
Other	....	....	....	....	18.2
Total	100	100	100	100	100

[1]Included in other.
[2]Included in manufacturing.

cost-of-living index increasing at extremely high rates in some years, for example, over 147 percent annually during the 1952–56 period. In other years, such as 1962 to 1964, the cost-of-living index rose by only 1.7 percent annually. From 1965 to 1968 the index rose by an average of 6.3 percent annually and by less than 4 percent annually from 1969 to 1971. The UN, however, characterizes the increases in the cost-of-living index as being only moderate when compared to Latin America as a whole. In 1967 the compilation of data for the cost-of-living index was revised to include a sampling of 158 basic articles. The previous formula was considered no longer representative of an average family's market basket. The new formula, however, is applied only to La Paz, and only the food items are sampled monthly; other commodities are priced semiannually.

ROLE OF GOVERNMENT

Before 1952 government involvement in the economy was not significant. Since the 1952 Revolution governmental policy has varied depending upon the philosophy of the president in power. During the period 1952 through 1964 there was increased public ownership in many sectors, particularly mining, petroleum, and transportation. From 1964 through 1969 there was a period of increased reliance upon private, mainly foreign, capital in developing the economy. After 1969, the public role again increased, but this trend was slowed in late 1971 under the government of President Banzer, who appeared to be attempting to achieve a more balanced mixture of state and private development. A new investment law of 1971 provided incentives and guarantees for private capital.

The central government and the seven largest public enterprises combined contributed about 30 percent to the GDP. With the scarcity of private employment, pressures to expand the ranks of civil servants were difficult to resist.

The largest single public enterprise is the Mining Corporation of Bolivia (Corporación Minera de Bolivia—COMIBOL), which earns about half the country's foreign exchange. The petroleum enterprise YPFB (see Glossary) is the second largest, but the government uses it to employ excess labor and to engage in nonrevenue activities, such as local road maintenance, thus reducing its profits. There are dozens of other government-owned agencies and enterprises, some of which are profitable and some of which are operated at deficits (see ch. 9).

The government's role is weakest in manufacturing. Most activity in this sector is left to private enterprise unless the government wishes to ensure an adequate supply of particular commodities, such as milk or cement. The Armed Forces Corporation for National Development (Corporación de las Fuerzas Armadas para el Desarrollo Nacional— COFADENA) has investments in several fields and will operate in projects not undertaken by private capital or other state entities.

An industrial incentives law of 1965, which replaced more than fifteen separate pieces of legislation on investment, was instrumental in stimulating some new industrial and mining investment until 1971. The Institute for the Promotion of Investment in Bolivia (Instituto Promotor de la Inversión en Bolivia—INPIBOL) was also created to supervise the administration of the development law and to promote and assist new ventures. On December 16, 1971, a new law of investments decreed by President Banzer replaced the previous law; it covered domestic and foreign investments in the fields of industry, mining (except hydrocarbons, which were covered by separate laws), agriculture, construction, and tourism (but no other service industry). INPIBOL was replaced by the National Investment Institute (Instituto Nacional de Inversiones—INI), a decentralized organization composed of public and private representatives under the Ministry of Industry and Commerce.

The new investment incentive law provided numerous fiscal benefits and a guarantee that the benefits granted would not be altered for at least seven years. General benefits included the liberalization or rebate of customs duties for raw materials, machinery, and equipment; exemption of export duties; special depreciation rates; a ten-year property tax exemption; free land for new plants; and protection against competition from imported commodities. In addition, each economic sector had special benefits for investments in that field. Further, investments made in the sparsely populated departments of El Beni, Pando, and Tarija received a ten-year income tax exemption.

The constitution makes it obligatory for the government to engage in development planning for all sectors of the economy. The first comprehensive planning was started after the 1952 Revolution. Between 1952 and 1962 plans were compiled piecemeal by different entities, but in 1962 the National Planning Board was created to oversee long-range economic planning policies. The National Planning Board met with initial resistance from the various ministries because the board's plans did not conform to the ministries' policies. In 1963, in order to overcome this problem, a new cabinet post was created—the Ministry of Planning and Coordination—to replace the planning board and give the planning authorities equal status among the ministries (see ch. 9).

The Ten Year Social and Economic Development Plan for the period 1962 to 1971 was deemed too unrealistic and ambitious by economic experts of the Alliance for Progress. The ten-year plan was not prepared in a manner for easy implementation—final goals were set without specific stages of achievement. Outside economists then recommended that biennial plans with detailed projects be developed within the framework of the ten-year plan. The biennial plans could not be put into effect, however, because of a lack of authority within the government for implementing them. For example, six different government agencies carried out agricultural colonization and resettlement projects without coordinating their activities.

The Five Year Plan for Economic and Social Development for the 1972-76 period was drawn up under the government of President Banzer but, instead of being made public in 1973 as forecast, it was postponed until 1974 with interim plans used for 1972 and 1973. The plan was said to project a GDP growth rate of between 8 and 10 percent annually, the creation of 22,000 new jobs, the raising of per capita income to the equivalent of US$270 by 1976, and the investment of about US$700 million. Almost US$589 million was to be invested by the government, and the balance was to be invested by the private sector. About US$494 million of the public investment would have to come from loans from foreign sources because of the inability of the government to raise the funds itself.

PUBLIC FINANCE

In 1973 the public sector consisted of the central government; forty-two decentralized institutions, such as the universities and social security administrations; thirteen public companies, such as COMIBOL and YPFB; four banks; and all prefectures, municipalities, and regional development organizations. Until 1965 the annual budget only included operations of the central government. Each of the decentralized institutions and state companies prepared its own budget, and the local governments had their budgets consolidated and approved separately. Since 1965 all budgets have been grouped together, and subsequent budget law revisions gave the Ministry of Finance greater control over the supervision of the budgets of the autonomous agencies, but the larger agencies still exercised some degree of independence.

Operations of the central government usually account for from 22 to almost 28 percent of the total public sector budget. The state companies combined account for the largest share, over 61 percent, and the decentralized institutions account for almost 11 percent; the local governments account for the small balance. A 1969 law made it mandatory for the profitable enterprises to turn over to the treasury 20 percent of their net profits and to start paying customs duties on goods imported for their operations. The law was slowly being enforced, and from 1973 onward it was hoped that various enterprises would be making significant contributions to central government revenues.

Although the budgets for the local governments are very small compared to those for the rest of the public sector, they affect a larger portion of the rural population and, therefore, are more meaningful in their everyday lives. Land taxes, road tolls, fees levied on market spaces, licenses, fees for water and cemeteries are more easily recognizable than national taxes, which are frequently included in the price of merchandise or levied on higher income groups by a remote authority. The municipality of La Paz alone accounts for over a third of total local expenditures, and the Public Works Committee of Santa Cruz accounts for 25 percent.

The fiscal year is identical with the calendar year. Budgets are usually submitted to congress for approval within thirty days after August 6 of each year. If the budget is not approved within sixty days after submission or if congress is not in session, the budget becomes law automatically. Extrabudgetary financing during the fiscal year takes the form of amendments to the budget law. An accounting directorate in the Ministry of Finance maintains records of budgetary transactions. A new draft budget law that would improve budgetary procedures was under discussion in 1973.

The size of the consolidated budget for the entire public sector has been growing rapidly. In 1968 the total budget was approved for $b4.4 billion, and in 1969 the figure was $b4.94 billion. The budget jumped to $b5.96 billion in 1970, fell to $b5.6 billion in 1971, and rose to $b6.4 billion in 1972. The total 1973 budget was not approved as of early 1973. The government decided to review the 1973 figures quarterly and adjust them in accordance with fluctuations in revenue. The central government portion of the 1973 budget was set tentatively at nearly $b3 billion. No figures were available for the rest of the public sector.

Bolivia has been faced with budgetary deficits every year since the early 1930s except for 1944 and 1945, when the budgets were nearly in balance. The deficits have been made up by borrowing from the Central Bank of Bolivia (Banco Central de Bolivia) by issuing bonds or borrowing from other domestic banks, by foreign loans, and by budgetary support from the United States. The government hopes that by improving budgetary procedures, reorganizing the tax collection administration, and following an austerity program begun in late 1972 it can bring deficits down to manageable levels in the future.

An analysis of the central government's budget indicates that the largest single share during the late 1960s and early 1970s went for education—about 24 percent, but mainly for salaries of educators and administrators. Amortizing the growing public debt accounted for the second largest share—from 16 percent to 20 percent annnually. About 15 percent was spent on defense, 12 percent on transportation and communication, and the balance on all other governmental services. No details were available for expenditure breakdowns of the autonomous agencies or local administrations.

The central government received most of its current revenue from taxes and a small amount from fees and the transfers of profits from the state entities. Extraordinary revenue comes from loans and the sale of public property. Historically there had been a multiplicity of taxes. The first president of the republic, Antonio José de Sucre, eliminated or reduced all colonial taxes and established a withholding personal income tax for government employees and head taxes and property taxes for other persons. Opposition to the withholding system, mismanagement of collections, and numerous exemptions eventually forced the abolition of the income tax and the introduction of numerous specific taxes. By 1970 there were over 1,800 taxes, many of which generated little or no revenue. The existing tax system was to be replaced by an entirely new one in late 1973, the details of which were not available in mid-1973.

The tax burden was not heavy; during most of the 1960s it was between 11 and 12 percent of GDP, and in 1971 taxes represented only 9 percent of GDP. The government recognized that the population could not assume much higher tax burdens, but that tax collections could be improved. Evasion was said to be high, especially among the self-employed and small retail merchants. In 1970 the government estimated that tax evasion represented between 40 and 70 percent of real taxable income. Tax delinquents are charged only current bank rate interest on the unpaid balance, and many who are delinquent receive reductions in their fines. A ten-member tax court was created in 1966 with jurisdiction over all tax claims, and a system is followed of refusing such governmental services as issuance of passports until taxes are paid.

It was assumed by the population that the major revenue-producing taxes in existence before the announced overhaul of the tax system in 1973 probably would be retained, although some features and rates would be changed or abolished. Import duties had provided the largest share of government revenue—one-third in 1971—but modification of the tariff schedules as part of the tax revision implied that customs would provide a smaller proportion of total revenue than in the past.

A modern income tax was introduced in 1928. Before the 1973 tax revision, businesses paid a flat rate of 25 percent on net profits, and individuals paid progressive rates depending upon taxable income. Miscellaneous sales taxes were another important source of revenue, but it was anticipated that a single rate general sales tax on goods and services would prevail after the tax revision. In 1973 the government reintroduced a sales tax lottery based upon sales slips. Every three months copies of sales slips are selected at random, and the holders of the originals are awarded prizes. The fear that one of his slips may be a winner and his books audited was expected to form the incentive for a merchant to turn in all his sales tax receipts to the government. Export taxes had not been contributing much revenue, but new export taxes on minerals, metals, hydrocarbons, and cotton, which were to form part of the revised tax structure, were established in late 1972.

The public debt of the country is relatively high. At the end of 1972 the foreign debt totaled over US$681 million. The extent of the domestic debt was unknown but was considered to be large. In addition to the advances made to the government by the Central Bank, bond issues, and other domestic loans contracted, there is a constantly accumulating floating debt composed of delayed payments to government employees and suppliers of services and equipment. At the end of 1969 the floating debt was estimated to be about US$25.4 million.

A goodly proportion of the foreign debt in 1973 was of short-term duration—under fifteen years. The government decided to limit the contracting of new short-term debt, but at the same time it was seeking long-term loans for the investment program envisaged by the economic and social development plan. Some of its long-term foreign debt was contracted at low interest rates with a grace period included. A few loans were even payable in Bolivian pesos. Although the government attempted to maintain a good international credit rating, there was about US$60 million in outstanding defaulted bonds dating back to 1917. Irregular payments had been made on the defaulted bonds from 1958 onward, and the government was trying to offer the bondholders a new payment schedule.

THE BALANCE OF PAYMENTS AND FOREIGN AID

Bolivia's balance-of-payments performance has been characterized by considerable fluctuation. From 1964 through 1966 there were annual surpluses, mainly because of high capital inflows from foreign loans during those years. In 1967 and 1968 net capital inflow could not counterbalance an outflow in the current account, and there were balance-of-payments deficits of US$9 million and US$4 million, respectively. Loans from the International Monetary Fund (IMF) were used to help support the peso in those years. In 1969 the balance of payments remained in near equilibrium as increased export earnings offset declining incoming capital, and in 1970 there was a small surplus. In 1971 there occurred a major deterioration in the balance of payments. A relaxation of restrictive domestic financial policies, a drop in the world price of major export minerals accompanied by the uncertainty of adequate exports, slower economic growth, rising governmental deficits, and a sizable increase in debt repayments were contributory factors. The political situation also deteriorated before the change of government in August 1971, and the new government, faced with a large budget deficit coupled with increased Central Bank credit, could not offset a balance-of-payments deficit of more than US$11 million (see ch. 10).

The balance of payments continued to deteriorate during the first nine months of 1972, and waning confidence in the strength of the peso resulted in a massive capital outflow by holders of foreign exchange. By the end of September 1972 the country had foreign reserves equivalent to only two weeks' imports of goods. The authorities were forced to devalue the currency on October 27. Support for the peso was then received from a standby arrangement with the IMF and loans from the United States. Exports started to increase, imports contracted sharply, foreign exchange holdings climbed to more than US$57 million, and it appeared by early 1973 that there was once again an improvement in the balance of payments.

Bolivia has received foreign aid in the form of loans, grants, and technical assistance from a wide variety of sources, including international organizations, foreign governments, and private foreign banks and suppliers. As of early 1973 the total amount received since World War II totaled more than the equivalent of US$1.1 billion, one of the highest amounts in Latin America. In early 1973 representatives of all suppliers of aid and credit met with the government in order to coordinate future aid programs and permit a more balanced development.

The United States has been the largest single provider of foreign aid. From 1942, when assistance first began with a public health program, through mid-1973 the United States supplied over US$620 million, US$330 million of which was in the form of grants. The Agency for International Development (AID) and its predecessor agencies had authorized about US$407 million; about US$102 million had been provided under the Food for Peace program; the Export-Import Bank had made loans of US$45 million; military grants totaled about US$25 million; US$16 million was given to the Social Progress Trust Fund administered by the Inter-American Development Bank (IDB); and the balance went for the maintenance of Peace Corps volunteers and other programs.

Assistance from the United States was for a wide variety of economic and social programs. Funds were supplied for budgetary support, mining and industry, railroads, highways, aviation, school construction, marketing cooperatives, improvement of civil service administration, health programs, potable water systems, school food programs, public safety, manpower training, agricultural credits, electricity, housing, petroleum, and rural communities. Until Bolivia terminated the Peace Corps program in 1971, after a ten-year relationship, there were more volunteers per capita in Bolivia than in any other Latin American country.

The IDB has become the second largest supplier of assistance—mainly in the form of loans. Through 1972 the IDB had provided Bolivia with about US$157 million in thirty-five different loans. The loans were for such purposes as industry, mining, transportation, communications, low-cost housing, rural colonization, and water supply and sewerage systems. Of the World Bank Group, the International Development Association has been the most active in Bolivia. As of early 1973 it had supplied over US$51 million for power projects, railroad rehabilitation, and livestock programs. The International Bank for Reconstruction and Development (IBRD—commonly known as World Bank) made one loan, in the amount of US$23 million, to construct a gas pipeline from Santa Cruz to the Argentine border (see ch. 13).

UN assistance programs began in 1950. They consisted mainly of technical assistance, including costs of consultants and studies of various projects, and also some road building, schools, and community action projects. As of 1971 the total cost of UN assistance had reached US$50 million. Some special studies of agrarian reform and public administration were carried out by technicians of the Organization of American States. The IMF had negotiated twelve standby arrangements between 1956 and 1972 for varying amounts to bolster the currency. The IMF also maintained a resident staff in Bolivia to provide technical assistance to the government in the fields of budgeting, expenditure control, cash management, and bank legislation.

Numerous foreign governments had lent or were committed to lending more than US$187 million as of early 1973. Argentina had supplied US$75 million for various projects; Brazil, US$21 million; the Federal Republic of Germany (West Germany), US$20 million; the United Kingdom, US$6 million; Canada, US$6 million; Czechoslovakia, US$4 million; Chile, US$2 million; and Venezuela, US$2 million. Three countries had negotiated loan agreements that were not yet drawn upon: the Soviet Union, US$27.5 million; Japan, US$12 million; and Bulgaria, US$12 million. The Soviet Union credit was to be used for mining and metallurgical equipment, the Bulgarian credit for factory machinery, and the Japanese credit for road-building equipment.

Private foreign banks and other financial institutions in the United States, the United Kingdom, West Germany, France, South Africa, Spain, Argentina, and Brazil had provided over US$35 million, mainly in short-term loans to the government and autonomous entities. From the mid-1960s through the end of 1972 foreign private suppliers in more than a dozen countries had extended credit to the government and other state organizations for purchases of supplies and equipment totaling over US$55 million, most of which was still owed in 1973.

There is not much foreign investment in Bolivia. The nationalization of Bolivian Gulf Oil Company and other foreign firms in 1969 and 1970 weakened the investment climate (see ch. 13). By the end of 1972 the government of President Banzer had made satisfactory arrangements to compensate all nationalized foreign firms in an effort to improve the image of Bolivia for foreign investors. At the end of 1971 there was an estimated US$56 million in foreign investment in the country, US$21 million of which was represented by the investments of the Bolivian Power Company, a Canadian corporation. In 1972 there were fewer than three dozen United States firms with Bolivian subsidiaries or affiliates, mainly in banking, mining, and telecommunications; and their total investment was about US$32 million.

CURRENCY, BANKING, AND CREDIT

The Bolivian peso, whose symbol is $b, was the unit of currency in 1973. It had been adopted as the monetary unit in January 1963, replacing the boliviano—the monetary unit used since June 1, 1928.

During the nineteenth century Bolivia followed a policy of bimetallism with both gold and silver as the standard. Coins had been minted as early as 1562 at the Royal Mint in Potosí. In 1872 copper coins and paper money started to circulate. The name of the unit of currency was changed several times before the boliviano was adopted. The official rate of exchange of the boliviano was altered thirteen times during its lifetime—the prime reason for its replacement by the Bolivian peso. Bolivianos were permitted to circulate along with Bolivian pesos at the rate of 1,000 bolivianos to 1 peso until the end of 1965, at which time the boliviano ceased to be legal tender.

Bolivian pesos are issued in banknotes of 1, 5, 10, 20, 50, and 100 units. The peso is equal to 100 centavos, which are minted in coins of 10, 20, and 50 centavos. An unusual feature of the monetary law is that coins are legal tender for private transactions only up to a limit of fifty coins of each value.

When the boliviano was the unit of currency, its initial par value, as agreed to with the IMF on December 18, 1946, was 43 bolivianos to US$1. Because of inflationary pressures the par value was changed to 60 bolivianos per US$1 on April 24, 1950, and then to 190 bolivianos per US$1 on May 14, 1953. On November 17, 1956, the Bolivian government informed the IMF that future currency transactions would no longer occur at the par value and a fluctuating exchange rate would be utilized instead. Fluctuating rates prevailed until January 1959, when the exchange rate was stabilized at a buying rate of 11,875 bolivianos per US$1 and a selling rate of 11,885 bolivianos per US$1. When the Bolivian peso replaced the boliviano, the buying and selling exchange rates decreased by a ratio of 1,000 to $b11.875 and $b11.885 per US$1, respectively.

On October 27, 1972, the Bolivian peso was devalued for the first time since its inception. The official rate became $b20 to US$1, but for IMF purposes a par rate was used instead of the official rate. The par rate became $b21.7143 per one Special Drawing Right (SDR) or $b760 per troy ounce of gold. The SDR is an artificial unit of currency created by the IMF on January 1, 1970, as a new international reserve money. One SDR is equivalent to 0.888671 grams of gold. Several countries' currencies, such as Bolivia's, are measured by the IMF in SDRs rather than in dollars, although dollar quotations are also given. Except for a period from November 1969 to October 1972 no exchange controls have ever existed. A black market grew up during the period when there were exchange controls, but it is believed to have ceased operating when controls were lifted.

The country's financial needs are served by a fairly large number of institutions relative to the population. Some of the credit institutions are state owned, but most are private enterprises. During the first half of the nineteenth century minerals-purchasing agencies called themselves banks, but they performed very few banking functions.

The first true bank, the Bolivian Bank, was founded in 1869 and was later absorbed by the private National Bank of Bolivia, established in 1871 and still in operation in 1973. The first banking law was promulgated in 1890; until then banks operated on the basis of corporation law. In 1928 a new general banking law was issued, which was still in force in early 1973, although a completely new banking law was in preparation in mid-1973.

The state-owned Central Bank of Bolivia was created by the 1928 banking law to replace a previous institution that was only partially owned by the government. As originally set up, the Central Bank was composed of two departments: the Monetary Department, designed to perform all functions of a central bank; and the Banking Department, which functioned independently and engaged in commercial banking activities. In November 1970 the Banking Department was separated from the Central Bank and made into a commercial and development bank called the State Bank (Banco del Estado). The State Bank's initial capital was the equivalent of US$4 million, and by 1973 it was the largest commercial bank in the country. The Central Bank continued to operate as a purely central bank. At the time of the separation of the Banking Department, the former autonomous agency the Superintendency of Banks was made the Supervisory Department of the Central Bank, which was then given the role of regulating the banking system.

The Mining Bank of Bolivia (Banco Minero de Bolivia—BAMIN) was founded in 1936 with government and private capital. It was nationalized in 1939 and reorganized in 1970 as a state corporation owned by the central government, the Central Bank, and COMIBOL. In addition to providing development and working capital funds to small private mines, BAMIN also markets and exports minerals (see ch. 13). BAMIN can purchase minerals from small producers at a stipulated price, pay 85 percent upon delivery by the producer, and pay the balance after export sale. BAMIN, unfortunately, has been continually handicapped by political influence from both the government and the private miners. By 1972 almost three-fourths of its entire loan portfolio was in arrears, and it had experienced several years of losses. In response to the growing vocal criticism of BAMIN's operations the government was studying the possibility of yet another reorganization in 1973.

The Agricultural Bank of Bolivia (Banco Agrícola de Bolivia) is another state development bank; it was founded in 1942 and reorganized in 1954. The Agricultural Bank is designed to promote agricultural development through credit, organization of cooperatives, purchase of subsidized crops, and the sale of seeds and fertilizer to farmers. The bank maintained about forty-five regional and provincial branches in 1970 and also engaged in regular commercial bank activities by accepting deposits from the public. Funds for its activities have come from several sources: the Central Bank, AID, IDB, the

International Development Association, private foreign banks, and foreign governments.

The Bolivian Development Corporation (Corporación Boliviano de Fomento—CBF), a semiautonomous agency that was created in 1942 with the help of the United States Export-Import Bank, has played an important role in financing economic development. From its inception until 1955 it primarily promoted the financing of infrastructure projects; but since 1955 it has been promoting production projects, such as a cement factory, a sugar mill, and mining and agricultural development. The CBF also helps generate new government entities to deal with specific problems. An Industrial Refinancing Fund (Fondo de Refinanciamiento Industrial) under the jurisdiction of the Central Bank, designed to lend funds to medium-sized or small firms producing goods for the Andean Common Market, was created in 1972 with the help of a loan from AID.

There were sixteen private commercial banks and one private development bank operating in 1973, several of which were subsidiaries of foreign banks. Many of the banks had several branches in the major cities. The largest was the Bank of the Argentine Nation (Banco de la Nación Argentina), established in 1958.

The private development bank is called the Industrial Bank (Banco Industrial, S.A.—BISA) and was founded in 1963. Most of its loans are for expansion, new plant construction, and working capital. Half of its portfolio was for loans to firms in the food and textile industries. In 1972 BISA started to lend to small firms processing raw materials for export.

A number of small home savings and loan associations operate in various parts of the country. Several of them have pooled their resources, although they operate independently. The associations also have sole access to the Central Fund of Savings and Loans for Housing (Caja Central de Ahorros y Préstamos para la Vivienda).

Strict controls on credit have been maintained for years in an effort to stem inflationary pressures, and the principal characteristic of credit is its extreme scarcity. Credit has expanded at less than 13 percent annually. Reserve requirements are kept high, and true interest rates are higher than in many other Latin American countries because special taxes must be paid when obtaining a loan. One estimate in 1972 was that the actual cost of a short-term commercial loan was between 30 and 40 percent annually.

More credit is extended to the central government and its independent agencies than to the private sector. At the end of 1971, for example, total outstanding bank credit to the public sector was the equivalent of US$170 million, but credit to the private sector totaled only US$100 million. The largest percentage of total credit is extended by the State Bank. When it was the Banking Department of the Central Bank it accounted for almost one-fourth of total loans in the banking system.

Almost all of the agricultural credit is granted by the Agricultural Bank; only two private banks grant agricultural loans. Private bank portfolios may have up to 70 percent of their loans in industry; in fact, less than 40 percent of bank credit has been made for industry in recent years. The principal source of credit for the medium-sized mines is the CBF.

About one dozen domestic firms and an equal number of foreign companies engage in insurance activities. The Supervisory Department of the Central Bank regulates all insurance firms and their premium rates. Although foreign firms may write any class of insurance, most of the insurance business is done by the domestic firms. Automobile insurance is the largest single type sold.

There was no stock exchange as of 1973, although the IDB financed a study in 1969 as to the feasibility of a securities exchange. The private firms desirous of raising capital either make private placements of securities with friends or relatives or promote the sale of stock by advertising in the newspapers. Private banks may serve as underwriters and may buy and sell stock of domestic corporations. There are about two dozen exchange houses, some with branches in several cities. They are authorized to buy and sell foreign exchange, but they may not engage in other banking activities. Some offer tourist services as an adjunct to their exchange dealings.

CHAPTER 13

AGRICULTURE AND INDUSTRY

Agriculture provided employment for about two-thirds of the economically active population but accounted for only about 20 percent of the gross domestic product (GDP) and about 10 percent of Bolivia's exports in the early 1970s (see ch. 12). Mining, which employed less than 3 percent of the labor force, provided about 11 percent of the GDP but about 85 percent of the exports (see ch. 14). Manufacturing, in an early stage of development, contributed about 12 percent to the GDP and employed 8 percent of the labor force. Very few manufactures were exported. Petroleum and natural gas accounted for about 3 percent of the GDP and the balance of the exports. This was expected to increase since gas exports to Argentina began in 1972.

Before 1900 agriculture produced sufficient food for the nation. Demand for more consumer goods, especially food, increased sharply when the export of minerals began to provide new sources of income to a rapidly growing population. The agrarian reform program introduced after the 1952 Revolution changed the land tenure system radically but had little effect on production and agricultural techniques; and large quantities of food, especially wheat, dairy products, and edible oilseeds, were still being imported in 1973. The indices of agricultural production in 1969 and 1970 were well below the average for Latin America as a whole. Although production of some commodities has grown considerably, the production of others has not kept pace with the growth of population. In fact, the acreage planted and the yield per acre declined from the late 1950s to the late 1960s for barley, corn, and potatoes. Vast, unused arable acreage in the eastern lowlands provides a potential that could easily feed the inhabitants, but settlement of that area is slow (see ch. 3).

Mining production of tin and a variety of other minerals, which is so vital to the country's foreign exchange earnings, is subject to fluctuations caused by world prices of metals, low capitalization of the mines, and labor unrest. The miners are tightly organized and constitute a political force that affects governmental mining policy (see ch. 10). The government owns all the large mines in the country, and private interests own the medium-sized and small mines. The private mines tend to be more efficient than the state mines, but some of the medium-sized companies are reluctant to increase their investment because they are apt to be nationalized if production exceeds a certain level.

The performance of the state-owned mines has not been very good; most have low-grade reserves that are not easily accessible, and production costs are high.

The output and export of hydrocarbons have grown rapidly since 1966. About three-fourths of the annual petroleum production and almost all of the natural gas are exported. An obstacle to a further increase in petroleum exports is the low level of reserves but, since much of the national territory had not been prospected for oil as of 1973, there were hopes of discovering additional deposits. Natural gas reserves, on the other hand, were estimated to represent more than fifty years' output at the 1972 production level.

The growth of manufacturing has been slow. The domestic market is limited, and local products are faced with competition from smuggled goods. Productivity is low because of extensive use of hand labor and obsolete equipment and machinery. The largest proportion of the workers engaged in manufacturing perform handicraft or artisan work.

Large investments were made in electric power generation during the 1965-71 period by both government and private suppliers. Despite the considerable investments, per capita consumption of electricity is low, and the mining industry absorbs the biggest share of generated electricity.

LAND USE, RESOURCES, AND PRACTICES

Although sources of data vary, the total land area of the country may be assumed to be about 271.2 million acres. The largest portion, almost 41 percent, or the equivalent of 110.9 million acres, was covered with forests in the early 1970s. Almost 38 percent of the total area, or 102 million acres, was considered unfit for agriculture. The balance, about 58.3 million acres, was under cultivation, in natural pastures, or idle but considered to be potentially arable. Of the 58.3 million acres, however, only 1.8 million acres actually was in crops during the late 1960s; the remainder was pasturage or idle land. The state owned about 157 million acres, and a large portion of this was available for new agricultural settlements.

A serious man-to-land-use imbalance existed between the main geographic regions. The Altiplano, constituting about 14 percent of the total area of the country, held over 56 percent of the population in 1970 and accounted for more than 43 percent of the land under cultivation; but only 34 percent of the total agricultural production by value originated there. Variations in daily temperatures are considerable on the Altiplano, and frosts and hailstorms cause substantial crop damage. Erosion is extensive, and the soils lack basic nutrients (see ch. 3).

The Valles and the Yungas, which cover about 16 percent of the total land area, held about 30 percent of the population in 1970 and accounted for one-third of the cultivated land but over 40 percent of the total value of agricultural production. The soils in the Valles and

Yungas are better, and climatic conditions are more stable and predictable, with generally more adequate rainfall than on the Altiplano. The Oriente, or lowlands, covering about 70 percent of the country, contained only 14 percent of the population but accounted for over 23 percent of cultivated land and 27 percent of agricultural production. The Oriente contains the major portion of the country's pastures and forests and is the area with the greatest agricultural potential.

Surprisingly few changes occurred in the pattern of cultivation with the coming of the Spaniards. Barley, alfalfa, sugarcane, and a few other crops were introduced; cattle, sheep, pigs, goats, and chickens were brought from Europe; but crops and livestock of the Indian cultures as well as traditional farming implements and techniques have continued to play a dominant role.

On the Altiplano a pointed digging stick is still the principal tool used for the cultivation of potatoes, and a wooden club called a *lampa* is used to break up earth clods. The principal instrument used in planting cereals is a wooden plow, which in some localities may have a steel tip. A foot plow, similar to a fork, is another common highland tool. Shovels, picks, steel poles, and axes are also used. Sowing of seeds is generally accomplished by hand-broadcast. Cereals are harvested with small sickles, and the grain is threshed by oxen and winnowed by the wind. Few large agricultural implements are used except on the larger farms in the lowlands. It is believed that the number of tractors and other pieces of machinery in use declined during the 1950s and 1960s because they were not being replaced when they deteriorated. About 90 percent of all farmwork was being done manually. In 1968 there were an estimated 1,600 tractors in the country, and Bolivia ranked last in tractor use in South America.

Little fertilizer is applied. Crop residue and animal manure are used on the Altiplano, but not enough animal manure is produced to fertilize all the Altiplano despite large numbers of animals. More manure is used for household cooking fuel than as fertilizer. All commercial fertilizers are imported and expensive. It is estimated that about 5,000 tons of chemical fertilizers are utilized annually in the country, one-third of the total being used by farmers in the Cochabamba Valley.

The only soil conservation method practiced by farmers is crop rotation. Potatoes are usually planted first. The field is then planted in legumes or quinoa and then with barley; finally it is left fallow. The exact length of the rotation cycle varies with soil fertility but is generally four to five years. Frequently, numerous farmers owning very small contiguous plots join their land into an *aynoka*, which is an ancient method of soil conservation. All owners of a plot in an *aynoka* agree upon planting the same crops in the same order of rotation followed by a period of fallowing. During the fallow period the landowners' sheep are commonly corralled in the *aynoka* plot to help fertilize the soil with their dung.

About 10 percent of the cultivated land was under some form of irrigation during the late 1960s. The various systems were mainly small-scale projects bringing water by gravity to lands in the valleys and near lakes Titicaca and Poopó. After 1939 various governments had plans for large-scale irrigation systems, but by 1973 the only major project completed was the Angostura Dam in the Cochabamba Valley, which irrigated about 10,000 acres. Irrigation is of particular importance on the Altiplano because of the irregular rainfall.

Certain agricultural ceremonies and practices related to pre-Columbian religion or social structure are still practiced by the highland Indians (see ch. 4). *Aini*, sometimes *ayni* (a reciprocal labor arrangement), exists whereby members of the *aini* group take turns working on one another's land, the recipient of that day's labor providing food and drink for all participants (see ch. 5). At potato planting time, usually in December, a llama is sacrificed and its viscera read to ascertain the outcome of the forthcoming harvest. Alcohol, coca leaves, and confetti are scattered on the four corners of the fields during February as a symbol of fertility. During changes in the phases of the moon certain agricultural work is not performed, and malevolent spirits are appeased to avoid agricultural misfortune.

Vocational education is of relatively recent origin and has had little impact on the average farmer (see ch. 6). The teaching of practical skills through government-operated extension service demonstrations and specialized training centers has been more successful, but the extension service is hampered by a shortage of personnel and funds. In the late 1960s there were only between seventy and eighty extension agents serving the entire country. During the same period less than 4 percent of the students in higher education were taking courses in agricultural sciences. Agriculture as a vocation is not popular because career possibilities exist only in government agencies, and new openings are limited.

Experimental stations, strategically located in the separate physiographical and climatic regions of the country, provide most of the technical information on which other projects are based. The experimental station at Belén, near La Paz, specializes in highland agriculture and develops new species, varieties, and breeds of crops and animals; that at General Saavedra, near Santa Cruz, concentrates on tropical and subtropical crops of the lowlands and on soil analysis; the Riberalta station in northern El Beni specializes in tropical crops, especially rubber, cacao, coffee, and various herbs. In addition to experimental stations, there are several demonstration stations, and development centers. One at Patacamaya, between La Paz and Oruro, specializes in livestock, mainly Corriedale sheep; the stations at Reyes and Trinidad specialize in livestock.

LAND TENURE AND AGRARIAN REFORM

Before the middle of the twentieth century the land tenure system in

Bolivia was described as being extremely unequal and nearly feudal. Under Inca rule landownership and cultivation were on a communal basis, and the concept of individual land titles was unknown. From the communal lands families were allotted an annual plot, which they were not permitted to cultivate until the land of the state and Inca clergy had been cultivated. Families helped each other on a communal basis and also took collective responsibility for the cultivation of land allotted to families whose menfolk were absent or incapacitated. When the Spanish conquered the Inca, they met with little resistance in transplanting the land tenure system of contemporary Spain. Under that system large tracts of land were granted to persons who had distinguished themselves in the service of the crown. Such land grants were theoretically restricted to use during the lifetime of the grantee, but corruption and the distance from Spain made it impossible to apply the law, and land was handed down from generation to generation as the permanent property of a family.

The Indians who were living on the land assigned to the Spanish conquerors remained there and were called *colonos*—persons who were given a plot of land in usufruct for their families, but for which they were obliged to perform three to five days of labor a week for the owner, both on the landlord's land and in his household. Female members of the family were assigned household duties on a rotating basis. *Colonos* were required to use their own implements, draft animals, and seeds. As far as the individual *colono* was concerned, there was not much change in his relationship to the land; he still had to till one piece for his superiors before he could till his own, which still did not belong to him.

Certain farmworkers on the owner's land were less well off than *colonos*. The farmworkers had to perform six days of work a week regardless of need. If the landowner did not have enough work for these individuals, he could rent out their labor to other landowners or to townsmen. The individual worker in this category could ease his own plight by having a member of his family perform his duties or by subletting relatives to a nonfamily member so that he would have time to work his assigned plot of land. In return he shared his produce with the other person. In 1945 such free personal services for the landowner were abolished, but many landlords failed to give remuneration for the services performed, and there was little change in land tenure. When farms were offered for sale the inventory usually included the number and quality of tenants, as if they were livestock.

Three other types of tenant resided on the large estates but with a relative degree of independence. There was the estate's horticulturist, who rented land for his own use from the owner for cash and one week's service per month. Another type of tenant was the cropland renter, who paid for the use of a plot of land either in cash or labor but had no other obligations. The remaining category comprised people who were given a small lot on which to construct their homes in return for three or four days of labor monthly. The rest of the time was their own. The lot was usually too small for crops, but some poultry and animals could be raised. The few truly independent farmers before the 1952 Revolution usually lived in small hamlets and made up the mobile labor force of the area. They may have owned small plots and also worked either as sharecroppers or as daily wage earners, who received wages both in cash and in kind.

In addition, self-sufficient Indian communities, whose lands had never been taken over by the Spaniards, continued to exist, dispersed through remote areas of the country. Such communities did not contribute to the market and remained almost unchanged from precolonial times; all residents, who were called *comunarios*, owned the land in common; plots were distributed annually to individual families for their use. At the time of Bolivia's independence in 1825 there were an estimated 11,000 such Indian communities, but numerous attempts by landowners were made to abolish the status of such communities, to seize their land, and to use their manpower on the large estates. Finally, in 1866 all Indian communities were abolished, and the land was distributed among their members. Unfamiliar with the concept of individual titles, most Indians sold their titles to whites and mestizos and lost their land. Social tension became so grave thereafter with threats of Indian violence that in 1871 the government ordered all community land to be returned, the cost of reimbursement to be paid by the government. Such repayments drained the government budget for decades. The reversal of the legislation, however, did not end the attempts to encroach on the Indian communal land and, as a result of numerous legal and extralegal movements, the number of Indian communities eventually fell to between 3,000 and 4,000 by the time of the 1952 Revolution.

Figures from the 1950 census indicate the extreme inequality of land tenure before 1952. There were only 82,600 landowners in the country, of which number 6.3 percent possessed almost 93 percent of all 80.9 million acres of privately owned land. Large estates of more than 2,500 acres were common, those of 25,000 acres were not unusual, and several had 50,000 acres or more. The two largest estates comprised 5 million acres and 4 million acres, respectively. Eight persons with the largest properties possessed one-tenth of Bolivia yet cultivated less than one-tenth of 1 percent of their landholdings. At the other end of the scale, nearly 70 percent of the landowners owned properties under twenty-five acres in size and accounted for only 0.4 percent of total farmland. The balance of the farmers possessed farms between twenty-five and 2,500 acres in size.

Regional differences in tenure relationships and attitudes between owners and workers were significant. On the Altiplano most land was held in large estates owned by absentee landlords and operated by managers while the owners devoted themselves to other professions.

Workers on the Altiplano estates suffered the severest terms of labor contracts in the country. The Valles and Yungas were areas of both large estates and fragmented landholdings. Over 50 percent of the farms in the Valles were worked by their owners, and labor contracts between owners and workers were somewhat more liberal than on the Altiplano. In the northeastern portion of the lowlands a few individuals and corporations owned most of the land but tolerated squatters and their families who provided paid farm labor in that sparsely populated region. In the Santa Cruz area large owner-operated estates had been maintained since colonial times, and there were few absentee owners. The relationship between owners and workers was more paternalistic in Santa Cruz than elsewhere, particularly since an ill-fated separatist movement of 1875-76, which resulted in peasants being offered pay for their labors as an inducement to lay down their arms. In addition to wages, Santa Cruz landowners usually provided housing, food, medical and welfare services, and occasional cash loans. Numbers of agricultural workers eventually were able to establish themselves as small farmers on purchased or rented land with the funds they had accumulated.

Some form of agrarian reform had been advocated by almost every political party and group since the 1930s, but no agreement existed on the best possible solution, and no plan was ever implemented. Beginning in 1936 in the Cochabamba Valley, however, Indian veterans of the Chaco War, who returned with new ideas of emancipation, started to form peasant leagues. These local associations eventually produced political leaders who inspired a grassroots national movement for agrarian reform, which grew beyond the control of the central government (see ch. 2; ch. 10). After taking power in 1952, the revolutionary government was immediately faced with spontaneous seizures of large estates by peasant groups in a situation that, in some areas, approached anarchy.

A government commission was hastily formed to establish a method of redistributing land in an orderly manner and on August 2, 1953, an Agrarian Reform Act was proclaimed, and the date was thereafter celebrated as "The Day of the Indian." The law brought a radical change to Bolivia's centuries-old land tenure system. It established the claim of the state to all land, water, and natural resources but recognized private property if it fulfilled useful purposes in the service of society. The law had six fundamental objectives: redistribution of land; abolition of unpaid labor; promotion of Indian communities; stimulation of agricultural production; preservation of natural resources; and internal migration to the less populated regions of the lowlands.

Six types of land tenure are defined and recognized by law: the farmer's homesite; the small farm property, which can be cultivated by the farmer and his family without assistance; the medium-sized property worked with hired labor or farm machinery; the large-scale enterprise requiring intensive capital investment, hired labor, and machinery; communal property of Indians (whose communities have the right to recover land lost since 1900); and common holdings of agricultural cooperatives or societies. The legal maximum size of each type of property varies according to location. The small family property, for example, varies from 7.5 acres in the valleys to 200 acres in the Chaco region; medium-sized properties range between 600 and 1,500 acres; and agricultural enterprises from 200 acres in the valleys to 5,000 acres in the tropical region. Properties designated as agricultural enterprises escaped expropriation and redistribution despite their size. For stock ranches the law recognizes private rights up to 124,000 acres, provided that at least one head of livestock is raised for each twelve acres. Additionally, the law provides that each beneficiary of agrarian reform can also obtain almost 150 acres of state-owned land in the Oriente in addition to what he received in his home community. Many peasants have taken advantage of this clause and are working their new lands on a commuting basis, although some have moved their families to the new sites for permanent residence.

The basic agrarian reform law was amended in 1963 and 1968. Administrative procedures were simplified, and some new features were added. For example, property abandoned by a landowner is to be worked as a cooperative by the new tenants rather than be redistributed to them. Sharecropping became illegal in 1968 because various arrangements had sprung up that were not in keeping with the philosophy of the agrarian reform law. Before then certain divisions of the crop were permitted between owner and tenant. Under the 1968 amendment all land use payments are required to be in money terms, and no crop division is made; the tenant receives the entire crop.

All of the properties under the various types of land tenure recognized by the law receive one of five types of titles. The most common title is called an affectation title and is that which is granted to each recipient when a large property is broken up and redistributed. Restitution titles are given for land being returned to Indian communities. Consolidation titles are those given to occupants of land whose squatters' rights have been recognized. Large estates, which are exempt from agrarian reform, receive titles of inaffectability, which serve as a legal defense against future expropriation. The last type of land title is called a grant and is given for the newly settled lands in the Oriente previously owned by the government. All recipients of any title must work the land and may not sell it. It can be passed on to heirs but reverts to the state if there are no heirs.

Under the law former owners of expropriated land are entitled to compensation in the form of twenty-five-year bonds paying 2 percent annual interest. In fact, however, very few owners have been compensated. As of 1973 the bonds had not been printed, and few owners had pursued the issue through the courts because the payment was to have been based upon the value of the land as declared for tax purposes in 1948. As a result of devaluation of the currency over the ensuing years, the owner would receive a very small amount. Simultaneously, the new owners were to pay the government five times the 1948 value in twenty-five annual installments, but this regulation had almost never been enforced as of 1973.

The administrative mechanism charged with implementation of agrarian reform is the National Agrarian Reform Service, a semi-autonomous agency, and the National Agrarian Reform Council, a dependency of the Ministry of Rural Affairs and Agriculture. The National Agrarian Reform Service has not always received sufficient funds to carry out its mandate, and some of its functions were assumed by other government agencies. In many cases the process of expropriation, redistribution, and granting of titles was only partially or inefficiently performed. Disputes have arisen between peasants and former landlords attempting to regain their lands and between peasants themselves over property lines and division of land, and many cases have to be reheard. Over 400,000 peasant families became owner-operators after the 1952 Revolution, and countless additional numbers of new farm families have submitted claims for land since then. As of the beginning of 1972, however, only about 320,000 families had received clear titles to their land.

A target date of 1975 was set by the government in 1968 to process all cases then pending, and mobile brigades were set up consisting of a land judge, a secretary, seven topographers, an agronomist, and a soil analyst. Cases were being resolved on the site, and computers were being used in processing the titles. The average size of the individual small family farms being distributed was about twenty-five acres but ranged from 2.5 acres to over sixty acres.

CROPS

Potatoes are the most important food crop and constitute the basic diet of the highland population. Potatoes originated in the Andes, and many varieties and species have been produced since pre-Inca times. About 260,000 acres were planted in 1970, mostly on the Altiplano but also in the valleys and near Santa Cruz. Production tends to fluctuate, but the country generally is self-sufficient (see table 4). The yield per acre was highest in the Cochabamba and Santa Cruz areas, and the government was attempting to encourage increased production in those areas rather than on the Altiplano, where large quantities of fertilizer and improved cultivation methods would be required to increase yields. Trial plantings of new varieties forecast increased yield if farmers would adopt the new seeds, but the most popular potato is a small, white variety with a low yield. Some sweet potatoes are raised, but production has never been more than 13,000 tons annually.

Corn is the second most important food crop in the country and is grown mainly in the valleys and lowlands. Harvested acreage has been steadily increasing and comprised about 555,000 acres in 1971—more than that for any other crop. Corn is consumed not only as a vegetable

Table 4. Estimated Agricultural Production of Bolivia Listed by Crop Year, 1967–72
(in thousand metric tons)

	1967	1968	1969	1970	1971	1972
Bananas	313.0	190.0	198.0	212.0	115.0[1]	125.0[1]
Barley	80.0	58.0	83.0	62.0	66.0	65.0
Brazil nuts	5.0	5.5	n.a.	n.a.	n.a.	n.a.
Cacao	4.0	1.5	1.5	1.5	1.5	1.5
Cassava	110.0	181.0	187.0	160.0	234.0[1]	250.0[1]
Citrus fruit	37.3	53.0	73.0	86.0	90.0	n.a.
Coffee	3.5	3.7	9.6	9.9	5.1	5.1
Corn	203.1	218.8	289.0	283.0	293.0	300.0[1]
Cotton	1.5	3.4	3.0	5.1	12.0	31.0
Dry beans	20.4	20.4	20.4	n.a.	n.a.	n.a.
Grapes	7.9	11.0	12.0	11.0	n.a.	n.a.
Meat (beef)	30.9	n.a.	n.a.	n.a.	56.1	n.a.
Miscellaneous fruits	55.4	73.0	n.a.	n.a.	n.a.	n.a.
Pineapples	7.6	7.0	7.0	n.a.	n.a.	n.a.
Potatoes	452.7	680.0	620.0	642.0	620.0	614.0
Quinoa	8.5	8.8	10.0	10.0	11.0	11.0
Rice	42.7	45.1	53.0	60.0	77.0	75.0
Rubber	n.a.	1.9	n.a.	n.a.	n.a.	n.a.
Sugar (refined)	96.7	108.7	124.0	123.0	116.0[1]	100.0[2]
Tobacco	n.a.	n.a.	n.a.	2.0	2.0	2.0
Wheat	27.0	45.0	47.0	62.0	69.0[1]	70.0[2]

n.a.—not available.
[1]Estimated.
[2]Projected.

but also in the form of flour and meal and as an ingredient in the popular fermented beverage called *chicha*. Some corn is fed to chickens and hogs.

Rice has become a standard item in the diet of lowland and valley people, and production has increased steadily since the end of World War II, stimulated by government price supports, increased use of machinery by rice farmers, and improved storage facilities. The acreage harvested averaged over 86,000 acres in the 1966–71 period and rose to 89,000 acres in 1972. Annual production had reached the level where the government was accumulating large stocks of rice under its price support program, and some exports were made in 1969. Most of the stocks were being retained, however, as a buffer supply to substitute for potatoes in years of lower potato production. Most of the rice is grown in the Santa Cruz area, one-third of the total production coming from the Japanese and Okinawan colonies.

Barley, well adapted to high altitudes, is an important highland crop; about 296,000 acres are planted annually. It is eaten roasted or milled and is used for beermaking. In some localities it is utilized as animal feed. Yields are low except on lands where fertilizers are used.

Quinoa and *cañahua* are small, hardy cereals, which require little attention and grow well at altitudes between 7,500 and 12,000 feet.

They have high protein and vitamin content, but quinoa contains a toxic substance called saponin, which must be removed before the cereal is used as a human food. Quinoa is prepared and eaten like rice, and *cañahua* is used in the form of toasted flour.

Wheat is raised in small plots with traditional methods in the departments of Cochabamba, Potosí, Tarija, and La Paz and is the food crop with the largest production deficit. Quantities of both wheat and wheat flour are imported annually despite the government's attempt to encourage increased production. A national wheat plan designed to eventually achieve self-sufficiency had stimulated the planting of about 316,000 acres by 1970, but at least 524,000 acres should have been planted in that year to meet domestic demand, and it appeared that imports would continue to be required for several years.

Sugarcane, an important crop and industry during the colonial era, declined in importance after independence, and the industry fragmented into many small home-type mills producing a brown sugar called *chancaca*. The first modern mill was installed in 1939, and the industry grew steadily thereafter until the country became self-sufficient in sugar in 1963. Almost all the sugarcane is raised in Santa Cruz Department with the largest concentration in Warnes Province. About 2,000 farmers were raising sugarcane in the late 1960s on a total of about 75,000 acres. Many of the sugarcane farmers had formed cooperatives, and a total of about 15,000 persons were dependent upon some aspect of the industry. Some sugarcane growers shifted to planting cotton in 1971, however, and sugar production declined in that year and also in 1972.

Spurred by high export prices in the late 1960s and early 1970s, cotton production increased rapidly. The acreage planted soared from 15,000 acres in 1968 to over 120,000 acres in 1972, and growers were planning to plant 250,000 acres in 1973. Cotton was recognized as being the most profitable crop in the country in the 1971–72 period. It is raised in Santa Cruz, Tarija, and Cochabamba departments on both small farms and on highly mechanized plantations. Although almost no fertilizer or irrigation is utilized by cotton farmers, the yield per acre is among the highest in the world because of excellent climatic conditions and a minimal amount of pest damage. An association of cottongrowers has been instrumental in obtaining foreign loans for its members, in coordinating planting, in marketing the crop, in distributing seeds, and in maintaining quality controls.

Coffee and tea thrive in the Yungas, and coffee also grows well in the Alto Beni and Santa Cruz areas. Farmers, however, give preference to other crops that bring faster returns, and coffee growing is a secondary activity. Despite the limited amount of coffee produced, the quality is high, and good export prices are received. Bolivia has a small export quota under the International Coffee Agreement, and export sales have been given priority over the domestic market with the result that in some years of low production, such as 1971, there is a temporary shortage of coffee for domestic sale. In 1972 about 10,000 farmers were growing some coffee on a total of about 37,000 acres. Small quantities of high-grade black tea are produced near Alto Beni, and the government is assisting producers in the hope that tea may become an export product.

Coca, which resembles a tea bush, is grown extensively in the Yungas and also near Cochabamba. Its leaves, when dried and chewed with vegetable ash, produce cocaine alkaloid, a stimulant having an anesthetic side effect, which has been used by highland Indians since prehistoric times. Attempts by the government and the church to reduce coca consumption have had little success, and farmers continue to grow it because it is easy to produce and profits are high. Its production is not illegal.

Low-quality cacao grows in the Yungas and in El Beni Department. Some farmers are attempting to increase the quality by the use of better varieties and application of improved processing practices. Most cacao is used domestically for making chocolate.

Oilseed production is low despite favorable climatic conditions. Sesame, castor beans, soybeans, sunflowers, peanuts, and cottonseeds are produced but not in sufficient quantities to meet demand. Therefore imports are required. There are large numbers of unexploited palm trees growing in Santa Cruz Department.

Fruits and vegetables are grown in small garden plots in La Paz, Santa Cruz, and Cochabamba departments. Apples, pears, grapes, peaches, plums, citrus, figs, pineapples, onions, chili, beans, and bananas are raised. Cassava is grown and used as an admixture of wheat flour. Tobacco is a minor crop; about 5,000 acres were harvested in 1972. Rye is grown in small quantities on the Altiplano, and oats are raised in small amounts in Cochabamba and Potosí departments. Alfalfa is produced on about 20,000 acres, mainly in Cochabamba. One unusual product is pyrethrum, a chrysanthemum-type flower whose dried leaves are a natural insecticide. Cultivation of the crop was begun in 1955 under the encouragement of the government. It is grown mainly in high altitudes and is found only in Bolivia, Ecuador, and a few other countries. It is usually planted by farmers on land being held fallow, and the flowers can be harvested every two months. A pyrethrum-processing plant has been built near Lake Titicaca.

LIVESTOCK, FISHING, AND FORESTRY

No reliable statistics are available regarding livestock numbers but a 1969 estimate gave a total of 2 million head of cattle with 820,000 in El Beni Department and 430,000 in Santa Cruz. There are almost 800 large cattle ranches in El Beni; 40 percent have between 400 and 1,000 head, and the largest ranch has about 18,000 head of cattle. Because of the favorable conditions in the Oriente for cattle production (El Beni alone has 37 million acres of open grasslands) and the possibility of fresh or frozen beef exports, the government started to provide funds in 1967, partly with outside financial assistance, to cattle ranches to help them improve their herds, pasturage, slaughtering methods, processing, grading, and marketing of beef. As of early 1973 three loans totaling US$10.4 million had been obtained from the International Development Association, and US$5 million had been received from the. Inter-American Development Bank for livestock improvement projects.

Between 200,000 and 220,000 head of cattle are slaughtered annually, producing about 32,000 to 36,000 tons of beef. Air transportation makes possible the shipment of the beef from the ranches to the consumers. Each slaughterhouse in El Beni has a landing strip, and several aviation companies are engaged in transporting meat to urban areas (see ch. 14). Some ranchers trail-drive their herds to Brazil where higher prices prevail, but the higher prices are offset by cattle deaths on the drive and a loss of weight by the remaining cattle. Sun drying is a popular method of curing meat. In fact, the expression "jerked beef" comes from a Quechua word meaning dried meat.

Of the large numbers of cattle only about 16,000 are dairy cows, most of which are found in the Cochabamba area. Smaller numbers are found near La Paz, Santa Cruz, and Sucre. As of 1973 there were two milk products plants—one in Cochabamba and one near La Paz—with a total capacity of 95,000 quarts of milk daily. Neither of the two plants was functioning at capacity, and milk had to be imported to fulfill demand. Many farmers process their own butter and cheese and deliver them directly to the consumer or marketplace. The products have varying degrees of purity.

There were an estimated 7.2 million sheep in 1970 with more than 5 million on the Altiplano. Most produce a low-quality wool, which is used mainly by the farmer and his family. Better quality wool must be imported to meet the requirements of the domestic wool textile industry. A good demand exists in the cities for mutton, however, and the sheep also provide the farmer with milk and with dung for fertilizer. Most sheep suffer from malnutrition and parasites, and their weak resistance causes losses during dry spells. A portion of the funds from one of the livestock loans is being utilized to improve techniques, pasturage, and herd management on about 150 sheep ranches on the Altiplano, mainly on cooperatives. In addition to sheep cooperatives, sheep share-herding is prevalent. Peasants who herd another farmer's flock receive one-tenth of the number of animals born during his stewardship.

Llamas and alpacas have been used by the highland Indians since prehistoric times. Sturdy domesticated animals with high resistance to insects, cold, and disease, they are as important to the highland people as camels to the Near East nomads or reindeer to the Lapps.

Similar to camels in endurance and in use for transportation, llamas and alpacas are never milked, but their dung serves as an important, often the sole, source of fuel. Their wool is used for the preparation of cordage and clothing; their meat is seldom consumed fresh but rather dried and conserved; bones are turned into household implements and musical instruments; and skins are made into good shoes and bags.

Although the total number was not known, there were an estimated 2 million llamas and 400,000 alpacas in the late 1960s. The increased use of trucks on the Altiplano since 1950 has caused a decrease in the use of llamas as beasts of burden. A Bolivian Committee for Wool Development (Comité Boliviano de Fomento Lanar—COMBOFLA) has been successful in organizing both the domestic and international marketing of llama and alpaca wool. Alpacas produce an average of four pounds of wool annually, and llamas provide between two and five pounds.

An unknown number of oxen are used as draft animals. Old oxen are slaughtered for meat. Saddle oxen are utilized for locomotion in the swampy areas of the Oriente. Estimates of other livestock as of 1973 were: hogs, over 800,000; goats, about 1.4 million; horses, under 300,000; mules and asses, over 700,000; chickens, over 3.1 million; ducks, over 250,000; and turkeys, around 100,000. Many farmers maintain bee-hives, and over 1,200 tons of honey are produced annually.

Bolivia is one of the best endowed countries in timber resources in the world (see Land Use, Resources, and Practices, this ch.). The forested lands contain about 2,000 species of trees and plants, many of which are used for medicinal purposes. Nevertheless, most of the vast timber resources lay beyond the reach of the available means of transportation in 1973. More than 40 percent of all forestry operations is carried out in Santa Cruz because of easier communications. Most of the cut wood is used for firewood; in 1968 for example, of an estimated 5.75 million cubic yards cut, around 5.2 million cubic yards were for firewood.

In 1969 there were about sixty-three sawmills in operation in the country, one plywood factory, and fifty-eight furniture factories. About twenty of the sawmills, employing about 1,700 workers, formed an association in 1972 to export wood products and received a line of credit from the Inter-American Development Bank to help finance export sales. The most popular woods exported are mahogany, quebracho, and walnut.

Rubber and Brazil nuts are two other important forest products. About 3,400 tons of natural rubber are produced annually, mostly in Pando Department and in parts of El Beni. There is one large rubber plantation near Riberalta in El Beni Department plus about 5,200 independent wild rubber collectors and families. Most Bolivian rubber is shipped to Brazil and enters world markets as Brazilian rubber.

Brazil nuts and almonds are gathered in Pando and El Beni by the wild rubber collectors who engage in these two activities from April through November. The rest of the time they plant subsistence crops, such as rice, cassava, and bananas. As in the case of rubber, much of the nut crop is exported to Brazil whence it is reexported as a Brazilian product.

Fishing is a minor economic activity, although the waters of the country are well stocked with a large variety of fish, which are caught and consumed by people living near lakes and rivers. Commercial fishing is practiced at Lake Titicaca and on the Pilcomayo River, particularly by young farmers who are waiting for their fathers to turn land over to them. After they receive land, fishing becomes a secondary activity. Lake trout and a species of bass or bream called *boga* are the most commonly caught fish and are supplied to the markets of La Paz, Tarija, Potosí, Sucre, and Cochabamba. Between 1,000 and 2,000 tons of fish are estimated to be sold annually. A fairly large number of alligators and caimans are caught in the eastern rivers for their skins, and wild animals are caught for food and live export.

MINING AND METALLURGY

In terms of export earnings mining has been the leading economic sector since colonial days. Mineral ores have been known since prehistoric times, and it is said that a sample of every known mineral occurs in the soil of Bolivia. In the sixteenth century large deposits of silver were discovered at Cerro Rico in Potosí, enabling Bolivia to become the leading silver producer in the world and Potosí to become the largest city on the continent at the time (see ch. 3). By the nineteenth century, however, the silver mines started to become exhausted, and tin replaced silver as the leading mineral by the beginning of the twentieth century. Other important minerals being mined in the 1970s were lead, zinc, copper, tungsten, bismuth, antimony, gold, and sulfur (see table 5).

Before 1952 the three largest mining enterprises, which represented about 67 percent of total production of the mining industry, were controlled by three families, who played a decisive role in the course of the country's political and economic development (see ch. 2). Divesting these families of their power had become a topic of political discussion as early as 1928. After the successful revolution of April 1952 the new government hastened to nationalize the major mines. On October 2, 1952, the Mining Corporation of Bolivia (Corporación Minera de Bolivia—COMIBOL) was created; and on October 31, 1952, the three large companies plus several smaller ones were nationalized and placed under COMIBOL's control. The remaining private mines fell under government control indirectly through taxation, through government mining policies, through decrees securing social benefits for their employees, and through the authority given to the Mining Bank of Bolivia (Banco Minero de Bolivia—BAMIN) to control most private mineral exports and the import of much mining equipment (see ch. 12).

The Mine Workers Federation of Bolivia (Federación Sindical de

Table 5. Minerals Production of Bolivia, Selected Years, 1961-72

Mineral	1961-63 (average)	1968-70 (average)	1969	1970	1971	1972[1]
Antimony[2]	7.0	11.9	13.1	11.6	11.4	10.6
Bismuth[3]	262.0	622.0	669.0	623.0	658.0	649.0
Copper[2]	2.5	7.9	8.0	8.8	7.4	8.9
Crude petroleum	0.4[2]	1.6[2]	1.9[2]	8.8[4]	13.4[4]	18.0[4]
Gold[5]................	2,932.0	1,359.0	1,350.0	1,219.0	690.0	822.0
Lead	21.7[6]	26.9[6]	27.8[6]	28.4[6]	21.2[2]	21.8[2]
Silver[3]	129.0	147.0	107.0	185.0	145.0	156.0
Sulfur[2]	8.7	29.3	36.2	16.3	10.5	18.8
Tin..................	21.6[7]	29.6[7]	29.6[7]	30.1[7]	29.6[2]	31.1[2]
Tungsten[2]	1.5	2.3	2.3	2.4	1.5	1.4
Zinc.................	5.0[6]	31.2[6]	29.2[6]	51.3[6]	44.1[2]	43.0[2]

[1]Estimate.
[2]In thousand metric tons.
[3]Exact number of metric tons.
[4]Millions of barrels.
[5]Kilograms (one kilogram equals 2.2 pounds).
[6]In thousand short tons.
[7]In thousand long tons.

Trabajadores Mineros de Bolivia—FSTMB) is the most disciplined and strongest labor union in the country and exerts such pressure on the government via strikes or political influence that governmental mining policy opposed by FSTMB is either altered or not carried out (see ch. 10).

The mining industry is divided into three sectors: large mines, medium mines, and small mines, each of which is governed by different regulations and laws. The large mining sector contains all government-owned mines and accounted for about 50 percent of all mineral production as of 1972. All state-owned mineral deposits are the responsibility of COMIBOL except for iron ore and manganese, which were transferred to a newly formed state entity in early 1973, the Bolivian Iron and Steel Corporation (Siderúrgica Boliviana, S.A.—SIDERSA), and radioactive minerals, which are under the control of another agency. COMIBOL, which employed about 23,000 persons in late 1972, was responsible for exploring, exploiting, and processing all mineral deposits assigned to it. In 1973 it operated more than two dozen mines and owned about 100 other mining properties. In addition, it could sell and export its own minerals and import machinery and equipment for either its own use or for the use of the rest of the mining industry. It also operates powerplants, hospitals, schools, railroads, and farms because it is obliged to provide certain social benefits to its employees and their dependents. In 1972 COMIBOL's nonmineral assets were valued at the equivalent of US$108 million.

From the time of its inception through 1964 COMIBOL suffered heavy losses totaling the equivalent of over US$51 million. Among the reasons for the losses were mismanagement and administrative shortcomings, nonmining social costs, excessive personnel hired for political or welfare reasons, high production costs because of lower mineral content of the ores, and inaccessibility of the major veins of ore. With outside financial assistance from the United States, the Federal Republic of Germany (West Germany), and the Inter-American Development Bank, COMIBOL was able to improve operations, install new equipment, and alter its cost structure. It had small annual profits from 1965 through 1971. Half of all profits are shared with the employees: part goes to the individual miners in the mines that had a profit and part is given to all COMIBOL employees.

Medium-sized mines are private mines producing between sixty and 400 tons of fine metal annually in concentrate form and meeting certain technological, capital, and social requirements. In 1972 there were almost three dozen companies in this sector, seven of which were foreign owned. Between 6,000 and 7,000 people were employed in the medium mines sector, which accounted for about 25 to 30 percent of the total mineral production. Small mines are legally defined as all those producing under sixty tons annually as well as all mining cooperatives regardless of amount of production. Most of the mining cooperatives have been formed by former COMIBOL employees who lease a COMIBOL property and market their production through COMIBOL. There are an estimated 30,000 people employed in the small mines sector, which comprises about 3,000 mines, including one-man operations. Some of the employees in this sector are part-time miners, who work on a daily wage basis with no social benefits. Many of the small mines use primitive mining methods, which are generally inefficient, but some of the small mines use modern equipment. The small miners must transport their ore themselves to one of the many collection points maintained by COMIBOL and the BAMIN.

In addition to COMIBOL, BAMIN, and SIDERSA, several other government agencies have been created to deal with mining matters, and some duplication of activities exists. The Ministry of Mining and Metallurgy sets all general policy in the mining and metallurgical field, which is then implemented by a specific agency. The National Smelting Company (Empresa Nacional de Fundiciones—ENAF) is in charge of most government metal smelters, foundries, and refineries, but COMIBOL operates a bismuth smelter. The Geological Service of Bolivia (Servicio Geológico de Bolivia—GEOBOL) is in charge of mapping, exploration, mineral analysis, and laboratory work. As of 1972 only 25 percent of the country had been mapped geologically, and only 5 percent had been explored for minerals because of inadequate funding. In mid-1972, however, a one-year program of geological mapping by satellite began in association with the United States space agency National Aeronautics and Space Administration (NASA), and a five-year exploration program was initiated in the Lipez area of Potosí, where large reserves of copper, lead, silver, bismuth, and tin are known to exist.

The Mining and Metallurgical Research Institute (Instituto de

Investigaciones Minero-Metalúrgicas—IIMM) is engaged in research and technical services pertaining to mining techniques and the processing of ores. The IIMM receives financial support from the United Nations Development Program, and its primary objective is to increase the recovery of metals from the ore in government-owned and private medium-sized mines. Some of the activities of the IIMM duplicated those of GEOBOL, and the government was forced to redefine their respective responsibilities in 1972. Finally, the Bolivian Nuclear Energy Commission (Comisión Boliviana de Energía Nuclear—COBOEN) is responsible for all activities related to the exploration and exploitation of radioactive ores.

Bolivia has long been known as a tin-producing country, and the mineral has been exploited on a large scale since 1861. Bolivia is the second largest tin-producing country after Malaysia, accounting for about 16 to 17 percent of annual world production, and is the only significant tin producer in the Western Hemisphere. There are ten types of tin ores in Bolivia, the most important of which is cassiterite, also called tinstone—a brownish black mineral. Tin is also found mixed with other ores, such as silver, copper, lead, tungsten, and bismuth. It is found in an arc, ranging in width from twelve miles to 130 miles, running from Puerto Acosta on the Peruvian border near Lake Titicaca to Villazón on the frontier with Argentina. About 90 percent of all tin ore comes from underground mines, many over 1,500 feet deep, and the balance is surface stripped, dug from shallow veins, dredged from alluvial deposits, or reclaimed from discarded tailings (refuse materials) of the concentrating plants.

There are over 1,000 tin mines in the country, but four of the most important are located near Oruro, and one-half of all tin is produced within sixty miles of that city. The mines of COMIBOL produce between 60 and 70 percent of Bolivian tin—one, the Llallagua mine, also called Catavi, alone producing 30 percent of it. By 1970 that mine, which had been operating steadily since 1903, had produced more than the equivalent of US$2 billion worth of tin from its 430 miles of galleries.

Since the beginning of the twentieth century the quality of the tin ore has been declining. From an assay of 16 to 18 percent tin content the ores were down to an average 1 percent by the time of the 1952 Revolution and nationalization. Many of the veins are less than ten inches wide and located at very low levels with accompanying intense heat and humidity so that the miners must work naked and under a continuous spray of water. The lower grade ores require milling and concentration, but as much as half of the tin is lost in the form of dust during the process of milling and concentration, the most serious technological problem of the industry. Beginning in 1968 and continuing through 1972 COMIBOL had been installing new equipment and improving existing facilities in order to increase the recovery rate of the low-grade ores to 85 to 90 percent. The tailings of the old concentration plants contain higher grade ore than many of the veins, and since 1970 the tailings have been reprocessed. Estimates of the amount of tin in all the accumulated tailings in the country in 1972 ranged from 300,000 to 600,000 tons. Known tin reserves in the mines at that time were only 1 million tons.

Successive governments since 1952 have been attempting to alter the export pattern from that of shipping mainly raw mineral ores to that of exporting processed metals, which have higher value. Several small tin-processing plants have been built, and a 7,500-ton-per-year tin smelter capacity was opened by ENAF in 1971. In 1973 the government had plans to expand the tin smelter to 20,000 tons.

Bolivia is also the second leading world producer of primary antimony, after the Republic of South Africa. About half of the antimony is produced by two private companies, whereas about thirty medium-sized companies and 300 small mines produce the balance. Construction on an antimony smelter located near the ENAF tin smelter began in 1973. It was planned to have a capacity of 5,000 tons annually and was scheduled for completion by 1975.

Silver, lead, and zinc ores are found combined in varying percentages and are mined together. Of the three metals the reserves of zinc are the largest, estimated at 1.1 million tons in 1970 and are followed by lead with 95,000 tons. From 1900 until 1930 Bolivia was the only producer of bismuth in the world and since 1930 has remained the single most important producer. Most bismuth comes from the Tasna mine in the southern part of the Cordillera Real, although part of the production comes as a secondary mineral in the tin mines. A bismuth smelter began operations in 1972 with a 400-ton-per-month capacity, and in the same year the world bismuth producers agreed to the establishment of an international bismuth institute in Bolivia in 1973.

There are 171 copper-bearing ores in Bolivia, but only ten were being exploited in 1973. COMIBOL accounted for about one-third of copper production but had 75 percent of the known reserves, which were about 174,000 tons in 1970. A 1972 government report forecast copper as the future leading mineral in Bolivia if the lower grade ores could be economically exploited.

Gold, found in rivers and mines, has been mined since colonial days, either by itself or mixed with other metals. The major gold mining area is along the Tipuani River in La Paz Department on the western side of the Cordillera Real. One large company operated a dredging facility, and about fifty small cooperative enterprises were also located there. The government has long acknowledged that much gold leaves the country illegally. In order to combat the illegal movement of gold, the government issued regulations in 1972 that provided new incentives for the gold miners to turn in their production to the BAMIN. Prices to be paid to producers were to be based upon the London international gold market, and royalties and fees paid to the state were to be lowered. In return the mining cooperatives must meet monthly production quotas; if the quotas are not met for three consecutive months the concessions could be lost.

Tungsten, or wolfram, is another valuable metal produced in Bolivia. The private mines account for as much as 75 percent of tungsten ore. Sulfur is mined in response to world demand. The sulfur deposits are of volcanic origin and are found in the western portion of the country near the Chilean border. Large concessions are owned by the Military Pension Fund (Caja de Pensiones Militares). Rich deposits of asbestos are found in the upper part of Chaparé Province in Cochabamba Department. Production until 1972 was about 900 tons annually from forty-seven small mines but was expected to be increased considerably afterward, stimulated by an asbestos-processing plant and the obtainment of foreign credits to expand the small mines.

Hopes were high in 1973 for the development of iron mining. Incredibly rich iron ore deposits overlaid with manganese were reported to exist at Mutún, which lies north of the point where Bolivia, Brazil, and Paraguay meet. The deposits were known to have existed for many years but had not been exploited or adequately surveyed. Finally, in late 1972 and continuing through mid-1973 trial shipments of the ore, eventually totaling 50,000 tons, were made to Argentina to ascertain if the ore was of the quality required by the Argentine steel industry.

PETROLEUM AND NATURAL GAS

Bolivians attach great hopes to the oil and natural gas reserves of their country. Oil has been known to exist since colonial days, but exploration was not initiated until the early part of the twentieth century. Before 1916 foreign firms were permitted to explore. From 1916 to 1920 all petroleum exploitation was nationalized, but the law was repealed in 1920 to encourage foreign investment. In 1937, after several years of successful operations by foreign firms, the industry was once again nationalized, and a newly established government company, known as YPFB (see Glossary), was given exclusive exploratory and exploitation rights.

Expansion of the industry by YPFB was gradual between 1937 and 1952. After the 1952 Revolution the government devoted itself with great vigor to the development of the petroleum industry. It reorganized YPFB, poured vast amounts of money into exploration and drilling, and had increased output by 500 percent by 1957. Realizing, however, that domestic financial resources were not sufficient to continue the aggressive expansion program, the government issued a new petroleum code in 1952 with liberal provisions designed to attract foreign firms once again. More than eighteen foreign companies responded and began drilling operations, but only one, the Bolivian Gulf Oil Company (known as Bolivian Gulf), a subsidiary of the Gulf Oil Corporation, had any measure of success. The others eventually withdrew after the termination of their initial concessions. By 1969

Bolivian Gulf had brought in 153 producing oil wells. The granting of concessions to foreign oil companies, however, had been under constant criticism by left-wing politicians since 1956, and the first act of the government of General Alfredo Ovando Candia on September 26, 1969, was to invalidate the law under which Bolivian Gulf had operated. Less than one month later, on October 17, 1969, the company was nationalized. An indemnification agreement called for twenty annual payments to begin in January 1973.

Under the government of Hugo Banzer Suárez, a new general law on hydrocarbons was approved on March 28, 1972. Under that law no petroleum or natural gas concessions could be granted to private companies. Instead YPFB was to carry out its own exploration and exploitation, but it might enter into service contracts with private oil firms for exploration, development, and production of petroleum. The private firms would be reimbursed for their services with a portion of YPFB's production. As of March 1973 one such service contract had been negotiated for exploration in La Paz and El Beni departments, and YPFB, on its own, had begun extensive explorations for petroleum in an area near the town of Vilque on the Altiplano west of Oruro where natural gas had been discovered.

As of mid-1972 there were 235 producing oil wells in twelve oilfields with an average daily production of 32,000 barrels. The fields were located in the departments of Santa Cruz, Tarija, and Chuquisaca. The field at Camiri was the oldest producing field, in operation since 1927, but those at Caranda, Río Grande, and Monteagudo were the three largest producing fields. In late 1972 YPFB estimated the recoverable reserves of petroleum at 200 million barrels, which would last about ten years at the then current exploitation rate. If new reserves are not discovered, Bolivia will have to import petroleum in the future.

Transportation of crude oil and oil products, a major problem under the existing topographical conditions, has been solved through the construction of an extensive pipeline system augmented by railroad tank cars and a fleet of tank trucks. The length of the entire pipeline was about 1,440 miles in 1972. The main network of pipes connected the three major oilfields with the refineries and the refineries to the consumption centers of La Paz and Oruro. One line runs to the Chilean port of Arica, from which crude oil is exported. Storage tanks with a total capacity of over 5.3 million gallons are available in the larger cities. A plant manufacturing 7,000 oil drums a day is located in Cochabamba.

YPFB operates eight refineries, including a portable one, which had a total capacity of over 23,000 barrels per day in 1973. The largest refinery, located in Cochabamba, had a capacity of 15,000 barrels per day after being expanded in 1972. Smaller refineries are located at Camiri, Sanandita, Santa Cruz, Sucre, Puerto Villarroel, and Bermejo. The

311

small portable refinery was located in Santa Cruz in 1972. The Cocha-bamba refinery has an adjacent plant for the production of lubricants, which meets most of the country's demand for lubricating oils and waxes. The Camirí refinery has a plant to manufacture liquid petro-leum gas.

Of perhaps greater importance to the country than petroleum are the vast reserves of natural gas. In 1970 the proven recoverable gas reserves were about 2.5 trillion cubic feet. Most of the seven gasfields were near the oilfields in Santa Cruz, but a large field was also discovered near Monteagudo in Chuquisaca Department, and there was one near Camirí. Small quantities of natural gas are being used in thermal plants to generate electricity, but far larger quantities are being ex-ported to Argentina and are earning much needed foreign exchange.

Argentina negotiated a long-term contract in the late 1960s for nat-ural gas, but construction of a gas pipeline was delayed following the nationalization of Bolivian Gulf, which had been the prime guarantor for a loan from the International Bank for Reconstruction and Develop-ment (IBRD—commonly known as the World Bank) to finance the pipeline. In 1971 YPFB created an autonomous Santa Cruz Division to operate the gasfields. The Santa Cruz Division could enter into foreign contracts, and its funds were segregated from YPFB's general funds. Under this arrangement, refinancing of the loan was negotiated with the World Bank and other lenders, and the 446-mile gas pipeline from Santa Cruz to Pocitos on the Argentine side of the border was finally inaugurated in April 1972. Exports commenced almost immediately.

ELECTRICAL ENERGY

Only a small portion of petroleum production is used for industrial fuel as distinguished from automotive and other uses. There is no coal in the country, and fuel used in rural households consists of firewood, llama dung (in the highlands), charcoal, and some resinous plants that burn like peat. The country's greatest energy source in 1973 was hydro-electricity. The potential has been variously estimated from 2.7 million kilowatts to over 21 million kilowatts, but most areas have not been adequately studied. Despite the potential, the country has a chronic shortage of delivered energy. Total installed electric energy capacity was only about 252,000 kilowatts in 1970, although several additional projects scheduled for completion in 1973 should raise that figure by perhaps another 25,000 kilowatts. About 171,000 kilowatts of the installed capacity in 1970 were hydroelectric, and the rest was thermal, the thermal plants being either gas or oil fueled.

Electricity is rarely found in rural areas. In 1972 about 90 percent of the urban population had access to electricity, but only 5 percent of the rural population was served, which meant that as much as 68 percent of the total population had no access to electricity. The mining industry is the largest user of electrical energy; in the late 1960s it was absorbing 47 percent of the total electricity generated. Residential use accounted for 30 percent of the total generated, industry took only 15 percent, and the balance was for other uses. The current produced is of the alternating type: fifty cycles in La Paz, Cochabamba, Oruro, Potosí, Santa Cruz, Sucre, and Tarija; and sixty cycles elsewhere. Voltage is 110, 115, 220, 230, 380, or 400, depending upon the locality.

Electricity is provided by private firms, state-owned companies, municipal plants, cooperatives, and self-users (individuals, groups, or firms that generate electricity for their own use). The largest producer is the privately owned Bolivian Power Company (Cia. Boliviana de Energía Eléctrica, S.A.), which has been operating since 1926. It serves La Paz and its environs and, through a subsidiary, Oruro and some of the adjacent mines.

The major government-owned power producer is the National Electricity Company (Empresa Nacional de Electricidad—ENDE), established in 1965 to develop electricity in areas of the country not served by other systems. ENDE is financially sound and competently managed and is constantly increasing its facilities so that eventually it may become the major producer in the country. Its plans include the electrification of the entire southern half of the country and the building of a gas pipeline to Sucre to provide a source of fuel for new thermal plants. ENDE also sells its power in blocks to other companies, such as COMIBOL and the Cochabamba Electric Company. COMIBOL operates two plants of its own, which serve the mining districts of Potosí. The Cochabamba Electric Company—owned jointly by ENDE, the municipality of Cochabamba, and private investors—serves that city and some outlying provinces.

In order to provide for more efficient utilization of electricity resources, the National Directorate of Electricity (Dirección Nacional de Electricidad—DINE), which sets rates throughout the country and implements the regulations of the electricity code, ordered ENDE and the Bolivian Power Company in 1972 to interconnect their systems. Engineering studies on the feasibility of such an undertaking were in process in 1973. In addition to ENDE and DINE, there are two other government agencies concerned with electricity. The National Electricity Council (Consejo Nacional de Electricidad—CNE) sets overall policy with regard to electricity, and the National Institute for Rural Electrification (Instituto Nacional de Electrificación Rural), formerly the National Directorate of Hydraulics and Electrification, installs small diesel units with less than a 500-kilowatt capacity in rural communities.

MANUFACTURING

The manufacturing sector, including registered and unregistered enterprises and artisans, contributed about 12 percent to the gross national product (GNP) during the late 1960s. No heavy industry exists, and plants are very small in size. Over 2,700 manufacturing establishments were registered with the Ministry of Economy in 1970, but more than 1,000 were small shops making handicrafts, and some of the remainder had ceased to function but were still being listed on the ministry's rolls according to the National Chamber of Industries annual report for 1970. Little is known of the firms not registered. An estimated 170,000 persons were employed in manufacturing in 1970, but only about 27,000 were working in factories; the large balance were individual artisans or small-shop craftsmen. An additional 40,000 persons were employed in the construction industry.

The market for manufactured goods is small; the National Chamber of Industries estimates that only half of the population in 1970 purchased any factory-made articles. The small domestic market is further constricted by the influx of a large volume of contraband commodities; it is estimated that 40 percent of the demand for manufactured products is met by imports, both legal and illegal (see ch. 12). A salient feature of domestic manufacturing is the high number of import substitution goods made from imported raw materials. Among the products manufactured domestically are some not usually found in countries on Bolivia's level of economic development. These are items needed by the mining and petroleum industries, such as cables, hoses, pipes, and drums. There was still room for additional growth in the manufacture of import substitutes for consumer goods and beginning in 1971 the National Chamber of Industries began to assess each member firm 10 percent of its annual profits to establish an industrial development fund with which new cooperatively owned factories could produce new products.

The major manufacturing industries in 1972 were cotton and woolen textiles, food, and beverages. Textiles (including clothing) manufacturing, constituted the leading sector in terms of the number of establishments—over 300—and number of employees, about 7,000, but second in terms of value of production (about 20 percent of the total). The modern textile industry dates only from 1928, when the first textile factory was established. Cotton textiles predominate. There are periods of oversupply compounded by problems of contraband items adversely affecting sales. Some manufacturers with modern equipment have been able to reduce prices and compete with the illegally imported articles.

Food processing is the second leading sector in the number of establishments—about 200—but first in terms of value of production. Many of the establishments are small bakeries. One of the more important elements of the food-processing industry is sugar refining. All the mills are located in Santa Cruz and have modern equipment; the largest of the five sugar mills is government owned. Other important segments of the food-processing industry are grain milling, fruit and vegetable canning, and meatpacking, along with the production of candy and chocolates, milk products, and vegetable oils.

About 150 beverage companies accounted for about 13 percent of value of manufacturing production in 1970. Production of beverages is concentrated in La Paz, where almost half the national output originates. Beer brewing is the leading component and one of the oldest industries in the country—the first brewery was established in 1875—and there are breweries in most major cities. Production of alcohol and aguardiente, a brandy made from sugar, has been stimulated by the expansion of the sugar industry. Another popular alcoholic beverage is *chicha*. Many small firms bottle soft drinks and mineral water, but only a few companies make wines and liquors.

Tobacco manufacturing is another important industry, although production is concentrated in a few companies. One match factory, partially owned by the government, holds a legal monopoly on the manufacture and sales of matches until 1980. The National Glass and Crystal Factory employs about 400 persons and mainly produces bottles for the beverage industry and drinking glasses for the public. More than 200 firms, all very small, are in the furniture and woodworking industries and make items to order. The leather goods industry is another sector with a large number of small enterprises. It uses domestic leather almost exclusively, but output is affected by the poor quality of the raw product and improper tanning of the hides. Leather goods are also faced with competition from imported and domestically made plastic articles that can be substituted for leather.

More than three dozen plants in La Paz, Oruro, and Potosí produce chemicals, soaps, and pharmaceuticals. Sulfuric acid, livestock vaccine, paints, and candles are also manufactured. Printing and paper products are offered by four dozen firms in the principal urban areas. Production is limited to a few varieties of paper and packing cartons. Two small rubber goods factories make footwear, raincoats, toys, and miscellaneous rubber products, including recapped tires. A large number of small shops are engaged in making and repairing metallic products. A state-owned factory in Cochabamba manufactures refrigerators, metallic tables, and kitchen utensils. One plant makes automobile batteries.

The construction industry was stimulated by a combination of new roadbuilding, other public works, and a residential housing boom in most cities throughout the 1960s and into the early 1970s. Three cement plants supplied the country's needs. They were located at Viacha, Sucre, and Coboce. The latter, near Cochabamba, initiated its operations in 1972.

A large number of urban artisans operate one-man shops, sometimes assisted by their families. Most of the urban artisans are mestizos or Indians, but almost all rural artisans are Indians. Artisans are not organized, formal training is unknown, and skills are learned in the family. Vocational school graduates do not usually become artisans but rather factory wage earners. Although the tools and equipment utilized by most artisans are rudimentary, they are able to meet the domestic need for handicrafts (see ch. 3).

In rural areas such craftwork as the spinning of thread from sheep or llama wool for sale in weekly markets is usually a supplemental economic activity. Most rural folk can make their own textiles and clothes, domestic utensils, and agricultural implements. Some of the more important handicrafts made for sale or barter are hats, home-brewed *chicha*, knitted goods, adobe bricks, dolls, figurines, fireworks, musical instruments, cord and rope, wooden combs, straw sleeping mats, and sandals. Dollmaking is a very old household activity in Bolivia, dating to pre-Columbian times. The dolls are made of rags, gypsum, straw, wood, rubber, ceramics, wax, candies, or bread. Figurines are sculptured or molded plaster and are used for household decorations. Fireworks are important because of the large number of village festivals. The most popular handmade musical instrument is the *charango*, made from the shell of an armadillo.

CHAPTER 14

TRADE AND TRANSPORTATION

According to available estimates, foreign and domestic trade accounted for 15 percent and transportation for 8 percent of gross domestic product (GDP) during the 1969-71 period. The economy of the urban segment of the population and the economic development of the entire country are heavily dependent upon foreign trade. Exports, particularly tin and other minerals, provide the earnings to pay for the import of needed consumer and capital goods. The country is extremely sensitive to world fluctuations in mineral prices, and its foreign policy is significantly influenced by economic considerations (see ch. 11).

With the exception of certain years after the 1952 Revolution Bolivia has had an annual foreign trade surplus, exporting more than it has imported. Because of its landlocked position its transportation system was initially directed outward to accommodate its foreign trade; a national transportation network was not developed until the middle of the twentieth century. It was still easier, in 1973, to travel to neighboring Chile, Peru, Argentina, or Brazil than to go from La Paz to certain parts of the eastern lowlands where much of the land of agricultural potential is located (see ch. 13).

Domestic trade patterns were altered by the 1952 Revolution and by the change in the socioeconomic status of the Indian. Before 1952 trade in rural areas was isolated from national activities and was generally self-contained. Only the trade of the cities, mining regions, and rural communities along the transportation networks was national in scope and conducted on an organized basis. Since 1952 the Indian has been brought into the domestic economy, and new trading patterns are being established.

DOMESTIC TRADE

The 1952 Revolution not only altered land tenure relationships, minerals ownership, and the basic social system but also caused a drastic change in marketing conditions. Before the revolution the marketing of agricultural products was controlled by the landowners, who sold commodities directly to wholesalers, to retailers, or even to individual consumers in the cities. After the revolution retailers and wholesalers no longer could obtain produce in quantities directly from the producer, and new marketing structures started to develop, which still were not definitive as of 1973.

Wholesale trade is found almost exclusively in the urban-industrial segment of the economy and is concentrated in La Paz. There are four broad categories of wholesaler: large importers, wholesaler-retailers of nonperishables, fruit and vegetable wholesalers, and meat wholesalers. The importers usually have their own warehouses and may also act as representatives of foreign manufacturers. The uncertainties of transport from the originating country make it almost impossible to specialize in the importation of any single line of merchandise, although five firms in the late 1960s specialized in importing foods. Rather, most importers handle a variety of goods so that those goods in ample supply will compensate for those not available at a given time. Importers need long lead times in ordering merchandise from abroad and must carry costly inventories if they wish to have an adequate supply on hand. Most wholesalers rely on middlemen or retailers to distribute their merchandise, but domestic manufacturers who do their own wholesaling may have respresentatives in many small towns who only take orders for direct delivery to consumers.

Some wholesalers are also retailers in that they may sell directly to consumers on a regular basis. This is particularly true of the marketing of dry and processed foods. More than three dozen such firms exist in La Paz. Numerous small firms are engaged in fruit, vegetable, and grain wholesaling and operate out of a market complex of three large buildings in the center of La Paz. The wholesalers of such perishables may also sell directly to consumers who come to the markets in addition to delivering to their regular retail customers.

Most meat comes from forty-three slaughterhouses located in El Beni (see ch. 13). The slaughterhouses are operated by the largest ranches for their own use and for that of their neighbors on a fee basis. All slaughterhouses are located near airstrips, and the cattle are slaughtered only when a cargo plane is on hand and weather will permit a takeoff. About 10 percent of El Beni cattle are moved live via riverboat to Cochabamba for slaughter in that city. Some of the larger ranches also maintain their own wholesale outlets in La Paz. In the late 1960s there were about thirty meat wholesalers in La Paz, sixteen of whom had cold storage facilities. Very few meat wholesalers sell directly to individual consumers. Meat is retailed via butcher shops and market stalls.

Retailing is accomplished through a multiplicity of units, most of which are small. A 1966–67 retail survey in La Paz found more than 10,000 retailers, fewer than 200 of whom could accommodate nine or more customers on the premises at the same time. About half of the 10,000 retail units in La Paz were stores; the balance were market stalls or street vendors—ambulatory or stationary. No department stores or supermarkets existed as of 1972. Many stores sold a variety of unrelated goods, but most retailers specialized in a few product lines. The 1966–67 survey indicated that half of all La Paz retailers sold only one product line. Stores in small towns carried limited quantities of a wider range of staples—alcohol, beer, soft drinks, matches, sugar, salt, pasta, rice, soap, and kerosine, and perhaps bread, wheat, candy, and cooking oil. Only the largest rural stores carried additional items.

Markets are found in all cities and in many smaller communities. La Paz has several large elaborately enclosed markets with separate stalls for each vendor and sometimes sanitary facilities for the customers. In Cochabamba the principal market is the open-air Concha market, which has a few enclosures. The wares are displayed on sidewalks, pushcarts, wooden stands, or on the ground. The city markets are monopolized by professional traders, mainly women. Smalltown markets attract farmers from the vicinity who sell or exchange their surplus agricultural produce. Itinerant vendors also frequent the smaller markets, selling small manufactured items. Some markets are free markets (*mercados libres*); vendors do not pay a fee for the right to sell their merchandise. This is common in many parts of the Altiplano and on special occasions in La Paz. Many local markets, particularly those near areas like Tarija and Sucre, are frequently saturated with the same produce, but inadequate transportation and lack of knowledge of the markets elsewhere in the country hinder the transfer of such local surplus to other consuming areas.

Many weekly fairs and markets have developed since the 1952 Revolution, and going to market is considered a pleasant break in the routine of the farmer's family. A 1967 survey indicated that as many as seventy-five towns on the Altiplano had weekly fairs. As many as 65 percent of all farmers in the country marketed their produce at such weekly fairs to truckers and other middlemen. Some farmers who are closer to the cities transport their produce directly to city retailers or to wholesalers. Farmers who do not frequent the markets usually take their produce to specified rural assembly points where the goods are purchased by truckers or other middlemen.

Both men and women participate in retail trade, but women predominate in the markets, and most street vendors are women. Children may assist their parents, but they may also engage in their own businesses—selling pencils, ball-point pens, or lottery tickets. Retailers do not constitute a cohesive, clearly identifiable group. They may range from the foreigner who operates a speciality shop to the upper class domestic tradesmen, mestizos, *cholos* (see Glossary), or Indians. The location of the shop usually reflects the class status of its owner and operator.

An unusual relationship exists between retailers and their clients. A survey in La Paz in the late 1960s indicated that more than 70 percent of the customers returned to the same retailer rather than shop around for a better price. Bargaining between the retailer and the returning customer has been replaced by a tacit understanding that the vendor will sell at the lowest price or advise the customer to wait for a better shipment. In turn the customer is expected to purchase with regularity from the same vendor. The very best customers may receive credit, but most retail establishments do not customarily extend it. On occasion an extra amount or another item is given free as a token of appreciation for the customer.

Basically the country has a free market economy in domestic trade with prices set locally by the law of supply and demand, although the prices vary regionally because of a lack of communication. A few commodities, such as rice and sugarcane, are subsidized by the government. The government also markets all the rice through the National Rice Company in order to keep prices uniform. The retail price of meat, but not the wholesale price, is controlled. In an effort to control prices, the government on occasion, as in late 1972, may sell basic foods in addition to rice directly to the people for a period of time. The products sold by the government are usually those confiscated from speculators. Most retail prices are not quoted in newspaper advertisements or in radio commercials; they are more often publicized by word of mouth or are not known until the shop is visited.

The metric system has been the official basis for weights and measures since 1893, and all official publications and many merchants use it. Traditional Spanish measurements and some English measures are also used, and some shops may quote prices in more than one system. There are also local variations of the old measurements, which cause considerable confusion to outsiders. Among the more common old Spanish measures still used is the *arroba*, which is usually equivalent to twenty-five pounds but varies with the product being weighed—it may also be 6.7 gallons. The *libra* is equivalent to 1.01 pounds; the *quintal*, to 101 pounds; the *cargo*, to 200 pounds of grain; and the *cajón*, to 5,000 pounds of mineral ore. A *vara* is usually equivalent to 32.9 inches but may vary if something other than land is being measured. An *almud* is either 1,000 square *varas* of land or thirty-two pounds of grain.

TOURISM

Tourism is a small but well organized segment of the economy. Fewer than 37,000 people visited Bolivia in 1971. Virtually all of the tourist attractions are found in the northern Altiplano—mainly pre-Incan ruins. Some of the tourist agencies provide trips into the valleys and lowlands. La Paz and the other large cities offer comfortable hotel accommodations, but outside these metropolitan areas lodging is difficult to find. In 1972 there were only seventy hotels in the entire country. In small communities travelers must find lodging in private homes or inns where rooms are available and where vehicles and merchandise can be safely kept in enclosed courtyards.

In 1973 Bolivia hoped to benefit from special decreased air fares for

320

tourists from countries of the Andean Common Market (ACM) beginning in May as part of a joint effort to encourage Andean tourism. In addition, the Bolivian Institute of Tourism was created in early 1973 to develop tourist centers and to alter an image of Bolivia held by many potential visitors based upon a history of political instability and the fear of altitude sickness. There are several thermal springs scattered over a wide area of the mineral belt that are frequented by many Bolivians. With a little more investment and promotion, these and other communities have the potential for developing into spas.

Restaurants are found in all principal cities but not in smaller communities. Barbershops in the hotels offer wholly adequate service, and less elaborate enterprises serve the residential areas of the cities and small towns. Beauty parlors are found almost exclusively in La Paz and Cochabamba. Commercial laundries and dry cleaners exist in the major cities only; in other areas laundering is the traditional responsibility of the housewife or servant.

TRANSPORTATION AND COMMUNICATION

Transportation has been a crucial problem ever since colonial days, when well-maintained lines of communication with Spain were required, especially after silver and other minerals were discovered. In early days, when Panama held a monopoly of all goods sent to the Spanish colonies, the main route of transport from there to Argentina was via Bolivia; but when Buenos Aires became an important seaport, a large portion of the overland traffic was diverted to Argentina. Roads were built to both Pacific and Argentine ports. The topography of the country and the formidable physical barriers make the building of surface transportation difficult and costly. Most Bolivian governments, however, visualize the costs as being justified if the various regions of the country can be linked and a sense of national identity increased while regional separatism diminishes (see fig. 5). Since September 1972 the Ministry of Transport, Communication, and Civil Aviation has been responsible for all transport policy. It receives proposals from the various government transport agencies and adjusts them to the nation's transport requirements.

Until the end of the nineteenth century, men, burros, and llamas served as the principal carriers of goods in the highlands. Very few wheeled vehicles, such as carts, were used except in the lowlands, where the terrain was more suitable. Men and women have hauled food, ores, and industrial goods on their backs over long distances and at high altitudes for centuries. Long llama pack trains were the prime means of moving merchandise between Bolivia and seaports until the twentieth century. Even in the 1970s transport by man and pack train prevailed along mountainous tracks and remained the only means of bringing agricultural products from outlying areas to collection points.

Until the middle of the twentieth century the principal roads of the

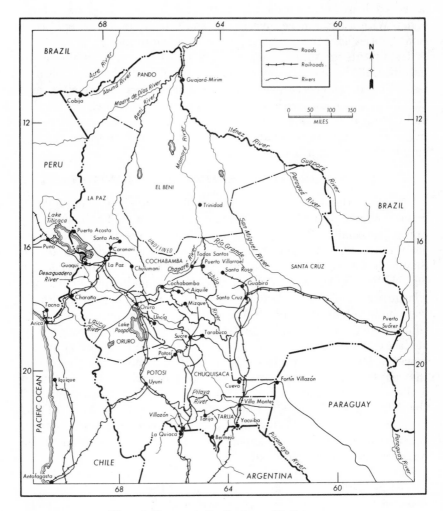

Figure 5. Transportation Systems of Bolivia, 1973

322

country consisted of widened tracks and dry riverbeds. Only since World War II have modern roads been built. The National Road Service, established in 1964 as a decentralized entity, is in charge of all matters relating to the construction, improvement, and maintenance of roads. Landslides are common in the mountains and cause frequent delays and costly maintenance. A road tax, levied on all males between the ages of eighteen and sixty and payable annually in either cash or from two to four days of labor, helps to maintain some local roads.

Lack of uniformity in criteria applied to the definition of roads makes it impossible to establish the length of the overall road network. Figures varied in 1973 from 12,000 miles to 17,500 miles, but in any event only 664 miles had been paved by that year. About 2,400 miles were all-weather improved roads, and the vast balance was passable only in dry weather. About half the agricultural area of the country is not served by roads, and large areas of the departments of El Beni, Pando, and Santa Cruz lack road connections with the rest of the country.

The principal road is the Pan American Highway, a 705-mile route, of which only thirty miles were paved as of 1973, from Desaguadero at the Peruvian border via La Paz, Oruro, and Potosí to Villazón on the Argentine border. The longest paved road is the 350-mile Cochabamba-Santa Cruz highway. Before that highway was built, the average driving time between La Paz and Santa Cruz was from two to four days, with delays of up to twenty days en route because of bad weather and landslides. It was cheaper to import agricultural commodities via the Pacific coast than to transport them overland from Santa Cruz to La Paz.

Road construction from the highlands to the fertile valleys and lowlands has been a most important contribution to the national economy. Thousands of settlers have opened up new lands in the Yungas and the Oriente along newly built roads. One such road, fully paved, was inaugurated in late 1972, extending from Cochabamba 125 miles northeast to Puerto Villarroel on the Ichilo River, a tributary of the Mamoré River, which eventually flows into the Amazon. It was hoped that this combined river-road connection would open up the relatively isolated El Beni Department. In late 1972 the National Road Service had drawn up impressive plans to build 1,800 miles of new roads and to improve and pave highly traveled sections of older roads in order to lower costs to users caused by wear and tear on their vehicles. Much of the financing of the new construction would have to come from foreign sources.

Results of the expansion of the road system are visible in the rising number of registered motor vehicles, which reached 53,000 in 1971. About 14,000 were heavy trucks; 2,000 were buses; 29,000 were automobiles; and the balance were other types of vehicles. Truckers have become an important element in the marketing process. Most of these operate on an organized and regular basis, plying between specific points. It was estimated that trucks carry 60 percent of all domestic freight but very little international cargo. Only one trucking firm maintains scheduled service between Bolivia, Argentina, Brazil, Chile, Paraguay, and Uruguay.

In addition to freight, truckers carry passengers. Time, cost, and points of departure are generally known to the local people, particularly on the Altiplano where the farmer may be taking produce to La Paz himself. In Cochabamba most of the truckers have formed a cooperative, which helps them obtain cargo and passengers on a more organized basis and also handles their accounts. Many rural persons prefer riding on trucks to riding buses because, although plentiful and inexpensive, the buses are slow and in poor condition.

Railroads, the primary means for moving goods in foreign trade, represent Bolivia's main lifelines to the rest of the world. In addition, they carry a significant, although declining, percentage of domestic freight and passengers. As of 1973 there were two major railroad systems, each with several lines, administered by the state-owned National Railways Company (Empresa Nacional de Ferrocarriles—ENFE), plus two short lines, one run by the Mining Corporation of Bolivia (Corporación Minera de Bolivia—COMIBOL). The oldest lines are those that are part of the Western System and were constructed by private interests between 1870 and 1920 for carrying ores to the various Pacific ports and bringing back imported machinery and equipment. In later years they were taken over by the government. The Western System was previously composed of six separate railroad lines, totaling about 1,400 miles. In 1964, when ENFE was founded, they were consolidated into an integrated system. The Western System provides access to the Pacific ports of Matarani in Peru, Arica and Antofagasta in Chile, and various Atlantic ports in Argentina.

The 730-mile Eastern System was built after 1937 with financial assistance from Brazil and Argentina. It has two main lines; one goes from Santa Cruz to Yacuiba on the Argentine border, and the other runs from Santa Cruz to Corumbá on the Brazilian border. A third line of the Eastern System under construction in 1973 by a joint Bolivian-Argentine commission was planned to reach Puerto Mamoré, 190 miles northeast of Santa Cruz, but early in 1973 only sixty-six miles had been completed. Further extension of this line from Puerto Mamoré to Trinidad also was under study, but its construction would be far in the future. The lines of the Eastern System were combined in 1967 and turned over to ENFE. The Eastern and Western systems are linked only by going through Argentina. Bolivia is a member, however, of the Latin American Association of Railroads, formed in 1964 to carry out joint projects, one of which is the eventual construction of a connecting line between the two systems in Bolivia. This would permit direct rail travel from Arica, Chile, to Santos, Brazil. In 1973 a joint Bolivian-Brazilian commission began studies of the feasibility of constructing

324

such a connection between Cochabamba and Santa Cruz.

In 1972 ENFE had over 1,800 freight cars, 200 passenger cars, and about 140 locomotives. Most of its equipment was obsolescent, however, and financial and managerial problems caused annual operating deficits and dependence on government subsidies. The Five Year Rehabilitation and Investment Plan was adopted by the government for the 1973-77 period to modernize ENFE at a cost of about the equivalent of US$37 million intended to eliminate the annual deficits by 1978. The costs were being partly financed by the United Nations Development Program and the International Development Association. ENFE also hoped to reduce a redundant portion of its 6,200-person labor force through attrition by 1977.

The two short lines are the 120-mile Machacamarca-Uncía Railroad, owned by COMIBOL, which connects Oruro with the mining areas around that city, and the sixty-mile La Paz-Guaqui Railroad, operated by the Peruvian Corporation as an extension of its Southern Railroads of Peru, via Lake Titicaca ferry. The track gauge for all railroad lines in Bolivia is one meter, which facilitates interchange of railroad cars.

Because of the landlocked position of the country and the absence of surface transportation to many outlying areas, air transportation had been developed extensively. Bolivia was one of the first Latin American countries to organize aviation and to use it as an important means of communication. As early as 1914 the Bolivian Air Club was functioning, and in 1925 the first scheduled domestic airline was formed, Bolivian Air Lloyd (Lloyd Aéreo Boliviano—LAB). In 1927 LAB established a school for pilots in Cochabamba that became the National Aeronautical Institute in 1954.

In addition to LAB, in 1973 there were seven unscheduled airlines, thirty-one air taxi companies, and a commercial branch of the armed forces, Military Air Transports (Transportes Aéreos Militares—TAM), which provided domestic air service in 1973. TAM took over scheduled flights between isolated towns in 1973, permitting LAB to restrict itself to the more profitable routes. LAB is a mixed state-private enterprise. The National Aeronautics Council, created in 1965, is a technical and administrative agency that carries out government aeronautical policy. Six of the unscheduled airlines are engaged in transporting meat from El Beni to the Altiplano (see Domestic Trade, this ch.) (see ch. 13). In addition to the commercial airlines, both COMIBOL and YPFB (see Glossary) operate their own aircraft, and seven civilian air clubs were in operation in 1972.

There was a total of about 200 registered aircraft in the fleets of all the airlines in 1972, ranging from small single-engine craft to helicopters and large jets, such as the Boeing 727. There were about twenty-five airfields and seventy landing strips in the country in 1972, only three of which had paved runways: La Paz, Cochabamba, and Santa Cruz. The La Paz airport has the reputation of being the highest commercial airport in the world: 13,400 feet. Feasibility studies began in 1973 regarding the possibility of constructing a new airport for Santa Cruz that would also serve as an international airport. All airports are built and managed by a state entity called the Administration for Airports and Auxiliary Services for Air Navigation.

International air service is provided on a scheduled basis by LAB and a number of foreign airlines: Braniff, Lufthansa, Iberia, the British Overseas Airways Corporation (BOAC), Aerolineas Argentinas, Varig, and Cruzeiro do Sul (Brazil). Some of the other domestic companies will handle charter international flights. LAB flies to Lima, Buenos Aires, and Salta in Argentina, Arica, Chile, and São Paulo, Brazil. Braniff has five flights weekly between La Paz and the United States via Lima.

The more than thirty large rivers of the Amazon drainage system that transect the Eastern Plains are navigable for thousands of miles. An estimate was made that there were more than 12,000 miles of navigable waterways in the country in 1972, although some sections of rivers require shallow-draft vessels. Some rivers constitute the main, and in some places the only, routes of communication between small settlements and the rest of the country. All river and lake waters, their navigation, and all vessels are under the jurisdiction of the Lake and River Force (Fuerza Fluvial y Lacustre), a subordinate agency of the Ministry of Defense.

The main rivers being used are the Beni and the Mamoré, followed by the Guaporé, Chaparé, and Ichilo. The Paraguay River may become important in the future as an outlet for the iron ore to be exploited at Mutún; and a new river port, Puerto General Busch, was under construction in 1973 for that purpose (see ch. 13). In the late 1960s there were about 200 registered boats in commercial use on the lakes and rivers; the largest was sixty registered tons. Hydrofoils and ferryboats connect Bolivia and Peru via Lake Titicaca.

Despite its landlocked position, Bolivia does have the use of seaports in other countries. Antofagasta in Chile is a free port for Bolivian merchandise, as are Santos, Belém, and Portovelho in Brazil. Under the terms of a 1969 agreement with Argentina, a twelve-acre site in Rosario, Argentina, was ceded to Bolivia in 1972 as a free zone seaport. The free zone began operations in early 1973 under a special mixed Bolivian-Argentine commission. A shipping line, Transmarine Bolivia (Transmarítima Boliviana), was established in 1969 by the government. It operated out of Chilean and Peruvian ports with chartered freight vessels. It was in financial difficulties from its inception, and its future was in doubt in 1973.

There were about 155 telecommunications systems in the country in 1972, but the majority were privately owned and used by the owner, such as a mining or industrial firm. The National Enterprise for Telecommunications was installing a national microwave system in 1973 that would permit telephone, telegraph, and television services to be supplied to most of the country by 1974 or 1975. Most of the local telephone companies were privately owned, and some were cooperatives, such as the telephone company of Santa Cruz. There were about 28,000 telephones in operation in all of the companies in 1970. Dial service was available in La Paz, Cochabamba, Oruro, Sucre, Potosí, and Santa Cruz. In 1971 Bolivia and Argentina were connected telephonically via satellite.

There were about 8,000 miles of telegraph lines in 1972. Domestic telegraph service was provided by the government. International telegraph service was provided by three private companies. There were over 400 post offices in the country in 1972, of which 200 also provided telegraph and telephone services to the patrons. Bolivia was a member of the Andean Postal Union, formed in 1973 to standardize postal rules and facilitate the introduction of modern mail-handling methods and equipment in the Andean countries.

FOREIGN TRADE

The government's foreign trade policy is to diversify exports and to decrease the importation of goods that could be produced in Bolivia. To stimulate exports the government sometimes exempts or rebates export duties, which are levied on specific products. The Bolivian Institute for the Promotion of Exports attempts to find ways to expedite exports and suggests approaches the government can make to other governments to help free the flow of Bolivian exports from undue paperwork. Sometimes, despite the government's desire to diversify exports, it has had to suspend exports of a particular product in order to satisfy domestic demand, as occurred with coffee and beef for short periods in 1972.

The government's import policy has been unrestrictive with certain exceptions. A limited list of goods may not be imported at all in order to protect domestic manufacturers; a 1971 decree prohibited the importation of any capital or consumer good that competes with locally made goods. Import quotas exist for a few commodities, and certain items require a prior import license. Otherwise, most import duties are low, although import surcharges may be applied on consumer goods on a temporary basis in response to balance-of-payments difficulties in some years.

The economy is disturbed by the extensive smuggling, which floods the market with goods that are imported illegally and often sold openly. For years the government's fight against smuggling has been unsuccessful, mainly because governmental efforts are sporadic and not continuous. Observers comment that the seemingly passive attitude toward contraband has had a deleterious effect upon domestic production and trade.

Historically, Bolivia had been an exporting country; a gradually expanding volume of trade produced a substantially higher income from exports than was spent on imports. Between 1900 and 1957, with the single exception of 1921, the balance of trade had been favorable. The sociopolitical uncertainties that followed the 1952 Revolution were reflected in a slackening export volume and a comparable reduction in imports. By 1957 the volume of imports exceeded that of exports, reversing the traditional trend and causing a sizable deficit. The negative balance of trade continued until 1964, when the balance was favorable. Imports surpassed exports again in 1965, but from 1966 through 1972 the country once more experienced a trade surplus. In 1972 exports soared to US$254 million, and imports only reached US$188 million. During the decade of the 1950s exports actually decreased by an average annual rate of 1 percent, but during the 1960s they grew by more than 11 percent annually, the highest growth rate for all of Latin America, and reached the equivalent of US$254 million in 1972 (see table 6).

The country's acquisition of foreign exchange has depended almost exclusively on the export of minerals. Historically, minerals made up over 90 percent of all exports; but since the mid-1960s the government's attempts at diversifying the export mix has had some success, and the share of minerals dropped to between 80 and 90 percent annually (see table 7). Tin is the leading single export; during the first sixty years of the twentieth century, it accounted for between 55 and 80 percent of annual exports, but in 1970 and 1971 the relative share of tin had dropped below 50 percent. Bolivia is a member of the International Tin Agreement, which is designed to offset adverse shifts in the world price of tin. The signatory members are assigned annual export quotas and jointly own a buffer stock of tin that is used to balance world supplies of the mineral.

Hydrocarbons (petroleum and natural gas) have been the second leading export since 1966, with the exception of 1970. The falloff in 1970 was caused by the need to find new markets for petroleum after the nationalization of the Bolivian Gulf Oil Company (see ch. 13). Natural gas exports began in 1972 and should contribute to increased export earnings. All of the natural gas exports as of 1973 were sold to Argentina via a newly built gas pipeline. Argentina contracted to purchase over US$300 million of natural gas during a twenty-year contract period.

Among the other significant minerals making up the spectrum of export commodities are antimony, tungsten, zinc, copper, silver, bismuth, and lead. Their relative shares vary annually, reflecting market prices and production. Gold, sulfur, mica, cadmium, gypsum, iron, and a score of minerals of minor importance make up the remainder of the mineral export list.

Cotton and coffee are the two most important nonmineral exports.

Table 6. Bolivian Exports by Value, 1967–72
(in million U.S. dollars)

Exports	1967	1968	1969	1970	1971	1972*
Minerals						
Tin	90.9	92.5	102.5	101.9	100.3	
Tungsten	8.0	9.7	11.1	17.6	13.2	
Antimony	6.4	6.0	11.0	31.0	9.3	
Zinc	4.4	3.0	7.8	14.3	14.5	
Copper	6.4	7.7	11.0	12.5	7.8	
Silver	6.7	11.2	10.8	10.5	7.9	
Lead	4.9	5.1	6.8	7.8	6.8	
Gold	...	...	1.5	0.2	...	
Other	3.6	3.8	4.7	8.9	6.9	
Subtotal	131.3	139.0	167.2	204.7	166.7	193.3
Hydrocarbons	22.9	24.3	23.0	10.2	24.7	
Agricultural Products						
Cotton	...	0.6	1.2	3.0	6.0	
Coffee	4.5	2.7	2.9	.3.6	4.8	
Timber and lumber	0.7	0.9	0.9	1.6	1.9	
Nuts	2.6	0.9	0.9	1.0	1.1	
Rubber	0.7	0.5	0.8	0.9	0.9	
Hides and skins	1.1	0.5	0.5	0.5	0.6	
Quinine	1.1	0.1	0.1	0.1	0.1	
Sugar	0.7	0.8	0.8	1.0	...	
Cattle and beef	...	...	...	0.1	...	
Subtotal	11.4	7.0	8.1	11.8	15.4	
Other exports	0.2	3.8	...	1.6	...	
Total	165.8	174.1	198.3	228.3	206.8	254.0

... not applicable.
*Breakdown of minerals and agricultural products for 1972 not available.

Coffee was the more important of the two, accounting for between 2 and 5 percent of annual exports, until 1971, when cotton surged ahead. Bolivia is a member of the International Coffee Agreement, which sets annual export quotas for producing countries. Bolivia has been able to meet its basic export quota in most years and often receives a supplemental quota. Its 1972 export quota was set at 65,000 bags (a coffee bag weighs 132 pounds). Cotton exports first commenced in 1968 and have been steadily increasing; in 1971 such exports accounted for 6 percent of the total. Even larger shares are anticipated for 1973 and for later years, as cotton grows well in the Bolivian lowlands and there is a good market for the product because of its high quality. Minor exports are beef, timber, nuts, rubber, hides, sugar, and miscellaneous products.

The emphasis on imports is on manufactured goods. Capital goods, the most dynamic import category, increased from under 33 percent of total imports in 1963 to over 48 percent in 1971. The most important

Table 7. Structure of Bolivian Exports, 1967–72
(in percent)

Export	1967	1968	1969	1970	1971	1972*
Minerals						
Tin	54.8	53.1	51.7	44.6	48.5	
Tungsten	4.8	5.6	5.6	7.7	6.4	
Antimony	3.9	3.5	5.6	13.6	4.5	
Zinc	2.6	1.7	3.9	6.3	7.0	
Copper	3.9	4.4	5.6	5.5	3.8	
Silver	4.0	6.4	5.5	4.6	3.8	
Lead	3.0	2.9	3.4	3.4	3.3	
Gold	...	...	0.7	0.1	...	
Other	2.2	2.2	2.4	3.9	3.3	
Subtotal	79.2	79.8	84.4	89.7	80.6	76.1
Hydrocarbons	13.8	14.0	11.6	4.4	11.9	
Agricultural Products						
Cotton	...	0.3	0.6	1.3	2.9	
Coffee	2.7	1.6	1.4	1.6	2.3	
Timber	0.4	0.5	0.5	0.7	0.9	
Nuts	1.6	0.5	0.4	0.4	0.5	
Rubber	0.4	0.3	0.4	0.4	0.5	
Hides and skins	0.7	0.3	0.2	0.2	0.3	
Quinine	0.7	0.1	0.1	0.1	0.1	
Sugar	0.4	0.4	0.4	0.4	...	
Cattle and beef	...	...	...	0.1	...	
Subtotal	6.9	4.0	4.0	5.2	7.5	
Other	0.1	2.2	...	0.7	...	
Total	100.0	100.0	100.0	100.0	100.0	100.0

... not applicable.
*Breakdown of minerals and agricultural products for 1972 not available.

categories of capital goods are mechanical equipment for the mining and petroleum industries and transportation equipment and vehicles (see table 8). Raw materials and intermediate goods are the next largest category, although the relative share fluctuates; in 1971 they accounted for under 30 percent of total imports. Consumer goods are mainly durables and foodstuffs. In spite of the numbers of persons who engage in agriculture, much food has to be imported, particularly wheat and flour, and fats and oils.

The United States can be considered Bolivia's major trading partner. It is the primary supplier of imports, providing about one-third of total imports before World War II and between 40 and 50 percent since 1942 and until the 1969-71 period, when the percentage fell to around one-third. The United States has been the second leading market for Bolivian exports, except for the 1942-56 period, when it was the primary export market (see table 9). The principal exports to the United States are minerals, petroleum, and coffee. The United States buys almost all

Table 8. Structure and Value of Bolivian Imports, 1967-71

Commodity	1967	1968	1969	1970	1971
Value[1]					
Mechanical equipment	22.0	29.9	27.1	26.1	28.1
Vehicles	21.6	19.7	18.9	20.4	21.5
Iron and steel	12.1	15.0	18.8	15.5	16.3
Wheat and flour	14.1	10.4	9.9	11.7	12.3
Electrical equipment	9.7	8.2	9.2	9.2	9.6
Fats and oils	5.5	4.6	6.3	5.5	5.8
Pharmaceuticals	3.7	4.1	4.3	4.1	4.3
Rubber products	3.3	4.1	3.5	3.7	3.9
Railroad equipment	0.5	1.5	9.2	3.7	3.9
Aircraft	1.0	1.5	4.2	2.2	2.4
All other products	57.4	53.7	53.7	56.0	63.2
Total...................	150.9	152.7	165.1	158.1	171.3
Structure of Imports[2]					
Mechanical equipment	14.6	19.6	16.4	16.5	16.4
Vehicles	14.3	12.9	11.5	12.9	12.5
Iron and steel	8.0	9.8	11.4	9.8	9.5
Wheat and flour	9.3	6.8	6.0	7.4	7.2
Electrical equipment	6.4	5.4	5.6	5.8	5.6
Fats and oils	3.7	3.0	3.8	3.5	3.4
Pharmaceuticals	2.5	2.7	2.6	2.6	2.5
Rubber products	2.2	2.7	2.1	2.4	2.3
Railroad equipment	0.3	1.0	5.6	2.3	2.3
Aircraft	0.7	1.0	2.5	1.4	1.4
All other	38.0	35.1	32.5	35.4	36.9
Total...................	100.0	100.0	100.0	100.0	100.0

[1] In million U.S. dollars.
[2] In percent.

the tungsten and antimony and most of the lead and silver. In turn the United States provides machinery, transportation equipment, wheat and flour, and a long list of miscellaneous products.

Except for the period when the United States was the primary export market, the United Kingdom has been the historic market for Bolivia. The United Kingdom buys from 75 percent to almost 90 percent of all tin exports, one-third of lead exports, and 20 percent of the silver. The major role played by the United Kingdom in Bolivia's export trade is not equaled by its share of imports, which averaged under 5 percent of the total during the 1968-71 period.

The Federal Republic of Germany (West Germany) and Japan have become the second and third leading suppliers of imports—West Germany since the mid-1950s and Japan since 1962. Both provide a variety of goods. Japan purchases most of the copper and zinc exports and a small portion of the lead. Argentina is the main trading partner in Latin America. Despite numerous trade agreements and aid offers by

Country	Exports				Imports			
	1968	1969	1970	1971	1968	1969	1970	1971
United States	34.7	30.7	36.8	35.6	43.4	31.1	38.6	37.5
United Kingdom	44.0	45.8	43.8	42.6	4.7	5.0	4.8	4.6
Japan	3.0	6.1	3.8	3.8	11.1	16.4	13.3	12.9
Federal Republic of								
Germany (West Germany)	3.3	2.6	3.6	3.5	11.9	12.4	12.0	11.7
Argentina	4.7	5.3	4.5	4.4	7.4	10.2	7.9	7.7
Netherlands	2.9	3.1	2.6	2.5	3.1	3.5	3.0	2.9
Brazil	0.5	0.5	0.6	0.5	1.6	1.9	1.8	5.2
Spain	1.6	1.8	1.2	1.2	1.1	1.1	1.2	1.2
Peru	1.3	1.7	1.4	1.3	1.4	1.3	1.3	1.2
Chile	0.8	0.8	0.7	0.7	1.3	1.2	1.3	1.3
Ecuador	...	...	...	...	0.1	0.1	0.7	0.7
Colombia	...	...	...	...	0.2	0.3	0.2	0.2
Paraguay	...	...	...	...	...	...	0.1	0.2
Uruguay	...	...	...	...	...	0.1	0.1	0.1
Others	3.2	1.6	1.0	3.9	12.7	15.4	13.7	12.6
Total	100.0	100.0	100.0	100.0	100.0	100.0	100.0	100.0

... not applicable.

the communist countries, actual trade with state trading countries has not been very important (see ch. 12).

REGIONAL ECONOMIC INTEGRATION

Bolivia was a member of the Latin American Free Trade Association (LAFTA), the Andean Common Market (ACM), and the River Plate Group in 1973. LAFTA was created on June 1, 1961, on the basis of a multilateral agreement known as the Montevideo Treaty of February 1960. The original founding members were Argentina, Brazil, Chile, Mexico, Paraguay, Peru, and Uruguay. Colombia and Ecuador joined in late 1961; Venezuela, in September 1966; and Bolivia, in January 1967. Although it had participated in the early negotiations for the establishment of LAFTA, Bolivia was reluctant to ratify the treaty. As originally conceived, LAFTA was to be a trading association with the objective of expanding member markets by the elimination of barriers to trade, particularly tariffs. Bolivia desired LAFTA to be more than a trading association and, during the negotiations, received assurances that all members would agree to create conditions favorable to the establishment of a Latin American common market with concomitant regional development. When LAFTA exhibited no movement toward regional development, Bolivia deferred joining. In addition, President Víctor Paz Estenssoro was opposed to joining LAFTA, because the country was dependent upon sales to non-Latin countries for its hard currency needs and because he did not wish to alter Bolivia's trading patterns.

After President Paz was overthrown in 1964, Bolivia indicated a renewed interest in joining LAFTA but requested special treatment as a condition of joining. Such treatment included the right to assume its obligations under LAFTA only on a gradual basis, special tariff rights for Bolivian exports, and financial assistance from the other members. The conditions were agreed to; Bolivia, along with Ecuador and Paraguay, received over 7,000 exclusive trade concessions as lesser developed members, and Bolivia received a further benefit in that other members would agree to cut tariffs on Bolivian exports of manufactured goods through 1973. It was also agreed to convert LAFTA from a free trade zone into a common market, the process to begin in 1970 and end in 1985.

Full free trade among members of LAFTA was to be achieved by 1972 through annual tariff negotiations. Over 11,000 tariff concessions had been negotiated by 1972, but many obstacles had developed, particularly over agricultural products, from 1965 onward, and the 1972 deadline could not be met. An amendment, called the Caracas Protocol, pushed back the free trade deadline to 1980, provided that all members ratify the protocol by the end of 1973.

Bolivia found that it benefited little from joining LAFTA; most of its exports still went to non-LAFTA countries, and it imported more from LAFTA members than it sold to them. Ninety percent of all intrazonal trade was in primary products, whereas most of the special tariff concessions made to Bolivia were for manufactured products that Bolivia did not produce. In fact, two-thirds of all tariff concessions made by LAFTA members were never utilized by any other member as of 1972.

Dissatisfaction with the rate of progress and benefits accruing to them as members of LAFTA led Bolivia, Chile, Colombia, Ecuador, and Peru to sign an agreement in May 1969 called the Andean Subregional Economic Integration Agreement, commonly known as the Cartagena Agreement, to form an association leading to an Andean common market. Venezuela participated in the original negotiations but did not join until February 1973, when it received certain assurances that its tariff-protected high-cost industries would not be endangered. The details of Venezuela's adherence were not made public.

The ACM proposes duty-free trade, with certain exceptions as requested by members, and a common external tariff for imports from nonmembers. Bolivia exempted 248 products from free trade. Chile, Colombia, and Peru started free trade on numerous products on January 1, 1971, and were to have complete duty-free trade by December 31, 1960. Bolivia and Ecuador were permitted to defer reducing their tariffs until 1976 and then could have until December 31, 1985, for their duty-free clauses to become effective. A common external tariff is to be agreed upon by the end of 1975 and is to be implemented by 1980.

Concerned with the creation of the ACM, the LAFTA executive committee announced that membership in the Andean group was compatible with membership in LAFTA and that the bloc would be considered a subregional grouping within LAFTA. Lima was chosen as the site for the headquarters of the ACM, and a permanent staff is located there. The highest body of the group is called the Commission of the Cartagena Agreement; it convenes three times a year on a regular basis and also holds extraordinary sessions.

Each member agreed to adopt certain limitations upon foreign investment; for example, foreign manufacturing firms would have to divest themselves of a majority interest within fifteen years in Peru, Colombia, and Chile and within twenty years in Bolivia and Ecuador in order to take advantage of any trade benefits in the ACM. As of April 1973 Bolivia had not yet implemented the regulations pertaining to limitations on foreign investment, and there was some indication that the country would be flexible in its actual negotiations with each foreign firm.

In addition to tariff cutting, the group assigns certain new industrial products to each member that the others agree not to manufacture but to purchase from the producing member. Bolivia has six years, and the other members five years, from the date of assignment to initiate production of the items. If manufacture of the items is not commenced during the period of time, then the product is assigned to another member.

The Andean Development Corporation (Corporación Andina de Fomento—CAF) was organized by the ACM members (Bolivia, Chile, Colombia, Ecuador, Peru, and Venezuela) and headquartered in Caracas, Venezuela. The corporation, with initial authorized capital of US$100 million (only US$25 million had been subscribed by 1973) has as its purpose the financing of multilateral investment and technical assistance projects that would lead to economic integration. The CAF was authorized to give priority to loans that would help either Bolivia or Ecuador as the two lesser developed members.

The members agreed that equal tax treatment would be accorded one another's taxpayers from January 1, 1973, onward. Individuals and firms will be taxed only on the income actually generated within the taxing country in order to avoid double taxation. Also, capital movements are to be facilitated between members.

Another subregional grouping of LAFTA of which Bolivia is a member, is the River Plate Group. Besides Bolivia, it is composed of Argentina, Brazil, Paraguay, and Uruguay. As early as 1941 a regional conference of the countries in the Río de la Plata basin (19 percent of Bolivia lies within the basin) met to discuss and negotiate agreements on a number of common economic matters in the fields of water, power, and transportation. The basic treaty was never ratified, but in April 1969 these countries signed the River Plate Basin Treaty for economic integration and joint development of the area, which is over 1.5 million square miles in size.

The Intergovernmental Coordinating Committee was established by the treaty to coordinate proposed projects for the development of the area and to serve as a central collection point for data. Each country also has a national commission, and there are numerous special commissions for specific projects. Some preinvestment studies were done by 1973 financed by a development fund pooled by the members, the Inter-American Development Bank (IDB), the United States Agency for International Development, and the United Nations. Bolivia has been a prime mover in the River Plate Group, and it wants to avail itself of the markets for its products in Argentina and Brazil and needs adequate transportation facilities in the basin.

In addition to the River Plate Group, Bolivia, Paraguay, and Uruguay have formed a permanent committee called URUPABOL (see Glossary) to coordinate their positions within LAFTA and to study common problems, such as interbank cooperation, improvement of telecommunications, and the exchange of commercial information.

SECTION IV. NATIONAL SECURITY

CHAPTER 15

NATIONAL DEFENSE AND PUBLIC ORDER

The country's history has been full of instances of strife, violence, and disorder that have taxed and frequently defeated attempts to contain and control them. In addition to criminal acts that result from the isolated actions of individuals, the government has been faced with politically inspired activists that, in its view, imperil its existence.

For matters of simple law enforcement the government's agencies include the Police and Carabineros of Bolivia, the Directorate General of Traffic and Travel, and the municipal police. The Carabineros operate primarily in the rural areas of Bolivia. Usually, violent disorder is countered by the armed forces, the Police and Carabineros of Bolivia, and an assortment of civilian militias.

Bolivia's armed forces have played a prominent part in the country's history and continued to do so in 1973. Apart from their responsibility for security, the approximately 17,000 men of the armed forces perceived themselves as playing an essential role in matters related to the development of the nation. Although there is a divergence of views among officers as to the military's proper role in development, the dominant element favors economic growth without the sweeping structural revisions of socioeconomic patterns that development has come to connote in Latin American developmental doctrines. During the last decade Bolivia has been under the leadership of military men at the expense of participation in the process of national decisionmaking by civilians (see ch. 2; ch. 10).

The legislative branch of the government makes or changes the laws governing relationships between individuals or between individuals and the state and appoints the judges of the Supreme Court and the district courts. The executive branch issues decrees that have the weight of law and directs their enforcement through the police forces and the Public Ministry, a quasi-independent arm of the executive that performs functions resembling those of an attorney general or public prosecutor. The judicial branch interprets and administers justice through the courts (see ch. 9).

337

POLICE

Legal Basis and Development

From the inception of the republic the police force and all its successors have been responsible to the national government rather than to lesser political authorities, as is the case in most Latin American countries. The persistence with which the concept of centralized police power has remained dominant is attested by the constitution.

The first significant change in enabling legislation covering law enforcement agencies was contained in a law of 1886, which superseded all previous enactments and defined and clarified many concepts of police organization and operation that had not been formally stated before. This system remained basically unchanged until 1950, when it was substantially revised in the Organic Law of Police and Carabineros of Bolivia—sometimes referred to simply as Law No. 311. Together with the law of 1886, it provides the legal basis for the present-day police system.

Until the Revolution of 1952, the police corps was subordinate to the regular armed forces. There was a tendency to look upon it as a nondescript appendage of the military, and most senior police posts were given to army officers. The army assumed most police functions and treated the corps as a reserve to be called upon only in times of dire emergency. This situation changed radically in 1952 with the rise to power of the Nationalist Revolutionary Movement (Movimiento Nacionalista Revolucionario—MNR). The corps sided with the revolutionaries and was rewarded by being given greater jurisdiction over the usual challenges to public law and order. Under the aegis of the United States Agency for International Development (AID) training mission, the corps has been developing into a technically qualified law enforcement agency.

Operational Organization

Under the constitution, the president of the republic is the commander in chief of the *carabineros* (rural police force) and all other police forces. In this capacity, he names the director general of police and *carabineros* and other key officials and formulates the policies under which the force operates. Moreover, during times of internal stress, when public order and safety are endangered, the president is empowered to administer directly the activities of the corps.

Within the national structure the Ministry of the Interior has jurisdiction over the police and the *carabineros*. The relationship between them is similar to that existing between the Ministry of National Defense and the regular armed forces in that both ministries stay aloof from operational matters and concern themselves exclusively with administrative supervision. In time of war the uniformed *carabinero* units and personnel may be transferred to the Ministry of National

Defense and their activities integrated with those of the regular armed forces, as though they were reserve units called to active duty for the duration of hostilities.

Operational control is vested in an appointive director general, who may be a civilian but is almost invariably a high-ranking, career police officer. Legally, this office is entitled to a general, as chief officer, but through the late 1960s no incumbent had been elevated beyond the rank of colonel.

The director general is also commandant of the National Police Academy; head of the National Identification Service; and chief of the Bolivian contingent that cooperates with the International Police (Interpol), all of which are separate administrative units within his office. International police cooperation is significant in that Bolivia is a prime producer of coca leaves, from which cocaine is derived, and Bolivian agents work closely with narcotics control agencies of other countries.

The office of the director general, which serves as national headquarters for all police and *carabinero* activities, consists of a command group and twelve numbered staff sections. Most staff sections are conventionally established. In 1960 a section was established with the mission of dealing with political control. It was integrated into the regular police organization. Whether or not it still exists is not known.

Under the firm centralized command of the Office of the Director General in La Paz, field elements are stationed in all sectors of the country, where they function without responsibility to departmental, provincial, or municipal governments. Subordinate headquarters, known as brigades, are established in the capital of each of the nine departments to coordinate and supervise operations. The brigade is divided into two commands, one urban and the other provincial. The urban command, at the departmental capital, has charge of the police stations and local jails and is divided into sections that have assigned personnel to patrol and carry out criminal investigations.

Most corps personnel and units within a department, regardless of their size, composition, mission, or station, are considered part of the brigade in the area they serve and are members of a single departmental unit. An exception is the city of La Paz, where two separate regiments of the police are kept under the direct control of the director general and the president. Other exceptions are made in sections of the country where dependence on the regular departmental brigade forces is not deemed advisable or feasible. Two such areas—San Ignacio de Velasco in Santa Cruz Department and Tupiza in Potosí—have independent *carabinero* detachments in addition to the department brigades.

Certain departmental brigade personnel of the rural command are on duty at a series of frontier posts scattered at twenty-seven critical points along the borders and at river and lake ports of entry. They include customs police now integral to the corps, as well as uniformed *carabineros* concerned with combating smuggling and other forms of illegal border crossing.

In 1970 the Police and Carabineros of Bolivia, including officers, enlisted personnel, and civilians, numbered about 5,000 men. Precise figures on the national distribution of corps strength were not available, but assigned strength is generally in direct proportion to the density of population and the nature and importance of governmental and economic activities in a given area. Most of the corps is concentrated in the La Paz area, where about 50 percent of its uniformed members and 60 percent of its civilian personnel are stationed.

Within the corps itself approximately 80 percent are uniformed *carabineros*, and 20 percent are civilian police investigators, specialists of the identification service, and minor functionaries. Both elements are undermanned, particularly in the field of routine police activities. In La Paz there is a rudimentary crime detection laboratory. When funds are available, some use is made of police informers, but reliance in solving crimes is chiefly on periodic massive roundups of known miscreants.

Recruitment and Training

In the early 1970s a career in the police or *carabinero* forces offered little that was attractive or rewarding. Pay scales were low, opportunities for personal betterment or advancement were rare, and little, if any, prestige was attached to members of the corps. Consequently, corps personnel are usually men between the ages of twenty-one and twenty-five, who have already completed their tours of obligatory duty in the army; they usually come from a relatively low economic stratum of Bolivian society and are, in most cases, illiterate. Conscious and deliberate efforts have been made to eliminate, or at least mitigate, these adverse factors, and improvement in both the quality and effectiveness of corps personnel is becoming evident.

In addition to the corps, two other official agencies are involved in the maintenance of public order. One is the Directorate General of Traffic and Travel, an agency involved with vehicular traffic and its control. The other is the strictly local municipal police.

The quality of officers and higher civilian employees, drawn mainly from the small urban middle class, is relatively higher. Officers receive their commissions regularly upon graduation from the National Police Academy; by transfer or after retirement from commissioned status in the armed forces; by direct political appointment for demonstrated ability; or by outright patronage. Civilians are nearly always political appointees. Specialized education is not a prerequisite to their appointment, but some degree of qualification is usually present and facilitates on-the-job training.

Cadets accepted for the National Police Academy are not subject to the age limitations for enlisted military service, and matriculation automatically exempts them from their military obligations. Entrance requirements are rather sketchy as far as education goes, but political reliability and unquestioned loyalty to the government are given great importance.

Since the arrival of the United States police training mission in 1956, specialized training in criminal law, personnel administration, police methods and techniques, and riot control tactics have been introduced. Upon graduation cadets receive a bachelor of humanities certificate, a saber that is symbolic of officer rank, and a commission as second lieutenant in the *carabineros*.

Personnel of the corps are classified in three distinct groups. The first is made up of the uniformed personnel, known as *carabineros*. The second includes all technical and auxiliary personnel, such as physicians, dentists, veterinarians, chaplains, communications and transportation specialists, and social service workers, who may be either uniformed *carabineros* or civilians. The third is made up of police investigators and identification personnel, who are almost exclusively civilians.

Uniformed personnel are grouped in four general classifications, with a graded system of rank within each class. In descending order the classifications are field officers (*jefes*); company officers (*oficiales*); noncommissioned officers (*clases*); and privates (*tropas*). Ranks generally correspond to those in the army.

Uniformed personnel are promoted on the basis of annual examinations given when they enter the zone of consideration. This zone is determined by time in grade, which is usually four years for all except captains and sergeants, who must spend five years in grade before becoming eligible for promotion. Classification of civilian personnel is based on a simple, nonmilitary two-category system composed of superiors (*funcionarios superiores*) and subordinates (*funcionarios subalternos*).

Before 1956 police and *carabinero* training was largely of the on-the-job type. Enlisted men received about four months' training in active units and were then assigned permanent duties. Officers had only the formal training they had received as cadets in the National Police Academy.

Since the arrival of the United States police training mission in 1956, the government considers both the training and the manner in which it is conducted to have been greatly improved. More of the in-service training is being taken over by the National Police Academy; special courses have been established for duty-time training of all types of personnel; special unit schools are being run by the brigades; and some officers are being sent abroad for special training.

One of the first special courses was an instructor's course conducted by United States mission members at the police academy. Students drawn from each brigade throughout the country received classroom instruction in detection and general police methodology, augmented by practical exercises. Students were required to pass an examination and, on graduation, returned to their brigades to organize local classes.

Other special courses at the police academy for both officers and enlisted personnel have since been established: for privates and agents the courses include use of the riot stick, unarmed combat, riot control, and police ethics; for noncommissioned grades there are the same subjects, plus public relations, preparation of reports, personnel relations, and leadership; for civilian detectives there are courses in scientific crime detection, criminal law and procedure, and methods of interrogation and identification; and for officers there are courses in tactics, leadership, control of riots, and many administrative functions.

The National Police Academy also offers a program of foreign training for officers. Personnel selected for training in the United States at official police schools, such as the International Police Academy, the Federal Bureau of Investigation, and the Special Warfare School at Fort Bragg, North Carolina, are first sent to the academy for English-language schooling. Others, who are scheduled for schools in Puerto Rico, Chile, or Argentina, report to the police academy for brief refresher and indoctrination lectures before leaving the country. On completing their courses abroad, these trainees return to Bolivia for duty, to lecture at the police academy, or to organize and conduct unit-level courses throughout the corps.

Other types of training, such as self-improvement courses, are also being stressed and encouraged. Officers are urged to attend off-duty classes in universities near their duty stations, and both officers and detectives are required to select, research, and present annually a paper on some aspect of police work. A special off-duty school for enlisted personnel, which offers a variety of courses in literacy, arithmetic, hygiene, geography, and history, has been established at the police academy (with branches elsewhere in the departments). These classes are taught by officially sponsored volunteer teachers, two of which are members of the United States police mission.

When the customs police was transferred from the Ministry of Finance to become an integral element of the corps, police officials soon realized they lacked experience and capability in this special form of police work and requested a training program to help them. The United States police mission responded by organizing a master course at the police academy, which graduated fifty-two officers the first year. The course is still in operation and is augmented by short courses run periodically at departmental capitals, such as Cochabamba, Oruro, and Santa Cruz. Another specialized course offered at the police academy is patterned on the counterinsurgency course of the Special Warfare School at Fort Bragg.

A United States training mission arrived in 1956 to help improve and modernize the Bolivian police system. Beginnings toward improvement were made in the fiscal and organizational areas and in traditional attitudes and concepts of police personnel. Lack of funds remained a major problem, despite the considerable aid that had been received from the United States. Formal training in new methods, techniques, and procedures has been greatly intensified, resulting in a corresponding advance in individual efficiency.

LAWS AND THE PENAL CODE

The Penal Code, as augmented and expanded by specific laws, policy regulations, and official decrees, constitutes the basis for Bolivia's legal system. The country's first president, Marshal Antonio José de Sucre, persuaded the National Congress to adopt the old Spanish Criminal Code of 1822. The first national code was proclaimed in 1832 and revised in 1834 under President Andrés Santa Cruz. Although its provisions have been modified by special legislation or constitutional amendment, it has remained basically unchanged in character and orientation.

Like all codes rooted in the Hispanic tradition, the Penal Code displays an unyielding rigidity. Specific punishable acts are minutely defined with maximum and minimum punishments established. Little discretion is permitted in interpreting the nature of an offense, and no latitude is allowed in assessing penalties other than the difference between maximum and minimum as stated in the code. The principles of case law and judicial precedent are not applied.

Every violation of the code is looked upon as both a criminal and a civil breach. On the criminal count, the objective is to determine whether or not the accused has actually broken the law; on the civil count, whether or not the accused caused damage or injury that requires compensation to the plaintiff. Usually, legal actions to make these determinations proceed concurrently, but sometimes they are tried before different judges and argued by different counsels. Verdicts and punishments are rendered separately and may differ radically.

Although the code was probably adequate and appropriate when drafted, it is currently acknowledged to be archaic, inadequate, and frequently inapplicable. Many attempts have been made to bring it up to date or to formulate an entirely new document, but no suitable or acceptable alternative has yet been found.

COURT AND CRIMINAL PROCEDURES

The courts and the criminal procedures are rooted in the old Spanish and Napoleonic codes and are unified into a single national system under the Ministry of the Interior. No juries are empaneled for trials, and the presiding judges base all decisions on their own evaluation of the data brought out during the proceedings.

The Public Ministry, within the Ministry of the Interior, is intimately involved in court procedures. It is headed by two attorneys general (*fiscales generales*) at the national level, who operate in the fields of criminal and civil law. Subordinate prosecutors (*fiscales* and *sub-fiscales*) are stationed throughout the country, where they serve in capacities similar to, but more wide-ranging than, those of state and district attorneys in the United States.

Apprehension of Offenders

Apprehension and arrest of criminals is a function of the police, although the constitution recognizes the validity of citizen arrest when offenders are caught in the act of committing a crime. The police may also take a suspect into custody on the basis of their own investigation, the formal accusation of a local public prosecutor, or the written deposition of any citizen. Persons so apprehended are held in local jails for twenty-four hours, pending a determination of facts before being charged with a crime. When this is accomplished, the police notify the public prosecutor, who lodges a complaint before an investigating judge, who then assumes cognizance of the case.

Pretrial and Trial Procedures

The public prosecutor is responsible for assembling the evidence and testimony and, with police assistance, for studying the complaint, visiting the scene of the crime, and locating and interrogating witnesses. Both questions and answers are recorded so that evidence is available in the form of depositions. When the evidence is assembled, an open hearing is held by the investigating judge before all interested parties. The public prosecutor makes an accusation and presents all witnesses and documents for the prosecution. Witnesses are not questioned directly or cross-examined but deliver their testimony as a continuous narrative. When the prosecution has finished, the judge interrogates the accused and receives depositions and statements from witnesses who may appear on behalf of the accused.

The trial judge reviews the investigating judge's summary and makes one of several possible determinations. In forming his decision the judge is required by law to consult the public prosecutor. He may decide that the indictment is not warranted, dismiss the case, and free the prisoner. If he decides that a trial is necessary, he may remand the case to the investigating judge for trial and disposition depending upon the seriousness of the crime.

The trial judge also acts as a court of second instance for actions taken by an investigating judge. When reviewing cases from a lower court, if he concurs in the decision, the action is ended; if he disagrees, he may direct a retrial. He also considers appeals from decisions of the lower courts.

In the event the trial judge decides to hear a new case himself, the proceedings are generally similar to those in the lower court, but there are several important differences. The defendant, for example, must be represented by an attorney, either his own or one appointed by the judge. In addition to witnesses already on record, new ones may be called—either for or against the defendant—if the judge feels they may contribute to a better understanding of the case. The judge may also call upon advisers, chosen by him, when he is ready to study the data developed during the trial. Within three days after the conclusion of the trial, he must confront the defendant, inform him of the decision, and pronounce sentence. Exactly the same procedures for reviews, appeals, and higher courts are followed by the district courts and the Supreme Court.

The Penal System

Conceptual and traditional considerations exert a strong influence on both the nature and the severity of the sentence finally imposed. Penalties and punishments are authorized for various types of offenses, and in arriving at a verdict the judge takes into consideration the nature of the crime committed and the existence of special circumstances surrounding the case.

Bolivian law makes a clear-cut distinction between felonies and misdemeanors. Any crime that is committed voluntarily and in a spirit of malice is considered by the code to be a felony; the same crime done without malice is considered a misdemeanor. In deciding a case the judge must give special attention to the intent of the criminal.

The Penal Code recognizes three types, or orders, of punishment that may be imposed on criminals, regardless of whether the offense was a felony or a misdemeanor. There are corporal punishments that involve some form of restraint or restriction on the person of the offender, for example, imprisonment; noncorporal punishments that call for nonphysical penalties such as deprivation of a civil right; and pecuniary punishments that exact a fine or other form of monetary payment.

Corporal punishments are usually the most severe and are imposed in various degrees that are difficult to differentiate because firm definitions are lacking and because all may be imposed for as long a time as ten years. There are a number of forms of noncorporal punishment: deprivation, surveillance, bonding, reprimand and warning, and public sentencing. Pecuniary punishment is used principally against offenders in civil suits but may also be applied in criminal convictions.

Capital punishment for any reason was abolished by the Constitution of 1961 but was held constitutional by the Supreme Court in August 1973. The second most severe punishment allowable is thirty years at hard labor with no recourse to pardon or clemency of any sort. This severe punishment is permissible only for the crimes of parricide, assassination, or treason in time of war; no other crime carries a greater penalty than ten years' imprisonment.

The Bolivian penal system also includes a statute of limitations. Severe criminal offenses may not be prosecuted unless the offender is brought to justice within ten years of the date of commission. In the case of lesser crimes the period during which action must be taken is shorter.

Judicial pardon does not exist in the Bolivian penal system, but both the president and the National Congress have this power in certain limited circumstances. Both are authorized to declare amnesty for political offenses, and the National Congress is empowered to pardon offenders in either criminal or civil cases provided the Supreme Court concurs.

Penal Institutions

Persons who receive sentences calling for imprisonment are committed to one of several penal institutions in the country. There is a national penitentiary at La Paz and one in each of the nine political departments. Most provinces have jails of their own to accommodate local offenders whose crimes are serious enough to warrant long-term imprisonment. Other facilities include a correctional farm at Caranavi, a reformatory for women at La Paz, and three reformatories for juveniles, one in La Paz and two near Cochabamba. These institutions, with the exception of the juvenile reformatories, are under the general supervision of the Ministry of the Interior, which assigns detachments of *carabineros* to provide guard and security forces.

Better conditions prevail at the correctional farm at Caranavi than in most penal institutions in Bolivia. Regulations there are strict, and prisoners are tightly secluded in their cells at night under enforced silence. Communication with the outside world is closely regulated, and families are rarely permitted to visit inmates. Nevertheless, during the day, prisoners engage in common work in the fields and, since they are at the source of supply, meals are better than in urban prisons. Most livable of all institutions in the system is the Women's Reformatory at La Paz. Small, with a capacity for only thirty women, it is operated under contract by a Roman Catholic order of nuns whose charity, dedication, and propensity for cleanliness and order have made it comparable to similar Catholic institutions elsewhere in the world.

INCIDENCE OF CRIME

Because of the lack of systematized records, the incidence of crime can be discussed only in very general terms. Most observers agree that it is not unusually high but appears to be on the increase, particularly in the urban areas. A survey of the public press suggests that petty thievery ranks high on the list of most common crimes. Also reported with considerable frequency are attacks upon persons, disorderly conduct, rape, and nonsupport. Young men seem to be involved more in thievery than in other forms of crime, whereas older men are more frequently arrested for acts of violence against other persons. The number of crimes seems greatest during holidays and festivals, when drinking to excess is common.

The national boundaries of Bolivia are among the most difficult in the world to police and keep secure because they are located in exceedingly rugged mountainous, jungle, and desert terrain, remote and inaccessible from centers of population. Twenty-seven frontier posts manned by *carabineros* at critical points of ingress and egress around the nation are a response to the recognized need to control smuggling, but their net restraining influence appears to be small.

INTERNAL SECURITY

The internal security of the country rests primarily on the ability of the government to cope with three types of challenges. The first is the high incidence of mob violence that periodically sweeps the country; the second is the spate of activities persistently carried out by opposition parties to undermine the government; and the third is the presence of guerrillas, whose numbers have decreased drastically since the death of Ernesto (Che) Guevara, the Cuban revolutionary, in 1967.

There seems to be a close relationship between mob violence and planned agitation. The violence does not usually occur haphazardly or spontaneously but in connection with strikes, demonstrations, and marches, which take place frequently and regularly. Of the strikes that were called during the past two decades, a large percentage resulted in violence and bloodshed.

Mob Violence and the People's Militias

The divisions that render the country's political life into so many bitterly contending opposition parties of the Right and Left appeared to be responsible for most of the mob violence that characterized the 1960s. The armed forces and the Police and Carabineros of Bolivia have played an active role in curtailing these activities.

The part played by the groups of armed civilians known as People's Militias, which in many ways has been the most active and decisive, warrants special attention. Although designated by the constitution as the "reserves of the armed forces," the function of the armed civilian militias has less to do with formal combat than with the preservation of internal security. These elements had their origin in the 1946 uprisings when unorganized mobs broke into the national arsenal and seized its store of arms and ammunition.

Fearing a counterrevolution, Víctor Paz Estenssoro launched a program of deliberate debilitation of the military and conscious strengthening of the civilian militias. Existing militias were legitimized, and weapons taken from the army were made available to new units sponsored by peasant, miner, and factory leaders. By 1953 the civilian militias were the strongest military forces in the country.

The numerical strength of the militias has fluctuated widely throughout the past decades. They probably reached their peak strength in 1956 (between 50,000 and 70,000 armed men), a gradual deterioration setting in shortly afterward under President Hernán

Siles Suazo. In the early 1970s the strength of the militias was estimated at 16,000, although some accounts would double or even triple that number.

The most important civilian militia units are those of the miners, peasants, and factory workers, in that order. Over the years the miners' militias, sponsored by the Mine Workers Federation of Bolivia (Federación Sindical de Trabajadores Mineros de Bolivia—FSTMB), have not been the strongest numerically, but they have been considered the most effective because they are better organized, trained, disciplined, and equipped. The peasant militias are the most numerous and—because of their intimate knowledge of local terrain, their ability to live off the land, and the ease with which they can merge with local populations—they could be particularly adaptable for employment as guerrilla units. The factory workers' units, formerly controlled by the Bolivian Labor Central (Central Obrera Boliviana—COB), are relatively small but are capable of effective vanguard action because of the speed with which they can be mobilized and because of their physical presence in urban areas where mob violence is most likely to occur.

Che Guevara's Guerrilla Warfare

Che Guevara's guerrilla movement is perhaps the best known revolutionary attempt at subversion in Bolivia. This campaign was designed, in part, to spread the Cuban revolution and to show that communism need not be accompanied by slavish obedience to Moscow and could be accommodated to Latin American sensibilities. Other leftist groups in Bolivia have been unsuccessful in promoting armed revolution. They included the pro-Peking faction of the Bolivian Communist Party (Partido Comunisto Boliviana—PCB), the National Liberation Army (Ejército de Liberación Nacional—ELN), the National Liberation Front (Frente Nacional de Liberación—FNL), and the National Leftist Revolutionary Party (Partido Revolucionario de la Izquierada Nacional—PRIN). Che Guevara's guerrilla movement, however, initiated in 1966, caused the Bolivian government significant difficulty.

In the middle of 1966 Che Guevara started the guerrilla campaign with the training of some forty men on a remote ranch that he used as a depot for supplies brought in by air or smuggled across the borders from neighboring countries. The guerrillas were able to construct— undisturbed—underground tunnels and refuges and a well-concealed field hospital. They also prepared other sites in accordance with guerrilla methods that Che Guevara had observed during a visit to the Democratic Republic of Vietnam (North Vietnam) after he disappeared from public life. Training for combat took the form of forced marches to teach the guerrillas how to live off the country and to familiarize them with the terrain.

The rising number of skirmishes between the guerrillas and the government forces caused increasing alarm to the government, despite public statements to the contrary in 1966. The Bolivian army was not in a position to mount a full-scale offensive against Che Guevara, as most of the untutored Indian conscripts who constituted the bulk of the forces had just begun their training and fewer than 2,000 were ready for combat. Moreover, captured evidence revealed that the guerrillas were led by experts in jungle fighting and that their equipment and arms were of the latest design. Therefore, the Bolivian commander in chief decided on a policy of containment. The southwest of Bolivia was declared a military area—the "Red Zone." Probing attacks were made to keep the guerrillas off balance, and they were also deprived of foods and supplies, although this meant moving peasants from their farms and destroying the crops of those suspected of selling produce to the guerrillas.

These tactics allowed time for a special force of 800 men to be trained and equipped at a camp near Santa Cruz. At the request of the Bolivian government for military assistance, experienced antiguerrilla fighters were provided by the United States Southern Command Headquarters in Panama to establish a jungle warfare school. Military supplies, including field radio sets and helicopters were also provided.

The government took immediate steps to deprive the guerrillas of civilian support, using information found in captured documents to round up underground agents and urban sympathizers. From June 1967 onward the guerrillas had to contend not only with repeated attacks by government troops, but also with a perpetual shortage of food and supplies and the cold rain of the Bolivian winter. By marching and countermarching, Che Guevara exhausted his men, and some of his units became separated when radio communications failed.

By the end of July 1967 well-equipped Bolivian antiguerrilla Ranger units were ready for action. On July 30 Che Guevara was involved in a violent engagement with an army detachment, and he realized that the army was now using his own surprise tactics against him. Moreover, as well as being perpetually short of food, his men were suffering from tropical diseases and from the hardships of the bush. They were also running short of ammunition and medical supplies and were not attracting the anticipated Bolivian recruits.

When the Bolivian Army put into operation their encirclement plans, the remaining guerrillas soon found it impossible to break out of the net; nor could they hope for assistance from the towns because large numbers of sympathizers were being rounded up by the government. The Bolivian government put a price of $b500,000 (for value of the Bolivian peso—see Glossary), or about US$41,667, on Che Guevara's head. On October 8, 1967, two fresh companies of Bolivian troops, probably acting on a peasant's tip, had the small guerrilla nucleus trapped. Che Guevara and Simón Cuba were captured, and Che Guevara's Bolivian campaign was over. The nature of Che Guevara's eventual death has been the subject of much controversy, but the official version is that he died as a result of wounds received during a five-hour battle with government troops on October 8, 1967, near Las Higueras.

Many explanations have been offered as to Che Guevara's defeat. Among the most prominent are: the overwhelming superiority of a 1,500-man Ranger force trained with United States military assistance; Che Guevara had been mistaken in thinking that he could repeat his Sierra Maestra experiences in a sparsely populated area of Bolivia, where the peasants ultimately betrayed him to the army; the PCB remained aloof and condemnation of Che Guevara's activities by both Moscow and Peking isolated him from possible communist supporters; Che Guevara's "apparatus" in the towns was not sufficient, and its leaders were easily rounded up by the police, especially after the army began to capture secret documents; the Bolivian miners failed to rally to Che Guevara's cause; the guerrillas failed to attract recruits because they were in large part Cubans, who were regarded as foreigners by the Bolivians; captured documents, deserters, and peasant spies had kept the army informed of Che Guevara's plans and movements; the Bolivian Ranger force was quite different from the Bolivian conscript army that Che Guevara expected to encounter; and Bolivia had already experienced a revolution in 1952.

Rightist and Leftist Activities

During the Hugo Banzer Suárez government, the political Right and especially the conservative Bolivian Socialist Falange (Falange Socialista Boliviana—FSB) were allowed a certain degree of criticism of the military. The activities of the Left, however, were considered subversive and therefore were officially banned. The political Left is split into at least three schools of thought by disputes as to the best method to establish a socialist society in Bolivia. Those who follow Trotskyite theories, holding that only by arousing the proletariat to armed revolt can the ideal state be brought into being, having organized themselves into the Revolutionary Workers Party (Partido Obrero Revolucionario—POR) and seem to follow the guidance of the Fourth International in Paris. Those who adhere to similar revolutionary concepts but who prefer to remain independent of all international affiliations have grouped themselves into the National Leftist Revolutionary Party (Partido Revolucionario de la Izquierda—PRIN). Those who are most orthodox in communist belief and practice have formed the PCB.

With little appeal to the peasants, the PCB has perforce relied on the few cities and the mining areas for its members. Before 1964 the party achieved some penetration of the government. Since the accession of René Barrientos Ortuño in 1964, however, this penetration has probably ceased entirely. In early 1964 a pro-Chinese faction was formed; in 1965 it withdrew from the orthodox party. The Moscow line has an estimated 4,000 members; the Peking faction, about 500. The orthodox faction supported the communist FNL in the 1966 elections. The Peking line did not favor electoral participation. The pro-Chinese POR is an old party of Trotskyites also weakened in past years by dissension. It chose not to take part in the 1966 elections. Its base is in part in the mines and factories; it has an estimated 1,000 members. The FNL dates from 1964 and is a Marxist party that draws upon students, miners, and urban workers and has been allied with the PCB. In the 1966 elections it drew 33,000 votes, or 3 percent of the total.

THE ARMED FORCES

The armed forces of Bolivia have played a prominent part in the country's history and continued to do so in 1973. Along with the church, the military became the bastion of conservatism and, after independence, it assured the landowning and merchant class that the revolution would not go beyond the achievement of independence. With the decline of the powers of the church in the late nineteenth century, the military came to wield even greater power; it was limited only by the advent of the liberal movement of the early twentieth century. But even during this era the military continued to exert a powerful influence on Bolivian politics.

The working relationship that had been crudely and imperfectly fashioned between the military and civilian leaders before 1932 broke apart under the impact of the Chaco War (1932–35) against Paraguay. This bitter, agonizing experience was a defeat not only for the German-trained Bolivian Army but also for the entire nation. As a consequence of the war, the army underwent a political awakening. The old roles were disappearing in that the army as an institution was ready to act in pursuit of its own political goals (see ch. 2).

After a brief period of cooperation between the MNR and the army, the earlier involvement of the army in politics was abruptly choked off and stifled, at least temporarily, following the Revolution of 1952. The Bolivian Army was drastically reduced in terms of numbers, budget, and power. For the next several years the military, police, and the civilian militias remained a neatly balanced constellation of forces while the MNR proceeded to initiate sweeping reforms in Bolivia's social and economic life. The army as an independent political force exercised little or no influence. Scanty financing limited even its contribution to Bolivia's economic development, although the military did some light roadbuilding and survey work, and soldiers were used to clear land for colonization.

A new army was created on the basis of permitting members of the lower class to enter the Military Academy. As a result of the increasing alienation between the miners' militia and the MNR and the deterioration of the enthusiasm and discipline of the peasant militia units, the relative power of the armed forces grew steadily, especially after the ascension of Barrientos, chief of the air force, to the presidency in 1964.

Finally, in the 1960s the army gained a measure of dominance over the irregular militias, a fact that coincided with the rise to a position of power by the elite nucleus of officers trained in the career school. Furthermore, the Bolivian military was affected by changes most convincingly articulated by General Alfredo Ovando Candia, who advocated a different role for the army, attempting to de-emphasize the traditional role of the armed forces and transforming it into an instrument of development and production.

In 1973 Bolivia's armed forces establishment exceeded the pre-1952 level. It totaled almost 17,000 men, not including the paramilitary force of about 5,000 armed policemen and frontier guards. Almost 13 percent, or about US$17.1 million of the total central government budget, was spent by the military in the early 1970s. The rise in the budget between the late 1950s and 1973 is indicative of the increasing role the military has played.

Mission, Organization, and Operations

The president of the republic, as captain general of the armed forces, is provided with a small personal staff known as the Military Household. At this highest level of government and presided over by the president is the Supreme Council of National Defense, which carries out general planning for matters of national defense, including matters of economic as well as international implications. There is also the permanent Tribunal of Military Justice. The president designates the commanders in chief of the armed forces, the commanders of the army, air force, and river and lake force, and the commandant general of police. The authorization of a river and lake force is unique. Although its establishment was forecast in the Constitution of 1961, it was not organized until 1963.

The Ministry of National Defense is charged with general supervision of the army, the air force, and the river and lake force. It confines its activities exclusively to the administrative sphere and does not become involved in operational and command matters. The minister has a small personal staff and two undersecretaries—one for the army and another for the air force. The officers are divided into directorates for specialized functions, such as personnel, logistics, air defense, meteorology, and territorial administration. The undersecretaries may be civilians but are usually military officers.

The legal basis for the armed forces of Bolivia is found in the Constitution of 1967. Under a minister of national defense, there is a regular establishment composed of an army, an air force and a river and lake force.

Banzer was assisted by a joint staff of conventional makeup in exercising full operational control over all elements of the Bolivian armed forces. Before June 1973, however, the position of commander in chief of the armed forces was occupied by a person other than the president, who was responsible directly to the president without recourse to the minister of national defense except in purely administrative matters.

Army Headquarters is headed by a commanding general who has a small personal staff of advisers and the General Staff under a chief of staff. The General Staff has five sections—personnel, intelligence, plans and operations, logistics, and a section concerned with history, cartography, and public relations. Army units are of several functional types, although all are generally organized along standard military lines. A considerable number of units perform essentially nonmilitary duties, or civic action. Practically all engineer troops are engaged in roadbuilding, land clearing, and colonization work. Other units are organized for conventional military duty but conduct civic action projects part of the time. All units have the task of raising the low literacy levels of the soldiers. Still others perform military school service duties. Some are elite units stationed in La Paz or its vicinity.

The total strength of the army has been estimated at 17,000 men. It is divided into twelve infantry regiments, one motorized regiment, three ranger battalions, one paratroop regiment, and three artillery regiments.

The air force is commanded by its own general who has headquarters in La Paz. His command is not broken down into districts but is unified for the country as a whole. Air Force Headquarters contains the conventional Air General Staff and a small complement of supporting staff personnel.

The air force has both a combat and a transport element. Combat planes are World War II varieties or trainers converted to combat purposes. The transport element, called the Military Air Transport Service, operates as an all-purpose supplementary cargo and personnel line and is used to reach remote and frontier locations where the commercial airlines find it unprofitable to maintain service. It, too, shares in the civic action kind of employment.

The Bolivian Air Force in 1972 had about 1,800 men. Of its twenty-five combat aircraft, twelve were F-51D Mustang fighters of World War II vintage, and thirteen, T-6D armed trainers. Of twenty-six transports, sixteen were C-47s and six were Cessna 172s. The air force also had seven PT-19s, eight Fokker T-21s, seven Cessna 185 communication aircraft, and about fifteen helicopters, including Hughes 500M and OH-23C/D. Bolivia's major air bases are in La Paz, El Trompillo, Charaña, Colcapima, Santa Cruz, La Florida, El Tejar, and Puerto Suárez.

Bolivia, being a landlocked country, has a tiny navy. It comprises a small patrol unit on Lake Titicaca on the border with Peru, a vessel providing medical services to residents of the lake region, and various river boats in the Amazon Basin.

Recruitment and Training

All personnel, other than officers, are conscripted into the armed forces. The first law requiring compulsory service was passed in 1904 and, though since amended, has not been changed to any large degree. The obligatory universal service of all males is a constitutional requirement, and existing law sets the period of military obligation between the ages of eighteen and forty-nine. Budgetary restrictions have placed stringent limitations on the number of men actually inducted.

The enlisted career service in the army (all noncommissioned officers) and the entire air force enlisted strength have historically been maintained at authorized levels by recruitment on a voluntary basis from among those completing conscript service. On the other hand, the great majority of Bolivian line officers are graduates of the Military Academy. Applicants to the prestigious academy enter between the ages of eighteen and nineteen after completing their secondary education. The secondary school degree may be waived if the applicant appears to be promising. Evidence of good moral character, a health certificate, and the sponsorship of an influential individual are additional prerequisites for entering the academy. The majority of the 800 to 1,000 applicants received by the academy each year come from members of the middle class (see ch. 5). Often the secondary education of potential applicants is planned so that they can successfully complete the academy's entrance examination. Between 100 and 150 applicants are selected for the academy each year, and seventy-five to eighty-five go on to graduate after four years.

A highly important mission of the armed forces is basic literacy schooling for conscripts. Although the results of this training are inconclusive, there are indications that levels of Spanish-speaking ability, reading, and writing skills have been raised. A number of noncommissioned officers attend a school in the main school center at Cochabamba, which has courses devoted principally to technical training in such subjects as communications and motor mechanics.

Professional preparation has become an essential element of the Bolivian armed forces and a prerequisite for any high-level promotion within the armed forces. The educational structure is quite elaborate. The four-year training for cadets of the Military Academy includes a variety of topics ranging from military-related topics to academic subjects. During the first two years the candidates are exposed to military training and to academic subjects, such as geography, history, algebra, and geometry. During the third year the cadets choose one of the following branches of service: infantry, artillery, cavalry, engineer, or signal. In the fourth year the curriculum is entirely devoted to branch training. Graduating as a second lieutenant, the graduating officer is expected to serve a minimum of eight years, five of which are likely to be in frontier postings. If he resigns before the eight years expire, he is required to repay the state for the educational costs incurred.

During the initial ten years of duty, officers attend the School of Arms (Escuela de Aplicación de Armas) at least twice. The school, located in Cochabamba, offers some academic courses, but most of the training is devoted to military history and geography, leadership, and battalion-level tactics and techniques. The courses are designed for about twenty-five to twenty-seven officers and are prerequisites for promotion in the armed forces. The professors are both civilian and military.

The Military Engineering School annually accepts about twenty-five to twenty-seven young officers who have passed rigorous entrance examinations. This full-fledged five-year engineering institution graduates annually between five and seven men with a degree in geodetic or construction engineering.

Graduates of the engineering school and the top graduates of the School of Arms may enter the Command and General Staff School. A graduate of the school, a general staff officer, thereby qualifies for command in tactical units or service on the army General Staff. This two-year course selects between twenty-five and thirty candidates annually, and twelve to fifteen complete the course. Taught by both civilians and military men, the curriculum in 1967 required forty-one hours of sociology, forty hours of international law, forty hours of political economics, and a 250-hour block on "revolutionary war" that included studies of political theory and development philosophy. The core of the nonacademic curriculum is devoted to operations at corps, field army, and theater levels. The school also teaches tactical employment and logistical support of military aggregations.

On a highly selective basis the most senior officers may attend the School of High Military Studies at La Paz, which is also open to government officials and distinguished persons in industrial and banking pursuits. Designed for persons with an interest in national security affairs, it is a prerequisite for promotion to general officer under the Organic Law. The program usually consists of twenty-five to thirty students. Like most institutions of advanced learning in Bolivia, it operates on an inadequate budget.

Selected officers and noncommissioned officers have attended United States Army and Air Force service schools in the United States and Panama. Others have studied in neighboring South American countries. These military representatives have probably been influenced to some degree by the doctrines encountered in these foreign schools and, in some instances, have become spokesmen for the philosophies espoused in the various countries. This is especially true for military men trained in Peru, Argentina, and Brazil.

Conditions of Service

Active commissioned officer ranks in the army and the air force are identical or correspond to ranks of the United States forces, with a few minor exceptions. For example, officers do not progress beyond major general except for the president, who is ex officio the captain general of the armed forces, popularly known as marshal. He presides over the Supreme Council of National Defense and appoints the service commanders as well as the commander in chief of the armed forces. This latter position, however, has also been occupied by the president since May 1973. Only combat officers become generals; supply and technical service officers (physicians and lawyers) are limited to the top rank of colonel.

Career enlisted men are found in four categories of warrant officers, two of sergeants, and one grade of corporal. Conscripts are all privates. Conscripts, found only in the army, receive no regular pay for their services. Instead they are provided with food, clothing, and lodging and, on rare occasions when funds are available, they may be awarded small monetary gratuities or issues of alcohol.

Details of the defense budget are not made known publicly. The rate of pay for junior officers in the early 1960s was $b40, about US$40 per month, but that could easily be tripled by allowances. It is known that a complicated system of increments and bonuses exists, but that the total, even when added to basic pay, amounts to a less-than-adequate amount. For that reason, it is official policy to permit service personnel sufficient free time to earn a supplementary income.

There are only two known orders in the Bolivian system of awards, of which the grades closely correspond to those of conventional European orders. The degrees range from the Grand Collar or Grand Officer to that of Knight. The circumstances in which military officers are admitted to the senior order, the Condor of the Andes, are unclear, but the junior order is exclusively military, as indicated by its title, the Order of Military Merit.

Three military medals are also among the decorations awarded servicemen. A Service Cross is awarded in three classes, according to length of service. The Iron Star is the Bolivian equivalent of the Purple Heart, and the War Medal is the campaign badge for Chaco War service.

Military Justice

The armed forces lost exemption of the military from the ordinary law codes and procedures in 1904. Consequently, for all crimes and misdemeanors not exclusively military in nature, men and officers come before the civil courts, though commanding officers may punish minor derelictions by command authority. There are no prisons exclusively for the military.

The Supreme Tribunal for Military Justice (Tribunal Supremo de Justicia Militar) is the highest of all councils and courts in the military organization. Composed of seven military officers with the ranks of general and colonel, it is subject to the minister of national defense only. The lower courts include disciplinary councils, war councils, and review boards. Under a law of 1958 special ranks and promotions have been given to men with legal training in order to attract them to the armed forces. For example, law students not yet graduated from law school are admitted as lieutenants.

BIBLIOGRAPHY

Section I. Social

Albo, Xavier. "Social Constraints on Cochabamba Quechua." (Dissertation Series No. 19.) Ithaca: Cornell University, Latin American Studies Program, 1970.

Alexander, Robert J. *The Bolivian National Revolution.* New Brunswick: Rutgers University Press, 1958.

————. *Today's Latin America.* (2d ed., rev.) Garden City: Doubleday, Anchor Books, 1968.

Altizarra Flores, Norma. "Intervención del servicio social para el cambio de actitudes de una comunidad." La Paz: Escuela Nacional de Servicio Social, 1961 (typescript thesis).

Anstee, Margaret Joan. *Bolivia, Gate of the Sun.* New York: Paul S. Eriksson, 1970.

Antezana, Fernando. *Los Braceros bolivianos.* Cochabamba, Bolivia: Imprenta Icthus, 1966.

Arguedas, Alcídes. *Raza de bronce.* Lima: Ediciones Nuevo Mundo, 1966.

Arnade, Charles W. "A Discussion of the Bolivian Indian," *Johrbuch des Museums für Volkerkunde su Leipzig* [Leipzig], Band 22, 1966, 75-84.

————. *The Emergence of the Republic of Bolivia.* Gainesville: University of Florida Press, 1957.

Bailey, Norman A. *Latin America in World Politics.* New York: Walker, 1967.

Bartholomew, Doris. "Boletín informativo sobre idiomas indígenas de Latino-américa," *América Indígena* [Mexico City], XXIX, No. 2, April 1969, 515-528.

Béhague, Gerard. "Music." Pages 466-482 in Henry E. Adams (ed.), *Handbook of Latin American Studies,* XXXII. Gainesville: University of Florida Press, 1970.

Bennett, Wendell C. "The Andean Highlands." Pages 1-60 in Julian H. Steward (ed.), *Handbook of South American Indians,* II. Washington: Smithsonian Institution, 1946.

Bills, Garland D.; Vallejo, Bernardo; and Troke, Rudolph C. *An Introduction to Spoken Bolivian Quechua.* (Offprint series No. 145.) Austin: University of Texas, 1969.

Blakemore, Harold. *Latin America.* London: Oxford University Press, 1966.

Bolivia. Consejo Nacional de Educación Superior. *Universidad Boliviana, Católogo—1973.* La Paz: Editorial Lux, 1973.

Bolivia. Instituto Boliviano de Estudio y Acción Social. "Ciclo de formación complementaria, I: Salud pública y salud ocupacional." La Paz. June 1967 (mimeo.).

———. "Ciclo de formación complementaria, II: La salud en las regiones bolivianas." La Paz: June 1967 (mimeo.).

———. "Ciclo de formación complementaria, III: Administración, procedimiento y socialización." La Paz: June 1967 (mimeo.).

Bolivia. Instituto Nacional de Estadística. *Plan, 1971.* La Paz: 1970.

Bolivia. Laws, Statutes, etc.
Código de la educación boliviana, edición oficial. La Paz: Ministerio de Educación Pública y Bellas Artes, 1955.

Bolivia. Ministerio de Planificación y Coordinación. *Estratégia socioeconómica del desarrollo nacional, 1971–1991.* La Paz: 1970.

Bolivia. Ministerio de Transportes, Comunicaciones y Aeronáutica Civil. Subsecretaría de Aeronáutica Civil. Dirección General de Aeronáutica Civil. *Aerocivil Bolivia: Bodas de plata, 1947–1972.* La Paz: Editorial Aeronáutica, 1972.

Bourne, Edward Gaylord. *Spain in America, 1450–1580.* New York: Barnes and Noble, 1962.

Bouroncle, Carreón A. "Contribución al estudio de los Aymaras," *América Indígena* [Mexico City], XXIV, 1964, 129–169, 223–269.

Buechler, Hans C. "The Reorganization of Counties in the Bolivian Highlands: An Analysis of Rural-Urban Networks and Hierarchies." Pages 48–57 in E.M. Eddy (ed.), *Urban Anthropology: Research Perspectives and Strategies.* (Southern Anthropological Society Proceedings No. 2.) Athens: University of Georgia, 1968.

———. "The Ritual Dimension of Rural-Urban Networks: The Fiesta System in the Northern Highlands of Bolivia." Pages 65–71 in W. Mangin (ed.), *Peasants in Cities.* Boston: Houghton Mifflin, 1970.

Buechler, Hans C., and Buechler, Judith Maria. *The Bolivian Aymara.* New York: Holt, Rinehart and Winston, 1971.

Butland, Gilbert J. *Latin America: A Regional Study.* New York: John Wiley and Sons, 1966.

Camacho Saa, Carlos. *Minifundia, Productivity, and Land Reform in Cochabamba.* (Research Paper No. 21.) Madison: University of Wisconsin, Land Tenure Center, December 1966.

Cámara Nacional de Industrias. *Memoria, 1969/70,* XXXIX. La Paz: Empresa Editora Universo, 1970.

Canfield, D. Lincoln. "Language." Pages 321–341 in Henry E. Adams (ed.), *Handbook of Latin American Studies,* XXXII. Gainesville: University of Florida Press, 1970.

Carter, William E. *Aymara Communities and the Bolivian Agrarian Reform.* (University of Florida Monographs—Social Sciences, No. 24.) Gainesville: University of Florida Press, Fall, 1964.

―――. *Bolivia, a Profile.* New York: Praeger, 1971.

―――. "Factores socio-económicos en el desarrollo de la personalidad Aymara." Pages 367-381 in *Congreso Internacional de Americanistas, 36, Sevilla, 1964, Actas y Memorias,* III. Sevilla, Spain: Editorial Católica Española, 1966.

―――. "El protestantismo como vehículo de cambio cultural en Sudamérica." Pages 245-252 in *Congreso Internacional de Americanistas, 36, Sevilla, 1964, Actas y Memorias,* III. Sevilla, Spain: Editorial Católica Española, 1966.

Castedo, Leopoldo. *A History of Latin American Art and Architecture from Pre-Columbian Times to the Present.* (Ed. and trans., Phyllis Freeman.) New York: Praeger, 1969.

―――. "Latin American Painting and Sculpture." Pages 795-801 in Claudio Véliz (ed.), *Latin America and the Caribbean: A Handbook.* New York: Praeger, 1968.

Céspedes, Augusto. *Bolivia.* Washington: Unión Panamericana, 1962.

Chase, Gilbert. *Contemporary Art in Latin America: Painting, Graphic Art, Sculpture, Architecture.* New York: Free Press, 1970.

Clark, Ronald James. "Problems and Conflicts over Land Ownership in Bolivia," *Inter-American Economic Affairs,* XXII, No. 4, Spring, 1969, 3-18.

Cleven, N. Andrew N. *The Political Organization of Bolivia.* Washington: Carnegie Institution of Washington, 1940.

Cohen, Alvin. "Bolivia: Internal Instability and International Dependence," *Current History,* LX, No. 354, February 1971, 78-83.

Cohen, J. M. (ed.) *Latin American Writing Today.* Baltimore: Penguin Books, 1967.

Comitas, Lambros. "Education and Social Stratification in Bolivia," *América Indigena* [Mexico City], XXVIII, No. 3, July 1968, 631-651.

―――. "Education and Social Stratification in Contemporary Bolivia." Pages 363-378 in Thomas La Belle (ed.), *Education and Development, Latin America and the Caribbean.* (Latin American Studies Series, Vol. 18.) Los Angeles: University of California, Latin American Center, 1972.

Dandler, Jorge. *El sindicalismo campesino en Bolivia: los cambios estructurales en "Uruceña."* Mexico City: Instituto Indigenista Interamericano, 1967.

Davis, Harold Eugene. *History of Latin America.* New York: Ronald Press, 1968.

―――. *Latin American Social Thought.* Washington: University Press of Washington, D.C., 1961.

―――. *Latin American Thought: A Historical Introduction.* Baton Rouge: Louisiana State University Press, 1972.

Davis, Kingsley. *World Urbanization, 1950-1970.* I: Basic Data for Cities, Countries, and Regions. (Population Monograph Series, No.

4.) Berkeley: University of California, Institute of International Studies, 1969.

Demographic Yearbook, 1970. New York: United Nations, 1971.

Douglas, William O. *Holocaust or Hemispheric Co-operation: Cross Currents in Latin America.* New York: Random House, 1971.

Dozier, Craig L. *Land Development and Colonization in Latin America: Case Studies of Peru, Bolivia, and Mexico.* New York: Praeger, 1969.

Editor and Publisher International Year Book, 1972. New York: Editor and Publisher, 1972.

Erasmus, Charles J. "Upper Limits of Peasantry and Agrarian Reform: Bolivia, Venezuela, and Mexico Compared," *Ethnology,* VI, No. 4, October 1967, 349–380.

Erasmus, Charles J., and Buechler, Hans C. *Land Reform and Social Revolution in Bolivia.* New York: Praeger, 1969.

Ertl, Hans. *Arriba Abajo.* Munich: F. Bruckmann, 1958.

Ferragut, Casto. "La reforma agraria boliviana," *Revista Interamericana de Ciencias Sociales,* II, No. 1, 1963, 78–151.

FIAT Concord S.A.I.C. Oficina de Estudios para la Colaboración Económica Internacional. *Bolivia: Síntesis económica y financiera, No. 2.* Buenos Aires: 1969.

Fifer, J. Valerie. *Bolivia: Land, Location, and Politics Since 1825.* London: Cambridge University Press, 1972.

Flornoy, Bertrand. *The World of the Inca.* Garden City. Doubleday Anchor, 1958.

Fonseca Mora, Jaime. *La Iglesia en América Latina.* Madrid: Marsiega, 1960.

Forbes, David. "On the Aymara Indians of Bolivia and Peru," *Journal of the Ethnological Society,* II, 1870, 193–305.

Foreign Broadcast Information Service. *Broadcasting Stations of the World,* Part I: Amplitude Modulation Broadcasting Stations According to Country and City. Washington: GPO, 1972.

———. *Broadcasting Stations of the World,* Part IV: Television Stations. Washington: GPO, 1972.

Fox, David J. *Tin and the Bolivian Economy.* London: Latin American Publications Fund, 1970.

Fox, Hugh. "Bolivia: New World Tibet," *North American Review,* V, No. 3, May–June, 1968, 2–4.

Franco, Jean. "The Spanish American Novel." Pages 764–771 in Claudio Véliz (ed.), *Latin America and the Caribbean: A Handbook.* New York: Praeger, 1968.

Francovich, Guillermo. *La Filosofía en Bolivia.* Buenos Aires: Editorial Losada, 1945.

Gamboa, Rubén A. "Literature: Bolivia, Colombia, Ecuador, Peru, Venezuela." Pages 378–383 in Henry E. Adams (ed.), *Handbook of Latin American Studies,* XXXII. Gainesville: University of Florida

362

Press, 1970.

García, Antonio. "La Reforma agraria y el desarrollo social de Bolivia," *El Trimestre Económico* [Mexico City], XXXI, No. 123, July-September 1964, 339-387.

Gerassi, John. *The Great Fear in Latin America.* (Rev. ed.), New York: Collier Books, 1968.

Glassner, Martin Ira. "The Río Lauca Dispute over an International River," *Geographical Review*, LX, April 1970, 192-207.

Goins, John F. "Huayculi." Doctoral dissertation, University of California. Berkeley: 1954 (typescript).

————. *Huayculi: Los indios quichua del valle de Cochabamba, Bolivia.* (Ediciones Especiales 47.) Mexico City: Instituto Indigenista Interamericano, Departamento de Antropología, 1967.

————. "The Present Distribution of Indian Languages in Highland Bolivia," *Kroeber Anthropological Society Papers* [Berkeley, California], II, November 1950, 17-34.

Greene, David G. "Revolution and the Rationalization of Reform in Bolivia," *Inter-American Economic Affairs*, XIX, No. 3, Winter 1965, 3-25.

Gunther, John. *Inside South America.* New York: Harper and Row, 1967.

Hanke, Lewis. *The Imperial City of Potosí.* The Hague: Martinus Nijhoff, 1956.

————. "Luis Capoche and the History of Potosí, 1545-1585," *Inter-American Economic Affairs*, XII, Autumn 1958, 19-51.

————. *The Spanish Struggle for Justice in the Conquest of America.* Philadelphia: University of Pennsylvania Press, 1959.

Haring, C.H. *The Spanish Empire in America.* New York: Oxford University Press, 1947.

Harp, Will. "Those High-Living Pacenos," *Travel*, CXXIX, No. 2, February 1973, 67-71.

Hawthorne, Harry B., and Hawthorne, Audrey E. "Stratification in a Latin American City." In Olen E. Leonard and Charles P. Loomis (eds.), *Readings in Latin American Social Organization and Institutions.* East Lansing: Michigan State College Press, 1953.

Heath, Dwight B. "The Aymara Indians and Bolivia's Revolutions," *Inter-American Economic Affairs*, XIX, No. 4, 1966, 31-40.

————. "Drinking Patterns of the Bolivian Camba." Pages 22-36 in David J. Pittman and Charles R. Snyder (eds.), *Society, Culture and Drinking Patterns.* New York: John Wiley, 1962.

————. "Hacendados with Bad Table Manners: Campesino Syndicates as Surrogate Landlords in Bolivia," *Inter-American Economic Affairs*, XXIV, No. 1, Summer 1970, 3-13.

————. *Historical Dictionary of Bolivia.* (Latin American Historical Dictionaries, No. 4.) Metuchen: Scarecrow Press, 1972.

————. "Land Reform in Bolivia," *Inter-American Economic Affairs*,

XXII, Spring 1959, 3–27.

Heath, Dwight, B. "Land Tenure and Social Organization," *Inter-American Economic Affairs*, XIII, Spring, 1960, 44–66.

———. "New Patrons for Old: Changing Patron/Client Relationships in the Bolivian Yungas." Pages 101–137 in Arnold Strickon and Sidney Greenfield (eds.), *Structure and Process in Latin American Patronage, Clientage and Power Systems*. Albuquerque: University of New Mexico Press, 1973.

———. "Peasants, Revolution, and Drinking: Inter Ethnic Drinking Patterns," *Human Organization*, XXX, Summer 1971, 179–186.

———. "Profiles of Acculturation," *Rocky Mountain Review*, XX, No. 1, Winter 1964/65, 29–33.

———. "Revolution and Stability in Bolivia," *Current History*, XLIX, No. 292, 1965, 328.

Heath, Dwight B., and Adams, Richard. *Contemporary Cultures and Societies of Latin America*. New York: Random House, 1965.

Heath, Dwight B.; Erasmus, Charles J.; and Buechler, Hans C. *Land Reform and Social Revolution in Bolivia*. (Praeger Special Studies in International Economics and Development.) New York: Praeger, 1969.

Heyduk, Daniel. *Huayrapampa: Bolivian Highland Peasants and the New Social Order*. (Cornell University Dissertation Series No. 27.) Ithaca: Cornell University, 1971.

Hickman, John M. "The Aymara of Chinchera, Perú: Persistence and Change in a Bicultural Context." (Cornell University Doctoral dissertation.) Ann Arbor, Michigan: 1963 (University Microfilms No. 64-3641.)

———. "Colonización y Movilidad Social en Bolivia," *América Indígena* [Mexico City], XXVIII, No. 2, April 1968, 389–403.

———. "Problemas y opiniones de la juventud en Bolivia." Pages 10–40 in John Hickman (ed.), *La Juventud evangélica y la Iglesia*. Montevideo: ULAJE, 1967.

Holmberg, Allan R. *Nomads of the Long Bow: The Sirionó of Eastern Bolivia*. (Institute of Social Anthropology, Publication No. 10.) Washington: Smithsonian Institution, 1950.

"La Iglesia ante los problemas bolivianos," *Estudios Americanos* [Seville], March 1954.

Inter-American Committee for Agricultural Development—CIDA. *Inventory of Information Basic to the Planning of Agricultural Development in Latin America: Bolivia*. Washington: Pan American Union, December 1963.

Inter-American Development Bank. *Socio-Economic Progress in Latin America, Annual Report, 1971*. Washington: 1972.

———. *Socio-Economic Progress in Latin America: Social Progress Trust Fund, Ninth Annual Report, 1969*. Washington: 1970.

————. *Socio-Economic Progress in Latin America: Social Progress Trust Fund, Tenth Annual Report, 1970.* Washington: 1971.

International Labor Organization. International Labor Office. *Labour Force Projections, 1965–1985, Latin America.* Geneva: 1971.

International Planned Parenthood Federation. *Family Planning in Five Continents.* London: 1969.

Introduction to Colonial Art in Latin America. (Colonial Art, I.) Washington: General Secretariat, Organization of American States, n.d.

James, Preston. *Latin America.* (4th ed.) New York: Odyssey Press, 1969.

Kantor, Harry. *Patterns of Politics and Political Systems in Latin America.* Chicago: Rand McNally, 1969.

Key, Harold, and Key, Mary. *Bolivian Indian Tribes: Classification, Bibliography, and Map of Present Language Distribution.* Norman: University of Oklahoma, Summer Institute of Linguistics, 1967.

Klein, Herbert S. *Parties and Political Change in Bolivia, 1880–1952.* (Cambridge Latin American Studies, V.) Cambridge: Cambridge University Press, 1969.

Kornfield, William J. "Concepto de cultura y cambio social en un pueblo bilingüe de los Andes," *América Indígena* [Mexico City], XXIX, No. 4, October 1969, 983–1027.

Koth, Marcia N.; Silva, Julio G.; and Dietz, Albert G.H. *Housing in Latin America.* Cambridge: Massachusetts Institute of Technology Press, 1965.

Kubler, George. "The Quechua in the Colonial World." Pages 331–410 in Julian H. Steward (ed.), *Handbook of South American Indians*, II. Washington: Smithsonian Institution, Bureau of American Ethnology, 1946.

La Barre, Weston. "Aymara Folklore and Folk Temperament," *Journal of Folklore Institute* (Indiana University), II, No. 1, June 1965, 25–30.

————. *The Aymara Indians of the Lake Titicaca Plateau Bolivia.* (American Anthropological Association Memoir No. 28.) Menasha, Wisconsin: 1948.

————. "The Uru-Chipaya." Pages 575–585 in Julian H. Steward (ed.), *Handbook of South American Indians*, II. Washington: Smithsonian Institution, Bureau of American Ethnology, 1946.

Lanning, John Tate. *Academic Culture in the Spanish Colonies.* New York: Oxford University Press, 1940.

Lara, Jesús. *La Literatura de los Quechuas.* Cochabamba: Editorial Canelas, 1960.

Leonard, Olen E. *Bolivia, Land, People, and Institutions.* Metuchen: Scarecrow Press, 1952.

————. *El cambio económico y social en cuatro comunidades del Altiplano de Bolivia.* (Instituto Indigenista Interamericano Serie Antropología Social, 3.) Mexico City: Instituto Indigenista Interamericano, 1966.

Leonard, Olen E. *Canton Chullpas: A Socioeconomic Study of an Area in the Cochabamba Valley of Bolivia.* (Foreign Agriculture Report No. 27.) Washington: U.S. Department of Agriculture, Office of Foreign Agricultural Relations, July 1948, 1-77.

―――. "Locality Group Structure in Bolivia." In Olen E. Leonard and Charles P. Loomis (eds.), *Readings in Latin American Social Organization and Institutions.* East Lansing: Michigan State College Press, 1953.

―――. *Santa Cruz, Bolivia: A Socioeconomic Study of an Area in Bolivia.* (Foreign Agriculture Report No. 31.) Washington: U.S. Department of Agriculture, Office of Foreign Agricultural Relations, October 1948.

Léons, Madeline Barbara. "Changing Patterns of Social Stratification in an Emergent Bolivian Community." (Doctoral dissertation.) Berkeley: University of California, 1966.

―――. "Land Reform in the Bolivian Yungas," *América Indígena* [Mexico City], XXVII, No. 4, October-December 1967, 689-714.

Linares, Adolfo. "Land Settlement in Bolivia," *Development Digest,* V, No. 1, April 1967, 89-100.

List, G., and Orrego-Salas, J. (eds.) *Music in the Americas.* Bloomington: Indiana University Press, 1971.

MacEoin, Gary. *Revolution Next Door—Latin America in the 1970s.* New York: Holt, Rinehart and Winston, 1971.

McEwen, William J. *Changing Rural Bolivia.* New York: Research Institute for the Study of Man, 1969.

―――. "Teoría y metodología del proyecto RISM de Bolivia," *América Indígena* [Mexico City], XXVII, No. 2, April 1967, 349-364.

McQuown, Norman A. "Indigenous Languages of Native America," *American Anthropologist,* LVII, No. 3, Part 1, June 1955, 501-570.

Mallet, Alfredo. "Diversification or Standardization: Two Trends in Latin American Social Security," *International Labour Review* [Geneva], CI, No. 5, January 1970, 49-83.

Malloy, James M. *Bolivia: The Uncompleted Revolution.* Pittsburgh: University of Pittsburgh Press, 1970.

Malloy, James M., and Thorn, Richard S. (eds.) *Beyond the Revolution: Bolivia Since 1952.* Pittsburgh: University of Pittsburgh Press, 1971.

Marschall, K.B. *Revolution and Land Reform in Chuquisaca and Potosí.* La Paz: Servicio Nacional de Reforma Agraria, Sección de Investigaciones, 1970.

―――. *Revolution and Land Reform in the Bolivian Yungas of La Paz.* La Paz: Servicio Nacional de Reforma Agraria, Sección de Investigaciones, 1970.

Martin, Michael Rheta, and Lovett, Gabriel H. *Encyclopedia of Latin American History.* New York: Bobbs-Merrill, 1968.

Masur, Gerhard. *Simón Bolívar.* Albuquerque: University of New Mexico Press, 1948.

Matos Mar, José. "The Oldest Andeans," *Américas*, VI, March 1954, 12-31.

Mautner, H. Eric. *Doctor in Bolivia.* Philadelphia: Chilton Company, Book Division, 1960.

Means, Philip A. *The Fall of the Inca Empire and the Spanish Rule in Peru, 1530-1780.* New York: Scribners, 1932.

Mecham, John Lloyd. *Church and State in Latin America.* Chapel Hill: University of North Carolina Press, 1934.

———. *A Survey of United States-Latin American Relations.* Boston: Houghton Mifflin, 1965.

Meggers, Betty J., and Evans, Clifford. "Archaeology: South America." Pages 67-101 in Donald E. J. Stewart (ed.), *Handbook of Latin American Studies: Social Sciences*, XXXIII. Gainesville: University of Florida Press, 1971.

Menanteau-Horta, Dario. "Conflicto social y la juventud en Bolivia," *Aportes* [Paris], XXIV, April 1972, 44-66.

Métraux, Alfred. "The Inca Empire: Despotism or Socialism," *Diogenese*, XXXV, Fall 1961, 78-98.

———. *The Native Tribes of Eastern Bolivia and Western Matto Grosso.* (Bureau of American Ethnology, Bulletin No. 143.) Washington: Smithsonian Institution, 1942.

Meyer, Gordon. *Summer at High Altitude.* London: Alan Ross, 1968.

Milne, Jean, *Fiesta Time in Latin America.* Los Angeles: Ward Ritchie Press, 1965.

Mishkin, Bernard. "The Contemporary Quechua." In J.H. Steward (ed.), *Handbook of the South American Indians*, II. Washington: GPO, 1946.

Monast, Jacques. *L'univers religieux des Aymaras de Bolivie*, IV. Cuernavaca, Mexico: Centro Intercultural de Documentación, 1966.

Munro, Dana Gardner. *The Latin American Republics: A History.* (3d ed.) New York: Appleton-Century-Crofts, 1960.

Muratorio, Blanca. "Changing Bases of Social Stratification in a Bolivian Community." (Paper presented at the 65th Annual Meeting of the American Anthropological Association, November 17-20, 1970, Pittsburgh, Pennsylvania.) Pittsburgh: American Anthropological Association (mimeo.).

Needler, Martin C. *Political Systems of Latin America.* (2d ed.) New York: Van Nostrand, Reinhold, 1970.

Nunn, Frederick M. "Chile and the Andean Republics: The National Period." Pages 73-102 in Roberto Esquenazi-Mayo and Michael C. Meyer (eds.), *Latin American Scholarship Since World War II: Trends in History, Political Science, Literature, Geography, and Economics.* Lincoln: University of Nebraska Press, 1971.

Organización de los Estados Americanos. *América en Cifras, 1970: Situación Cultural:* Educación y Otros Aspectos Culturales. Washington: 1971.

Organización de los Estados Americanos. *América en Cifras, 1972: Situación Demográfica:* Estado y Movimiento de la Población. Washington: 1972.

――――. *América en Cifras, 1972: Situación Física:* Territorio y Clima. Washington: 1972.

――――. *Datos básicos de población en América Latina, 1970.* Washington: n.d.

Organización de los Estados Americanos. Instituto Interamericano de Estadística. *América en Cifras, 1970. Situación Social:* Hogar, Habitación, Mejoramiento Urbano, Previsión Social, Asistencia Médica y de Salud, y Trabajo. Washington: 1971.

Organization of American States. *Statistical Compendium of the Americas.* Washington: 1971.

Organization of American States. General Secretariat. *Bolivia.* (American Nations Series, No. 3.) Washington: 1970.

――――. *21 Latin American Meals.* (641.5-E-7488.) Washington: n.d.

Ortuño, René. *Bolivia y la integración económica de América Latina.* Buenos Aires: Instituto para la Integración de América Latina, Banco Interamericano de Desarrollo, 1969.

Osborne, Harold. *Bolivia—A Land Divided.* (3d ed., rev.) London: Royal Institute of International Affairs, 1964.

――――. *The Indians of the Andes: Aymaras and Quechuas.* London: Routledge and Kegan Paul, 1952.

Otero, Gustavo Adolfo. *Life in the Spanish Colonies.* New York: Bertrand, 1955.

――――. *La Piedra mágica: Vida y costumbres de los indios callahuayas de Bolivia.* (Ediciones Especiales, No. 5.) Mexico: Instituto Indigenista Interamericano, 1951.

Palza, Humberto. "La Clase media en Bolivia: Nota para el estudio y comprehensión del problema." Pages 1-17 in Theo Crevenna (ed.), *Materiales para el estudio de la clase media en Latino-américa,* III. Washington: Pan American Union, n.d. (mimeo.).

Pan American Health Organization. *Annual Report of the Director, 1969.* Washington: 1970.

――――. *Annual Report of the Director, 1970.* Washington: 1971.

――――. *Health Conditions in the Americas, 1965-1968.* Washington: 1970.

Paredes Candia, Antonio. *Artesanías e industrias populares de Bolivia.* La Paz: Ediciones ISLA, 1967.

Patch, Richard W. *Agriculture and the Supernatural.* (American Universities Field Staff Reports, West Coast of South America Series, XVIII, No. 4.) Hanover, New Hampshire: AUFS, June 1971.

――――. *An Anthropologist's Approach to Economic Aid.* New York: American Universities Field Staff, October 1961.

――――. *Attitudes Toward Sex, Reproduction, and Contraception in Bolivia and Peru.* (American Universities Field Staff Reports, West

Coast of South America Series, XVII, No. 11.) Hanover, New Hampshire: AUFS, 1970.

———. *Bolivia: Decision or Debacle.* New York: American Universities Field Staff, April 18, 1959.

———. *Bolivian Background.* New York: American Universities Field Staff, June 1958.

———. *Bolivia's Developing Interior.* (American Universities Field Staff Reports, West Coast of South America Series, IX, No. 3.) Hanover, New Hampshire: AUFS, 1962.

———. *Bolivia Today: An Assessment Nine Years After the Revolution.* (American Universities Field Staff, VIII, No. 4.) New York: AUFS, March 17, 1961.

———. "Bolivia: U.S. Assistance in a Revolutionary Setting." Pages 108–176 in R.N. Adams, et al. (eds.), *Social Change in Latin America Today.* New York: Vintage Books, 1961.

———. *Charazani: Center of Supernatural Beliefs of the Andes.* (American Universities Field Staff Reports, West Coast of South America Series, XVIII, No 5.) Hanover, N.H.: AUFS, 1971.

———. *The Concept of Luck in Indigenous and Hispanic Cultures.* (American Universities Field Staff Reports, West Coast of South America Series, XVII, No. 4.) Hanover, New Hampshire: AUFS, 1970.

———. *The La Paz Census of 1970.* (American Universities Field Staff Reports, West Coast of South America Series, XVII, No. 12.) Hanover, New Hampshire: AUFS, 1970.

———. "Peasantry and National Revolution: Bolivia." Pages 95–126 in K.H. Silvert (ed.), *Expectant Peoples —Nationalism and Development.* New York: Knopf, Vintage Books, 1967.

———. *Population Review 1970: Bolivia.* (American Universities Field Staff Reports, West Coast of South America Series, XVIII, No. 1.) Hanover, New Hampshire: AUFS, 1971.

———. "Social Implications of the Bolivian Agrarian Reform." Doctoral dissertation, Cornell University Microfilms, June 1956.

Pattee, Richard. *El Catolicismo contemporáneo en hispanoamérica.* Buenos Aires: Editorial Fides, 1948.

Pérez Velasco, David. *La Mentalidad Chola en Bolivia.* La Paz: n.pub., n.d.

Picón-Salas, Mariano. *A Cultural History of Spanish America; from Conquest to Independence.* (Trans., Irving A. Leonard.) Berkeley: University of California Press, 1962.

Plummer, John S. "Another Look at Aymara Personality," *Behavior Science Notes,* I, No. 2, 1966, 55–78.

Ponce García, Jaime, and Uzin Fernández, Oscar. *El Clero en Bolivia, 1968.* Cuernavaca, Mexico: Central Internacional de Documentación, 1970.

Population Reference Bureau. "La Fuga de talentos: un círculo vicioso,"

Población [Bogotá, Colombia], II, No. 8, 1971, 1.

Porter, Charles O., and Alexander, Robert J. *The Struggle for Democracy in Latin America.* New York: Macmillan, 1961.

Prescott, William H. *The Conquest of Peru.* Garden City: Dolphin Books, n.d.

Preston, David A. "New Towns—a Major Change in the Rural Settlement Pattern in Highland Bolivia," *Journal of Latin American Studies* [London], II, Part 1, May 1970, 1-27.

Price Waterhouse. *Information Guide for Doing Business in Bolivia.* Chicago: 1967.

Publishers' World—1968-69. New York: R.R. Bowker, 1968.

Rippy, J. Fred. *Latin America: A Modern History.* Ann Arbor: University of Michigan Press, 1968.

Robertson, William Spence. *History of the Latin American Nations.* New York: D. Appleton, 1930.

———. *The Rise of the Spanish-American Republics; as Told in the Lives of their Liberators.* New York: Collier Books, 1961.

Robinson, Harry. *Latin America—A Geographical Survey.* New York: Praeger, 1967.

Rodríguez, Humberto. "Cambios sociales en una comunidad del Altiplano, Bolivia." Pages 331-346 in *Congreso Internacional de Americanistas, 36, Sevilla, 1964, Actas y Memorias.* Sevilla, Spain: Editorial Católica Española, 1966.

Rowe, John H. "Inca Culture at the Time of the Spanish Conquest." Pages 183-330 in Julian H. Steward (ed.), *Handbook of South American Indians,* II. Washington: Smithsonian Institution, Bureau of American Ethnology, 1946.

Sangines Uriarte, Marcelo. *Educación rural y desarrollo en Bolivia.* La Paz: Editorial Don Bosco, 1968.

Saucedo, Sevilla. *Matrimonio civil y divorcio absoluto: doctrina, legislación y jurisprudencia nacional y extranjera.* Santa Cruz: Editorial Santa Cruz, 1963.

Schweng, Leonard P. "An Indian Community Development Project in Bolivia." Pages 44-57 in Arthur H. Niehoff (ed.), *A Casebook of Social Change.* Chicago: Aldine, 1966.

Slater, Charles, et al. *Marketing Processes in La Paz, Bolivia.* (Marketing in Developing Communities Series, Research Report No. 3.) East Lansing: Michigan State University, Latin American Studies Center, 1970.

Sotomayor, Marcelo Peinado. "Land Reform in Three Communities of Cochabamba, Bolivia." (Research Paper No. 44.) Madison: University of Wisconsin, Land Tenure Center, August 1971 (mimeo.).

Statistical Yearbook, 1971. New York: United Nations, 1972.

Stebbins, Richard P., and Amoia, Alba (eds.). *Political Handbook and Atlas of the World, 1970.* New York: Simon and Schuster, 1970.

Stein, William W. *Mothers and Sons in the Andes: Developmental*

Indications. Buffalo: State University of New York, Buffalo, 1972.

Stephansky, Ben S. *Latin America—Toward a New Nationalism.* (Headline Series, No. 211.) New York: Foreign Policy Association, June 1972.

Steward, Julian H., and Faron, Louis C. *Native Peoples of South America.* New York: McGraw-Hill, 1959.

Suárez Arnez, Cristóbal. *Desarrollo de la educación boliviana.* La Paz: Editora Universo, 1970.

Summer Institute of Linguistics. *Bolivian Indian Grammars.* 2 vols. Norman, Oklahoma: SIL, 1967.

Terry, Edward Davis (ed.). *Artists and Writers in the Evolution of Latin America.* University: University of Alabama Press, 1969.

Torres-Rioseco, Arturo. *Antología de la literatura hispano-americana.* (2d ed.) New York: Appleton-Century-Crofts, 1941.

Trask, David F.; Meyer, Michael C.; and Trask, Roger R. *A Bibliography of United States-Latin American Relations Since 1810.* Lincoln: University of Nebraska Press, 1968.

Travel and Trade Publications. *The South American Handbook, 1973.* (49th ed.) London: 1973.

Tschopik, Harry S. "The Aymara of Chucito, Peru," *Anthropological Papers of the American Museum of Natural History,* XLIV, No. 2, 1951.

―――. "The Aymara." Pages 501-574 in Julian H. Steward (ed.), *Handbook of South American Indians,* II. Washington: Smithsonian Institution, Bureau of American Ethnology, 1946.

Uhle, Max. *Wesen und Ordnung der Altperuanischen Kulturen.* Berlin: Colloquium Verlag, 1959.

United Nations. *Compendium of Social Statistics, 1967.* (Series K, No. 3.) New York: 1968.

―――. *Population and Vital Statistics Report: Data Available as of 1 October 1972.* New York: 1972.

United Nations Educational, Scientific and Cultural Organization. *World Survey of Education,* II: Primary Education. Geneva: 1958.

―――. *World Survey of Education,* III: Secondary Education. New York: International Documentation Center, 1961.

―――. *World Survey of Education,* IV: Higher Education. New York: UNESCO Publications Center, 1966.

―――. *World Survey of Education,* V: Educational Policy, Legislation and Administration. Paris: 1971.

U.S. Agency for International Development. "Land Reform in Bolivia." In *Land Reform in Bolivia, Ecuador, Peru; A.I.D. Spring Review of Land Reform,* VI. (2d ed.) Washington: AID, 1970.

―――. *Population Program Assistance.* Washington: 1970.

―――. *Summary of Economic and Social Indicators, 18 Latin American Countries: 1960-1971.* Washington: n.d.

U.S. Department of Commerce. Bureau of International Commerce.

"Basic Data on the Economy of Bolivia." *Overseas Business Reports.* (OBR 69-61) Washington: GPO, 1969.

U.S. Department of Defense. Office of the Assistant Secretary of Defense. *Bolivia: Nutrition Survey—A Report by the Interdepartmental Committee on Nutrition for National Defense.* Washington: June, 1964.

U.S. Department of State. *Foreign Relations of the United States, 1945—Diplomatic Papers: The American Republics,* IX. Washington: GPO, 1969.

————. *Republic of Bolivia: Background Notes.* Washington: GPO, September 1972.

U.S. United States Information Service. *Country Data: Bolivia.* Washington: February 1, 1972 (mimeo.).

Urquidi, Arturo. *Las Comunidades indígenas en Bolivia.* Cochabamba: Los Amigos del Libro, 1970.

Valda, Roberto. "Bolivia: Bishop's Case of Conscience," *America,* CXXVIII, No. 2, January 20, 1973, 37-38.

Vetrano, Vicente. "Algunas reflexiones sobre la Iglesia en Bolivia," *Criterio,* [Buenos Aires], XXXIX, No. 1517, February 9, 1967, 80.

————. "La Iglesia en Bolivia," *Criterio* [Buenos Aires], XXXIX, No. 1515-1516, January 19, 1967, 15.

Villarroel Claure, Rigoberto. *Bolivia.* (Art in Latin America Today.) Washington: Pan American Union, 1963.

————. "Medio siglo de pintura boliviana," *Separata de la Revista de Arte y Letras "Khana,"* II. Nos. 31 and 32, July 1958.

Viscarra Monje, Humberto. "La Música en Bolivia," *Bellas Artes,* November 1953.

Whitaker, Arthur P. *The United States and South America: The Northern Republics.* Cambridge: Harvard University Press, 1948.

————. *The United States and the Independence of Latin America, 1800-1830.* Baltimore: Johns Hopkins University Press, 1941.

Whitaker, Arthur P. (ed.) *Latin America and the Enlightenment.* New York: Appleton-Century, 1942.

Whitehead, Laurence. "Bolivia," *Current History,* LXII, No. 366, February 1972, 86-90, 117.

Wilgus, A. Curtis. *The Development of Hispanic America.* New York: Farrar and Rinehart, 1941.

————. *Historical Atlas of Latin America.* New York: Cooper Square, 1967.

Wilgus, A. Curtis (ed.). *South American Dictators During the First Century of Independence.* Washington: George Washington University Press, 1937.

Wilgus, A. Curtis, and D'Eca, Raul. *Latin American History—A Summary of Political, Economic, Social, and Cultural Events from 1492 to the Present.* (5th ed.) New York: Barnes and Noble, 1967.

Williams, Mary Wilhelmine; Bartlett, Ruhl J.; and Miller, Russell E.

The People and Politics of Latin America. (4th ed.) Boston: Ginn, 1958.

Wilson, George, et al. *The Impact of Highway Investment on Development.* (Transport Research Program.) Washington: Brookings Institution, 1966.

Woodman, James Monroe. "Ecuador." Pages 154–157 in Eugene Fodor (ed.), *South America, 1972.* New York: David McKay, 1972.

Worldmark Encyclopedia of the Nations: Americas. New York: Worldmark Press, Harper and Row, 1967.

World of Learning, I. (23d ed.) London: Europa Publications, 1971.

World Radio-TV Handbook, 1972. (26th ed.) (Ed., J.M. Frost) Hvidovre, Denmark: Billboard A.G., 1972.

Yearbook of Labor Statistics, 1971. Geneva: International Labor Organization, International Labor Office, n.d.

Yearbook on Latin American Communist Affairs, 1971. (Ed., William E. Ratliff.) Stanford: Hoover Institution Press, 1971.

Zook, David H., Jr. *The Conduct of the Chaco War.* New York: Bookman Associates, 1960.

(Various issues of the following periodicals were also used in the preparation of this section: *El Diario* [La Paz], April–May 1973; *New York Times*, February 1973; *Presencia* [La Paz], December 1970.)

Section II. Political

Agor, Weston H., and Suárez, Andrés. "The Emerging Latin American Political Subsystem," *Changing Latin America*, XXX, No. 4, 1972, 153-166.

Alba, Victor, *Politics and the Labor Movement in Latin America*. Stanford: Stanford University Press, 1968.

Alexander, Robert J. *The Bolivian National Revolution*. New Brunswick: Rutgers University Press, 1958.

———. "Bolivia: The National Revolution." Chapter 16 in Martin C. Needler (ed.), *Political Systems of Latin America*. (2d ed.) New York: Van Nostrand, Reinhold, 1970.

———. *Communism in Latin America*. New Brunswick: Rutgers University Press, 1957.

———. *Prophets of the Revolution*. New York: Macmillan, 1962.

Allen, Robert Loring. *Soviet Influence in Latin America: the Role of Economic Relations*. Washington: Public Affairs Press, 1959.

"An 'Alliance' Problem in Depth—Bolivia's Paradox," *Economic World*, IV, February-March 1962, 1.

"Andean Bloc Seeking Accords with EEC and Japan," *Business Latin America*, October 14, 1971, 328.

Andrade, Joaquín. "Entrevista con Juan Lechin," *Marcha* [Montevideo], XXXIV, No. 1615, October 20, 1972, 16, 22.

Andrade, Victor. *Bolivia—Problems and Promise*. Washington: n.pub., 1956.

Antezana E., Luis. "La Reforma agraria campesina en Bolivia (1956-1960)," *Revista Mexicana de Sociologia* [Mexico City], XXI, No. 2, April-June 1969, 245-321.

Arguedas, Alcídes. *Historia general de Bolivia, 1809-1921*. La Paz: Arnó Hermanos, 1922.

———. *Obras Completas*. 2 vols. Mexico City: Aquiler, 1959.

Arnade, Charles W. "Bolivia in Early 1959," *Vital Speeches of the Day*, XXV, 1959, 465-468.

———. *The Emergence of the Republic of Bolivia*. Gainesville: University of Florida Press, 1957.

Bailey, Norman A. *Latin America in World Politics*. New York: Walker, 1967.

Ball, Margaret M. *The OAS in Transition*. Durham: Duke University Press, 1969.

Barcelli S., Agustín. *Medio siglo de luchas sindicales revolucionarias en Bolivia*. La Paz: Editorial del Estado, 1956.

Beatty, Donald W. "Bolivia: An Uncertain Future," *Current History*, XXXII, April 1957, 216–222.

Blanksten, George I. "The Politics of Latin America." In Gabriel A. Almond, et al. *The Politics of Developing Areas*, Princeton: 1960.

Bolivia. *La Revolución nacional a través de sus decretos más importantes*. La Paz: E. Burillo, 1955.

Bolivia. Dirección Nacional de Informaciones. *Bolivia: 10 anos de revolución*. La Paz: April 1962.

Bolivia. Laws, Statutes, etc.
Las Constituciones de Bolivia. (by Ciro Félix Trigo.) Madrid: Instituto de Estudios Políticos, 1958.
Las Constituciones de Bolivia. (by Ramón Salinas Mariaca.) N.pl.: n.pub., 1947.
Constitución Política del Estado. (11th ed.) (With notes and concordances by Dr. Ciro Félix Trigo.) La Paz: Gisbert, 1961.
Constitution of Bolivia, 1967. Washington: Organization of American States, General Secretariat, 1968.

Bolivia. Ministerio de Relaciones Exteriores y Culto. *La Desviación del Río Lauca (antecedentes y documentos)*. La Paz: Imprenta "Nacional," 1962.

"Bolivian Government Tightens Economic Belt," *Latin American Digest*, VII, No. 2, January 1973, 5.

"Bolivia: Surgery in the Mines," *Economist* [London], CCXIX, No. 6397, April 2–8, 1966, 32–33.

Bonifaz, Miguel. *Legislación agrario-indigenal*. Cochabamba: Universitaria, 1953.

Borgono, L. B. *Problem of the Pacific and the New Policies of Bolivia*. Baltimore: Johns Hopkins University Press, 1924.

Bowen, J. David. "Bolivia's Revolution Comes of Age," *Reporter*, IV, September 26, 1963, 34–36.

Brice, Angel Francisco. "Constitución Bolivariana," *Revista de la Sociedad Bolivariana* [Caracas], XVII, December 17, 1958, 514–563.

Brill, William H. *Military Intervention in Bolivia: The Overthrow of Paz Estenssoro and the MNR*. Washington: Institute for the Comparative Study of Political Systems, 1967.

Burr, Robert N. "The Balance of Power in Nineteenth-Century South America: An Exploratory Essay," *Hispanic American Historical Review*, XXXV, 1955, 37–60.

Canelas L., René. *Constitución política del estado*. Cochabamba: Imprenta Universitaria, 1950.

Carrasco, José. *Estudios Constitucionales*, I–IV. La Paz: González y Medina, 1923.

Carroll, Thomas F. "The Land Reform Issue in Latin America." Pages 161–201 in Albert O. Hirschman (ed.), *Latin American Issues—Essay and Comments*. New York: Twentieth Century Fund, 1961.

Carter, William E. *Aymara Communities and the Bolivian Agrarian*

Reform. (University of Florida Monographs—Social Sciences, No. 24.) Gainesville: University of Florida Press, Fall 1964.

Céspedes T., Antonio (ed.). *Guía de legislación nacional, julio 1953–agosto 1960*. Sucre: Instituto de Socialogia Boliviana, n.d.

Chávez Ortiz, Nuflo. "Bolivia's Land Reform: An Agrarian Revolution," *New Leader*, XXXVII, December 27, 1954, 23, 24.

Clagett, Helen L. *The Administration of Justice in Latin America*. New York: Oceana, 1952.

———. *Anti-Subversive Legislation in Latin America, Current as of 1959*. Washington: Library of Congress, n.d.

———. *A Guide to the Law and Legal Literature of Bolivia*. Washington: Library of Congress, 1947.

Clark, Ronald James. "Land Reform in Bolivia." (*AID Spring Review of Land Reform*, VI. 2d ed.) Madison: University of Wisconsin, Land Tenure Center, June 1970 (mimeo.).

———. "Problems and Conflicts over Land Ownership in Bolivia," *Inter-American Economic Affairs*, XXII, No. 4, Spring, 1969, 3-18.

Cleven, N. Andrew N. *The Political Organization of Bolivia*. Washington: Carnegie Institution of Washington, 1940.

Cohen, Alvin. "Bolivia: Internal Instability and International Dependence," *Current History*, LX, No. 354, February 1971, 78-83.

Columbia University. Sixteenth American Assembly. *The United States and Latin America*. New York: Columbia University, December 1959.

Connell-Smith, Gordon. *The Inter-American System*. London: Oxford University Press, 1966.

Corbett, Charles D. *The Latin American Military as a Socio-Political Force: Case Studies of Bolivia and Argentina*. Coral Gables: University of Miami, Center for Advanced International Studies, 1972.

Davis, Harold Eugene. *History of Latin America*. New York: Ronald Press, 1968.

Davis, Harold. *Government and Politics in Latin America*. New York: Ronald Press, 1958.

del Castillo Avendaño, Walter. *Compilación legal de la reforma agraria en Bolivia*. La Paz: Fénix, 1955.

de Vecano, Máximo J. *Bolivia: Su desarrollo y progreso*. Berlin: Dietrich Reimer/Ernest Voksen, 1925.

Díez de Medina, Eduardo. *Apuntes sobre tópicos internacionales*. La Paz: Arnó Hermanos, 1919.

———. *Bolivia: Breve resumen histórico, fisico y politico*. La Paz: Issac Palza Soliz, 1926.

———. *Problemas Internacionales*. La Paz: 1936.

di Natale E., Remo. *Revolución agraria en Bolivia*. Cochabamba: Universitaria, 1953.

Douglas, William O. *Holocaust or Hemispheric Co-operation: Cross Currents in Latin America*. New York: Random House, 1971.

Duncan, W. Raymond. "Soviet Policy in Latin America Since Khrushchev," *Orbis*, XV, No. 2, Summer 1971, 643-669.

Duran P., Manuel. *Bibliografía jurídica boliviana (1825-1954)*. Oruro: Editorial Universitaria, 1957.

Erasmus, Charles J. "Upper Limits of Peasantry and Agrarian Reform: Bolivia, Venezuela, and Mexico Compared," *Ethnology*, VI, No. 4, October 1967, 349-380.

Ferragut, Casto. "La reforma agraria boliviana," *Revista Interamericana de Ciencias Sociales*, II, No. 1, 1963, 78-151.

Fifer, J. Valerie. *Bolivia: Land, Location and Politics Since 1825*. London: Cambridge University Press, 1972.

Finot, Enrique. *Nueva Historia de Bolivia*. Buenos Aires: Imprenta López, 1946.

Fitzgibbon, Russell H. (ed.) *The Constitutions of the Americas (as of January 1, 1948)*. Chicago: University of Chicago Press, 1948.

Flores, Edmundo. "Land Reform in Bolivia," *Land Economics*, XXX, May 1954, 112-124.

Flores Moncayo, José. *Legislación boliviana del indio. Recopilación 1825-1953*. La Paz: Editorial Fénix, 1953.

Fox, Hugh. "Bolivia: New World Tibet," *North American Review*, V, No. 3, May-June 1968, 2-4.

Francovich, Guillermo. "El Marxismo." Pages 169-175 in *La Filosofía en Bolivia*. Buenos Aires: Editorial Losada, 1945.

———. *El pensamiento boliviano en el siglo XX*. Mexico City: Fonda de Cultura Económica, 1956.

Galarza, Ernesto. *The Case of Bolivia*. (Inter-American Reports, No. 6.) Washington: n.pub., 1949.

García, Antonio. "La Reforma agraria y el desarrollo social de Bolivia," *El Trimestre Económico* [Mexico City], XXXI, No. 123, July-September 1964, 339-387.

Gil, Federico. *Latin American-U.S. Relations*. New York: Harcourt, Brace Jovanovich, 1971.

Glassner, Martin Ira. "The Río Lauca Dispute over an International River," *Geographical Review*, LX, April 1970, 192-207.

Goodrich, Carter. "Bolivia: Test of Technical Assistance," *Foreign Affairs*, XXXII, April 1954, 473-481.

———. *The Economic Transformation of Bolivia*. (New York State School of Industrial and Labor Relations, Bulletin 34.) Ithaca: Cornell University, October 1955.

Gray, Richard B. (ed.) *Latin America and the United States in the 1970s*. Itasca, Illinois: F. E. Peacock, 1971.

Green, David. *The Containment of Latin America: A History of the Myths and Realities of the Good Neighbor Policy*. Chicago: Triangle Books, 1971.

Guerrant, Edward O. *Roosevelt's Good Neighbor Policy*. Albuquerque: University of New Mexico Press, 1950.

Hauberg, C. A. "Challenge in Bolivia," *Current History*, XXXVIII, 1960, 78–81.

Heath, Dwight B. "Hacendados with Bad Table Manners: Campesino Syndicates as Surrogate Landlords in Bolivia," *Inter-American Economic Affairs*, XXIV, No. 1, Summer 1970, 3–13.

―――. "Land Reform in Bolivia," *Inter-American Economic Affairs*, XII, Spring 1959, 3–27.

Heath, Dwight; Erasmus, Charles J.; and Buechler, Hans C. *Land Reform and Social Revolution in Bolivia*. (Praeger Special Studies in International Economics and Development.) New York: Praeger, 1969.

Herring, Hubert. *A History of Latin America*. (3d ed.) New York: Knopf, 1968.

Holland, James E. "The Foreign Relations of Bolivia." Chapter 17 in Harold E. Davis and Larman C. Wilson (eds.), *Latin American Foreign Policies: An Analysis*. Washington: 1971 (manuscript).

Houston, John A. *Latin America in the United Nations*. (United Nations Series, No. 8.) New York: Carnegie Endowment for International Peace, 1956.

Hunter, Robert E. "Bolivia." Chapter 12 in Ben G. Burnett and Kenneth F. Johnson (eds.), *Political Forces in Latin America: Dimensions of the Quest for Stability*. Belmont, California: Wadsworth, 1968.

Institute for the Comparative Study of Political Systems. *Bolivia: Election Factbook, July 3, 1966*. Washington: 1966.

Ireland, Gordon. *Boundaries, Possessions and Conflicts in South America*. Cambridge: Harvard University Press, 1938.

Jose, James R. *An Inter-American Peace Force Within the Framework of the Organization of American States*. Metuchen: Scarecrow Press, 1970.

Kantor, Harry. *Patterns of Politics and Political Systems in Latin America*. Chicago: Rand McNally, 1969.

Karaz, Arthur. "Experiment in Development: Bolivia Since 1952." Pages 256–280 in Frederick B. Pike (ed.), *Freedom and Reform in Latin America*. Notre Dame: University of Notre Dame Press, 1959.

Klein, Herbert S. *Parties and Political Change in Bolivia, 1880–1952*. (Cambridge Latin American Studies, V.) Cambridge: Cambridge University Press, 1969.

Knudson, Jerry W. "Bolivia's Popular Assembly of 1971 and the Overthrow of Juan José Torres." Brookings: South Dakota State University, 1972 (Unpublished research paper.).

Law and Judicial Systems of Nations: Bolivia. Washington: World Peace Through Law Center, 1968.

Leonard, Olen E. *Bolivia: Land, People and Institutions*. Metuchen: Scarecrow Press, 1952.

Levinson, Jerome, and de Onis, Juan. *The Alliance That Lost Its Way: A Critical Report on the Alliance for Progress.* Chicago: Quadrangle Books, 1970.

Loftstrom, William L. "Attitudes of an Industrial Pressure Group in Latin America: The Asociación de Industriales Mineros de Bolivia, 1925-1935." (Dissertation Series, No. 9.) Ithaca: Cornell University, Latin American Studies Program, September 1968 (Unpublished Ph.D. dissertation.).

López Avila, J. Hugo. *Reforma Agraria.* La Paz: Ediciones Nueva Era, 1957.

Lord, Peter P. "The Peasantry as an Emerging Political Factor in Mexico, Bolivia and Venezuela." (Land Tenure Center No. 35.) Madison: University of Wisconsin, LTC, May 1965 (mimeo.).

Lucha Obrero [La Paz], No. 119, May 7, 1962.

Lumpkin, T. D. "Bolivia: Gulf Oil's Experience." (Paper presented April 30, 1970, at Symposium on Recent Trends Affecting Trade and Investment in Latin America, Bates School of Law, University of Houston, Texas.) Houston: n.pub., 1970.

MacDonald, N. P. "Bolivia's Revolution," *Quarterly Review* [London], No. 295, January 1957, 46-59.

McEwen, William J. *Changing Rural Bolivia.* New York: Research Institute for the Study of Man, 1969.

Maldonado, Abraham. *Derecho agrario historia-doctrina-legislación.* La Paz: n.pub., 1956.

Malloy, James M. "Bolivia's MNR: A Study of a National Popular Movement in Latin America." (Special Studies No. 8.) Buffalo: State University of New York, Council on International Studies, 1971 (mimeo.).

———. *Bolivia: The Uncompleted Revolution.* Pittsburgh: University of Pittsburgh Press, 1970.

Malloy, James M., and Thorn, Richard S. (eds.) *Beyond the Revolution: Bolivia Since 1952.* Pittsburgh: University of Pittsburgh Press, 1971.

Marsh, Margaret Alexander. *The Banker in Bolivia: A Study in American Foreign Investment.* New York: Vanguard Press, 1928.

Martin, Louis Deicke. *Bolivia in 1956.* Palo Alto: Stanford University, 1958.

Mecham, John Lloyd. *The United States and Inter-American Security, 1889-1960.* Austin: University of Texas Press, 1961.

Mendoza, Jaime. *El Factor geográfico en la nacionalidad boliviana.* Sucre: n.pub., 1925.

Mendoza, Samuel. *La Revolución Boliviana.* Santiago: Publicación de Acción Democrática Boliviana, 1955.

Mercado Moreira, Miguel. *Historia Internacional de Bolivia.* (2d ed.) La Paz: Imprenta "Atenea," de Crespi Hermanos, 1930.

Merryman, John H., and Ackerman, Edgar D. *International Law, Development, and the Transit Trade of Landlocked States: The Case of*

Bolivia. (Werkhefte 14.) Hamburg: Institut für Auswärtige Politik in Hamburg, 1966.

Meyer, Gordon. *Summer at High Altitude*. London: Alan Ross, 1968.

Millington, Thomas M. "Bolivia Under Barrientos," *Current History*, LVI, No. 329, January 1969, 25-30, 51-52.

Montenegro, Carlos. *Nacionalismo y coloniaje; Su expresión histórica en la prensa de Bolivia*. (3d ed.) La Paz: Alcaldía Municipal, 1953.

Movimiento Nacionalista Revolucionario. Secretaria Ejecutiva. Comité Político Nacional. *El Pensamiento revolucionario de Paz Estenssoro*. La Paz: 1954.

Ocampo Moscoso, Eduardo. *Reflexiones sobre la historiografía boliviana. La Antítesis: Arguedas-Mendoza*. Cochabamba: n.pub., 1954.

O'Connor D'Arlach, Tomás. *Los Presidentes de Bolivia desde 1825 hasta 1912*. La Paz: González y Medina, 1918.

Ordóñez López, Manuel (comp.). *Constitucion política de la República de Bolivia: leyes y disposiciones más usuales*, I and II. La Paz: González y Medina, 1917.

Ortuño, René. *Bolivia y la integracion económica de América Latina*. Buenos Aires: Instituto para la Integración de América Latina, Banco Interamericano de Desarrollo, 1969.

Osborne, Harold. *Bolivia: A Land Divided*. (2d ed.) London: Royal Institute of International Affairs, 1955.

Ostría Gutiérrez, Alberto. *The Tragedy of Bolivia: A People Crucified*. New York: Devin-Adair, 1958.

Pan American Union. *Bolivia in Brief*. Washington: PAU, 1955.

Pando Gutiérrez, Jorge. *Bolivia y el mundo geografía económica*. 2 vols. La Paz: Féniz, 1947.

Paredes, Manuel Rigoberto. *Politica Parlamentaria de Bolivia*. La Paz: n.pub., 1911.

Partido Obrero Revolucionario. XIX Congreso Nacional. *Desintegración del desgobierno movimientista y tareas del partido obrero revolucionario* (Tesis Política). La Paz: April 1962 (mimeo.).

Patch, Richard W. *Bolivia's Nationalism and the Military*. (American Universities Field Staff Reports, West Coast of South America Series, XVI, No. 3.) Hanover, New Hampshire: AUFS, October 1969.

———. "Bolivia: The Restrained Revolution." Pages 123-131 in *Latin America's Nationalistic Revolutions* (The Annals of the American Academy of Political and Social Science, CCCXXXIV), March 1961.

———. *Bolivia Today: An Assessment Nine Years After the Revolution*. (American Universities Field Staff, VIII, No. 4.) New York: AUFS, March 17, 1961.

———. "Bolivia: U.S. Assistance in a Revolutionary Setting." Pages 108-176 in R. N. Adams, et al. (eds.), *Social Change in Latin America Today*. New York: Vintage Books, 1961.

———. *The Last of Bolivia's MNR? Tensions Between Personalism and Party in Politics*. (American Universities Field Staff Reports, West

Coast of South America Series, XI, No. 5.) Hanover, New Hampshire: AUFS, June 1964.

———. "Social Implications of the Bolivian Agrarian Reform." Doctoral dissertation, Cornell University Microfilms, June 1956.

Paz Estenssoro, Víctor. *Discursos Parlamentarios*. La Paz: n.pub., 1956.

———. *Mensaje al pueblo del Excelentísimo Presidente Constitucional de la República Dr. Víctor Paz Estenssoro.* La Paz: Subsecretaria de Prensa Informaciones, 1954.

———. *Mensaje del Presidente de la República Dr. Víctor Paz Estenssoro al H. Congreso Nacional, 1956.* La Paz: 1956.

Paz, Luis. *Constitución política de la República de Bolivia: Su texto, su historia y su comentario.* Sucre: M. Pizarro, 1912.

———. *La Corte Suprema de Justicia de Bolivia: Su historia y su comentario.* Sucre: n.pub., 1912.

Petras, James. "Bolivia Between Revolutions," *Monthly Review*, XXIII, No. 2, June 1971, 11-24.

Ponce García, Jaime. "El sindicalismo boliviano: Resumen histórico y perspectivas actuales," *Desarrollo Economico* [Buenos Aires], IX, No. 33, April–June, 1969, 3-32.

Preston, David A. "New Towns—A Major Change in the Rural Settlement Pattern in Highland Bolivia," *Journal of Latin American Studies* [London], II, Part I, May 1970, 1-27.

Reed, Irving B.; Suchlicki, Jaime; and Harvey, Dodd L. *The Latin American Scene of the Seventies: A Basic Fact Book.* (Monographs in International Affairs.) Coral Gables: University of Miami, Center for Advanced International Studies, 1972.

Richards, Allan R. *Administration—Bolivia and the United States.* Albuquerque: University of New Mexico, Department of Government, Division of Research, 1961.

Rippy, J. Fred. *Latin America: A Modern History.* Ann Arbor: University of Michigan Press, 1968.

Rosenbaum, H. Jon, with Glen M. Cooper. *Arms and Security in Latin America: Recent Developments.* (International Affairs Series, 101.) Washington: Woodrow Wilson International Center for Scholars, December 1971.

Royal Institute of International Affairs. *The Republics of South America.* London: Oxford University Press, 1937.

Ruddle, Kenneth, and Gillette, Philip (eds.). *Latin American Political Statistics* (A Supplement to the Statistical Abstract of Latin America.) Los Angeles: University of California, Latin American Center, 1970.

Salinas Baldivieso, Carlos Alberto. *Historia Diplomática de Bolivia.* Sucre: Editorial Charca, 1938.

Salinas Mariaca, Ramón. *Códigos Bolivianos.* (3d ed.) La Paz: Gisbert, 1955.

Sergio, Fernández Larrain. *El Comunismo en Bolivia.* Santiago: n.pub., 1956.

Sigmund, Paul E. *Models of Political Change in Latin America.* New York: Praeger, 1970.

Siles Salinas, Jorge. *La Aventura y el Orden.* Santiago de Chile: n.pub., 1956.

Smith, Peter Seaborn. "Bolivian Oil and Brazilian Economic Nationalism," *Journal of Inter-American Studies and World Affairs,* XIII, No. 2, April 1971, 166–181.

Sotomayor, Marcelo Peinado. "Land Reform in Three Communities of Cochabamba, Bolivia." (Research Paper No. 44.) Madison: University of Wisconsin, Land Tenure Center, August 1971 (mimeo.).

Spain, August O. "Bolivia: Case Study of Welfare-State Politics." In John M. Claunch (ed.), *Case Studies in Latin American Politics* (Arnold Foundation Monographs IX.) Dallas: Southern Methodist University, 1961.

"The Stabilization Plan in Bolivia," *Bolivia,* XIV, May–June 1957.

Statesman's Year-Book, 1972–1973. (Ed., John Paxton.) London: Macmillan, 1972.

Stokes, William S. *Latin American Politics.* New York: Crowell, 1959.

———. "The 'Revolución Nacional' and the MNR in Bolivia," *Inter-American Economic Affairs,* XII, Spring 1959, 28–53.

Thayer, George. *The War Business: The International Trade in Armaments.* New York: Simon and Schuster, 1969.

Trigo, Ciro Félix. *Derecho constitucional boliviano.* La Paz: Editorial "Cruz del Sur," 1951.

U.S. Agency for International Development. *U.S. Overseas Loans and Grants and Assistance from International Organizations: Obligations and Loan Authorizations, July 1, 1945–June 30, 1971.* Washington: GPO: May 24, 1972.

U.S. Congress. 86th, 2d Session. Senate. Committee on Foreign Relations. *Latin America: Venezuela, Brazil, Peru, Bolivia and Panama.* (Report of Senator George D. Aiken on a Study Mission.) Committee print, February 2, 1960.

U.S. Congress. 89th, 2d Session. Senate. Committee on Foreign Relations. *South America: Argentina, Bolivia, Brazil, Chile, Colombia and Venezuela.* (Report of Senator Wayne Morse on a Study Mission.) Committee print, February 20, 1960.

———. *United States-Latin American Relations.* (Document No. 125.) Washington: GPO, 1961.

U.S. Department of State. *Background Notes: Bolivia.* Washington: GPO, December 1972.

———. *Foreign Relations of the United States, V: The American Republics.* Washington: 1942.

———. *Treaties in Force. A List of Treaties and Other International Agreements of the United States in Force on January 1, 1962.* Washington: GPO, 1962.

U.S. United States Information Service. *Country Data: Bolivia.* Washington: February 1, 1972 (mimeo.).

Urquidi, Carlos Wálter. *Régimen legal boliviano.* La Paz: n.pub., 1947.

Urquidi, José Macedonio. *Compendio de la historia de Bolivia.* (4th ed.) Buenos Aires: 1944.

Valda, Roberto. "Bolivia: Bishop's Case of Conscience," *America,* CXXVIII, No. 2, January 20, 1973, 37–38.

Valencia Vega, Alipio. *Desarrollo del pensamiento político en Bolivia.* La Paz: n.pub., 1953.

———. *Fundamentos de derecho político.* La Paz: Librería Editorial "Juventud," 1954.

Wainhouse, David W., et al. *International Peace Observation.* Baltimore: Johns Hopkins Press, 1966.

Whitehead, Laurence. "Bolivia's Conflict with the United States," *World Today* [London], VIII, No. 1, January 1970, 167–178.

———. "Bolivia Swings Right," *Current History,* LXII, No. 336, February 1972, 86–91, 117.

Wilkie, James Wallace. *The Bolivian Revolution and U.S. Aid Since 1952; Financial Background and Context of Political Divisions.* (Latin American Studies, 13.) Los Angeles: University of California, Latin American Center, 1969.

———. "Recentralization: The Budgetary Dilemma in the Economies of Mexico, Bolivia, and Costa Rica." Gainesville: University of Florida,1971 (Unpublished paper, mimeo.).

Wolpin, Miles. *Military Aid and Counterrevolution in the Third World.* Lexington, Massachusetts: D.C. Heath, 1972.

Wood, Bryce. *The Making of the Good Neighbor Policy.* New York: Columbia University Press, 1961.

Zondag, Cornelius H. *The Bolivian Economy, 1952–65: The Revolution and Its Aftermath.* New York: Praeger, 1966.

(Various issues of the following periodicals were also used in the preparation of this section: *El Diario* [La Paz], March 1973–April 1973; *Latin America* [London], July 1968–March 1973; *New York Times,* September 1969–February 1973; *Noticias: Weekly Digest of Hemisphere Reports* [New York], March 1973–April 1973; *Times of the Americas* [Washington], May 1968–January 1973; and *Washington Post,* February 1971–April 1973.)

Section III. Economic

Abercrombie, K. C. "Agricultural Mechanisation and Employment in Latin America," *International Labour Review* [Geneva], CVI, No. 1, July 1972, 11-46.

Abrams, Charles. *Report on Housing Financing in Bolivia.* UN Technical Assistance Administration, 1959 (mimeo.).

Adams, Dale W. "Agricultural Credit in Latin America: A Critical Review of External Funding Policy," *American Journal of Agricultural Economics,* LIII, No. 2, May 1971, 163-172.

"Agricultural Policy in the Countries Signatory to the Andean Subregional Integration Agreement," *Economic Bulletin for Latin America,* XVI, No. 2, 1972, 91-119.

Ahlfeld, Federico. *Los Yacimientos minerales de Bolivia.* Bilbao, Spain: Imprenta Industrial, 1954.

Alexander, Robert J. *The Bolivian National Revolution.* New Brunswick: Rutgers University Press, 1958.

Anaya Oblitas, Ivan G. *Breve intento de análisis económico de Bolivia.* Cochabamba: Universitaria, 1958.

Anaya, Ricardo. *Nacionalización de las minas de Bolivia.* Cochabamba: Imprenta Universidad, 1952.

The Andean Common Market. New York: Business International, December 1970.

Antezana, E. Luis. "La Reforma agraria campesina en Bolivia (1956-1960)," *Revista Mexicana de Sociología* [Mexico City], XXI, No. 2, April-June, 1969, 245-321.

Aramayo Avila, Cesareo. *Ferrocarriles bolivianos: Pasado-presente-futuro.* La Paz: Imprenta Nacional, 1959.

Aramayo, Carlos Víctor. *Memorandum sobre las problemas de la industria minera de bolivia.* Buenos Aires: Patagonia, 1947.

Ayala Mercado, Manuel. *El Crédito agrícola y el plan de desarrollo agropecuario de Bolivia.* La Paz: n.pub., 1963.

Baerresen, Donald W.; Carnoy, Martin; and Grunwald, Joseph. *Latin American Trade Patterns.* Washington: Brookings, 1965.

Baer, Werner. "The Inflation Controversy in Latin America: A Survey," *Latin American Research Review,* II, No. 2, Spring, 1967, 3-25.

Banco Boliviano Americano. *Annual Report, 1970.* La Paz: n.pub., 1971.

Beals, Carleton. *Fire on the Andes.* Philadelphia: Lippincott, 1934.

Bell, Harry H. *Tariff Profiles in Latin America.* New York: Praeger, 1971.

Bennett, Wendell. *Ancient Arts of the Andes.* New York: 1954.

Bennett, Wendell, and Bird, Junius B. *Andean Culture History.* (Handbook Series, No. 15.) New York: American Museum of Natural History, 1949.

Bolivia. Banco Agrícola de Bolivia. *Vigésima sexta memoria, julio 1968–junio 1969.* La Paz: 1970.

Bolivia. Banco Central de Bolivia. *Boletín estadístico, enero-marzo, 1972.* La Paz: Imprenta Naviana, 1972.

Bolivia. Comisión Nacional de Estudio de la Caña y del Azúcar. *La industria azucarera boliviana.* La Paz: Editorial del Estado, 1969.

Bolivia. Consejo Nacional de Establización Monetaria (National Monetary Stabilization Council) *Report by George J. Eder* (Director). La Paz: April 17, 1957 (mimeo.).

Bolivia. Dirección General de Minas y Petroleo. *Memorandum of Tin Mining Industry in Bolivia.* La Paz: February 1950.

Bolivia. Dirección Nacional de Informaciones. *Bolivia: 10 años de revolución.* La Paz: April 1962.

Bolivia. Empresa Nacional de Ferrocarriles. *Estadística de los ferrocarriles de Bolivia, 1970.* La Paz: n.pub., n.d.

————. *Memoria, 1969–1970.* La Paz: Imprenta Quelco, n.d.

Bolivia. Junta Nacional de Planeamiento. *Plan de desarrollo económico y social de Bolivia, 1962–1971.* La Paz: July 1961.

Bolivia. Laws, Statutes, etc.
Código del petroleo y su reglamento. La Paz: Yacimiento Petrolíferos Fiscales Bolivianos, 1956.

Bolivia. Ministerio de Economía Nacional. Dirección General de Minas y Petroleo. *Mapa de los yacimientos minerales de Bolivia.* (Con una memoria explicativa por Federico Ahlfeld.) Buenos Aires: Peuser, 1946.

Bolivia. Ministerio de Hacienda. Dirección General de Estadística y Censos. *Boletín Estadístico, 1966.* La Paz: 1967.

Bolivia. Ministerio de Planificación y Coordinación. *Estratégia socioeconómica del desarrollo nacional, 1971–1991.* La Paz: 1970.

Bolivia. Ministerio de Transportes, Comunicaciones y Aeronáutica Civil, Subsecretaría de Aeronáutica Civil. Dirección General de Aeronáutica Civil. *Aerocivil Bolivia: bodas de plata, 1947–1972.* La Paz; Editorial Aeronáutica, 1972.

Bolivia. Ministry of Industry and Commerce. National Institute of Investments. *Law of Investments.* La Paz: Publicaciones ISAP, n.d.

Bolivia. Secretaría Nacional de Planificación y Coordinación. *Cuentas nacionales de Bolivia, período 1958–1965.* La Paz: Editorial Cassigoli y Cía., 1966.

Bolivia. Subsecretaría de Prensa. Informaciones y Cultura. Departamento de Publicaciones. *El Libro blanco de la independencia economía de Bolivia.* La Paz: 1952.

Bolivia. Superintendencia de Bancos. *Memoria Anual, 1969.* La Paz: Empresa Editora Universo, 1970.

Bolivia. Yacimiento Petrolíferos Fiscales Bolivianos. *Estatutos y decretos-ley de creación de la entidad.* La Paz: 1959.

———. *Petroleo en Bolivia.* La Paz: August 1958.

"Bolivia: Agreements Concerning Indemnification for the Nationalization of Bolivian Gulf Oil Properties," *International Legal Materials,* November 1971, 1113-1150.

"Bolivia: Legislation Concerning Nationalization of Bolivian Gulf Oil Properties," *International Legal Materials,* November 1971, 1201-1223.

Bowmann, Isaiah. "Trade Routes in the Economic Geography of Bolivia," *Bulletin of the American Geographical Society,* XLII, 1910, 90-104, 122-137, 180-192.

Brown, Robert T. *Transport and the Economic Integration of South America.* (Transport Research Program.) Washington: Brookings, 1966.

Burke, Melvin. "Does 'Food for Peace' Assistance Damage the Bolivian Economy?" *Inter-American Economic Affairs,* XXV, No. 1, Summer 1971, 3-20.

———. "Land Reform and Its Effect Upon Production and Productivity in the Lake Titicaca Region," *Economic Development and Cultural Change,* XXVIII, No. 3, April 1970, 410-450.

Cale, Edward G. *Latin American Free Trade Association: Progress, Problems, Prospects.* Washington: GPO, 1969.

Camacho Saa, Carlos. *Minifundia, Productivity, and Land Reform in Cochabamba.* (Research Paper No. 21.) Madison: University of Wisconsin, Land Tenure Center, December 1966.

Cámara Nacional de Comercio. *Comentarios y sugerencias en torno a algunas problemas de la economía nacional.* La Paz: Empresa Editora Universo, 1972.

———. *Memoria LXXVII, 1971-1972.* La Paz: July 1972.

Cámara Nacional de Industrias. *Memoria, 1969/1970,* XXXIX. La Paz: Empresa Editora Universo, 1970.

Cardenas, Martin. *Contribuciones a la flora económica de Bolivia.* Cochabamba: n.pub., 1941.

Cardenas, Martin, and Cutler, H. C. "Chicha, a Native South American Beer." *Botanical Museum Leaflets* (Harvard University), XIII, No. 3, 1947.

Carroll, Thomas F. *Report on the Latin American Seminar on Land Problems.* Rome: Food and Agriculture Organization, 1953 (mimeo.).

Carter, William E. *Aymara Communities and the Bolivian Agrarian Reform.* (University of Florida Monographs, Social Sciences No. 24.) Gainesville: University of Florida Press, Fall 1964.

Centre de Recherches Socio-Religieuses. *Programme d'Aide Sociale à la Bolivie.* Brussels: 1962 (mimeo.).

Céspedes, Augusto. *Bolivia.* Washington: Unión Panamericana, 1962.

Chaves, Fernando. "Cooperatives: A Force for Social Change,"

Américas, XIII, August 1961, 6-12.

Clark, Ronald James. "Land Reform and Peasant Market Participation on the North Highlands of Bolivia," *Land Economics*, XLIV, No. 2, May 1968, 155-172.

―――. "Problems and Conflicts over Land Ownership in Bolivia," *Inter-American Economic Affairs*, XXIII, No. 4, Spring 1969, 3-18.

Clark, Sydney A. *The West Coast of South America*, New York: Prentice-Hall, 1941.

Claunch, John M. (ed.) *Case Studies in Latin American Politics*. (Arnold Foundation Monographs IX.) Dallas: Southern Methodist University, 1961.

Cohen, Alvin. "Bolivia: Internal Instability and International Dependence," *Current History*, LX, No. 354, February 1971, 78-83.

"Commodity Problems and Policies," *Economic Bulletin for Latin America*, XVII, No. 1, first half 1972, 1-40.

Corporación Boliviana de Fomento. *La Corporación boliviana de fomento, sus orígénes, su organización y su actividad*. La Paz: Universo, 1943.

Cratacap, Maurice. *Recomendaciones generales para el sector de la minera estatizada en Bolivia*. Santiago de Chile. United Nations, 1960.

Davila Michel, Oscar. *El Estaño*. La Paz: Corporación Minera de Bolivia, 1960.

Davis, L. Harlan. *United States Assistance to Agriculture in Latin America Through the Agency for International Development*. (Land Tenure Center No. 7.) Madison: University of Wisconsin, LTC, June 1970.

Dell, Sidney. *The Inter-American Development Bank: A Study in Development Financing*. New York: Praeger, 1972.

Dion, H. B. *Agriculture in the Altiplano of Bolivia*. (Food and Agriculture Organization Development Paper No. 4.) Washington: FAO, 1950.

Dorner, Peter (ed.). *Land Reform in Latin America: Issues and Cases*. Madison: University of Wisconsin, Land Economics, 1971.

Dozier, Craig L. *Land Development and Colonization in Latin America*. New York: Praeger, 1969.

Echeverri Herrera, Carlos. *Tendencias económicas de América-Latina*. Madrid: Sucs. de Rivadeneyera, 1958.

Economist Intelligence Unit. *The Crisis in Latin American Integration*. (Quarterly Economic Review, Q.E.R. Special No. 1.) London: 1968.

―――. *Quarterly Economic Review: Peru, Bolivia*. (No. 1, 1973.) London: 1973.

Edelmann, Alexander T. "Colonization in Bolivia: Progress and Prospects," *Inter-American Economic Affairs*, XX, No. 4. Spring 1967, 39-54.

Eder, George Jackson. *Inflation and Development in Latin America: A*

Case History of Inflation and Stabilization in Bolivia. (Michigan International Business Studies, No. 8.) Ann Arbor: University of Michigan, 1968.

Erasmus, Charles J. "Upper Limits of Peasantry and Agrarian Reform: Bolivia, Venezuela, and Mexico Compared," *Ethnology,* VI, No. 4, October 1967, 349–380.

Fehmerling, G. B. "Survey of the Food Industry in Bolivia." (Prepared for the Industry Office, USAID/B), December 1961 (Unpublished typewritten manuscript.).

Ferragut, Casto. *Principles características de la colonias agrícolas de Bolivia y surgerencias para una política de colonización.* La Paz: Food and Agriculture Organization, July 1961 (mimeo.).

————. "La reforma agraria boliviana," *Revista Interamericana de Ciencias Sociales,* II, No. 1, 1963, 78–151.

FIAT Concord S.A.I.C. Oficina de Estudios para la Colaboración Económica Internacional. *Bolivia: Síntesis económica y financiera, No. 2.* Buenos Aires: 1969.

Fifer, J. Valerie. "Bolivia's Pioneer Fringe," *Geographical Review,* LVII, January 1967, 1–23.

Fisher, Frederic R. *Tax Reform in Latin America.* Washington: U.S. Agency for International Development, January 24, 1962 (mimeo.).

Flores, Edmundo. "Agrarian Reform and Economic Development," *Proceedings of the Conference on World Land Tenure Problems, Part 1.* Madison: n. pub., 1951.

————. "Land Reform in Bolivia," *Land Economics,* XXX, May 1954, 112–124.

Food and Agriculture Organization. *Government Marketing Policies in Latin America.* Rome: FAO, 1967.

————. *The State of Food and Agriculture, 1970—Preliminary Version.* Rome: FAO, September 1970.

Ford, Bacon, and Davis. *Continuation Studies at Selected Mines.* New York: Ford, Bacon, and Davis, April 1958 (mimeo.).

————. *Report Mining Industry of Bolivia.* 9 vols. New York: Ford, Bacon, and Davis, December 3, 1956 (mimeo.).

Fox, David J. *The Bolivian Tin Mining Industry: Some Geographical and Economic Problems.* London: International Tin Council, 1967.

————. *Tin and the Bolivian Economy.* London: Latin American Publications Fund, 1970.

Fox, Hugh. "Bolivia: New World Tibet," *North American Review,* V, No. 3, May-June 1968, 2–4.

Frias Alvarez, Ricardo. *El Puerto para Bolivia y la paz mundial.* Cochabamba: Editorial Canelas, 1971.

Garbacz, Christopher. *Industrial Polarization Under Economic Integration in Latin America.* (Studies in Latin American Business, No. 11.) Austin: University of Texas Press, 1971.

García, Antonio. "La Reforma agraria y el desarrollo social de Bolivia,"

El Trimestre Ecónomico (Mexico City), XXXI, No. 123, July-September 1964, 339-387.

García Godoy, Cristián Raul. "Planificación y Organizacion en Bolivia," *Revista de Administración Pública* [Buenos Aires], IV, No. 13, April-June 1964, 48-62.

Glade, William. "Social Backwardness, Social Reform, and Productivity in Latin America," *Inter-American Economic Affairs*, XV, No. 3, 1961, 3-32.

Goncalves de Souza, Joso. "Aspects of Land Tenure Problems in Latin America," *Rural Sociology*, XXV, March 1960, 36, 37.

Gonzales, Heliodoro. "The Domestic Political Effects of Foreign Aid: Case: The Failure in Bolivia," *Inter-American Economic Affairs*, XV, No. 2, 1961, 77, 78.

Goodrich, Carter. "Bolivia: Test of Technical Assistance," *Foreign Affairs*, XXXII, April 1954, 473-481.

————. *The Economic Transformation of Bolivia.* (New York State School of Industrial and Labor Relations, Bulletin 34.) New York: Cornell University, October 1955.

Greene, David G. "Revolution and the Rationalization of Reform in Bolivia," *Inter-American Economic Affairs*, XIX, No. 3, Winter 1965, 3-25.

Griffin, Keith B. (ed.) *Financing Development in Latin America.* London: Macmillan, 1971.

Grunwald, Joseph; Wionczek, Miguel S.; and Carnoy, Martin. *Latin American Economic Integration and U.S. Policy.* Washington: Brookings, 1972.

Guevara Arze, Wálter. *Plan de politica económica de la revolución nacional.* La Paz: Ministerio de Relaciones Exteriores, 1955.

Heath, Dwight B. "Commercial Agriculture and Land Reform in the Bolivian Oriente," *Inter-American Economic Affairs*, XIII, Autumn 1959, 35-46.

————. "Hacendados with Bad Table Manners: Campesino Syndicates as Surrogate Landlords in Bolivia," *Inter-American Economic Affairs*, XXIV, No. 1, Summer 1970, 3-13.

————. *Historical Dictionary of Bolivia.* (Latin American Historical Dictionaries, No. 4.) Metuchen: Scarecrow Press, 1972.

————. "Land Reform in Bolivia," *Inter-American Economic Affairs*, XII, Spring 1959, 3-27.

————. "Land Tenure and Social Organization," *Inter-American Economic Affairs*, XIII, Spring 1960, 44-66.

Hirschman, Albert O. *Latin American Issues.* New York: Twentieth Century Fund, 1961.

Hoselitz, Bert F. *Theories of Economic Growth.* Glencoe: Free Press, 1960.

Hughlett, L. J. *Industrialization of Latin America.* New York: McGraw-Hill, 1946.

"Hydro-Electric Resources in Latin America: Their Measurement and Utilization," *Economic Bulletin for Latin America,* VII, No. 1, 1962, 73-113.

"Inflation and Growth," *Latin American Business Highlights,* II, No. 2, 1961, 14-17.

Instituto Boliviano de Estudio y Acción Social. *Bolivia y la Cuenca del Plata.* La Paz: 1968.

Instituto para la Integración de América Latina. *El Régimen de las sociedades anónimas en los países de la ALALC.* Buenos Aires: Inter-American Development Bank, 1971.

———. *The River Plate Basin: A Summary Report.* Washington: Inter-American Development Bank, 1969.

Inter-American Development Bank. "Argentina to Provide Special Funds Through Bank for Projects in Bolivia, Paraguay, and Uruguay," *News Release,* No. 51/70, November 24, 1970, 1-2.

———. *The Mobilization of Internal Financial Resources in Latin America.* Washington: n.d.

———. *Socio-Economic Progress in Latin America, Annual Report, 1971.* Washington: 1972.

Inter-American Economic and Social Council. *External Financing for Latin American Development.* (OEA/SER.H/X.14 CES/1382.) Washington: Pan American Union, May 19, 1969.

International Bank for Reconstruction and Development. *Transportation: Sector Working Paper.* Washington: IBRD, January 1972.

International Bank for Reconstruction and Development and International Monetary Fund. *The Problems of Stabilization of Prices of Primary Products,* Part I. Washington: IBRD-IMF, 1969.

International Bank for Reconstruction and Development. Economic Department. *The History and Present Position of the External Debt of Bolivia.* Washington: IBRD, July 1950 (mimeo.).

International Labor Organization. International Labor Office. *Las Agricultures sin Tierras en América Latina.* Geneva: ILO, 1957.

———. *Indigenous Peoples.* Geneva: ILO, 1953.

———. *The Landless Farmer in Latin America.* Geneva: ILO, 1957.

International Monetary Fund. *International Financial Statistics: February, 1973.* Washington: 1973.

Johnson, William Weber (ed.). *The Andean Republics: Bolivia, Chile, Ecuador, Peru.* (Life World Library.) New York: Time, 1965.

Kearns, Kevin C. "The Andean Common Market: A New Thrust at Economic Integration in Latin America," *Journal of Interamerican Studies and World Affairs,* XIV, No. 2, May 1972, 225-250.

Klein, Herbert S. "American Oil Companies in Latin America: The Bolivian Experience," *Inter-American Economic Affairs,* XVIII, No. 2, Autumn 1964, 47-72.

Kohli, Atul. "Costs and Benefits of Direct Foreign Investment in the Process of Development: The Case of the Andean Countries."

(Occasional Papers, No. 17) Ottawa: Carleton University, School of International Affairs, February 1972 (Unpublished paper.) (mimeo.).

Kostishack, John. "A Comparison of the Administrative Capacities for Land Reform in Bolivia, Ecuador, and Peru." Madison: University of Wisconsin, Land Tenure Center, 1972 (mimeo.).

Legg, H. J. *Bolivia, Economic and Commercial Conditions in Bolivia.* London: HMSO, 1956.

Leonard, Olen E. *Bolivia: Land, People and Institutions.* Metuchen: Scarecrow Press, 1952.

————. *Canton Chullpas: A Socioeconomic Study of an Area in the Cochabamba Valley of Bolivia.* (Foreign Agriculture Report No. 27.) Washington: U.S. Department of Agriculture, Office of Foreign Agricultural Relations, July 1948, 1-77.

————. *Santa Cruz, Bolivia: A Socioeconomic Study of an Area in Bolivia.* (Foreign Agriculture Report No. 31.) Washington: U.S. Department of Agriculture, Office of Foreign Agricultural Relations, October 1948.

Léons, Madeline Barbara. "Land Reform in the Bolivian Yungas," *América Indígena* [Mexico City], XXVII, No. 4, October–December 1967, 689-714.

Lofstrom, William. "Attempted Economic Reform and Innovation in Bolivia Under Antonio José de Sucre, 1825-1828," *Hispanic American Historical Review*, L, No. 2, May 1970, 279-299.

López Rivas, Eduardo. *Esquema de la historia económica de Bolivia.* Oruro: Universitad, 1955.

————. *La Minera y la economía de Bolivia.* Oruro: Universitario, June 1958 (pamphlet).

Lora, Guillermo. *La Establización, una impositura.* La Paz: Masa, 1960.

Lumpkin, T. D. "Bolivia: Gulf Oil's Experience." (Paper presented April 30, 1970, at Symposium on Recent Trends Affecting Trade and Investment in Latin America, Bates School of Law, University of Houston, Texas.) Houston: n.pub., 1970.

McBride, George M. *The Agrarian Indian Communities of Highland Bolivia and Peru.* (American Geographical Society, Research Series, No. 5.) New York: Oxford University Press, 1921.

Malloy, James M. *Bolivia: The Uncompleted Revolution.* Pittsburgh: University of Pittsburgh Press, 1970.

Malloy, James M., and Thorn, Richard S. (eds.) *Beyond the Revolution: Bolivia Since 1952.* Pittsburgh: University of Pittsburgh Press, 1971.

Manzon, Jean; Asturias, Miguel-Angel; and Díez de Medina, F. *Bolivia, an Undiscovered Land.* London: G. G. Harrap, 1961.

Maritano, Nino. *A Latin American Economic Community.* Notre Dame: University of Notre Dame Press, 1970.

Marsh, Margaret Alexander. *The Banker in Bolivia: A Study in American Foreign Investment.* New York: Vanguard Press, 1928.

Martner, Gonzálo. "Un Análisis estructural de la inflación en Bolivia,"

El Trimestre Económico [Mexico City], XXIX, No. 116, October-December 1962, 599-621.

Merryman, John H., and Ackerman, Edgar D. *International Law, Development and the Transit Trade of Landlocked States: The Case of Bolivia.* Frankfurt am Main: Alfred Metzner Verlag, 1969.

Milenky, Edward S. "Developmental Nationalism in Practice: The Problems and Progress of the Andean Group," *Inter-American Economic Affairs,* XXVI, No. 4, Spring 1973, 49-68.

––––––. "From Integration to Developmental Nationalism: The Andean Group," *Inter-American Economic Affairs,* XXV, No. 3, Winter 1971, 77-91.

––––––. *The Politics of Regional Organization in Latin America: The Latin American Free Trade Association.* New York: Praeger, 1973.

Minerals Yearbook, 1969, IV: Area Reports: International. Washington: GPO, U.S. Department of the Interior, Bureau of Mines, 1971.

Moller Pacieri, Edwin A. *El Cooperativismo y la Revolución.* La Paz: Dirección Nacional de Cooperativas, n.d.

––––––. "Interpretación histórica del cooperativismo en Bolivia." La Paz: Dirección Nacional de Cooperativas, 1962 (mimeo.).

Monroy Gardenas, Arturo. *Historia aduanera de Bolivia y tratados comerciales con los paises vecinos, 1825-1958.* La Paz: Nueva, 1959.

Morales, Jose Augustín. *El Oro verde de los Yungas.* La Paz: Instituto de Readapción y Reeducación de Inválidos, 1938.

Morawetz, Davis. *Common External Tariff for the Andean Group.* (Economic Development Report, No. 209.) Cambridge: Harvard University, Center for International Affairs, Development Research Group, February 1972.

––––––. *Economic Prospects for the Andean Group.* (Economic Development Report, No. 217.) Cambridge: Harvard University, Center for International Affairs, Development Research Group, May 1972.

––––––. *Equitable Distribution of Benefits in Integration Schemes Among Less Developed Countries: The Andean Group.* (Economic Development Report, No. 216.) Cambridge: Harvard University, Center for International Affairs, Development Research Group, April 1972.

––––––. *Harmonization of Economic Policies in Customs Unions: The Andean Group.* (Economic Development Report, No. 202.) Cambridge: Harvard University, Center for International Affairs, Development Research Group, December 1971.

––––––. *Problems of Transport and Communications in the Andean Group.* (Economic Development Report, No. 204.) Cambridge: Harvard University, Center for International Affairs, Development Research Group, February 1972.

Navarrete, Jorge E. "Latin American Economic Integration: A Survey of Recent Literature," *Journal of Common Market Studies* [Oxford], IV, No. 2, December 1965, 168-177.

Nwaneri, V. C. "Income Distribution Criteria for the Analysis of Development Projects," *Finance and Development*, X, No. 1, March 1973, 16-19, 37.

Organización de los Estados Americanos. Instituto Interamericano de Estadística. *América en Cifras, 1970. Situación Económica:* I, Agricultura, Ganaderia, Silvicultura, Caza, y Pesca. Washington: Secretaría General de la OEA, 1970.

Organization of American States. Advisory Office on Integration. *Latin American Economic Integration: Organizations and Their Financing Institutions.* Washington: General Secretariat, 1972.

Organization of American States. Department of Economic Affairs. *Latin America's Foreign Trade Problems and Policies.* Washington: Pan American Union, 1966.

Organization of American States. Department of Legal Affairs. General Legal Division. *Mining and Petroleum Legislation in Latin America.* (2d ed.) Washington: Pan American Union, 1969.

Organization of American States. General Secretariat. *Bolivia.* (American Nations Series, No. 3.) Washington: 1970.

————. *Copper.* (Commodity Series.) Washington: Pan American Union, 1971.

————. *Estudio sobre transporte aereo en las Américas,* III. Washington: Pan American Union, n.d.

————. *The Pan American Highway System.* Washington: Pan American Union, 1971 (reprint).

————. *A Statement of the Laws of Bolivia in Matters Affecting Business.* (3d ed.) Supplement No. 1. Washington: Pan American Union, 1967.

Organization of American States. Pan American Union. *Tin.* Washington: Pan American Union, 1966 (reprint).

Orrego-Vicuña, Francisco. *The Dynamics of the Subregional Agreements Within the LAFTA Movement.* (Paper presented to the Conference on the Economic Integration of Latin America: The Movement Toward Latin American Unity, at the California Institute of International Studies, Palo Alto, California, May 9-11, 1968.) Palo Alto: California Institute of International Studies, n.d. (mimeo.).

Ortuño, René. *Bolivia y la integración económica de América Latina.* Buenos Aires: Instituto para la Integración de América Latina and Banco Interamericano de Desarrollo, 1969.

Osborne, Harold. *Bolivia: A Land Divided.* (2d ed.) London: Royal Institute of International Affairs, 1955.

————. *The Indians of the Andes: Aymaras and Quechuas.* London: Routledge and Kegan Paul, 1952.

Ostría Gutiérrez, Alberto. *The Tragedy of Bolivia: A People Crucified.* New York: Devin-Adair, 1958.

Otero, Gustavo Adolfo. *La Piedra mágica: Vida y costumbres de los indios callahauas de Bolivia.* (Ediciones Especiales, No. 5.) Mexico: Instituto Indigenista Interamericano, 1951.

Pan American Coffee Bureau. *Annual Coffee Statistics.* (No. 35, 1971.) New York: 1972.

Pan American Union. *La estructura agropecuaria de las naciones americanas.* Washington: Instituto Interamericana de Estadística, 1959.

Pan American Union. Stanford Research Institute. *Air Transport Development and Coordination in Latin America; A Study of Economic Factors.* Washington: PAU, 1961.

Pando Gutiérrez, Jorge. *Bolivia y el mundo geografía económica.* 2 vols. La Paz: Fénix, 1947.

Paredes Candia, Antonio. *Artesanías e industrias populares de Bolivia.* La Paz: Ediciones ISLA, 1967.

Parson, Kenneth H.; Penn, Raymond J.; and Raup, Philip M. (eds.) *Land Tenure.* Madison: University of Wisconsin Press, 1956.

Patch, Richard W. *Agriculture and the Supernatural.* (American Universities Field Staff Reports, West Coast of South America Series, XVIII, No. 4.) Hanover, New Hampshire: AUFS, June 1971.

————. *Bibliography of the Andean Countries.* New York: American Universities Field Staff, 1958.

————. *Bolivian Background.* New York: American Universities Field Staff, October 10, 1958.

————. "Bolivia: U.S. Assistance in a Revolutionary Setting." Pages 108-176 in R. N. Adams, et al. (eds.), *Social Change in Latin America Today.* New York: Vintage Books, 1961.

————. *A Note on Bolivia and Peru.* New York: American Universities Field Staff, July 1959.

————. "Social Implications of the Bolivian Agrarian Reform." Doctoral dissertation, Cornell University Microfilms, June 1956.

Payne, Joseph E., Jr. "Foreign Trade Regulations of Bolivia." *Overseas Business Reports.* (OBR 69-36.) Washington: GPO, for U.S. Department of Commerce, Bureau of International Commerce, July 1969.

Peinado Sotomayor, Marcelo. *Land Reform in Three Communities of Cochabamba, Bolivia.* (Land Tenure Center Research Paper No. 44.) Madison: University of Wisconsin, LTC, 1971.

Penaloza, Luis. *Historia Económica de Bolivia.* La Paz: Artística, 1946.

Pick's Currency Yearbook, 1972. New York: Pick, 1972.

Pike, Frederick B. *Freedom and Reform in Latin America.* Notre Dame: University of Notre Dame Press, 1959.

Pommier Aguilar, Rolando, and Pommier, Gaby Saavedra de (eds.) *Guía nacional de Bolivia comercial e industrial, 1972.* La Paz: Imprenta y Librería Renovación, 1972.

Power Aliberti, Alejandro. "El Desarrollo industrial del Grupo Andino," *Boletín de la Integración* [Buenos Aires], VI, No. 69, September 1971, 475-480.

Press, Heinrich. *Gutachten Uber Wasserwirtschaftliche, Wasserbauliche und Wasserkraftliche Projekte auf Grund einer Studienreise nach Bolivien.* Berlin: 1957.

Preston, David A. "New Towns—A Major Change in the Rural Settlement Pattern in Highland Bolivia," *Journal of Latin American Studies* [London], II, Part I, May 1970, 1-27.

———. "The Revolutionary Landscape of Highland Bolivia," *Geographical Journal* [London], CXXXV, No. 1, March 1969, 1-16.

Price Waterhouse. *Information Guide for Doing Business in Bolivia.* Chicago: 1967.

"Les Produits Tropicaux et Méditérranéens," *Marchés Tropicaux et Méditérranéens* [Paris], (Special Issue) XXVIII, No. 1415, December 22, 1972, entire issue.

Pryor, Donald. "Livestock: The Recognition of a Stepchild," *Finance and Development*, VII, No. 3, September 1970, 19-25.

Puga, William B. (ed.) *Electrical World: A Directory of Electric Utilities in Latin America, Bermuda, and the Caribbean Islands, 1969–70 Edition.* New York: McGraw-Hill, 1969.

Rens, Jef. "The Andean Programme," *International Labour Review* [Geneva], LXXXIV, No. 6, December 1961, 423-461.

Rice, E. B. *Extension in the Andes: An Evaluation of Official U.S. Assistance to Agricultural Extension Services in Central and South America.* (Evaluation Paper 3A.) Washington: Agency for International Development, 1971.

Richard, Allan R. *Administration—Bolivia and the United States.* Albuquerque, University of New Mexico Department of Government. Division of Research, 1961.

Rippy, J. Fred. "Bolivia. An Exhibit of the Problems of Economic Development in Retarded Countries," *Inter-American Economic Affairs*, X, Winter 1956, 61-74.

Rudolph, W.E. "The Railroad from Corumbá to Santa Cruz," *Geographical Review*, XXXIV, 1944, 329, 330.

Ruiz Gonzales, Rene. *La Economía boliviana y el comercio exterior.* Oruro: Universitaria, 1955.

Salgádo, Germánico. *El Grupo Andino: Un concepto nuevo en la integracíon económica.* (Hackett Memorial Lecture Series.) Austin: Institute of Latin American Studies, University of Texas, 1972.

Salmon Baldivieso, Luis. *Las Industrias en Bolivia.* La Paz: Editorial Fénix, 1947.

Sampson, Henry (ed.). *Jane's World Railways, 1971-72.* London: B.P.C. Publishing, n.d.

Sanders, Thomas G. *Andean Economic Integration.* (American Universities Field Staff Reports, West Coast of South America Series, XV, No. 2.) Hanover, New Yampshire: American Universities Field Staff, 1968.

Santos, Joâo Oliveira. "Latin America's Export Earnings." (Paper prepared for Symposium on Contemporary Economic Problems and Issues in Latin America.) Washington: Georgetown University, Latin American Forum, November 23, 1968.

Sariola, Sakari. "A Colonization Experiment in Bolivia," *Rural Sociology*, XXV, March 1960, 76-90.

Sautter, Hermann. "LAFTA's Successes and Failures," *Inter-Economics* [Hamburg, Germany], No. 5, May 1972, 149-152.

Schmidt-Schlegel, P. *Die Gutachten der 1956-57 nach Bolivien Endsandten Deutschen Sachverständigen und ihre Auswertung.* Cologne West-Deutscher Verlag, 1959.

Schulman, Sam. "The Colono System in Latin America," *Rural Sociology*, XX, March 1955, 34-40.

Scott, P.H. *Bolivia: Economic and Commercial Conditions.* (Overseas Economic Surveys.) London: HMSO, 1956.

Scott, Rebecca. "Economic Aid and Imperialism in Bolivia," *Monthly Review*, XXIV, No. 1, May 1972, 48-60.

Slater, Charles, et al. *Market Processes in La Paz, Bolivia.* (Marketing in Developing Communities Series, Research Report No. 3.) East Lansing: Michigan State University, Latin American Studies Center, 1970.

Sloan, John W. "Dilemmas of the Latin American Free Trade Association," *Journal of Economic Issues*, V, No. 4, December 1971, 92-106.

Smith, Peter Seaborn. "Bolivian Oil and Brazilian Economic Nationalism," *Journal of Inter-American Studies and World Affairs*, XIII, No. 2, April 1971, 166-181.

Smith, Stephen M. "The Potato Market of La Paz, Bolivia, and the Effects of the Agrarian Reform." (Land Tenure Center, No. 76.) Madison: University of Wisconsin, LTC, 1971 (mimeo.).

The South American Handbook, 1973. London: Trade and Travel Publications, 1973.

Statesman's Year-Book, 1972-1973. (Ed., John Paxton.) London: Macmillan, 1972.

Stokes, William S. "The 'Revolución Nacional' and the MNR in Bolivia," *Inter-American Economic Affairs*, XII, Spring 1959, 28-53.

"Surgery in the Mines," Economist [London], CCXXIX, No. 6397, April 2, 1966, 32-33.

Switzer, Kenneth. "The Andean Group: A Reappraisal," *Inter-American Economic Affairs*, XXVI, No. 4, Spring, 1973, 69-82.

Szokoly, Endre. *Hét év Bolíviában* (Seven Years in Bolivia). Budapest: Bibliotheca, 1958.

Taboada Calderón de la Barca. José. *Economía Boliviana,* I. La Paz: n.pub., 1966.

Teichert, Pedro M. *Economic Policy Revolution and Industrialization in Latin America.* Oxford: University of Mississippi, Bureau of Business Research, 1959.

Thomas, Alfred B. *Latin America: A History.* New York: Macmillan, 1956.

Tilemans, Willy. "Bolivie, declin de la production dans les mines et les manufactures," *Bulletin Commercial Belge* (Office Belge du Commerce Exterieur), February 2, 1961, 53–61.

United Nations. *Patterns of Industrial Growth, 1938–1958.* N.pl: UN, July 1960.

———. *World's Weights and Measures.* New York: UN, 1966.

United Nations. Asistencia Técnica de las United Nations. *Los Transportes en Bolivia, Bolv 1., Ferrocarriles.* La Paz: UN, April 1957.

United Nations. Economic and Social Council. Economic Commission for Latin America. *Analyses and Projections of Economic Development, IV:* The Economic Development of Bolivia. Mexico City: ECLA, 1958.

———. *Development of Agriculture in Bolivia.* Mexico City: ECLA, May 28, 1951 (mimeo.).

———. "The Economic Development of Bolivia," *Economic Bulletin for Latin America,* II, No. 2, 1957, 19–72.

———. "The Economic Policy of Bolivia in 1952-64," *Economic Bulletin for Latin America,* XII, No. 2, October 1967, 61–89.

———. *Economic Survey of Latin America, 1970.* New York: UN, 1972.

———. "Hydro-electric Resources in Latin America: Their Measurement and Utilization," *Economic Bulletin for Latin America,* VII, I, February 1962, 73–113.

———. *La industria textil en América Latina: Bolivia.* New York: UN, 1964.

———. "Latin America's Hydroelectric Potential," *Economic Bulletin for Latin America,* XII, No. 1, May 1967, 56–62.

———. *Recent Events in the Latin American Free Trade Association.* (General El CN-12/887.) Santiago: UN, 1971.

United Nations. Industrial Development Organization. *El Desarrollo industrial de América Latina. Bolivia.* (International Symposium on Industrial Development, Athens, November 29–December 20, 1967.) N.pl.: UN, 1967.

United Nations. Technical Assistance Administration. *Report of the Technical Assistance Mission to Bolivia.* New York: UN, 1951.

United Nations. United Nations Conference on Trade and Development. *Insurance Legislation and Supervision in Developing Countries.* New York: UN, 1972.

U.S. Agency for International Development. "Land Reform in Bolivia," In *Land Reform in Bolivia, Ecuador, Peru: A.I.D. Spring Review of Land Reform,* VI. (2d ed.) Washington: AID, 1970.

U.S. Agency for International Development. Bureau for Program and Policy Coordination. Office of Statistics and Reports. *A.I.D. Economic Data Book: Latin America.* Washington: July 1971.

————. *U.S. Overseas Loans and Grants and Assistance from International Organizations, July 1, 1945–June 30, 1971*. Washington: AID, 1972.

U.S. Congress. 86th, 2d Session. Senate. Committee on Government Operations. Permanent Subcommittee on Investigation. *Administration of U.S. Foreign Aid Program in Bolivia*. Washington: GPO, 1960.

U.S. Congress. 87th, 2d Session. Joint Economic Committee. Subcommittee on Inter-American Economic Relations. *Economic Development in South America*. Washington: GPO, 1962.

————. *Economic Policies and Programs in South America*. Washington: GPO, 1962.

U.S. Congress. 89th, 2d Session. House of Representatives. Committee on Banking and Currency. Subcommittee on International Finance. *Food for Progress in Latin America*. Washington: GPO, February 1967.

U.S. Department of Commerce. Bureau of Foreign and Domestic Commerce. *Investment in Latin America, IV: Bolivia*. (By Frederic M. Halsey and James C. Carliss.) Washington: 1927 (pamphlet).

U.S. Department of Commerce. Bureau of International Commerce. *Trade List—American Firms, Subsidiaries, and Affiliates*. Washington: GPO, October 1971.

U.S. Department of Commerce. Bureau of International Commerce. Office of International Marketing. "Marketing Profiles for Latin America and the Caribbean." *Overseas Business Reports*. (OBR 73-03.) Washington: GPO, February 1973.

U.S. Department of State. Bureau of Public Affairs. Office of Media Services. *Republic of Bolivia: Background Notes*. (Department of State Publication No. 8032.) Washington: GPO, September 1972.

U.S. Department of the Treasury. *Foreign Credits by the United States Government. Status of Active Foreign Credits of the United States Government and of International Organizations as of June 30, 1971*. Washington: GPO, 1972.

U.S. Embassy in La Paz. *Industrial Outlook Report: Petroleum, 1971*. (Airgram A-111.) La Paz: May 12, 1972.

————. *Post Report: Bolivia*. La Paz: September 1970.

————. *Post Report—La Paz, Bolivia*. La Paz: Agency for International Development, 1968.

U.S. Federal Power Commission. *World Power Data: Capacity of Electric Generating Plants and Production of Electric Energy, 1969*. Washington: GPO, 1972.

U.S. Office of Inter-American Affairs. *Bolivia: Natural Regions*. Washington: 1945 (mimeo.).

U.S. United States Operations Mission. *Latin American USOM Seminars or Agrarian Reform, February 21-24, 1961*. (Papers prepared by Raymond J. Penn and Solon Barraclough.) Santiago: 1961.

U.S. United States Operations Mission. Engineering and Transportation Division. "Red de caminos nacionales de Bolivia." N.pl.: USOM, 1961 (mimeo.).

U.S. United States Tariff Commission. *Mining and Manufacturing Industries in Bolivia.* Washington: USTC, 1945 (pamphlet.)

Universidad Mayor de San Andrés. Instituto de Estudios Internacionales. *Bolivia v los problemas de la integracíon andina.* La Paz: UMSA, 1970.

University of Wisconsin. Land Tenure Center. *The Progress of Land Reform in Bolivia.* (Discussion Paper No. 2.) Madison: University of Wisconsin, LTC, May 1963.

Urquidi Morales, Arturo. *Bases sociologicas de la reforma agraria.* (Revista Jurídica, No. 63–66.) Cochabamba: Universidad Mayor de San Simón, n.d.

————. *Plan general para el estudio de la reforma agraria.* Cochabamba Imprenta Universitaria, 1953.

Valcárcel, Luis E. "Indian Markets and Fairs in Peru." In Julian H. Steward (ed.), *Handbook of South American Indians*, II. Washington: GPO, 1944, 477–482.

Violich, Francis. *Cities of Latin America.* New York: Reinhold, 1944.

Volmuller, J. "Transportation in Bolivia," *U.N. Transportation and Communication Review,* April 1954, 14–27.

vonHagen, Victor W. *The Ancient Sun Kingdom of the Americas.* New York: World, 1957.

Walle, Paul. *Bolivia: Its People and Its Resources.* London: Unwin, 1914.

Whelan, James R. "Latin Mart May Freeze Out U.S.," *Washington Daily News,* December 1, 1970, 21.

Whitehead, Laurence. "Basic Data in Poor Countries: The Bolivian Case," *Oxford University Institute of Economics and Statistics Bulletin* [Oxford], XXXI, August 1969, 205–227.

————. "The Bolivian Peso," *International Currency Review* [London], III, No. 3, November–December 1971, 30–33.

————. "El Impacto de la gran depresión en Bolivia," *Desarrollo Económico* [Buenos Aires], XII, No. 1, April–June 1972, 49–80.

Wilkie, James Wallace. *Bolivian Foreign Trade: Historical Problems and MNR Revolutionary Policy, 1952–1964.* (Special Studies, Council on International Studies.) Buffalo: State University of New York, Buffalo, 1971.

Wilson, George W., et al. *The Impact of Highway Investment on Development.* (Transport Research Program.) Washington: Brookings Institution, 1966.

Wionczek, Miguel S. (ed.) *Economic Cooperation in Latin America, Africa, and Asia: Handbook of Documents.* Cambridge: Massachusetts Institute of Technology Press, 1969.

―――. *Latin American Economic Integration.* (Praeger Series on International Economics and Development.) New York: Praeger, 1966.

Wish, John R. *Economic Development in Latin America: An Annotated Bibliography.* New York: Praeger, 1966.

The World and Its Peoples: Brazil, Peru, Bolivia. New York: Greystone Press, 1965.

"The World Bank Atlas: Population, Growth, Rate, and GNP Tables." *Finance and Development*, X, No. 1, March 1973, 25-27.

World Bank Operations. *Sectoral Programs and Policies.* Baltimore: Johns Hopkins University Press, 1972.

"Worldwide Production," *Oil and Gas Journal*, LXX, No. 52, December 25, 1972, 102-121.

"Worldwide Refining," *Oil and Gas Journal*, LXX, No. 52, December 25, 1972, 89-102.

Woytinsky, W.S. *The United States and Latin America's Economy.* New York: Taniment Institute Public Service Pamphlet, 1959.

Zamora, Hernando. "La Establzacion monetaria y el crédito bancario," *Industria*, X, July 1962, 5-8.

Zimmerman, Eric. *World Resources and Industries.* New York: Harper, 1951.

Zondag, Cornelius H. *The Bolivian Economy, 1952-65: The Revolution and Its Aftermath.* New York: Praeger, 1966.

―――. *Problems in the Economic Development of Bolivia.* La Paz: November 1, 1956 (mimeo.).

(Various issues of the following periodicals were also used in the preparation of this section: *Alliance for Progress Weekly Newsletter* [Washington], January 2, 1967-April 30, 1973; *Boletín de la Integracion* [Buenos Aires], August 1972-April 1973; *BOLSA Review* [London], May 1968-April 1973; *Business Latin America* [New York , February 20, 1969-April 5, 1973; *Christian Science Monitor*, April 9, 1970-April 9, 1973; *CIAT Informativo-Newsletter* [Panama City], January 1968-March 1973; *El Diario* [La Paz], March 12-April 12, 1973; *IMF Survey* [Washington], January 22, 1973-May 14, 1973; *Inter-American Bulletin on Taxation* [Washington], July 1971-December 1972; *Latin America* [London], December 29, 1967-April 6, 1973; *Latin American Digest* [Tempe, Arizona], November 1972-January 1973; *Latin American Studies Center Newsletter* [East Lansing], December 1972-March 1973; *Monthly Bulletin of Agricultural Economics and Statistics* (FAO, Rome), December 1972-March 1973; *New York Times*, June 17, 1969-May 9, 1973; *Noticias: Weekly Digest of Hemisphere Reports* [New York], January 15, 1969-May 2, 1973; *Presencia* [La Paz], December 3, 1970-January 5, 1971; *Times of the Americas* [Washington], July 17, 1968-April 18, 1973; U.S. Embassy in La Paz, miscellaneous reports,

May 29, 1971–January 31, 1973; *Washington Post,* September 11, 1970–April 10, 1973; *Washington Star and Evening News,* December 1968–May 10, 1973; and *World Agricultural Production and Trade: Statistical Report* [Washington], December 1972–February 1973.)

Section IV. National Security

Alexander, Robert J. *The Bolivian National Revolution.* New Brunswick: Rutgers University Press, 1958.

Arnade, Charles W. *The Emergence of the Republic of Bolivia.* Gainesville: University of Florida Press, 1957.

Brill, William H. *Military Intervention in Bolivia: The Overthrow of Paz Estenssoro and the MNR.* Washington: Institute for the Comparative Study of Political Systems, 1967.

Corbett, Charles D. *The Latin American Military as a Socio-Political Force: Case Studies of Bolivia and Argentina.* Coral Gables: University of Miami, Center for Advanced International Studies, 1972.

Cramer, James. *The World's Police.* London: Cassell, 1964.

Institute for the Study of Soviet Affairs. *Annual Proceedings, 1962.* Bonn: 1962.

Johnson, Cecil. *Communist China and Latin America, 1959–1967.* New York: Columbia University Press, 1970.

Johnson, John J. (ed.) *The Role of the Military in Underdeveloped Countries.* Princeton: Princeton University Press, 1962.

Kantor, Harry. *Patterns of Politics and Political Systems in Latin America.* Chicago: Rand McNally, 1969.

Klein, Herbert S. *Parties and Political Change in Bolivia, 1880–1952.* (Cambridge Latin American Studies, V.) Cambridge: Cambridge University Press, 1969.

Kolarz, Walter. "Communism's Global Strategy," *NATO Letter,* IX, December 1961, 4–7.

Macdonald, Austin F. *Latin American Politics and Government.* (2d ed.) New York: Crowell, 1954.

Malloy, James M., and Thorn, Richard S. (eds.) *Beyond the Revolution: Bolivia Since 1952.* Pittsburgh: University of Pittsburgh Press, 1971.

Markham, Clemets R. *The War Between Peru and Chile, 1879–1882.* New York: Worthington, 1883.

The Military Balance, 1972–1973. London: International Institute for Strategic Studies, 1972.

Millington, Thomas M. "Bolivia Under Barrientos," in *Current History,* LVI, No. 329, January 1969, 25–30, 51–52.

Munro, Dana Gardner. *The Latin American Republics: A History.* (3d ed.) New York: Appleton-Century-Crofts, 1960.

Needler, Martin C. *Political Systems of Latin America.* (2d ed.) New York: Van Nostrand, Reinhold, 1970.

Osborne, Harold. *Bolivia: A Land Divided.* (2d ed.) London: Royal

Institute of International Affairs, 1955.

Ostría Gutiérrez, Alberto. *The Tragedy of Bolivia: A People Crucified.* New York: Devin-Adair, 1958.

Patch, Richard W. *Bolivia's Nationalism and the Military.* (American Universities Field Staff Reports, West Coast of South America Series, XVI, No. 3.) Hanover, New Hampshire: AUFS, October 1969.

Stark, Harry. *Social and Economic Frontiers in Latin America.* Dubuque: Brown, 1961.

Stokes, William S. *Latin American Politics.* New York: Crowell, 1959.

Urquidi, Carlos Wálter. *Régimen legal boliviano.* La Paz: n. pub., 1947.

——. *A Statement of the Laws of Bolivia.* (3d ed.) Washington: Pan American Union, 1962.

Walle, Paul. *Bolivia: Its People and Its Resources.* London: Unwin, 1914.

Wilgus, A. Curtis. *The Development of Hispanic America.* New York: Farrar and Rinehart, 1941.

Wilgus, A. Curtis (ed.). *South American Dictators During the First Century of Independence.* Washington: George Washington University Press, 1937.

Zook, David H., Jr. *The Conduct of the Chaco War.* New York: Bookman Associates, 1960.

(Various issues of the following periodicals were also used in the preparation of the section: *El Diario* [La Paz], March 1973–July 1973; *New York Times*, February 1973–July 1973.)

(In Addition, extensive use was made of the La Paz newspapers *El Diario, Ultima Hora, La Nación,* and *Presencia* for the period 1952–1962, as well as of both United States and Bolivian government documents.)

GLOSSARY

Altiplano—Literally, high plateau. Geographic region; the high plateau of Bolivia.

ayllu(s)—A form of social organization in pre-Columbian Bolivia based on collective agriculture.

barrio(s)—Urban working-class residential neighborhood.

Bolivian peso—Unit of currency as of mid-1973. Symbol is $b. Established in January 1963 to replace the currency that had been in use since 1938. The buying rate for the Bolivian peso originally was set at $b11.875 equal US$1. On October 27, 1972, the Bolivian peso was devalued. The official rate became $b20 equal US$1, but for purposes of the International Monetary Fund (IMF) a par rate was established at $b21.7143 per one Special Drawing Right, the artificial unit of currency created by the IMF.

caja(s)—Literally, a box. A fund of money maintained by the government for a particular purpose of public interest.

campesino(s)—Peasant farmers; also the term that officially replaced *indio* (Indian) in everyday usage.

cholo(s)—A term that has a variety of definitions and social implications. During colonial times, was equivalent to mestizo but has evolved to include persons of mixed or pure Indian ancestry who are trying to move up the social and economic ladder. *Cholos* speak Spanish in addition to an Indian tongue and often act as vendors or economic middlemen in rural areas.

compadrazgo—Literally, copaternity. A system of ritual coparenthood that links parents, children, and godparents in a close social or economic relationship.

empleado(s)—The white-collar worker(s) or employer(s), as contrasted with the blue-collar worker or *obrero* (*q.v.*).

facultad(es) (faculty)—A college within a university offering degree programs in a single discipline or in two or more related disciplines.

fiesta—Festival; it may be a religious celebration on a holy day or a festival honoring the patron saint of the community. It may also be held to celebrate important civic or family occasions, such as independence, baptism, or marriage.

gente buena or *gente decente*—Literally, good or decent people. The upper class in rural areas.

machismo—Literally, maleness. Complex of beliefs and attitudes defining the concept of masculinity.

nucleo(s) escolar(es)—Nuclear school(s); a rural unit offering all six grades of primary school and surrounded by smaller satellite units that usually offer only a few grades.

obrero(s)—The blue-collar or manual worker(s) as contrasted to the white-collar worker or employee.

Oriente—Literally, East. Geographic region; the tropical lowlands that make up two-thirds of the country.

patron(es)—Literally, patron(s). The term used for *boss* or *master*; formerly applied to the Bolivian landowning class. Aside from its generic usage, is also a behavioral concept implying a paternalistic relationship between two persons of unequal status.

patronato—Special privileges granted by the state to the military and to the church.

rosca—Literally, the screw. National elite class whose basis of power was strongly shaken by the 1952 Revolution.

sindicato(s) campesino(s)—Peasant syndicate(s) or leagues formed after the 1952 Revolution, usually of a political nature but sometimes performing important social roles.

URUPABOL—An acronym for an economic coordinating committee of representatives of Uruguay, Paraguay, and Bolivia. The acronym comes from the first letters in the names of the countries.

Valles—Literally, valleys. Geographic region, a series of valleys and basins on the eastern slope of the southern Andes.

YPFB—Yacimientos Petroliferos Fiscales Bolivianos—The state oil company. Name is variously translated as Bolivian State Petroleum Enterprise, or Bolivian Government Oil Deposits.

Yungas—Geographic region; a series of narrow valleys on the eastern slope of the northern Andes.

INDEX

academic freedom: 155,156
Achá, José Mariá de: 24,218
Acosta, José de: 194
Acre: territory, 27, 259; War of, 198
adult education: 158
advertising: 213, 214, 320
Agrarian Reform Act: 63
Agricultural Bank of Bolivia: 287, 289
agricultural reform (see also expropriation of estates): ix, 36, 37, 38, 61, 167, 291, 294-299; agrarian courts, 224
agriculture (see also crops): ix, 3, 63, 280; employment, 46, 70, 71; exports, 329, 330; production, 276, 277
Aguilar, Aníbal: 237
Aguirre, Nataniel: 197
air force: ix, 352, 353, 355
air transport: viii, 318, 325, 326
Alacitas Festival: 92, 189
alcohol: 185, 186, 294
Alliance for Progress: 41, 253, 279
Almagro, Diego: 14
Almagro, Diego de: 13
Almaraz, Hugo: 207
alpacas: 57, 303, 304
Altiplano: 292, 320; geography, 50, 54, 57; markets, 319; people of, 107, 118, 166, 297
altitude, effects of: 29, 55, 66, 187
Alto Beni: 65, 66, 301, 302
Alto Perú: 12, 15, 16
Amaru, Tupac: 18
Amazon River: 53
Anaya, Ricardo: 204
Andean Common Market: viii, 267, 288, 321, 332, 333
Andean Development Corporation (CAF): 334
Andes mountains: 48, 49, 50, 203
Anti-Imperialist Revolutionary Front (FRA): 245
antimony: 306, 309, 328, 331
aparapita: 72
Aramayo mining company: 27, 36
Arapata: 64
Arawakan language: 78, 82
Arce Carpio, Alfredo: 246
archeology: 9, 79, 206, 210

architecture: 193, 197, 208
area: vii, 45, 292
Argentina: ix, 47, 68, 285; border with, 46, 259; cultural influence, 213, 214; relations with, 30, 265, 266, 267, 288, 332, 334, 355; trade, 291, 310, 312, 321, 324, 326, 331, 332
Arguedas, Alcides: 26, 199
Arguedas, Antonio: 240
Arica, Chile: 48, 311
armed forces (see also military persons in politics; and under United States): viii, ix, 2, 7, 28, 29, 223, 284, 338, 351-357; housing, 172; pensions, 182
Armed Forces Corporation for National Development (COFADENA): 278
army: ix, 352, 353, 355
arts (see also folkloric tradition): 153, 191-192; National Academy, 201, 206, 207; National Museum, 210
Arze, José Antonio: 204, 235
Aspiazu, Augustín: 198
Authentic Nationalist Revolutionary Movement (MNRA): 39, 40, 41
Authentic Revolutionary Party (PRA): 40, 41, 235, 236, 240
Aymara Indians: vii, 81-85, 87, 89, 128; religion, 133, 135; social class, 118, 120, 121, 122, 123
Aymara language: 2, 145, 157, 159, 194, 214
Azapa Valley: 263

balance of payments: 283-284, 327
Ballivián, Adolfo: 25
Ballivián, Hugo: 35
Ballivián, José: 24, 196, 218
balsas: 56
BAMIN. See Mining Bank of Bolivia
banking: 286-289
Banzer Suárez, Hugo: armed forces, 352; biography, viii, 3, 74, 230, 234, 242, 243, 245, 250, 266; church and state, 132, 133; development plans, 278, 311; education under, 144, 155, 246; foreign relations, 258, 271, 273; government of, 173, 182, 229, 271, 350
Bárbara, Gesta: 200
barter. See domestic trade

407

Barrientos Ortuño, René: 42, 43, 220, 221, 238, 239, 240, 248, 250, 255, 256, 264, 269, 350, 351
Barrigan, Raul: 209
beef: 167, 300, 303, 318, 327, 329, 339
Belgian teaching mission: 138
Beltrán de Oliveira, Humberto: 201
Belzu, Manuel Isidoro: 24, 218
birds: 58
birth control: 69
birth rate: 67
bismuth: 59, 60, 306, 309, 328
blanco(s): (*see also* white population): 96
Bolívar, Simón: 21, 22, 216; church and state, 131, 217
Bolivian Air Lloyd (LAB): viii, 31, 325, 326
Bolivian Catholic University: 152, 157, 213
Bolivian Communist Party (PCB): 34, 38, 41, 235, 242, 348, 350, 351
Bolivian Development Corporation (CBF): 288, 289
Bolivian Gulf Oil Company: 233-234, 241, 266, 269, 285, 310, 311
Bolivian Iron and Steel Corporation (SIDE RSA): 306, 307
Bolivian Labor Central (COB): 38, 40, 239, 242, 249, 250, 348
Bolivian peso: 245, 250, 285, 286; exchange rate, 38, 405
Bolivian Socialist Falange (FSB): 3, 32, 38, 39, 41, 223, 229, 233, 235, 236, 244, 251, 252, 350
Bolivian State Petroleum Enterprise (YPFB): 278, 310, 311, 312, 325
boliviano: 38, 285, 286
books: 142, 213
border police: ix, 340, 342
borders (*see also* treaties): xiv, 29, 46, 266
Brazil: 30, 46, 266, 270, 285, 332, 334, 355; migrations, 47, 68; trade, 303, 304, 305, 324, 326, 332; treaties, ix, 27, 28, 259, 260, 264
budget: 141, 280, 296; armed forces, 354, 356
bullfighting: 187
Busch, Germán: 29, 31, 219, 232
Bustamante, Ricardo José: 196

Caba, Eduardo: 208
Calacoto district: 171
Calahumana, María: 23
Calancha, Antonio de la: 195
Callahuaya Indians: 89, 179
Camacho, Eliodoro: 26
Cambas: 95, 96, 118, 125, 126, 129
Campero, Narciso: 25, 26
campesinos: 84, 118-124; connotation, 64, 78, 95; political influence, 247-249

Canada: 285
cantons: 225
Capac, Huayna: 10
Capac, Manco: 14
Carabineros (*see also* police): 337
Caracas Protocol: 333
Caranavi correctional farm: 346
Casas, Bartolomé de las: 13
censorship of the press: 35, 192, 210, 211, 244
censuses: vii, 16, 61, 66, 80, 296
Central Bank of Bolivia: 281, 287
Cerro Rico: 16
Cerruto, Oscar: 203
Céspedes, Augusto: 203, 204
Chácobo Indian language: 82
Chacaltaya ski run: 187
Chaco: 55, 57, 60
Chaco War: 2, 7, 8, 28-30, 202, 261, 262, 351
Chaparé Province: 310
Chaparé River: xiv, 65
Charangas area: 88
Charcas, Audiencia of: 12, 14, 15, 20, 195
Chávez Ortiz, Nuflo: 38, 245
chicha: 189, 300, 315
children: 121, 319
Chile (*see also* War of the Pacific): ix, 23, 68, 246, 266, 267, 273, 285, 332; border with, 46, 49; diplomatic relations with, 28, 30, 198, 332, 333, 334; trade, 263, 324, 326
China, People's Republic of: 246, 350
China, Republic of: 5, 271
chinchilla: 57
Chipaya Indians: 79, 82, 88
Chiriguano Indians: 93, 94
Chirveche, Armando: 199
cholo(s): 90, 98, 104, 114, 116, 122, 129
chuño: 167
Chuquisaca Department: xiv, 21, 49, 65, 311; arts, 194; capital, 19; health services, 174, 176; people, 86, 87, 94, 112, 124; university, 152
church and state: 27, 130, 132, 133, 245, 253-254
cinchona tree: 56
civil liberties (*see also* censorship of the press; freedom of religion): 36
Claure, Villarroel: 206
clergy: 130, 131, 135, 221, 346; foreign, 132, 133
climate: vii, 54-55
clothing and dress: 84-85, 87, 88, 89, 95, 168-169
COB. *See* Bolivian Labor Central
Cobija: xiv, 61, 62

408

COBOEN. *See* nuclear energy commission.

coca leaves: 56, 168, 185, 294, 302, 339

Cochabamba Department: xiv, 15, 21, 48, 49, 172, 189, 212, 247, 311, 319, 325; agriculture, 293, 299, 301, 303; people, 61, 62, 63, 74, 79, 86, 104, 107, 118, 119; university, 152, 153

Code of Education: 140, 143, 149, 156, 158; language used, 157

coffee: 300, 301-302, 327, 328, 329, 330

Coipasa, Lake: 49

Colombia: 30, 267, 332, 333, 334

colonization: 1, 65-66, 74, 323, 351; in Brazil, 47; near Santa Cruz, 62, 63, 280; new towns, 105, 106

COMIBOL. *See* Mining Corporation of Bolivia

communication: viii, 5, 192, 210-214, 326-327

communism. *See* Bolivian Communist Party; subversive organizations and literature

condor: 58

conscription: 353-354, 356

Conservative Party: 26

constitutions: vii, 2, 23, 24, 31, 216-220; of 1826, 211, 216; of 1961, 253; of 1967, viii, 215, 220-221, 352

construction: 72, 277, 314, 315

consumer goods: 107, 108, 166, 168, 185, 186, 314; imports, 327, 330

cooperatives: 298, 301, 303

Copacabana: 209

Copacabana Peninsula: 46, 47, 74

Cordova, Jorge: 24

corn: 299-300

Corumbá, Brazil: xiv, 46, 47

costumbrismo: 203

cotton: 300, 301, 328, 329, 330

courts: 218, 224, 225, 343, 345

crime and punishment: 340-347, 356

crops (*see also* food): 56, 75, 299-302

Cuba: 270, 272, 348

Cuba, Simón: 349

currency (*see also* Bolivian peso): ix, 245, 250, 283, 405

Czechoslovakia: 214, 271, 285

dance: 201, 206, 209, 210

Darío, Rubén: 200

Day of the Indian: 139, 184, 297

Daza, Hilarión: 25

death rate and causes: 67, 174

Delanze, Sebastián: 196

departments (*see also* individual names): viii, 48, 152, 225; police, 339, 346

Desaguadero: region, 88, 323; river, xiv, 51,

63

development plans: 165, 223, 325, 335; ten-year plan, 41, 279; use of armed forces, 278, 352, 353

Díaz Romero, Belisario: 199

Díaz Vilamil, Antonio: 201

diet and nutrition (*see also* food): 73, 165-168, 181

Diez de Medina, Fernando: 198, 203, 204, 205

diseases: viii, 4, 94, 167, 174-176; miners, 175, 308

dollmaking: 316

domestic trade: 75, 282, 317-320; barter, 185, 186

Don Bosco school: 150

droughts and floods: 52, 54, 55

economy (*see also* domestic trade; foreign trade; inflation): 275-289

Ecuador: 267, 302, 332, 333, 334

education (*see also* higher education; vocational and technical schooling): vii-viii, 4, 137-163; budget, 281; middle class and, 115; upper class and, 110

Eisenhower, Milton: 268

El Alto airport: 62, 325

El Beni Department: xiv, 48, 49, 53, 92, 94, 178, 323; agriculture, 294, 302, 303, 304, 318; development, 279, 311; university, 152

El Comercio: 212

elections: 36, 226-227, 248, 252; lack of suffrage, 216, 217, 219

electricity: 171, 223; generation of, 263, 292, 312-313

elevations (*see also* altitude, effects of): vii, 45, 49, 50, 51

ELN. *See* National Liberation Army

emigration: 47, 68, 69; of educated class, 4, 36, 153, 177

employment. *See* labor force

ENAF. *See* National Smelting Company

encomienda system: 13, 14, 17, 80, 102

ENDE. *See* National Electricity Company

ENFE. *See* National Railways Company

English language: 68

Escobar Uría, Armando: 241

ethnic groups and languages (*see also* Aymara Indians; Indians; Quechua Indians): vii, 78-96

eucalyptus trees: 56

Export-Import Bank. *See* United States Export-Import Bank.

exports (*see also* tin): ix, 282, 327-330; agriculture, 57, 62, 300, 301, 303; minerals, 306, 311, 328

expropriation of estates: 2, 3, 63, 298

family and kinship ties: 83, 86, 107, 122, 127-129, 182
Fellman Velarde, José: 205
fertilizers (*see also* War of the Pacific): 260, 293, 304
festivals: 87, 108, 135, 165, 188, 189, 192, 209, 316, 346
fiesta sponsorship: 107, 121, 123, 125, 188
Finot, Enrique: 205
fish: 58, 166
Fiver Year Rehabilitation and Investment Plan: 325
FNL. *See* National Liberation Front
folk medicine: 89, 178-179
folk religion: vii, 83, 92, 133-135, 179; ceremonies, 294
folkloric tradition: 192, 202, 206, 210
food (*see also* names of specific items): ix, 75, 293; costs, 166, 187; imports, 37, 330; processing, 301, 314
foreign affairs: 5, 253, 257-274
foreign aid: ix, 274, 283-285; from United States, 28, 41, 262, 284
foreign political ideologies (*see also* Marxism): 31-32, 235
foreign trade (*see also* exports; imports): 265, 270, 317, 324, 327-332
forestry: 53, 56, 57, 275, 292, 304, 329, 330
Fortún Sanjines, Federico: 238
France: 214, 272, 285
Francovich, Guillermo: 206
freedom of religion: vii, 27, 131, 218
Freyre, Ricardo Jaimes: 200
Frías, Tomás: 25
FSB. *See* Bolivian Socialist Falange
FSTMB. *See* Mine Workers Federation of Bolivia

Gabriel René Morona Higher University: 152, 199
Gamarra, Agustín: 2, 23, 24
Geological Service of Bolivia (GEOBOL): 307
German immigrants: 68
gold: 58, 59, 306, 309, 328
Gosálvez, Botelho: 204
"Gospel and Violence": 132, 133, 254
government, national (*see also* budget): viii, 221-225, 277; employment in, 71; price control, 320; public finance, 28, 36, 280-283, 287; role, 278-280
Goyeneche, José Manuel de: 20, 21
Great Britain: 258, 270, 271, 285, 331, 332
gross domestic product (GDP): 276, 277, 291, 317
Group of 77: 274

Guaranian linguistic group: 78, 82, 92, 93, 94
Guardio, Alejandro: 201
Guaycuruan language: 82
guerrillas. *See* internal security
Guevara Arze, Wálter: 39, 41, 42, 236, 237
Guevara, Ernesto (Che): 240, 266, 269, 273, 347, 348-350
guinea pigs: 57, 166, 185
Gutiérrez Gutiérrez, Mario: 40, 236
Guzmán, Augusto: 203, 205
Guzmán de Rojas, Cecilio: 201, 206, 207

habeas corpus: 219
handicraft employment: ix, 72, 73, 314, 315, 316
hats: 168, 169
health (*see also* diet and nutrition; diseases; folk medicine; medical care and personnel): viii, 173; services, 70, 174, 178
hematite ore: 47, 60
Herrera, Joaquín: 206
Hertzog, Enrique: 34, 236
Higher and Autonomous Juan Misael Saracho University: 152
Higher and Autonomous Tomás Frías University: 152, 210
higher education (*see also* emigration; unemployment and underemployment; and names of individual universities): 145, 152-157, 162; agricultural science, 294; public universities, 141, 143, 144; universities closed, 243-244, 253
Higher University of San Andrés: 23, 70, 143, 152, 154, 155, 206, 210; students in politics, 243, 253
Higher University of San Simón of Cochabamba: 152, 204
history (*see also* Spanish colonial rule): 2, 7-43, 47-48, 79-81; arts, 193, 197; education, 138-140; foreign relations, 258-263; literature, 4-5, 194-196, 199, 206; social structure, 101-104, 120; Spanish criminal code, 343
Hochschild mining company: 27, 36
holidays (*see also* festivals): 183-184
horses: 89, 304
hospitals: 177-178
hotels: 320
housing: 4, 169-173, 315
Huarisata: 139, 151

Illampu (mountain): 50
Illimani (mountain): 50
immigrants: 65, 68
imports: ix, 37, 318, 327, 329, 330; food, 301, 302, 303; minerals, 306, 311
Incas: 8, 9-11, 13, 23, 79, 101, 194, 295; reli-

410

gion, 133, 209
Indagadores: 198, 199
independence: 20-23, 24
Indian communities: 226, 297, 298
Indians (see also Aymara Indians; Quechua Indians): vii, 1, 13, 82, 226; education, 138, 139; in literature, 199, 200, 203; in political life, 230, 231; religion, 129, 133; social status, 7, 18, 26, 30, 32, 64, 78, 102-103, 115
Industrial Bank (BISA): 288
infant mortality: viii, 67, 174
inflation: 37, 38, 229, 252, 276, 286, 288, 320
inheritance: 128, 298
Institute for the Promotion of Investment in Bolivia (INPIBOL): 279
insurance: 289
Inter-American Cooperative Education Service (SCIDE): 139
Inter-American Development Bank (IDB): viii, 143, 172, 178, 284, 287, 303, 307, 335
Inter-American Treaty of Reciprocal Assistance: viii, 272
interest rates: 288
internal security (see also Guevara, Ernesto): ix, 3, 255, 351; insurgents, 273, 347-350
International Development Association: 284, 288, 303, 325
International Monetary Fund (IMF): 38, 237, 274, 283, 285
international organizations (see also individual names of organizations): viii, 272-274
iron: 59, 60, 310, 328
Israel: 5, 214, 271
Italy: 214
Japan: 5, 258, 271, 285; immigrants from, 65, 68, 300; trade, 331, 332
"jerked beef": 303
José Ballivián University: 152
judicial system (see also courts; military justice): 217, 224, 343, 344
Kellogg, Frank B.: 262
kolla: 96
Kolla: 96
Korea, South: 5, 271
labor force (see also unemployment and underemployment): ix, 45, 70-75, 275; agriculture, 3, 291; artisans, 292, 315; government employees, 183, 222, 227-228, 234; industry, 307, 314, 325
labor unions: 32, 35, 37, 219; in politics, 245, 249
LAFTA. See Latin American Free Trade

Association
lake and river forces: 222, 326, 352
land tenure system: ix, 10, 85, 294, 297; title granting, 39, 295, 296, 299
languages (see also Aymara language; ethnic groups and languages; Quechua language; Spanish language): vii, 2
La Paz: xiv, 1, 14, 18, 27, 50, 166, 184, 318; airport, 325; climate, 54; cost of living, 278; employment, 74, 187; housing, 171; police, 339, 340; population, 61-62, 66, 112; press, 192, 212; radio and television, 213, 214; water supply, 180
La Paz Department: xiv, 21, 48, 49, 52, 281, 346; agriculture, 301; mining, 309, 311; population, 82, 89; universities, 152, 153
Lara, Jesús: 203, 204, 205, 206
Laredo, Jaime: 209
Lastra de Suárez, Yolanda: 206
Latin American Free Trade Association (LAFTA): viii, 267, 332, 333
Latin American Nuclear Free Zone Treaty: viii, 272
Lauca River: 257, 263, 264
Lechín Oquendo, Juan: 34, 35, 39, 40, 41, 42, 187, 220, 237, 238, 239, 241, 249, 250
legal codes (see also Code of Education; Penal Code): 11, 23, 338; investment incentives, 279; labor, 73; social security, 181
legal tender: 286
Liberal Party: 26, 27, 28, 131, 236
libraries: 142, 154
life expectancy: 67, 68
Linares, José María: 24
literacy: 66, 69, 91, 137, 157-160, 192; army, 353; police, 340; rural dwellers, 4, 137, 147; urban areas, 117; voting and, 219, 227
literature: 4-5, 196, 198-200, 202-205
livestock: 62, 293, 294, 298, 302-304
Llallagua (Catavi) mine: 308
llamas: 47, 57, 166, 303, 304, 321
Loa River: 49
local government: 180, 225, 280
lower class (see also Indians): 118, 249
Lujan Sandoval, Emiliano: 208
machismo: 110, 111
Madeira River: 27, 53
magazines: 198, 203
malnutrition: viii, 73, 166
Mamoré River: 46, 53, 326
manganese ore: 59, 60, 310
manufacturing: ix, 62, 71, 276, 277, 278, 313-316; GDP, 291, 292
markets and fairs: 105, 106, 107, 122, 185, 319; market towns, 64, 316; marketing of goods, 317

marriage: 119, 127, 128; civil 27
Martínez Arsanz y Vela, Nicolás: 194–195
Marxism: 158, 200, 204, 234, 249, 252
masks for carnival: 189
Matilde mine: 269
medical care and personnel: 176–178
Medinacelli, Carlos: 200
Melgarejo, Mariano: 25, 206, 218, 260, 270
Mendoza, Alonso de: 14
Mendoza, Jaime: 199
Mendoza Nava, Jaime: 208
mestizos: vii, 1, 77, 81, 90, 93, 97, 116, 230, 231; education, 137; social class, 103, 115, 118
Mexico: 202, 270, 332
middle class: 100, 114–116, 127; army, 354; police, 340; political power, 252
migration (see also colonization; emigration; immigrants): 62, 72, 74, 297
militias (see also miners; People's Militias): 3, 7, 219, 229, 247, 337, 348, 351
military academy: 242, 255, 351, 354–355
Military Air Transports (TAM): 325
military justice: 352, 356
military persons in politics: 32, 35, 222, 230, 239–247, 254–256, 337
Military Vanguard of the People (VMP): 242
milk: 181, 303
Mine Workers Federation of Bolivia (FSTMB): 34, 249, 250, 305–306; militia, 348
mineral resources (see also petroleum): ix, 58–61, 305, 306, 328, 329, 330; exports, 241, 292, 329
miners: 32, 35; militias, 239, 348, 351
Mining Bank of Bolivia (BAMIN): 287, 305, 307, 309
Mining Corporation of Bolivia (COMIBOL): 239, 278, 287, 305, 306, 307, 308, 309, 313, 325; railroad, viii, 223, 324
mining industry (see also nationalization of industry): 1, 3, 16–18, 26, 27, 59, 71, 305–310, 312; ownership, 278; production, 277, 291
ministries: 222–223, 234
Ministry of Agriculture: 276
Ministry of Defense: 180, 326
Ministry of Economy: 314
Ministry of Education: 222
Ministry of Education and Culture: 140, 144, 145, 153, 209, 210, 223
Ministry of Education and Fine Arts: 140
Ministry of Finance: 222, 227, 280, 281
Ministry of Foreign Affairs and Worship: 222
Ministry of Health and Social Welfare: 70

Ministry of Industry and Commerce: 279
Ministry of the Interior: 222, 223, 338, 343, 346
Ministry of Labor and Social Security: 181
Ministry of Labor and Trade Union Affairs: 145
Ministry of National Defense: 338, 352
Ministry of Peasant Affairs and Agriculture: 222, 223
Ministry of Planning and Coordination: 65, 142, 223, 279; data, 276, 277; housing, 173
Ministry of Rural Affairs: 140
Ministry of Rural Affairs and Agriculture: 299
Ministry of Social Service and Health: 180, 223
Ministry of Transport, Communications, and Civil Aviation: 321
Ministry of Urban Affairs and Housing: 172, 223
Miraflores General Hospital: 177
Miranda, Rogelio: 242
missionaries: 12, 13, 146; Jesuits, 19, 93, 94
mita system: 13, 14, 17, 31, 80, 102, 103
MNR: See Nationalist Revolutionary Movement
Mojoan (Arawakan) Indian language: 82, 92, 94
molybdenum: 60
Montenegro, Carlos: 204
Morales, Agustín: 25, 218
Morales D'Avila, Mariano: 205
motion pictures: 165, 187, 188, 214
motor vehicles: 323, 324, 331; tractors, 293
Moxos (Mojos) Indians: 92, 94
mozo: 118
museums: 210
music: 192, 198, 316; folk, 206, 208, 209
Mutún iron mines: 47, 60, 326

names: 12, 22
narcotics: (see also coca leaves): 179, 338
National Agrarian Reform Service: 222, 299
National Bank of Bolivia: 262, 287
National Confederation of Rural Workers of Bolivia: 248
National Council for School Construction (CONES): 143
National Council on Higher Education: 141
National Electricity Company (ENDE): 223, 313
National Family Center: 69, 70
National Housing Council (CONAVI): 172
National Investment Institute (INI): 279
National Leftist Revolutionary Party (PRIN): 238, 242, 348, 350
National Liberation Army (ELN): 254, 348

National Liberation Front (FNL): 348, 351
National Planning Board: 279
National Police (*see also* police): 35
National Police Academy: 339, 340–341, 342
National Popular Front (FPN): 244
National Potable Water and Sewerage Corporation (CORPAGUAS): 180
National Railways Company (ENFE): viii, 324, 325
National Smelting Company (ENAF): 307
National Social Security Fund (CNSS): 181, 182
National Socialist Party: 31
nationalism: 197, 198, 200, 202, 205, 232
Nationalist Revolutionary Movement (MNR): 2, 3, 7, 32, 33, 34, 35, 36, 37, 38, 39, 41, 42, 220, 221, 223; church and, 131; dominant party, 112, 140, 229, 234–238, 242, 248, 251, 252, 255; foreign affairs and, 259, 268, 272
nationalization of industry: 36, 285, 305, 310, 311
natural gas: 59, 275, 291, 310, 312
navy (*see also* lake and river forces): ix, 353
negroes: 17
Netherlands: 332
news services: 213
newspapers: 192, 211–212
nitrate deposits: 260
Nogales, Avelino: 201
nuclear energy commission: 308
Núñez del Prado, Jorge Carrasco: 207
Núñez del Prado, Marina: 207, 208
nursery schools: 145

occupational prestige: 89, 91, 108, 121; law, 115; medical personnel, 176; police, 343; retail trade, 319; teachers, 161; white elite, 97, 110; work ethic, 110
Olañeta, Pedro de : 21
Ollagüe (volcano): 60
Olmos Algreda, Angel: 206
Organization of American States (OAS): viii, 258, 285
Orbegoso, Luis José de: 23
Oriente: 50, 51, 53, 57, 58, 293, 298; education, 146; health, 167, 178; society, 113, 118, 126
Oruro Department: xiv, 15, 48, 49, 59; capital, 54, 212; festivals, 209; people, 61, 62, 86, 88; university, 152
Ovando Candia, Alfredo: 43, 220, 221, 234, 238, 239, 240, 241, 250, 256, 266, 269, 311, 352

Pachakutismo Party: 203
Pachamama: 83, 134
Pacheco, María Luisa: 207

painting: 194, 197, 207
paja brava: 56
Pan American Highway: 323
Pando, José Manuel: 26
Pando Department: xiv, 47, 48, 49, 53, 265, 323; agriculture, 304; development, 279; health services, 174, 178
Panoan language: 82, 94
Paraguay (*see also* Chaco War): 5, 266, 267, 324, 332, 333, 334, 335; border with, 46, 257
Paraguay River: 27, 47, 264, 326
Paredes, Rigoberto: 199, 206
Paredes Candia, Antonio: 206
Party of the Revolutionary Left (PIR): 32, 33, 34, 204, 234, 235, 240
Pastorelo, Jusepe: 194
Patacamaya: 52
Pathfinder Fund: 70
Patiño, Simón: 204
Patiño mining company: 27, 36, 261
Paz Estenssoro, Víctor: 32, 33, 34, 35, 36, 39, 42, 43, 211, 219, 220, 234, 237, 238, 244, 255, 265, 268, 272, 332, 347; on education, 143, 229; son, 245
PCB. *See* Bolivian Communist Party
peasant leagues. *See sindicatos campesinos*
Pedro Domingo Murillo National Industrial School: 150
Penal Code: 343, 345
Peñaranda, Enrique: 29, 31, 33, 262
People's Militias: ix, 347
Pérez de Holguín, Melchor: 194, 207
personalismo: 110, 233
Peru (*see also* War of the Pacific): ix, 46; migration to, 47, 68; relations with, 30, 266, 267, 273, 332, 333, 334, 355; trade, viii, 332
Peru-Bolivian Confederation: 23, 218, 259
peso. *See* Bolivian peso
petroleum (*see also* Chaco War): 1, 59, 60, 61, 310, 328, 329, 330
petroleum industry (*see also* Bolivian State Petroleum Enterprise; natural gas): 268, 269, 275, 278; GDP, 277, 306; political influence, 306; private schools, 140, 142; social insurance, 181
Philippines: 5, 271
Pilcomayo River: xiv, 53, 58, 166, 305
PIR. *See* Party of the Revolutionary Left
Pizarro, Francisco: 2, 8, 13, 14
Pizarro, Gonzalo: 14
Poland: 271
police (*see also* militias; National Police; and United States): ix, 337, 338–343, 344, 346, 352

413

political parties (*see also* Nationalist Revolutionary Movement; and names of specific parties): viii, 26–43, 229–256
Ponce, Wálter: 209
Ponce Sanginés, Carlos: 206
Poopó, Lake: 50, 79, 88
Popular Christian Movement (MPC): 239–240
population: vii, 45, 50, 61, 66–69, 94, 99
POR. *See* Revolutionary Workers Party
ports: ix, 1
Portuguese language: 47, 68
postal system: 227, 327
Potosí (town): 172, 194; architecture, 193; university, 152
Potosí Department: xiv, 21, 49, 339; agriculture, 301; history, 8, 12, 15, 16–18; mining, 58, 305; mint, 286; people, 61, 62, 63, 86
PRA. *See* Authentic Revolutionary Party
Presencia: 212, 213
presidency: 2, 216, 217, 221, 224, 226; military forces and, 338, 355, 356
primary schools: vii–viii, 145–148
PRIN. *See* National Leftist Revolutionary Party
private schools: 140, 141, 149; university, 141
Problems of Peasant Women Seminar: 123
Protestantism: 135–136, 146
provinces (*see also* departments): 48, 225
Prudencio, Roberto: 203
PSC. *See* Social Christian Party
public health: 173, 284
public housing: 172
publishing: 194, 210
Puerto General Busch: xiv, 46, 47, 326
Puerto Suárez: xiv, 46, 47, 353
Puquina language: 88, 89
pyrethrum: 302

quebracho tree: 56
Quechua Indians: vii, 118, 128, 133, 157, 159
Quechua language: 2, 10, 66, 85–88, 145, 160, 194, 206, 214, 303
Quintanilla, Carlos: 31

radio: 5, 159, 192, 213
railroads: viii, 27, 28, 259, 260, 261, 264, 322, 324
rainfall: 54
Ramírez Velarde, Fernando: 205
Reason for the Fatherland (RADEPA): 32, 33, 254
recreation (*see also* festivals): 187–190
regionalism: 77, 96, 97, 99, 118, 233; economic integration, 334; in literature, 203, 205
religion (*see also* folk religion; freedom of religion; missionaries; Roman Catholic Church): vii, 129–136
René-Moreno, Gabriel: 198–199
Republican Socialist Union Party (PURS): 236
research: mining, 307–308; science, 206
Revolution of 1952: 2, 7, 35, 131, 219, 247; consequences, 78, 84, 90, 236, 254
Revolutionary Workers Party (POR): 32, 33, 34, 38, 234, 242, 350, 351
Reyes Ortiz, Serapio: 197
Ricci, Lorenzo: 17
rice: 300, 320
River Plate Group: 267, 332, 334, 335
rivers (*see also* lake and river forces): 46, 53, 322, 326
roads and highways: viii, 72, 322–324
Roche de Ballivián, Elisa: 201
Rojas Guevara, José: 247
Roman Catholic Church (*see also* church and state): vii, 18, 129, 193, 218, 346; education and, 138, 146, 150, 152, 159; radio stations, 213–214
Romero, Gonzalo: 206
rosca: 112, 251
Rousseau, Jean-Jacques: 195
Royal and Pontifical Higher University of San Francisco Xavier of Chuquisaca: 19, 152, 195, 213
rubber: 27, 300, 304, 315, 329
rural areas: 169, 170, 177, 180; electricity, 312, 313; police, 339; schools, 139, 146, 147, 151

Saavedra, Bautista: 199
Sajama peak: 49
Salamanca, Daniel: 28, 29
saltpans: 52, 60
Sánchez Bustamante, Daniel: 198
sanitation: 174, 179–181
Santa Cruz, Andrés: 23, 196, 218, 343
Santa Cruz (town): xiv, 15, 61, 62, 113–114, 136, 209, 281; newspapers, 212; politics, 233, 251, 252; sewerage, 180; transportation, 325, 326; university, 152
Santa Cruz Department: 21, 48, 49, 53, 189, 266, 277, 323; agriculture, 294, 299, 300, 301, 304; health care, 176; livestock, 302; oil, 311; people, 92, 95, 97
sapo: 188
savings and loan institutions: 172, 288
savings patterns: 187
sculpture: 193, 197, 207, 208
secondary education: 148, 253
securities exchange: 289
Seleme, Antonio: 35

414

Selich, Andrés: 230, 244, 245, 246
Sène, Henri: 201
Seoane, Manuel A.: 200
Seventh Day Adventists: 135, 136
sharecropping: 298
sheep and wool: 294, 303
Siles, Hernando: 28
Siles Salines, Luis Adolfo: 240-241
Siles Suazo, Hernán: 32, 35, 38, 39, 220, 237, 238, 242, 268, 347-348
silicosis: 175
Silva, Alfredo da: 207
silver: 8, 16, 26, 58, 59, 305, 306, 309, 328, 331
sindicatos campesinos: 85, 87, 88, 101, 104, 105, 107-108, 119, 124, 125, 127; education and, 151; political power, 232, 233, 247, 249, 297; social services, 183
Sirionó tribe: 82, 132
slavery: 94
smuggling: 265, 292, 314, 327, 340, 347
soccer: 108, 117, 187
Social Christian Party (PSC): 41, 235, 251, 252
Social Democratic Party: 240
social mobility: 100, 109, 114, 126
social security. *See* welfare and social security
social status (*see also* fiesta sponsorship; occupational prestige): 18, 73, 86, 90-92, 98, 124, 125, 168, 188; *machismo*, 110, 111; upper class, 109-114, 251
soils: 52, 53, 275, 292, 293
Solón Romero, Wálter: 208
Soviet-bloc countries: 270, 271, 272, 285, 332
Soviet Union: 209, 246, 271, 285, 350
Spain: 5, 271; aid, 285; trade, 213, 332
Spanish colonial rule: 11-20, 79-81, 96, 102-104, 130, 193, 197
Spanish language: vii, 5, 66, 97; used by Indians, 86, 91, 95, 157
spirits and demons. *See* folk religion
Standard Oil Company of New Jersey: 30, 261, 266
State Bank: 287, 288
students in politics: 155-157, 230, 235, 240, 252-253, 254, 255, 264
Suárez, Isla de: 46
subversive organizations and literature (*see also* Guevara, Ernesto; Marxism): 32, 230, 246, 256, 348, 350
Sucre: xiv, 112, 172; legal capital, 27, 62, 224; people, 61, 62, 63, 79
Sucre, Antonio José de: 21, 22, 196, 281
sugar: 300, 301, 314, 320
sulfur: 59, 60, 306, 310, 328

Summer Institute of Linguistics: 94
supernatural. *See* folk religion
Tacanan language: 82, 94
Tacora (volcano): 60
Tamayo, Franz: 200, 231
Tarija Department: xiv, 48, 49, 65, 147, 279; agriculture, 301; capital, 15, 61, 62, 63; industry, 311; people, 86, 94, 97, 112, 124; university, 152, 153
taxes: 222, 281, 282, 323, 333, 334
teachers: 115, 151, 160; housing, 172; pay, 161; pensions, 182; training, 138, 140, 145, 147, 153
Technical University of Oruro: 152
Tejada Sorzano, José Luis: 29
telephone and telegraph systems: viii, 184, 326-327
television: 214, 327
theater: 196, 197, 201, 210
Tiahuanaco: 79, 206, 209, 210
tin: 8, 31, 37; deposits, 58-59, 305, 306, 309; exports, ix, 26, 263, 268, 308, 328
Titicaca, Lake and region: ix, 46, 51, 54, 265, 294, 326; fish, 58, 305; health care, 178; industry, 302; people of, 47, 63, 79, 88, 135, 188
tobacco: 301, 302, 315
Toro, David: 29, 31, 232, 263
Torres Gonzáles, Juan José: 3, 155, 211, 229, 234, 242, 243, 250, 256, 266, 269
tourism: 320-321
Tracy, Destutt de: 196
trade. *See* domestic trade; foreign trade
transportation: 317, 321-327
treaties: viii, 25, 27, 28, 272; border, 46, 259, 260; common market, 332, 334; use of ports, ix
Trinidad: xiv, 61, 62, 113-114, 294
truckers: 91, 114, 323
tuberculosis: 175, 177
tungsten: 31, 59, 60, 306, 310, 328, 331
unemployment and underemployment: ix, 4, 46, 70, 74; university graduates, 69, 148
United Nations: 150, 258; aid, 284-285, 335; member, viii, 273-274
United Nations Development Program: 308, 325
United States: 5, 30, 261, 265, 267-270; aid from, 28, 150, 237, 239, 283, 284, 307; attitude toward, 213, 236, 240, 253, 256, 257-258; emigration to, 68; military aid, 241, 244, 245, 255, 268, 270, 350, 355; police training, 341, 342-343, 349; trade, 285, 330, 332
United States Agency for International

415

Development (AID): 227, 284, 287, 335, 338
United States Export-Import Bank: 284, 288
United States Information Service: 214
United States National Aeronautics and Space Agency: 307
United States Peace Corps: 209, 284; terminated, 3, 269
universities. *See* higher education
Unzaga de la Vega, Oscar: 38, 235, 236
upper class: 81, 100, 109–114, 127; mobility, 109, 111; political power, 216, 230, 251
uranium: 60
urban areas: 169, 171, 277; crime, 346; schools, 140, 145, 146, 147
urban society: 105, 106, 114, 136; health care, 173, 180; working class, 116–118
Urquidi, Arturo: 204
Urriolagoitia, Mamerto: 34, 236
Uru Indians: 79, 88
Uruguay: 267, 324, 332, 334, 335
URUPABOL committee: 335

Vaca Guzmán, Santiago: 196, 198
Valles: 50, 51, 52, 55, 56, 146, 166, 292; labor force, 74, 297; population, 63, 69
vegetation: 55–57
Velasco, José Miguel de: 23, 24, 218
Velasco Maidana, José María: 208
Venezuela: 267, 285, 333
Victoria, Queen: 270
vicuña: 57
Villalpando, Alberto: 209
Villarroel, Gualberto: 33, 232, 259, 263
Vincenti, Benedetto: 196
Virgin Mary: 134
vixcacha: 57
vocational and technical schooling (*see also* military academy; National Police Academy): 138, 142–143, 144, 149, 150, 153, 159, 315, 354, 355; agriculture, 294; seminaries, 131
Voice of Bolivia: 213
volcanoes: 49

wages and income (*see also* inflation): 277; civil service, 227; nurses, 177; military, 356; police, 340
War of the Pacific: 5, 8, 25, 29, 48, 198, 259, 260, 264
water for drinking: 52, 54, 55, 179–180, 284
water transport (*see also* lake and river forces): ix, 53, 54
wealth (*see also* wages and income): 99, 109, 112, 115, 126
weights and measures: 320
welfare and social security (*see also* sindicatos campesinos*): 132, 135, 181–183; military pension fund, 310; social security program, 165, 172, 174, 178, 223
West Germany: 28, 29, 270; aid, 214, 285, 307; trade, 31, 258, 271, 272, 331, 332
wheat: 300, 301
white population (*see also* upper class): 96, 102, 109, 137
wildlife: 57–58
windows: 171
women: crime and, 346; dress, 88, 95, 120, 168, 169; education, 66, 122–123, 138, 145, 146, 148, 149–150, 152, 157, 161, 162; employment, 45, 70, 71, 73, 319, 321; social role, 110, 111, 116, 122, 128, 129; suffrage, 201
World Bank (IBRD): 274, 284, 312
Yacuiba-Santa Cruz railroad: 259
Youth Athenaeum: 201
YPFB. *See* Bolivian State Petroleum Enterprise
Yugoslavia: 214
Yungas: 50, 51, 52, 55, 64, 65, 292, 293; agriculture, 56, 301, 302; diet, 166, 168; education, 146; employment, 72, 74, 297; people, 63, 69, 107, 118, 123
Zamucoan language: 82
Zenteno Anaya, Joaquim: 246
Zilveti Calderón, Luis: 207

PUBLISHED AREA HANDBOOKS

550-65	Afghanistan		550-50	Khmer Republic (Cambodia)
550-98	Albania		550-81	Korea, North
550-44	Algeria	·	550-41	Korea, Republic of
550-59	Angola		550-58	Laos
550-73	Argentina		550-24	Lebanon
550-66	Bolivia		550-38	Liberia
550-20	Brazil		550-85	Libya
550-168	Bulgaria		550-163	Malagasy Republic
550-61	Burma			
550-83	Burundi		550-45	Malaysia
550-166	Cameroon		550-161	Mauritania
550-96	Ceylon		550-79	Mexico
550-159	Chad		550-76	Mongolia
550-77	Chile		550-49	Morocco
550-60	China, People's Rep. of		550-64	Mozambique
550-63	China, Rep. of		550-35	Nepal, Bhutan and Sikkim
550-26	Colombia		550-88	Nicaragua
550-67	Congo, Democratic Rep. of (Zaire)		550-157	Nigeria
			550-94	Oceania
550-91	Congo, People's Rep. of		550-48	Pakistan
550-90	Costa Rica		550-46	Panama
550-152	Cuba		550-156	Paraguay
550-22	Cyprus		550-92	Peripheral States of the Arabian Peninsula
550-158	Czechoslovakia			
550-54	Dominican Republic		550-42	Peru
550-155	East Germany		550-72	Philippines
550-52	Ecuador		550-162	Poland
550-150	El Salvador		550-160	Romania
550-28	Ethiopia		550-84	Rwanda
550-167	Finland		550-51	Saudi Arabia
550-29	Germany		550-70	Senegal
550-153	Ghana		550-86	Somalia
550-87	Greece		550-93	South Africa, Republic of
550-78	Guatemala		550-95	Soviet Union
550-82	Guyana		550-27	Sudan, Democratic Republic of
550-164	Haiti		550-47	Syria
550-151	Honduras		550-62	Tanzania
550-165	Hungary		550-53	Thailand
550-21	India		550-89	Tunisia
550-154	Indian Ocean Territories		550-80	Turkey
550-39	Indonesia		550-74	Uganda
550-68	Iran		550-43	United Arab Republic
550-31	Iraq		550-97	Uruguay
550-25	Israel		550-71	Venezuela
550-69	Ivory Coast		550-57	Vietnam, North
550-30	Japan		550-55	Vietnam, South
550-34	Jordan		550-99	Yugoslavia
550-56	Kenya		550-75	Zambia

☆ U.S. GOVERNMENT PRINTING OFFICE: 1974 O—541-139 (P.O. 20)